D1510317

A MATTER OF CONSCIENCE

OPERATION RAUSIM KWIK

GENERAL JERRY SINGIROK

PARTRIDGE

To order additional copies of this book, contact
Toll Free +65 3165 7531 (Singapore)
Toll Free +60 3 3099 4412 (Malaysia)
orders.singapore@partridgepublishing.com

www.partridgepublishing.com/singapore

PART A

CONTENTS

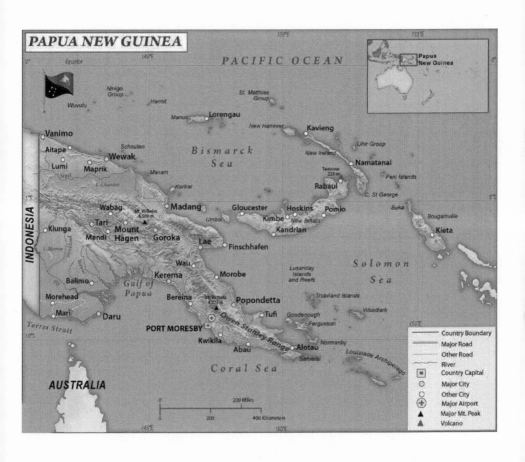

OPERATION RAUSIM KWIK

Chronology of Important Events

August 1994   The then prime minister Paias Wingti resigns. The Supreme Court rules against him, and Sir Julius Chan is nominated as the new prime minister.

                         Sir Julius immediately announces the Bougainville crisis as his top priority.

October 1994   Peace talks in Arawa fail to get Bougainville Revolutionary Army (BRA) hardliners, although Ishmael Toroama does attend but only as an observer.

19 October 1995   Col. Jerry Singirok is promoted to the rank of brigadier general and appointed commander of the Papua New Guinea Defence Force.

1996

March   Sir Julius lifts the ceasefire and warns of increased security actions against BRA and the blockade of the PNG/Solomon Island international maritime border.

5–7 April	The defence council departs for Cairns. Defence Minister Mathias Ijape, Sec. James Melegepa, and Gen. Jerry Singirok will meet with Tim Spicer and Tony Buckingham, who have introduced themselves as executives of Executive Outcomes.
15 April	Singirok and Deputy Secretary of Finance Vali Iamo meet with Tim Spicer and Michael Grunberg in London to discuss the military assistance package for combined operations with Executive Outcomes and the defence force for Operation Contravene in Bougainville.
10–15 July	Operations High Speed II in central Bougainville is launched by the First Battalion but aborted a few days later as ordered by the commanding officer.
8 September	Kangu Beach massacre occurs, where twelve security force members are killed, two missing, and five hostages taken to Laguai.
12 October	Premier Theodore Miriung is assassinated at Tonu, South Bougainville.
	Sir Julius orders an enquiry into the assassination of Theodore Miriung. A commission of enquiry is held under retired Sri Lankan judge Thiruvukkarasu Suntheralingam, which has found in December 1996 that the murder was allegedly committed by several members of the security forces with their allies, the Siwai Resistance.

27 November	Deputy Prime Minister Haiveta meets with all the heads of financial institutions including Singirok to identify and channel funds to PNGBC and Central Bank to fund the Sandline contract.
3 December	Tim Spicer and Anthony Buckingham arrive to meet with Prime Minister Chan, Deputy Prime Minister Chris Haiveta, and Defence Minister Mathias Ijape and discuss the contract with Sandline, and a consultancy fee for Tim Spicer is signed for USD 350,000.
	Tim Spicer visits Bougainville for a reconnaissance with Lieutenant Colonel Sasa and Capt. Siale Diro.

1997

5 January	Sir Julius departs for Majuro, capital of the Marshall Islands, for the state funeral of the late president Amata Kabua with Bob Nenta, Singirok, and Peter Eka.
14 January	The defence council meets and prepares submission for Defence Minister Ijape to present to the National Executive Council (NEC) submission for approval for the engagement of Sandline International to deploy into Bougainville with the defence force.
15 January	NEC approves the contract for Sandline International on Project Contravene.

20 January	Sir Julius directs NEC secretary Peter Eka to instruct Singirok to transfer the Special Forces Unit (SFU) under the command of the police force but administratively under the prime minister's department.
30 January	Four other department heads with Singirok write to the PM's secretary Noel Levi and inform him of the serious security implications of the engagement of Sandline with the state. Sir Julius does not respond.
31 January	Haiveta signs the contract for USD 36 million with Vele Iamo, acting deputy secretary of the Finance Department, and Tim Spicer and Nic van den Bergh for Sandline International.
4 February	PNG transfers USD 18 million into Sandline's Hong Kong operating account number 600774426, 50 per cent of the Sandline contract.
10 February	First batch of Sandline mercenaries arrives with hardware, weapons, ammunition, and explosives and deploys to Urimo Jungle Training Camp, East Sepik Plains.
12 February	Ijape and Haiveta depart for Hong Kong.
13 February	Tim Spicer and Nick Violaris depart for Hong Kong via Cairns to join up with Haiveta and Ijape.
14–15 February	Sandline mercenaries complete on the ground at Urimo Jungle Training Camp with SFU.

15 February	Singirok departs for an official trip to Manila, Philippines, at the invitation of General Acedera, chief of staff of the Philippine Armed Forces, through Amb. James Pokasui, who is the PNG's ambassador to the Philippines.
22 February	An Australian newspaper leaked the story about the contract between the Papua New Guinea government and Sandline International, deploying a mercenary entity into Bougainville to open the Panguna mine with SFU. The story is by Mary-Louise O'Callaghan.
	Singirok makes a decision while in the Philippines to cancel the contract and abort the operation with Sandline and expel the mercenaries from Papua New Guinea, inspired by the stories of the People Power in 1986 that ousted Pres. Ferdinand Marcos, led by Catholic cardinal Jaime Sin and Gen. Fidel Valdez Ramos.
8 March	Singirok discusses the general outline plan of Operation Rausim Kwik with key officers: Walter Enuma, Gilbert Toropo, Michael Tamalanga, Tokam Kanene, Alois Tom Ur, Max Aleale, and Kamona Falaniki.
14 March	Orders for Operation Rausim Kwik are distributed to key officers including Lt Col. Walter Salamas (who did not read as it was in his in tray until after the operation was launched).

15 March	Team bonding and range practice with Operation Rausim Kwik team happen at Goldie River Barracks with Singirok and final briefing to officers and hand-picked troops.
16 March	D minus 1 Operation Kwik launches.
	Hand-picked junior officers and troops swear and take an oath of secrecy in Singirok's office and are being briefed about the operation commencing at 7 p.m.
	Tim Spicer and his command team are arrested and detained in HMPNGS *Salamaua*, captained by Capt. John Wilson.
17 March	Bob Nenta is informed of the operation by Singirok and invited to attend the briefing for senior officers at the defence force conference room.
	Muster parade for Port Moresby–based military units occurs for Singirok to address troops about the cancellation of the Sandline contract and the conduct of Operation Rausim Kwik by selected offices and troops.
	Singirok meets with Sir Wiwa Korowi, governor general.
	Singirok is on national radio, NBC's *Talk Back Show*, with Roger Hau'ofa.
	News conference happens with diplomatic corps and media at Murray Barracks.

Mercenaries are rounded up in Wewak, ready for repatriation overseas.

18 March

Singirok is terminated by NEC as commander of PNGDF, and navy captain Fred Aikung is appointed as acting commander.

19 March

Soldiers and public demonstration and civil unrest are mainly organized by NGOs and student representative councils (SRCs) throughout the country.

Walter Enuma appears on national TV (EMTV) and appeals for calm but reminds the public that Sandline will be expelled from PNG and that the contract for Bougainville has been cancelled by Singirok.

Tim Spicer is relocated to Taurama officers' mess, and Salamas attempts to rescue Spicer but gets confronted by Enuma, Torop, and Chris Mora and is detained again. Salamas returns to Murray Barracks without Tim Spicer and his pistol after being slightly bruised.

Singirok relocates all confidential files to a confidant at Goldie River Barracks for safekeeping.

Sir Julius announces the establishment of a commission of enquiry with a wider scope of investigation to cover other aspects of the defence force like the Kangu massacre, Operation High Speed II, and the assassination of BTG premier Theodore Miriung.

20 March	Australian prime minister John Howard's emissary arrives to meet with Sir Julius to discuss the implication of the Sandline engagement and assess the current revolt by a faction of the military and wider security implications. They are Philip Flood from Department of Foreign Affairs and Trade (DFAT); Dr Hugh White, assistant secretary of defence; and former Australian high commissioner to PNG Alan Taylor.
	Civil unrest and demonstrations start in Port Moresby and elsewhere in the country.
	Prominent leaders visit Singirok to broker the peace, including MP Kilroy Genia, Sir Peter Barter, and Gabriel Dusava, but General Singirok maintains that Prime Minister Julius must step down or resign with his two key ministers.
	Soldiers get a signed petition with hundreds of signatures for the reinstatement of and support for General Singirok's action to expel Sandline and call for the prime minister to resign or step down.
21 March	Singirok calls a news conference, and copies of the Sandline contract are passed to journalists and the public to view the contents.
	Acting Commander Aikung's vehicle is confiscated and burnt by soldiers.

Aikung spends a night hiding at Parliament House and asks the prime minister to relieve him of command and appoint an acting commander. Col. Jack Tuat is appointed.

Tim Spicer is relocated by troops to Landcron on HMPNGS *Salamaua* again so he is separated from his men, to be charged and handed back to British high commissioner Brian Low.

22 March

Sandline mercenaries' main body is expelled and departs on Air Niugini bound for Singapore.

Tim Spicer remains on board *Salamaua*, and arrangements are made to take him to Boroko Police Station and press several criminal charges against him before handing him over to Brian Low.

Australian high commissioner David Irvine arrives at Flagstaff House to present Australia's official potion for the impasse and its citizens.

MP Kilroy Genia, Sir Barry Holloway, Dame Meg Taylor, Mr John Paska, and Richard Kassman arrive to speak to General Singirok on his demand for Sir Julius to step down. There is no change to the original demand, and the message is conveyed to Sir Julius by Singirok.

Capt. Ben Sesenu and a foreign affairs officer are caught at Lamana Hotel with US dollars in their possession and detained at a Murray Barracks military cell.

23 March	A combined church service is held at the Murray Barracks parade ground. In attendance are officers, soldiers, and their families including the prominent public figure Paulias Matane, who will be appointed the next governor general. Singirok attends with troops and others to find spiritual comfort and find a path of reconciliation as the nation is facing difficult times ahead.
24 March	Gov. Gen. Sir Wiwa Korowi appeals to all constitutional office holders to pray and find ways forwards.
	Riots, looting, and demonstrations continue in Goroka and elsewhere in PNG.
	Tim Spicer is asked at Boroko District Magistrate Court to answer charges of possessing illegal weapons and not disclosing a large amount of US dollars in his possession.
	A teleconversation is conducted by Sir Rabbie Namaliu and Singirok for a possible compromise.
25 March	Commonwealth secretary general Chief Emeka Anyaoku arrives to meet with Singirok and Maj. Walter Enuma at Flagstaff House, accompanied by Andrew Ogil, consulate general of Cairns.
	All present are Dame Meg Taylor, Sir Barry, John Paska, and Richard Kassman.

Singirok maintains that Sir Julius must step down as prime minister and allow a commission of enquiry to ascertain the circumstances surrounding the engagement of Sandline. There is a stalemate.

Troops, university students, public servants, and civil society lead a protest march into Parliament to witness the 2 p.m. Parliament sitting, hoping that Sir Julius will step down as prime minister.

Capt. Charlie Andrews and Lt Eddie Miro fly the Huey very low over Parliament to show support for the crowd building up at the Parliament House.

Sir Julius wins by majority vote to remain as prime minister (58–39), and the crowd is upset and increases by numbers to provide vigil at the Parliament House overnight.

Sir Rabbie Namaliu, the speaker, opens dialogue with Singirok, Enuma, Sir Barry, Perter Donigi, Dame Meg Taylor, and Richard Kassman for a compromise with Sir Julius.

Sir Julius escapes from Parliament precinct dressed in police uniform, and Chris Haiveta also escapes from the soldiers and the crowd. Other members of Parliament jump over the fence late at night to escape from the crowd. Others with Sir Michael Somare remain in Parliament and allow Major Enuma, Toropo, Namah, Renagi, Sir Barry, and Peter Donigi to meet with them and guarantee their safety. They do emphasize that Sir Julius must step down as prime minister and guarantee the safety of the MPs who are confined to the Parliament precinct.

26 March   PA for Sir Julius calls Singirok, saying that Sir Julius has prepared a speech to the Parliament that he will stand aside as prime minister and will instruct Haiveta and Ijape to also do the same and allow the commission of enquiry to begin.

Capt. Charlie Andrews and Lt Eddie Miro fly the Huey over the Parliament again.

Sir Julius informs the Parliament and addresses the nation that he has instructed his deputy and defence minister to step aside pending the outcome of the commission of enquiry.

The crowds outside Parliament and elsewhere throughout the nation are jubilant, and celebrations are held throughout the nation.

27 March   Singirok and family and Sgt Chris Mora depart for Wewak to be with close relatives Balim (sister) and Francis Sumanop and speak to officers and senior non-commissioned officers at Second Battalion under Lt Col. Michael Tamalanga.

The Bulgarian-hired transport carrier Antonov is intercepted by two RAAF jets and diverted to Tindal Air Force Base, Northern Territory. It is carrying missiles, attack helicopters, and thousands of ammunition. The intercept is being ordered by the chief of defence force Gen. John Baker.

Cabinet appoints member for Henganofi, Hon. John Giheno, from Pangu Pati as acting prime minister. Hon. Andrew Baing was appointed acting deputy prime minister.

30 March   Singirok and family return to Port Moresby from Wewak.

1 April   The commission of enquiry convenes, and Donigi, counsel for Singirok, applies for expansion of the terms of reference to cover additional contract aspects such as the establishment of an illegal army, arguing that Sandline is not a military entity as it does not have a state and as such is an illegal entity.

2 April   Singirok appears before Andrew's commission of enquiry and meets Tim Spicer at the lobby. The commission adjourns till Monday, 7 April, for Tim Spicer to be cross-examined.

4 April   *Operation Rausim Kwik is officially called off.*

Haiveta and Ijape make peace with Major Enuma and the troops involved in Operation Rausim Kwik.

7 April   Acting PM John Giheno refuses additional terms of references for the commission of enquiry.

8 April   Singirok tenders USD 400,000 in cash as court exhibit taken from Tim Spicer's safe at Fort Williams, Boroko Drive.

Spicer tells the commission that the strike force capability consisting of Mi-24 and Mi-17 attack and transport helicopters is made in Russia.

Spicer's charges at Boroko District Court are dismissed, and he departs Port Moresby unannounced for Australia and then goes to London and tells the media that he came very close to death when he was detained by PNG troops.

9–10 April   Singirok tells the enquiry that Sandline was only targeting the opening of the Panguna mine by use of excessive force.

Singirok also tells the enquiry that four departmental heads opposed the engagement of Sandline but that the prime minister and his two ministers refused to take bureaucratic advice.

16 April   Singirok unexpectedly exits the witness box during cross-examination for being called a liar by QC Marshall Cooke for Sir Julius.

Justice Andrew agrees and tells Marshall Cooke that it is not appropriate to call Singirok a liar as he has fully cooperated in the past week in the witness box.

22 April   The government announces it will not fund Singirok's legal fees.

Singirok appeals to the public for legal fees and tours the highlands, Madang, and Wewak to raise funds, and a trust account is established by Dame Meg Taylor and Sir Barry Holloway.

14 May	Peter Donigi calls for Sir Julius, Haiveta, and Ijape to be criminally charged in the media for various breaches of the constitution, particularly raising, aiding, and abetting of an illegal entity like Sandline mercenaries and when only one member of Parliament signs a multimillion-dollar contract on behalf of the state without proper processes.
29 May	Justice Andrew completes the enquiry and hands the report to Acting PM John Giheno.
2 June	Sir Julius announces that he will resume his post as prime minister and that John Giheno is no longer acting prime minister.
4 June	Sir Julius immediately announces the appointment of Col. Leo Nuia as commander of the defence force and promotion to rank of brigadier general. The appointment draws critique from the Australian media and from Bougainville.
6 June	John Giheno refuses to transfer the prime minister post to Sir Julius.
7–17 June	Singirok, Donigi, and Sir Barry commence the public awareness and fundraising campaign at Wapenamanda, Mount Hagen, Kundiawa, and Goroka with members of NGO Fr Robert Lak, Fr Louis Ambane, Peti Lafanama, and Jonathan O'ata.
26 June	Legal counsel for General Singirok changes from Peter Donigi to Ralph Saulep and then to Moses Murray.

5 July	Justice Mark Sevua rules against Singirok not to remain in a military housing and orders him out of Murray Barracks. Singirok departs Flagstaff House for private residence.
10 July	Five hostages are released by rebels in Bougainville with assistance from Commonwealth secretary general Sir Don McKinnon, Grand Chief Sir Michael Somare, and Sir Peter Barter.
July	Sir Julius and Mathias Ijape lose their respective national Parliament seats during general election.
22 July	Bill Skate is nominated as the new prime minister.
	Meaningful peace talks with the BRA, Bougainville Interim Government (BIG), and Bill Skate's government commence with unprecedented desire for reconciliation and everlasting peace on Bougainville without use of force. Skate's cabinet orders security forces to commence withdrawal from Bougainville.
4 August	The prime minister announces the second commission of enquiry, to be headed by Justice Kubulan Los.
21 August	Sir Julius publicly announces that he has sued Singirok for K1 million for defamation.
12 September	Singirok is being charged with sedition under Criminal Code section 54(1)(b).
13 October–3 Nov	The second commission of enquiry commences.

1998

28 August   Los' commission of enquiry report in draft is submitted to the prime minister and remains in draft to this date.

18 October   Singirok is reappointed as commander by Bill Skate's government and promoted to the rank of major general.

1999

18 March   Singirok makes a public apology to Sir Julius on national newspaper for making defamatory remarks against his family and himself for the Sandline engagement. Sir Julius drops charges against Singirok for defamation.

April   Singirok attends peace talks in Rotorua, New Zealand, with Skate, John Momis, Sir John Kaputin, Sec. Bill Dihm, and BRA commanders led by Ishmael Toroama.

5 August   Singirok is charged under sections 27(1), 27(2), and 27(5)(b) of the Constitution of the Independent State of New Guinea and sections 12(1)(a) and 4(6)(b) of the Organic Law on the Duties and Responsibilities of Leadership.

November   The leadership tribunal headed by Justice Moses Jalina finds Singirok guilty of leadership breach and recommends his dismissal from office.

March 2000   The curtains are drawn for Singirok in his military
               career and is officially discharged from the defence
               force after serving for twenty-five years.

CHAPTER 1

Background to the Engagement of Sandline Mercenaries

Carl von Clausewitz tells us that there are two indispensable qualities for military command:

First, an intellect that, even in the darkest hour, retains some glimmerings of the inner light which leads to truth; and second, the courage to follow this faint light wherever it may lead.[1]

I turned 40 on 5 May 1995, having served as a volunteer soldier for my beloved country, Papua New Guinea (PNG), for just over twenty years after enlisting on 5 January 1975 into the Papua New Guinea Defence Force (PNGDF). That was the year of political independence for PNG, the newest independent state in the world. I was singled out among the senior ranks of the military by the government of PM Sir Julius Chan, who promoted me from colonel to brigadier general and appointed me as commander of the PNGDF. This was on 18 October 1995. Sir Julius Chan had made it clear to me that he was looking for a young and competent

---

[1]   Quoted in Michael Howard and Peter Paret, eds., *On War/Carl von Clausewitz* (Princeton: Princeton University Press, 1984), 102.

career officer who could 'hit the rebels hard'. He told me that Bougainville was his number one priority. In my first conversation with him in his office, he asked me to provide him a new military operational concept that would bring an end to the conflict.

The operational concept that I provided was relatively straightforward. It involved landing a battalion-sized group to create a beachhead at Aropa Airport in central Bougainville. From a firm base, the battalion would conduct a series of patrols into Sipuru, Kongara, and Koromira with a view of neutralising any rebel opposition and restricting their movement and resupply via their traditional sanctuaries in the Solomon Islands and the east coast of central Bougainville. There would be a need for patrol boat and helicopter support, together with a rear echelon unit at Loloho, to support operations, followed by the seizure of the Panguna mine. The estimated cost of a month-long operation of this nature was PGK 10 million (around AUD 7 million at 1996 rates).

A few days after I was appointed commander, I gave a copy of my operational concept and budget for Operation High Speed II to the Prime Minister's Office and waited for a response. Nothing happened. I assumed that budgetary difficulties were the problem or coalition politics that the prime minister needed to work through.

The new year came and went. Towards the end of February 1996, the Defence Council—which comprised of the Minister for Defence Mathias Ijape, Secretary of Defence James Melegepa, and myself as commander—decided, on the initiative of Defence Minister Ijape, that we should go to Hong Kong via Malaysia. The purpose of the trip was not explained, but Defence Minister Ijape wanted all the members of the council to travel.

Before we could get the trip organised, Minister for Foreign Affairs and Chairman of the Bougainville Ministerial Advisory Committee Kilroy Genia asked me to meet him at the old foreign affairs office at the Central Government Office complex at Waigani. This was in the first week of March. I arrived and met him in his office. Genia was an impressive politician, well spoken with an air of natural authority. He wanted to know if I was able to mount a concentrated military operation into central Bougainville. I said yes, we could exert additional military pressure on the rebels. But we would need funding and logistical support and time to train. And I added that the government also needed increased collaboration with political leaders on Bougainville if we were to make any progress with peace efforts.

From Genia's remarks, I sensed that the government was looking for increased military pressure as an adjunct to renewed peace efforts and that the onus was on me to deliver the military part of the package. He asked me for a time frame for intensified operations, and I replied that it could take up to three months to ensure the availability of fresh troops, as well as mobility and logistical support.

From this initial discussion, events moved quickly. Genia convened a full ministerial advisory committee meeting on 8 March. The members were Mathias Ijape, minister for defence; Castan Maibawa, minister for police; and Paul Tohian, minister for state, assisting the prime minister. There was no politician from Bougainville to represent its people, which was a concern to me.

Genia began the meeting by noting that the prime minister had tasked the committee with surveying the government's current approaches to Bougainville, the government's current plan to resolve the conflict, and other available and sustainable options for moving forwards. The committee was to report back on the situation on Bougainville and make recommendations on the preferred options, taking into account the costs and possible casualties associated with any intensified military effort that might be recommended.

The committee considered three options: (1) political settlement, (2) independence, and (3) intensified security operations. After considering all the options in detail, the committee advised that options 1 and 3 be followed. Independence for Bougainville was ruled out. The committee recommended that:

- the government endorse intensified security force operations on Bougainville,

- the prime minister direct the secretary and the minister for finance to allocate PGK 10 million to the defence force for the operations,
- the current ceasefire be lifted for the period of the offensive,
- operations commence at the end of April,
- the commander be given specific approval to plan and effect the operations,
- the Ministerial Advisory Committee on Bougainville reassess the options for a political settlement following military action.

The prime minister received the Ministerial Advisory Committee's report on 15 March. His secretary, Noel Levi, was asked to obtain from me a comprehensive breakdown of the proposed PGK 10 million budget. The Defence Council was asked to submit an operational plan to be approved by the National Security Council and the National Executive Council (NEC). Finally, the prime minister asked why the military operation could not begin before the end of April. Why not sooner?

After receiving the prime minister's comments, I discussed the committee's recommendations with Ijape. I observed that I had advised both the prime minister and Genia that I needed three months to mount a properly resourced operation, but the report had cut the time to half of that, and despite promises of additional funding, none had been forthcoming. Genia noted that the military operations were important as the prime minister had committed his government to making progress on Bougainville. The prime minister, he said, was getting increasingly agitated at the lack of military progress on Bougainville and was beginning to question the ability of the PNGDF to resolve the crisis militarily.

At this point, I had been commander for a little less than four months. Political expectations were clearly set out in the Ministerial Advisory Committee's report. As I reflected on the experiences I had gained in the field as the senior commanding officer on Bougainville during the state of emergency in 1989 and again in 1993 and 1994, I knew that it was not going to be an easy job. The military option that the government was banking on might very well prove counterproductive, especially given the likelihood of political interference coupled with inadequacies in our logistical supply chain and the financial constraints under which the defence force was operating.

Meanwhile, Ijape's planned trip to Hong Kong had been organised, and we departed Port Moresby via Singapore and Kuala Lumpur. It was only over breakfast in Kuala Lumpur that Ijape revealed to me the reason for the rushed trip to Hong Kong. It was to meet Alastair Morrison from Defence Systems Limited (DSL). This was the first I had ever heard of DSL.

Ijape explained that DSL was a UK-based company that he had dealt with, along with another company called Plaza 107, as minister for police. He said these were very wealthy companies that made money from mining investments. He added that if we handled the Panguna mine well with DSL and Plaza 107, we could each end up very well off. He said that DSL had already been in PNG and that Minister for Police Maibawa, who had replaced Ijape as police minister, had also been to Hong Kong for initial talks.

As it turned out, our trip to Hong Kong was aborted when an insider in the Prime Minister's Office (who we suspected could have been Emos Daniels, an executive to the prime minister and the secretary general for Sir Julius Chan's party, the People's Progress Party [PPP]) suggested that we should be ordered to return to PNG. I do not know what transpired between Ijape and Sir Julius, but it soon became obvious that the issue of engaging DSL or Plaza 107 was fixed in Ijape's mind.

Ijape instructed me to reschedule a separate trip to visit our defence suppliers in Singapore, London, and the United States and to meet up with a firm called Executive Outcomes (EO) while I was in London. He explained that they were linked to DSL and were working up a proposal that he wanted the Defence Council to consider.

On 21 March 1996, the prime minister addressed the nation on Bougainville. He made the following points:

One of my first actions when I became Prime Minister of Papua New Guinea on 30 August 1994 was to seek personal dialogue with leadership of the so-called Bougainville Revolutionary Army [BRA]. I travelled to Honiara on 3 September 1994, just three days after assuming office as Prime Minister and I met with Sam Kauona. Out of the meeting came the Honiara Agreement. There was [a] surge of optimism on all sides. My mission was undertaken for one purpose only—to help resolve a conflict which for five years had been eating away at Papua New Guinea's soul . . . The rebel leaders have completely lost control of what is happening today in Bougainville . . . They kill, they burn, and they destroy for no real purpose . . . It is time to consider new options. It is time to face the truth that continued talking is not working. For the last 18 months, the Government has left no stone unturned . . . travelled down every path . . . tried every legal means at its disposal . . . to resolve this conflict, to find peace.

I am now convinced that we have exhausted all human tolerance. Every time an agreement of any sort was reached, then the rebels reneged, defaulted and continued killing and destroying. I restate the Government's position:

a) Above all else, the national Constitution of Papua New Guinea must be upheld and respected.
b) Bougainville is an integral part of Papua New Guinea.
c) The overwhelming majority of the people of Bougainville want peace and normalcy.
d) The rest of Papua New Guinea is distressed at the continuing slaughter of innocent people and fed up with being held to ransom by the BRA's various groups and their small bands of supporters.

e) Peace and normalcy must be restored with no further delay.

I have always been prepared to give concessions in the name of peace but hopes of a political settlement cannot be translated into reality unless there is equal goodwill on either side.

As of this morning, the National Executive Council has directed the lifting of the Ceasefire, to enable the Security Force to take preventative measures. The legal effect of the 'lifting of the Ceasefire' is that the Defence Force will now once again be operating under full powers and responsibilities imposed upon it by the Constitutional Call-Out of 23 December 1988. They are once again being directed to actively assist the civilian authorities in the restoration of public order without the restriction which the NEC imposed upon them in 1994, in a hope of achieving negotiated peace. The NEC has further directed that our Security Force be greater and better equipped, and that we deal with BRA elements inside and outside Papua New Guinea.

Every offensive killing that has taken place since May 1995 has been a criminal act of murder. And it will be as an act of murder that prosecution will proceed. As Prime Minister, I urge the leadership of the Bougainville rebellion to clean out its house. Purge your ranks of all the criminal elements and senseless killers you have attracted—before it's too late. Ona, Kabui and Miriori, Foster and Havini: these men have selfish and evil motives. They are fighting out of greed, and for power. They themselves are not physically fighting a battle. They command from [a] distance. The blood that is being spilled is not their own—that blood comes from innocent people, from women and children.

When I took office, I declared Bougainville as my Government's top priority. It remains so. It will have number one priority until the whole conflict is resolved. Whilst I continue to listen and be receptive to all constructive peace moves, I must also now act decisively. And this is exactly what I am doing.

To those criminals who continue to kill, destroy and destabilise the peace longed for [by] all—let me say just this. Your darkest hours have arrived. Your number has been called and you are now facing the full force of the law.

The government's message was clear. It would now do everything in its power to destroy the Bougainville Revolutionary Army (BRA) and its command structure. Ijape used the prime minister's address to impress on the Defence Council the need to bring sufficient military force against the BRA, to neutralise them and make way for further political negotiation with the central government. The onus was now on me as commander to accomplish the desired military outcomes as reinforced by the prime minister.

While planning for a new military offensive got underway, Ijape instructed the secretary and me to travel to Cairns, Australia, on Easter Friday for a meeting with a team from London associated with DSL and EO. I flew to Cairns after lunch on Friday, 5 April, with James Melegepa and checked in at the Cairns Travel Lodge to meet the delegation from London. Ijape was travelling via Brisbane. I had no idea who the DSL team were. But at 9 a.m. on Easter Saturday, two gentlemen met us in the lobby and introduced themselves as Tim Spicer and Tony Buckingham. Spicer was about 170 cm (5 feet 7 inches) in height and Buckingham was quite tall, maybe 183 cm (6 feet). There was an air of confidence about them. Both were wearing dark glasses. After introductions, I suggested we adjourn to a more private area in the cafeteria for our meeting. I was conscious that Australian security and intelligence might well take an interest in the presence of a PNG minister, military commander, and secretary for defence meeting for some unknown purpose with so-called military consultants from the UK.

During the meeting, we were given a rundown on EO. This was a South African–based security outfit with an office in London. They were capable, they said, of providing additional military assistance drawing on all aspects of combat power. Spicer explained how he envisaged providing such assistance and concluded by giving us videos and other marketing material on EO. As Buckingham said little during this first meeting, it was not clear to me where he fitted. After a few questions, we parted. It was agreed that the trip to London in mid-April would enable me to follow up, if necessary, on any proposed military consultancy with Spicer and EO.

After the meeting, Ijape continued to talk about Plaza 107 and DSL. He said he had dealt with them over a proposal to assist the police force to establish a rapid response unit. They could be used to open the Panguna mine and render other services. This was complete news to me as was the whole concept of PNG hiring private armies. With my experience on defence funding shortfalls and our continual scrimping and saving, I doubted if PNG would be able to find the money to hire firms like Plaza 107 and EO. Thinking about the aborted trip to Hong Kong a month earlier, it seemed likely that Ijape must have organised with DSL for Spicer and Buckingham to travel from London to Cairns to meet us. And Ijape must have known that, because it was the Easter weekend, the prime minister and his aides were less likely to find out what the Defence Council was up to.

On my return to Port Moresby, I glanced through EO's profile. It appeared that they were a private military security company based in South Africa and that they offered military services mainly to failed African states with natural resources that could be provided on concessionary terms in return for military assistance.

EO was formed by Lt Col. Eeben Barlow, a South African Army special forces officer. Founded in 1989, the organisation claimed to have fought in South and West Africa, South America, and Indonesia. An example of one of its initial tasks was to assist a South American drug enforcement agency conduct operations against local drug producers.

Other EO operations were in Angola and Sierra Leone, where their services had been paid for with a combination of cash, mining licences, oil rights, access to geological deposits, and logging concessions.

EO's military specialisations included the provision of military combat forces, electronic surveillance and telecommunications, military skills, training and intelligence, and technical and logistical support. EO was controlled from the Bahamas by a company called Strategic Resources Corporation. This company, in turn, was closely associated with Buckingham, who controlled Branch Energy Ltd, which owned diamond concessions in Angola and Sierra Leone. Buckingham was also a director of EO. The nature of EO's relationship to DSL was not made clear.

While I could see a number of immediate objections to the employment of a private military company in PNG, I was not too concerned as it appeared that EO was just another consultancy company trying to take advantage of the crisis on Bougainville with an eye on the Panguna copper mine. So it was not a surprise that Buckingham from Branch Energy was included in the Cairns meeting. Reflecting on the glossy profile of EO on my desk, it was obvious that former British Army officers smelt a bigger prize in Bougainville than just a military consultancy or taking on the suppression and elimination of a rebel army.

Mid-April found me in London, as planned, for calls on a round of defence suppliers and for a call on the Ministry of Defence. Towards the end of my visit to the UK, on 19 April, I met with Spicer and a financial colleague of his, Michael Grunberg, in my room at the Royal Horseguards, where they had tracked me down after I had failed to call on them at their Plaza 107 offices. We spent nearly two hours going through a document they had drawn up for a military assistance package they called Project Contravene. The document gave an overview and background to the Bougainville crisis and a military estimate, including what services and equipment they could offer. In introducing the package, Spicer freely admitted that his thinking had moved on significantly since the Cairns meeting a couple of weeks previously. At that point, he and Buckingham had talked about the possible supply of helicopters, which had been the focus of Ijape's interest. But since then, he had broadened his thinking to propose a package to 'win the war'. Project Contravene was the result of that thinking. They glossed pretty quickly over the estimated contract price, though I saw that the sum of USD 32 million was included in the proposal. That kind of money, I knew, would be well out of the reach of PNG. In fact, I thought the whole thing a childish fantasy.

As Spicer was preparing to leave, I cautioned him on the use of telephones and facsimile machines. Operational security was extremely important. I said that, providing there were long-term benefits for the PNGDF and if the problems of cost were not, as I supposed, insurmountable, I would not oppose further exploration of the package.

Arriving back in Port Moresby on Saturday, 24 April, I pondered the results of my overseas trip. While the government was wanting a quick-fix military solution in Bougainville, I knew that even the best army in the world could not win that war. With its exclusively military focus, I thought that Project Contravene made little sense as a stand-alone proposal.

Before briefing Ijape, I went through the draft copy of Project Contravene. The use of mercenaries by failed and failing African states was common enough. And they were now knocking on the door to enter PNG. Their modus operandi had already attracted the attention of Ijape, whose personal motivations were clear enough. Spicer gave me two copies of the Project Contravene proposal titled 'Military Support Package for the Government of Papua New Guinea'.

Here are the summary notes taken from the proposal by EO as presented by Spicer:

> **Concept.** There is a military requirement to carry out specific counter-insurgency operations in a short timeframe. The operation is highly sensitive, and needs to be carried out with minimum collateral damage to make it acceptable to the Government and the people of PNG. To achieve this the military imperative is the ability to gather high-grade, specific intelligence about

the location, capacity and intentions of the enemy force, particularly their C3I assets and match that intelligence with a strike capacity, the key ingredients of which are: firepower, mobility, precision, speed and surprise.

The combination of a strategic EW [electronic warfare] capability and a helicopter force comprising both attack and support helicopters can generate a massive increase in combat power out of all proportion to the cost and gives the Commander the capacity to carry out his operation in a timely, effective and publicly acceptable way. In addition the assets can be used for other strategic operations and will greatly enhance the capacity of the Armed Forces of PNG.

Security. It is understood that security is vital to the project. Other than mission operators and the project coordinators, only four key personnel within our organisation will be aware of the details of this project.

Time and Cost. The objective is for the full package and all personnel to be in theatre by 15 May 1997. The total cost of the proposal is USD32.7m; however we are prepared to quote a fixed price at USD30m, including the provision of all personnel and management support with appropriate training resources for up to one year. A detailed breakdown of the equipment, personnel and costs is provided below.

The above cost of the payment is payable by electronic funds transfer to our bank in the following stages: (a) on confirmation of order 50%, and (b) on delivery of the assets to theatre 50%. Upon receipt of your decision to proceed we will immediately provide our banking information to you.

Summary. We will provide Government of PNG a surveillance and strike package to enable the Commander to carry out the operations with little collateral damage, thus satisfying the political imperative. In addition the package has many other national uses, not limited to the scope of initial operations, e.g. national intelligence gathering, marine surveillance, fisheries protection. We will operate the package for a minimum contract period of one year. In addition, we will train PNG personnel to take over the operation of the equipment. The equipment becomes the property of the PNG government and the personnel are under full command of the Commander for the contract period. The sensitivity and security of this project is accepted and understood.

Equipment to be supplied. (a) 2 x Mi-24 Attack helicopters for night operations, gunship, and weapons system and rocket launchers. USD 8.2m; (b) 2 x Mi-17 troop carrying helicopters equipped for support, including night operations. Winch fitted if required. USD 3.0m; (c) All the ordnances for the Mi-24 and Mi-17 helicopters. USD 1.9m; (d) Surveillance Platform to include jet aircraft and pressurised environment. USD 2.4m; (e) EW suite. USD 4.85m; and, (f) Spares for helicopter and surveillance platform; USD 2.1m.

The Project Contravene document was marked 'Secret'. In my debrief to Ijape, I ran through what was proposed. He was delighted at the prospect of a long-term engagement with EO. He did not seem troubled by the circumstances surrounding the hire of mercenaries, nor did he seem the least bit worried about where the money would come from. As I would touch on later, no issues were raised regarding a range of obvious command, control, and legal issues.

As mid-1996 approached, we were still preoccupied with the security situation in Bougainville. More soldiers were returning in body bags, and more civilians were either being killed, injured, or mistreated at the hands of the rebels or by the security forces. Sir Julius had promised close cooperation with Bougainville's leaders, but he underestimated the extent of the damage already done and the suspicion the Bougainvilleans had for the central government. The gap was widening. Clearly, there was a disconnect among the national government, the Bougainville Transitional Government, the rebel faction, and the security forces. All the major players were on different wavelengths. The command and leadership by the government in Port Moresby was sporadic and often misdirected.

As commander, I had inherited a host of problems that were preoccupying my time and thinking. Mobility was my single biggest headache. The lack of funds to sustain the war effort in Bougainville was a close second. We were operating on an absolute shoestring budget with just enough to see our troops through monthly. Even meeting the cost of basic services like power and telephones at Murray Barracks was a continual preoccupation. Most days, we kept the lights and air conditioning off to conserve power. Access to working telephones was strictly rationed. We were barely limping along.

It was against this unpromising reality that Ijape instructed me that an operation into the central heart of Bougainville had to be launched soon and that I should present a brief to the Defence Council. He, in turn, would provide an information paper to the cabinet. He reminded me that Sir Julius had already made his address to the nation, that the BRA had been warned, and that we must act now to show that the government was serious in its intentions.

Despite the instructions by the prime minister and the letter to the Department of Finance, the PGK 10 million in funds promised for Operation High Speed II had not been allocated. I would be forced to launch the operation using funds from my recurrent budget, undermining the integrity of the operation in just about every respect. I was mindful that I had undertaken to the prime minister that the operation would be launched in mid-March. The deadline had not been met as we were preoccupied with trying to find, and fund, a new strike force capability to meet the prime minister's intentions.

Meantime, Spicer had been sending faxes to the prime minister seeking his agreement to an early visit to Port Moresby by himself and his chairman, Buckingham, regarding Plaza 107's military capabilities and investment interests. These faxes, sent on 16 July and 21 August, were prompted by a wall of silence from both Ijape and myself in response to his various faxes and phone calls.

In my case, I was preoccupied by operational matters, including fallout from the failure of Operation High Speed II when the First Battalion withdrew prematurely from conducting operations into the Kongara area in central Bougainville; the Kangu Beach massacre in September, in which rebels killed twelve members of D Company, First Battalion, along with their commanding officer, Maj. Paul Panau, and took five hostages; the loss of weapons and ammunition; and the assassination of Premier Theodore Miriung by members of the resistance force supported by element of the security forces. In Ijape's case, he had received so little encouragement from the prime minister to earlier suggestions of obtaining overseas military help to take the war to the rebels that he had not even briefed the prime minister, as it turned out, on anything to do with Spicer, Grunberg, and Buckingham's Project Contravene.

In these circumstances, the faxes from Spicer to the prime minister in July and August advising him that he had been in regular touch with both his minister for defence and his military commander on proposals for 'winning the war' might well have come as a considerable surprise. No doubt to get the matter off his desk, Sir Julius scrawled a note to his departmental head, Noel Levi, on the second of the two faxes: 'I would *not* be taking this too seriously. Check and *advise*.'

Levi, who had been PNG's high commissioner in London in 1991–95 and had also served as PNG's first secretary of defence in 1974–77, spoke to the British high commissioner in Port Moresby and also sought confidential information from a barrister in London who had been one of his contacts there. In a memo to Sir Julius dated 19 September, he set out a starkly worded warning about Plaza 107:

> The above organisation Plaza 107 with which the Minister for Defence has been corresponding with a view to assist Papua New Guinea on Bougainville is a London based affiliate of HERITAGE OIL, registered

and operating in Sierra Leone in Africa. It is part of an international network which specialises in exporting military equipment together with mercenary soldiers. The network is headed by a former South African military officer by the name of Eeben Barlow who runs the operation under the umbrella of a mining and petroleum company called Heritage Oil. This company has extensive interests in Sierra Leone after they were invited by the Government to put down the rebel movement in that country.

As a mercenary outfit, Barlow's organisation is regarded as the best in the world. They are professional, efficient and are known for doing their job effectively. Their method of operation however leaves very little room for any meaningful dialogue between the host Government and the people whom they help to pacify. In other words, they are not concerned about the aftermath of their operations and very often have left long term ill feeling behind in countries where they have been engaged to put down rebellious opposition to the elected Government. Their operations often leave very little room for dialogue and negotiations.

The price a country pays for their services is a substantial upfront cash payment and participation in mining and petroleum industry as well as other investments. The London operations are run by Tim Spicer and Tony Buckingham. Tim Spicer is the military man but, according to my contact, he is not highly regarded as a military strategist by his former military colleagues. Tony Buckingham is an economist and is highly regarded as a financing and investment expert.

Based on the foregoing and my conversation with my contact, I would suggest that the government should consider this matter carefully with the view to reject it. Our aim on Bougainville is not to completely alienate the people and therefore engaging this organisation would be contrary to our long term political and constitutional interest.

(Signed) Noel Levi, CBE

Sir Julius read Levi's memorandum the following day, 20 September, and wrote on it one word: 'reject'. This might well have been the end of the Plaza 107/EO story but for the entrance, stage left, of a brand-new player, Deputy Prime Minister and Minister for Finance Chris Haiveta. On the same day that Sir Julius was rejecting the approach from Spicer and Buckingham, Haiveta was in Hong Kong in connection with a planned float of the government's oil and mining interests in a new global investment vehicle called Orogen Minerals Ltd. The adviser for this float was Rupert McCowan of Jardine Fleming Securities Ltd. To promote the float, McCowan was planning a travelling roadshow that would take place in London in October. Spicer, upon hearing about this, got in touch with McCowan, briefed him on Project Contravene, and asked him to arrange for a meeting with Haiveta when he was in London. According to a file note kept by McCowan on this call, Spicer mentioned that the name Plaza 107/EO had been changed to Sandline International. This was the point at which Sandline International first entered the story, though I did not know it at the time.

Before Deputy Prime Minister Haiveta left for London, he contacted me, and we had lunch. He informed me that he would be seeing Spicer, and I gave him some background on Plaza 107/EO and Project Contravene. I cannot recall what transpired in London during Haiveta's visit there, but a copy of Project Contravene was handed to Haiveta by Spicer. At this stage, neither Haiveta nor I knew of Noel Levi's advice to Sir Julius or of the prime minister's direction to reject their approach.

When Haiveta returned from his roadshow, he called me for a late meeting on his workboat at the Royal Papua Yacht Club. He asked me where matters stood with Project Contravene and Plaza 107. I replied that neither the defence minister nor I were actively pushing the project as securing funding for the employment of external military forces was a likely stumbling block. Haiveta assured me that, during his visit overseas, outside funds had been identified and that he would seek cabinet approval for the release of the funds. He had both the Bank of Papua New Guinea and the Papua New Guinea Banking Corporation (PNGBC) establishing facilities to access funds.

On 27 November, Haiveta called a business lunch meeting of the heads of PNG's financial institutions, including Sir Brown Bai, chairman of PNGBC; Rupa Mulina, managing director of PNGBC; Koiari Tarata, governor of the Central Bank; and Gerea Aopi, former finance secretary and now a director of PNGBC and executive manager for Oil Search. The purpose of the lunch meeting, as Haiveta explained it, was to find ways to consolidate the funds required so that they could be sent out through PNGBC or the Central Bank to Jardine Fleming in Hong Kong to be disbursed to Sandline. It appeared from the discussion that critical banking procedures laid down in legislation would need to be sidestepped to enable the money, now identified as North Fly Development Corporation funds, to be transferred to Hong Kong. From this technical finance and banking discussion, it was very apparent that ministers were effectively committed to Sandline. Whereas I had been assuming all along that the money would never be found to employ 'military consultants' (as the prime minister had instructed that Sandline personnel must be called, not mercenaries), it was apparent that funding was no longer an issue, provided the bankers could find a way around the legal and legislative constraints.

Haiveta reminded me that the prime minister had already warned the rebels and the people of Bougainville that he had given them many chances and turned every single stone. He also noted that 1997 was an election year and that the government was determined to reopen the Panguna mine before it went into the elections. I asked Haiveta to remember that the previous month had been a very difficult time for the defence force with many soldiers killed and hostages still in the jungle. It had not been easy for me. I felt that Chris Haiveta was a good and generous man who tried his best to help with our funding issues. But he, too, was under considerable pressure to find additional funding for the defence force, and no doubt this was what disposed him to look favourably on talk of external funding lines in return, no doubt, for mineral concessions.

Spicer arrived back in Port Moresby in early December at the invitation of Haiveta and held a series of meetings with Haiveta, Ijape, myself, and Gilbert Toropo from my Special Forces Unit (SFU). When meeting with me, he announced that he was no longer associated with EO or Plaza 107. He had registered another company called Sandline International Holdings. I asked him how this had come about and why the name Sandline. His explanation was clear so far as it went. Sandline used EO for their profile as they were well established in dealing with failed states in Africa, mainly Angola and Sierra Leone. Sandline would use EO's soldiers and equipment, which would be deployed to PNG once the government agreed to the contract. Plaza 107 was based in London, and they were sharing their office and related services, which explained why facsimiles arriving from Sandline still had Plaza 107 on the letterhead. It was obviously something of a stretch for Spicer to claim that he no longer had any association with EO or Plaza 107. In fact, he was still intimately tied up with both corporate entities and dependent on EO for any combat manpower that might be required.

Spicer said that, when trying to find a name for this new entity, he was on a family holiday in the Bahamas. He was standing on a beach and drew a line on the sand and thought about the connotations of the line 'this far and no further'. B-grade movie though that sounded, that was how he came up with the name Sandline. He had registered Sandline International Holdings Ltd by changing the name of a dormant company known as Castle Engineering in the Bahamas.

During our meeting, Spicer announced another name change. He had decided to rename Project Contravene as Operation Oyster. He had accepted my advice that 'contravene' had some negative connotations, whereas 'oyster' was more acceptable sounding. He explained that he had chosen this name because the Panguna mine, which was seen (wrongly in my view) as the key to the whole affair, reminded him of an oyster. Of course, the actual keys were the attitudes of the civilian population on Bougainville. While they remained opposed, the mine would never open.

The first fruit of the early part of the December visit was an agreement by Haiveta to a suggestion from Spicer that the PNG government fund a short consultancy that would allow him to carry out a full military appreciation of the situation on Bougainville, on the basis of which he would flesh out the Project Contravene proposal and put it into a form that could be considered by cabinet. The amount sought by Spicer to carry out the consultancy was USD 350,000. This was obviously exorbitant, but James Melegepa managed to reduce the fee by USD 100,000 in negotiation with Grunberg. The consultancy fee was still exorbitant but was to be paid. A fee of USD 250,000 was invoiced by Sandline for the consultancy agreed to by Haiveta. The first 50 per cent was to be paid to a holding bank account in Hong Kong on 10 December and the balance in the first week of January 1997. Spicer was informed by Haiveta, I learnt later, that the Sandline contract of engagement would be signed and executed by the middle or end of January 1997, subject to a satisfactory consultancy report.

Meantime, on Tuesday, 3 December, I had been asked to go to the Prime Minister's Office at short notice. Arriving at Morauta Haus, I was surprised, shocked even, to see Spicer and Buckingham standing in the corridor outside the Prime Minister's Office. I asked them what they were doing there. Spicer, seeing that I was taken aback and obviously had not been briefed by Haiveta or Ijape on their invitation to visit, said he was there to brief the prime minister. In a tone of voice that I took exception to, he added that this meant 'there was no need for me to be worried'. I stared at him hard, anger boiling up inside me. I snapped, 'At least you could have told me of your visit. So now you think you can act as the commander having direct contact with the prime minister, do you? And I will get directions and orders from you? Is that it?'

I was so angry that it was all I could do not to start a fracas right then and there outside the Prime Minister's Office. I kept my temper and left. I was not going to attend a meeting with the prime minister on which I had not been properly briefed. As the lift doors closed in front of me, Spicer and Buckingham looked stunned. I walked out in protest. I did speak to Sir Julius that morning. Fuming, I thought, *That's it—Spicer can run the effing PNGDF on behalf of Sir Julius, if that is what the damn prime minister wants. And good luck to him and Sir Julius. The mess they create in Bougainville will be on their heads!*

Of course, I cooled down quickly, but this incident was absolutely the last straw. Something had to be done about Sandline. What exactly, I did not know—not at that moment at least. But the prime minister and other ministers needed to be protected from their collective flights of fancy. That much I owed them. And I owed it to my friends on Bougainville not to let them be exposed to some African-style idiocy that would tear PNG apart.

I took the midday flight to Goroka, where I was the guest speaker at a graduation ceremony at my former high school, Asaroka Lutheran. As I flew, I reflected on my encounter with Spicer and the tension that was now looming between us. Col. Jack Tuat could stand in for me during the final negotiation stages with Spicer. I did not want anything more to do with the man.

When I arrived and checked in at the Bird of Paradise Hotel in Goroka, the phone in my room rang. It was Ijape on the line. He said, 'Commander, I have a complaint from Spicer about your behaviour at the Prime Minister's Office this morning. What is going on between you two?' I explained that I had been caught by complete surprise. Spicer had not had the courtesy to tell me that he and Buckingham were visiting Port Moresby. I was angry that no one had thought to brief me on the visit and that Spicer had told me not to worry about him seeing the prime minister in tones that were supercilious, condescending, and downright rude.

Ijape started to interrupt, but I cut him off. 'Sir,' I said, 'I just met Buckingham and Spicer by chance. We do not have two defence forces and two commanders. The least that your office and Tim Spicer could have done is to keep me informed. Now that Sir Julius is getting involved with Spicer, we will be overwhelmed by his schemes. If he is to be involved here, the very least that has to be done is to put in place an arrangement so that I know what he is up to and when he is visiting and who he is seeing. I remind you that I report to the Defence Council and the National Security Council, and I work in the interest of 6 million Papua New Guineans, including over 300,000 Bougainvilleans and our soldiers. Spicer doesn't do any of those things. He works for himself. And if you are looking for an apology, I am absolutely not offering one.'

I hung up and disengaged the phone. *Ministers*, I thought, *effing . . . bloody morons! Who needs them?*

I cooled down after that, but it felt good to get that lot off my chest. But anger was not going to solve anything. I needed to give serious thought to what to do next. Shouting at my minister was not a long-term strategy, not even a short- or medium-term one. But something had to be said, if only to clear the air.

The pressure for Spicer to be actively engaged was growing under the watchful eyes of Minister Ijape and Deputy Prime Minister Haiveta, so I (reluctantly) agreed to a reconnaissance trip for Spicer into Bougainville, not that I had any choice. But to facilitate the consultancy, I agreed—with the best grace that I could manage—to organise a covert trip into Bougainville for Spicer to get an overview of what he would be dealing with if Operation Oyster ever got government approval. Spicer travelled to Bougainville under the fictitious name of Simon Brown. He was accompanied by Lt Col. Yaura Sasa and Capt. Siale Diro, who was now the intelligence officer for the Special Forces Unit. This visit was an opportunity for Spicer to assess the terrain, the people, and the physical features of Bougainville. His trip to central Bougainville and the PNGDF forward operations base at Loloho would give him additional insight into possible bases and staging areas.

When Spicer returned to Port Moresby from his reconnaissance, he introduced me to Rupert McCowan, a rather short, chubby British man who was also staying at the Holiday Inn. Spicer said that McCowan was assisting in the financial package for the money transfer from the PNG government to Hong Kong for the contract to employ Sandline. I had no idea what this arrangement was. All I could think about was the remarkable speed at which the Sandline contract was moving, especially given all the new players turning up in Port Moresby.

After briefing me on his Bougainville trip, Spicer—as he was leaving Port Moresby—presented me with an unfinished bottle of Johnnie Walker Blue Label, bidding me to celebrate the new year with it as 1997 was going to be 'a very good year for all of us'. *Sure, whatever,*

I thought. It was more likely a very tough year, certainly tougher than anything either of us had encountered until then.

Before Spicer left, he also gave me a copy of a document called 'Sandline Profile'. This was essentially a marketing prospectus. Sandline claimed to be able to provide military consulting and combat assistance across the entire military spectrum, vet all requests carefully to ensure that the company only worked for legitimate governments or international organisations, conduct military operations on behalf of client governments, and create 'own force' combat groups of any size but typically 150 men equipped with their own organic helicopter lift and helicopter gunships.

Looking through the profile, some points were very obvious. Sandline was using EO to resource its capabilities. The company had never been an independent entity, and the name Sandline had only been registered when the possibility of engagement by the PNG government was becoming more likely. Sandline was no different from other private military companies—its involvement was contingent on gaining access to the host country's natural resources as a concession for its services. Sandline was assuming that the PNG government, in its handling of the Bougainville crisis, was no different from the failing states it had dealt with in Africa; and if engaged, the company would purchase all its weaponry, ammunition, and attack helicopters second-hand from ex-Soviet states. It was also very apparent that the ultimate aim of Sandline/EO/Branch Energy Ltd and Heritage Oil was to use PNG government resources to become beneficial owners of the assets and mineral resources of copper, gold, and silver in the Panguna mine.

At the back of the profile was Spicer's curriculum vitae. Spicer had commanded First Battalion, the Scots Guards, in Belfast; had been operations officer for Second Battalion, the Scots Guards, in the Falklands War; had worked as a press officer for Gen. Mike Rose in Bosnia; and had been military assistant to Gen. Sir Peter de la Billièr in a wide-ranging Middle Eastern role. He was a graduate of the Royal Military Academy at Sandhurst, where he was the top honour student in his year, and had tried out, unsuccessfully, for selection into the

British SAS. He had also served as an instructor at the British Army Staff College at Camberley.

As I reviewed the possible engagement of Sandline, a number of questions that had been bothering me from the outset struck me with some force. The 'Sandline Profile' that Spicer was handing around looked attractive at first glance. But there were some obvious problems that needed addressing. First, what was the legal status of Sandline personnel if deployed within the jurisdiction of PNG? Were they to be subject to PNG laws, the PNG Criminal Code, and the PNGDF Code of Military Discipline? If a Sandline personnel was in breach of the laws of armed conflict, would that person be subject to trial and the possibility of a lengthy prison term in PNG?

Second, what would the command arrangements be? In Western military doctrine, there is a universal belief in the need for unity of command. There can only be one commander for any operation. Command cannot be shared or divided. And the commander of a military operation in PNG needed to be a PNGDF officer. It would be unacceptable for Sandline, a mercenary outfit, to have operational control and command over elements of the PNGDF. In fact, it would be not only unacceptable but also illegal under the PNG's constitution. Would I be granted operational command over Sandline forces, and how would that command arrangement be made to work? Would Sandline need to be sworn in as an integral part of the PNGDF or as special constables under the Royal Papua New Guinea Constabulary as seemed to be the requirement? And what would the result be if a Sandline operative refused to accept a legitimate command from a PNGDF officer?

Third, and in some ways most worryingly, how would the principles of proportionality of force be laid down and insisted on? How would the obvious prospect of heavy collateral damage associated with attack helicopters and high-powered munitions be contained and minimised? How acceptable would it be, for example, if a Sandline helicopter gunship, under the operational command of a PNGDF officer, razed an entire village in Bougainville with high explosives, rocket fire, and heavy machine-gun fire just because some people in the village were suspected of being BRA operatives? Did we really want to risk having a My Lai incident, or a series of such incidents, on our hands? How many William Calley–type court martials did we want to preside over? How many ordinary civilians in Bougainville would have to die before the senior leadership of the BRA could be made to lay down their arms? Did we really want to regard the leadership of the BRA, or even the rank and file, as our enemy when, in fact, they were citizens of PNG and entitled to the rights and protections of the constitution? Even if BRA military leaders were to be regarded as criminals, as described by Sir Julius, they were entitled to a fair trial, not to be hunted down and machine-gunned indiscriminately.

These were the moral, political, legal, and military operational and command issues that any responsible military officer would want answered. And in some ways, these issues dwarfed in importance the issue that the politicians seemed to be focusing on. They only seemed to be concerned about where the money was to come from to hire their private military company. I was aware that there had been some airy assurances given to the effect that Sandline operatives could be sworn in by the police commissioner, if required, as special constables. But this was hand-waving only. There was never any serious discussion of the legal and constitutional issues involved in employing foreign mercenaries to hunt down Papua New Guinean citizens for a fee. And I had no wish whatsoever to have a bunch of special constables of any foreign nationality operating under either my command or that of the police commissioner. Worse still, if that can be imagined, was the prospect of having my soldiers operating under the command of Sandline. This was the stuff of nightmares—or comic opera, were it not for the fact that it was the lives of Papua New Guinean citizens that ministers were contemplating putting under the hired guns of African bounty hunters and English soldiers of fortune.

The next day, I received a message that Ovia Rauka, director general of the National Intelligence Organisation (NIO), wanted to speak to me about an urgent matter. I made my way to the Prime Minister's Office, where Rauka was waiting for me in the conference room. He raised two issues. The first was the fact that two foreigners, brothers Mark and

Cedric Rodrigues from Australia, who were persons of interest to the police and immigration authorities, were now working for Byron and Vanessa Chan's security company, Network International. He handed me a file to read and take back with me.

The Rodrigues brothers were also shareholders and directors of Network International, which meant that two foreigners on tourist visas were doing business in PNG in contravention of their visas. He asked me if I could throw any light on the matter. I said that I could not as they had had no dealings, so far as I knew, with the PNGDF. I said that I thought it would be advisable to inform the prime minister's secretary, Noel Levi; the police commissioner; and the secretaries for labour and foreign affairs. They would be able to talk to Sir Julius and suggest that his offspring remove the Rodrigues brothers from their business so that they could leave the country quietly. If not, both Australian subjects could cause a lot of damage to Network International, and Sir Julius's name would get dragged in.

The other issue on his mind concerned Col. Leo Nuia. Rauka said that the colonel, as I well knew, was a controversial figure who had admitted on Australian television that troops under his control had been involved in extrajudicial killings on Bougainville in 1991 and had dumped the bodies at sea from Australian-supplied helicopters. Rauka was hearing that Nuia could be appointed chief of operations at any time; he might even be appointed as commander. Rauka said Sir Julius had been openly stating that he was not happy with my performance to date, citing the Kangu Beach massacre, the taking of the five hostages, and Theodore Miriung's assassination. The prime minister thought that I had lost control of the defence force.

I responded by saying that if the prime minister was not happy, he should tell me face to face and replace me. Further, if he thought that a change of commander would make any difference on Bougainville, he was mistaken. Bougainville was a struggle for hearts and minds. Military pressure could play a role, but Bougainville was a political problem, not a military one. It needed a lot of tolerance, a sustained approach from the central government, and an understanding of Bougainville customs and traditions to bring peace.

Rauka agreed that there was no military solution. He said that the NIO had done a thorough check on Plaza 107 and EO and had concluded that the methods used in Africa were inhumane and not appropriate in the PNG context. What did I propose to do about it? I said that, ultimately, it was a matter for cabinet. Personally, I doubted that, despite Haiveta's confidence on that score, the government would be able to find the sort of money required by Sandline International. And even if they found the money for the initial period that was being proposed, they would find it very expensive to sustain an externally sourced military operation. Costs aside, there was a raft of legal and constitutional issues to consider, quite apart from the ethical, moral, political, and reputational issues at stake. Many of these issues were outside my strict area of competence. But as far as the military issues were concerned, my view was that, while additional military pressure might bring limited results on the negotiating front, there was no such thing as a military solution insofar as that phrase was generally understood. One only had to consider the Russian experience in Afghanistan, the French experience in Algeria, or countless other examples to understand the futility of military solutions to deep-seated problems such as what we were experiencing in Bougainville.

Therefore, when ministers asked if Project Contravene would work, they had to be brought to understand that, while it was impossible to say with any certainty what would happen in the event that an EO-type operation was mounted, the odds were that it would make the Bougainville crisis very much worse, not better. Indeed, the likelihood was that machine-gunning and rocketing suspected BRA locations on Bougainville would bring about precisely the opposite result than the one government wanted. Lots of innocent deaths and the permanent alienation of Bougainville from PNG—no sane person could want that.

Rauka said that he completely agreed with me. But had I spoken to key ministers in those terms? I said I had not. Ijape was a lost cause as Rauka well knew. Ijape was the sort of person who only understood a knuckle fight, and he had probably been bought off. Haiveta and Chan might listen. They were a lot more sophisticated than Ijape would ever be. But it appeared that they had also bought Spicer's particular brand of snake oil. They had made a political commitment to make progress on Bougainville. Chan had even gone on TV and radio to promise the rebels that their darkest hour had come. So no, I had not spoken in those terms, but then I was a military man, not a political adviser. And I was still hoping that the whole Sandline fantasy would fall over at the funding hurdle.

As I thought about my meeting with Rauka in the weeks leading up to Christmas, I reflected on the danger posed by the EO/Sandline people. I had patched up some sort of working relationship with Spicer since the threatened fracas in the hallway outside the Prime Minister's Office in early December. But we were wary of each other, and there was very little trust or, in my case at least, professional respect. I thought it very likely that Spicer would produce a sales document for Sandline International masquerading as a military consultancy report very early in January. Haiveta had already assured Spicer that, assuming his consultancy report was satisfactory, a contract of engagement would be signed with Sandline by mid- to late January. I would need to find some other way to try to convince ministers of the fiasco that they were likely to land themselves in if they decided to try for an outright military solution in Bougainville. This might well be my most urgent task in the new year, given that ministers were committed to making progress on Bougainville before the national elections scheduled for June 1997.

Spicer's consultancy report, due in less than a couple of weeks, would be the key. My days as commander seemed numbered. I knew that I had a solid professional reputation as the soldiers' commander. I knew also that Sir Julius had been warned that my popularity was such that any effort to replace me could lead to widespread industrial action and even a shutdown of essential government services. This prospect might buy me a little time with Sir Julius but possibly not much.

CHAPTER 2

The Crisis Deepens, January–
February 1997

To every thing there is a season, and a time to every purpose
under the heaven:
    A time to be born, and a time to die; a time to plant, and a
time to pluck up that which is planted;
    A time to kill, and a time to heal; a time to break down,
and a time to build up;
    A time to weep, and a time to laugh; a time to mourn, and
a time to dance;
    A time to cast away stones, and a time to gather stones
together; a time to embrace, and a time to refrain from embracing;
    A time to get, and a time to lose; a time to keep, and a time
to cast away;
    A time to rend, and a time to sew; a time to keep silence,
and a time to speak;
    A time to love, and a time to hate; a time of war, and a
time of peace.

—**Ecclesiastes 3**

Friday, 3 January 1997, was my first day back at work after the New
Year break. Sadly, the Papua New Guinea Defence Force was greeted

by a controversial newspaper article published in the *National* alleging
that HIV and AIDS were prevalent throughout the defence force.
It was written by my senior high school classmate Neville Togerewa
from Milne Bay, a veteran reporter. It rocked the morale of the defence
force once again, with soldiers at the Port Moresby Supply Company
demanding to go to the management of the *National* to make them
justify their claim. I called the newspaper in protest and demanded an
explanation and justification of their claim or an apology and retraction
of the story as it was completely lacking in evidence.

I got a call that day from Sir Julius Chan's office instructing me
to travel with the prime minister and the police commissioner, Bob
Nenta, to the Marshall Islands for the funeral service of Amata Kabua,
president of the Republic of the Marshall Islands from 1979 to 1996.
We departed on Sunday, 5 January, on the Government Flying Unit
Beechcraft Super King Air, a turboprop aircraft called the *Kumul*. We
stopped at Nauru to refuel and then arrived at Majuro, the capital of
Marshall Islands. The state funeral was held on Monday, 6 January,
at Parliament House with hundreds of local and overseas mourners.
Sir Julius, being a prominent leader in the Pacific, was given special
recognition during and after the funeral.

On the way back to the hotel after the burial, I was seated with
Sir Julius in the back seat of our official car, and he raised the issue
of the joint operations with Sandline. He asked me what I thought
about the choice of helicopters Sandline were talking about. I said that
the helicopters were Soviet-era military-issue Mi-17 troop transports
and Mi-24 gunships. The obvious downsides were the difficulty of
ongoing technical support, conversion for our aircrew (given their lack
of familiarity with the helicopters), and the probability that cockpit
instrumentation and technical manuals would all be in Russian. Sir
Julius agreed that this could cause difficulties and instructed me to see
Gabriel Dusava, the foreign affairs secretary, to ask for help to organise
a visit to the Philippines. 'Get hold of Papua New Guinea's ambassador
James Pokasui in Manila,' he said. 'And ask him to explore if there is any
scope for getting the Philippines' assistance with helicopter support.

After all, Gen. Eddie Ramos is a friend of ours, and he will be only too willing to assist us.'

As I sat through dinner that evening, I knew that Sir Julius—who owned a helicopter company, Islands Nationair—shared my concerns about Soviet military helicopters and their operability and sustainment. Sir Julius also raised the issue of the five hostages in Bougainville and wanted more information about what we were doing to get them released. We flew back the following day, Tuesday, 7 January, to Port Moresby, where I was greeted with the prospect of more meetings with Tim Spicer and a long checklist of provisional planning in the event that Operation Contravene went ahead.

The year 1997 was a general election year for Papua New Guinea. The mood of the politicians changed as the political parties were manoeuvring and plotting their respective campaign strategies, identifying candidates, and more importantly looking to raise funds to support their election campaigns. Sir Julius had floated the kina in mid-1994, and already, there were signs of a failing fiscal management strategy. Other investment sectors, like agriculture, remained dormant, while fisheries and logging were left unmonitored as they were manipulated by foreign investors, and tax revenues were limited. The World Bank had a tough management strategy in place for restraining public sector expenditure. One of the few bright spots heading into the election year was the successful float of the Orogen shares issue.

In the meantime, back in London, Spicer had been working overtime through the Christmas holidays to produce his consultancy report on Project Contravene. He had completed this by New Year's Eve and caught an immediate flight back to Port Moresby. Sir Julius's first full day back in his office after the state funeral at Majuro was on Wednesday, 8 January. Spicer suggested to Minister for Defence Mathias Ijape that the two of them go over to the Prime Minister's Office unannounced that day and give him his copy of the Project Contravene consultancy report. Sir Julius, surprised and more than a little annoyed by this unannounced call, refused to see them that day but tasked Spicer, through Ijape, to write him a brief two-page note on what Contravene could do for the government, including how to deal with the rebel factions on Bougainville and reopen the Panguna mine.

This was the chance Spicer had been hoping for. Noel Levi was away on leave, so Spicer could get at the prime minister without the normal filter that the prime minister's departmental secretary would have provided. Spicer found himself an empty office and handwrote a brief intended to secure the prime minister's attention. He summarised Sandline's proposals in a couple of brief paragraphs. They were that Sandline was proposing to carry out the main part of the military operation, to destroy the rebel leadership and to reopen the mine, using its own operatives but possibly with the involvement of the Special Forces Unit and that the defence force could then be used to mop up any remaining opposition and guard the mine. Spicer concluded his handwritten brief with the advice that the cost of Sandline's involvement could be recoverable from mine revenues and that Branch Minerals (Buckingham's company) might be interested in purchasing the mine. Sandline's involvement in subsequent operations was open for discussion, including the provision of military services to hold the mine open.

Spicer followed this up with a more formal two-page brief:

Prime Minister Sir Julius Chan
JUSTIFICATION OF A MILITARY OPTION FOR BOUGAINVILLE
Sir,

You asked me to prepare a briefing note about how you can justify the implementation of a military option involving the employment of high tech equipment and outside specialists to support the Forces of PNG, in the time frame January to June 1997. To date the 4,500 men of the Defence Force, some having done 8 tours of duty in Bougainville have archived minimum objectives. This primarily is due to lack of the right technical support.

WHY USE OF MILITARY OPTION?

For nine years successive governments have failed to resolve the crisis either by military means or by negotiation. This has given the BRA terrorists psychological advantages; and the political astuteness between negotiation and military action when it suits them. They have appealed to the international community as an oppressed minority in a totally unscrupulous and manipulative way. They have continually pretended to wish to negotiate and then immediately reverted to military action when it suited them. Therefore it is time the problem was resolved once and for all in order to achieve the stated aim of Restoration, Rehabilitation and Reconstruction. The Government must do this from the position of strength hence a quick, precise military action with minimum collateral damage to innocent life.

WHY NOW?

Prior to Christmas it was felt that there might be a political break through with MP's visit to hostages etc. Today the government has heard that 3 of the 8 hostages held by the BRA have been murdered in cold blood. This demonstrates a total lack of concern for human life, an attitude of total lawlessness and a total disregard for government efforts to negotiate for a peaceful settlement.

This combined with massive loss of life during the last nine (9) years, the damage to the fabric of PNG Society and the drain on resources that could have been spent on health, education and infrastructure have led to a situation where the government cannot allow this to continue and as a final gesture to the people of Bougainville and PNG, it is this administration's duty to resolve the crisis immediately. The BRA gives the administration no alternative but military action.

HOW TO ACHIEVE IT?

Conventional military operation is costly in life and money and has been ineffective. A radical solution is called for, that involves precise military action to destroy the leadership of the BRA, fragmenting their organisation, with minimum loss of life on both sides. This will involve the acquisition of technical enhancements to the forces of PNG to enable them to achieve this in the time frame.

HOW DO YOU JUSTIFY THE COST?

In order to achieve this requirement funds must be available. The armed forces of PNG have seemingly failed to achieve significant results against a small poorly armed but cleverly led revolutionary group. Their morale has suffered. The cost of this operation is insignificant in comparison to what it has cost the country to date, in lost revenue, expenditure, human misery, the dislocation of PNG society and the standing of the country in the eyes of the world.

WILL THIS HAVE ADDITONAL BENEFITS?

It will have the following additional benefit for the country:

- Creation of climate of stability—attracts foreign investments.
- Possibility of cost recovery.
- Reopening of Panguna mine—Jobs, wealth etc. in Bougainville.
- Unification of society and prevention of further suffering in Bougainville.

- An end to cynical terrorism.
- Enhanced capacity for national forces and strengthening position of PNG regionally.

WHY BEFORE THE ELECTION?

Is this cynical electioneering? No. It is the administration's duty to solve this problem particularly in view of the murder of the hostages. The administration has One last chance to complete what it has to do.

Tim Spicer, OBE
Sandline International
8 January 1997

Having absorbed these two briefs and forgetting his earlier decision to 'reject' (see chapter 1), Sir Julius was now thoroughly engaged. After a long conversation with the prime minister the next day, Spicer called Michael Grunberg and assured him that Sir Julius had taken the bait. He directed Grunberg to contact Executive Outcomes (EO) in South Africa and to warn Brig. Gen. Nic van den Bergh, EO's chief operating officer. The instruction was to get ready and commence putting his team together. Spicer then suggested to Grunberg that he should come to Port Moresby as soon as practical so that he could draw up a draft contract. Spicer also contacted Ijape that day and told him that the prime minister was very impressed and happy with the brief. According to Spicer, Sir Julius had described it as the best brief he had ever had on a proposed military solution for Bougainville. Ijape, in turn, assured Spicer that all was on track in terms of financing.

By now, Ijape—who presumably did his own checks—was so completely sure that the prime minister was convinced by Spicer's brief that he issued a ministerial direction to the secretary of defence and myself as commander. Ijape called me into his office and said, 'Commander, we only have this week to complete our submission to the NEC on Project Contravene. I want you and Secretary Melegepa to work on the NEC submission as soon as possible. The cabinet is waiting.'

Between 14 and 15 January, I was sick with the flu and so was at home when Stephen Raphael, the legal officer for the Department of Defence (later deputy secretary), came to see me at Flagstaff House. With some considerable misgivings, we wrote the NEC policy submission in my study. Project Contravene had, by now, become Project Oyster. In drawing up the submission, we based our recommendations on the Sandline consultancy report:

NEC POLICY SUBMISSION
TOP SECRET
SUBJECT: PROJECT OYSTER JOINT MILITARY OPERATIONS SPECIAL FORCES UNIT AND SANDLINE INTERNATIONAL

The Purpose of the Submission:
a) To seek approval from NEC and Security Council to officially engage Sandline International with the PNGDF and Special Forces Unit (SFU).
b) To approve the use of SFU in-depth operations in Central Bougainville.
c) Seek approval to conduct pre-emptive strikes on selected targets in Bougainville.
d) To seek approval for the funding of Sandline International of USD 36 million for the Project including 50% down payment for the services.
e) To seek funding for Special Forces Unit operations and sustainment of K6.0m.
f) To seek approval for foreigners to be engaged in consultancy work including training and technical support.
g) To approve as part of Defence Force development as contained in the White Paper the acquisition of new high tech capabilities through Sandline International.

To achieve high level operational success specific military intelligence about locations, capacity, and enemy intentions will be gathered in order to match intelligence with a strike capability having the following ingredients:

- Firepower;
- Mobility;
- Precision;
- Speed; and
- Surprise.

Surveillance Package

The Surveillance package will provide capability consisting of:

- Electronic platform;
- Fixed wing fitted with Electronic Warfare (EW) package that will consist of sensors and processors that can gather and pinpoint intelligence information. The VHF and UHF have intercept and directional finding, voice and statistical analysis capability to track beacons and transmitters;
- Night Vision Equipment will use the latest generation of night vision equipment and goggles to detect and destroy targets at night;
- Ground Intelligence handling will consist of computer system process, store and retrieve operational intelligence gathered and imagery interpretation and enhancement packages;
- Air Crew for continuous operations to fly both day and night;
- Trainers. Implicit to the package is a Training team who will train the SFU members in the use

of technology and other close quarter operations, demolitions and advanced medical skills; and,

- Ground Staff. These will be technicians and computer operators including a small administrative team.

Strike Package

The strike package will operate effectively with the surveillance package and consist of the following assets:

- Two Mi-24 Attack helicopters;
- Two Mi-17 Support helicopters;
- One fixed wing electronic and surveillance platform; and,
- Support and ground staff to keep the helicopters and electronic and communications operational.

There are also options to train and hand over these assets to the PNGDF and at the same time the additional assets will provide a strategic capability to enhance operational posture after the major military operations.

The continuous application of military pressure on the rebels will force the rebels to re-negotiate with the national government as their main sources of support have been impaired through military operations at minimum cost.

Financial Implications
- Sandline International–
  Air and technical support   USD 29.17m
  and capabilities:
  Training of SFU: USD 7.10m

Communications   USD 1.1m
Equipment:
Total: USD 37.37 million

- SFU–
  Operational Sustainment: K 2.5m
  Additional capabilities: K 1.5m
  Charters: K 0.5m
  Contingencies: K 1.5m
  Total: K 6.0m
  Total Costs: Sandline: SFU: K 6m
  USD 37.37m

Sandline payment is to be paid 50% on confirmation of order and 50% on delivery of assets in the country.

SFU, who will be in the actual frontlines must also be provided for as the cost of sustaining them even after the operations is equally important.

While the initial outlay will be expensive, the benefits will be:

- Longer term financial gains through investment and mining revenue.
- The repayment of some costs by the mine owners is possible.
- Acquisition of significant force multiplier for the government and the PNGDF.
- Stability attracts good and future investment which in turn increases government revenue.
- International financial support would be more forth coming.

If approved, the funding will come from the government's contingency funds and not from the PNGDF 1997 recurrent budget.

Political Implications

The whole operations will give the government control of Bougainville and prevent those who intend to prolong the crisis from success. It will indicate that the government is effective, tough, but clear in its objectives to achieve lasting peace on the island. It will impress international opinion and warn potential enemies to be wary of taking on PNG.

The views of the Prime Minister and other Members will be sought in cabinet.

Recommendations

The following are the recommendations:

- NEC and Security Council approve the engagement of Sandline International to undertake Operation Oyster with the government of PNG.
- The Council approve the use of SFU with Sandline International on operations in Bougainville.
- Council approve the Commander to deal directly with Sandline on all operational matters.
- The Council approve USD36 million to engage Sandline International for the operations, with 50% to be paid and the remainder to be settled once operations commence.
- The Council approve K6m for the sustainment of SFU.
- That the funds be made available from national government contingencies funds.
- The Council approve the PNGDF on behalf of the national government to keep the extra military hardware and the arsenal that are supplied by Sandline International.

- NEC approve the engagement of foreigners as consultants, trainers and technical officers to work alongside the PNGDF members; and
- The NEC approves Sandline International members to gain entry visas without undue delay.

HON. MATHIAS IJAPE, MP, LLB
Minister for Defence, January 1997

Although very deficient—among other notable omissions, it did not specify a time frame or duration for the operations, had no advice on the command arrangements, and was silent on the legal and constitutional implications of employing mercenaries—this submission was, nonetheless and much to my surprise, approved by Sir Julius's cabinet on 16 January without amendment. The approval meant that I had to begin the process of mobilising troops and resources to prepare for the joint operations with Sandline International, which was a dilemma. I had thought that the NEC paper would be bounced back for more work, including in the legal and constitutional area. But from Ijape's perspective, it was just a 'tick the box' submission.

Chris Haiveta also had a dilemma: where was the money going to come from, and what kind of contract was to be put in place to cover the proposed services? Despite cabinet having given its approval, there was no contract to cover the engagement of Sandline. Rather than asking State Solicitor Zachary Gelu to prepare the contract on behalf of the state, per the normal procedure, in the interests of speed and to minimise unwanted questions, Haiveta asked Spicer and Grunberg to prepare the contract on behalf of the government and Sandline Holdings. This was a highly irregular way to proceed. Never before had potential clients been asked to prepare a contract on behalf of the state and themselves. When copies of the draft contract were circulated to Melegepa and me, it was noticeable, if hardly surprising, that all the clauses and conditions weighed very heavily in Sandline's favour.

Spicer arrived back in town on Sunday, 19 January. He called to advise me that he planned to speak to Haiveta and Ijape about the contract. I had no idea at that point that the state solicitor was not to be involved in the drafting of the contract, and I remained ignorant of that fact until a few days later. When I finally realised the situation, my concern was that neither the state solicitor nor Melegepa nor myself was consulted or given an opportunity to take ownership of the contract on behalf of the state. The reality of the situation began to set in for Sir Julius and Haiveta as well. There was no money to pay Sandline. Neither the cost of the earlier consultancy (ignominiously enough, the cheque given to Spicer before Christmas had bounced as it turned out) nor the 50 per cent down payment required under the terms of the draft contract could be covered.

In anticipation of Operation Oyster being launched before the end of March, I issued a commander's intent to the operations branch with specific guidelines and instructions. This was handed to Acting Chief of Operations Lt Col. Walter Salamas to turn into an operations order. Operation Oyster involved a good deal of high-level planning. My commander's statement of intent was set out broadly as follows:

> Introduction
>
> The Government intends to launch an in-depth operation into BRA and BIG strongholds using a combined force of Special Forces Unit and Sandline operatives. The following guidance is to be observed:
>
> a) Operation Oyster to be completed by end of May '97;
> b) Sandline and SFU to provide a combined 120 man team;
> c) Transport and attack helicopters to be used to strike and knock out targets as acquired by electronic detection and directional location identification;
> d) Coordinate airborne elements with contingency elements on the ground;
> e) Operations to be conducted swiftly on preassigned targets with minimum collateral damage; and,

f) With an overall view to seizing and holding the Panguna mine and associated assets.

The Mission of Operation Oyster

SFU and Sandline supported by Forward Tactical Units are to conduct in-depth overt operations on targets followed by a *coup-de-main* operation to seize Panguna mine.

General Outline

After pre-deployment training, the operations team will move into Assembly Area (AA) ready for deployment into Area of Operations (AO). The Operations will be a combination of air mobility plus fire power using a combined total of 120 men using helicopters, attack gunships, mortars and high explosive rockets to knock out targets as acquired by electronic means.

There will be four phases of Operations:

- **Phase One.** Pre-training at Urimo Jungle Training Range, East Sepik to be completed by 20th March '97.
- **Phase Two.** Mission Preparation and movement into Assembly Area in Area of Operations. To be executed immediately after Phase 1.
- **Phase Three**. Conduct Operations for thirty days. First week of April to first week of May.
- **Phase Four.** Mopping up operations. Remainder of May '97.

Ending Statement and Targets

The following are the targets:

- BRA/BIG Communications to be destroyed.
- BRA and BIG organisation destroyed. Leaders arrested wherever possible and brought to trial.

- Secure and hold the Panguna mine (including its power supply, access road and port facilities).

Ensure that

- National government 3R Strategy, Reconciliation, Restoration and Rebuild is maintained uninterrupted and government services to flow to the Bougainville people.
- Return of normalcy; and
- High degree of Combat Power in the PNGDF through acquisition of Sandline contracted assets is retained.

Administration and Logistics

Main logistics support will be from Murray Barracks and Air Transport Squadron through Joint Operations Command (Rear).

Forward Operations base will be at Loloho and Buka respectively to support efforts in central Bougainville.

Command and Communications

- *Operation Oyster* is a high level operation controlled by National Security Council.
- The Commander PNGDF is the Commander of all deployed forces.
- Land Force Commander, taking orders from Commander PNGDF, will be Sandline.
- Ground Tactical Commander is OC SFU.
- Joint Force HQ will be manned by SFU and Sandline joint operations team operating out of Air Transport Squadron (ATS) and an operations room at ATS HQ is to be established to control

and monitor all operations carried out by *Operation Oyster.*

- Force Operations Room at HQPNGDF will continue to monitor all other normal operations in Bougainville and the rest of PNG.
- Joint Forward Tactical HQ will be established at Loloho.
- Joint Training HQ at Second Battalion, Moem Barracks.
- Electronic Counter Measures. TBA.
- Rules of engagement. TBA.

I was desperate to pin down the six million in kina for SFU funding agreed to in the NEC submission; however, no sooner had I completed this commander's intent than I got a thoroughly disturbing letter from the Prime Minister's Office that momentarily eclipsed my funding concerns. This letter came to me through NEC secretary Peter Eka, who was acting secretary to the prime minister at the time. The letter concerned the future of the SFU. It read:

20th January 1997
My dear Commander

I write in reference to the above subject **(PNGDF RAPID REACTION FORCE)** and wish to convey the direction of the Prime Minister on the same.

Firstly, let me convey to you the Prime Minister's expressed appreciation on the manner in which our security forces reacted to the most recent threats made on his personal safety. The Prime Minister was impressed with the arrangement set up by our two security agencies during the time of his arrival from Solomon Islands on Tuesday 7th January 1997.

Secondly the Prime Minister having been made aware of the existence of the PNGDF Rapid Reaction

Force has directed that this unit be formalised, strengthened and commanded by the Police. For administrative convenience, he suggests that it be brought under Department of Prime Minister and NEC. I am aware of the previous government direction on the establishment of a Protective Security Unit within the Department to respond to threats against VIPs.

I intend to put this matter on the NSAC agenda on the practicality of the concept. I have written to the Attorney General seeking his advice on the legal and constitutional implications (if any) of the intention of the Prime Minister. In the meantime, while I await response from the Attorney General, I would appreciate very much if you could provide your initial thoughts on the same. I have written to the Commissioner for Police requesting the same. Please forward your comments as soon as possible.

Yours sincerely
Peter M. Eka, OBE
Acting Secretary

I was stunned. How on earth could the prime minister think to bring a strategic force such as the SFU, which is intrinsically a military force requiring command by a military officer, under his direct command?

I called the officer commanding SFU, Major Toropo, and discussed the implications of the letter. It was obvious to both of us that the letter represented the views of officials in the Prime Minister's Office who were envious of the capabilities being developed in the SFU. We agreed that we would ignore the letter in the hope that it would blow over or be buried in the aftermath of Operation Oyster.

It was now approaching the end of January, and I was assailed by issues on a variety of fronts—from uncertainties around funding for Operation Oyster to inadequate information about the helicopters being brought in from the former Soviet Union, the hostages in Bougainville, and the proposed transfer of the SFU to the prime minister's department.

I knew that Sir Julius had the nation to worry about, including the repercussions on the economy of not opening the Panguna mine after he had floated the kina. The economy was not stable. Where would the money come from to fund the Sandline contract, and how would the prime minister micromanage the SFU? I began to worry about Sir Julius's mental state as many of the decisions that he was making did not seem right.

That night, just before I turned into bed, I was surprised to see Haiveta drive up to Flagstaff House. He was always an easy person to talk things over with, so we sat under the house, discussing the forthcoming operations. He assured me that the funds had been secured and that Sandline would be paid to do the job with the defence force. I had no issues, as such, with Sandline having its funding line secured. However, by then, the defence force was completely strapped for cash. The funding situation under my regular budget allocation was so bad that, with hardly any funding coming through, I could barely pay my phone and power bills at Murray Barracks. Yet a foreign company could be awarded USD 36 million for three months of operations with an option to renew their services. Something was definitely wrong when a foreign military company was favoured over our own national requirements.

On Tuesday, 21 January, I arrived at my office and my aide-de-camp (ADC) brought me the Bougainville operations file with notice of casualty (NOTICAS) of two more soldiers killed in Bougainville: Lt Jonathan Sembisan and Private Bayape. I had served with Lieutenant Sembisan, and I felt the pain that was already in me as more men I knew were falling and more body bags were returning to Port Moresby. There had to be a stop to this somewhere. We could not continue to endure the suffering. Bougainville was crying, and the nation was bleeding. We were all in trouble. I shut my office and told the ADC that I needed some time to myself. I disengaged the phone. I asked the Lord, 'How long must we endure?'

Then James Loko, acting finance secretary, called and wanted us to meet with Haiveta and the governor of the Central Bank in his office. I departed in haste, still preoccupied with the loss of a private soldier and Lieutenant Sembisan.

When I arrived at Vulupindi Haus in Waigani, I realised that my presence was needed mainly to impress on the governor of the Central Bank that the funds identified were required for Operation Oyster and, as agreed by the National Security Council (NSC), were to be transmitted to the Sandline account in Hong Kong. Then I was given a copy of the draft contract for the engagement of Sandline. I still had no idea, even at this late stage, that the contract had been prepared by Spicer and Grunberg rather than the state solicitor.

Rumours of the government's agreement to the hiring of foreign mercenaries were now circulating widely in Port Moresby. Retired general Ted Diro, his counsel Peter Pena, and Kevin Conrad, a United States–born PNG environmental lawyer who was the son of American missionaries who had lived and worked with the Arapesh tribe near Wewak in East Sepik Province, came to my office to confirm the engagement of Sandline. Diro was particularly concerned about the cost factors and the long-term implications of having mercenaries in the country, although in 1989 it was he himself who had put a bounty on Francis Ona's head, dead or alive.

On 23 January, I met Rupert McCowan in James Loko's office with senior finance official Vele Iamo. McCowan explained that he was from Jardine Fleming Securities Ltd in Hong Kong and that he was there to ensure that the first 50 per cent of the contract (USD 18 million) would be disbursed to Sandline International in Hong Kong. From James Loko's office, we departed for Jacksons International Airport to see Sir Julius off on a trip to Australia. Nick Violaris, whom I recognised as Sir Julius's long-time associate, was also at Jacksons and started raising questions with me about Sandline, asking for verification on finer points of the contract of engagement. I never discuss matters of national security with anybody, let alone somebody as completely unauthorised as Violaris. But from what he was saying, I was dismayed that even those not privy to state secrets were already in the loop. In PNG, nothing stays secret for long, even the most sensitive of matters.

On Sunday, 26 January, before Spicer left for overseas, we had a briefing on all the operational estimates and projections, as well as the concept of operations, with the Project Oyster team. Spicer and Grunberg departed for London with an air of extreme confidence about them, but I could see that there was resistance growing over the engagement of Sandline among senior government officials. These included the prime minister's highly respected secretary, Noel Levi; National Intelligence Organisation director general Ovia Rauka; State Solicitor Zachary Gelu; Vele Iamo; and Secretary of Defence James Melegepa. There were a variety of concerns expressed, but the overall belief was that the engagement of Sandline would quickly prove to be massively counterproductive.

That evening, well past midnight, Haiveta and Zachary Gelu arrived at Murray Barracks' main gate and wanted to see me at Flagstaff House. The duty officer called my extension. I was too tired to see them and excused myself until the morning. Disengaging my phone, I thought of Ecclesiastes 3:

> To every thing there is a season, and a time to every
> purpose under the heaven . . . A time to love, and a time
> to hate; a time of war, and a time of peace.

And for me, it was a time for sleep. I could be spoken to in the morning unless it was something very important. It was not. By then, I was too tired anyway and slept soundly, despite all the troubles gathering on multiple fronts.

On Friday, 24 January, Rupa Mulina—the managing director of the Papua New Guinea Banking Corporation—called me and said that, from his perspective, there was not enough documentation being offered to justify the transfer of USD 18 million to Sandline. I called Vele Iamo. He told me there was a problem both with the availability of the funds and the procedural aspects and that PNGBC did not want to undermine due process, diligence, and transparency.

With Rupa Mulina standing firm, Haiveta impressed on him, 'If we do not make the payment, the government stands to lose the equipment because there are other buyers for it.' But both the governor of PNG's Central Bank, Koiari Tarata, and Rupa Mulina said there was not enough documentation to contemplate such an extravagant payment. Haiveta explained that the equipment schedule was not attached to the documents due to the top-secret nature of the operations. There was a stalemate.

Haiveta attempted to break the stalemate by writing a letter confirming that the government of PNG irrevocably guaranteed the payment of the contract sums in accordance with the schedule set out. This letter was sent to Jardines in Hong Kong despite the fact that no contract was in place and no terms of the proposed contract had been performed. That being the case, this letter would obviously carry no weight in a court of law should Sandline subsequently attempt to sue for non-performance by the government.

On Monday, 27 January, James Forrester—executive manager of PNGBC's Treasury and International Division who had been away on leave while all this was unfolding—was back in town. Rupa Mulina asked him to take over the question of the Sandline contract payment. Quickly studying the files, Forrester confirmed that there was insufficient documentation concerning the transaction. He said that it required Central Bank approval and informed Rupa Mulina and the governor of the Central Bank. It also needed contract invoices and other documentation before he could approve a foreign exchange payment of the magnitude being discussed.

In the meantime, having had an opportunity to look at the draft contract more closely, the four of us most closely concerned (Gelu, Iamo, Melegepa, and myself) put in a conference call to Grunberg in London in an attempt to renegotiate aspects of the contract that had already been signed by Haiveta on behalf of the government. Grunberg was completely inflexible. The contract had been signed. It was not up for negotiation. Sandline was already assembling the operatives and the equipment called for under the contract. Time was of the essence. No changes were possible.

In response to this, the four of us met in Vele Iamo's office to discuss the implications for the engagement of Sandline. We all agreed that Sandline had left us very little room to negotiate. In fact, there seemed to be no room. We resolved to write a memo to Noel Levi urging him to try to persuade Sir Julius to renegotiate the contract with Sandline. The letter was written by James Melegepa on our behalf:

TOP SECRET
30 January 1997
Brief to: Secretary, Department of the Prime Minister
IMPLEMENTATION OF NEC/NSC – DECISION NO 1/97

While telephone negotiations with Sandline on the Contract are progressing, certain information has now come to our notice which needs to be brought to immediate attention of the Prime Minister, Deputy Prime Minister, Minister for Defence, Minister for Planning and Minister for Justice for their further directions and instructions. We are aware that the Prime Minister may already be well aware of this information.

As advisers, we will not be seen as doing our jobs in fully advising the government over this transaction and any serious ramifications should this project somehow backfire on the government in future. Whilst we all have maintained the confidentiality of this project at its highest level and therefore our acceptance of a 'deep feed' information flow, we are not satisfied with the Contract and therefore strongly recommend that it be re-negotiated to justify the level of payment to be made. Given that the Contract is still unsigned, it is therefore not binding on the State at this stage.

1. **Background   Information   on   Sandline
   International**

We now have information that Sandline is a subsidiary of a Sierra Leone based company Heritage Oil, whose purpose is to be involved in the mining and petroleum industry. We are aware that while militarily they are very effective in their assignments they are usually very insensitive about the consequences of their actions on the host government and the people. They normally require upfront payment in full or participation in mining and petroleum ventures from the client's government prior to the engagement of their military services.

2. **Implementation of the NEC/NSC Decision**

Having noted the signed copy of the NEC/NSC decision Zachary Gelu the State Solicitor is generally satisfied to provide clearance once the Contract is finalised and all the State's concerns relating to the implementation of the project are fully addressed in the Contract. On that note, you should be assured that we are continuing discussions with Sandline via conference call to finalise the Contract by today or tomorrow.

It should however be noted that the following deviations have since occurred rendering inconsistencies with NEC/NSC decision as follows:

a)   Although it is implied that the project funding will be an ex-budget item, the K33.6 million transfers from the Bank of PNG have recently entered the Waigani Public Accounts from which a cheque for the same amount has been raised payable to Roadco, the proposed vehicle to be used for the project. This occurrence now puts at risk maintenance of secrecy of the project and any implications arising there on in terms of World Bank/IMF conditions with government. We should get EPU to immediately advise on any such implications;

b) The decision is also silent on the source of funding and the vehicle to be used for the implementation of the project. It is our understanding that MRDC at that point was being considered initially as the vehicle. In order to maintain the secrecy of the project, we changed to Roadco which was now a shelf company and the directors were all government officials. As a company incorporated under the Companies Act, Roadco would be more flexible and faster in making decisions compared to any Statutory Authority which will require compliance with all normal government requirements with implications on timing and the speed of implementing the project. An NEC/NSC decision will therefore be required to formalise the above changes, including rewording of the Contract in favour of Roadco and Sandline International.

3. **Concerns of the Contractor**

We have since yesterday communicated with Sandline to make amendments to sections of the Contract deemed unsatisfactory to the state. They are as follows:

a) The 3 months period in the contract is far too short to justify the USD36 million payment from the State. We have advised that the Contract be extended to 12 months, inclusive of the 3 months for the specific operational assignment and an additional 9 months for the training purposes. Sandline indicated that such extension will cost an additional US$9.00 million in the Contract price but this counter bid was rejected. Sandline insists that it uses the helicopters as proposed by them.

b) We also raised with Sandline the concern that the timing of the second payment is not satisfactory. It needs to be tied to the primary mission objective being achieved and not just the delivery of the equipment. This follows concern that if Sandline leave the country after 3 months without achieving their mission objectives the state will still be obliged to pay. Sandline however insisted that normally they would require upfront payment for their type of cost but in the PNG case they have already made concessions by allowing the second payment within 30 days of their arrival in the country.

Other than minor concessions on cosmetic matters, our team was generally disappointed that on substantive issues Sandline's positions were mostly nonnegotiable. In view of the foregoing we are not convinced of the advisability of executing the Contract without at least some attempt at your level to secure further negotiations with Sandline for concessions on the concerns raised. Having given our views and concerns, we recommend that the proposed arrangements per NEC/NSC Decision No 1/97 are not implementable unless and until these concerns are addressed substantially.

James Melegepa, Secretary for Defence
Jerry Singirok, Commander PNGDF
Zachary Gelu, State Solicitor
Vele Iamo, Acting Deputy Secretary, Finance

This top-secret memo to Noel Levi, secretary of the prime minister's department, was signed by us as heads of the responsible government departments in an attempt to ensure that the nation's interests were protected. We wanted the Sandline contract in its present form to be stopped by the prime minister or, at the very least, substantially renegotiated. When Sir Julius got the memo, he made no comments; and instead, he sat on it, which was most unusual for him.

Zachary Gelu, the state solicitor, confirmed to Vele Iamo that he was not prepared to give legal clearance for the execution of the contract because, quite apart from the technical deficiencies identified in the memo to Noel Levi, he had not seen the NEC decision. Gelu spoke to Michael Grunberg, who was the author of the draft contract, for a couple of hours. Over the phone, Grunberg made it very clear to Gelu that Sandline was not willing to renegotiate any of its terms. This made Gelu angry, and he advised Grunberg that, as far as he was concerned, the government would be advised against executing the contract in its present form.

We also agreed that I must contact Tim Spicer and Michael Grunberg about our concerns on the Mi-17 helicopters and the long-term technical implications. This was based on staff advice from the directors of Technical Services and Air Operations and the commanding officer of the ATS. The concerns I raised in my letter were as follows:

SERIOUS CONCERNS ABOUT MI 17 SUSTAINMENT DURING AND POST OPERATION OYSTER

During the review of the Contract I expressed to the Contract Committee serious problems of having in my inventory two additional Mi-17 helicopters. My reasons are as follows:

a) Costs for running in terms of fuel, spare parts, training are beyond budget.
b) More importantly, I already have four UH I H Iroquois of which three are operational, two Bell 212 are being purchased with down payment already made to Hevi Lift Mount Hagen. The two Bell 212

are already painted and require only the completion of payment and other Contract provisions to be fulfilled.

c) I do not see having more than three different types of helicopters in my inventory as it is totally unacceptable in terms of various skills, maintenance and sustainment issues.

I would suggest at the earliest to reduce costs and address the long term benefits to the PNGDF that we can make do with helicopters already in the country for transportation while Sandline negotiates with Hevi Lift Mount Hagen for the acquisition of the remaining Bell 212s. While the Mi-24s are important for the operations. This will be reflected in the Contract as we fax it back to you today.

I hope my reasons are appreciated by you to allow time to make necessary changes.

Jerry Singirok, MBE
Brigadier General, Commander

Spicer replied that they would not negotiate with Hevilift for the Bell 212 as it was far too late and too difficult to undertake the necessary technical evaluations of the machines and ownership validation. As he put it, pursuing the Bell 212 option would seriously affect the agreed timescales for the operation. He further stated that the Bell 212s were not suitable for the type of operations envisaged. He added that if the contract was not signed, he would have no choice but to disband the manpower team that had been assembled and subsequently rehire the necessary team members, including redrafting the specialists needed for this type of operation if and when the green light was given. He sent an urgent fax to underline his advice:

Jerry please urgently reconsider your evaluation and, if you agree with our analysis, advise the contract team that the question of the Bells be dropped so that we continue on already predetermined path. I look forward for your confirmation to the above.

This fax was dictated by Spicer from Port Moresby, where, as it turned out, he was now moving between the offices of Haiveta and Vele Iamo in an effort to get the contract signed without further delay. He was successful. On 31 January, the contract was signed by Haiveta, along with Acting Deputy Secretary for Finance Vele Iamo. Against all the provisions of the Financial Management Act and with no parliamentary approval, Haiveta signed the contract on behalf of the Independent State of Papua New Guinea, committing USD 36 million. A draft copy of the contract is attached as annex A.

On Saturday, 1 February, I was attending a mourning ceremony at the residence of Lieutenant Sembisan at Taurama Barracks when Haiveta called me on my analogue phone to advise me that the contract was signed and that the funds were being transferred to Hong Kong. He asked me to ensure that the operational planning remained on schedule. He also reminded me that it was an election year and that his party, Pangu Pati, were anticipating returning more new members to the next Parliament in August 1997 to form the new government.

I called the commanding officer (CO) of Second Battalion (2RPIR), Lt Col Michael Tamalanga, to alert him that I would be visiting him later in the day. At the same time, I contacted Indonesian Embassy defence attaché Lieutenant Colonel Ruru to request airspace clearance for a flight from South Africa with the first batch of arms and a Sandline training team into PNG. This done, I got on an Air Niugini commercial flight for Wewak. On board the flight was my relative Bernard Narokobi, who was the local member for Parliament for Wewak Open. He was sitting next to me in business class. He said, 'Commander, what is this I hear that Chan has hired a private army from Africa to come and bomb our people on Bougainville?'

I thought quickly about what I should say to Narokobi, if anything. My mother was from the Aropes-speaking language and came from the same area as Bernard, so I was reasonably confident about my reply.

'Only three MPs are handling this operation on Bougainville: the PM, his deputy, and the minister for defence. Haiveta called me the other night and said the contract was signed, and the first contract instalment was being transferred to Hong Kong. It was for USD 18 million.'

Narokobi replied, 'You know what this will do to our nation?'

I said, 'Yes, I have a fair idea.'

I inspected the facilities at Moem Barracks with the CO. This was the regiment that built my earlier military career. However, today the facilities lacked maintenance, the grass was overgrown, and the golf course was all gone. This was the reality of the neglect of our defence force facilities throughout the country. The government was spending too much money on Bougainville with too little left over to maintain the barracks. But the CO was optimistic that he could accommodate the Sandline training team and the SFU members in transit to the Urimo jungle training range. On my way out of the barracks, I inspected a quarter guard at the main gate and then caught the afternoon commercial flight back to Port Moresby.

On Tuesday, 4 February, the international division of the Central Bank of PNG electronically transferred to Shanghai Banking Corporation in Hong Kong a cheque from PNGBC (cheque number 436597 from North Fly Development Company Pty Ltd) in the amount of PGK 24,657,535.00, dated 24 January 1997. This cheque had been issued to Tim Spicer earlier, but he had been told not to present it until the funds were made available. The amount was the kina equivalent at that day's rate of USD 18 million, the 50 per cent deposit as stipulated in the Sandline contract. So USD 18 million was now credited to account number 600774426, Sandline's operating account in Hong Kong.

It was Friday, 7 February. I was being driven from Jacksons Airport to Murray Barracks when Sir Peter Barter called me. 'Jerry', he said as he always addressed me.

I replied, 'Yes, sir.'

'I hear these Africans are arriving, and Sir Julius is not backing off. You know what you're doing to the people of Bougainville and Papua New Guinea?'

I said, 'Yes, sir, I understand your concern.'

He asked me again, 'Did you inform the PM about the serious consequences of a major military offensive on innocent people, and what are you personally doing about it?'

I was uptight, upset, and on the spot, not with Sir Peter but with the way all these events were unfolding, seemingly beyond anyone's control. It had become a living nightmare. I said, 'Sir, we have already written to the PM about our concerns and are awaiting his response. I was with member for Wewak, Bernard Narokobi, a few days ago, and he expressed the same concerns as you. Sir, I am looking at other avenues to get assistance, but it appears it may be too late as the contract has already been signed.'

He asked who had signed the contract. I said, 'The deputy prime minister, Chris Haiveta.'

I sensed that Sir Peter was upset. He knew me well enough to speak frankly. 'Madness', he said and hung up. Sir Peter was my local member of Parliament, and he had every right to speak his mind to me. He represented our people of Madang. We were both from the same province, and besides, he was the member of Parliament most closely associated with the government's peace efforts on Bougainville.

It was way past five, and I went home and changed before I returned to the command officers' mess for the usual Friday happy hour, when officers and friends get together for drinks and a catch-up. I was not a serious drinker by any means but had always seized the opportunity to mingle with subordinate officers and departmental officials. It was good to catch up with navy captain Reginald Renagi, who seemed to be there most Fridays at a particular corner of the mess, along with navy commander Alois Tom Ur.

After an hour or so, I departed with my ADC, Capt. John Keleto, back to Flagstaff House. I had some very important concerns to discuss with my wife Weni, who had seen me disillusioned over the handling of Bougainville and had assisted me in nursing my war injuries. She was concerned about my state of mind, and she knew that the recent death of Lieutenant Sembisan and the signing of the contract had been weighing on me. With a few moments free, it was a good time for a talk.

Weni told me that she was worried about the Bougainvilleans and that she did not like the look of the Sandline operatives, Spicer and Grunberg, who had come to Flagstaff House. She said they looked very unfriendly and that she could not stand them. At that moment, as Weni was expressing her reservations, an important realisation came to me. 'Weni,' I said, 'you know what? I do not think I can be part of these upcoming operations with Sandline. I have seen enough suffering. I am contemplating leaving the force. The government can appoint another commander.'

There was a long silence. I told Weni about what Sir Peter Barter had said to me earlier in the day. He had asked what the outside world would think of us. Sir Peter held Weni in high regard and was an admirer of her work with the National Broadcasting Commission and now the Australian Broadcasting Corporation. She said, 'Jerry, Sir Peter is right. I just do not know how you can justify all the killings of innocent people. There are no smart bombs in this world, only stupid and dumb people. When people talk about smart bombs, I think dumb generals.

'Weni,' I said, 'if only Sir Julius had allowed me to study in the USA in 1996, as I was hoping for, I would not be in this dilemma. The last thing that I want to do in the world is to leave the military. But I am now forced to consider doing just that, to leave on my own accord, as the whole Sandline deal is so outrageous and criminal.'

We talked well into the night. We discussed our children and our future. Futua had just settled in at Wesley College in Auckland. Maib and Moka were at primary school, and Alfred was schooling in Madang. We had a mortgage to pay off on our property for the next ten years. Our future looked bleak—full of uncertainties and very far from promising. In the meantime, Sir Julius wanted me to go to the Philippines to explore the possibility of getting more assistance with military training and hardware.

The next day, Saturday, 8 February, Tim Spicer called me mid-morning to inform me that arrangements were now complete for the Sandline training team to arrive along with other technical staff. I called David Sode in his office at Internal Revenue Commission House as he had asked me to drop by for a chat. Sode was from Ialibu in the Southern Highlands; he had a law degree from the University of Papua New Guinea and was commissioner of customs, having been appointed in 1994. He, too, was upset that things were moving much faster than expected. As we stood in his office, looking down at people wandering about aimlessly in the street, Sode said, 'You know, bro, these people have no future. We need to save this nation from going to the dogs. We have set up a regime where the foreigners always seem to get the upper hand. Sandline is just another example. None of us want them, only the politicians thinking about the national elections.'

I agreed. Sode said he had to give his concurrence after a ministerial direction to waive tax and duties on imports of Sandline military assets and hardware and cash transfers. 'It's all tax-free, bro. We are losing big time. Thirty-six million in US dollars in less than a few months, not bad for a company who can just turn up on our doorsteps and make such money. But at whose expense?' he went on. 'And what are you going to do about it?'

'Bro,' I said, 'believe me, it's been tough just being in the front line of all this as commander. I have to live with the failures of High Speed II, the Kangu Beach massacre, and the hostages. And now I will also have to live for the rest of my life with the trauma that will result from all the killings that will be facilitated by those tax and customs exemptions you have been issuing. The responsibility will not be mine alone. But I may be the one who has to resign. For now, though, it's too early. I will vie for time.'

Sode took me to the lift, and we shook hands as I left. That made one more departmental head to oppose the Sandline engagement.

I spent the remaining afternoon with Sir Barry Holloway at his Paga Hill flat. I told Sir Barry about my predicament, and he listened intensely. He said, 'Jerry, you do realise that this is an election year, don't you?'

'Yes, sir.'

'Well,' Sir Barry continued, 'all these politicians and their political parties need money to fund their elections in June. I can already see the pattern of their behaviour in soliciting for contracts where there are loose ends.'

I said, 'Please explain.'

'Well,' he said, 'if you look at the US$36 million paid out in Hong Kong, our politicians will have already discussed with Tim Spicer how much they will get out of the deal. The banks in Hong Kong are liberal and many times do not carry out due diligence and just transfer money into hidden accounts as long as the funds are available on instructions.'

Sir Barry continued, 'Very few politicians will put the people's welfare before their personal interest. In Papua New Guinea, it's hard to find honest leaders.'

Although Sir Barry had promised me and others umpteen times that he would quit smoking, he lit another cigarette before asking the obvious question. 'So what are you going to do about the operations in Bougainville with Sandline?'

I replied, 'Sir, too many bad things have happened in the past eighteen months. I am contemplating resigning from the defence force.

He nodded and asked. 'Have you read what mercenaries do in Africa? These are hired killers, ruthless and barbaric murderers. They are bloodthirsty when it comes to securing diamond and gold mines and gas fields and kill innocent people near and around the mines with attack helicopters and missiles. They will destroy anything that moves. I have been to Rhodesia and South Africa, and I know what they are capable of doing. They have a very bad history.'

'Sir Barry,' I said, 'I am going to the Philippines on Friday next week and will be away for just over one week.'

As I bade him goodbye and he shook my hand, I said, 'You will be the first one to know about my future when I return from the Philippines.'

On the way home, I was comforted to know that at least Sir Barry, who had come here as a young patrol officer from Australia and had made his permanent home here, was one of the few pioneer settlers who cared about PNG. A distinguished politician, the first speaker of the National Parliament, a minister of finance in the government of Sir Michael Somare and, until 1982, in Sir Julius Chan's first government,

Sir Barry had become my closest confidant. I would never go past him if I needed advice on how to handle an issue that affected the defence force or the nation at large. I was indeed thankful to have unprecedented access to Sir Barry. He was more than a friend. He was a very special mentor.

For my part, as long as I remained the commander of the defence force, I had no choice but to obey directions from the duly elected executive government. That is what we were always taught, and that is what was required of our military service by the Defence Act and by the constitution that I was sworn to uphold. Of course, if an order was manifestly illegal, then I had a duty to refuse it, but could it be said that the engagement of Sandline was illegal under the constitution? From any ordinary reading of the constitution, which expressly prohibits the engagement of foreigners on combat duties within the Independent State of Papua New Guinea, the Sandline contract was a clear breach of the constitution and was therefore an illegal act. But a definitive ruling on this was a matter for the solicitor general, not me. When I had discussed the matter with Zachary Gelu in late January during the negotiations over the draft contract, his view was that the time for such considerations was long past since the government was already committed to the engagement of Sandline. I was not optimistic, nor did I think this was an adequate response from the solicitor general to a government that had signed an illegal and unconstitutional contract.

On Monday, 10 February, the first Sandline-contracted aircraft, an Antonov cargo carrier from Air Sofia, landed with the initial batch of mercenaries, weapons, and ammunition. After clearance from customs and immigration, they commenced setting up at Kiki Barracks on the opposite side of the main runway at Jacksons International Airport. In the meantime, Tim Spicer and his command element had rented a flat at Fort Williams along Vaivai Street in East Boroko. Spicer was very happy as things were now moving much faster; the initial payment of money was in the bank, and he had all the resources that he needed available to him.

On Wednesday, 12 February, I had a very important visitor from Canberra. Col. Mark Radford was the UK defence attaché in Canberra, accredited also to PNG. He was a well-spoken career officer in the British Army. I hoped that he would not raise the issue of Sandline International. He did not. We spoke about our nomination of Officer Cadet Dalos Umul to attend Sandhurst and my hope that, every year, PNG would be able to send an officer cadet to Sandhurst. This was an important investment so that PNG and the UK could build personal contacts that could be drawn on when our officers operated as coalition partners on peacekeeping or enforcement missions globally.

On the same day, I got a call from the CO of Air Transport Squadron to advise that both the CASA CN-235 and the Israeli IAI Arava 201 transport aircraft had been serviced and that airworthy certificates had been issued for them to fly. This was good news for us as we needed air mobility urgently to continue sustaining the defence force as well as our efforts in Bougainville.

I walked down the staircase to the adjourning floor where Minister Ijape's office was located to inform him of the arrival of the Air Sofia flight. I knocked on his door. His personal assistant answered. 'Sorry, sir, you just missed him as he is checking in to go overseas.'

I asked, 'Where to?'

She replied, 'Hong Kong.' This surprised me, but then I recalled what Sir Barry had told me over the weekend about ministers running around for commissions and election funds. On the same day, Tim Spicer also left, ostensibly for Cairns, but Cairns was just a cover. It turned out that he was transiting from Cairns to Hong Kong so that he could team up there with Haiveta and Ijape. Spicer, we later learnt, had arranged for the travel of Haiveta and Ijape to Hong Kong. It is not difficult to imagine what transpired.

On Thursday morning, 13 February, Nick Violaris—of Greek origin—boarded Air Niugini PX 060 at eleven thirty and arrived at Cairns in time to check in at the international counter by 1.25 p.m. He was comfortably seated in QF 085 bound for Hong Kong also. Hardly a coincidence. In Hong Kong, the three main Sandline executives were all gathered together—Tony Buckingham, Michael Grunberg, and Tim Spicer—while the PNG delegation comprised Haiveta, Ijape, and Violaris. For all six to be in Hong Kong at the same time was unusual, to say the least. But the obvious conclusion was that Spicer had the money and the access to the Sandline account with its USD 18 million from the PNG government. It was no trouble for one of the Sandline bank account signatories to walk into the bank and withdraw USD 1.5 million from the account to share among Sandline's new clients. The PNG delegation departed Hong Kong on about 17 February for Singapore.

On the same day, we had arranged to host the Israeli ambassador, who was accredited to PNG from Canberra. James Melegepa and I gave the ambassador a brief on our bilateral relationship with Israel and assured him that we looked forward to developing the defence relationship further. The Israeli company Elbit Systems was already installing satellite communication facilities throughout the country in collaboration with the PNG Fisheries Board. During the meeting, James Melegepa confirmed what I had already established, that Ijape was out of the country, travelling with Haiveta to Hong Kong.

I asked Melegepa to follow up on the PGK 6 million for SFU sustainment funds that had been approved along with Sandline's first USD 18 million. He said he would talk to the Department of Finance. The next day, he advised that no such funds would be made available. We were told to draw our counterpart expenses from our recurrent funds. This was a massive and wholly unexpected kick in the gut. It put our ability to work alongside Sandline in jeopardy and meant, in effect, that Sandline would have an almost completely free hand in implementing Operation Oyster. A less desirable outcome would be difficult to imagine.

Later that day, I made an appointment to see Gabriel Dusava, the secretary for foreign affairs, to confirm with him my official trip to the Philippines. It was always good to meet with Dusava as he was a smart and articulate career service officer. He said, 'Commander, Ambassador Pokasui is our man on the ground in Manila. He is not new to you, having served with you in the defence force. He has your itinerary worked out, and all will be in order for your trip.'

My official team for the visit included navy captain Alfred Aikung, chief of logistics; Fred Punagi from Defence Intelligence and Policy,

Department of Defence; Jake Bentegui from the defence housing project and a Philippine national; and my ADC, Capt. John Keleto. Our date for travel was set for Saturday, 15 February. It was a casual Friday evening, so I called on Sir Barry, who was at his son Joe Holloway's business centre at Gordon.

Over a few glasses of wine, he asked how things were, and I reminded him what he had told me about the cut the politicians would be taking out of the Sandline payments. Well, that was happening right as we spoke in Hong Kong. I said it had been confirmed that Haiveta, Ijape, and Violaris were in Hong Kong with Spicer, Grunberg, and Buckingham. Sir Barry was visibly upset at this news. He asked, 'You mean Nicholas Violaris, that Greek hanger-on and a close associate of the PM, is also in the pack?' I said I believed so as I had been reliably informed that he transited through Cairns as a decoy and teamed up with Tim Spicer, who had departed for Cairns the day before. From what I had been told by airline sources, they boarded the same Qantas flight from Cairns to Hong Kong.

I asked, 'So who do you think he was representing?'

Sir Barry replied, 'Why would Violaris be there in the first place? It's so suspicious and outrageous. Only in Papua New Guinea. When will they learn, these lunatics?'

The conversation then turned to the question of my immediate future. 'Have you decided on quitting the military when you return from the Philippines?'

'I think so,' I said. 'Weni and I have talked about my future for some time, and it is becoming more and more evident that the upcoming operations in Bougainville are likely to have a serious impact on innocent civilians. Weni is worried about my emotional and psychological well-being. I have taken recent defence force casualties and deaths very hard, and I don't know if I can go on like this.'

'Let me know when you return,' he replied. 'And we will talk further.' We had a few more rounds of drinks, and I offered Sir Barry a lift home to Paga Hill.

The next day, Saturday, 15 February, Maj. Gilbert Toropo was with me at the check-in at Jacksons International Airport as we went through a last-minute 'to do' list together. I could see among serious concerns the uncertainty in him as a result of the prime minister's most recent direction to transfer the SFU to the prime minister's department. I assured Toropo that many decisions being made at the political level would be overshadowed and quite possibly reversed or forgotten after the general elections in June.

In the meantime, I planned to make use of the training and operational opportunities Sandline had promised as a means of transferring knowledge, skills, and technology to the SFU. I reminded him that I was interested in making sure that Sgt Francis Jakis, other up-and-coming junior non-commissioned officers, and other junior soldiers whom he could identify were exposed to additional training opportunities. I wanted them to be groomed, and I was hoping that new opportunities would emerge to train them with the Philippines Special Forces Training School at Fort Andres Bonifacio as the US Army only offered one space per year at Fort Benning, Georgia.

I said, 'Sandline trainers and aircrew are here, and more will be arriving. Along with Lt Col. Yaura Sasa, our liaison officer, you are my representative with the Sandline team. Good luck, Gilbert, and please take care of them.'

As I waited with the four other members of my team for the flight to be called, I reflected on how we had got ourselves into this position with Sandline. Should I have taken a more forthright line with the ministers on the purely military aspects of Operation Oyster? The ministers knew that I had long ago concluded that there was no prospect of a military solution to Bougainville at any acceptable level of force. But had I done enough to lay out the thinking behind this conclusion, driven as it was by long years of my leading military operations on Bougainville, both as a junior officer and as the senior military commander on the ground, and reinforced by the military disasters of Operation High Speed II, the Kangu Beach massacre, and the constant stream of dead and wounded soldiers coming back from Bougainville?

It is easy to say that decisions such as that behind the engagement of Sandline are ultimately a political responsibility. But it was also true that Stephen Raphael and I were the ones who had drawn up the NEC submission that led to the engagement of Sandline in the first place. The more I thought about this, the more conflicted I felt, and the more that my early resignation as commander seemed like the only honourable path.

Conversely, it was also true, I thought, seeking comfort in the words of the scriptures, that there was a time for war and a time for peace and a time for every purpose under heaven. If only I could bring myself to believe that, I thought, I might find some comfort in the words of Ecclesiastes. But the larger truth was one that I could not escape. The larger truth was that, increasingly, this looked like it was turning into a story in which there would be no good guys—only deeply flawed human beings, of whom I was evidently one, a truly humbling and deeply disturbing thought.

CHAPTER 3

Military Appreciation of Sandline's Operation Oyster

I know it is my disposition, that difficulties and dangers do but increase my desire of attempting them.

—Horatio Nelson

As I settled into my flight to Singapore from Port Moresby on Saturday, 15 February 1997; and then onto Manila the next day, I set my mind to a reappraisal of the military aspects of Sandline's Operation Oyster. For some considerable time, I had been saying—with my long operational experience as the senior military commander in Bougainville—that I did not believe there was a military solution to the Bougainville crisis at any acceptable level of force. In contracting Sandline to launch a fresh military offensive in Bougainville, the prime minister and his senior ministerial colleagues were saying, in effect, that I had got it wrong. They had accepted Sandline's sales pitch that there was a military solution, that the rebel leaders *could* be 'neutralised' or be forced back to the negotiating table, and that the Panguna mine *could* be reopened. Could they be correct? Could I, as the government's senior military adviser, be wrong? Was I guilty of being frightened off by the obvious difficulties and dangers that Admiral Lord Nelson might have relished had he been in my shoes?

To examine my thinking, I pulled out the government's contract with Sandline and looked through it again with as much dispassion as I could muster. I also had with me the consultancy report that Spicer had written over the Christmas break. The obvious beginning point for any military appreciation was to confirm what it was that Sandline had contracted with the government to deliver. Apart from two training and intelligence gathering objectives, the key outcome was defined in the preamble of the agreement as 'conducting offensive operations in Bougainville in conjunction with PNG Defence Force to render the BRA [Bougainville Revolutionary Army] militarily ineffective and repossess the Panguna mine'. The primary objective was again defined as 'the rendering of the BRA militarily ineffective'.

What did these terms mean? To render the BRA militarily ineffective was to force it to cease all military operations, hand in its weapons, and submit itself to the mercy of the government, in this case the normal judicial processes of arrest, detention, and trial or a general amnesty as the case may be. To repossess the Panguna mine was not just to secure a very big hole in the ground since, on its own, the hole was worthless. Spicer claimed that the Panguna mine had psychological value, and in his consultancy report, he went so far as to argue that retaking and holding the mine was the 'key element to the problem—the cause of it, the symbol of it and probably the end of the conflict'.

He saw Panguna mine as the 'centre of gravity' of the Bougainville conflict. There was a time, as a much more junior and inexperienced officer, and at a much earlier point in the conflict when I might have thought in similar terms. But I no longer shared that view. The mine and its associated infrastructure, running all the way from Panguna down to Loloho, might well be considered 'ground of tactical importance', but it was not the centre of gravity in any serious attempt to resolve the Bougainville conflict. The political, social, and environmental situation on Bougainville was the true centre of gravity, not the mine.

Seen in this light, the mine was only worth anything to anybody if it could be put back into production. So the necessary military aim must be to create the conditions under which the mine could be reopened and start producing again. In the case of the Panguna mine, this *could* be the flow-on from forcing the BRA to give up its weapons and surrender itself to the civilian authorities since, if there was no longer an enemy force, there would be no threat to the reopening of the mine. In practice, however, it was important to remember that reopening the Panguna mine was not just about securing the actual mine. It was also about rehiring, and providing protection to, the workforce that would need to be reintroduced to the mine and ensuring the physical security of its heavy excavators, ore crushers, and trucks. It was also about securing the entire length of the 35 km-long port-mine access road that was needed to service the mine and the port at Loloho Bay, from which the ore needed to be shipped. Also vulnerable to sabotage and needing to be secured was the power supply and the associated pylons carrying power to the mine for the ore crushers, the other mining machinery, and the accommodation blocks. Reopening the mine was a very tall order that required not just the application of enough military force to provide the necessary security for mine operations, road and port security, power generation, electricity supply, and a functioning pipeline but also the agreement of affected landowners and the involvement of the Bougainville Transitional Government (later the Bougainville Autonomous Government), none of which was impossible but all of which extraordinarily difficult. One recent estimate puts the investment required to reopen the mine at a very conservative figure of USD 5 billion. Still, the starting point to all this was undoubtedly the requirement to deal with the BRA, which brings me back to the primary objective in the contract.

How difficult was it, from a military perspective, to neutralise the BRA? Spicer, in his consultancy report that led to the government's decision to hire Sandline to undertake the task in conjunction with the SFU, estimated the BRA's strength as being 'up to 1,000'. Of these, he estimated that the hard core of fighters 'probably number 200–300'. This was as good an estimate as any, though it needed to be remembered that the population of Bougainville was around 300,000, of whom upwards of 50,000 might be fighting-age males, a proportion of whom provided a potential recruitment base for the BRA.

The BRA forces were highly dispersed, operating typically in no more than section-sized units (ten to eleven men each) or less. They were lightly armed, generally with World War II–era Japanese leftovers—second- and third-hand weapons—reinforced by more modern rifles and ammunition captured from the Papua New Guinea Defence Force and the Royal Papua New Guinea Constabulary (RPNGC). They did not operate on any centralised basis of command and control. Rather, they were better thought of as a collection of largely independent, loosely organised, criminal or quasi-military gangs. For a lightly armed and highly dispersed enemy force, the BRA had proved remarkably effective for their size. They were aided by the jungle and the mountainous terrain in which they operated and the fact that, as a non-uniformed force, they were completely indistinguishable from the local population.

Spicer's military concept was to apply 'precision, cohesion, surprise, speed, mobility, firepower and security' to the operation. The key to his concept was the ability to locate enemy targets by intercepting airborne signals and communications intelligence and analysis, plus high-frequency (HF) and ultra-high frequency (UHF) direction finding. This concept relied heavily on the enemy revealing their locations through their use of HF radios to communicate with one another. Once the targets were located, Spicer relied on mobility and overwhelming firepower to take them out. I made some notes against each of Spicer's headings:

> **Precision.** Accuracy of target location. The ability to pinpoint enemy locations and then to distinguish between enemy forces and the civilian population. And then to use that knowledge to capture or destroy the enemy without incurring heavy civilian casualties. Spicer proposes to use signals intercept and communications intelligence (ELINT and SIGINT) and analysis plus electronic direction finding as his primary tool. This may be effective if the enemy is unaware that his electronic emissions are being captured, analysed and

pinpointed. If the enemy is aware that there is a risk of his signals being monitored, he will simply maintain radio silence and rely instead on foot messengers. In which case, so much for target acquisition. There are two other assumptions that need testing. First, the assumption that all electronic emissions are likely to be enemy-based. A handful of civilians in Bougainville have access to two-way radios and computers, and so do many of the missionary stations, schools, hospitals and government care centres. So careful discrimination to separate the wheat from the chaff will be necessary. The second assumption is that enemy transmissions will always be in English and susceptible to transcription and analysis by Spicer's electronic warfare operators. But Bougainvilleans use a wide variety of local dialects, none of which would be familiar to English speakers. A radio call in the Nasioi language, say, would need to be translated before there would be any chance of working out whether it was an enemy transmission or that of an innocent person. How many non-Bougainvilleans speak Nasioi? Or Korokoro Motuna, Telei or Halia to name just a few of the many independent languages on the main island of Bougainville. Of course, if we are lucky, enemy transmissions might sometimes be in Tok Pisin, the lingua franca of PNG, but it is very unlikely they would be in English, much less Africaans.

Cohesion. The ability to hit multiple targets simultaneously for the purpose of throwing the enemy off balance and gaining the upper hand. This could be through the use of both airborne and ground forces attacking one or more targets to a pre-arranged schedule. This requires multiple, real-time target identification. This is very much easier to achieve on paper or in the military classroom than in the real world. I am doubtful that a high degree of cohesion is achievable in the difficult terrain and foreign language environment of Bougainville. Spicer describes the ability to hit multiple targets simultaneously as a 'must'. Realistically, I would judge this ability as being near to impossible to achieve in the context of Bougainville where the BRA and civilians blend so perfectly into one another because they are, to all intents and purposes, one and the same.

Surprise. Requires the enemy to be unaware that government and mercenary forces are in the act of closing in and targeting them. Special Forces are the classic means of achieving stealth and surprise. Tactical level surprise is certainly a possibility, but Special Forces have much the same difficulties as the rest of us in distinguishing between enemy fighters and civilians. Unlike the Vietcong, the BRA do not wear black pyjama pants. But, certainly, carrying a gun is not a good idea if Special Forces are in the vicinity. Therefore, the assumption has to be that enemy forces will cache their weapons in secure prearranged hiding places if they think a large scale military operation is in prospect.

Speed and mobility. This is the domain of helicopter transports and gunships. Two Mi-17 helicopter transports are to be assigned to the troop mobility task. They are to be escorted by two Mi-24 helicopter gunships. Helicopters are wonderful for troop mobility in jungle terrain. But, as we saw in Operation High Speed II, helicopters are also very vulnerable to rotor damage and various types of equipment failure. The PNGDF lost both of its assigned UH-1H Iroquois helicopters from gunfire damage to their rotors early in Operation High Speed II. It cannot be assumed that the Sandline Mi-17 helicopters will be any more immune from gunfire damage than the UH-1H helicopters. The Mi-24 Hind gunships on the other hand are armour plated and have titanium rotor blades so are reasonably resistant to ground-based rifle and heavy machine gun fire. But they are not totally immune to ground attack. In the Iraq–Iran War, for example, the Iraqis lost over a hundred helicopters from ground attack, including 40 Mi-8s, 15 Mi-17s and 32 Mi24/25s. In the Second Chechen War, the Russians lost 23 Mi-8s and 16 Mi-24s, some to anti-tank missiles and some to heavy machine gun fire. In the Sri Lankan Civil War, the army lost 7 Mi-17s, all to rifle fire. The BRA are not thought to have anti-tank or shoulder-fired MANPAD (man-portable air defence systems) missiles such as the American Raytheon Stinger that was used to such devastating effect in Afghanistan against Soviet Mi-17s and Mi-24s. However, the Stinger missile or its Chinese and Russian variants can be purchased on the black market, as can anti-tank weapons, so if the BRA have enough advance notice of the likely appearance in theatre of helicopter gunships it is to be expected that they will try to up-gun their weaponry.

Firepower. Sandline are certainly not stinting in the supply of ordnance under the agreement. For the 2 Mi-24 gunships they are providing 1,000 rounds of 57 mm high explosive, 20,000 rounds of 23 mm ball, 5,000 rounds of 23 mm tracer and 12,500 23 mm links. For the Special Forces, they are providing 500,000 rounds of 7.62 x 39 and 250,000 rounds of 7.62 x 54 ammunition, plus 100,000 rounds of 12.7 mm ball and 25,000 rounds of 12.7 mm tracer. To supplement these stocks, Sandline are also providing 2,000 40 mm grenades, 2,500 rounds of 60 mm HE and 2,500 rounds of 82 mm HE for their mortars. In addition, 250,000 ammo links are to be supplied along with 1,000 AK-47 magazines, plus illumination flares and smoke/frag grenades. This is a massive quantity of ordnance to

target a lightly armed, irregular enemy force estimated
to be in the low hundreds and travelling mainly on
foot and at night. Evidently, Sandline is provisioning
for a much more protracted conflict than ministers are
bargaining for. Possibly years rather than months.

Later, looking through these notes, I jotted down some further
points. First, it was extremely concerning that Sandline had paid so
little attention to the maintenance of operational security (OPSEC). As
long ago as April the previous year, I warned Spicer not to use fax or
phone to discuss any aspects of Operation Contravene, as it was then
called. Since then, he had completely ignored my caution. He had been
a regular telephone caller to Minister Ijape and had sent numerous
detailed faxes to both myself and other interested parties in Port
Moresby about Sandline's plans and intentions. It was a near certainty
that Australian Intelligence had, by now, built up a very detailed picture
of what was being planned from its signals intelligence (SIGINT)
capabilities, if from nothing else. They would have noted the arrival of
the Air Sofia Antonov flight at Jacksons and had probably secured a
complete breakdown of its weapons load and other equipment.

Further, as comments made to me by Bernard Narokobi and Sir
Peter Barter suggested, knowledge that Chan was planning a large-
scale military operation in Bougainville was now widely talked about
in Port Moresby. It had to be assumed that Bougainville sympathisers
in the capital would have tipped off the BRA, in general terms at least,
to the forthcoming offensive, and they may even have obtained copies,
by now, of the consultancy report and the agreement between the
government and Sandline International. It would at least be prudent
to assume so. I concluded that the achievement of the operational
surprise on which Spicer had pinned so much of his own as well as the
government's expectations could not be depended on and had indeed
largely evaporated.

Almost certainly, this meant that the BRA—knowing of the
government's intentions—would counter Operation Oyster by
maintaining strict cell phone and radio silence during the period that

Sandline and the SFU were on the island. It was also possible that BRA operatives would cache their weapons for the duration and take up the appearance of farming or some other civilian occupation until the threat passed. A passive response such as this would be very effective in denying targets to the Sandline and SFU forces. If the BRA were looking for a more active response to the mercenary threat, two obvious possibilities presented themselves. They could decide that the Mi-17 and Mi-24 helicopters were the key to both firepower and mobility and attempt to destroy them while they were parked on the ground at the Loloho forward tactical base. Any crude anti-tank gun, mortars, satchel charges, or even heavy machine guns could do sufficient damage to ground the helicopter force. And, as there were only two of each type and no reserves back in Port Moresby, this would represent a serious impediment to the Sandline/SFU force. A second option, if the BRA had appreciated the extent to which the government forces were planning to depend on ELINT/SIGINT/EW and radio direction finding to locate enemy forces, was that they might choose to try to spoof Sandline by placing the Radio Free Bougainville transmitter in or near a village that they were happy to have strafed to try to create civilian casualties on a mass scale. Or they could try for the same result by making spoof mobile phone calls in the name of one or more of the BRA commanders in or near a village that they were happy to sacrifice. Their calculation might be the obvious political one that the government could not long withstand the international condemnation that would result from mass civilian casualties occurring as a result of indiscriminate mercenary action.

Second, the initial contract period for Operation Oyster was set at three months from the date that the first contract payment was banked into Sandline's account. The payment went off to Hong Kong last thing on Friday, 31 January, and the funds were presumably lodged to Sandline's account overnight, suggesting that Saturday, 1 February, marked the start of the three-month contract period. This meant, in turn, that the operation would run until 30 April, whereupon it would either conclude or be the subject of an extension. If the BRA were to find out the contract termination date, they could presumably choose to wait it out before re-emerging as an effective military force in May, thus frustrating the prime minister's electoral ambitions.

What, then, were my conclusions? For Operation Oyster to prove a success, a great many things needed to go right for Sandline and the SFU. Rendering the BRA 'militarily ineffective' required the ability to pin down the locations of the principal enemy commanders (Ona, Kabui, Kauona, Tsiaripi, Toarama, and Tari) and their forces and then kill or capture them and recover their weapons. This required three things: effective intelligence gathering, mobility, and lethal firepower. Looking at these, I was doubtful of the intelligence aspect for the reasons already noted. The BRA knew we were coming. The element of surprise had been thrown away by prolonged carelessness over maintaining OPSEC on the part of Sandline command and leadership elements and by the inability of PNG's ministers and their staff to respect confidentiality.

I was also doubtful of the ability to maintain mobility over the three-month period of the contract. The two Mi-24 Hind gunships were a superb military asset. But like all helicopters, they were vulnerable to mechanical breakdown; and despite their advanced armour and lethality, they were subject to enemy action, particularly when on the ground. The two Mi-17 troopships were also great military assets, but they would be more vulnerable than the Mi-24s. And there was no strategic reserve of helicopters in theatre or back in Port Moresby to call on for replacements in the event of mechanical breakdown or outright loss. This was a key vulnerability. And loss of the Mi-24 gunships would mean loss of much of the lethality of firepower.

This left me to consider the special forces element. This was to comprise a total of 120 men, 70 of whom were Sandline operatives while 50 would come from the PNGDF Special Forces Unit (SFU) augmented and specially trained for the operation. The seventy-strong Sandline strike force were mercenaries hired for the operation; they comprised mainly black South Africans but also included some Australians, Ukrainians, French, and other miscellaneous soldiers of fortune. The Sandline strike force was responsible, according to the agreement, for the accomplishment of the primary objective of the contract, which was to render the BRA 'militarily ineffective'. They were to be aided by the PNG SFU, but responsibility for success rested squarely on African shoulders.

How much confidence could I place in them? To be honest, not much, maybe none. I had a mental picture of a section of African soldiers dropped by helicopter into a remote Bougainvillean village somewhere deep in the bush. I imagined them trying to work out which of the villagers they were interrogating at gunpoint were BRA elements or sympathisers and which were just ordinary farmers getting on with their lives. Few, if any, of the villagers would speak English. Many would have some Tok Pisin, but would the Africans? It felt like a nightmare, all the more so as I had been in exactly the same situation myself many times in Bougainville—and I speak Tok Pisin. Imagine for a minute how the conversation might go. An eleven-man section of Africans holds a group of frightened men who they have rounded up at gunpoint. Perhaps they have an SFU interpreter with them who can at least converse in Tok Pisin. 'Ask them, "Which of you is Francis Ona?"'

'Who?'

'Ona. O-N-A.'

'No, no. We don't know Ona. Ona is not here.'

'Where is he?'

'Don't know. In the bush maybe. Up at the mine maybe. Not here.' The interrogation goes round and round in circles. No one knows anything. No one ever knows anything. If there are any BRA enemy elements around, they are not in the village. But maybe they are down the jungle path leading back to the helicopter clearing, waiting there in silent ambush for the African soldiers.

The projected ground operations were likely to be very frustrating and very unproductive. The rebel leaders would not be seeking a military confrontation unless they saw an opportunity to impose an embarrassing defeat on an isolated section of Sandline and SFU troops somewhere. Their strategy would almost certainly be to wait out the contract period. Time was on their side. The mercenaries were only in it for the money, so they would not be putting their lives on the line. Sandline would be paid its entire contract fee within one month of deploying its sixteen-man command, administration, and training team (CATT), which itself was to be deployed within one week of the initial contract payment. There was nothing in the contract that hinged on the accomplishment of the primary military objective of neutralising the BRA. In this circumstance, the likelihood, I estimated, was that Sandline would engage in some military theatrics with the gunships, perhaps demonstrating the lethality of their armament with some demonstration firing. They might even go after a suspected enemy target with an aerial strike; however, the probability was high that this would result in mass civilian casualties in some unfortunate village and little or no damage to the BRA. In fact, the most likely outcome would be a rush of young men to sign up to the BRA as has occurred in comparable counter-insurgency operations elsewhere.

With the element of operational surprise thrown away, with doubts over intelligence gathering and Sandline's ability to pinpoint the enemy, and with questions about mobility and the likely failure of the Sandline strike force to make effective progress in ground operations, my overall conclusion came back to where I started. I remained convinced that Operation Oyster had no chance of military success.

In preparing this military appreciation, I glossed over many elements, which also concerned me. The question of who exactly was to command the operation was one such concern. The question had been fudged in the agreement with Sandline. The contract envisaged that 'the operational deployment of Sandline personnel and equipment was to be jointly determined by the Commander, PNGDF and Sandline's Commander'. It stated:

> The State recognised that Sandline's commanders would have such powers as were required to efficiently and effectively undertaken [sic] their given roles, including but not limited to the powers to engage and fight hostile forces, repel attacks therefrom, arrest any persons suspected of undertaking or conspiring to undertake a harmful act, etc. etc.

None of this placed me in overall command. Rather, the language of these two sections gave Sandline commanders full freedom to carry out their military objectives regardless of any views that I may have. I noted also that the concept of joint command applied only to *deployment* and not to *employment*. This was thoroughly unsatisfactory, though no doubt it accorded exactly to the wishes of the drafters of the contract (i.e. Sandline, not the state).

Legality, including constitutionality, was another concern. The contract spoke of all Sandline personnel being enrolled as 'special constables', but no provision had been made for the RPNGC to make this happen, and even if they tried to make it happen, large legal and constitutional issues would be raised since the constitution specifically prohibits the employment of foreign citizens in a conflict role.

This was not just a narrow legality. The question would become important and pressing in the event that Sandline personnel, wittingly or otherwise, abused the Geneva Convention and the laws of armed conflict, which takes us back to the actions of Sandline strike force members in the bush. They could arrest elements of the population conspiring to undertake a harmful act, but they could not indiscriminately injure or kill unarmed civilians (the Geneva Convention). However, if they did, in whose court of law would they be tried?

Mine was a military appreciation, not a political, moral, or ethical one. Strictly speaking, as commander of the PNGDF, I was responsible only for military appreciations; yet I could not ignore the political, legal, social, moral, or ethical dimensions of military operations under my command or those carried out by the state, to which I owed my duty, my honour, and my responsibility. With this troubling thought, I set aside my aircraft jottings and looked ahead to the week's official visit to the Philippines.

CHAPTER 4

The Planning Process

Don't delay. The best is the enemy of the good. By this I mean that a good plan violently executed now is better than a perfect plan next week.

—George S. Patton, Jr.

With many calculations, one can win; with few one cannot. How much less chance of victory has one who makes none at all!

—Sun Tzu

It was Saturday, 22 February 1997, three weeks before D-Day. I had come to the end of an official trip to the Philippines to explore the possibility of establishing closer defence cooperation between the Papua New Guinea Defence Force (PNGDF) and the Philippine Armed Forces. I was being hosted at an official send-off dinner by Arnulfo Acedera, a charming gentleman who was a four-star general, chief of staff, and head of the Philippine Armed Forces. Also at dinner was His Excellency James Pokasui, a former minister of defence and Papua New Guinea's ambassador to the Philippines. James had a background of service in the PNGDF, having been an adjutant in the maritime forces at Lombrum Naval Base, Manus Island, before entering Parliament.

With dinner pleasantries over, I retreated to my room to ponder the issues surrounding the engagement of Sandline International. I was concerned at developments earlier in the day back in Port Moresby. Weni had called to say that news of the Chan government's secret deal to engage mercenaries in a last-ditch attempt to take out the rebel leadership on Bougainville had been broken that morning in the *Weekend Australian* by Honiara-based Australian journalist Mary-Louise O'Callaghan.

This major security breach destroyed any chance the Chan government might have had of mounting a surprise attack on the BRA leadership. During the day, Brig. Gen. Ted Diro—the first PNGDF commander and former deputy prime minister—had phoned me. He had wanted to discuss the implications of the security breach and to share thoughts about the wisdom of the entire Sandline affair. As it turned out, he also had serious concerns over the use of mercenaries.

The story in the *Weekend Australian* was particularly troubling because I had warned Tim Spicer not to use faxes for his communications with Sandline International in London and Hong Kong or telephone calls or emails as I knew there was a very high chance of them being intercepted by the Australian signals intelligence network. Whether it was lax communications security by Spicer or others in his advance sixteen-man CATT or the careless and highly public use of Bulgarian-flagged heavy transport aircraft to move Sandline military assets into Jacksons Airport or a deliberate leak by Australian defence intelligence to O'Callaghan was now largely beside the point. We had lost the element of surprise.

But the compromising of operational security was only the latest in a series of issues that had been troubling me over recent weeks in relation to the secret contract between the PNG government and Sandline. These issues were a mixture of moral and ethical concerns. I was worried about military efficacy; the likely impact on the people of Bougainville, whom I had come to respect and care for as a result of my own military experiences on successive operational deployments as a young major; the impact on PNG's international reputation of hiring African mercenaries; the potential implications for PNG's sovereignty; evidence of corrupt payments to key ministers by Sandline; irregularities in trading in Conzinc Riotinto of Australia (CRA) stock, a major shareholder in Bougainville Copper Ltd (BCL); and the sidelining and disrespect shown towards my own defence force by key ministers.

These were all troubling enough. But there were also other factors. For a start, I had long since ceased to believe in the possibility of achieving an outright military result in Bougainville. Further, I did not think—despite the impressive array of heavy weaponry that Sandline had promised to deploy as part of their secret contract with government—that Sandline had any better chance of achieving the reopening of the Panguna copper mine than our own efforts by the PNGDF over the last nine or more years of civil war in Bougainville.

On a personal level, I had begun to develop a serious, deep-seated, and abiding dislike for Tim Spicer, a lieutenant colonel and former British Army officer whose personal characteristics of downright ignorance, arrogant bumptiousness, and ill-concealed feelings of superiority grated on me the more I had to deal with him. And I was growing increasingly unhappy with my own defence minister, Mathias Ijape, whose support, understanding, and interest in the funding and other issues faced by the PNGDF were close to zero. As a defence minister, he was a complete write-off.

As I thought about my possible options for dealing with Sandline, it was perfectly clear to me that none of them were very attractive. In fact, despite the advice offered in self-help books about the powers of positivity and self-confidence, the more I thought about it, the more I was convinced that what I was confronted with was nothing but a series of thoroughly bad options. There is nothing particularly new in this for the military commander. Often enough, what we are faced with is a choice among a set of unappealing, if not shockingly bad, options (think North Korea). Bad options are a reality that go with the territory of military command. It is a reality that most civilians are not required to confront and typically do not understand.

In the aftermath of the Sandline crisis, plenty of commentators asked me why, if I disagreed with the Sandline option, I did not simply resign as commander of the PNGDF. After all, if a government chief executive is faced with a directive from government that appears thoroughly wrong-headed and ill-advised, isn't that what we are supposed to do?

Are we not supposed to resign? To be honest, I did think about this as the first option. Certainly, it was the most straightforward of the possible options and the one least likely to result in personal criticism. But to resign as commander was not ever likely to be an effective option for dealing with the presence of Sandline International, let alone a mercenary outfit in our region. The government would simply look for a substitute commander who was prepared to support them in the implementation of the Sandline contract. And there were plenty of potential candidates waiting in the wings to replace me. These were senior officers who had been passed up when I was appointed over their heads as commander in October 1995.

Then there was the 'do nothing' option. In other words, let events take their course; let the government find out for itself what was likely to happen if Sandline was let loose over the jungles of Bougainville. Another Bay of Pigs fiasco was in the making, and I was in no doubt who would get the blame for yet another military disaster. It would be the government's favourite punching bag, the PNGDF and me as its commander—not the politicians.

This unappealing prospect aside, doing nothing is not in my nature. I am an activist and a proven enforcer. I believe in the power of human agency. My military instincts, hardened by long years in the field, told me that Clausewitz was perfectly correct. Military leadership can never be a passive affair. A commander needs to hold on to that glimmering light that tells one where the truth lies and be prepared to follow that light wherever it leads and at whatever cost.

The more I reflected, the more it appeared to me that the only way to prevent the Sandline operation going ahead was for me to put my career and my life on the line. I had to come up with a military plan to arrest and deport the heavily armed mercenaries, some seventy of them all up, effectively cancelling the Sandline contract with the government of PNG.

The decision to expel the Sandline mercenaries, and the first detailed planning, started right there on my final night in the Philippines, Saturday, 22 February, at the Dusit Thani Hotel in the Ayala Center, Makati, Manila. The rest of the planning was completed thousands of feet above the earth while flying between the Philippines, Malaysia, Singapore, and Port Moresby. By the time I arrived in Port Moresby on Friday, 28 February, I had completed a handwritten, highly secret draft of planning notes for Operation Rausim Kwik—the operation to arrest and deport the Sandline mercenaries.

In approaching my planning, I had in mind Gen. George Patton's advice. He was a great believer that 'a good plan violently executed now is better than a perfect plan next week'. I agreed with that. I was not after perfection. I was after a good plan, not a perfect one. Speed, shock, surprise, and total efficacy were what I wanted. A bloodless operation, if at all possible, would suit me best; but ultimately, that would be up to the mercenaries and the extent to which they might attempt to avoid arrest and deportation. Certainly, if Spicer was to be so ill-advised as to resist arrest, he would bear the consequences. And the same was true for the rest of his senior command team. But a peaceful deportation, and a hurried one that would not give the government time to react, was what I was seeking.

As a young PNGDF officer on exchange at the Australian Army's Land Warfare Centre, Tactics Wing, some years previously, the art and science of military appreciation and planning was my area of command and instructional speciality. I was now going to put my experience and knowledge in this area to immediate use.

The military appreciation process (MAP) is a structured procedure used by the Australian Army as the first step in its operational planning. A well-conducted MAP leads to the development of course of action (COA) proposals and their analysis, after which operation orders can be developed that consider all the planning factors and assumptions that have been identified. All Western armies—including the American, British, Canadian, Australian and New Zealand armies (ABCA) grouping, plus the NATO (North Atlantic Treaty Organisation) armies more broadly—follow similar approaches in their military appreciation and options analyses processes, so I knew that I was in very solid company in adopting a classical MAP and COA approach to my operational planning for Operation Rausim Kwik.

Far from being just some form of academic exercise dreamed up to fill in instructional hours at military command and staff courses, a classical MAP and COA analysis has immediate and solid practical benefits. A MAP process will identify and consider all the major risk factors that could affect the operation. This enables the commander to take the necessary steps to minimise the risks including loss of lives and equipment. It must take into consideration what actions to take if the initial steps in a mission fail and how to recover lost ground. It must contain and specify the aim and the objective of the operation; the general outline that is proposed, including which troops and units are to be deployed; and the coordination instructions, which outline all aspects of coordination such as timings, dates, marshalling areas, and so on. Administrative and logistic considerations must be considered including the provision of meals and the issuing of weapons and other specialist equipment. And then there are the entire array of command-and-control, communications, and signals matters that need attention. In short, every factor critical to the success of the operation needs to be considered and planned for.

While at the Dusit Thani Hotel, Manila, I took out my field notebook and started a handwritten appreciation to clarify my thinking and explore the options and military consequences of each of them.

Mission Aim

The first and most important issue was to clarify, as precisely as possible, the intended purpose of the operation. This was the easy part—or at least it was the most straightforward part.

My primary purpose was to force the cancellation of Operation Oyster—the operation to destroy the Bougainville Revolutionary Army as an effective fighting force and to reopen the Panguna mine. Operation Oyster was to be based around the deployment into the Bougainville operational area of Sandline International mercenaries, their attack helicopters, and other weaponry, supported by PNGDF special forces, infantry, maritime, and logistic assets. To achieve this purpose, I needed to arrest and detain the Sandline personnel and expel them from PNG as soon as practical. I also needed to deal with the pending arrival of the assault and transport helicopters, the specialised communications gear and the heavy weapons and ordnance ordered under the Sandline contract, and the surveillance aircraft, communications equipment, weaponry, and other assets already in the country.

A secondary but important purpose was a political one. I wanted to expose the real purpose of the Sandline contract to the public and condemn the engagement of Sandline mercenaries by the prime minister and two of his most senior ministers: the deputy prime minister and minister for finance and the defence minister. To that end, I needed to seek media opportunities to speak to the nation, in which I would call for the resignation or stepping aside of the ministers concerned and the installation of a caretaker government pending results from an independent judicial enquiry to examine all aspects of the Sandline contract. Importantly, in calling for the ministers to resign or step aside, I was not proposing to conduct a military coup. I would respect the PNG constitution and avoid, at all costs, any attack on PNG's democratic institutions including its loyalty to the Crown.

Enemy

Having identified my mission aims, I now needed to consider the nature of potential opposing forces (the 'enemy' in classical military planning terms) and the planning implications for dealing with each of these. First in order of importance was Sandline International because they had the weaponry and the military training to oppose me and the most immediate commercial incentives to do so. But there were other actual and potential opposing forces that I needed to account for in my planning. These included Network International, a security company that was suspected by the National Intelligence Organisation of being supported by rouge soldiers; the potential involvement of dissident groups within the senior ranks of the PNGDF; the Royal Papua New Guinea Constabulary, the possible response of which had to be taken as an unknown; and the potential involvement of political opportunists of various types who might seek to take advantage of any public turmoil and disorder that resulted from the arrest and expulsion of Sandline.

Depending on how events played out, the potential involvement of external military forces—including most immediately the Australian Defence Force (ADF)—was also a factor that I needed to keep to the front of my mind. Taking each of these actual and potential opposing forces in turn, I outlined my planning assumptions and the operational consequences arising from them.

Sandline International

The first priority was to ensure that mercenaries remained concentrated. The main body would be at Urimo training range upcountry from Wewak, and the sixteen-man CATT would be in Port Moresby. Two series of arrests and detention would be required, one for the main body of mercenaries in Wewak (the Africans) and one for the CATT headed up by Tim Spicer in Port Moresby.

A separate place of detention was needed for the CATT. Spicer would need to be detained and secured out of sight in a separate holding area. As the senior figure in Sandline and the one closest to ministers, it was important that he not be held in custody together with his operations commander (van den Bergh) and intelligence officer (Deats).

All communications or access between Spicer and the prime minister, the deputy prime minister, and the minister for defence must be denied. All contact with any other government officials who could compromise the mission must also be denied. No consular access would be permitted. Likewise, no communications between Spicer and Sandline International were to be allowed. In short, he was to be held absolutely incommunicado. Spicer's physical location was to be kept absolutely secret until he was deported. His whereabouts would only be known to the immediate members of the Rausim Kwik operational team and those responsible for his security.

Further considerations included cutting off all electronic and mobile communications with and between Sandline signallers, electronics operators, and other Sandline team members and organising air support to lift Sandline personnel from Wewak to Port Moresby and outward bound from Port Moresby to overseas. The main body of Sandline personnel at Wewak would be supervised by our own troops as they would pose no threat after their personal weapons had been removed from them. All equipment—including communications facilities, aircraft, helicopters, weapons, and ammunition—would be removed.

Another priority was to ensure that the heavy transport Antonov An-124 aircraft arriving with the Mi-17 transport helicopters and Mi-24 gunships, rockets, bombs, mortars, and other weapons and military equipment was detained upon arrival and that access was denied to all but authorised PNGDF personnel. It would also be important to establish a communications channel between the defence transport directorate and Air Niugini's head office at Air Niugini House, Jacksons International Airport, to facilitate airlifting the mercenaries out of PNG. Finally, an effective media campaign needed to be mounted to explain to the wider public the reasons for cancelling Operation Oyster and the arrest and deportation of the mercenaries.

Network International

Network International was owned by Sir Julius Chan's children, Byron James Chan and Vanessa Pelgen Chan, together with Mark Gregory Rodrigues and Cedric Jude Rodrigues, former members of the Australian police and defence forces. The office was located at Allotments 10 and 11, Section 33, Waigani Drive.

Network International was closely monitored by both PNG's NIO and the police and was a subject of discussion at the National Security Advisory Council. According to a confidential file detailing the alleged involvement of the Rodrigues brothers in a suspected illegal raid at Wolupu joint-venture mine, they were both subject to criminal investigation and proceedings by the police. While Network International was not an enemy in the traditional military sense, their possible involvement in a mission to rescue Sandline detainees, ill-advised though that would be, could seriously jeopardise the fulfilment of the mission. I was aware through Defence Intelligence that Network International could pose a serious threat to the success of our overall operation.

With these considerations, I set down the following operational requirements:

- Monitor and prevent Byron Chan and either of the Rodrigues brothers from communicating with any rogue solders from the First Royal Pacific Islands Regiment (1RPIR) with a view to denying them the opportunity to link with the police force and other elements loyal to the government of Sir Julius Chan.
- Request the commissioner for police to prevent Network International from deploying in the event that public safety and order gets out of hand.
- Require all PNGDF units in Port Moresby to ensure that neither Byron Chan nor either of the Rodrigues brothers or any of their employees have access to any military units in Port Moresby. Required all PNGDF units in Port Moresby to ensure that Rodrigues brothers or any other of their employees have access to any military units in Port Moresby,
- If events make it necessary, PNGDF units are authorised to arbitrarily detain the Rodrigues brothers and hand them over to the police on suspicion of crimes committed at Wolupu mines and for suspected immigration irregularities.

The Corps (PNG) Ltd

The Corps had overseas and British interests in the security industry in PNG and may be used by elements of Sandline or other security entities to seek their support. It is important that, while they do not pose immediate threat, we monitor their activities, especially when the operations and subsequent phase commence.

Dissident Groups within Senior Levels of the PNGDF

With regard to potential opposition coming from within the PNGDF, my greatest concern was a number of officers within the officer corps who were envious of my appointment and openly working against my command. One very disillusioned officer was Maj. Geoffrey Wiri from Western Highlands Province. He was one of the last batch of PNG officers to graduate from Portsea Officer Cadet School in 1972. Having risen to the rank of lieutenant colonel, he was then demoted. As a result, he had become embittered and was openly preying on the loyalty of junior officers and his peer group from Portsea to gain support for my removal. I had served under him in previous postings as a junior officer, and now that I outranked him, he took my success personally. He was obsessed with his situation and was involved in a personal war against me.

Among others who openly questioned my appointment was Col. Leo Nuia from East New Britain and Lt Col. Carl Marlpo, director of transport. Colonel Nuia was removed from his post by the previous commander, Brig. Gen. Robert Dademo, after a proposed posting as defence adviser in Indonesia was turned down by Jakarta after the airing of a controversial ABC *Four Corners* programme in 1991 in which Nuia was branded the 'butcher of Bougainville', having admitted on air that men under his command had dumped the dead bodies of executed rebel suspects into the sea using Australian-supplied helicopters. This was in mid-February 1990 (the so-called Valentine's Day massacre). Now unattached, he was soliciting with factions in the officer corps and the Prime Minister's Office for my removal. In this, he was ably assisted by Lt Col. Carl Marlpo, a medically downgraded and unfit officer who, like Geoffrey Wiri, preyed on the vulnerabilities of subordinates in an effort to have me removed.

These three officers would be a serious threat to us if they recruited or enticed other professional officers to join them. Nuia, Marlpo, and Wiri collectively had the ability to mobilise a group of dissident junior officers and soldiers. From a planning perspective, the obvious conclusion was to ensure that they remained in their residences and that defence intelligence officers should be tasked with closely monitoring their movements until the mission was accomplished.

Political Opportunists

There was a risk that various politicians could seek to cash in on any civil unrest that occurred and mobilise the civilian population to gain political mileage for themselves. While possibly unlikely, it was worth considering. Rogue soldiers could be used by politicians, for example to attempt to stir up trouble including riot and civil unrest.

Publicising details of the Sandline contract would give the opposition—including highly respected politicians such as Sir Michael Somare, Bill Skate, John Momis, Sir Peter Barter (who was in the government but sided with the opposition over the military exploits in Bougainville), Bernard Narokobi, and Sir Rabbie Namaliu—a great deal of ammunition with which to criticise Sir Julius Chan and other senior ministers involved in negotiating the Sandline contract. The whole issue around the engaging of mercenaries had the potential to become a very sensitive and important item on the floor of Parliament, particularly given the fact that March and April would be the last sitting weeks before the 1997 general elections.

In addition to the possibility of politicians stirring up trouble, two NGO groups openly discussing issues of good governance and corruption were the Melanesian Solidarity Group (MELSOL) and the Individual and Community Rights and Advocacy Forum (ICRAF). While they would be expected to be responsible and careful in their actions, they should nonetheless be monitored.

Other Players (Forces)

The RPNGC is the only other uniformed, organised armed force available to the government in addition to the PNGDF. It was important that I make early personal contact with Police Commissioner Bob Nenta; Ludwick Kembu, the chief of operations; and Samson Inguba, the metropolitan commander of Port Moresby, including other very senior officers like Gari Baki, Peter Aigilo, Joseph Kupo, and Giosi Labi. I have personally worked with these senior police officers in many joint operations, and the PNGDF has fostered close relations with them over the years. Policemen and women have operated with us since 1989 on Bougainville and many other security operations, so many of them would be sympathetic to our cause. Sam Inguba was one year my senior at the Joint Services College at Igam Barracks, and we have a sound personal basis on which to address security issues together.

My biggest concern was the possibility of a joint operation being mounted between Network International, the police, and dissident groups in the PNGDF under the command of the Police Special Services Unit. They might seek to launch counter-operations to disarm Special Forces Unit members and release Tim Spicer, thereby allowing the government to continue Operation Oyster with the Sandline mercenaries on Bougainville. It was important to get the police commissioner involved and hopefully supportive of Operation Rausim Kwik. Police would be asked to monitor Rausim Kwik until all the Sandline mercenaries had been deported.

External Military Forces Including the Australian Defence Force

In my appreciation, I considered that the most likely external military force that might be put on immediate notice to move after the launch of Operation Rausim Kwik would be the Australian Army's Third Brigade, operating out of Townsville. The perceived threat that the Australian government would be seeking to meet would be the potential for harm to Australian citizens in PNG and Australia's investments in the event that the law and order situation got out of hand.

At the Land Warfare Centre, the lessons learnt from Operation Morris Dance between 14 and 29 May 1987 in response to the coup d'état led by Col. Sitiveni Rabuka in Fiji was on our lecture schedule. Morris Dance featured a deployment by a flotilla of Royal Australian Navy (RAN) ships with B Company 1RAR from Third Brigade in

Townsville embarked. The troops were deployed by Royal Australian Air Force C-130 to Norfolk Island and then transported by ship to Fiji but remained on board the flotilla while they waited to see if the situation in Fiji was going to be normalised. In the course of the operation, one of the RAN's helicopters crashed on HMAS *Tobruk*, but there were no fatalities.

A light infantry brigade, Third Brigade, formed part of the ADF. It was supported by armour, artillery, and aviation units and consisted of over 3,000 troops stationed at Lavarack Barracks, Townsville, with supporting units spread across northern Queensland. It had the capability, in theory at least, to respond within two hours of a notice to move, and its role was to be ready for insertion in hotspots within Australia's territory and jurisdiction.

I had the privilege of serving in the Third Brigade in 1984 under its then commanding officer Lt Col. Peter Cosgrove, 1RAR. I was on an exchange company programme with the Second Battalion and got to know the operational command and structure of the brigade. The exercise in which I was involved was code-named Wantok Warrior, an annual deployment that brings together company-sized units of the ADF and the PNGDF to conduct field exercises and training with the aim of building familiarity, interoperability, and high levels of trust in each other's forces.

If the Third Brigade was deployed to Port Moresby, we could expect that their deployment would be similar to Operation Morris Dance. But this time, it would be more effective as lessons learnt from the Fiji deployment had since been addressed. From my familiarity with the Australian Army, there was no doubt in my mind that, in relative terms, the ADF was one of the world's top militaries in terms of leadership, technology, readiness, deployment platforms, and overall capability to meet security challenges and threats to Australia's national interests. And depending on how it unfolded, Operation Rausim Kwik could be seen in Canberra as a threat.

Having the Third Brigade put on notice to move was a contingency I had to expect. In itself, such a development would not unduly concern me. What would rip my nightie, though, as the Aussies like to say, would be having to deal with an actual deployment of the Third Brigade into Port Moresby. That would seriously up the stakes, not that the Australians would necessarily seek to reverse the outcome of Rausim Kwik. In fact, my assessment was that they would be more than happy to go along with the planned deportation of the mercenaries. It was more the possible aftermath of an Australian deployment that concerned me in terms of potential consequences for PNG's sovereignty and international reputation.

In thinking this through, two operational consequences were immediately apparent. First, whatever else we did, it was vitally important that the operation did not result in widespread civil unrest, including a threat to Australian lives and commercial interests. Second, we had to move in complete secrecy and with utmost speed. A bungled arrest attempt on the Sandline command elements leading to a long-drawn-out operation that could end up in street warfare between various armed groups in Port Moresby was exactly the scenario in which Australia would feel it had no choice but to act.

The need for secrecy was one of the more difficult operational requirements to meet. A range of junior- to middle-ranking officers in the PNGDF who worked closely with the SFU and Sandline might, unwittingly or otherwise, say something that could compromise the operation. Many PNGDF officers are close to Australian High Commission defence and civilian staff. In normal circumstances, this was to be encouraged. But Rausim Kwik was anything but normal. In a gin-soaked town like Port Moresby, there was a very high risk that someone might talk out of turn. My selection of key members of the operational team would need to take these risks into account.

Australian Signals Directorate (Formerly the Defence Signals Directorate)

Australian signals intelligence capability was another concern. My working assumption was that Australian SIGINT would have already obtained a copy of the Sandline contract through its massive multibillion-dollar satellite and intercept facilities at Kojarena, near Geraldton in

Western Australia, or through New Zealand's parallel signal intercept capabilities run by a very capable and powerful organisation called the Government Communications Security Bureau. My time with the ADF—including one year as a student at the Army Command and Staff College at Queenscliff, Victoria, and another year and a half posting at the Land Warfare Centre at Canungra, Queensland, where the Australian Military Intelligence School is based—had given me a broad perspective on the type of sophisticated intelligence network that the ADF and the Australian Security Intelligence Organisation (ASIO) have developed between them.

Even though New Zealanders often have the appearance of being very laid back compared with their louder and more aggressive neighbours across the ditch, in working alongside both armies over the years, I have learnt that such appearances can be deceiving. The Kiwis play an important role in intelligence collection for ABCA countries through their membership in a multilateral organisation informally known as the Five Eyes network. This network was established to facilitate joint cooperation in signals and other forms of intelligence gathering and analysis, making it the most effective and comprehensive intelligence gathering network in the world.

With this background knowledge, my core assumption was that, well before Mary-Louise O'Callaghan's story on the Sandline engagement broke in the *Weekend Australian*, the Australians already knew the basic outline—and quite possibly every element of the actual detail of the contract arrangements between Sandline International and the PNG government. Indeed, that was precisely what would explain the increasing levels of anxiety being shown on the part of Australian prime minister John Howard and Foreign Minister Alexander Downer, including Downer's trip to Port Moresby and Howard's subsequent invitation to Chan to visit him for dinner at Kirribilli House in Sydney's North Shore. This situation made Sir Julius Chan's repeated assurances to both men that the mercenaries were only in PNG to offer training to the PNGDF and that there were no plans to use them in any operational context in Bougainville all the more ridiculous.

The leak to O'Callaghan and the *Weekend Australian* was, I assumed, inspired by ASIO, on the direction of Canberra, to put public pressure on the Chan government to come clean about Operation Oyster. In her later book about the Sandline affair, O'Callaghan explained that she stumbled on the story through a chance observation of an Air Sofia aircraft unloading mercenary supplies at Jacksons Airport, together with stray comments picked up from government contacts in Port Moresby. While plausible, I think this was a convenient cover story for what was, more likely, a deliberate plant by Australian intelligence.

My Relationship with Gen. John Baker

An important consideration, as I went through my appreciation and planning phase, was my personal relationship with the Australian chief of defence force Gen. John Baker. In previous encounters, when we were both chiefs of defence intelligence in our respective defence forces, I had developed a close relationship with General Baker. Since then, both of us had been promoted, but we kept our lines of communication open and continued our personal contact. With General John Baker's official and private phone numbers in my possession, I knew I could always call on him if the situation warranted it.

In light of my reflections on the possibility of an ADF deployment, my operational conclusions were to

- open a direct line with ADF chief of defence force Gen. John Baker;
- open lines of communication with the Australian high commissioner and veteran diplomat David Irvine;
- update the Australian head of defence staff Col. Charles Vagi on an ongoing twenty-four-hour basis (after the initial arrests of the Sandline command team);
- conclude Operation Rausim Kwik as quickly as possible and desirably within five to seven days of the initial strike;

- keep the media informed, especially the ABC and other Australian media representatives covering Operation Rausim Kwik;
- require Maj. Walter Enuma to establish regular and direct contact with Lt Col. Gary Hogan, deputy head of Australian defence staff.

Having completed my military appreciation, the next step in my planning process was to jot down my summary conclusions, including an initial run-through of operational aspects. These notes, developed somewhere in mid-air as I travelled back to Port Moresby from the Philippines, took the following form:

Aim

The aim of Operation Rausim Kwik is to expel Sandline International from PNG and cancel Operation Oyster.

How Will I Execute My Aim?

The operation will be code named Operation Rausim Kwik. In Pidgin English 'Rausim Kwik' means 'Remove them quickly'.

The Operation will be conducted in four phases:

- Phase 1. Detention of the Sandline command team in Port Moresby and the rest of the mercenaries at Urimo Training Camp near Wewak.
- Phase 2. Demand that Sir Julius Chan, his Deputy Chris Haiveta and Defence Minister Mathias Ijape resign or step down pending the conduct of an independent judicial enquiry into all aspects of the Sandline contract.
- Phase 3. Deportation of the Sandline mercenaries.
- Phase 4. Consolidate and damage control for Operation Rausim Kwik.

Phase 1

The detention of the Sandline command team including Tim Spicer must be in Port Moresby.

Disarming all the mercenaries in Wewak and securing them at Moem Barracks in preparation for them to be flown to Port Moresby and out on the same day to their overseas destination.

All personal belongings to be searched and weapons, explosives, communications, bugging devices and other equipment to be confiscated, accounted for and retained in unit armouries awaiting further instructions.

A place for the detention and the separation of Tim Spicer from other members of the command team is important. It is also important to cut off all communication links between Tim Spicer and Sir Julius Chan, Chris Haiveta and Mathias Ijape or any person who might intend to communicate with or rescue Tim Spicer and other members of the command team.

Phase 2

Use national media to denounce what Sir Julius and his senior ministers have done in relation to the engagement of Sandline mercenaries.

Expose details of the Sandline contract to the Governor-General, the Chief Justice and to TV, radio and other forms of media. Write letters to the Prime Minister and the Defence Minister outlining my reasons for the cancellation of the contract.

Expose details of the Sandline contract to the public.

Phase 3

Coordinate efforts between Director Transport, Logistic Branch and Air Niugini to transport Sandline mercenaries from Wewak to Port Moresby and into the Air Niugini Airbus out of PNG on the same day.

Phase 4

Consolidation and damage control will involve return of troops and any weapons to barracks and any liaison that may be required with media, and with organisations such as MELSOL and the ICRAF. Also, any legal matters that may need attention including the provision of comment on the terms of reference for the proposed Independent Judicial Enquiry into the Sandline contract, and the provision of evidence to the enquiry.

Troops to Task

In military planning where more than, say, ten people are to be involved in an operation and where there are lots of moving parts to consider, it is important to formally assign 'troops to task'. If this is not done through a series of orders, often called an 'orders group', nothing is likely to happen. It could be as simple as making sure someone thinks of providing a key to the armoury, assuming weapons are to be involved. And it will be likely to involve all manner of other aspects including specific tasks, responsibilities, resources, and timelines.

Normally, a commander at my level would delegate all that to an operations officer; and indeed, that was exactly my intention on my return to Murray Barracks. But in an operation as politically sensitive as Rausim Kwik, I had a responsibility to map out as much as I could in advance as a guide to more detailed lower-level planners. On my flight back to Port Moresby, I made notes about who to involve in the operation.

Operations Team, Rausim Kwik

Maj. Gilbert Toropo was my obvious first choice and key figure for Rausim Kwik, but because he was the officer commanding the SFU, which I needed to retain as a strategic reserve in the event of matters not going to plan, I needed to appoint another able and skilful middle-ranking officer at the rank of major or lieutenant colonel. I also needed to hand-pick a small number of very brave and committed officers of junior rank who had served with me under my command on Bougainville or in the two regiments. They would be needed to make the initial arrests and secure the detention of the Sandline command team.

The operations team needed to be focused, determined, and not easily distracted. They would be up against two very tough operators in van den Bergh and Deats, white South African officers who had a reputation for ruthlessness and military effectiveness. Spicer was a bit more of an unknown quantity. A former military officer in the British Army with extensive operational and combat experience, he might put up a tough fight, or he might collapse like a pricked balloon. Either way, I was not going to take any chances. Spicer, van den Bergh, and Deats would be up against the toughest set of combat-experienced people I could find. And I had a good set to pick from.

Selection of Operation Rausim Kwik Team

The first thing on my mind was to appoint an operations officer for Rausim Kwik. I made a list of officers who had served with me from the time I was commissioned in 1976 until 1997. The list was made up mainly from the rank of major to lieutenant colonel. As I eliminated from the list senior officers on the basis of family considerations and the fact that many had reached an age where an adventure of this nature was not even on their minds, I decided to hand-pick officers at the rank of major and below to make up my core team for the operation.

Maj. John Walter Enuma

In considering a shortlist of majors, John Walter Enuma stood out. In every important respect, he was an officer ahead of his time. Fearless, brave, aggressive, articulate, intelligent, physically fit, loyal, and most importantly a proven field and tactical leader with operational experience, Enuma was well respected by his troops. He was nicknamed 'Walker' after the *Phantom* comic ghost as he had a remarkable ability during operations in Bougainville to infiltrate himself into locations infested by rebels and still come out alive, many times fighting his way out.

I had served with Enuma in 1978 at the Second Battalion, Royal Pacific Islands Regiment (RPIR) when he was a platoon commander with the D Company. The highlight of his subaltern days was when he was appointed aide-de-camp to the third governor general of PNG, Sir Kingsford Dibela, in 1983. Having served with Enuma along the PNG-Indonesian border and later in Bougainville and having seen his abilities first-hand, I had no doubt that my choice of operations officer for Operation Rausim Kwik was, in effect, made for me. All I needed was to confide in him about what I had in mind and offer him the position. In doing so, I planned to make it clear that nothing would be used against him if he turned it down.

Maj. Gilbert Toropo

Gilbert Toropo was a graduate from the PNG Defence Academy in 1986 and served with me as a subaltern at the Second Battalion when I was the operations officer. He was selected for special forces training and attended US Army Ranger School at Fort Benning, Georgia. This sixty-one-day combat leadership course has been described as the most physical and mentally demanding course in the US Army. After Ranger School, Toropo was attached to Battle Wing at the Australian Army Land Warfare Centre at Kokoda Barracks, Canungra, in 1992, where I was instructing at the Tactics and War Administration Wing.

Toropo later took up a two-year posting as an instructor at the Australian Army Duntroon Officer Cadet School in Canberra and was then posted back as company commander, D Company, 1RPIR. Like Enuma, he had served a number of tours on Bougainville and was a thoroughly seasoned soldier.

In December 1995, just a few months into my appointment as commander, I was able to get Defence Council approval to raise an SFU. I issued Commander PNGDF Directive Number 04/95 for the raising and the establishment of an SFU to be based at Goldie River Barracks. The obvious choice for the founding officer commanding position was Capt. Gilbert Toropo. He was promoted to the rank of major and posted to command SFU with instructions to raise the unit. The task of raising the SFU was difficult, but given the priority and the importance of the role, he was able to raise a platoon-sized unit with support staff and an intelligence cell.

Stocky in build, physically strong, and at about 167 cm (5 feet 6 inches) tall, Toropo was ready for any confrontation. He was from the Southern Highlands, Ialibu-Pangia District, as was the sitting member of Parliament and former prime minister Peter O'Neill. Toropo had over thirty men under his command, who would be a valuable strategic reserve for Operation Rausim Kwik.

Capt. Belden Norman Namah

Capt. Belden Namah was from West Sepik/Sandaun Province. He graduated from the Australian Army's Royal Military College, Duntroon, in 1990 and—after attending a language course at James Cook University, Queensland, to learn and speak Bahasa Indonesia— was posted as platoon commander in the First Battalion. It was there that he served with me between 1993 and 1994.

He was singled out by me to join the SFU as a platoon commander and assistant operations officer because of the great determination and courage he showed when I was operations officer (1RPIR) in 1993 on Bougainville. He was platoon commander of C Company under Maj. Michael Kumun. Major Kumun was operating out of Arawa Township, and he told me of Lieutenant Namah's tactical and leadership skills and how he would conduct ambushes in areas infested with the BRA completely without fear. Namah built such confidence in his troops that he was considered one of the most outstanding battlefield junior commanders that the PNGDF had ever seen. He was nicknamed 'Skull' by troops in Bougainville for his unusual haircut that left only his skull exposed with hardly any hair on.

Capt. Bola Renagi

Capt. Bola Renagi joined as an ordinary soldier but applied for officer cadet school when I was the senior instructor at the PNG Defence Academy in Lae in 1989. He was shortlisted to go to Officer Cadet School at Waiouru, New Zealand, in 1990.

After he returned, he was posted to the Second Battalion, where he was put in charge of the reconnaissance platoon. His skills were further advanced when he attended special forces training in the United States in 1991, after which he completed a tour as acting officer commanding on Bougainville. He was the ideal choice to be operations officer and second in command of the SFU, where he would work directly under Maj. Gilbert Toropo.

With these officers identified, all I needed were another two officers to beef up the Rausim Kwik team to detain Tim Spicer and his command team in phase 1. The subalterns I had in mind were Lt Nick Henry, another New Zealand Army Waiouru graduate, and Ben Sesenu, a Duntroon graduate serving in defence intelligence.

As for the supporting elements, which were mainly in the maritime area, I had to confide in navy commander Tom Ur, who was my director of maritime operations and both a schoolmate and a graduate friend of mine from the PNGDF officer intake class of 1/75. I also needed to take into my confidence the commanding officer of the landing craft base, Cdr Max Aleale, who was also in Tom Ur and my officer cadet intake and was another close colleague of mine.

From the air element, I needed Capt. Charlie Andrews as he was the most daring as well as the safest helicopter pilot the PNGDF had ever graduated and trained. He had shown his flying prowess many times on operations with me in Bougainville and was the best pilot for me to rely on for air support to Operation Rausim Kwik.

First Royal Pacific Islands Regiment

Lt Col. Jethro Tokam Kanene was a schoolmate of mine as we had attended Sogeri Senior High School together in 1973–74. He enlisted in 1978 as a maritime cadet but switched to the land element after he experienced difficulty in handling rough sea conditions. He scooped the tactics prize on graduation in 1979 and was posted to Second Battalion, RPIR, where we served together. In 1980, he was posted to the mortar platoon and served under me as my second in command.

A well-trained officer, having just graduated from the US Army Command and Staff College at Fort Leavenworth, Kansas, he was my choice for CO of First Battalion. This was after I demoted the previous commanding officer, Seki Berapu, for incompetence in Bougainville on Operation High Speed II, when Berapu and Commander Ilau decided to establish the battalion command post on a patrol boat off Aropa Airport with the aim of directing operations from the sea. In June 1996, upon recommendation to the Defence Council, we approved Kanene's promotion to lieutenant colonel just before he graduated from Fort Leavenworth.

Second Royal Pacific Islands Regiment

Lt Col. Michael Tamalanga was the CO of Second Battalion. He also was in the class of 1/75 along with Commanders Tom Ur, Max Sundei Aleale, and me. Michael Tamalanga and I shared many tales from our experiences together, and these had built close bonds between us over the last twenty years.

Other Commanding Officers

I also needed to have an important understanding with Lt Col. Blaise Afara, who was the CO of Murray Barracks garrison. He was the landlord of all the assets in Murray Barracks and had enough support soldiers under his command to provide security at the main gate as well as at Flagstaff House. An element of his troops would also be called on to provide protection at NBC studios when I went on air to address the nation.

The last CO I had to instruct was Lt Col. Patrick Waeda, CO of the Air Transport Squadron. He was a close relative of Blaise Afara from Sandaun Province and was responsible for the entire air assets of the PNGDF. I consulted him on the availability of the Iroquois, and he gladly replied that it was available and serviceable and that Capt. Charlie Andrews and some other chopper pilots were available for tasking.

Detailed Planning Notes and Operational Orders

The actual operational orders for Rausim Kwik were classified 'secret' and derived from the military appreciation and the planning notes. Having considered all the factors and the main framework of the operation order for Operation Rausim Kwik, I needed to confirm the provisional start date and that the timings and other factors were all in order. It was now 1 March 1997, and time was running out. I needed to move fast.

Other Important Considerations

Operational Security

As mentioned earlier, maintaining operational security over the first phase of the operation, in particular, was a major preoccupation. Instructions restricting the use of phones and high-frequency radios would be issued as part of the operational orders for Rausim Kwik.

Media Strategy

The best medium to explain my actions and to voice my opposition to the Sandline contract was via radio, TV, and print media. My policy, once Operation Rausim Kwik had gone public, would be to make myself available to journalists on a twenty-four-hour basis. To achieve this, I would ensure that all my contact numbers were given out during the first day's press conference. A common venue for follow-up press conferences would be established during and after Operation Rausim Kwik. It was vitally important to me, and to the success of the operation, that I win the media over and swing favourable public support to my side.

Address to the Troops

One of the keys to the success of Operation Rausim Kwik would be to address the troops as their understanding of the implications of using Sandline in Bougainville was important. Operation Oyster, if not cancelled, had the potential to affect them and their families and later their children and the provinces they came from. The same address must be conveyed to other units like Igam Barracks, the Engineer Battalion, the Defence Academy, 1RPIR and 2RPIR, and the patrol boat base at Lombrum. As we still had troops on Bougainville, my address would be passed on by messenger to the forward tactical commander there as well.

Address to the Nation

My planned address to the nation on the morning of the first day of Operation Rausim Kwik was vitally important. I had to hit exactly the right note if I was to galvanise public support for what I was trying to do. As the Bougainville crisis had affected every home in PNG, I didn't think it should be too difficult to get public support throughout the country. Universities and colleges would be especially important in raising support. And in Port Moresby, all the major settlements would be targeted through my networks as this was where many working-class people resided.

As seen in Manila just ten years earlier, people power could be a potent weapon against even the most entrenched government as President Marcos's military government had been. In 1986, Roman Catholic cardinal Jaime Sin led street protests of two-million-plus Catholics that were so effective that they ultimately resulted in President Marcos and his wife, Imelda, abandoning the presidency and seeking asylum in Hawaii.

So there was a precedent elsewhere in the region in the event that Sir Julius refused to step aside. By the time I completed my military appreciation and planning, I was ready to draft the operational orders for Rausim Kwik. A copy of Operations Rausim Kwik is included herewith as annex B.

Legal Aspects

It may seem ironic, considering that I was, by now, committed to an operation that was almost certainly going to be described by the government as illegal and an abuse of my power as commander of the PNGDF, but I nevertheless paused to think through some of the legalities of what I was planning. In particular, I wondered what powers of arrest and detention I actually had over people from an irregular foreign-based military force such as Sandline. As a military commander, I certainly had powers of arrest and detention over members of the PNGDF. But foreign mercenaries, or 'military consultants' as Sir Julius preferred to call them, were another matter.

Normally, when a foreign military force is invited into another country for exercises, or indeed for any purpose, the deployment will be subject to a carefully negotiated status of forces agreement between the host nation and the guest nation. Such agreements routinely cover what is to happen in the event of crimes being committed by members of a visiting force or other acts of indiscipline. But a mercenary force, by its nature, is not a military force in the normal sense of the word. A mercenary is someone who is not a national involved in the conflict and whose participation is motivated by the expectation of monetary gain. Mercenaries are not entitled to the status of a combatant or a prisoner of war. But they are entitled, under international law, to be given adequate conditions of detention and a fair trial if captured.

The government's agreement with Sandline International specified at paragraph 2.2 that all Sandline personnel would be signed on for the duration of Operation Oyster, by Sandline, as 'special constables' and that they would carry ID cards identifying them as such. This provision of the contract was never carried out, but had it been, it would have been in strict violation of PNG's constitution, specifically division 5, section 200, which deals with the raising of unauthorised forces. Part (3), subsection 200(3) provides a potential waiver but only for the armed forces of another country and then only if duly authorised by an act of Parliament. However, Sandline was not an armed force from another country; it was a contracted group of irregulars not subject to the discipline and control of an armed force belonging to another state. Therefore, it was well outside anything envisaged by the framers of the constitution, whether sanctioned by act of Parliament or not. In the simplest of terms, the Sandline contract was illegal in terms of PNG's constitution, and it could not be rendered legal by the device of signing Sandline personnel in as special constables, by act of Parliament, or by the pretence, much depended on by Sir Julius Chan, that Sandline was only a group of military *consultants* involved in training activities.

While these were all important points, the constitutionality and legality of the Sandline contract was, of course, always likely to be overtaken by a much larger set of issues once Operation Rausim Kwik was launched and became public. All this served to underline the wisdom, if not necessarily the complete legality, of moving with utmost speed and secrecy to effect the arrests and detention of Sandline personnel and to keep their locations of confinement confidential for as long as practicable. Denying Sandline personnel access to consular or legal representation would probably be difficult to insist on for very long; however, as they would not be granted access to phones or other means of communication, they would have no practical means of seeking consular or legal access in any case. Again, this was yet another reason for trying to ensure the quickest possible means of their deportation and onward travel.

Getting the public to demand the resignation of PM Sir Julius Chan; his deputy, Chris Haiveta; and the minister for defence would be a challenge involving the military and people power. As with all good plans, it would be tested on the day. I envisaged it would be the most difficult aspect to achieve as it involved multiple considerations and implications that I, as a military officer, had no expertise in. In this, I relied on God by faith and common sense and would keep a cool head.

CHAPTER 5

Decisions Made: Completing the Plan, 23 February–15 March 1997

Gentlemen, saddle up. The game is on.

On Sunday, 23 February, I said goodbye to Amb. James Pokasui and departed Manila for Singapore. On the two-hour flight, I had in my hand Joey Manalang's book *People Power, an Eyewitness History: The Philippine Revolution of 1986.* This was an account of how Cory Aquino, the widow of the assassinated opposition leader Benigno 'Ninoy' Aquino, and Cardinal Jaime Sin worked together to mobilise the mass public demonstrations that forced Pres. Ferdinand Marcos from office. Hundreds of feet over Southeast Asia, as I read about the peaceful application of a force of two million people in the Philippines, my mind was all but made up. I began to see how a peaceful protest might be put together that would force Sir Julius Chan; his deputy, Haiveta; and Defence Minister Ijape to resign over their decision to engage the Sandline mercenaries.

From Sunday to Thursday that week, I had a series of defence-related meetings in Kuala Lumpur and Singapore. But during that week, my mind did not stray far from the possibility of using people power in Port Moresby as Cory Aquino and Cardinal Sin had done in Manila just over ten years earlier. A few hours before midnight on

Thursday, 27 February, my delegation boarded Air Niugini PX 393 from Changi International Airport bound for Port Moresby. With a flight time of six hours and fifteen minutes, there was plenty of time to start working on specifics. As I sat comfortably in my business-class seat, I took out my notebook and a biro and commenced working up a military appreciation of how I might go about the task of arresting the Sandline mercenaries and forcing the cancellation of the Sandline contract.

The flight arrived at 6.30 a.m. and I was met at Jacksons International Airport by Col. Jack Tuat, my chief of staff, and military adviser Lt Col. Joseph Fabila. Tuat informed me that Sir Julius was aware of my opposition to the engagement of Sandline mercenaries on Bougainville. However, what neither Jack Tuat nor Sir Julius knew, as I had not spoken of it to anyone at that point, was just how far my opposition had progressed.

Back at Flagstaff House, I rested until after lunch before returning to my office to go through a backlog of correspondence. I then headed to Jacksons Airport to visit the Special Forces Unit operations room. The SFU intelligence officer was Lt Eddie Yodu, a very promising junior officer who had been wounded on Bougainville. He briefed me on current issues including his encounter with an ABC crew who went to Jacksons and commenced filming without permission. Their tape had been confiscated.

On Saturday, 1 March, I contacted Sir Barry Holloway to arrange an evening meeting at the Ponderosa Hotel, owned by his son Joe Holloway, at Nuana Road in the suburb of Five Mile. I arrived with my bodyguard, Cpl John Koraia, and took a quiet table in the far corner of the restaurant. It was good to see Sir Barry, and I took him into my confidence, telling him about the ousting of President Marcos and how I was thinking of using people power in Port Moresby. He heard me out but said, 'Port Moresby is not Manila, Jerry. What you plan to do against Sir Julius, Haiveta, and Ijape will have little or no impact.'

He continued, 'If I were Sir Julius, I would use the powers vested in me as prime minister to isolate, humiliate, ostracise, and physically remove you from office. I would then appoint a senior colonel as commander who would go ahead and launch the operations. And God knows, there are plenty of such colonels ready to take your place. The plan is crazy. You have too much to lose. Do this, and Sir Julius will destroy you.'

'Wait,' I said to Sir Barry. 'I am not finished yet. Plan A is to do a people power protest and force Sir Julius to resign. But plan B is to expel the Sandline mercenaries and then, in the ensuing chaos that is bound to erupt, force Sir Julius, Haiveta, and Ijape to resign. And plan C is to just resign and walk away from everything. But if I simply resign, another commander will execute Operation Oyster. And I will have achieved nothing.'

Sir Barry nodded at that but commented that, at the end of the exercise, the sad reality was that I was bound to lose more than I gained. But I would have saved my integrity.

We sat into the night and discussed all the pros and cons with Sir Barry, drawing on his experience as finance minister to Sir Julius. 'You know, Jerry,' he said, 'the kina couldn't have been floated at a worse time. And look at the quality of the advisers around Sir Julius. With the exception of his head of department, Noel Levi, and a very few others, they are nonentities or worse.'

He continued, 'Jerry, the worst thing is that this is election year. And by talking tough on Bougainville, Sir Julius has tied his own noose. Time is against him, and to engage a private army to solve the Bougainville crisis in ninety days or less is suicide, in fact completely mad. My goodness, it could only happen in PNG.'

Sir Barry then asked me a key question. 'Jerry, setting aside the ethical, moral, and legal questions for a moment, how much confidence do you have in the technology, the firepower, and the precision that Sandline are promising to bring into the battlefield in Bougainville?'

I replied, 'History is full of examples where even the best army in the world gets defeated by a ragtag, untrained militant group such as the BRA. Look at Vietnam. The Americans were done over by the Vietcong. The Soviets got their bums kicked in Afghanistan and the French in Algeria and Vietnam and the Brits in the Khyber Pass and Khartoum and Zululand. So no, I have absolutely no confidence that

Sandline can deliver. They will be too thin on the ground. They won't be able to distinguish between the BRA and the local population. Their helicopters will get hit, there will be no backup, and the terrain is completely unlike most parts of Africa. Plus, no one in Bougainville I have ever met speaks Afrikaans.'

I continued, 'You were a patrol officer in Buin once upon a time, Sir Barry, and you know what it is like patrolling into the hills of the Crown Prince Range. I have spent many months on Bougainville trying to pinpoint the exact location of the BRA. But we continue to fail. Because the BRA has an upper hand in terms of the terrain, they live off the land. And more importantly, they have support from the villagers. They feed off the locals. It's a long and tedious process trying to win hearts and minds in Bougainville. In straight military terms and quite apart from the humanitarian aspects, I would rather physically arrest and expel Sandline than risk another humiliation at the hands of the BRA. Despite everything Spicer has fed to Sir Julius, it's flat out impossible to achieve a military solution in Bougainville at any acceptable level of casualties or maybe at any level, period. The BRA will fight to the last man and then the last woman. Will the mercenaries? Of course not. They only fight for their monthly pay. They are not in the game to get killed. They are in the game to make money, to get rich. Tim Spicer is just a salesman. He has fed this notion to Sir Julius that just because we will have Mi-24 gunships and Mi-17 troop transports in theatre and all the ammunition and missiles in the world, they will eliminate the BRA leadership structure and win militarily in thirty days. It is a complete fantasy.'

Sir Barry nodded at this. He said that he was off to Brisbane the following day for a week and then would be back. We finished our drinks, and I got up to leave. Sir Barry said in parting, 'Jerry, I wish I could be of greater help to you. Sorry, General, but the burdens of the nation, including Bougainville, are on your shoulders. I can only anticipate the long road ahead. Good luck.'

Driving home to Flagstaff House, I lay down on the couch in the living room to watch TV before dozing off to sleep.

It was early Sunday morning, 2 March, when Weni and the children awoke. After breakfast, we attended the Protestant church service at Murray Barracks chapel and then went shopping before returning to Brigadier Hill. Weni knew something was wrong; she had picked up on the anxiety in my face and my behaviour, and I was spending more and more time downstairs in my private study. She joined me later, and I confirmed with her my final decision over the engagement of Sandline. I said I had considered all the odds and all the advantages and disadvantages and had decided that I would expel Sandline, cancel the contract, and demand that Sir Julius, Haiveta, and Ijape resign. Weni, although relieved at my decision, was naturally worried about how we would sustain the family and endure a long uncertain future.

I explained to Weni my thinking. Why force Sir Julius to resign and not do anything about the Sandline mercenaries? I may as well expel Sandline and, at the same time, force Sir Julius to resign. It was better that way. At least I would have achieved something to justify my sacking or a long prison term.

I gave myself seven days to complete all the necessary documentation. The base document would be a refined military appreciation, fleshed out from my outline sketch prepared on the flight back from Singapore. The operational orders covering the arrest of the mercenaries, the detention of the Sandline command team, the securing of their equipment, and their subsequent expulsion from PNG would be based on this. I also needed to draft my address to the nation and my letters to Sir Julius Chan, to Gov. Gen. Sir Wiwa Korowi, to Minister for Defence Mathias Ijape, and to CJ Sir Arnold Amet, a fellow Karkar Islander. I also needed to prepare my address to the troops and the SFU. The remaining seven days would be set aside for consolidation and dealing with issues arising. I pencilled D-Day in for 16 or 17 March 1997, two weeks away.

I was expecting Maj. Gilbert Toropo after dinner, and sure enough, he arrived and was greeted by my two dogs, Saribi and Rocky. Major Toropo was a very humble but committed military officer in whom personal loyalty was deeply ingrained. Toropo would be the first person in the military whom I confided in about my plans for the expulsion of Sandline. I elected to talk to him first because of the direct consequences for the SFU, the unit we co-founded and raised. We sat in the office for a long time, and he agreed with me that, at the end of the day, I was the commander, and it would be my call. He appeared concerned, in fact very concerned, but he understood the consequences and the longer-term implications not only for my professional career but also for that of the PNGDF, the SFU, and the nation.

On Monday, 3 March, I called the CO of 1RPIR, Lt Col. Tokam Kanene, to come to my office for a chat after morning tea. He arrived as expected, and I briefed him on the imminent cancellation of the Sandline contract and told him that I would need his personal commitment and that of the regiment if and when this was required.

Tim Spicer called me at about three o'clock and said he had spent nearly an hour on the phone with the prime minister (more detailed grist to the mill of Australian intelligence, I reflected). He confirmed that Sir Julius had every confidence that Sandline would deliver. There was plenty of optimism by now and a complete air of confidence between Tim Spicer and Sir Julius. Spicer then asked me if I could visit Fort Williams to see his operational commander, Nic van den Bergh, and intelligence officer, Carl Deats, that evening. This I agreed to.

I arrived at Fort Williams with my security team. As they parked in the dark on Vaivai Street, I entered Flat 2 at Fort Williams. Tim Spicer was seated near the table with his favourite Johnnie Walker Blue Label Scotch whisky that, even purchased duty-free, runs at around five times the cost of Johnnie Walker Red. Spicer must be feeling flush, I thought. Spread across the table were newspaper cuttings and a set of highly confidential BRA intelligence reports shared from our own joint intelligence organisation. For a soldier of Spicer's seniority and long operational experience, his approach to operational security bordered on criminal negligent.

After a few pleasantries, Spicer said, 'Well, General, we have lost the tactical element of surprise, but I have given it thorough thought and have come up with a new strategy. The prime minister also agrees that we should conduct a coup de main on the Panguna mine using surprise and a massive demonstration of firepower instead of going into Kongara and central Bougainville. Let's capture and secure the Panguna mine on D + 1 and let the rebels come to us, and we will eliminate them.

I asked how. He said, 'Well, General, we clear the Espie Highway and clear it from small arms range on both sides, and we patrol the highway using helicopters and bulletproof vehicles. And if anything moves within small arms range of the road, we instantly engage and destroy. It is that simple. By then, all the equipment and workers should be arriving to get the mine operational. We will be shipping ore out before you can count to ten.'

During all my military training and experience, I doubt that I had ever been as dumbfounded as I was in hearing such a bizarre proposition. Tactically, it was the most unsustainable solution to fighting the rebels I had ever come across. I thought, *Here is this clown from the East End of London, a city dweller who has only spent two days of his life in Bougainville. He's cut out a few newspaper cuttings and, over a glass of Blue Label whisky, claims to have solved a tactical problem that we have been unable to solve in over eight years of flogging ourselves in the jungles of Bougainville.*

He said, 'You know what, Jerry? Sir Julius even agrees with me that we should not waste time chasing the rebels in the countryside. Let them come to Panguna, and we will have them mowed down.'

He continued, 'You know what the Australians will think?'

I said, 'I have a pretty fair idea, but go on.'

He said, 'They will respect the PNGDF because what they would not assist you with, we will provide. And you will win.'

'Another thing commander', he continued.

'Yes, Tim.'

'We will cripple the radio station in Solomon Islands, and they will not be able to transmit for a long time.'

I said, 'Are you capable of doing that?'

'Absolutely', he said. 'We have the expertise, and believe me, Solomon Islands will be silenced.' I could not believe what I was hearing. We had shifted our focus from the rebels on Bougainville to planning the disruption, through a clandestine operation, of the smooth running of another sovereign country.

'We will definitely need a battalion group for such operations,' Spicer said, waving his glass in the air to make his point.

Listening to Spicer as he laid out his new operational approach over several glasses of Blue Label whisky, I judged that the whole operation would be an absolute disaster from start to finish. A coup de main operation against a bloody great hole in the ground with nobody there even to witness a firepower demonstration was completely pointless. What were we going to do? Issue free admission tickets to the BRA to come and watch? And then following up with operations to try to keep an access road and port open was absolutely begging for military failure. Who was going to keep the power pylons to the mine from being blown up one by one? Who would prevent trees being felled across the 35 km-long access road to stop supplies from reaching the mine and ore being crushed and shipped out? Who would keep the mine open and running? Spicer was talking glibly about a battalion worth of troops, say, 1,200 men all up. But Sandline was bringing less than a hundred men to the operation, in fact no more than about seventy men, a good deal less than a company, and two gunships and two helicopter troopships. No armoured vehicles to patrol the access road; no ready reaction force to speak of; no engineering troops to clear obstacles such as felled trees and to restore downed power lines; no troops to guard the helicopters, bearing in mind that helicopters spend the vast majority of their time on the ground where they are extraordinarily vulnerable; and no helicopters in reserve. A more amateurish plan would be hard to conceive.

Spicer's plan flew in the face of the long years I had spent operating and commanding troops on Bougainville, as well as lecturing in tactics at one of the finest and most prestigious military institutions in the Commonwealth of Australia. At the Land Warfare Centre, we analysed lessons learnt from insurgencies such as those seen in the Malayan campaign, Borneo, the Philippines, and now Bougainville. In all those examples, putting down an armed insurrection involved winning the hearts and minds of the local population, not strafing them with high explosive rockets Hollywood-style.

The biggest concern I have always had as a field commander is when politicians want to be battlefield commanders and armchair strategists. Now with Spicer waving his bottle of snake oil around, it was all set to go as far as Ijape, Haiveta, and Sir Julius were concerned. They were already sold on his new notion of clearing and keeping open the Espie Highway from Panguna to Loloho. From a military perspective, keeping open a steep and mountainous jungle highway with dense vegetation coming down to the very edge of the road seal for 35 km was an unthinkable proposition. And it would remain so unless every village and jungle trail in the surrounding countryside was also secured, which was not part of Spicer's solution and, in any event, could not be delivered at any conceivable level of force. I was also troubled at his suggestion of crippling the Solomon Islands Broadcasting Commission with some kind of covert military action. A clandestine military operation not sanctioned by the National Security Council to cripple a radio station in a friendly neighbouring country was tantamount to an illegal declaration of war on another Melanesian nation.

Earlier that day, I had been visited by retired general Ted Diro, Kevin Conrad, and counsel Peter Pena. They were interested in exchanging thoughts on the implications of Operation Oyster. I expressed doubts, but I did not tell General Diro that I was cancelling the contract. Instead, I told them that I was off to play golf, which was true, but I had never played golf before. I would have liked to have taken Diro into my confidence, but operational security was uppermost in my mind, and Port Moresby was a very small town.

The golf was organised by my military adviser, Lt Col. Joseph Fabila, and Australian training adviser Lt Col. Larry Holmes. It was a long-awaited game that had been planned by Joseph for many months. Having never played golf in my life, I thought this would be an excellent chance for me to learn something new; besides, I needed a break. I had a new golf set that I had recently bought in Singapore. As I placed the golf ball to tee off, I felt very clumsy. It was frustrating as neither my hits nor my putts went particularly well. As we played the round, I felt very tempted to tell Larry Holmes about my plan but decided against it. Again and as with Ted Diro, there was too much at stake to risk operational security being compromised.

Back in my office and working on my own operational planning, I could not help pondering Spicer's advice to the prime minister on his revised strategy for capturing and reopening the Panguna mine and securing its access road and port, with all other military considerations to be made secondary. This was all because the element of surprise had been squandered through basic lapses in operational security, for which Spicer himself was the main culprit due to his extraordinarily careless handling of phones and faxes. He obviously had no appreciation of Australia's intelligence capability, or if he did, he was careless to the point of negligence. I worked into the evening and by midnight had completed my first very rough draft of Operation Rausim Kwik, my address to the nation, and my address to my soldiers.

On Thursday, 6 March, Haiveta, Sir Pita Lus, and Emos Daniels from the Prime Minister's Office and an ABC crew departed on the CASA for Wewak to see the training and field firing. They wanted to see how the small and medium weapons would perform in Bougainville. When Sir Pita Lus was given an AK-47 to shoot at Moem Barracks Open Range, he said no human being could survive the ferocity and the lethal effect of the weapon; he warned the BRA that their days were numbered.

I did not travel with the team to Wewak as I had to attend an important National Security Advisory Committee (NSAC) meeting that day. Among the many security issues raised at the NSAC meeting, the one that stood out the most was the Rodrigues brothers' connection to Network International. This agenda item was raised jointly by Police Commissioner Bob Nenta and the director general of the National Intelligence Organisation, Ovia Rauka. The issue of Sandline was also raised as an agenda item. I informed the committee that, as we spoke, the deputy prime minister and Sir Pita Lus were at Moem Barracks, testing weapons and seeing the training in progress. I said that we were almost all set to go as the attack helicopters and missiles and many thousands of rounds of ammunition and recoilless rifles and bombs would arrive mid-March. There was more briefing regarding

Bougainville in relation to rebel activity and the government's 3R strategy—reconciliation, restoration, and reconstruction—that was being implemented.

After the meeting, Secretary of Defence James Melegepa, Police Commissioner Bob Nenta, and I walked across to the Golden Bowl for lunch. This is a moderately priced Chinese restaurant on John Guise Drive, Waigani. Over lunch, I raised the issue of Sandline, saying that I was very doubtful of it achieving military success and that the contract looked like it bordered on corrupt deals and kickbacks. James Melegepa agreed with me on the basis of on our earlier letter to Secretary Levi in relation to the credibility of Sandline and their reputation. As we departed, I sensed that they agreed in principle that the Sandline contract was probably not in the best interests of PNG, but they did not know how to put a stop to the contract, especially when the country's three most senior politicians were all for the engagement.

On Friday, 7 March, my lunchtime official engagement was with the British high commissioner, His Excellency Bob Low, to officially farewell Officer Cadet Dalos Umul to attend Sandhurst Royal Military Academy in the UK. Dalos was an economics graduate from the University of Papua New Guinea in 1995 and had enlisted as a recruit, having spent six months in recruit training. He came from Kebasob, a village in the hinterland of my home island of Karkar off Madang. The lunch was attended by Acting Director of Training Maj. Francis Agwi and Michael Kwandi. As we dined, I noted that the high commissioner kept the issue of Sandline away from the discussion, which either was very diplomatic and kind of him or meant that he already knew all that he needed to know courtesy of our friends in Australian intelligence. He was more focused on the future of officer cadet training. Officer Cadet Dalos was a test case to see if our cadets could endure the training intensity and cold climate of the UK. Back at the office, I asked my military assistant, Joseph Fabila, to inform Lt Col. Kamona Falaniki (Frank), who was the task force commander on Bougainville, to fly to Port Moresby for a briefing early the following week as the planned cancellation of Operation Oyster would inevitably have some effect on the overall operations on the ground on Bougainville.

On Saturday, 8 March, I called Major Enuma to Flagstaff House. I outlined what I was planning and invited him to take on the role of operations officer for Operation Rausim Kwik. Like me, he was perplexed by the decision to engage Sandline and really concerned, especially at the long-term consequences of engaging mercenaries in PNG. Enuma was an enforcer and also a deep thinker; he was also very intelligent. He asked for time to ponder his projected role as operations officer. As he departed, he assured me that he would be back within twenty-four hours to let me know of his decision. It was late at night, and I heard dogs barking deep in the valley as he left. I went through all the prepared documents once again. I was content that all the documents were printed and saved to my floppy disk. For additional security, I erased all the files on my computer.

The next day, Sunday, 9 March, we had just arrived home from church when I got a call from Gus von Schweinfurt, a long-time former administrator for Morobe Province. German by origin, Schweinfurt had migrated to Australia and spent most of his early days in PNG. He was with the convener of the German Project (a proposed helicopter acquisition project that Haiveta had been pushing before Sandline came along), Mr Mansfield from Germany. Schweinfurt asked me to dinner that night at Bacchus Restaurant at the Airways Hotel off Jacksons Airport.

I was in my study at Flagstaff, glossing through the draft operation plan, when Major Enuma arrived in his jogging shorts. I asked him into the office and closed the door. There was nobody in sight, and Enuma went through the pros and cons of his appointment as operations officer for Rausim Kwik. After a few minutes of discussion, he arrived at the point. 'Sir,' he said, 'I am deeply honoured to be the operations officer for Operation Rausim Kwik. I know that what we will do is unconventional and may well be seen as being mutinous. But if we do not stop Sir Julius and the cabinet and Tim Spicer and his schemes, who else will?'

We went through the operational concept, from isolation to deportation of the mercenaries and mobilisation of the civil community to force Sir Julius, Haiveta, and Ijape to resign. I then passed Enuma the first blueprint copy of Operation Rausim Kwik, and he took a much longer time to go through it, together with my appreciation notes. The most significant threat that Enuma saw were the dissident groups within the defence force and the security company, Network International, especially the presence of the Rodrigues brothers. As he was on secondment to the Electoral Commission, he would speak to Michael Malabag, the deputy electoral commissioner, to ask for his release for a month of social leave.

I was delighted to have Enuma on board. He carried considerable physical presence—more than most officers of his rank—and commanded genuine respect from everyone he worked with. As we parted, he assured me that he would be available on an analogue phone 24/7. We agreed to a simple voice code if we needed to speak to each in person; however, other than arranging to meet as and when required, we would maintain complete cell phone silence. We also agreed that D-Day was Monday, 17 March, in eight days' time, and that D - 1 would be Sunday, 16 March, for phase 1. Enuma and I agreed that only I would have the authority to cancel Operation Rausim Kwik. We also agreed that the operation would only be called off by me for the following reasons:

a. if we lost the element of secrecy, in which case Sir Julius would dismiss me and order intervention by the National Security Council (in which case I would resign—I had already prepared my letter of resignation)
b. if we were faced with a counter-operations group that was markedly superior in numbers and firepower
c. if the Sandline command team and mercenaries were used by elements of the PNGDF and police to counter us and if this threatened large-scale loss of life

We then discussed those we considered as major threats within the PNGDF: Col. Leo Nuia, Lt Col. Carl Marlpo, and Maj. Geoffrey Wiri. While there were question marks over a few others, these were seen as the main threats. We agreed that most middle- and junior-ranking officers were either loyal to me or too timid to take us on. As Enuma departed, I reflected that, even with the best military plan, success or failure depends on the operations commander leading in the field. In this case, I knew that I could have complete confidence in Enuma to have the courage and personal determination to see it through.

In the evening, I went to the Bacchus Restaurant at Airways Hotel. It was a typical Greek restaurant with a well-stocked central bar, hanging lights, and a well-lit dining area. In the corner of the restaurant were Schweinfurt and Mansfield. As we ordered dinner and commenced our conversation, I could see Nic Violaris through the glass entry door. He seemed to be trailing me everywhere in Port Moresby as he was indeed up to something big, I calculated. He had a big grin on his face as he shook hands around our table. Sitting briefly to join us, he whispered to me, 'If you have problems with this German helicopter project, please let me know as we have already identified funds for it from Public Officers Superannuation Funds and Defence Force Retirement Funds.' I was not surprised with the role Nic Violaris was playing as he had been in Hong Kong with Haiveta and was now acting on behalf of those in power, attempting to be a broker for the German government in a defence capabilities acquisition project. At the end of the dinner, I told Mansfield that—Violaris's confidence notwithstanding—the government's ability to find a source of funding for the purchase of German helicopters currently appeared very unlikely.

On Tuesday, 11 March, Lt Col. Kamona Falaniki arrived and dropped by my office. It was good to see him. Many years earlier when I was a young captain, he had been operations commander of D Company, 2RPIR. I went through the whole issue and the implications of hiring Sandline mercenaries to operate on Bougainville. I explained that their assessment of the mission had changed to that of securing the mine and patrolling and keeping open the Espie Highway. He agreed with my review and promised to instruct his troops to remain vigilant during the conduct of Operation Rausim Kwik. He assured me of his personal loyalty and departed back to Buka.

It was now Thursday, 13 March. The week leading up to D-Day was an anxious and stressful time. Ovia Rauka rang and asked me to get members of the SFU and PNGDF Operations Branch and Defence Intelligence to sign a secrecy oath to keep the details of Operation Oyster secret. I told Rauka that all PNGDF members had already taken an oath to keep state secrets and that we had never been put in any security situation in which we were required to take an oath in the presence of another civilian head, let alone the director general of NIO.

The real scare came when Peter Niesi, a very capable and respected reporter from the *Post Courier* newspaper, called to interview me about rumours of a possible coup and a planned operation to evict the Sandline mercenaries. I always maintained an open line with journalists and so took the call. I denied any such plots. I said that, yes, we had some concerns about the credibility of Sandline International but that Sir Julius and his senior cabinet ministers had made up their mind to be fully engaged with Sandline. I suggested to Niesi that perhaps some junior- and middle-ranking officers were not happy with the decision and, now that the engagement had been made public, that it was they who were expressing their opinion against Sandline. That was the last time he called me until the launch of the operation.

On Friday, 14 March, Major Toropo arrived back from Wewak after briefing his second in command, Capt. Bola Renagi, on the specifics of Operation Rausim Kwik. He confirmed what I had already heard—that Sandline troops in Wewak were unfamiliar with close jungle operations, totally unfit physically, and very clumsy during night operations and lacked field discipline. He said they openly smoked during training and on mock operations at night. They also had a policy that they called 'no trace'. Sgt Francis Jakis, who had trained with Sandline, told Toropo that the mercenaries spoke openly of taking no prisoners and leaving no trace. After they captured the enemy and civilians, their policy was to kill them all. No one's life was spared.

I called Toropo and Enuma to my office before the end of the day. I said, 'Gentlemen, we have a problem, and it is a very serious one. The executive officer for Sandline International, Tim Spicer, is out of the country, and therefore, Rausim Kwik will need to be placed on hold until his return. At this stage, I don't know when that will be. Otherwise, we are all set to go. Another issue concerns the arrival of the final consignment of weapons on the Antonov, now expected around 27 March. If Tim Spicer is not here by 26 March, before the arrival of the final consignment, we will have to readjust our plans. In any case, we have to re-scope our mission analysis. And if we need to delay that long, the whole of Operation Rausim Kwik may be at risk as I have had to brief too many of our people in advance of the operation, and maintaining operational security that long may well prove to be impossible.'

We agreed to make a final assessment the following day, Saturday, 15 March. This was the day of final bonding as we needed to do a final head count with junior officers and selected soldiers and determine where we stood. Shooting practice at the twenty-five-metre range at Goldie River Barracks opposite the SFU base and Warrior Training Wing was the perfect place to regroup and do a final assessment.

On the way to Goldie River Barracks, I got the call I was hoping for. Tim Spicer, in a very excited and positive voice, said, 'General Singirok, Commander, I have just arrived from Hong Kong. Thank you for the foreign affairs officer who was able to assist me through immigration. I am at East Boroko, Fort Williams. And just to confirm, I'll see you with Nic and Carl in your office at seven tomorrow evening for a final run-through of our plans.' Little did the foreign affairs official know that in Tim Spicer's carry-on bag from Hong Kong was just under half a million in US dollars of undeclared cash.

After the shooting practice and having tested all our personal weapons, I informed Enuma and Toropo that Tim Spicer was back in Port Moresby. 'Gentlemen,' I said, 'saddle up. The game is on.'

CHAPTER 6

D-Day - 1

Moderation in War is imbecility. Hit first. Hit hard. Keep on hitting.

—Lord John Fisher

The result of the operation would almost certainly be my immediate removal as commander PNGDF, followed by a trial for sedition- or worse high treason or even death by bullet from the opposing force.

—Jerry Singirok

The time was four thirty, Sunday morning, 16 March 1997. Flagstaff House, Murray Barracks, was the official residence of the commander of the Papua New Guinea Defence Force. We were asleep upstairs in the main bedroom. A rooster crowing outside the louvred windows was answered from somewhere farther down the hill. I woke up from a fitful night's sleep and looked over at Weni, who was still sound asleep. It had been a restless humid Port Moresby night; the bedroom air stirred lazily by a slowly turning ceiling fan. The chrysanthemum-scented remains of a couple of pyrethrum mosquito coils, Fish brand, were smouldering on either side of the bed. My left arm and wrist were aching from an old bullet wound sustained while trying to retrieve the body of a dead colleague officer and his batman at Guava Village,

Panguna mine, on Bougainville in 1994. Despite several attempts at surgery at the finest hospitals in Australia, the wounds had not yet healed completely and probably never would.

Don't let anyone about to authorise a major military operation tell you that they slept well the night before its launch—particularly an operation that could cost lives; that had as one of its aims the removal from office of a prime minister, deputy prime minister and treasurer, and defence minister; and that involved the arrest at gunpoint of a seventy-strong team of black African mercenaries and their white South African and English commanding officers. They were the most notorious of all mercenaries and private armies, highly sourced by corporate giants, and feared in sub-Saharan Africa. The result of the operation would almost certainly be my immediate removal as commander of the PNGDF, followed by a trial for sedition—or worse high treason or even death by a bullet from the opposing force.

Sunday morning or not, I realised that more sleep was beyond me. As I took a long cold shower to wake up, I went through the operation in my mind. There was still time to call it off. But that was no longer a real option. Too much was now at stake. Apart from anything else, a Bulgarian-flagged Antonov An-124 aircraft, the largest military transport aircraft in the world, loaded with two Mi-24 helicopter gunships and hundreds of thousands of rounds of ammunition, high explosives, mortars, and rockets was in the air, heading towards Port Moresby's Jacksons International Airport. If I did not move to abort the mercenary operation, it would be too late. Having a heavily armed pair of mercenary gunships on the ground was not going to make my life any easier. Not for the first time in my life as a military officer, I accepted that there was much truth in the old saying 'Boldness is best. And speed, resolution, and absolute secrecy are everything.'

I made a stiff cup of instant black coffee and grabbed some toast and a bowl of cereal. Looking in at the kids' room, I saw Maib and Moka fast asleep. It was too early to wake them. I told Weni that I needed to go down to the office to pick up some documents.

Weni was just as anxious as I was. We both understood the consequence of the impending operations on our family and our children. We had also discussed the impact on our son Futua, who was attending Wesley College in Auckland, New Zealand.

There was always comfort in action. Slipping into my maroon Landcruiser four-by-four support vehicle, I headed out down the hill and into town. I drove myself to avoid drawing attention to my presence. After a hot and humid night, the dawn air was crisp and refreshing. Few people were still about. Some dogs were nosing through street rubbish. In thinking through what was to unfold later that day, I accepted that there were two main threats to the success of what was being planned. If there was to be an armed confrontation with the men carrying out my orders, it would likely come from the security company Network International or from one or more mobile police squads of the Royal Papua New Guinea Constabulary.

Intervention from Australia's Third Brigade based out of Townsville was also a very real possibility that I needed to plan for, particularly if there was a widespread breakdown in law and order as a result of the operation to arrest the mercenaries. But first things first. While the Australians could become an issue, especially if the lives of Australian nationals were perceived to be at risk, I hoped to negate that by hitting hard, moving fast, and taking the mercenaries and the government by complete surprise and then deporting the mercenaries before they could become a further issue. In this, I hoped to secure the cooperation of the police or at least their neutrality. But Network International, being owned and controlled by the prime minister's family, was another matter.

Network International was located at Section 61, Allotment 7, Gordon, Port Moresby. I wanted to see again for myself their precise location and fix in my mind the routes in and out of there and the nature of surrounding properties in case my tactical commanders needed to throw a security cordon around their headquarters to keep Byron Chan and his boys off the street and out of our hair. They were reported to also hang out at a clubhouse on Garden Hills along Waigani Drive. I was satisfied that there was no unusual movement at either place and that they could be contained at both locations should that become necessary.

I headed back to Murray Barracks and Flagstaff House. Traffic was very light at this hour on a Sunday morning, and I knew I had drawn no undue attention by my early morning drive. High up on Brigadier Hill, Flagstaff House enjoys extensive views out over Basilisk Passage and the lush suburb of Boroko. It had been my home since my appointment as commander of the PNGDF in late 1995.

As I entered the kitchen, I found Weni preparing breakfast. Sunday mornings in the Singirok household were normally relaxed affairs with family gathered around and a chance to catch up on one another's news from the week. But that morning, I was feeling anxious. It was less than ten hours to the start of an operation that, whatever its outcome, would change PNG's history forever and seal my fate as commander. I feared the consequences for my wife and family. But I needed to act, regardless of the personal consequences.

I joined my family for breakfast but found it hard to eat. In my mind, I went over the details of the operational plan as I sipped hot black coffee and thought about the evening and the uncertainties of the days ahead. Rising from the family table, I went upstairs to the en suite off the main bedroom to shave and prepare for the day. At 40 years of age, when I was appointed commander of the PNGDF, I was one of the youngest brigadier generals the PNGDF had ever had and possibly the youngest commander of armed forces anywhere in the region at that time. I looked at myself critically in the mirror. I looked a lot older that morning than my 41 years of age. Command at the top was a lonely business and an extremely ageing one. It required political courage just as much as military courage. I could have still called off the operation, and nobody but those closest to me would be the wiser. But I would have been the poorer, and so would my country.

The moment of weakness and doubt passed almost as soon as it arose. I rinsed off the last of the soapsuds and dressed quickly in my working uniform, pausing only to check my appearance in the bedroom mirror. Command was as much about appearances and theatre as it was about substance. I needed to look the part of a military commander who knew his mind and was in control of events, which was not always easy.

I went downstairs to my study and retrieved my copy of the operational orders for Operation Rausim Kwik. I made some last-minute amendments to reflect what I had seen in my early morning reconnaissance and then went over the orders one last time. I was due to brief my hand-picked team later that day.

Outside my study, some dogs were still barking, and the noise of children playing filled the air. I shut these sounds out as I retrieved the disc with my draft orders on it and fired up my personal computer. As it came to life, I looked around my study. Class photographs lined the walls from my early days at the Joint Services College, the Royal Pacific Islands Regiment, Australian Army Command, and Staff College and as an instructor in the Tactics Wing at the Australian Army Land Warfare Centre, Kokoda Barracks, Canungra, in the early 1990s. I glanced along the rows of books on command and leadership, military history, literature, and philosophy that had shaped my thinking and professional development. Now as I thought about what lay ahead, I found myself falling back on my infantry training, my years of operational experience in the field as a young captain commanding at Vanimo and as a major appointed twice as operations officer for both infantry battalions and on Bougainville, and subsequent staff appointments including very importantly my years as chief of defence intelligence at PNGDF headquarters. I thought about my exchange experiences with the US Army and the British Army and friendships built there and in Australia and New Zealand. All these played their part as I reviewed and made last-minute amendments to my operational orders.

I printed out a single hard copy of the finished operational order. I also retrieved the computer discs with my address to the nation, my letters to PM Sir Julius Chan, the chief justice, the governor general, and the minister for defence, advising them of my actions. Finally, I prepared a distribution list to help ensure that my letters reached the right people at the right time.

By now, it was late morning. I slipped down the hill to my office in the headquarters building, Murray Barracks, and prepared for a round of afternoon briefings and the administration of a secrecy oath to those officers whom I had hand-picked to carry out the operation. The building was deserted as I pulled into my official carpark. My office was located upstairs at the southern end of the building, up an outside flight of concrete stairs to the second-floor corridor that contained various staff offices and a conference room.

I let myself into my office and took a quick look around. On the wall behind my desk and directly opposite the entrance door was a large PNG flag. On the right-hand wall, as seen from the door, a presentation copy of a Singaporean assault rifle, the SR 88A, manufactured by Chartered Industries of Singapore, was mounted.

Elsewhere around my office were a variety of service plaques from units that I had served in or visited over the course of my career. On my desk, as a symbol of authority, was my carefully polished swagger stick on a stand and a carved marble nameplate specially made in the Philippines and presented to me by my sister, Balim. It had a brass ferrule at one end made from a .303-calibre rifle casing.

I went over to the louvred glass windows above the couch and drew the curtains so that I could see down into the car park and across to the parade ground on the lower level. I liked to be able to see out as I worked. I turned on the air conditioning. Settling behind my desk, I hit the power button on my computer. I typed in my password and fed in my discs. I then started printing out the letters and documents that were to be distributed across government tomorrow.

Around midday, my aide-de-camp, Capt. John Keleto, arrived along with my bodyguard, Cpl John Koraia. Both soldiers were looking on edge as if knowing that something was brewing. With Corporal Koraia standing by outside, I briefed Keleto on the operation and told him that I wanted four subalterns to report to my office precisely at 1500 hours: Capt. Belden Namah, Capt. Ben Sesenu, Lt Nick Henry, and navy lieutenant Augustine Emba. I told Keleto that it was very important that he find each of these men as the timing and secrecy of the entire operation depended on them reporting to me as ordered. I also told him that no substitutes were to be permitted.

Then I briefed my personal bodyguard, Corporal John Koraia. Koraia was one of the most honest, reliable, and dependable soldiers I had ever known. He had become close to me as commander and was extremely protective of my personal safety. He was the first PNGDF military policeman to be issued with a maroon-coloured British paratroop regiment 'red' beret, which he wore with pride everywhere. Koraia was of mixed parentage, Central and Gulf Provinces, from a fishing village at Domara down the coast from Port Moresby. At 175 cm (5 feet 9 inches) tall and weighing 90 kg, John was in excellent physical form to serve as my personal bodyguard. He reacted to my brief on the operation exactly as I had hoped. Straightening his beret and snapping to attention, he said he would stand by me to the end, regardless of the outcome. I could see that he meant every word of what he said. Loyalty at its best.

Walking over to my office safe, I drew one of my two personal weapons, an Israeli Galil ARM submachine gun. This was the sniper variant, called the Galil Tzalafim or 'Galatz', that used 7.62 × 51.00 mm NATO ammunition for additional accuracy. Giving it to John along with a couple of twenty-five-round magazines, I instructed him to clean and oil it thoroughly and check that all the working parts were fully operational. Not that either of us was expecting to have to use it; however, planning for the worst was always a good military principle. John's broad smile as he took the submachine gun from me was worth more than words could express.

At 1400 hours, Maj. Walter Enuma and Sgt Chris Mora arrived. It was good to see them. Both men had served alongside me on operations on Bougainville. They were among the bravest and most capable soldiers I had ever known—tough, resolute, reliable, unswerving in their determination, and thoroughly dependable. If you were caught in an ambush in the middle of a tropical downpour, you couldn't wish for anyone better to fight your way out with. They were excellent soldiers whose tactical ability and leadership skills had been tested time and again in the jungles of Bougainville against a tough and equally resolute enemy.

Just over a week earlier, I had sent a message to Major Enuma, then on secondment to the PNG Electoral Commission for the forthcoming 1997 national elections, asking him to call on me quietly at Flagstaff

House that weekend. Taking Major Enuma into my confidence, I had briefed him on what I intended and asked him to take on the role of operations officer for Operation Rausim Kwik. He had asked for twenty-four hours to think it over. The next day, he came on board, taking over the task of drafting the detailed operational orders. Sgt Chris Mora, also on secondment to the Electoral Commission, had joined him. Both had taken leave from the commission to draw up the plans for the operation. Enuma said he was honoured to serve me as operations officer. Knowing him as well as I did, I had no doubt that he would execute the operation effectively.

One other officer whom I had briefed on the operation, in fact the very first officer whom I had taken into my confidence, was Maj. Gilbert Toropo, the first officer commanding PNGDF's Special Forces Unit. Toropo, who I am proud to say has since risen to the rank of major general and is the current chief of the defence force, was another extraordinarily capable soldier whose quiet abilities, military efficiency, and natural authority spoke for themselves. I did not want to place Toropo in the direct line of operations. Rather, I wanted him to keep a quiet eye on things as the operation unfolded, ready to step in with other soldiers from the SFU if and when the situation demanded. Major Enuma and I went through the operational orders and then discussed a range of command and control issues as well as how to deal with the various contingencies that could arise.

At 1445, my ADC knocked on the door to advise that the subalterns had arrived and were waiting for my instructions. 'Bring them,' I said. They marched in smartly in single file, halted, came to attention, and saluted.

'Thank you, gentlemen,' I said, smiling. 'Relax and take a seat, and Major Enuma and I will brief you on why you are here.'

I paused and looked over at the subalterns, now sitting stiffly on my office couch. It was a squeeze for the four of them, especially Capt. Belden Namah, a fearsome-looking, militarily efficient, bullet-headed man his troops called him 'Skull'. Namah had been my intelligence officer when I was the commanding officer of the First Battalion (1RPIR). He was a graduate of the Royal Military College, Duntroon,

Australia, and a natural-born enforcer whom you definitely would not want to encounter in a urine-lacquered alley on a dark night. Typical of the many military exploits credited to Namah was a helicopter extraction from enemy-held territory east of Panguna mine at a village called Paruparu on Bougainville in 1994. As his CO, I had ordered his rescue and extraction, but there was no cleared helicopter landing zone near Namah where the chopper could be put down. Undaunted and with the helicopter hovering immediately overhead, Namah slung his rifle over his back, did a standing jump, took hold of the helicopter skids with his bare hands, and—hanging there in mid-air and savagely buffeted by the helicopter's downwash—was extracted to safety. It was a feat of skill, raw determination, and brute strength that has probably never been equalled.

Squeezed in next to Namah was Capt. Ben Sesenu, another RMC Duntroon graduate. Alongside Sesenu was Lt Augustine Emba, a private soldier who, as an enlisted officer cadet, had switched streams from land to maritime. He was sent to the US Coast Guard Academy in New London, Connecticut, to complete his training as a midshipman before returning to become the executive officer on board HMPNGS *Salamaua*, a Balikpapan-class heavy landing craft powered with twin diesels and armed with 2.00×0.50 inch machine guns.

Next to Emba was Lt Nicholas Henry, a New Zealand Army–trained soldier who had also shown fearlessness in conducting numerous fighting patrols with me on Bougainville. Like me, he had ended up with a serious bullet wound, in his case to the buttocks and intestines, and was lucky to have survived.

Looking over the four subalterns, I was confident that Major Enuma and I had picked the right men for the task we had in mind. 'Gentlemen,' I said, 'tonight you are to be charged with an operation that will likely change the course of this nation and make history. Details of the assignment will be given to you later, once you have been sworn to secrecy. But before I administer the oath, I want to outline why you are here and what it is that, as your commander, I want you to accomplish in my name.'

I paused and glanced over at my men. They remained silent, but I could see the anticipation in their eyes. Looking quickly at my notes, I ran through my outline. 'Gentlemen, you have been personally selected by me as your commander for an important assignment. The history books will be rewritten because of what we are about to do. Tonight we are going to put a stop to the government's plan to employ the Sandline mercenaries to wipe out the leadership of the Bougainville Revolutionary Army. You are going to arrest and forcibly detain Tim Spicer, the commanding officer of the Sandline mercenaries, and his senior officers when they come to this office at 1900 hours this evening. Separately, we have taken steps to round up all seventy or so of the remaining mercenaries at their various training and deployment locations around PNG. They will be deported back to Africa as soon as we can arrange their transport.

'It has been twenty-two years since PNG gained its independence. For the last nine years, we have been trying to resolve the Bougainville crisis with various peace initiatives supported by military operations against the BRA. It has become very clear to me as your commander that, at any acceptable level of force, there is no prospect of finding a military solution to the Bougainville crisis. The government's initiative in hiring the Sandline mercenaries to do its dirty work does not alter this fundamental truth. As we have ourselves seen through repeated attempts at imposing a military solution, any such approach is doomed to failure.

'There are many reasons why I believe that the use of mercenaries is both ill-advised and unlawful. And apart from the illegality, the introduction of African mercenaries into the Pacific region, with the certainty of outright failure and the loss of many lives, risks making our country look ridiculous and is an insult to our sovereignty.

'Moreover, the use of mercenaries at the force levels proposed will risk permanent alienation of Bougainville as well as changing the whole spectrum of security in the region. Once Sandline personnel are here in the country, usurping the constitutional role of the PNGDF, we can forget the sovereignty of our beloved country. The consequences of our government's decision to engage Sandline are far more damaging than we can comprehend. Our constitution and our sovereignty will mean nothing to us.

'As your commander, I will not be used by our politicians nor allow a foreign security company or even a military force to go against our people. This government's dream of imposing a quick-fix military solution on Bougainville to reopen the Panguna mine is farcical. I will not be answerable to the people about their actions, and therefore, I have made this decision to cancel the operation and evict the mercenaries out of this country. They can go back to Africa, where they belong.

'I have selected each of you personally, knowing very well that you will conduct the operation in the most professional manner and with minimum loss of lives. I have explained the background to this operation in the simplest possible way as it is important for you, as the key players, to be fully conversant with the rationale for it. This operation is not a military coup. Let me say that once again. This is not in any way a military coup. It is no more than the cancellation of a military operation that I believe is both illegal and extremely ill-advised and that, if it were to go ahead, would alienate our people and permanently damage our reputation as a country.

'You will be allocated specific tasks in this operation, the full details of which will be detailed to you once you have taken a secrecy oath that I will administer to you personally. I should add that there is no withdrawal for any of you now that you are aware what is about to unfold.

'The operation is code-named Operation Rausim Kwik. It is classified top secret. There are to be no landline communications by anyone and no emails, radio, or other electronic conversations that could be intercepted and used to abort the operation. We need to achieve complete surprise tonight, and to do that, I am demanding the maintenance of absolute operational and communications security. I want this to be very clearly understood. Families are not to be informed, nor are any members of the police or politicians of any stripe whatsoever. And needless to add, there are to be no leaks to the media.

'Your operational commander for Rausim Kwik is Maj. John Walter Enuma, and he will brief you on the full operational details as soon as you are sworn to secrecy.' I could see the excitement in everyone's eyes now that they had been briefed—and a measure of anxiety too.

'Are there any questions, gentlemen?' Some questions of administration were raised and also how best to keep what was about to unfold from the rest of the barracks. I said that I would be addressing the troops and going on nationwide radio in the morning, but until then, it would be best not to mix with those yet to be briefed on the operation. It was agreed that a takeaway meal would be provided for everyone involved so as not to risk families picking up on the impending operation.

Capt. John Keleto and I then administered the secrecy oath. Each officer came forward to my desk, placed his left hand on the Bible in front of them, and raised their right hand to repeat after me the following oath:

> I [name] of the Papua New Guinea Defence Force hereby on Sunday 16 March 1997, pursuant to the provisions of the Constitution of the Independent State of Papua New Guinea and the Defence Force Act Chapter 74 and by virtue of the Oaths, Affirmation and Statutory Declaration Act Chapter no. 317 of the revised Laws of the Independent State of Papua New Guinea do solemnly and sincerely swear that I will not divulge by word, deed or cause to be divulged any official secrets in whatever form to any person without lawful authority whether during or after my service in or with the Papua New Guinea Defence Force and I do swear that I will truly serve the Independent State of Papua New Guinea and the government in all matters pertaining to my service and I will faithfully discharge my duties according to the law. So help me God.

> Sworn this day before me.
> Brigadier General Jerry SINGIROK, MBE,
> Commander PNGDF

Each officer came forward to my table and took turns with the oath, starting with ADC Capt. John Keleto, then Capt. Ben Sesenu, Lt Augustine Emba, Lt Nicholas Henry, Capt. Belden Namah, Sgt Chris Mora, and finally Cpl John Koraia.

As we shall see, out of the subalterns selected for the operation, one would turn out to be a Judas Iscariot. Not only did he betray us but he also looted from his enemy, Tim Spicer. More of this later.

In our choice of the operational team, we took a gamble. As I said to Walter Enuma, the important thing was that Operation Rausim Kwik was now launched, and there was no way we would cancel it. From this point onwards, it was merely a question of stage management, determination to succeed, speed, toughness, and our military training and skills kicking in.

For his part, Enuma reaffirmed his commitment to the operation by making a short but very significant statement to everyone in my office. 'Gentlemen, thank you for taking your oaths. Whatever happens this evening and from tomorrow onwards, it is now a matter of duty. We are committed to saving our nation and the constitution from being exploited by foreigners who are misleading and using our leaders for their own selfish ends. I have, for the past week, considered all the pros and cons of what we are up against. I strongly support the commander in his decision. We will ensure that the whole operation is executed and accomplished exactly as we have planned. We have all operated and worked alongside General Singirok in the field and on numerous operations where our lives have been on the line. We know that we can depend on each other. I have both admiration and the deepest respect for the general. We will not let him down or our nation. As the operations officer for Operation Rausim Kwik, I will ensure, with your help, that we achieve our mission at whatever price it takes.'

Major Enuma's remarks to the team were important as a demonstration of his willingness to lead the team for a cause he believed in. There were no senior officers of the rank of lieutenant colonel and upwards involved in the operation because some senior officers were upset and envious of my sudden rise and appointment as commander over them, and their involvement could compromise the success of our operation. The men in my office were all hand-picked, young career officers with years of service life still in them. What made them stand out were their proven tactical and leadership abilities. They were not political. They were highly intelligent and motivated, as well as being operationally experienced. Most were not married. Why were they so committed? I asked myself. I could think of two reasons: loyalty and respect. Loyalty is earned once we respect each other based on our professionalism. Each of us in the room had respect for one another, drawn from the various operational assignments we had been on together. They all reassured themselves, and me, that we were a solid team and that there was no way we would be broken up.

With that, I bade them good luck and dismissed them. After the subalterns departed my office, I went through the concept of operations one more time with Enuma. This would be the last time we would be together before the planned encounter with Sandline executives at seven o'clock that evening in my office.

The general operational concept of Operation Rausim Kwik was as follows:

a. Tim Spicer and his two executives would come to my office at 1900 hours for a prearranged meeting to discuss the operational details of what had become known as Operation Oyster. They would be met by Lt Col. Walter Salamas, acting chief of operations. He had not been briefed on our operation and so could not unwittingly tip off the Sandline team that anything unusual was about to unfold. After handing the party over to my ADC and bodyguard stationed outside the door of my office, Salamas would be released from duty for the evening and instructed to go to his house immediately and not to leave the camp. Tim Spicer would be detained, forcibly if necessary, and searched, physically secured, and stripped of his analogue phone and any weapon on him before being transported by a security party to the landing craft base where HMPNGS *Salamaua* would be waiting for him, with Capt. John Wilson and his executive officer Augustine Emba in the wheelhouse to handle the ship. Cdr Col. Max Aleale, CO of the landing craft base and of *Salamaua*, would be responsible for this phase of the operation. Spicer would be locked into a cabin on board *Salamaua*. The *Salamaua* would sail in a southerly direction out of the harbour and stay out of sight of land until I instructed it to return. The intention was to separate Tim Spicer from the two other members of his team and prevent him from getting to the prime minister and other cabinet ministers or communicating in any way with the rest of his Sandline operatives. In short, this was to be a classic decapitation mission designed to disrupt and disorient the rest of the Sandline executive team and prevent them from mounting an effective response to the arrests.

b. The Sandline operational ground commander, South African brigadier general Nic van den Bergh, and intelligence officer Carl Deats, would be detained in my office, by force if necessary, and taken to First Battalion RPIR officers' mess at Taurama Barracks, where they would be held securely until deportation formalities were completed. A section of infantry troops from the First Regiment RPIR would take over the security duties and transport requirements once Nic van den Bergh and Carl Deats had been detained, and disarmed if necessary, in my office.

c. A security party led by Lt Col. Yaura Sasa would go to the Sandline executive flat at Fort Williams on Vaivai Street in Boroko, where Tim Spicer and some of his colleagues had been staying. There, they would detain Sandline logistics officer Michael Edwards and transfer him securely to Taurama Barracks. Lt Ben Sesenu and his troops would then mount a twenty-four-hour guard at Tim Spicer's flat as key documents and money were suspected to be in the flat along with the possibility of personal sidearm and ammunition.

d. For my part, I would go with a party of three soldiers to the Australian Broadcasting Corporation correspondent Sean Dorney's residence and detain Michael Ashworth, the Sandline press officer, and have him transferred to Taurama Barracks.

e.   The following day, on 17 March, I would speak personally to Police Commissioner Robert Nenta and Gov. Gen. Sir Wiwa Korowi and dispatch letters advising the cancellation of Operation Oyster (as the mercenary operation is termed) to PM Sir Julius Chan, CJ Sir Arnold Amet, and Minister for Defence Mathias Ijape.

f.   I would then address the troops who would be paraded for me at Murray Barracks before going to the National Broadcasting Commission (NBC) radio station. I would use their nationwide FM and medium-wave services to inform the nation about my decision to cancel Operation Oyster and my subsequent denouncement of Sir Julius Chan, his deputy, and the defence minister. A very strong section of troops were to hold the NBC grounds and buildings while I talked on the radio.

g.   An Iroquois helicopter was to be airborne over the NBC, and a special services Land Rover with SFU security detail would also be present to assist my evacuation in case there was an attempt to shoot or arrest me.

h.   I would end my day with a press conference at the force conference room at Murray Barracks around midday.

i.   In the meantime, immediate plans would be made to extract the Sandline mercenaries in Wewak and return them to Port Moresby for their deportation out of PNG.

My address to the troops on 17 March was a top priority. The men had to be informed of the major operation under way and the reasons for it, especially as it would affect them directly. As for outlying units of the PNGDF, we would dispatch two couriers, Majors Michael Kupo and John Boino, to the patrol base in Lombrum and the Engineer Battalion in Lae, respectively, to inform the COs, troops, and sailors of my message. They would be asked to remain vigilant but to continue their normal tasks as most of the operations connected with Rausim Kwik would be centred on Port Moresby, including the detention and deportation of Sandline troops in Wewak, East Sepik Province.

I had given my personal issue SIG Sauer P226 MK25 semi-automatic combat pistol, serial number AD 43260, to Major Enuma a week earlier. I figured that he would need it more than me. Besides, I would have my cleaned and oiled Galil submachine gun back from John Koraia before the evening was over. I reminded Enuma once again of the importance of maintaining and achieving our objectives. Then we went through a worst-case scenario analysis in which lives were lost, law and order broke down, and the Australian Army's Third Brigade intervened.

We agreed that the effective use of the media was the key to achieving our outcomes. The public must be informed in a manner that would leave no doubt in the minds of Papua New Guineans about the reason why we were arresting and deporting the mercenaries. The same was true of the importance of informing the troops. I reiterated that, after my address to the nation, the task would not be easy as we had to expect a swift and furious reaction from ministers. They would seek to have us put under immediate arrest, and we would be charged with mutiny.

I looked at Major Enuma and felt for him. I knew that, in appointing him as operations officer, I was asking him to make a huge personal sacrifice. But deep down, I also felt a sense of comfort in having Walter Enuma lead the operation. As he had shown on Bougainville, he was fearless, loyal, and a true warrior. He was the living embodiment of his tribesmen, the great warriors of Mambari, where his forefathers were renowned fighters. They had achieved prominence in World War II operations against the Japanese along the Kokoda track, and Enuma was from the same mighty stock. He was a soldier's son from Popondetta, a dusty little town in Oro Province. He was an asset not only to the defence force but also to the country.

Major Enuma feared neither evil nor foe. To me, he was, and always will be, my mentor and hero. His actions that day and in the following days would confirm my trust and confidence in him.

Both Enuma and I were concerned about the police and what their reactions would be. I said it was important that the police commissioner was contacted at the earliest moment so that he did not deploy his mobile squads without being briefed. We agreed that the key to the success of the operation was an effective media strategy to be controlled by me and the smooth conduct of the operation by Major Enuma. In all our planning, both of us were committed to the use of two of the key principles of war: absolute secrecy and surprise.

It was time for Enuma to make his final preparations, including briefing his men. Before he left, I had a final word for him. 'Walter,' I said, 'tonight you will be up against three tough and very determined characters. I have not the slightest doubt in your ability to take them down. But don't underestimate them. Both van den Bergh and Deats have a reputation in South Africa for absolute ruthlessness and a killer instinct. They have been recruited by Executive Outcomes, the parent company of Sandline, for their ability to achieve results, whatever the cost. Brigadier van den Bergh is their top operator in South Africa, and Deats is a hard man also. They will resist your efforts to arrest them. And they may be armed.

'Tim Spicer is another matter. He was a top cadet and took out the Sword of Honour in his year at Sandhurst. So he may be good at writing essays. But he is a bit of a gasbag, he doesn't have the slightest knowledge or feel for PNG, and he suffers from a very high opinion of himself that he makes no effort to hide.

'Admittedly, there is some reason for his self-regard. As a former British Army officer, he has extensive operational experience. He was battalion operations officer for the Second Battalion, the Scots Guards, in the Falklands Campaign, and he served several tours in Northern Ireland and as a press officer to Sir Michael Rose in Bosnia. When Haiveta checked on Spicer with one of Spicer's former bosses, Gen. Sir Peter de la Billière, Sir Peter described Spicer, who had been his military assistant on Middle East matters after the Gulf War, as 'very go' and 'something of a salesman'. This may or may not be a recommendation coming from Sir Peter, considering his own reputation among the British Special Forces community. On the whole, I suspect it was intended as a bit of a put-down. To be called a salesman by the special operations community sounded like a distinctly British insult.

'Spicer could cave in quietly, or he may try to give you some trouble. Like van den Bergh, he could be carrying a concealed weapon. In his case, most likely a 9 mm Browning, which the Brits tend to favour, though goodness knows why, and possibly a knife. Don't put up with any crap from him. I don't want him killed, but if you have to, a bullet in his knee will slow him down—or both knees if he is slow to get the message, which he shouldn't do as he knows from his days in Northern Ireland what a kneecapping can do. But try not to get a lot of blood on my carpet or all over my office walls. And instead of using a gun on him, I'd back either Namah or you to take him down one on one if he starts to fancy his chances. But however you do it, take all three of them down you must. Without them, I am pretty sure the rest of the mercenaries will fold without any trouble.'

Enuma heard all this with a big smile on his face and a bulge in his pocket, where he had tucked my SIG Sauer. 'Don't worry, sir,' he said. 'We'll have it sorted, no problem. And the carpet should be fine.'

My acting chief of operations, Lieutenant Colonel Salamas, dropped into my office before I departed for home. I asked him to confirm if Tim Spicer was aware of the meeting at 1900 hours. He said that Spicer was aware of the meeting and that he would come separately from van den Bergh and Deats as he had an appointment with the prime minister at 1700 hours in the Prime Minister's Office. News of this prior meeting bothered me. Had the planned operation been compromised? Why was Tim Spicer seeing the prime minister on the quiet and on a Sunday evening when I should be informed of such meetings? What were the two of them planning to discuss? Without showing my concern, I reminded Salamas to ensure that they were all at my office by 1900 hours. He said he would send an immediate message to remind Spicer, van den Bergh, and Deats.

I looked closely at Salamas as he spoke. I wondered whether Salamas knew what was being planned as I was not sure where his loyalties lay. It worried me about a possible compromise if he went straight to Sir Julius Chan as both were from New Ireland and, I assumed, would know each other personally. I could only hope for the best, and his body language suggested that all was well. I had, in fact, dropped a copy of the operations order for Rausim Kwik into his in tray on Friday afternoon, but it appeared he had not taken the time to read it before he left for the weekend. That was the only copy I sent other than the one given to Major Enuma.

I informed Enuma, who had stepped out when Salamas came by, what Spicer was up to. We concluded that there was nothing to be alarmed about. Sir Julius had fallen into the habit of inviting Spicer to drop by for a glass of wine of an evening and a chat, and that was probably all that was involved. Nonetheless, it grated that the prime minister was, by now, obviously putting more confidence in this fly-by-night showman than in his own commander.

Sir Julius was a past master at the use of the media to reinforce his position as prime minister. I knew that the success of what Enuma and I were planning would come down to my ability to get inside the domestic and international news cycle. Starting tomorrow, when news of the arrests became public, I could expect to be at the centre of regional and worldwide news coverage. Sir Julius would use all the powers of his office to wrest ownership of the news cycle off me. The key to the whole operation was which of us could make the most effective use of the media. I was privileged to have completed a media course at Australian Army Staff College in 1991. We were taught three important rules that I always remembered:

1. Be natural.
2. Be in control of yourself and the content of what you intend to communicate.
3. Be onside. Remember, reporters are only interested in a good piece of news. If you can help them, they will be on your side.

I kept these fundamental rules foremost in my mind, and they helped me throughout my career after I returned to PNG.

However, the most important factor behind my ability to handle the media was Weni. She was not only a caring wife and the mother of our children but also a career journalist. After nearly fifteen years in the job, she had gained a significant reputation as a professional, investigative, and ethical journalist. Her journalistic advice had assisted me in many sensitive situations in the past, and for these critical operations, she undoubtedly was very well prepared to assist me in controlling and managing my media strategy.

Operational security was another pressing issue. By 1600 hours on D - 1, only the key players knew what was being planned. Enuma and I listed those who had been briefed. Apart from Maj. Gilbert Toropo, commander of the SFU, these were the COs of the First and Second Battalions; CO of the landing craft base, Max Aleale; second in command of the SFU, Capt. Bola Renagi; the two dispatchers, Majors Kupo and Boino; and, of course, the four subalterns. The task force commander on Bougainville, Lt Col. Kamona Falaniki, had also been briefed.

As I prepared to leave the office, I was fully confident that the operation would be executed with minimum fuss as it was in the capable hands of two of the best officers the defence force had ever produced, Majors Walter Enuma and Gilbert Toropo. However, before going, I couldn't resist a last gesture of confidence in Enuma. Breaking military tradition and protocol, I informed him—with all the solemnity that the occasion demanded—that he was now personally responsible for the conduct of the operation commencing in my office in just under an hour and a half. He could now sit at ease in the commander's big black leather chair and, for the first time in history, play an acting role as commander. With a huge grin, Enuma acknowledged the challenge. Rotating himself around in the chair to get used to his new seniority, he took it all in. Rehearsals for the arrest and detention of the Sandline executives would start as soon as I left.

The plan for the arrest of the Sandline executives was a simple one. But as Clausewitz observed over a hundred years ago, just because something is simple does not mean it will necessarily be easy. Three soldiers, along with Capt. Belden Namah and Lt Ben Sesenu, would hide in the bathroom in an alcove off the commander's office. They were to be armed with semi-automatic rifles. Major Enuma was to be seated in the commander's chair, and he would have my SIG Sauer pistol on display on the desk in front of him. Upon arrival of the

Sandline team, the three soldiers, Namah, and Sesenu were to spring from the toilet and inform Spicer and his two colleagues that there had been a junior officers' coup. They were now under arrest and were to offer no resistance. They would not be harmed if they followed instructions.

The basis of the plan of arrest was to strike an immediate psychological blow to the Sandline team. Events were to unfold very fast—so fast that they would suffer immediate and extreme disorientation. There would be no time allowed for reaction. We were seeking maximum surprise and the appearance of a massive and imminent personal threat to their lives. We would hit them first, hit them hard, and keep on hitting until any resistance they offered was completely overcome.

The first thing that would throw them off balance was the apparent absence of anything unusual. Outside my office, all would appear perfectly normal. My ADC, Capt. John Keleto, and my personal bodyguard, Cpl John Koraia, would be there, as expected, and in uniform. The Sandline team would have been greeted by Lt Col. Walter Salamas, also in uniform and also as expected. All would be perfectly normal. But when they were ushered into my office, they would be hit by the unexpected. None of them had ever met Enuma. They would be expecting to see me. Instead, they would see an unknown but wild-looking person in civilian clothes sitting casually in my chair with a military-issue pistol lying menacingly on the desk in front of him. There would be a moment of total confusion as they tried to work out what was happening.

At that moment, the door behind them would be slammed shut, using maximum force. They would hear it being locked, cutting off their retreat. They would spin around to look at the door. At that moment, the door to my bathroom would burst open, and five armed men would be upon them, shouting in their faces and demanding that they get down on the floor or risk being shot. One of those men would be the bullet-headed Belden Namah, a scary-looking person at the best of times. And Enuma, when he is worked up, has wild staring eyes that make him look perfectly crazed. He would leap around from behind my desk, waving his pistol and yelling at them, 'Get down!

Fucking get down! All of you! On the fucking floor! Now!' In the face of this massive surprise, I didn't expect there would be much effective resistance put up—just shock and awe.

Below, in the car park, would be the special service vehicle (SSV). Using Tim Spicer's hired vehicle, they would split the executives into two groups. Spicer was to be separated and driven to the naval base, where he would be taken out to sea and anchored out of sight of land. Nic van den Bergh and Carl Deats were to be detained and taken to Taurama Barracks, a short ten minutes away from Murray Barracks. There, they were to be accommodated at the officers' mess under armed escort. A section of troops from Taurama Barracks were tasked for this, and they would be pre-positioned at the Difco Canteen, only metres way from the commander's office.

By now, the famous late-afternoon monsoon rains had arrived. This was a godsend as the downpour would provide extra cover for us. When the late afternoon rain arrives, visibility in Port Moresby is cut to just a few feet, which was a blessing for us this afternoon.

Arriving home, I found myself unable to relax. I tried to occupy myself in my study, but I wasn't taking in anything that I was trying to read. As the time ticked by from 1800 hours towards H-hour, 1900 hours, it seemed like an eternity. As I waited, I ran over my objectives for the day one last time to make sure I hadn't overlooked anything. These objectives were

- to arrest and secure the Sandline command team, isolating Tim Spicer from his other colleagues;
- to prevent a rapid regrouping of the main body of Sandline mercenaries currently at the jungle training facility near Wewak, stopping them from returning to Port Moresby to locate and free their command team;
- to keep the location of the command team secret so as to strengthen my hand in my dealings with Sir Julius Chan and his cabinet colleagues;
- to ensure that the police and other possible threats to the success of the operation were suppressed and neutralised;

- to maintain an effective media operation to garner maximum support both internally and internationally;
- to get the three key ministers responsible for the Sandline mercenaries to resign or step aside pending an independent enquiry: the prime minister, the deputy prime minister and treasurer, and the defence minister;
- to get the government to approve the cancellation of Operation Oyster, the contract to employ the mercenaries;
- to maintain public law and order so as not to provide any justification for the Australian Army to get involved;
- most importantly, to get government agreement to restart the peace process on Bougainville.

Back down the hill and near my office block, the activity was building up. By around 1830 hours, an unusual number of troops were positioned near the headquarters building but concealed out of sight. A section plus of troops in jungle fatigues were waiting in the dark on the lawn at Operations Branch, covering the commander's car park only a few metres to the north-west of the commander's office, while civilian-clothed intelligence operators waited behind the headquarters building to add an extra layer of security.

Exactly as scheduled, at 1855 hours, Brig. Gen. Nic van den Bergh and intelligence specialist Carl Deats arrived in their hired Toyota four-wheel drive and pulled up alongside the commander's car park. As their car came to a stop, all eyes in the dark were focused on the two Sandline executives. There was a momentary break in the downpour. Opening the car doors, they retrieved their field briefcases from the back seat and pocketed their mobile phones. They appeared relaxed. Captain Namah, observing this from the commander's bathroom, rushed out to Major Enuma to report that Tim Spicer was absent. There was a short silence. Then Enuma said, 'No problem. We will deal with these two executives first and take care of Spicer when he gets here.'

Within minutes, the two Afrikaners had climbed the steps to my office, where they were met by Captain Keleto and Corporal Koraia. They were shown immediately into my office. Coming around from behind my desk, Major Enuma pointed the pistol at them and said, 'Welcome, gentlemen. There has been a junior officers' coup. You are under arrest. Cooperate and follow instructions, and you will not get hurt.'

As he was speaking, Namah and his fellow soldiers burst into the office from their hiding place, armed with rifles and draped with ammunition belts. Both Sandline officers were too stunned to react. Neither offered any resistance. They were checked for concealed weapons and had their briefcases, wristwatches, wallets, car keys, and phones removed. Both were ushered quickly down to the car park and pushed into the SSV, where a waiting security party drove them straight down to the landing craft base at Fairfax Harbour.

This was the first mistake. Up until now, everything had gone completely to plan. However, to keep them apart from Spicer, whom we wanted to isolate completely, they were supposed to have been taken to Taurama Barracks, not the landing craft base.

Meanwhile, back at Murray Barracks, Lt Col. Walter Salamas was too dumbfounded and shocked by what he had seen to say anything when Timothy Spicer drove in. He arrived only minutes after his colleagues had been driven away under armed guard. By now, a massive downpour of rain had started up again. The noise was terrific as the tropical rain pounded down. Spicer was looking flustered at being late. Glancing at his watch and gathering up his black leather briefcase, he rushed up the steps through the downpour to the commander's office, where he arrived dripping with rain and perspiration.

Meanwhile, the security party near the office had instructed Salamas, in my name, to go home and to remain in his house and forget everything he had seen. The lieutenant colonel obliged without further questions and appeared relieved to go home.

Back upstairs, Captain Keleto and Corporal Koraia were trying to calm Tim Spicer, who was flustered from being late. Keleto informed Spicer that I was waiting, and he was shown into the office via a heavy sliding door that was immediately slammed shut and locked behind him.

The scene by then was one of high tension and drama. Enuma left the commander's chair and stood up near the computer table, holding a firm grip on the pistol. Spicer, hearing the door slam behind him, must have wondered where his colleagues and the commander were and who the wild-looking civilian was who was waving a gun at him.

Spicer apologised for his lateness and expressed surprise that I was not there. Major Enuma told Spicer that I was in the toilet and invited Spicer to take a seat. Enuma walked to the toilet and knocked, and immediately, the door burst open, and Captain Namah and his fellow soldiers leapt into the room with their rifles levelled at Spicer. Namah aimed his carbine at Spicer and said, 'Welcome to the land of the unexpected.' At this point, Spicer probably thought that he was the victim of a practical joke and that I was still in the toilet.

But to his astonishment, this was not a joke, and he immediately realised that he had to fight his way out of the situation now confronting him. Spicer's military training switched on, and he started moving towards Enuma and Namah. Enuma yelled at Namah, 'Do something!'

Namah rushed towards Spicer and grabbed him in a judo hold by the collar of his shirt. He hit Spicer so hard and fast that it was hard to tell if Namah was using the *uchi mata*, the so-called throw of kings, or the double leg takedown, a move banned by the International Judo Federation. Whichever it was, and it might have been Namah's unique blend of both, Spicer was swept off his feet and thrown high in the air before crashing to the floor with Namah on top of him. Spicer was pinned to the floor. 'One wrong move, mate,' Namah said, 'and you will be fucked. You will be dead meat.'

With Namah locking Spicer on the floor in a vicious death grip, Enuma told Spicer not to resist. 'Cooperate, and your life will be spared. Try to escape, and I'll happily shoot you. I've fucking killed before, and I will kill again.'

Namah's exuberant throwing of Tim Spicer cost the defence force four broken glass louvre blades from Spicer's feet hitting the window above the couch and left Spicer with a very sore back and elbows and concussed. He was also dealt the psychological blow of knowing that his dream of earning millions of dollars from ownership of the

Panguna mine was over. Spicer momentarily blacked out on the floor with Namah still on top of him.

Spicer was searched. His belt and shoes were removed, along with his watch, wallet, cell phone, and car keys. With a jacket over his head and his sleeves tied, he was immediately rushed barefoot down the steps and into a 4 × 4 Land Cruiser Prado, where he was secured in the back seat between Major Toropo and Captain Namah. With Sgt Chris Mora and a small convoy party for security, the Land Cruiser disappeared into the dark, heading for the landing craft base.

I had warned Enuma earlier of the chances of security being compromised by the Australians as they had a series of flats and accommodation on Port Road for their diplomatic and military staff. This accommodation, as it happened, was strategically situated to monitor activities at the landing craft base and Fairfax Harbour. I had said to Enuma, 'When you get to the wharf, act as normally as you can, and they will not detect anything.' They did exactly that. Of course, it was dark, and the downpour of rain also helped cut visibility to a minimum.

The time had ticked by to just H + 20, meaning the first phase of the operation took a mere twenty minutes and had been accomplished without a single shot having been fired. The Toyota Prado vehicle with Spicer in it reversed when it arrived at the wharf, and Tim Spicer was forced out onto the wharf immediately adjacent to the landing craft. He still had a jacket over his head. He refused point-blank to get onto the landing craft, demanding instead to see me. Belden Namah instructed him to cooperate and get onto the landing craft. Spicer started to complain again about his mistreatment, but before he could finish, he was given a rough kick in the small of the back that landed him face first on the well deck of the landing craft. From there, he was dragged to a cabin and locked inside. He was warned not to attempt to escape as the harbour was infested with sharks and saltwater crocodiles that would make short work of him if he landed in the water.

On board *Salamaua* was the commander, Max Aleale. Lt John Wilson was in the wheelhouse, giving sailing instructions. I had chosen to use *Salamaua* as Spicer's place of concealment as there were no problems over a potential clash of loyalties. Aleale and I were college mates who had graduated together from the 1/75 officer cadet intake. Aleale had always been a solid team member on operational duties and socially. He had been confidentially briefed the previous week to get the ship fully stocked and operationally ready for deployment within Port Moresby waters. He had reported to me at 1600 hours on 14 March that the ship was 80 per cent operationally ready. 'No task too difficult,' he confirmed.

As for Lt John Wilson, I had instructed him as a student at the Officer Cadet School in Lae in 1982, and we had later developed a good and professional relationship in operations on Bougainville.

Nic van den Bergh was not supposed to be on board *Salamaua*. The ship was specifically and only meant for Tim Spicer. However, in all the drama that took place at Murray Barracks, the troops who formed the security detail mistook van den Bergh for Spicer and took him to the ship. Nic van den Bergh was relocated from the ship back to shore, where he joined his Afrikaner mate Carl Deats in the much friendlier environment of the officers' mess at the First Battalion, Taurama Barracks. With Tim Spicer securely locked on board, the *Salamaua* sailed with the ship's company at 1945 hours towards Gemo Island. Spicer wasn't going anywhere apart from where the ship took him.

Meanwhile, back at Flagstaff House, I was receiving my first reports. Capt. John Keleto was the first to give me an update. Looking pretty shaken, he reported that all went as planned with the arrests except that four glass louvre windows had been broken in my office when Namah threw Spicer on the floor. My office was now secured, and the next update expected was from Major Enuma down at the wharf.

Because I had imposed a complete communications blackout, we could not communicate to either the ship or the wharf. Therefore, there was nothing for it but to wait as patiently as possible. While waiting for Enuma, the two security details arrived at Flagstaff with the hired vehicles belonging to Tim Spicer and Nic van den Bergh. Enuma arrived shortly afterwards, looking very focused and determined. Once he had settled down, he gave me a quick debrief on the progress of the first part of the operation.

Enuma reported that van den Bergh, Deats, and Spicer had all been arrested, with only Spicer providing any real opposition. Through a mix-up, both van den Bergh and Spicer had ended up on the ship, but this had now been straightened out with the timely intervention of Gilbert Toropo, assisted by Belden Namah and a security party. Everyone was now safely secured where they were supposed to be—Spicer on board *Salamaua* and heading out to sea, van den Bergh and Deats under guard at Taurama Barracks. All cell phones had been removed, so there was no chance of any one of the three Sandline executives communicating with one another or alerting either their men in the field or getting in touch with ministers or consular representatives.

Enuma then referred to the rest of our plan. The immediate next step was to arrest Michael Edwards, the senior logistics officer for Sandline. He was staying at Sandline's accommodation at Fort Williams. This was where Spicer had rented a flat belonging to Atlas Steel at Vaivai Avenue in the Fort Williams suburban area of Boroko. The issue was how Edwards could be arrested from a flat in the middle of Boroko without raising any suspicions from neighbours or others.

I came up with a simple plan. I sent for Lt Col. Yaura Sasa, the PNGDF liaison officer attached to the Sandline command team. Yaura Sasa, two years my senior, had served with me at 2RPIR. Knowing his abilities and operational experiences on Bougainville, I had appointed him as the liaison officer for Sandline. He was thoroughly familiar with their senior staff, including Edwards. I briefed Sasa about the operation and ordered him to go to Fort Williams with a security party to inform Edwards about the cancellation of Operation Oyster. Edwards was to cooperate and follow instructions. He was to be accommodated alongside his colleagues at the officers' mess, Taurama Barracks.

This Sasa did with some reluctance as he had developed close relations with Sandline. Like a number of other senior officers, he had happily gone along with the whole planning phase of the Sandline operation without stopping to think about the long-term consequences of accepting mercenaries into the country. As Sasa and the security team drove into the darkness towards East Boroko to execute their snap order, I saw that Sasa was torn between his immediate loyalty and duty to me and allegiance with the mercenaries with whom he had been liaising. I was concerned about the possibility of betrayal and the compromising of Rausim Kwik, but it was too late now to call Sasa back.

Sasa and his security detail arrived at Fort Williams and knocked on the door. Edwards opened the door and, after he was informed of the fate of his cohorts, obediently collected a change of clothes and was escorted to Taurama Barracks. He would spend the next few days in detention with his two colleagues until the rest of the mercenaries were rounded up and expelled.

Immediately after Edwards's detention, a section of troops occupied the Sandline executive flat. In the party was Capt. Ben Sesenu. He had been given the task of collecting any briefcases and loose documents for me and disconnecting all communications at the flat. This he did. A section of B Company troops remained behind to secure the flat—and enjoy high-end alcohol and luxury food courtesy of Sandline—before they were relieved.

At about eight thirty, we all gathered in my study at Flagstaff House for a quick debrief. No plan ever works out exactly as expected. For example, there had been the earlier mix-up about who was to go on board the landing craft and who was to go to Taurama Barracks. The distinction was very important. I wanted Spicer to be held well out of the way, and being secured on board a landing craft out at sea was the ideal location. I also wanted him to be physically isolated from his colleagues so that he would be disoriented and unable to plan anything that could disrupt our own operation. He was the key Sandline executive, and with him as our prize, we had every chance of succeeding. But if he escaped and was able to get back alongside the ministers with whom he had been working, our chances of success would be very minimal.

Capt. Belden Namah and Sgt Chris Mora were selected to guard Tim Spicer on board *Salamaua* as they were the stars of my crack team. I could be confident that, with Namah and Mora looking after his security, Spicer had no chance of escape. I went so far as to instruct Namah that if Spicer attempted any tricks, he was to take the necessary steps to neutralise him as Spicer was the centre of the Sandline operation, and it was imperative that we retain hold of him at all costs. He was our prize.

In this regard, I was very conscious of the capabilities of the Australian intelligence network. We knew, from our own surveillance capabilities, that Spicer had been in regular contact with Lt Col. Gary Hogan, the assistant military attaché at the Australian High Commission. We were aware that Hogan was sending detailed, near-daily briefs on Sandline, based on his contacts with Spicer, to Russell Hill in Canberra (Australian Defence Headquarters). It was important that the Australians remained ignorant of Spicer's precise whereabouts now that he was under our care as any Australian counterintelligence or rescue operation would be a critical blow to us. The Australians could cooperate with the PNG authorities either through the local police or through troops loyal to Sir Julius Chan. Indeed, it was not beyond contemplation that the Australians might be tempted to use their own special force capabilities to spring Spicer, and they could certainly attempt to do that while Spicer was at sea. That would be well within the capabilities of an Australian SAS boat squadron or through a HALO (high-altitude, low-opening) aircraft-based parachute insertion, at which Australian (and New Zealand) special forces were expert and well practised.

The briefing to my operations team was simple. If there was any suspicion of a compromise in Tim Spicer's location, he was to be relocated every second day. I had, by then, come up with four separate locations for Spicer as potential alternatives. In addition to keeping him at sea, these alternative locations were Taurama Barracks, Signal Squadron HQ Hill at Murray Barracks, or up in the mountains where the Kokoda Trail finishes.

We were also concerned that one of the Sandline aircraft, a CASA-212 equipped with electronic surveillance equipment, had been airborne, testing its instruments and communication intercept capabilities while today's operations were being conducted. The dilemma was more to do with whether they were monitoring what we were doing and, if so, whether they would inform the prime minister and the police or their training team at the jungle training facility near Wewak, which would mean that the follow-on phases of Operation Rausim Kwik could be jeopardised. I did not think this likely as we had been punctilious in not using radios, cell phones, text messages, email, or other electronic means of communication to stay in touch with various aspects of the operation. We knew that operational security was an absolute requirement, but what we could not know was whether there had been an unauthorised leak that the Sandline CASA aircraft could have picked up.

The Special Force Operations Room at the Air Transport Squadron apron at Jacksons Airport was tasked to monitor the movements of the CASA-212 upon its landing. A security team was ordered to immobilise all their vehicles and communications systems immediately after midnight. This team was composed of a small party of communications operators at the PNGDF Air Transport Squadron, assisted by an SFU component, to cripple or otherwise immobilise all Sandline air and ground transport and communications assets and place them under a security cordon.

The first phase of Operation Rausim Kwik was now effectively over. It had taken exactly one and a half hours to complete, despite the delay caused by the need to relocate Nic van den Bergh from the ship to Taurama Barracks.

Back in the study at Flagstaff House, over hot cups of coffee, I conducted a thorough debrief. The key players present were Maj. Walter Enuma, Maj. Gilbert Toropo, and a small number of senior non-commissioned officers. I congratulated my operations team on what they had achieved. The key Sandline personnel were all under arrest and accounted for. No weapons had been fired, injuries were minor, and not a single life had been lost. Property damage to date was, so far as we knew, confined to some windows in my office.

At the same time, successful though all this had been, we had to accept that, by now, the secrecy of the operation might have been compromised. The movement of troops at Fort Williams in East Boroko and the extra activities at the officers' mess at Taurama Barracks and the landing craft base at Fairfax Harbour might all have been noticed.

We also suspected that Lieutenant Colonel Salamas might, by now, have phoned his colleagues in the police force, with whom he was thought to be close, and maybe even Sir Julius Chan or his key staff to inform them of the detention of the Sandline personnel. If he had done that, his telephone calls would have been picked up by the SIGINT teams at the Australian High Commission, though whether these intercepts would have been transcribed already and sent to Canberra was another matter.

Major Enuma remained with me as we went through various issues like damage control once there was a news breakout and the rolling effect on the troops in Bougainville and the families. After brainstorming, I sent messengers to the CO of the Air Transport Squadron, Lt Col. Patrick Waeda, and Lt Col. Blaise Afara, CO of the Murray Barracks area, to come at once to see me at Flagstaff along with Capt. Charlie Andrews, a helicopter pilot.

By now, it was time for an evening meal. Weni had prepared a typical PNG dish consisting of coconut rice and steamed chicken with mixed vegetables. But I could not finish my dinner as I was in the middle of a military operation and preoccupied by everything that needed attending to. Weni was hovering within call distance, not knowing what to say or do. I felt for her because this was no longer a simple operation. It involved a multitude of people and lives and would affect the future of the constitution and the well-being of generations to come.

I found it very hard to comfort Weni throughout the whole operation. As a very perceptive woman, she knew all too well the possible implications for the well-being of our family and the future of the children. All that we could do was reassure each other that we had committed the whole matter to God, our Creator, and from here on, we would let him guide us.

The operations team were charged with a number of specific tasks to follow up with overnight: the securing of Sandline transport and communications assets at the Air Transport Squadron, the detention of the remaining Sandline personnel at Kiki Barracks, and ongoing arrangements for the security of the Sandline executives at Taurama

Barracks and Tim Spicer on HMPNGS *Salamaua*. I dismissed the team and awaited the arrival of new players who would be required for sustainment and damage control. Their assistance would likely be needed as, by dawn, it was very probable that information on the arrests the night before would be in the public domain.

While I was waiting for Waeda, Afara, and Andrews to join me, I went through the copies of my addresses to the nation and the troops and considered again how I could present my case to the people of PNG. I was confident of my media strategy. If I was to succeed in what I was hoping to achieve, handling the media had to be my counterstroke against the politicians led by Sir Julius Chan. The prime minister was a past master in his ability to use media, and that was a battle I needed to win. I knew it would not be easy.

However, in my short and, so far, limited encounters with Sir Julius Chan, I knew some of his vulnerabilities. For example, I knew that he surrounded himself with media gurus for rehearsals on sensitive issues well before he faced the media. I had no media advisers around me except for Weni. I knew that, even if I was not successful in accomplishing all aspects of the military mission, I must win the media war. This was the first time in history that a single person would take on a prime minister head-on. The issue was my ability not only to make skilful use of the media but also to engage the psychological aspects to ensure that the population understood and supported my statements.

Just then, Waeda and Afara arrived. Both officers had been professionally associated with me since our early days. They came from the same village, Lido in the Sandaun Province of West Sepik. Lieutenant Colonel Afara was one year my senior at Joint Services College; he graduated in June 1975 and joined the logistics stream. We both served at the Second Battalion, where he was the quartermaster, and we had spent many days in the field together including on Bougainville. He was promoted to the rank of lieutenant colonel in 1996 and given the massive task of being the CO for Murray Barracks area, a task and a responsibility that only a few could handle confidently.

Lieutenant Colonel Waeda was one year my junior. He had enlisted as a pilot cadet and later graduated as a pilot from the Royal Australian

Air Force Flying School at Point Cook. A maverick pilot, he had flown with me along the Indonesian border, inserting troops for patrols or air resupply, and was well known for crashing a DC-3 with Capt. Charlie Andrews in 1987. The crash happened in the run-up to a handover parade to mark a change of COs at Igam Barracks in Lae. The new national CO was Lt Col. Ignatius Lai, replacing the last Australian CO. The plan was for the DC-3 to conduct a ceremonial fly past. Unfortunately, despite a perfect rehearsal the day before, on the actual day of the handover, the DC-3 was nowhere to be seen. Major Waeda and Charlie Andrews, his co-pilot, had crashed their DC-3 aircraft minutes after take-off from Nadzab. With only a few scratches and disorientation, both officers and their two-man crew were found safe in the same thick grass that, in WWII, the American 503rd Parachute Regiment had used for practising their parachute jumps.

That night, some ten years after the crash, both officers would report to me. However, this time, their roles would be very different. There would be no fly past, no ceremony. These would be military operations. Charlie Andrews, also known as Cyclone Charlie from the broken beer bottles and upturned furniture that he used to leave behind at officers' messes around the country whom I recalled. Back into the military from a civilian flying career after I was appointed commander. He had an excellent flying record with both fixed and rotary wing aircraft and had flown me in some extremely risky operations.

Afara, Waeda, and Andrews arrived at my house looking rather anxious, but they settled down in my study, where we had some coffee before my brief. The brief was simple. I informed them that Operation Rausim Kwik had been launched, and the first phase was now complete. The second phase would commence the following day at about 0730 hours. Because of the significance of the operation, I was concerned that things might go wrong if the troops were not briefed properly. To achieve what was required, I issued two sets of instructions.

Lieutenant Colonel Afara, CO of Murray Barracks, was

- to ensure that all his troops were on parade at 0730 hours;

- to provide a security platoon of workshop and supply members to establish a security cordon at the NBC while I was on air during the Roger Hau'ofa *Talk Back Show*;
- to use the same troops to secure a helipad on the high ground of NBC residence of the chairman from where I could be extracted by helicopter back to Murray Barracks if there was an armed confrontation with the police or dissident groups;
- to enforce a closed camp at Murray Barracks once I returned from NBC to keep the troops in and the public, police, and politicians out;
- to place an armed guard on the armoury and ensure that no unauthorised weapons were issued;
- to ensure that the security party was fully briefed with a thorough set of rules of engagement to follow if the lives of the troops were in danger.

Lieutenant Colonel Waeda, CO of Air Transport Squadron, was

- to ensure that all Sandline personnel at the air transport base were detained and confined under guard at Kiki Barracks,
- to secure all Sandline aircraft in the hangar and not on the apron,
- to provide immediate security for the aircraft and the air assets at the squadron,
- to provide a Huey helicopter airborne over the NBC studio to effect my extraction back to Murray Barracks if there was a confrontation with the police or dissident groups.

The pilot responsible for my rescue, if I was to be detained or arrested at NBC, was Capt. Charlie Andrews. Andrews had had a long personal and professional relationship with me, including initial officer cadet training in 1983 and extracting me in his helicopter when I was shot and wounded during Operation High Speed I on 26 August 1994. He listened carefully to my description of his stand-by role in the operation the following day. I have always trusted him.

In the meantime and just before Walter Enuma and Gilbert Toropo were dismissed, we were informed that Deputy PM Chris Haiveta and veteran politician Sir Pita Lus had turned up at Murray Barracks and were trying to contact me. As the troops on guard at the main gate were under strict orders not to allow any unauthorised persons entrance to the barracks, Weni reported that they had tried to ring me from the gate directly several times.

Weni spoke to Chris Haiveta and said I was already asleep. Haiveta asked her to wake me up, but she refused. Haiveta and Lus had called past the Fort Williams flat to have a chat to Spicer, only to find Spicer gone and the flat under guard, so they suspected that all might not be well between Spicer and the defence force. Fortunately, however, they did not insist on gaining access to the barracks. Nor did they think to alert the prime minister. Therefore, it would be quite a few hours before matters would unveil themselves.

With my operations team now gone for the evening, there were two key phone calls that I needed to make before turning in for the night. Before beginning my preliminary planning for Rausim Kwik, I had taken political advice and guidance from two senior and very well-placed civilian mentors and colleagues of mine. The first was Sir Barry Holloway, and the second was David Sode, the tax commissioner.

Sir Barry, whom I code-named Stone in my diary (after Peter the Rock in the New Testament), was a veteran politician with a deep love and knowledge of PNG. He had come to the country as a patrol officer from Australia while still a young man, became a naturalised citizen of PNG, and eventually served as speaker. Sir Barry had special knowledge of, and expertise in, the constitution and politics of his adopted country, and he had become my closest friend, mentor, and political adviser as commander. He shared my growing disquiet over the involvement of the mercenaries, and while he left all operational details to me, I knew that he supported my broad objectives. Without compromising his position in the community in any way, I had briefed him in general terms about my plan to arrest and deport the mercenaries, and now I needed to give him a quick heads-up that Operation Rausim Kwik was under way and would hit the press the following day.

David Sode, whom I nicknamed Muno in my diary, which means 'brother or mate' in the East Sepik Yangoru dialect, was the second person I had taken into my confidence. I had done so because I knew that he, too, was concerned about the constitutionality of Operation Oyster and its long-term impact on the people of Bougainville as well as the international reputation of PNG. He was concerned also about the tax implications of providing tax exemption to all the weaponry that Sandline had been contracted to bring into the country. He had been deeply shocked when he saw the tax exemption certificates he was being asked to sign for the hundreds of thousands of rounds of ammunition that Sandline were planning to use in annihilating the leadership of the Bougainville Revolutionary Army. So as I had done with Sir Barry, I gave David a quick call using a prearranged code to let him know that the operation was under way.

It was now well past midnight and time to turn in. I was relieved that phase 1 had gone well. Not one shot had been fired. We had maintained a high level of operational security through to D-Day, and this was very pleasing given the number of service personnel who had been involved. But I knew that this was only the start of what would be a very long haul. Operation Rausim Kwik had only just begun. Nonetheless, it had been a good beginning.

CHAPTER 7

D-Day, 17 March 1997

He who desires but acts not, breeds pestilence.
—William Blake

I'm just very wary that once you start military operations in any country, it's difficult to predict what the outcome is.
—Abdallah II

Monday, 17 March 1997, was D-Day for Operation Rausim Kwik. Thanks to the previous day's quick series of arrests, we now had the Sandline command team safely detained and carefully secured. Now it was time to go public over my decision to cancel Operation Oyster, the government's plan to use African mercenaries to wipe out the Bougainville Revolutionary Army. I knew to expect a furious reaction from PM Sir Julius, whose baby this was, when he heard the news.

My sleep was quite short as I had stayed up late, discussing the day's events with Maj. Walter Enuma and Maj. Gilbert Toropo. We discussed a number of worst-case scenarios, focusing mainly on the possibility of counter-operations led by the police, possibly supported by a faction from the Papua New Guinea Defence Force. We were also concerned about the possible role of Network International, a security company owned and managed by the prime minister's son, Byron Chan. We concluded that, because I had always had a strong loyalty base with ordinary soldiers, having served with them in the field most of my career, any resistance within the PNGDF was probably manageable and could be contained until after Operation Rausim Kwik was completed.

Of course, we also had a wary eye out for possible intervention from the Australian Defence Force's Ready Reaction Force, the Third Brigade operating out of Townsville. The Third Brigade was a combined arms unit that consisted of a brigade headquarters and the First and Third Battalions, Royal Australian Regiment, based at Lavarack Barracks, with various other supporting units, including combat engineers, combat signals, artillery, and armoured cavalry. Having the Australians arrive in force would be a major complication for our handling of what was bound to be a delicate operation, no matter how it unfolded. But our assessment was that Australia would not want to commit troops to an urban peacekeeping or peace restoration operation in Port Moresby provided we were able to keep civil unrest and loss of life to an acceptable minimum. That was one reason for us to keep the most careful control possible over our troops.

It was 0445 hours when I woke up, ready to face what was likely to be the most difficult and important day in my life. I prayed for wisdom and strength. I prayed that nobody would lose their lives and that God would guide me so that we would achieve our mission of deporting the mercenaries and preventing more needless loss of life on Bougainville.

In my time and space appreciation, 17 March 1997 was selected as D-Day for various reasons. One of the more pressing was that an Air Sofia Antonov An-124 cargo lifter, a massive aircraft leased by Sandline and carrying two Mi-24 Hind twin-engine attack helicopters and two Mi-17 twin-engine transport helicopters, was expected to arrive in Port Moresby on about 18 or 19 March, in other words tomorrow or the day after. In addition to helicopters, the An-124 was also carrying massive amounts of ordnance, including 1,000 rounds of 57 mm high-explosive rockets, 20,000 rounds of 23 mm ball ammunition, 5,000 mortar rounds, 750,000 rounds of 7.62 ammunition and 2,000 40 mm grenades. This quantity of ordnance, agreed to and purchased by the government through the Sandline contract, gave the lie to the prime minister's claim, repeated both to the press and in private talks with

Australian ministers, that this was just a 'training' mission. Clearly, the intention was to use the mercenaries to lacerate the jungle in a sea of fire and destroy the BRA as an effective fighting force once and for all.

Monday, 17 March, was selected for another reason. After the weekend, politicians and bureaucrats were often slow at getting back into their work routines. Many of them would have returned to their villages for the weekend and would not be back to work until sometime late on Monday morning. The earlier the operations were launched, the longer it would take them to react.

The series of interviews and public appearances I had planned for the day were critical to the success of my mission of expelling the Sandline mercenaries and forcing Sir Julius, his deputy, and the defence minister to resign or step down. First on my visit list of planned meetings for the day were Robert Nenta, the police commissioner, and Sir Wiwa Korowi, the governor general, both of whom I planned to speak to personally. I would send a letter to Sir Arnold Amet, the chief justice of PNG, and also to Sir Julius Chan and Minister for Defence Mathias Ijape, advising them of my decision to cancel the Sandline contract. The most important of the day's activities would be meeting with my senior staff, addressing the troops at Murray Barracks and informing the nation through Roger Hau'ofa's *Talk Back Show* on NBC radio. The last of my planned meetings would be with representatives from embassies and high commissions and with the media. I had them all covered.

Our daughter Maib Kumai and son Moka woke up not knowing what was planned for the day. None of us knew how events would play out over the days, weeks, and months ahead. As our children were preparing for school, Weni and I took them into our room and told them that they would not be going to school today. Maib was seven years old and Moka five, and they sat motionless on the bed as we explained what was going on. I said, 'Daddy is not happy with the way the government is handling the Bougainville situation. Daddy has seen enough suffering and dead soldiers coming back from Bougainville. Over the past few days, you have seen foreigners come and speak to Daddy in our house. These are the people preparing to go to Bougainville and kill many more innocent people.'

Maib listened carefully to this and said, 'Daddy, this is not good. You must do something about it.'

I replied, 'Yes, and that is why today I will be telling the PM to resign or step down, and I will tell our people on the radio about the bad things these foreigners intend to do, and it means I may end up in jail or lose my job as a soldier and commander. But as for this week, both Moka and you will stay home and not go wandering around outside the Flagstaff House.'

They both nodded as I left the room. Weni stayed with them to explain further what I had said to them.

Much earlier in the morning when we had woken up, Weni and I had discussed whether she should go back to her village of Saroa Babaga in Rigo District, a few kilometres into Central Province. But in the end, we agreed that it was best for her and the children to stay at Murray Barracks and see how things unfolded. Weni assured me that we were in this together and that we would take matters as they came. Having settled my children and Weni, I was set to face the most important part of the day. It was 0700 hours.

My breakfast was abrupt as Walter Enuma arrived early. Over coffee, he confirmed that Tim Spicer was isolated and on board HMPNGS *Salamaua* with Belden Namah and Chris Mora, and three other operators were taking care of him. Carl Deats and Nic van den Bergh were at the Taurama Barracks lock-up. The success of phase 1 of Operation Rausim Kwik now set the stage for phase 2. From our immediate planning perspective, the most important consideration was that Tim Spicer and his Sandline command team must not be allowed anywhere near Sir Julius Chan or his cabinet colleagues. This meant that we needed to keep news of their precise locations completely secure. Alert observers might, of course, note that *Salamaua* was no longer at the landing craft base, and they might put two and two together. But we had a cover story worked up if we should be asked questions about the absence of *Salamaua* from its usual base.

By this time, all my support staff, drivers, and bodyguards were present at Flagstaff House. I came downstairs to physically check who was present and what vehicles were available. I had earlier instructed Cpl John Koraia to report to me before seven in the morning as we had to go to East Boroko, behind Bavaroko Community School, to talk to Police Commissioner Robert Nenta.

I hadn't yet dressed in my uniform and was still in my tracksuit when John Koraia drove me to Nenta's residence at Karu Street in East Boroko. As we drove into his compound, he was just driving out. Signalling to him that I was there to see him, I opened the car door and asked if we could talk. He led me to the chairs under his house, and with his wife watching from a distance, I spoke to him in a low but serious tone. I said, 'Bob, remember your appointment and promotion to commissioner rank? I think that you know very well that I had a lot to do with persuading the PM to make your appointment. I am now asking you for a return favour.

I saw that he was deeply concerned. I continued, 'Do you recall our lunch at Golden Bowl Restaurant with Defence Secretary James Melegepa last week, where we both expressed deep concerns about private security firms and armies from other countries taking over from our constitutional roles?

He replied and said he did. Then I went straight to the point. I said, 'Bob, last night I launched Operation Rausim Kwik. Defence personnel acting under my direct orders have detained all of Sandline's command team and other personnel in Port Moresby. The mercenaries at the training facility near Wewak have been confined to barracks. The aim of the operation is to deport all Sandline personnel out of Papua New Guinea as soon as possible. I have given my staff until Friday this week, 21 March, for them to be expelled from the country. I am also going to demand that the PM, Sir Julius Chan; his deputy, Christopher Haiveta; and the defence minister, Mathias Ijape, step aside or resign and allow an independent judicial enquiry to investigate all aspects of the Sandline contract. I believe that, apart from ministers plotting with Sandline to commit mass murder on Bougainville, there may also be corrupt dealings involved in the granting of the Sandline contract and the aim to reopen the Panguna mine. I want to get to the bottom of the whole contract, and I will be demanding straight answers from ministers on all their financial dealings with Sandline. Besides, this is the election year, and I suspect the ministers of state are engaged in corrupt deals to fund their election campaign in June.'

Bob Nenta nodded as I was talking, but he was too shocked to say anything yet. His surprise confirmed to me that phase 1 of Operation Rausim Kwik had been a complete success as it was quite apparent that no one had called him in the past twelve hours to tip him off. I said that I needed his support. I told him that I was planning to address my senior staff officers at the Murray Barracks at 0800 hours and that I would appreciate his coming along together with his deputy commissioner for operations, Ludwick Kembu, and the commander of the National Capital District, Samson Inguba.

Recovering from his shock at what I had been saying, he assured me that he would personally support me and that he would organise for a couple of his senior officers to attend with him at Murray Barracks. I said that if it became apparent that it was too much for the police force to work alongside the defence force, it would be helpful if he could at least monitor the planned expulsion of Sandline mercenaries from PNG and have his staff avoid confronting those members of the PNGDF involved in Operation Rausim Kwik.

Commissioner Nenta listened intently to all this. He was a well-respected and seasoned policeman with many years of both field and command experience. In 1996, Sir Julius had asked my opinion of Nenta when we were touring New Ireland together. We were spending a few days at his home at Huris, and Nenta was acting police commissioner at the time. I replied that I thought Nenta was a good choice as commissioner as he was a professional police officer with sober habits and was well respected by his peers and subordinates. No doubt, even after all his years of policing, this early morning encounter with me in which I explained my decision to expel the mercenaries would be remembered by him for years to come.

After our discussion, Nenta went upstairs to his house to change into his police uniform while Corporal Koraia drove me back to

Flagstaff House. If the police force were sympathetic and onside, that meant that I might only have to deal with Byron Chan's security company, Network International, as a possible block to the expulsion of the Sandline mercenaries if they chose to take us on.

Back at Flagstaff House, I changed into my army jungle fatigue uniform and put on my black jungle boots. Picking up my swagger stick with brass ferule, which I normally liked to carry with me, I slipped down to my waiting official car to be driven down to HQ PNGDF. As normal, I was driven by Cpl Paul Kam, my faithful official driver from Enga Province. A copy of my address to the officers and men, as well as my speech to the nation, was in my field bag, a grubby, much-used old olive green TEWT bag (TEWT is an abbreviation for 'tactical exercise without troops', also sometimes more sardonically referred to as 'total waste of time'). I have carried my TEWT bag for many years in the field and regard it as my faithful companion.

As I got into my official vehicle, Weni, Maib, and Moka looked on from the small balcony of the staircase above. Corporal Kam fired up the commander's blue Mazda sedan, registered plate ZDZ 007, denoting that I was the seventh commander of the PNGDF in order of succession. A pennant on the bonnet of the vehicle with a small flag and a single star meant that the commander was being driven in his official vehicle. As we drove down to the HQ office complex, my bodyguard, Cpl John Koraia, was in the front seat and my aide-de-camp, Capt. John Keleto, sat with me in the rear seat.

I broke the silence by explaining to Cpl Paul Kam what had transpired in the past twelve hours. Corporal Kam nodded as I spoke, not that he would do anything else, but sometimes it is worthwhile to share a few moments like this with people who are close to you since they need to hear your thoughts to assist them in their own judgement. As we drove down the hill, I reflected that this aspect of my daily routine, driving to work with my ADC and bodyguard, was almost certainly coming to a close. This would likely be my last such morning.

Arriving at the commander's official car park, I looked towards the assembly area on the parade ground. Troops in formation in their respective units were being organised into place by their senior non-commissioned officers, ready for my address as they mustered. My official vehicle was to be used to deliver my formal letters to Gov. Gen. Sir Wiwa Korowi, CJ Sir Arnold Amet, the prime minister, and the defence minister this morning. All the letters were to be delivered by my military adviser, Lt Col. Joseph Fabila.

Calling Fabila to my office, I instructed him to go to the governor general and brief him personally on my decision to evict the mercenaries. He was to hand him my letter and advise him that I would call on him at his office at about nine o'clock. I had to brief Fabila separately because I had left him out of earlier briefings on Rausim Kwik—not through any lack of confidence in him but because I needed to keep the initial circle of operational staff as small as possible. Fabila assimilated my brief very quickly. I told him it was important that he see the governor general personally and allow him time to go through the letter. He was further tasked with delivering my letter to the prime minister through Noel Levi and to CJ Sir Arnold Amet at the National Courthouse. Sir Arnold is a fellow Karkar Islander.

It was not long before the police commissioner and his deputy arrived. They were met by my chief of staff, Col. Jack Tuat, and taken to the force conference room. Before joining them, I called Force Sergeant Major (FSM) Warrant Officer Class 1 Raymond Maisu. He was in charge of organising the main parade. I briefed him on what had transpired in the past twelve hours. He was an excellent soldier with a field engineering background. He had served many good engineer commanding officers and had proven leadership qualities. But today he would be organising a different type of parade. This was to be a parade that would involve an address that defied the orders of the executive to execute Operation Oyster in Bougainville. Field Sergeant Major Maisu understood my explanation and gave some orders to his deputy before waiting to accompany me into the conference room.

By then, Jack Tuat had assembled all the staff officers along with Department of Defence staff in the conference room on the top floor of the operations centre. Jack Tuat was a well-respected colonel from East New Britain and a field engineer by background before becoming my chief of staff. The conference room was packed to capacity, news of Tim Spicer's arrest having already spread throughout the defence establishment.

There were some points raised before we went to the conference room. When I came out of my office and into the corridor, I looked down on the road below and could see hundreds of soldiers, sailors, and airmen gathered in their respective units to go on parade to hear what I had to say. I continued walking along the corridor to the conference room in company with the police commissioner and his deputy.

Following established military protocol, staff were brought to attention by the chief of staff. I told the assembled officers to sit easy and instructed the force chaplain Rosi, a Bougainville Catholic priest, to open the conference with a prayer. This he did. His prayer reminded me of all the pain and suffering that Bougainvilleans had gone through over nine or more years of civil conflict. Today he prayed for God's hand and intervention and asked for wisdom and grace to be granted to us all so that the Bougainville crisis could be concluded without any more killings.

I then briefed the officers about the background to Sandline International and what the Sandline contract amounted to. I told them that I had been silent up until then over the wisdom of the government's decision to contract Sandline International. But having considered all aspects of such a decision, including the implications for both Bougainville and the country at large, I had decided that the contract had wider and longer-term consequences that were extremely unwise. I explained that I also suspected that the contract had aspects to it that were corrupt and that I believed that it was more than likely that some politicians were making significant commissions on the side.

I further stated that, although I had been included as a key player in the project from its earliest beginnings until now, my conscience had been affecting me for some time, and it had become very clear to me that my duty to the PNG constitution and the country required me to take this action against Sandline and the government.

I challenged every officer in the conference room. 'What is wrong with this defence force?'

'Nothing is wrong,' came the reply.

'That is the issue,' I said. 'Our government, instead of spending money on us, has decided to hire mercenaries from, of all places, the failed states of Africa to come and do our jobs. All of you gathered here are landowners in one way or another. What if there are minerals and other natural resources found in your land or sea and there are disagreements between you as landowners and the government and the developer? The cheaper option to put an end to such disputes is to get mercenary companies like Sandline International in and shut you up with lethal weapons. Panguna mine in Bougainville is a test case for the government. I, as your commander, will not allow this mercenary operation to take place, and I am putting my career and life on the line to prevent such use and abuse of power by ministers using the constitution as the front.'

My approach and style of presentation was aimed at gaining a psychological effect, not unlike what is demanded of a military leader talking to his troops before an attack on a known fortified enemy camp. From many years of practice and experience as a military leader, I was aiming to get as many officers psyched up, motivated, and educated in the quickest time possible because I knew all too well that the real test would come in the second and third phases of Operation Rausim Kwik when ministers reacted to news of the arrest of the Sandline operatives.

The police commissioner assured us of his cooperation. While there had been small skirmishes between police and military personnel in the past, both forces worked hard at maintaining cordial and respectful relations, and I was banking on that understanding today. I reiterated to all present that this was not a military coup, even if my approach was decidedly unorthodox. This was unavoidable, given the circumstances.

We ended the brief with another concluding prayer. My officers clapped as I walked out of the room. I knew from their reaction that I had achieved an overwhelming level of support from most of those present. I also knew that getting as many officers onside as possible was one of the most important keys to the success of the operation.

It was now time for me to address the men, the people who can make officers and leaders look good or, conversely, look bad. I was already psyched up. As I had final discussions with the police commissioner and his deputy in my office, I sensed hesitation on the part of the deputy commissioner, Ludwick Kembu. However, his doubts, if that was what they were, didn't matter to me as long as I was able to achieve what needed to be achieved by Friday, 21 March—the expulsion of all the mercenaries.

Cpl John Koraia reported that the parade was ready to hear me and that the public address system was installed and working. I said goodbye to the police commissioner as he was on the phone with his staff officers at police headquarters at Konedobu. As it turned out, this would be the last time I saw the commissioner until a year later when we met briefly outside the second commission of enquiry at the Waigani National Court.

I crossed the road by the parking lot. Instead of arriving at the parade in my official vehicle, I walked to the dais on foot, where I was given a salute by the FSM. I liked Raymond Maisu as he had always stood by me in both good and bad times. It was my choice to get him appointed as FSM when I retired the previous FSM, Paul Kuia.

I reminded myself that, if there was to be a major impact on the men, this parade was the chance for me to make that impact. I needed all the support that I could get from the men. They needed to understand from me what the government had done to the defence force and what the future for our country would be if we allowed foreign security companies to take over our constitutional roles.

I had written out and carefully memorised my address to the troops so that I could dwell on the key issues. However, just as important as the content of my speech, possibly more important, I knew that the method and style of my delivery had to be appropriate for the men and the bystanders. Therefore, I had decided to deliver the address in Pidgin English as this was the language most men used at working level in the defence force despite English being the official language.

Ordering the men to stand at ease and easy, I took the microphone from its stand. I paused to make sure that I had everyone's attention. A complete silence fell across the parade ground as the men looked in my direction. I began by speaking quietly and slowly. 'Men, most of you will recall that it was 17 October 1995 when I was appointed commander. I said to you at that time, and I said as much in public, that there is no military solution to Bougainville. One year and three months later, I still have not changed my position on Bougainville.

'In my time as your commander, we have made little progress on Bougainville. The massacre at Kangu Beach in September last year, 1996; the loss of lives of many of our fellow soldiers, sailors, and airmen; the taking of hostages; and the loss of many innocent lives on Bougainville have haunted all of us. How many more will lose their lives all because we are hell-bent on opening the mine at Panguna and make money for the government?

'In a desperate move, the government has engaged Sandline International to impose a military solution on Bougainville. The government has turned to a bunch of African mercenaries because they have lost confidence in the defence force and the police. This decision to turn to mercenaries is not only demoralising for all of us. It also seriously undermines our potential.

'You know, and I know, that it is wrong for the government to hire foreign mercenaries to destroy our country. It is Papua New Guineans who will be made to suffer the consequences and nightmares of atrocities and sufferings. Many innocent lives will be lost during the heavy strikes and bombardment that Sandline are planning. There are many failed states in Africa. Now we are looking at the possibility of our own state failing.'

Not only in Bougainville but also throughout PNG, people will turn against the government and the defence force when civilians are killed in large numbers as a result of this operation. The people will no longer trust the government. And they will not trust us.

'The government has a constitutional duty to protect its citizens and not slaughter them as will happen under the Sandline contract. I remind you that the defence force has an obligation under the constitution to protect its people and our sovereignty, not to kill them.

'The contract with Sandline does not provide for the transfer of technology from Sandline International to the PNGDF. There is no financial commitment by government to the defence force that would allow us to sustain the newly acquired equipment and capabilities.

The money spent on the mercenaries could be spent on much-needed logistical support to sustain our current efforts on Bougainville, strengthening existing capabilities such as our helicopters, patrol boats, uniforms, dressings, and field equipment.

'Under the contract, the Sandline mercenaries will be paid a total of US$36 million over three months. They have already been paid the first half of that sum. What do you suppose will happen after the three months is up?

'Since 1989, despite all our efforts as a defence force in Bougainville, we have never been defended by the government against accusations of human rights abuses. In these coming operations with Sandline, there will be more abuses and more condemnation. There is no guarantee that the government will support us as it should. We will be left as the fall guys. As your commander, I cannot accept any responsibility if we conduct ourselves outside our constitutional roles and responsibilities.

'The conflict in Bougainville requires winning the hearts and minds of the people. The people who have been opposing us must be brought to negotiate. We have not exhausted all the avenues of negotiations and rebuilding of trust. Any further destructive acts will just prolong the conflict. Killing more innocent people on Bougainville just to reopen the Panguna mine is unethical and immoral.

'It appears that we have a government that is more interested in the revenue of the country and not the lives and welfare of the people. We know that the only durable strategy to bring everlasting peace on Bougainville is the 3R strategy: reconciliation, restoration, and reconstruction. Instead, the government has torn up this strategy and has now engaged the most notorious of all people, a bunch of paid killers and mercenaries from South Africa, to open the Panguna mine.

'The government is following a completely contradictory path. On the one hand, it has taken an initiative to extend the term of the Bougainville Transitional Government while it looks at past peace initiatives with a view to finding a solution to the long-running conflict. This initiative has brought about a positive response from the warring factions on the island. This proves that there is genuine hope for peace that will take time to bed in and become permanent. And this is good.

On the other hand, it is now sponsoring a major military operation by outsiders that can only set back the peace process. In my professional military opinion as your commander, the whole Sandline contract is crazy.'

Then came the inevitable political part in the last segment of my speech. 'In the past ten years or so, we have seen a drastic drop in the standards of conduct and management of our country by our leaders. There is widespread corruption and bribery amongst our leaders. The Sandline International deal is yet another example of a contract that involves corrupt behaviour on the part of key government ministers acting in the name of the defence force.

'As your commander, in the space of only a very short time in office, I have seen and experienced incompetence by our political masters who are corrupt in their dealings and who will continue to sell our country to foreigners. We have lost our national identity and pride. We have compromised our national interest by relying on foreign donors, foreign advisers, and now a foreign mercenary force. It means that the next generation will have to deal with foreigners who have been given all the opportunities by our leaders to do business, and we will be marginalised. This must be prevented. I call on all you, soldiers, standing here before me to make your own judgement while in uniform as soldiers or when you leave the defence force.

'I grieve and my heart bleeds when I cannot properly care for your operational, training, and welfare needs. We have many disabled soldiers who require specialist medical attention or repatriation. We have many mothers and children who have lost their fathers in Bougainville and who now require financial assistance and repatriation to their homes. How can we, as a national institution, assist the widows and fatherless children?

'Any person who thinks that they can solve Bougainville militarily is a fool. History is full of examples. One cannot put a timetable on Bougainville and say we will do it. Let us not be fooled by short-term initiatives such as the Sandline involvement as this is about political expedience. Only those of us who have been to Bougainville know how it needs the total cooperation from all the people so that we can reach amicable solutions and compromise. Sandline has infiltrated into our highest decision-making bodies including our two financial institutions and various agencies of state. For example, Sandline executives now have direct access to the PM and his deputy and the finance and defence ministers.

'Now, men, you tell me, what is wrong with this defence force that we need to engage African mercenaries to do our jobs?'

And to this, they all responded, 'Nothing, nothing.' And by then, they were clapping, and some were already crying with what they had heard so far.

I continued, 'There is another issue I want to talk to you about. Moving away from our traditional partners to seek new possibilities for military assistance is good. Our long-standing friends have to accept the fact that we are a sovereign country, and we need to make independent decisions and develop our strategic capabilities according to our specific needs and circumstances. Of course, the views of our friends must be respected. However, we cannot blame other countries for the current state of Papua New Guinea or the PNGDF. We must blame ourselves.

'The current state of the defence force is a result of many years of neglect and empty promises by successive governments. Our men deserve better than the cheap politics played by our politicians. Rather than allow the politicians to sell the defence force to foreigners, I am making this public statement to you now. I want to allow the four million Papua New Guineans and all officers, men, and their dependents in the defence force to judge for themselves. Our new generation needs to be as one, and we must maintain an indigenous defence force. We need to demonstrate our cry and our call for nationalism, unity, and *ahebou*, which in the Motu language means "unity".

'I now make my final plea to all of you, Officers, men, and dependents. We have come under a lot of public and political criticism. Despite this criticism, we are still a credible defence force. For all of us, the PNGDF is our lifeblood. It is our way of life. We can change the image of the defence force while we pursue Operation Rausim Kwik. During this operation, I want you all to be patient. I want you to continue to demonstrate a high standard and to uphold the name of our defence force.

'My plea to all of you is that there must be no rioting or protesting. We will all remain in the barracks while Operation Rausim Kwik plays out. As your commander, I will undertake the protesting on your behalf. If anybody has to be disciplined for any wrong against the state, I would rather it be me than you. I will fight for your rights and your well-being against an unjust group of politicians.

'Lastly, I want you to know that all COs have been ordered to impose closed camp. All members of the defence force are to remain in the barracks and conduct daily routines such as physical training, drills, and area cleanliness while I take the issue on with the authorities.

'Let me fight this fight with only a handful of brave young officers like Major Enuma, Major Toropo, Captain Namah, and Captain Renagi. I thank you for your patience, and may God bless you all.'

As I finished and brought the parade to attention, I could hear some men crying and rejoicing that maybe there would be no more loss of lives on Bougainville. I believed that the result that I wanted had been achieved. I took them to a height and a level of feeling that was such that they were prepared to stand beside me all the way. I knew it. I could tell from their body language and from my years of dealing with men; the rough and tumble had taught me the skills and techniques needed in such situations.

I went back to my office and prepared to give follow-up guidance to my senior officers, a number of whom appeared confused and unsure what to do next. I told them that, in effect, from here on, it was a question of damage control. They were to ensure that our men did not go out on the streets, that COs knew to get a firm hold of their respective units, and that situations should be controlled as they presented themselves. 'The operation has just started,' I said. 'Those in charge are already at work. If you can assist them, then do so. Otherwise, stay out of the way.'

At the same time as my own address to the troops, at around 0830 hours, the two dispatchers in Manus and Lae and the CO at Moem Barracks in Wewak all delivered the same message in front of the men.

Maj. Michael Kupo gave the same speech to the CO and the sailors at the patrol boat base in Lombrum, and Maj. John Boino, who was also a field engineer officer, gave the same speech to the CO Lt Col. Miri Osi and the Engineer Battalion troops.

Meanwhile, at Second Battalion, the CO, Lt Col. Michael Tamalanga, with a platoon of troops, made the one-and-a-half-hour drive to the jungle training camp on the Sepik Plains at Urimo, disarmed the Sandline mercenaries, removed all their personal weapons, and escorted them back to Moem Barracks to await further instruction for repatriation out of PNG. Tamalanga was assisted by SFU troops headed by Capt. Bola Renagi, who was operations officer and second in command of the SFU.

This being achieved in the first part of the morning, I was well within the schedule of phase 2. I had only the governor general to see, my talk on NBC radio, and then the news conference at Murray Barracks. About midday, I called the governor general's ADC, Capt. Alphonse Sangi. I had selected Alphonse Sangi out of many good subalterns as he had demonstrated a high standard of conduct along with maturity and respect. He was concerned as I spoke to him but, as usual, did not say much as my military assistant, Colonel Fabila, had already briefed the governor general. Captain Sangi would have sat in on this briefing and so was familiar with the outline of what I was wanting to achieve.

Captain Sangi said the governor general was awaiting my arrival. I took a copy of my letter to the governor general and a copy of my address to the nation and departed through the middle gate of Murray Barracks as the main gate was now closed for public access in accordance with my instructions. I passed Colonel Fabila as we drove through the gate. He gave me a thumbs up. Corporal Kam was driving and said little, while my ADC, Capt. John Keleto, and Cpl John Koraia reassured me that so far, so good and encouraged me to keep my cool composure at Government House.

Meanwhile, in the rear mirror, I saw a troop-carrying vehicle (TCV) loaded with troops following me. I felt secure as it was only a matter of time before we met with opposition. For me, it was a matter of speed and the method of delivery of my message. If you have to beat your foe, what matters most are speed and surprise. I was achieving that, and more importantly, I was still comfortably on schedule.

We arrived at Government House at Konedobu overlooking Port Moresby Harbour and Hanuabada Village. My car stopped at the steps leading up to the front balcony. The red carpet leading from the car park to the steps and up to the balcony reminded me that the governor general was the head of the nation and the leading symbol of democracy.

The rich history of Government House goes back to the turn of the last century. It was built by the British government in 1900, just sixteen years after the British flag was first raised over what was then known as British New Guinea.

The first governor general of the new Independent State of Papua New Guinea was the late Sir John Guise, who served from 1975 to 1977, when he resigned in a bid to re-enter politics. Sir John was born in 1914 in Gedulalara Village, Milne Bay Province, the son of an English adventurer and trader and a Papuan mother. He was also a leading member of the Royal Papua New Guinea Constabulary, rising to the rank of sergeant major.

Sir Wiwa Korowi was appointed governor general in 1991, when the previous incumbent, Sir Vincent Eri, resigned after only one year in office. This was Sir Wiwa's last year in office, and I could imagine that the Sandline crisis might be the most challenging issue that he would face during his term as viceregal representative. One of my most important messages that morning was to assure Sir Wiwa that his status as governor general was absolutely protected and that there was no military coup. I was not a power-hungry general but an advocate for peace and humanity. I was determined to put my case to him as simply and as comprehensively as possible.

I was met by Capt. Alphonse Sangi and Sir Wiwa's chief of staff and then shown into the visitors' room. Sir Wiwa came in at once. He was a tall man and, with his long beard, had the typical appearance of a southern highlander. He was calm and relaxed but also looked troubled.

I only came to Government House on very special occasions, and this time around, it was my own schedule I was following. But the stakeholders were waiting. I had to be more tactful, I thought, as I saluted the governor general. He had huge palms and just about crushed the knuckles of my right hand as he invited me to accompany him to an adjoining room away from public view.

Sir Wiwa and I had previously discussed problems in the defence force when on operations in Bougainville, including issues of logistics support and lack of funding. Before talking to him about my decision to cancel the Sandline contract, I had given him ample time to assimilate my letter and my address to the nation. He seemed very concerned about the Sandline contract and the implications for the nation in the long term, especially with mining concessions, but he now seemed even more worried about Operation Rausim Kwik and my demands. He asked why I hadn't discussed my concerns with him before I took action. I replied, 'Sir, you know what it is like. We can all raise our concerns, but as with many other things, the whole exercise will continue regardless. Nothing will change.'

He was also concerned because the prime minister and cabinet had not consulted him as they should have, given the need for multimillion-dollar contracts to go to his office for endorsement. The Sandline contract had not been discussed with him, and he had not seen the contract. He was equally concerned about the financial and humanitarian consequences of the engagement of Sandline mercenaries and the impact on PNG's regional and global reputation.

Sir Wiwa pleaded that, whatever I planned on doing, I had to uphold the constitution, respect the democratic government of PNG, and exercise restraint, even if it meant losing my job. Before I left the governor general, I reaffirmed my position:

- Sandline personnel must be deported from PNG by Friday, 21 March.
- Sir Julius Chan; his deputy, Christopher Haiveta; and Minister for Defence Mathias Ijape must resign or step aside from office.
- A full commission of enquiry must be established to investigate all aspects of the Sandline contract.

I assured Sir Wiwa Korowi that this was not a military takeover as I strongly believed in a civilian democratic government. I understood the consequences of my actions and was prepared to face whatever the ministers decided to do with me. My conscience was clear.

Before I departed Government House, I informed Sir Wiwa that I was off to the NBC to explain my actions to the public. I thanked him for his time. He offered a word of prayer for me, and I felt reassured.

I was escorted to my vehicle by his staff. Captain Sangi appeared very concerned about me based on what he had heard. I told him not to worry and to take care of himself and his family. I said I was able to handle whatever the prime minister threw at me.

Departing Government House with an armed escort following me, I headed to the NBC studio to speak on the *Talk Back Show* hosted by Roger Hau'ofa. Joseph Ealedona was assisting in holding open my time slot as it was already well past ten. It was a hot and humid morning. As my convoy tracked along Sir Hubert Murray Highway to the studio at Five Mile, I was treated like a VIP—a crowd was already out and cheering as I passed. The news had spread. Roger Hau'ofa had been telling his listeners to tune in to FM100 as the commander would be on the *Talk Back Show* to address the nation on the Sandline contract.

The NBC studio buildings were ancient—brick walls with white paint splattered on top, giving them a colonial look. Indeed, the building hailed from the time when the Australian regional station for Papua and New Guinea, 9 PA, ran its studio for the Australian community in the territory. The NBC was once a proud and important organisation. It had been used extensively before and after independence in 1975 to disseminate news and information to thousands of Papua New Guineans who were isolated from the rest of the world. Its new chairman was none other than Prof. Renagi Lohia. It was Lohia who, in 1995, had rung me in Singapore when I was travelling in the region as part of a US-sponsored security forum to inform me of my appointment as commander. At that time, he was chief of staff to Sir Julius Chan.

Lohia had attempted to bring new life to the NBC, but apart from improving the security fences, and building two native huts on the lawn, he was just as constrained by lack of funding as his predecessor had been. He had closed down most of the studio's operations. The whole place needed much more work than the new white paint job it had received. Despite this, NBC produced many talented broadcasters who went on to become prominent public figures.

I knew that while I was in the studio, I would be at my most vulnerable. Among other security concerns, I was worried that the police might be directed to arrest me in the studio. If they did, it could lead to a firefight between the police and my security detail while I was on air. I wanted to avoid such an incident at all costs. Apart from any other consideration, I did not want any interference with the programme while I was on air as this was the fastest and the most effective means to reach thousands of Papua New Guineans. I was committed. I had to go on air as this was the only way to communicate to ordinary people in the many remote parts of PNG. I reassured myself that the officers responsible for my security would be capable of handling the security situation outside the studio.

My party walked through the studio where Roger Hau'ofa had been waiting since ten o'clock for the *Talk Back Show*. As I was late, he had been telling his listeners that the programme was reserved for me and that I would be arriving at the studio very soon. He had kept his listeners in suspense for nearly two hours. It was nearly eleven when I settled into the cramped studio. Also in the studio was an EMTV camera crew and presenter John Egins. Egins had been one year behind me at Sogeri National High School and had become renowned for his TV show. Egins, like Hau'ofa, was in a buoyant mood. Both would scoop the Sandline and Rausim Kwik story for the six o'clock national news. Outside the studio, scores of print media journalists and photographers were waiting among my armed troops, who were holding their ground.

Roger Hau'ofa, who passed away in March 2017, was an icon in broadcasting services in PNG for over forty years. He was known as 'the voice of Papua New Guinea'. A tall and big man, born to Tongan Christian missionary parents who had lived and preached in the Milne Bay area, his commanding physical presence in the studio made it seem as if there was no room for other guests. He was a strong advocate for democracy, the rule of law, and good governance; and as such, he was the perfect radio host for my message. He was known for being above narrow partisan politics, and there was no doubt that he commanded respect the moment anyone went into his studio. I admired him for his work and contribution to journalism. He was a good man, and we got along well.

I felt for Roger as he would not have anticipated the method and style of my presentation; neither did he expect a military commander to condemn the government. He was, for want of a better word, shocked by my exposition. But he would live to share his experiences about which guests gave him thrills and shock waves. I would be one he would remember for a long time.

The troop's security presence outside the building made the workers at the radio station nervous. Some fled, hearing of the address and seeing a platoon of heavily armed troops outside the studio. The security party was not tasked with seizing the studio; they were directed by me to provide my personal security until the address was completed. In the background as I talked, the distinctive deep 'whop, whop, whop' noise of the helicopter hovering overhead, awaiting my possible extraction should a threat develop, could be heard.

The pilot was Capt. Charlie Andrews, my faithful friend who had never failed me on Bougainville and who was now, at my request, undertaking a task he had had barely any time to consider. As I came to the end of my address, I knew that I had achieved the first leg of my media campaign. I had barely finished my address to the nation when scores of phone calls came flooding in to support me. One caller, a woman from East New Britain, cried when she came on air to say that this was the answer to her prayers. Her family had suffered loss of life and property and, until my address, had had nothing to look forward to. I suspected she was a Bougainvillean.

Another caller, Gabriel Ramoi, a former politician and student activist, wanted to find out if this was a military coup. I was able to reassure listeners that this was not a military coup. It was the cancellation of an ill-advised military operation involving the Sandline mercenaries, a call for an independent judicial enquiry into how and why cabinet had made the decision to hire Sandline in the first place, and a demand for Sir Julius Chan, Chris Haiveta, and Mathias Ijape to resign or step aside pending such an enquiry. If they refused, I would mobilise the whole nation to force them to do so.

The *Talk Back Show* concluded at twelve. I went to the car park and got into my SSV, a bulletproof Land Rover that was being used for operations in Bougainville and manufactured by Shorts Brothers of Belfast. With a long convoy of trucks full of troops following, I drove back to HQ Murray Barracks, arriving without any interference just after midday. From the looks of civilians on the streets as my convoy speed past, it was obvious that there was anxiety and uncertainty in the air.

I checked to see if my staff had informed media and diplomatic representatives about the news conference scheduled for 1300 hours. They confirmed that they had. I then held a series of discussions with senior officers about the implications of the radio address and what was happening.

I was informed by Major Enuma that the mobile police squad that had been assigned to raid Network International had not proceeded. As we would learn later, the squad commander was ready, but Deputy Commissioner Samson Inguba had not approved the raids at Network International. Enuma also advised me that a police riot squad had been flown in from the highlands to boost police manpower in Port Moresby.

After hearing me on the radio and seeing troops around NBC and manning the gates at Murray Barracks, the police commissioner had retreated to the Prime Minister's Office at Waigani, where he set up a liaison team to be with the prime minister. He also put the squad of policemen at Parliament House on full alert to beef up security there.

These developments were the first sign of resistance to Rausim Kwik developing from the police force. The police had a very important job to do to preserve law and order and protect lives and properties. But I dreaded the possibility that they might decide to conduct counter-operations against Operation Rausim Kwik. If they were to do that, then all hell could break loose, forcing me to take action to prevent

Sir Julius from trying to free the Sandline command team and get Operation Oyster back on track.

Many of my senior officers had been caught completely off guard and were in a state of panic, if not shock. Some of them thought that the whole country could be crippled as a consequence of my address. Reassuring them, I said it was damage control from here on. How we handled our men in the barracks would dictate the conduct of the civilian population outside the military barracks, both in Port Moresby and in other major centres.

Port Moresby, the capital of PNG, was linked by road to Gulf Province, but the rest of the provinces were only accessible by air. As this offered many challenges, the centre of our operations was around Port Moresby, which was a great relief. Government HQ, Parliament House, and all commercial activities were centred in Port Moresby. If Port Moresby was controlled by the military and if entry and exit points to the capital were secured along with the main communications facilities, then the whole country could be controlled, not that we were seeking to do that, but it could be seen from this that control of Murray Barracks and parts of Port Moresby was central to controlling what was to happen in the next few days to achieve our mission objective.

Meanwhile, at Urimo military training camp in East Sepik Province, SFU members had been secretly briefed the previous evening (16 March) by the second in command, Captain Renagi, after the day's training. So SFU members were fully aware of what was to happen and had taken precautions just in case the mercenaries resisted. Just after ten o'clock, Lieutenant Colonel Tamalanga arrived at the Urimo camp with my address in his hands to inform the Sandline personnel of the cancellation of Operation Oyster. He called in all the members of the SFU and the Sandline mercenaries and informed them that their contract had been cancelled. He instructed them to surrender all their weapons and pack up their equipment and return to Moem Barracks, where they would receive further orders. The Afrikaners appeared apprehensive but could not do much as all communications with Tim Spicer and Nic van den Bergh had been disabled.

Turning on the twelve thirty news on medium wave, it was obvious that my address on Roger Hau'ofa's *Talk Back Show* was dominating the news headlines. As I expected, the news that I had cancelled Operation Oyster and arrested the Sandline mercenaries and their command team was being played nationwide. My call for the prime minister and the two other ministers to resign or step aside pending a judicial enquiry was also headline news.

I was now set to face the press and the diplomatic corps in the force conference room. Stepping into the room at one o'clock sharp, I saw that every seat was taken. I recognised most of the media personnel present along with defence attachés Col. Charles Vagi from Australia and W/Cdr Athol Forrest from New Zealand.

I began by giving the background to what had happened over the past twenty-four hours. I confirmed that we were holding the command team of Sandline International in secure military confinement along with the main body of the mercenaries and that we would continue to do so until Sir Julius acknowledged my demands, including the immediate expulsion of Sandline. I assured them that this was not a military coup and that there was no danger to citizens from other countries.

I then discussed the probable consequences of Sandline being allowed to conduct military operations in PNG. I said that, in my view, with many years of conducting military operations in Bougainville, the best way to resolve the Bougainville crisis was not by guns or the imposition of a military solution but by the Melanesian way of negotiation and people-to-people dialogue.

At least one reporter asked about the safety of the Sandline personnel. I said that they were under military confinement and had been warned not to try resisting or escaping from custody. If they did not obey these instructions, the troops had been instructed to use such force as was necessary to prevent them from escaping or resisting. Another reporter asked where the Sandline operatives were being kept. I replied that they were under our custody and were safe for the time being.

At the conclusion of the press conference, I invited Australian head of defence force staff Col. Charles Vagi, New Zealand defence adviser W/Cdr Athol Forrest, and a US Embassy representative who was present to join me in my office for a separate follow-up briefing. Apart from the political and strategic interests of the three countries concerned in PNG, I wanted Charles Vagi and Athol Forrest to have a one-on-one discussion with me as both gentlemen had had a lot to do with me at official and personal levels. I knew that personal channels are sometimes more effective than official ones. Besides, my personal reassurance that this was not a military coup might come as a useful, if perhaps only partial, reassurance to Washington, Canberra, and Wellington.

Two other factors were on my mind. First, I was aware that more than 27,000 troops from the United States and Australia were deployed on exercise Tandem Thrust in the Shoalwater Bay training area, central Queensland, between 10 and 22 March. The exercise involved a USN carrier battle group based around USS *Independence* (CV-62) and an amphibious ready group built around USS *New Orleans* (LPH-11), the III Marine Expeditionary Force, and the Eleventh Marine Expeditionary Unit exercising alongside Australian ground, air, and naval forces. Given this major concentration of forces in Australian waters, it was obviously of extreme importance that the security situation in PNG was not seen by anybody in the region as possibly warranting an external military response.

Second, I had very recently received a copy of a confidential telegram sent from Washington to its embassy in Canberra. The telegram had been handed to Lt Col. Joseph Kewa, acting defence adviser for PNG in Canberra. It conveyed Washington's disapproval of the decision to engage the Sandline mercenaries and its decision, as a result, to cancel a pending defence training exercise between US forces and the PNGDF (Exercise Balance Passion 97-1 and 97-2). The text of the telegram read as follows:

CONFIDENTIAL

THE USG IS DEEPLY CONCERNED WITH THE STATEMENTS PRIME MINISTER CHAN MADE FEBRUARY 25 TO AUSTRALIAN TELEVISION THAT FOREIGN PERSONNEL WORKING FOR SANDLINE INTERNATIONAL WOULD BE USED ON BOUGAINVILLE AS ADVISORS.

WE NOTE THAT THESE STATEMENTS CONFLICT WITH THE BRIEFING PROVIDED BY THE DEPARTMENT OF FOREIGN AFFAIRS AND TRADE TO THE DIPLOMATIC COMMUNITY ON FEBRUARY 25. IN THAT BRIEFING WE WERE INFORMED THAT THE FOREIGNERS WOULD BE EMPLOYED ONLY FOR THE PURPOSE OF TRAINING PNGDF PERSONNEL AND ASSISTING THE GOVERNMENT OF PAPUA NEW GUINEA IN PROCURING MILITARY EQUIPMENT, AND WOULD NOT BE USED IN BOUGAINVILLE.

WE ASK FOR FURTHER CLARIFICATION AS TO HOW MUCH SUCH A USE OF FOREIGN PERSONNEL ACCORDS WITH THE PRIME MINISTER'S EARLIER, PRINCIPLED REITERATION OF SUPPORT FOR A POLICY OF PEACEFUL SETTLEMENT OF THE BOUGAINVILLE CONFLICT. THE USG BELIEVES THAT THAT POLICY HOLDS THE BEST PROMISE FOR RECONCILIATION AND LASTING PEACE.

THE USG CONTINUES TO VALUE RELATIONSHIP WITH PNG, INCLUDING ITS MILITARY COOPERATION.

NEVERTHELESS, WHILE A COMMERCIAL COMPANY IS TRAINING PNGDF FORCES IN

PAPUA NEW GUINEA AND THE POSSIBILITY OF CONFUSION IN PUBLIC MIND REGARDING THEIR ACTIVITIES EXISTS, THE USG IS CANCELLING PLANS TO HOLD JOINT EXERCISE BALANCE PASSION 97-1.

UNTIL IT BECOMES CLEARER HOW LONG SANDLINE INTERNATIONAL WILL BE IN PNG, NO DECISION WILL BE MADE REGARDING BALANCE PASSION 97-2.

WE STAND READY TO DISCUSS WITH PNGDF COMMANDERS THE TYPE OF TRAINING WE ARE PREPARED TO OFFER UNDER PRESENT CIRCUMSTANCES.

CONFIDENTIAL

With these matters as background, the three foreign representatives and I had a good discussion of the whole Sandline affair and how I intended to pursue my objectives over the coming days. I reiterated again that this was not a military coup in any sense of the word. I supported the constitution and was a firm believer in democracy. At the same time, I also believed that a full and independent judicial enquiry into the awarding of the Sandline contract was necessary, and I was determined that, pending the outcome of that enquiry, the three ministers most directly involved in the awarding of the contract–namely the prime minister, his deputy, and the defence minister— should all resign or step aside from office. After half an hour or so, the representatives departed. Although they appeared apprehensive, I thought that they also appeared relieved. I hoped that, at a minimum, I might have reassured them that, in me, they were not dealing with some kind of power-hungry general.

I still had a few hours left before the end of the day, so I decided to do some last-minute paperwork on outstanding issues and then get into the desktop computer to erase confidential files. I opened the office safe and took out the original copy of the agreement between 'the

Independent State of Papua New Guinea and Sandline International'. I extracted all the working files on Operation Oyster.

While I was gathering up my papers, telephone calls started coming in from friends who had known me a long time, asking me what I had done and what I intended as my next move. I answered as many questions as possible, believing that transparency and openness was the best way to achieve understanding and acceptance of what needed to be done.

By then, it was ticking towards three thirty. I rang Weni at Flagstaff House to check up on her and the two children. She said they were fine and that she had had the transistor radio on for most of the day. She urged me to return to Flagstaff as soon as I could and allow events to unfold there.

I downloaded most of my reserved files onto floppy disks and retrieved all the confidential files in the safe. I got my ADC, Capt. John Keleto, to pack my files and personal belongings into cardboard cartons and to arrange for them to be moved up to Flagstaff House. I then called a few senior officers into my office and informed them that my position as commander was no longer tenable. The government was already meeting in an emergency session, and it was to be expected that an acting commander would be appointed any time after the revocation of my appointment and Queen's commission.

As I looked around my office for the last time, I reflected on what I had achieved in my short time as commander. I had established new opportunities for middle-ranking officers and for men to progress in rank and had emphasised the need for upskilling and multi-skilling. A defence housing scheme had been completed, and a new satellite communications capability had been introduced with the help of an Israeli company, Elbit Systems Ltd, which specialised in international defence electronics. A heavy weapons replacement programme with a Singaporean government company, Unicorn International, was under way. I had also been successful in opening new opportunities for overseas studies at military and staff colleges in the UK (the Royal Military Academy, Sandhurst), Singapore, India, China, and other countries.

I had served my God, my Queen, and my beloved country for twenty-two years as a volunteer soldier and officer with no other motives than a commitment to duty, honour, and loyalty. I had always tried to serve to the best of my ability and to be fair to my subordinates, my peers, and those superior to me, including their families. It had taken me less than eighteen years to rise to the rank of brigadier general, not counting the two-year training I had at Joint Services College, Igam Barracks. In relative terms, I had been lucky; the defence force had shown confidence in me and had invested in me. I had travelled the world and been to places I had never dreamed of visiting. Some of the more interesting places I had visited were Belfast in Northern Ireland, the South Korean Demilitarized Zone at Panmunjom on the border of South and North Korea, Cambodia, South Korea, Japan, Hawaii, and mainland USA and many Pacific countries.

I reassured myself that my service to the Crown had made my people from Madang and East Sepik proud. My mother was from East Sepik, and I was the first commander appointed to lead the PNGDF from my province. Now I had created my own battle for which I alone was accountable. I had put the people and my troops first, and now I had to face the consequences of my decisions. The choice to expel Sandline International was mine alone.

I bowed my head as I sat for the last time in the commander's black leather chair and paused for a word of prayer to the Lord to thank him for the strength, grace, and wisdom that he had given me. I asked for comfort and forgiveness for any that I had hurt in the execution of Operation Rausim Kwik. But most of all, I prayed for my family, for the defence force, and for peace in Bougainville.

I closed the door to the commander's office for the last time and walked down the stairs to the car park. Officers who were anticipating and monitoring my movements came out and saluted me as a sign of respect. I walked out into whatever was to become of my future.

In the meantime, back in his parliamentary offices, the prime minister had been briefed by his staff and had talked to a range of departmental heads. He had also consulted his deputy, Chris Haiveta, and Minister for Defence Mathias Ijape. He then called an emergency cabinet meeting to address my challenge to the future of the Sandline contract and to consider my future in the defence force. Chief of Staff Emos Daniel, whom I had replaced as chief of defence intelligence in late 1994, was busy getting in touch with his own contacts at Murray Barracks to underline the gravity of the operations now in full swing. The prime minister was determined to take all necessary steps to countermand Operation Rausim Kwik and whatever countermeasures were necessary to make me as permanently irrelevant as possible.

Within Murray Barracks, a number of senior officers got together to solicit for the opportunity of replacing me and to condemn my actions. I was informed that the Prime Minister's Office wanted names of the colonels who were branch heads so that a decision could be made on who would replace me. Hearing this reminded me of occasions in the past when the commander's job was on the line, and potential candidates for the commander's post were described as the runners for the 'Murray Barracks Cup'.

The cabinet sat for part of the evening, considering what to do. The prime minister's advisers underestimated the impact of my address to the nation and the broader political implications of the challenge that I had laid down. At this point, the prime minister evidently thought that he would have no difficulty riding out the political storm.

I hadn't been home long at Flagstaff House and was still catching up on the day's developments with Weni and the kids when Sir Barry Holloway's car came screaming up our driveway and screeched to a halt, gravel flying. Sir Barry unfolded himself from the driver's seat. He was a tall man, but at 62 years of age, his back had become slightly stooped. He walked into my study downstairs, sat himself down, and as had always been his way, got straight to the point. 'Jerry,' he said, 'now that you have injured Sir Julius Chan, he is hurt. You know what happens to a boar if you injure it?'

'Yes', I said. 'A boar that has been knifed but not finished off will gouge you with its tusks and try to rip your guts out. So he's angry?'

Sir Barry replied, 'Yes. Right now, Sir Julius is a very angry PM, angrier than I have ever seen him. I have served with him as a minister, and I know the type of person he is. He has Chinese blood in him as I am sure you know. He is not just some ordinary guy from New Ireland. He will do everything to destroy you. He will not rest for a single moment until he has ripped your integrity to pieces. He will stake his political future on making sure that you will be in the lock-up for a very long time. If he could string you up, he would.

By then, I was getting angry myself. 'So', I snapped back, 'what is your point?'

'The point is, get a lawyer,' he said. 'Get a counsellor and not an ordinary one. We can talk about other matters later, but you need a lawyer who is conversant with the constitution and international law and who understands the Criminal Code of Papua New Guinea and other Commonwealth jurisdictions.

'Anybody in mind?' I asked.

He said, 'Yes. Peter Donigi, one of Papua New Guinea's most elite lawyers.' I said that I knew Donigi's name as he came from my mother's area from a village called Lowon in Dagua in East Sepik Province. But I had never met him before. Sir Barry said that, with my permission, he would bring him up to Flagstaff House later that evening or whenever he was available. I agreed.

Sir Barry left as quickly as he had arrived, tyres spinning, rubber smoking. Sir Barry, I reflected, was an absolute one-off. An Australian who came to PNG as an 18-year-old patrol officer or *kiap*, he had settled at Kainantu in the Eastern Highlands and taken out Papua New Guinean citizenship as soon as he was able. He was elected to the House of Assembly in 1968, was the first speaker of Parliament when PNG became independent in 1975, and was minister of finance under both Sir Michael Somare and Sir Julius Chan. He had three children by his first wife, an Australian, and nine more by two Papua New Guinean wives (and possibly as many as thirteen more children by some accounts). Clearly, he was a man who would have acknowledged the truth of William Blake's eighteenth-century epigram that 'the nakedness of women is the work of God'. In the Eastern Highlands, they say of him that there may be many big men, but Sir Barry was the only great man. He was a giant in PNG political life, a vigorous defender of the constitution, and a sworn enemy of corruption in all its forms. He was generous and unstinting to his last dollar—a very good man to have at my side. He died in January 2013, and with his death, PNG lost a friend and an icon in every sense of the word.

By then, Weni had prepared a meal, which was just in time for when Majors Enuma and Toropo arrived for a briefing. As Enuma listed them, the issues immediately on hand were

1. maintaining the aim and integrity of Operation Rausim Kwik,
2. gauging the reaction of the troops once I was dismissed from command,
3. bringing the Sandline personnel from Wewak to Port Moresby and arranging for their deportation,
4. dealing with Tim Spicer,
5. dealing with senior officer resistance within the PNGDF,
6. ensuring that accurate information was provided to the media and the public so that the whole purpose of the mission was not misconceived,
7. reappraising the strategy for damage control,
8. anticipating the political backlash of Operation Rausim Kwik.

There were too many issues confronting me for now. I needed to analyse the events of the day and think through the commitment of our resources as it was important that we remained focused. Realistically, the whole operation could still turn against us. Most importantly, we needed to remove the mercenaries from our shores without doing them any harm. Then we could deal with matters internally.

We reappraised the situation. The CASA aircraft that had been sent to extract the Sandline mercenaries and the SFU had been ordered back to Wewak and grounded for reasons unknown to us. So we had to find alternative means. The solution to this was simple. We had to hire an Air Niugini aircraft. Lieutenant Colonel Sasa and Maj. William Bartley could handle the charter question as there were funds in the Sandline and Bougainville vote sufficient to extract them to Port Moresby. Their outward travel would be the responsibility of Sandline working with Air Niugini.

I contacted Moses Maladina to make the preliminary arrangements. He was not in his office, but his staff assured me that they would make immediate arrangements for the extraction of the mercenaries from Wewak as well as for their outward-bound flights. Maladina was a very good and experienced lawyer who had taken up the executive position as general manager of Air Niugini. He had always been on good terms with me, so I was confident of air support from Air Niugini. I left the finer details to Enuma and Toropo to deal with.

With dinner over, all three of us listed our key assumptions. First, a new acting commander would be appointed. Information reaching us suggested that this would be navy captain Fred Aikung and that he would be supported by either Maj. Geoff Wiri from Western Highlands, who had been an anti-Singirok man from way back, or Marlpo and Nuia. We concluded that the New Guinea Islands faction of the defence force would use officers from the highlands to do their dirty work. Second, we assumed that, very shortly, Network International, possibly with assistance from the police, would attempt rescue operations as Tim Spicer was still in our custody, as were van den Bergh and Deats.

I told Enuma that we could not hold Tim Spicer much longer on the *Salamaua*. We needed to relocate him. Both Enuma and Toropo agreed that that was an immediate priority and that Spicer should be relocated as soon as practicable under the CO of First Battalion, Lt Col. Tokam Kanene.

An informant in the National Executive Council then called to say that it was confirmed that navy captain Chief of Logistics Fred Aikung was nominated to be appointed acting commander. This decision was apparently the work of a strong lobby from Markham member of Parliament (MP) Andrew Baing from Morobe Province, supported by other members of the ruling party, Sir Julius's People's Progress Party and Kavieng MP Ben Micah (later to be minister for public enterprises and state investment in the first Peter O'Neill cabinet, where he was allied with Byron James Chan, MP for New Ireland Province and minister for mining). In making this appointment, Sir Julius was obviously acting in haste and under immense pressure, opting for the short-term palliative of appointing a colonel who had neither operational skills nor management and battlefield leadership.

The choice of Aikung as acting commander came as a surprise to me. Aikung had an engineering and naval background and had spent most of his earlier days in the directorate of technical services. As a result, he had no prior command experience. Nonetheless, he was promoted to the rank of captain in the navy, which carried a colonel-equivalent rank. But he was a 'stay behind' colonel who never served on Bougainville and had never held a command position.

As chief of logistics, he had overseen a multimillion-dollar housing scheme for the defence force. This was built by a Malaysian consortium, YTL Corporation Berhad, one of Malaysia's leading construction and infrastructure companies, named after its founding owner and director, Yeoh Tiong Lay. YTL, which had a market capitalisation of USD 10 billion, was looking for a turnkey project to establish itself in PNG. The project was spearheaded by Benais Sabumei, a former MP and previous minister for defence.

There were suspicions of inducements for those involved in the housing project. Colonel Aikung ended up driving a YTL project vehicle, a sleek air-conditioned 4×4 Mitsubishi Muso, while his official government-issued Mazda 626 was put into the reserve pool. This extravagance, plus other lifestyle excesses, angered the troops, whose own conditions of service had deteriorated markedly as a result of increases in the cost of living exacerbated by the devaluation of the kina in 1994 by Sir Julius Chan.

In the meantime, a group of senior officers at Murray Barracks, knowing of my impending sacking, had convened a meeting that Chief of Staff Col. Jack Tuat was chairing. The issue they were grappling with was how to go about cancelling Operation Rausim Kwik. Major Enuma, hearing about the meeting, fronted up to the officers and demanded to know on whose direction they were meeting and on whose authority they were talking about cancelling Operation Rausim Kwik. The senior officers were too timid to tell Major Enuma. Before Enuma left, he reminded the senior officers that I was still their commander and that, in any such discussions, the direction must come from me. Though only a major in rank and therefore very much his junior, Enuma instructed Colonel Tuat to go and see me. Colonel Tuat never came to Flagstaff House that night.

As news of the appointment of a new acting commander reached the soldiers from Murray Barracks, some of them, plus remnants of the SFU, packed up a TCV. Led by a young Duntroon graduate, Lt John Werauri, who was also former member of SFU, they drove to Government House to try to prevent the governor general from signing Fred Aikung's commission of appointment. Just before ten o'clock, the acting secretary for the NEC and prime minister's department, Peter Eka, accompanied by Fred Aikung, arrived at the governor general's main gate. I have never known any commander-designate, acting or otherwise, to turn up at Government House to witness the signing of the instrument for his appointment by the governor general. Colonel Aikung had the nerve to do so, only to suffer the humiliation of being refused entry by the soldiers at the gate of Government House.

The Prime Minister's Office intervened, calling Government House to arrange access for Eka and Aikung. But Lieutenant Werauri refused to budge, saying that he was not taking any orders except from Major Enuma. Leaving his troops to guard the gate, the young officer drove the shortest route back to Flagstaff House to pick up Enuma and Toropo and take them back to where the armed stand-off was taking place.

Meanwhile, the police commissioner and the metropolitan commander, Sam Inguba, had both arrived at the gates of Government House. With Enuma and Toropo now present, it was quickly agreed that the signing of the commission should proceed as it had been duly authorised by the competent authority, namely cabinet. Aikung was therefore duly signed into office as acting commander.

The night was still young when Enuma and Toropo and my support staff returned from Government House. They advised me that I had been replaced by navy captain Fred Aikung. There was a long silence while they waited to see my response. I said I had expected not to last even a few hours in office after today's events, so my replacement as commander came as no surprise.

Now that I had been replaced as commander, my biggest concern was how to sustain and see through Operation Rausim Kwik. Just past midnight, an 11 × 11 metre tent was erected on the lawn in front of Flagstaff House; high-frequency communications were installed, and full-time soldiers with command post (CP) experience were rostered to man the CP. The idea was to use the CP to monitor the movement of Sandline personnel and SFU members from Wewak to Port Moresby and, most importantly, to ensure that we continued to have Tim Spicer secured and contained and the remaining phases of Operation Rausim Kwik properly monitored and controlled.

With the CP erected and manned, it was time to sleep. It was now well into the small hours. But with a fully armed section of soldiers now camping in the grounds of the Flagstaff House for my personal protection, dogs barked into the night. I was still concerned about the police refusal to raid Network International where the National Intelligence Organisation had suspected there may be illegal caches of firearms stashed. I was also concerned about Tim Spicer's security, the timely provision of transport for the Sandline mercenaries, and the emergence of resistance within senior levels of the defence force, with new players coalescing around Fred Aikung. However, as all these were continuing problems, they were problems for the morning.

As the fan circulated the warm, humid air in the bedroom, I went through the issues I had discussed with Sir Barry and thought about what he had said about injuring Sir Julius and hiring a good lawyer. I was concerned about the possibility of the operation failing if troops loyal to Sir Julius Chan combined with the police force and rogue elements of the population. In that case, the whole operation would have been worthless, and Operation Rausim Kwik would fail.

The next day would be Tuesday, 18 March 1997. I would no longer be the commander of the defence force. I would no longer be in a position of authority to complete the remaining phases of Operation Rausim Kwik. I would need to rely on the loyalty of my team: Walter Enuma, Gilbert Toropo, Tokam Kanene, Belden Namah, Bola Renagi, Alois Tom Ur, Max Aleale, Blaise Afara, Patrick Waeda, Michael Tamalanga, John Wilson, Charlie Andrews, Chris Mora, John Keleto,

John Koraia, and the SFU troops soon to arrive from Wewak. That was the whole reason why I chose middle- and junior-ranking officers for Rausim Kwik. They were the best and the most revered officers the PNGDF had ever produced, the best of the best. With that bit of comfort about the integrity, quality, and loyalty of my team, I finally dozed off. It had been a long day.

CHAPTER 8

Everyone Had 'Gone Finish', Tuesday, 18 March–Monday, 31 March

Loyalty to country always. Loyalty to government when it deserves it.

—Mark Twain

Conscience is the inner voice that warns us that someone may be looking.

—H. L. Mencken

I woke up early on Tuesday, 18 March, ready to face a day that I knew would be filled with anxiety and anticipation. The cabinet of Sir Julius Chan had sat late into the previous night and, as expected, had dismissed me from office as commander and appointed navy captain Alfred Aikung, chief of logistics, as the acting commander. Notice of the revocation of my appointment was served by Chief of Staff Col. Jack Tuat. The governor general's advice of dismissal was based on special National Executive Council meeting 8/97, Statutory Business Paper No 13/97. This formalised my revocation of office and the appointment of Alfred Aikung as acting commander based on section 6 chapter 74 of the Defence Act. I wished Fred Aikung well. I knew that the task ahead of him would be daunting not only because of the enormity of the issues on hand but also because of the vacuum of leadership I would be leaving behind and the unprecedented following I enjoyed throughout the rank and file in the force.

Majors Walter Enuma and Gilbert Toropo were the first to arrive at Flagstaff House that morning. The immediate task of D-Day + 1 was to consolidate and review our progress. My priorities were

- to ensure that the Sandline command team remained secure, under arrest, and separated from Sir Julius and his cabinet;
- to commence repatriation of the mercenaries in Wewak to Port Moresby and arrange for their outbound travel from PNG;
- to deal with the crowd control issues already building up around Murray Barracks;
- to strategise and deal with the political implications.

With the momentum of events now beginning to pick up, Lt Col. Walter Salamas, acting operations officer, called an urgent meeting of senior officers at the force conference room to establish a crisis centre to manage events as they unfolded. The meeting was Co-chaired by Lt, Col. Yaura Sasa. Major Enuma, informed of the meeting, confronted the senior officers armed and in full battle dress. He said that, as far as he was concerned, Operation Rausim Kwik was still in progress. He noted that no orders had been given to terminate the operation and told the senior officers that their meeting was illegal as it was being held in defiance of orders from the commander's office. Until he was given formal notification of the cancellation of Operation Rausim Kwik, he said that the operation would continue unabated. The Salamas meeting broke up in disarray.

After lunch, Capt. Belden Namah brought me a handwritten letter from Tim Spicer, still being detained on HMPNGS *Salamaua* off Fairfax Harbour and sailing towards the coast off Taurama Point. The letter, described by Spicer in his autobiography as being 'pretty strong in tone', read:

18 March 1997

Dear Jerry

I am writing to you formally to protest about my illegal imprisonment and to suggest to you that we need to have detailed discussions about the current situation. Regardless of the outcome of your dispute with the government there are considerable logistics and administrative tasks to be carried out.

On Sunday Nic van den Berg and I were asked to come to your office at 1900 hours for a meeting. I was late due to a long meeting with the PM. On arrival at your office I was speedily ushered upstairs by Chief of Operations and once in your office was set on by a number of armed men in civilian clothes who assaulted me, confiscated my possessions including government papers, personal effects, cash, credit cards etc. At one point one of them threatened to kill me. There was no sign of Nic but I assume he was also assaulted, detained and arrested as I saw Major Toropo driving his vehicle later.

Subsequently I was taken to the naval base in POM, put on HMPNGS Salamaua and have been kept prisoner here for 36 hours with no access to communications, to a lawyer, the British Embassy, my family, my office, my colleagues. Nor have I been given my personal effects such as washing kit, bed and shoes etc. I should also mention that during my transfer from vehicle to the boat one of those men who kidnapped me gave me a severe kick in the back. This has aggravated an earlier back injury for which I am taking medications. This was in my briefcase which was removed. I have requested this medication on three occasions with no success.

However my main concern is my employees. It is obvious that with your opposition to our being here we have to sort out what is to be done. I have to make arrangements with London for their repatriation etc. There is also the question of the equipment, spares, aircraft which must be sorted out, handed over or removed from the country. Therefore I have the following request:

1. I am immediately brought ashore to have discussions with you and the government.
2. I am immediately reunited with my employees so that I can look after their welfare.
3. I am given access to communications so that I can get in touch with my office and family.

This matter of kidnapping was illegal. Detention is severe enough but is put into insignificance with the problem of extracting ourselves from this mess. Please will you adhere to my requests forthwith so that we can discuss this together and make progress.

Yours sincerely
Tim Spicer

Having read Spicer's letter, I confirmed to Enuma and Toropo that he was to remain isolated from his command team until we sorted out the transport of the mercenaries from Wewak and their outbound travel. Sir Julius had all the resources of the state at his direction. We did not. So we had to remain focused on the mission. If Spicer tried to escape, we would deal with him. I reminded Enuma and Toropo that this was not Africa. Just because we were brown, black, or whatever, it did not give Sandline the right to treat us as if we were a failed African state. Sgt Chris Kalik Mora and three other intelligence operators were directed to remain on board HMPNGS *Salamaua* to ensure that Spicer stayed put until further notice.

Our mission was to expel the mercenaries and force Sir Julius Chan, Haiveta, and Ijape to resign. We put Tim Spicer's letter away. We had to continue to give Spicer tough but fair treatment but within limits so that he was not tempted to return to PNG again with new ideas about employing his private army.

The troops, by then, had turned up at Murray Barracks headquarters in numbers and were openly stating they would not work with the new acting commander, whom they only knew as the 'stay behind' colonel. He had always managed to avoid service in Bougainville and was no more than an administrator. They circulated a petition for my reinstatement.

While we were dealing with handling the media, maintaining unity of purpose with members of the defence force, and witnessing unprecedented public support for Operation Rausim Kwik, the first signs of dissidence within the senior ranks of the force were also becoming evident. A group of officers I elected to call the Special Operations Group (SOG) were coming together to try to counter and disrupt Operation Rausim Kwik. The first sign of action from this group was an initiative by a middle-ranking officer from the navy who organised two speedboats manned by armed sailors to track down HMPNGS *Salamaua* off Taurama Point and attempt to rescue Tim Spicer. This attempt came to nothing, but in response to it, I ordered Enuma to take Spicer off the naval vessel and relocate him to Taurama Barracks with Nic van den Bergh and Carl Deats so that we could have immediate control over them until the main body of mercenaries arrived from Wewak. This transfer was completed by three o'clock.

It was evident that the defence force was beginning to divide into two groups, one comprising officers from the mainland of PNG and the other made up of New Guinea Islanders. While this growing split was unfortunate, it reflected the nature of PNG society, where ethnic loyalty is far more important and prominent than military loyalty. The SOG aimed to neutralise the SFU and engineer the appointment of a new commander from the New Guinea Islands region who could take care of their interests. This plan was not without its prospects.

Despite this development, my personal support and loyalty throughout the ranks was still intact and growing, and those collaborating to try to counter Rausim Kwik were being monitored by our informants. We had to quickly reorganise. First, I had to encourage the commanding officer of 1RPIR to play a more prominent role in taking in and securing the three principals in the Sandline command team (Spicer, van den Bergh, and Deats), holding them at Taurama Barracks officers' mess, and maintaining the tightest possible security both at the mess and at the main gate.

I recognised that we needed the SFU platoon at Moem Barracks to come to Port Moresby as soon as possible to help us counter any moves to disrupt Operation Rausim Kwik. SFU had its integral command-and-control system in place. They were highly trained and disciplined. It was easier for us to use the SFU than other units in Port Moresby. But we needed them back in Port Moresby to support and enhance our operation.

The plan was for the SFU platoon to return to Port Moresby that day on the defence force CASA. The CASA was captained by Capt. Terry Togumagoma and Vince Tongia. They were flying over Goroka Township en route to Port Moresby when Operations Branch radioed them to return to Wewak and ground the CASA. The reason for this was quite obviously to prevent the SFU platoon from reaching Port Moresby. Sgt Francis Jakis, who was in the aircraft jump seat, was informed by the pilots that they were instructed to return to Wewak and to remain on the ground until further notice.

Hearing this from Sergeant Jakis, we quickly secured the help of other loyal soldiers who volunteered from the rank and file at Murray Barracks to assist Major Enuma to continue the operation. One such person was Cpl Alan Nangurumo from Supply Company. His nickname was 'the Terminator'. He arrived at Flagstaff House with a section of ten soldiers and happily confirmed that they would take charge of operations within Murray Barracks to support Operation Rausim Kwik until the SFU arrived.

In the meantime, concerned about all the secret files and confidential information I had in my study, I packed all the documents and plans in a briefcase and sent it to Goldie River Barracks with a close relative who was a middle-ranking commission officer with specific instructions not to disclose to anybody that he had my briefcase.

Acting Chief of Operations Walter Salamas—carrying out orders from Minister for Defence Ijape, Acting Commander Alfred Aikung, and Chief of Staff Jack Tuat—drove out to Taurama Barracks in a defence force minibus to release Tim Spicer and his command team and bring them back to the minister's office. Our contacts at Taurama Barracks informed Enuma as soon as Salamas turned up and made his orders known. This was the last thing we needed. Enuma, Toropo, Namah, and Mora drove to Taurama Barracks as fast as they could to stop Salamas. Fortunately, Salamas was slow off the mark, and Enuma's team caught up with him at the boom gate just as he was about to exit the barracks with Spicer, van den Bergh, and Deats packed in the back of the minibus in a solemn row, looking for all the world like a bunch of very self-satisfied ladies going to a dance. They had won. Or had they?

The soldiers on duty at the gate were suspicious and halted Salamas to get confirmation of his orders. And sure enough, Enuma arrived with his team and had what could best be described as a 'very serious discussion' that led to a confrontation in which Salamas was disarmed and sent on his way back to Murray Barracks without Spicer and his command team. Spicer tried to put up some resistance, which was a bit hard to do in bare feet and wearing only loose-fitting chinos without a belt; plus, he was up against four of my toughest operators. He got a whack on the side of his head with the flat of a pistol butt for his efforts and, with his colleagues, was returned to the Taurama Barracks military police cell and locked up.

My instructions were reiterated to the guards that the command team was not to be allowed to leave the barracks until we gave express permission to do so, noting that Operation Rausim Kwik had not been officially cancelled yet (evidently, a fairly basic oversight on the part of the acting commander, Alfred Aikung). Lieutenant Colonel Salamas, who returned to PNGDF headquarters humiliated and without his sidearm, had the unenviable job of reporting back to Ijape's office and Emos Daniel from Sir Julius's office that he had failed in carrying out his orders to release the Sandline executives.

When Emos Daniels called his contacts at Murray Barracks to see if Tim Spicer and his colleagues had been released, he was informed that they were still in detention at Taurama Barracks and that nothing could be done about it. Sir Julius was angry and frustrated at this news and questioned the leadership of Acting Commander Fred Aikung and Salamas. Earlier that day, Sir Julius had informed a news conference that I was no longer commander and that all orders were to come from the new acting commander. This announcement did little but infuriate already discontented troops, which in turn did nothing to help Aikung's personal standing.

Because Salamas failed to rescue Spicer and his command team from Taurama Barracks, a daring and highly risky rescue operation was planned by Rodrigues brothers in collaboration with rouge soldiers at Taurama, Two brave operatives volunteered for a late night rescue mission. So they thought. The plan was to execute a covert rescue operation in collaboration with former reconnaissance soldiers. This was to be a late-night operation launched from the Network International office at Gordon. Two Network International security men were volunteered for this high-risk operation, issued with sidearms and briefed by Mark and Cedric Rodrigues on how to execute the plan. The operation to rescue Tim Spicer and his command team was set for ten o'clock that night. We were tipped off about this secret plan by an informant at Network International.

By now, Enuma was worried that his forces were too thin on the ground and that officers assigned to Operation Rausim Kwik were showing signs of switching sides or going underground in fear of future reprisals. He decided to take some pre-emptive action on his own initiative to shore up support. Going to EMTV, the local TV station, he went on air to inform his officers and soldiers that Operation Rausim Kwik had not been officially cancelled and that all hands assigned to Rausim Kwik were required to reassemble and ensure that Sandline was expelled. This was the first time that ordinary viewers had had a chance to see Walter Enuma in action. Until then, he had been a virtually unknown major in the force whose reputation for toughness and determination had been established within the operational arms of the PNGDF as a result of a series of exploits in Bougainville. A true warrior, Enuma got more support and public attention in a couple of minutes of national TV coverage than either Sir Julius or I had gained in half an hour (or Aikung would ever achieve in a lifetime). From then on, Enuma continued his media campaign, and public support for Operation Rausim Kwik never faltered.

Enuma and I were at Flagstaff House watching the seven o'clock news when Michael Grunberg from Sandline International called from Hong Kong and asked to speak to me. Enuma took the phone and said, 'Good evening, sir, Major Enuma here. How can I help you?'

Grunberg said, 'I want to speak to General Singirok.'

Enuma replied, 'If you want to speak to the general about Sandline matters, then you speak to me. I have been placed in charge of this operation. What is your question?'

'I want to know how we can get our men out of PNG, and I want to know where Tim Spicer is, please.'

Enuma replied sharply to Grunberg, 'You don't need to worry about Tim Spicer. He is OK, but he and the other members of the command team are being held under our control. You just find the money to charter an airbus from Air Niugini and get all your men out. You have until Friday mid-afternoon to get the main body of mercenaries from Wewak to Port Moresby and until Saturday morning to get the whole lot of them out of Papua New Guinea to wherever you want to send them.'

'But—' Grunberg stammered.

'Don't give me excuses,' Enuma interrupted. 'We paid you all the money. Just get the fuck on with it.' Enuma hung up on Grunberg.

At seven thirty, I relocated to the house of one of my closest colleagues, Maj. Francis Agwi, on Milne Bay Circle in Murray Barracks to give a live interview to Kerry O'Brien on ABC TV. Keeping the Australian media informed and onside was an important objective that I never lost sight of, no more so than at the present. And it was good to see Francis Agwi again. He would become the ninth commander of the PNGDF and, at time of writing, has a well-deserved appointment as PNG's high commissioner in New Zealand.

At about ten thirty two operatives known to Byron Chan at great personal risk, at great risk to their personal safety, attempted to free

Tim Spicer and his colleagues. They were John Butler, of mixed East New Britain and New Zealand descent, and Richard Alden, of mixed New Britain and Australian descent. Having made contact with rogue elements at Taurama Barracks, they arrived at the main gate in a white-tinted Mazda 626 sedan, registration number BAN 653. They were immediately stopped and searched. Sure enough soldiers manning the gate found a 9 mm SIG Sauer pistol, serial number B 157826, with twenty-two rounds of ordinary 9 mm ammunition and one dumdum (hollow-point expanding bullet), the use of which is ordinarily considered to be illegal under the International Laws of Armed Conflict. They also had equipped themselves with a microcassette recorder, though why or who they thought they were going to record was not clear. Butler and Alden were disarmed and arrested as they had no legitimate reason to be in a military barracks and were handed over to the police.

I was informed of the failed rescue mission by officers on duty at Taurama Barracks. I sat through the night with Enuma, Toropo, and Belden Namah for company. As predicted in my earlier military appreciation, our immediate security concerns were concentrated on dissident elements in the defence force and on Network International. We concluded that these had now materialised. The forming of the resistance group SOG within the military and the abortive rescue attempt by Network International were to be expected. I knew that we could deal with SOG as most of the officers were too timid to face us; instead, they would attempt to use the cover of Walter Salamas and Jack Tuat so as to be seen by the government as trying to do a legitimate job even if no effective action was undertaken.

While Network International in itself was by now not a serious concern, I retained some concerns about the Rodrigues brothers. If not countered, this had the potential to complicate our operations. I asked Enuma and Toropo to track down the Rodrigues brothers at all costs and do whatever was necessary to get them out of PNG. Both brothers had entered PNG on tourist visas and had been illegally employed while in PNG. They were overdue for deportation.

By then, we had already made a good working alliance with the riot police who had come down from the highlands to assist the Port

Moresby police in keeping law and order. Their commander was Senior Inspector John Baiagau. Both Baiagau and his senior non-commissioned officers had worked closely with us in Bougainville, and we enjoyed a lot of professional respect for each other. They gave us their word that they would oversee the expulsion of the Sandline mercenaries. They also pledged not to confront or interfere with Operation Rausim Kwik. This was a very important and timely pledge as the cooperation, or at least the neutrality, of the police was critical to the entire operation. And they kept their word until the mission was accomplished.

As we were discussing the failed rescue by one John Butler and Richard Alden at Taurama Barracks the CO of 1RPIR, Tokam Kanene arrived and urged us to relocate Tim Spicer as his presence would bring other issues to the regiment. I told Tokam that I needed him to hold Tim Spicer and his team for another night until we figured out when the main body from Wewak would be arriving. I said that Taurama Barracks was the only place I trusted for this task due to my long association with the regiment. Tokam had worked under me as operations officer and understood my stand. He agreed and assured me that he would comply.

I got a call later that evening from Bob Lowe, the British high commissioner. He was getting worried about Tim Spicer's well-being and asked me if I could release him to his care. He sounded distraught when I spoke to him. I told him that Spicer was safe and not too much the worse for wear. Nothing that a Scots Guards' officer shouldn't be able to handle. But until we were able to finalise the repatriation of the whole body of Sandline mercenaries out of PNG, we would not release either him or the rest of his command team. I told him that it was up to the PNG government and Sandline's chief financial officer, Michael Grunberg, to organise their outbound travel. My reasoning, I thought, would have been self-evident to Lowe. I did not want any risk of personal contact between Spicer and Sir Julius, Haiveta, or Ijape since, even at this late stage, there was a possibility that the government could try to reverse the actions we had taken.

Thursday 20 March 1997

In the meantime, the Australian government had sent three 'personal emissaries' from PM John Howard to discuss with Sir Julius possible ways out of the Sandline crisis. The emissaries were Phillip Flood, head of Australia's Department of Foreign Affairs; Hugh White, deputy secretary of defence; and Alan Taylor, a former Australian high commissioner to PNG. They travelled by a Royal Australian Air Force (RAAF) VIP flight and arrived in Port Moresby at 8.20 p.m. on Wednesday, 19 March.

There were different perspectives on what the Australians hoped to achieve. Sir Julius hoped that the Australian government might soften its stance towards military cooperation and offer some real alternatives to the Sandline deal, perhaps by indicating a preparedness to work with PNG on a military solution to the Bougainville civil war. Counter-insurgency training, military hardware, and electronic surveillance capabilities were all part of what Sir Julius may have been hoping for. For the Australians, however, it appears that their message was very straightforward. Australia deplored the introduction of mercenaries into the region and believed that Sir Julius had only one practical option: to cancel the Sandline agreement and deport the mercenaries. If Sir Julius was not prepared to do that, then Australia, for its part, would have no choice but to review its aid and Defence Cooperation Program with PNG. The implication was clear. Australia could not continue in a close aid relationship with PNG if it persisted in the proposed use of mercenaries to put down the rebellion on Bougainville.

The meeting between Sir Julius and the Australian emissaries went for four hours on Thursday morning and involved a fair bit of straight-talking. When it was over, it was unclear what would happen next, but the two sides agreed to meet again on Friday morning. I was disappointed with the Australian visit for two reasons. First, I thought that the emissaries, if they wanted to hear the full story, should have arranged to call on me. Second, it seemed to me to be far too late for the Australians to offer military assistance. I did not see how they could change the emphasis under the Australian-PNG Defence Cooperation

Program from training to capability development. This had always been Australia's dilemma. They wanted to help rebuild the defence force but had always been very selective in their assistance.

We had been told the previous night that Lt Col. Carl Marlpo had been pretty busy on the phone to the Prime Ministers' Office in Waigani discussing the progress of Operation Rausim Kwik. Marlpo, along with Colonel Nuia and junior officers from the New Guinea Islands region, was coordinating efforts to disrupt Rausim Kwik. Hearing this report, I was tempted to detain Marlpo; however, because of his health, I decided against it. Also, the last thing I wanted to do was to confront fellow soldiers and officers outright as it was not my nature.

So far, the police had handled crowd control very well. But standing on Brigadier Hill, I could see massive crowds gathering near the soldiers' barracks on Wards Road. It worried me that there might be a confrontation looming as relationships between the soldiers and police had historically not always been the best. We had to contain this public mood and do what we could to channel it in a positive direction.

By then, soldiers were signing a petition for my reinstatement. They arrived in truckloads at Flagstaff House to seek my views. I said it was the prerogative of the government to dismiss me for any reason, or for no reason for that matter, and that they could not get me reinstated based on public demand. I knew that too much damage had been done and that the gap of confidence between the government and me had further widened. I was already described as a mutinous general and my actions were being described as bordering on treason. The way in which Sir Julius was describing me in public was dividing the Parliament, the defence force, the public service, the universities, and the nation.

By then, the first lot of student representatives from the University of Papua New Guinea (UPNG) and non-governmental organisations (NGOs) had arrived and informed us of their support for me. The more vocal ones were John Napu and Patricia Kassman. A protest march would be staged outside the Australian and British high commissions and Parliament House to be led by the university students.

After the evening EMTV news show, members of Parliament (MPs) Peter Barter and Kilroy Genia visited me at Flagstaff House to seek a compromise between Sir Julius and myself. I told both politicians that the time for compromise had passed. There was no way I would change my demands. My message was clear. I knew Sir Julius was desperate for a compromise before the next sitting of Parliament. He had to resign or step aside pending the results of the independent judicial enquiry I was calling for and fresh elections. There was no possibility of compromise with him. I stood my ground.

The next caller at Flagstaff House was Gabriel Dusava, the foreign affairs secretary. Dusava had had a lot to do with recommending my appointment to the commander's position. When I saw him, I knew at once that Sir Julius had sent him. Dusava told me that Sir Julius had been advised to suspend the Sandline contract and that a judge would be appointed to head the enquiry the next day. I thanked Dusava for coming and restated my position and that of those who were supporting me as well as the thousands of ordinary people who had come out on the streets in a show of support. Sir Julius had no choice but to resign or step aside for the good of the public. Dusava departed and went back to Sir Julius with the same message.

By late evening, I was informed that Sir Julius had agreed to suspend the Sandline contract and to set up a commission of enquiry. This was not bad, I thought, but would he resign or step aside? One other matter that was troubling me was the absence from duty of Capt. Ben Sesenu. Reports stated that he had not made himself available to coordinate the operations and monitoring at Fort Williams or movement of the mercenaries from Wewak, which was scheduled for the following day. It was also reported that he had large sums of money in his possession.

Discussing matters with Enuma and Toropo that Thursday evening, I stressed the importance of not letting the whole operation become messy. The dissident groups within the defence force had been identified, and because they were essentially passive bystanders, we could work around them and carry on as if they did not exist. My instructions that evening to my officers were clear. The sooner we got the mercenaries out, the better. Then Sandline would be neutralised and the mercenary threat dealt with. We could deal with local issues as they developed after that.

The one exception to this was the imminent arrival in Port Moresby of the Antonov An-124 with its cargo of gunships, helicopter transports, and heavy weaponry. I had heard from my contacts that Grunberg had been holding the aircraft, first in Bangkok and now at Pulau Langkawi, a group of islands in the Andaman Sea belonging to Malaysia. The aircraft charter was costing Sandline USD 100,000 a day, and Grunberg, always sensitive to cost issues, was becoming obsessed with the issue of getting the aircraft charter off his hands. The PNGDF was not sure that it wanted the shipment delivered in the middle of the current crisis, but the government had paid for the weapons. Australia was offering to give the shipment a temporary home at the RAAF base at Tindal, some 15 km south-east of Katherine in Australia's Northern Territory, until the current crisis had passed and the PNG government could make a decision on how best to proceed. Chan, I later heard, had made a half-hearted enquiry of the Australian emissaries about whether the Australian government might like to buy the weapons and, not surprisingly, had received an emphatic no.

With the PNG government agreeing to cancel the Sandline contract and with the mercenaries expected in Port Moresby, we agreed to the release of Tim Spicer to Kiki Barracks. This being done, the stage was now set for a mass expulsion on Saturday, 22 March. I told Enuma that I wanted a show of force at the international departure lounge, Jacksons Airport, and the car park secured. Efficient as always, this was done, the force at the airport being composed of the SFU and supporting units.

In the evening, after a discussion that included Sir Barry Holloway, the decision was made that it would be in the public interest to release copies of the contract between the Independent State of Papua New Guinea and Sandline International to the media. Media outlets were advised that there would be a press conference at Flagstaff House on Friday, 21 March, at ten in the morning. Our small printer in the office at Flagstaff House went into overdrive as we printed out as many copies of the Sandline contract as we could. Many local reporters as well as foreign journalists turned up to the press conference at ten o'clock: Ray Martin from Channel Nine, Stan Grant from Seven Network, Lucy

Palmer, Mary-Louise O'Callaghan from the *Australian*, and veteran reporter Sean Dorney from the ABC.

After reading a statement confirming that all the Sandline mercenaries were set for deportation the following day, I reiterated my intention of ensuring that Sir Julius, Haiveta, and Ijape stepped down from office. I explained that if they did not, we would mobilise the people to remove them. Questions focused on whether my actions constituted a military takeover, how I intended to remove Sir Julius, and how I expected to be able to prove that the Sandline contract had elements of bribery. Copies of the Sandline contract were handed out to the press and a handful retained for student leaders who had volunteered to mobilise hundreds of protesters to march on Parliament for the last sitting day in March.

The operations team was boosted by the arrival of the SFU on the chartered Air Niugini flight from Wewak to Port Moresby along with the Sandline mercenaries. The SFU came straight to Flagstaff House to show their support.

Earlier, on the night of Tuesday, 18 March, Major Enuma had instructed Chris Mora and his team to go to Fort Williams and take immediate possession of the safe that had been found there and bring it to Murray Barracks. This being done, the safe was held in a secure place at the Trade Training Unit. On the night of 21 March, Sgt William Eremas along with Sgt Sip Kasu used cutting torches to open the Sandline safe, and the following items were retrieved:

- one Russian Makarov 9 mm pistol, fully loaded
- two spare pistol cases
- one spare pistol magazine
- two boxes of thirty-two 9 mm rounds
- confidential documents
- one black zippered bag containing USD 400,000 all in 100-dollar notes
- PGK 1,500

Sgt Chris Mora supervised the opening of the safe and brought the items to me, which we would later use to lay criminal charges against Tim Spicer.

After realising that nearly half a million US dollars had been in Tim Spicer's hands, I informed Enuma and Toropo that he was not to be allowed to leave with the rest of the mercenaries. He needed to explain to the courts how he was able to bring hundreds of thousands of US dollars into PNG without declaring them on arrival. Something was obviously not right. They had operating bank accounts in PNG and Hong Kong if they needed to obtain cash for their personal use. Enuma agreed to take Tim Spicer off the morning flight.

In the meantime, Sir Julius held a press conference and made public the appointment of Justice Warwick Andrew to head an enquiry into the matter of the engagement of Sandline International by the state. Sir Barry and Peter Donigi, my lawyer, protested at the appointment of Justice Andrew given his long association with Sir Julius and his business partners.

In another development, Acting Commander Aikung's SsangYong Musso vehicle was taken from his house by troops loyal to me, driven out of the barracks and set alight opposite the single quarters on Wards Road with the following inscription:

IN MEMORY OF THE LATE COLONEL MUSSO AT THE AGE OF 5 MONTHS. EUOLOGY GRADUATED FROM THE UNIVERSITY OF PACIFIC ENGINEERING MAJORING IN CORRUPTION, BRIBE, POWER HUNGRY WITH YTL, BY HIS UNPOPULAR EXCELLENCEY SIR JAY. LEST WE FORGET. RIP.

Fearing for their personal safety, Aikung's family fled from their house, and Fred Aikung spent the night at Parliament. He told Sir Julius early the next morning that, while it was an honour to be appointed as acting commander, the issues on hand were beyond him and that he did not have the following of the troops or the ability to command. He feared for his family and his own personal safety, and he strongly recommended that Chief of Staff Col. Jack Tuat be appointed as acting commander in his place. So Col. Fred Aikung set a new short-distance record as commander of the PNGDF for a mere seven days.

Early the next morning, Tim Spicer was arrested and removed from the main Sandline body by Lt Edie Yodu, intelligence officer for SFU, and other members of the SFU and taken back on board HMPNGS *Salamaua* so that he could be held out of touch until Sunday or Monday morning. The news of the Sandline mercenaries' expulsion from PNG was relayed on EMTV and NBC Radio. Before midday on Saturday, 22 March, Jacksons International Airport was packed to capacity with students from the UPNG and NGOs with placards denouncing the mercenaries. Soldiers in full combat gear supervised the expulsion, and as the Sandline mercenaries were boarding, the crowd booed them and waved placards. Soldiers took up pivotal positions with machine guns mounted just in case of a last-minute change of plan by the government.

As the Air Niugini airbus took off and headed out over the harbour, it flew directly over Tim Spicer, who was once again being held prisoner on board HMPNGS *Salamaua*. If the mercenaries had known where to look, instead of marvelling at the coral reefs, they might have seen a lone naval craft anchored off Fairfax Harbour. It was a sunny afternoon as the Air Niugini flight flew overhead. Little did they know that their executive officer was seeing out his last days in PNG as an unwanted foreigner and a lone fugitive. Spicer had chosen PNG as the venue for his private army services, but all his dreams and plans ended there and then. The expulsion of the Sandline mercenaries from PNG made headlines throughout the region for the next few days.

In the afternoon, I was visited by Australian High Commissioner David Irvine, a tall and very respectful diplomat who wanted to give me the Australian position regarding the primacy of the legitimate government and the discouragement of soldiers from involving themselves in politics. He handed me a diplomatic note from Canberra spelling out their concerns with Operation Rausim Kwik:

1. We note from your media statement that you intend to rely upon the Constitutional process to achieve the goals you have set.
2. The Australian government unequivocally supports the right of duly elected government of PNG to govern and the legal and constitutional processes which supports it.

3. We strongly believe that it is essential that the PNGDF obey the directives of the PNG government and cease any illegal or unconstitutional activity.

4. The future of the government should be decided constitutionally.

5. We would urge you to use your influence to support and uphold the constitutional processes.

6. The situation in PNG is clearly volatile and the government is extremely concerned about the safety and welfare of Australian citizens and would not want that further threatened.

7. Any use of force especially by the PNGDF or parts of the PNGDF against the duly elected government, would undoubtedly lead to disastrous consequences for PNG and its future as a constitutional democracy. If force is used against the elected government that would have extremely serious consequences for PNG's relationship with Australia.

Running through the note, Irvine stressed that the Austrian government urged all parties to the present crisis to seek ways of resolving the matter internally, to respect the constitutional processes of PNG, and to refrain from violence. Australia's principal concern remained the safety of Australian citizens, and in this context, as the Australian prime minister had mentioned the day before, the readiness of some elements of the Australian Defence Force had been increased. This did not reflect any decision to deploy. It was simply a prudent and sensible measure in the circumstances.

I acknowledged the diplomatic note and assured the high commissioner that what I had done was seen by me as being in the best interest of the country. Although I knew I was personally responsible for creating a new precedent, I would explain my position at a later date once the operation had concluded in an appropriate forum. I told the high commissioner that I still maintained my position that Sir Julius, Haiveta, and Ijape must resign or step aside. David Irvine looked worried when he departed, but I did my best to reassure him that we were doing our utmost to ensure that the crisis was resolved without loss of life and that there was no threat to the safety of Australian citizens.

The second phase of Operation Rausim Kwik was now a complete success. All the mercenaries, with the sole exception of Tim Spicer, had been expelled, and no lives had been lost. And the Sandline contract had been cancelled.

We were unaware, as we celebrated the expulsion of the mercenaries, that a little of the gloss of an otherwise successful operation was being rubbed off as we spoke. It was reported to us that Capt. Ben Sesenu, along with the liaison officer from foreign affairs who had provided immigration assistance over the arrival of the Sandline personnel, had decided to celebrate at the upmarket Lamana Hotel Gold Club. They cashed USD 1,000 out of the USD 10,000 they had stolen from Tim Spicer's briefcase at the club cashier. With money in their pockets, they entered the Gold Club and showered everyone with drinks. The party continued into the early hours of the morning and adjourned to a room at the hotel, which they had booked earlier. The following day, Ben Sesenu was arrested for looting and locked up in military custody. To date, he has not disclosed how he spent the USD 10,000 from Tim Spicer's briefcase. I am happy to say that he is no longer in the PNGDF.

Sir Julius Chan, Chris Haiveta, and Mathias Ijape Step Aside

With the removal of the mercenaries and the cancellation of the Sandline contract, our attention now focused on the three ministers who had played the key roles in engaging the mercenaries. At last light on Saturday, 22 March, the day the mercenaries were expelled, Sir Barry Holloway arrived at Flagstaff House, accompanied by lawyer Peter Donigi and three other eminent Papua New Guineans: Dame Meg Taylor, a prominent PNG diplomat and lawyer; John Paska, secretary general for the PNG Workers Union; and Richard Kassman, a member of Transparency International and an insurance broker. I dubbed these five visitors the 'Eminent Persons Group', and they played a key role as events then unfolded.

Meg Taylor received her LLB from the University of Melbourne, Australia, and her LLM from Harvard University. She practised law in PNG and served as a member of the Law Reform Commission. From 1989 to 1994, she was PNG's ambassador to the United States, Mexico, and Canada, resident in Washington, DC. She was on leave in Port Moresby in March when Rausim Kwik was launched, and she immediately made her time available through Sir Barry as they had been long-time family and professional acquaintances.

Peter Donigi graduated from UPNG in 1972 and was a career public servant before being appointed ambassador to Brussels from 1976 to 1979 and to the United Nations in New York from 1991 to 1995. He returned to PNG and was working for Maladina Lawyers when Sir Barry asked him to represent me. As a specialist in constitutional law, he was just the quality of counsel and lawyer we needed to address the constitutional and legal implications of the engagement of Sandline by the government and the legal quagmire I had created with Operation Rausim Kwik. Sadly, Donigi passed away in January 2014.

The aim of this group was to mediate between myself and Sir Julius Chan. I began by explaining my position on the Sandline contract, which I believed had been entered into illegally. I also told them that aspects of the deal appeared potentially corrupt, especially in that immediately after the contract was signed, Haiveta, Ijape, and Nick Violaris travelled to meet Tim Spicer in Hong Kong. What were they doing in Hong King immediately after USD 18 million had been credited to the Sandline account if not seeking to feather their own or their associates' nests?

I informed the group that I was not going to back down from my demand that Sir Julius, Haiveta, and Ijape resign or step aside while a commission of enquiry determined whether the contract was legal and whether it had involved any corruption. While this continued to be my position, I advised the group to assure Sir Julius that I would not overthrow him as I believed in the democratic processes of government.

The Eminent Persons Group agreed to open a dialogue with Sir Julius and the speaker for Parliament, Sir Rabbie Namaliu. This being done, Sir Barry and I called Sir Rabbie, who was in his electorate at

Kokopo in East New Britain, and spoke to him on the phone. He was a trusted politician whom we both knew and respected.

Contrary to many critics who were claiming at the time that I would break down under the pressure or go crazy, the reverse was true. My long years of military training and operational experience stood me in good stead. As I had already sacrificed my career, I wanted to complete the operation without a single life being lost. Fulfilling my mission was my sole focus.

At eleven on Sunday morning, 23 March, an interdenominational church service was arranged for the troops. I attended with the key players from Operation Rausim Kwik. Also in attendance was Sir Paulias Matane, who would later be appointed the country's eighth governor general (2004–10). He was a generous and hard-working citizen who brought much hope and peace to the combined church service. At lunchtime, we had to return to Flagstaff House as Sir Rabbie Namaliu was arriving for a chat. Sir Barry and I informed Sir Rabbie that, as the last scheduled sitting day of Parliament was to be held on Tuesday, 25 March, we intended to mobilise a peaceful march to Parliament for ordinary citizens to air their views and put pressure on Sir Julius, Haiveta, and Ijape to resign.

At three in the afternoon, student leaders from UPNG arrived at Flagstaff House. Together, we planned a coordinated protest march that would mobilise the entire population of Port Moresby, using the National Student Association and students from UPNG, Lae University of Technology, the University of Goroka, the University of Vudal, the Popondetta campus, and other state tertiary institutions. UPNG student president Kevin Kepore, along with John Napu and Patricia Kassman, undertook to liaise with members of the defence force and civil society to coordinate a peaceful march to Parliament House. Another very vocal and influential group, MELSOL, headed by a former UPNG activist, Peti Lafanama, and former soldier Jonathan Oata also attended the briefing. This augured well for a large public protest during the last sitting of Parliament. The stage was now set to implement the 'people power' model of 1986 from the Philippines. D-Day for this would be Tuesday, 25 March, at two o'clock.

The news headlines in Monday morning's papers centred on the destruction of Acting Commander Aikung's vehicle. It was not good news. Acting on cabinet's advice, the government appointed Col. Jack Tuat as acting commander to replace Aikung.

At ten in the morning, Tim Spicer—who had been returned to Port Moresby the previous day after a further period of incarceration on HMPNGS *Salamaua*—appeared at the Boroko District Court on a series of charges including illegal possession of a firearm and the importation of large amounts of undeclared cash. He was represented by Michael Wilson of Warner Shand Lawyers. This was what I had wanted to achieve, to put additional pressure on Tim Spicer before he was free to leave PNG. I wanted to make it clear that, while we had some problems in our government system and were struggling with some social issues and while we had not yet resolved the conflict on Bougainville, we were not a failed state. Let Tim Spicer face the courts and see if he could extricate himself. I was determined to expose as much of the Sandline deal through the media as I could, and Spicer's court appearance and the media publicity around that was an important ingredient in the whole affair.

I attended another parade at Murray Barracks around the same time that Spicer was appearing in Boroko District Court. This time, the SFU turned up in full force on their camouflage motorbikes, leading the parade. I had not deviated from my earlier calls for the prime minister to resign or step aside. By expelling the Sandline mercenaries and by Sir Julius agreeing to suspend the Sandline contract, we had achieved a psychological advantage. What we had to do at this critical moment was keep up the pressure on the ministers in the run-up to the next day's sitting in Parliament.

In the evening, Major Enuma had a final briefing with the NGO groups, UPNG representatives, and community leaders about how best to mobilise the population to march on Parliament House. The owners of the public transport system had agreed to provide free transport from suburbs and settlements to Waigani before the march to Parliament. The stage was well and truly set to show the power of the people to PNG's parliamentarians and the rest of the world.

As mentioned, Tuesday, 25 March, was the last scheduled sitting day of Parliament. It was to be a big day for me as Commonwealth secretary general Chief Emeka Anyaoku of Nigeria was due to call on me at Flagstaff House in an attempt to close the stand-off. He visited the governor general and Sir Julius in the morning, and his visit to me was the last of his appointments before returning to Australia.

In attendance for this meeting was the Eminent Persons Group: Sir Barry Holloway, Amb. Meg Taylor, Peter Donigi, John Paska, and Richard Kassman. Major Enuma was also present when Chief Anyaoku arrived with his entourage, which was led by Andrew Ogil, PNG's consul general in Cairns. We sat in the lounge of Flagstaff House. I thanked the secretary general for his time, especially his initiative to reschedule his visit to Australia so that he could come to PNG. I said that, as an African from Nigeria, he would appreciate the issue of mercenaries and their use to open mines and destroy people's lives and livelihood. I explained that Sandline was based on the African model and that most of the mercenaries were from Africa, though they were led and financed by British subjects and South Africans.

I repeated my claim that Sir Julius, Haiveta, and Ijape must step down and allow a properly instituted commission of enquiry to establish the background to the Sandline engagement, including whether there was any corruption. I said we were not pleased with the current terms of reference and wanted these broadened to include all aspects of the deal, including financial dealings, the possible illegal trading in shares, and possible breaches of the constitution.

In response, Chief Anyaoku made the following points:

- It was difficult to challenge the grounds for objection to the Sandline contract, and he was not in Port Moresby to do that.
- His concern was with how PNG would get out of the current constitutional crisis as the consequences of failing to do so were enormous.
- He was worried about what the military could do in the future under another general who did not believe in democracy.

- He did not want to leave the public with the impression that the military had pressured the government into making any decisions. This was vitally important.
- The military must not determine the political outcome.

He further suggested the following:

- A committed democratic country such as PNG should choose their government and do so quickly because there was a lot more air to be cleared.
- In the forthcoming elections, commonwealth observers were available if requested to ensure the process was free and fair and to allow the people to choose their own leaders.
- The commission of enquiry should be independent.
- The defence force should reaffirm and rededicate itself to its constitutional obligations.
- We must save the country from what could be an unfortunate future.

I thanked him, and he spent a few minutes getting to know Major Enuma. Chief Anyaoku encouraged Enuma to uphold the constitution and democracy. In reply, Enuma said, 'People of this country should be allowed to vote for who they want to govern them. We will uphold the constitution. That is why I ensured that Operation Rausim Kwik continued after the commander was removed. This was to protect democracy in PNG.'

Parliament commenced at two o'clock that afternoon, and the main issue was the government's decision to engage Sandline. Some politicians criticised me. However, Sir Michael Somare and former speaker Bill Skate, governor of the National Capital District, took the opportunity to discredit Sir Julius, Haiveta, and Ijape. Skate then sought leave to move a motion without notice, which Sir Rabbie Namaliu granted. This was a motion calling on Chan, Haiveta, and Ijape to resign their portfolios.

Speaking to the motion, Bill Skate initiated a series of attacks on Sir Julius and demanded that he take ownership of the Sandline contract, which was seriously flawed, and resign in disgrace. He accused Sir Julius of lying to the people when he claimed that Sandline had been engaged only to act as trainers and advisers. They were, in fact, here to lead a new and high-powered offensive on Bougainville, operating helicopter gunships equipped with hundreds of thousands of rounds of munition, missiles, and high explosives. He added that, in his view, what Chan, Haiveta, Ijape, and his cabinet had done made Richard Nixon's Watergate scandal look like a leaking tap.

Defending the Sandline decision, Minister for Defence Ijape attempted to shift the blame onto the Australian government. Their policy of depriving the PNGDF of any real capability had given the government no choice but to look elsewhere for the means to tackle the rebellion on Bougainville. The four Iroquois helicopters provided by the Australian government were a good example. The Australians had attached so many conditions to the gift that they had no offensive capability, and anyway, all four of them were now out of action. Ironically enough, at that very moment, Capt. Charlie Andrews, with co-pilot Edie Miro, was flying one of the Australian Iroquois overhead, keeping watch on the Haus Tambaran (Parliament House) from just a few feet above its roof. The noise created by the hovering helicopter made Ijape's remarks difficult to hear, and he was subsequently shouted down by the opposition.

Sir Michael Somare was next to speak. But before doing so, he moved an amendment to Bill Skate's motion, which was carried. The amendment softened the demand for resignation and replaced it with a call for the three ministers to step down from office for the duration of the commission of enquiry. In speaking about his proposed amendment, Sir Michael went straight to the heart of the matter. The Sandline agreement, he said, 'empowered these people to go out and kill people on Bougainville. Bougainvilleans are our people, and we should not hire other people to kill them.'

After a lengthy debate, Sir Julius and his supporters defeated the Skate-Somare motion by a margin of thirty-nine votes in favour, fifty-nine votes against. The nation was visibly shocked and surprised that Sir Julius survived the vote requiring him to step aside. The crowd outside Parliament was particularly upset as they had been expecting the prime minister's resignation. Instead of retreating, people from all walks of life started converging, mounting a vigil outside, while Parliament was still in session.

After the vote, Chief Ombudsman Simon Pentanu—a Bougainvillean from Pokpok Island near Kieta—branded the engagement of Sandline mercenaries a 'criminal act' and a decision by leaders who were 'quite mad'. 'Sandline proved conclusively that, in PNG, truth is stranger than fiction. How could such a stupid, costly decision—such as engaging Sandline—be made?' Pentanu asked.

John Momis, veteran politician and governor for Bougainville, also made his position clear on the engagement of Sandline. 'The issue is much more serious than hiring Sandline and sacking General Singirok. The issue is whether the prime minister can legitimately claim to have the political mandate to remain in office after the decision he made to hire private armies from overseas using public monies without the knowledge and approval of Parliament.'

Momis continued, 'The prime minister; his deputy, Haiveta; and Minister for Defence Ijape must know very well by now the flip side of the coin to executive authority is executive accountability.'

Meanwhile, the crowd outside Parliament was still growing as news of Sir Julius's defeat of the vote to stand aside was aired on EMTV and NBC Radio. Troops in Port Moresby and community elders and their followers started to converge on Parliament. As the number of protesters swelled, most if not all the parliamentarians were physically confined inside Parliament House.

By ten in the evening, Sir Julius was getting visibly agitated. Aided by police bodyguards, he was put into a black police riot squad uniform and boots, bundled into the back of a police riot squad van, and driven out through the back gate under police escort. Haiveta also escaped with the assistance of the police; in his case, because of his massive physique, brown cardboard was used to cover him as he was driven out of the heavily barricaded gates surrounded by soldiers and university students.

The news of Sir Julius's and Haiveta's escape spread through the Parliament, and other MPs began planning their own escape. One group, led by the member for Port Moresby North East, David Unagi, deputy speaker, made their way to the back of Parliament House and scaled the three-metre barbed wire fence under extreme physical constraints, weighed down as they were by kilos of fat, clothing, and personal belongings. Tumbling down the far side of the fence, they retreated into the safety of the night and the green pastures of the golf course behind Parliament to a prearranged rendezvous.

When David Unagi told me the story years later before his passing, he said, 'You know, General, the Port Moresby golf course has many ponds and billabongs infested with crocodiles. But that night, they slept well and did not bite us. The worst thing was when we got to the other side of the golf course on the Morata side of the road to a predesignated spot. I took my shirt off and displayed it on a stick as close as possible to the road so that my pickup will see me and stop while my gang was hiding amongst the tall grass. I was sweating furiously while others were breathing heavily. The mosquitoes feasted on me big time. I have never been bitten so many times in my life by mosquitoes. But worse still, our pickup did not see the shirt and drove right past it. He returned fifteen minutes later slowly, and when I flagged him down, I was so upset with him that I pushed him out of the driver's seat. How my colleagues, the highlands' politicians, squeezed into the back of the van was amazing. But that was how we escaped from the Parliament.'

We had a good laugh. I liked David Unagi. He was a true people's leader and always advocated for their welfare in the sprawling settlements of Port Moresby North East.

The crowd around Parliament House continued to swell into the night. The MPs who had not escaped were left without clean clothes, toothbrushes, shaving gear, and food for the evening. When news reached Sir Barry, Peter Donigi, and me at Flagstaff House, we dispatched Donigi with Walter Enuma and Gilbert Toropo to link up with Namah and Renagi at Parliament House to speak to the parliamentarians. Sir Michael Somare was at the main gate and received Enuma, Donigi, and the rest. They met with Sir Rabbie and assured him that we respected the constitution and the democratic process. However, they reiterated that Sir Julius had to do the right thing and step down pending the outcome of the commission of enquiry into the engagement of Sandline.

When Enuma and Donigi returned to Flagstaff House, we reviewed the day's events and agreed that Sir Rabbie Namaliu, as speaker, had saved the day by agreeing to accept the Skate-Somare motion. Sir Julius had survived the vote. But our mission was not complete until he stepped aside.

An additional sitting day had been added to the parliamentary schedule for Wednesday, 26 March, at the conclusion of the previous day's tumultuous sitting. In the morning, I got a surprise call from Miss Louise (Lulu) in the Prime Minister's Office. She said she was typing Sir Julius's statement to the Parliament advising of his decision to step aside to allow a commission of enquiry into the engagement of Sandline International to preserve democracy and protect the constitution. This act by Louise was most unexpected—it was indeed a predestined goodwill gesture that helped ease the tensions over the political developments in Parliament.

Out at Jacksons Airport, Capt. Charlie Andrews and Lt Edie Miro from Madang refuelled the Iroquois helicopter; and by lunchtime, it was serviced and ready to fly over Parliament when it resumed its afternoon sitting at two o'clock. Parliament House is less than two minutes flying time due west from the airport.

The crowd overnight had retained its vigil around Parliament. Bill Skate and David Unagi had arranged for businesses to supply refreshments—bread, biscuits, scones, and cartons of soft drink. The crowd zeroed in to hear what Sir Julius would say. At 2.50 p.m. after a delay while a quorum was assembled, the parliament bell rang to announce the commencement of the afternoon sitting. As members arrived, it was very clear who was on the government side and who was seated in the opposition. Sir Peter Barter, always a man of his words, was now seated with the opposition.

As EMTV had exclusive rights to film the sitting, we crowded around our TV set to watch the speech by the prime minister. Sir Julius stood and said, 'Mr Speaker, I have made up my mind, and I will step aside for the good of Papua New Guinea. I must take account of some pain and trouble and security that have happened in the past week. I want people to return to their normal lives as quickly as possible. I call on all sections of the community to help restore peace. Democratically elected government must not be dictated or forced by a section of the community at the barrel of the gun or other forces. I have watched the public unrest in the past ten days but have reserved my decision until the preliminary procedures were carried out.

'I stand up to protect the constitution and the supremacy of the Parliament, which was demonstrated on the floor yesterday when the motion calling for me to step aside was defeated. I am stepping aside not because of public pressure but to uphold the democratic process and the constitution of the country. The vote taken yesterday maintained the supremacy of Parliament. We need to respect this institution and exercise it when the government numbers stood firm to protect the integrity of Parliament.

'I will ask my deputy, Hon. Chris Haiveta, and Defence Minister Hon. Mathias Ijape to also step aside. I will ask cabinet to appoint a judge for an enquiry and confirm the terms of reference.'

Sir Julius's address to the Parliament was welcomed throughout PNG. As jubilant soldiers and policemen started to make their way back to their barracks, hundreds of people who had spent the night around Parliament House also started dispersing. There was nationwide jubilation.

Major Enuma told reporters that the soldiers were pleased to hear the prime minister's decision to step aside and allow the commission of enquiry into the Sandline issue. He praised Sir Julius for his decision as it was in the best interest of the nation.

When ABC's Sean Dorney and Channel 7's Stan Grant asked me my views, I said I did not want people to see me as a hero. The real winners were the people of PNG, including Sir Julius and all the MPs, because they voted according to the parliamentary process. I had taken a calculated risk in speaking out against Sir Julius's plans to send foreign advisers and operatives into Bougainville. This was because I could see a major disaster coming. So as a responsible commander, I did what I had to do to save our brothers, sisters, children, and future generations on Bougainville.

A few days earlier, I had called Gen. John Baker and asked him to do something. He assured me that I could leave the matter in his hands. Baker's contribution towards the expulsion of Sandline was for him to arrange for the interception of the Sandline flight and its diversion to Australia. Meantime, the head of Australian Defence Staff in Port Moresby, Col. Charles Vagi, and his deputy, Gary Hogan, were in personal damage control as they had not informed Canberra ahead of time about Operation Rausim Kwik.

On Thursday, 27 March, Gen. John Baker ordered two RAAF McDonnell Douglas F/A-18 Hornets to intercept Sofia Airlines Antonov An-124, loaded with gunships, missiles, ammunition, and other weapons, and directed it to land at Tindal Air Force Base in the Northern Territory to discharge the arsenal. This occurred as a result of Michael Grunberg informing me that the Antonov was arriving from overseas. Grunberg was warned, in no uncertain terms, that if the aircraft arrived in PNG, it would be disabled and destroyed with all its consignment.

Reflections on Operation Rausim Kwik

It was now the end of March 1997, and everyone touched by Rausim Kwik had 'gone finish': Sandline, Spicer, Aikung, the prime minister, his deputy and finance minister, the defence minister, and me. Reflecting on the lessons learnt, I told the operations team that I hoped that, one day, Operation Rausim Kwik would be used by military planners as a textbook case in military planning and the application of the joint military appreciation process. It served as an important reminder that, sometimes, as military officers, none of the choices facing us were very palatable. When this occurred, deciding what to do was a matter of choosing the least worst option among a sea of bad options.

Maj. Walter Enuma, as my operations officer for Operation Rausim Kwik, understood precisely what had to be done and walked my path for me in the best military tradition of personal loyalty. He displayed absolute determination and personal sacrifice to successfully complete the mission. Major Enuma was a match for any military officer anywhere in the world. He had what it took to be an officer fully capable of enforcing his superior commander's intent. Without his calibre of dedication and foresight, neither I nor we would have achieved our goal: the arrest and deportation of the mercenaries and the Sandline command team, the cancellation of the Sandline contract, the setting up of an independent judicial enquiry, and the stepping aside of the prime minister, the finance minister, and the defence minister.

As I conclude this chapter, I realise that a man's destiny is shaped by his dreams and aspirations. If he is part of a team, as in a military operation, there must be unity of command to arrive at the desired destination. From the outset, the leader must own the issue close to his heart. He must be passionate and emotional in his commitment to it. As we bring others into our confidence, those new to our dreams must be brought to embrace the same vision. The mission will only succeed if there is unity of purpose and a belief in the team's mission.

The Sandline crisis occurred because, as a nation, we did not exhaust all the options to solve the Bougainville crisis in our traditional way. We opted for an easier way out, or rather our politicians were naive and reckless and were spending millions on weapons as we continued to send our troops to their graves, making hundreds of families fatherless and homeless. We even went abroad to import a private mercenary army while neglecting our own.

I have gained no credit from my actions over precipitating the Sandline crisis, and I do not expect any. I sacrificed my job, my future, and my family's well-being for an outcome that was forced on me by the actions of others. I was a soldier following orders until the point at which those orders turned against the interests of my country. I deemed them to be illegal and unconstitutional. Under such circumstances, personal sacrifice becomes inescapable. Whether what we did was right or wrong will be a matter of debate for many years to come. I believe that, collectively, we provided a circuit breaker that helped create the conditions for a durable peace on Bougainville.

The wellspring for our collective actions was based on the examination of our consciences. I am pretty sure that every soldier who participated in Operation Rausim Kwik did so after examining their own conscience. This is not a matter that is taught in military institutions, law schools, faculties of humanities, or seminaries. A conscience is a trait and a quality that each of us possesses. We must nurture, develop, consult, reason, analyse, and act on our own reasonable judgement as we see fit when confronted with life-threatening matters or those that are delicate and difficult.

CHAPTER 9

Aftermath: The Two
Commissions of Enquiry

Veritas liberabit vos: *Ye shall know the truth, and the truth shall set you free.*

—John 8:32

This verse from the King James Bible is buried deep in the Western consciousness. John 8:32 appears as two simple lines of text in my family Bible. It is inscribed as a single line in foot-high letters cut deep into the marble above the entranceway to the Central Intelligence Agency (CIA) in Langley, Virginia, USA. Its architect evidently hoped the text would become the driving force behind the work of the CIA. In a more modest setting, it was also intended to be the animating spirit behind the two commissions of enquiry set up by the Papua New Guinea government to examine the engagement of Sandline International by the state.

The first of these commissions, held before Justice Warwick John Andrew, was convened under the PNG Commissions of Inquiry Act (ch. 31) in March 1997. The terms of reference, set by the prime minister before he stepped aside from office in favour of Acting Prime Minister Hon. John Giheno, were dated 21 March. As seen by Justice Andrew, the aim of the enquiry was not to adjudicate between the parties to the dispute. Rather, the aim was to establish the facts and arrive at the truth surrounding the engagement by the state of Sandline International.

The Andrew commission held its first preliminary hearing on 25 March, barely a week after my radio address to the nation on 17 March, in which I had called for an enquiry to establish the truth about suspected irregularities and possible corrupt dealings in relation to Sandline's contract of engagement. The main hearings before Justice Andrew commenced on 1 April and concluded on 15 May. The report of the enquiry was submitted to the acting prime minister on 29 May under the title 'Report of the Commission of Inquiry into the Engagement of Sandline International'.

The enquiry began by establishing that there were five people with bona fide interests who needed to be heard and who were entitled to be represented by legal counsel: Sir Julius Chan, Brig. Gen. Jerry Singirok, Chris Haiveta, Mathias Ijape, and Timothy Spicer. The state of PNG was also a party to the enquiry. Others who wished to appear could do so after establishing their reasons for attending. One such party was Jardine Fleming, the Hong Kong–based investment bank that was the joint lead underwriter for Orogen Minerals, the company being set up and funded by public subscription to take over a portion of PNG's interests in oil and mining assets.

Counsel assisting the enquiry was Ian Molloy. Counsel assisting me was Peter Donigi. Counsel appearing for Sir Julius were Marshall Cooke, QC, and Mal Varitomos, QC. Peter Donigi and I paid several calls on Acting PM John Giheno's office before the enquiry commenced. Our objective was to get the terms of reference widened and to have the state meet my legal costs. Both requests were summarily rejected. The enquiry remained narrowly focused on the engagement of Sandline, and I would have to pay my own legal bills or go unrepresented.

To help meet my legal costs, a trust account was opened, with Dame Meg Taylor, Sir Barry Holloway, and Richard Kassman agreeing to act as trustees. A nationwide appeal was launched, and we made numerous visits around PNG to take my case to the people. This was a wild success. The appeal resonated with people in all walks of life, and a significant sum of money was raised. We heard many touching and heartfelt stories of corruption in government and how it affected the lives of everyone we talked to. If the government felt that my dismissal from office and its refusal to meet my legal expenses would shut me down, it was very much mistaken. The outpouring of public support around the country wherever I travelled was enormous. Indeed, it may have been the most significant factor in Sir Julius losing his parliamentary seat in the June elections, along with Mathias Ijape and many other members of Parliament deemed to be tarred by the same brush.

Despite widespread public support wherever I travelled, the Andrew commission was a disappointing and bruising experience both for me personally and for my supporters, the 'little and poor' people of PNG politics. Sir Julius Chan and Mathias Ijape got completely free passes in the final report, no evidence of corruption or improper payments being found. Both ministers would have been extremely pleased with the commission's findings were it not for the fact that publicity surrounding the work of the commission resulted in an enormous public backlash. In stunning political upsets, both men were removed from office in the national elections that followed. Chris Haiveta retained his seat but received very heavy criticism at the hands of the commission as did I.

Copies of the Andrew commission's report are now very difficult to locate. It is not available online, but a single copy is held at the Department of Justice and Attorney General Library. Before discussing the criticisms levelled at Haiveta and myself, it is useful to provide a brief summary of points made in the report as background to why the enquiry had been called. These included the following:

- On 22 February, Australian newspaper reports revealed that the PNG government had hired Sandline International to provide personnel ('mercenaries') to assist the PNGDF in conducting operations in Bougainville.
- On 24 February, the Australian government described the use of 'mercenaries' as 'totally

unacceptable'. Other countries expressed similar objections.

- On 12 March, the World Bank and the Asian Development Bank were said to be reviewing their financial assistance to PNG if mercenaries were used.
- On 17 March, the PNGDF commander, Brigadier General Singirok, made a radio address to the nation in which he said, among other things:

There have been many false and misleading statements made by the prime minister, his deputy and the defence minister about the engagement of Sandline . . . I have [this morning] officially informed the prime minister that I have cancelled all further activities involving the PNGDF with Sandline International . . . and I have called on the prime minister, his deputy and the minister of defence to resign immediately.

The commander also observed that Sandline equipment had been sold to the government at exorbitant prices 'allowing the potential for sizeable percentage for commissions'.

- Later that day, the prime minister responded by dismissing Brigadier General Singirok from his command.
- On 18 March, the prime minister reiterated that the Sandline contract would stay in place and that Sandline personnel would be used on Bougainville. The Australian prime minister warned of serious consequences and sent a team of senior officials from Canberra to discuss matters further.
- On 19 March, there was widespread civil unrest in Port Moresby. Parliament was 'under siege'.

- On 20 March, the prime minister suspended the Sandline contract and announced an enquiry into how the Sandline contract had been entered into.
- On 26 March, the prime minister agreed to stand aside pending the results of the commission of enquiry. The deputy prime minister and the minister of defence also stood aside.

Justice Andrew's report, while narrowly confined by its terms of reference and rushed by an extremely tight reporting deadline imposed by the prime minister, was nonetheless a fair attempt to set out all the circumstances surrounding the government's quite extraordinary decision to engage Sandline International. It remains worthwhile reading, if personally discomforting, even at this distance in time.

The main criticism levelled at me in the report was that I should have done more to make my opposition to the Sandline deal known to key ministers earlier in the piece. There were opportunities to do that, but I did not. As the government's most senior military adviser, I should have made my doubts much more evident. In not speaking up, I let my ministers down, and I regret that. Indeed, in viewing my responsibilities too narrowly through a military rather than a political-military lens and in assuming that funding difficulties would scupper the deal, I made two serious mistakes.

I see these mistakes as major learnings that should be taken on board in staff and administrative colleges around the world and not just in PNG. These learnings are about military leaders not viewing their military responsibilities too narrowly and the need to be scrupulously open and honest in voicing doubts on professional military matters to ministers before it becomes too late. Related to this is the constant need to be aware of assumptions, to bring them to the surface and make them an explicit part of the military planning and decision-making cycle, and to keep them under constant review.

So yes, I do have regrets, and I accept the criticisms on this matter in Andrew's report. On the other hand, it should be acknowledged that I took the lead, along with James Melegepa, Zachary Gelu, and Vele

Iamo, the government's other key advisers on the proposed engagement of Sandline, in sending a last-ditch memo to Noel Levi, secretary to the prime minister's department, advising that we were 'not satisfied' with the draft contract with Sandline. We urged that the contract be substantially renegotiated as, in our view, it was 'not implementable' in the form in which it had been presented by Sandline to the state.

This memo, which should have rung loud alarm bells with ministers, was prompted after examining the draft contract that had been prepared by Grunberg and that we found to be seriously deficient on numerous counts. The memo was written and signed by Melegepa as secretary of defence and countersigned by myself as commander, Gelu as state solicitor, and Iamo as the finance department's acting deputy secretary. It was sent to Noel Levi on 30 January. It was classified top secret, and we urged that it be sent immediately to the prime minister, the deputy prime minister, the minister for defence, the minister for planning, and the minister for justice.

Noel Levi passed it to Sir Julius, who, so far as I am aware, took no action on it. Haiveta saw it that evening and was briefed on its contents but waved off the concerns. Despite receiving this advice and apparently agreeing with key parts of it, Haiveta nonetheless went ahead in signing the contract the following day, 31 January. No further effort was made to renegotiate the contract. The first tranche of money due under the contract, USD 18 million, was sent that same day to the Sandline holding account at the Hong Kong and Shanghai Bank, Queens Road, Hong Kong.

Haiveta came in for the heaviest criticisms levelled by the Andrew commission. It found that much of the minister's evidence was unreliable. ('Untruthful' was the word used by Justice Andrew.) Haiveta had put undue pressure on banking officials and finance and legal advisers to get the contract monies assembled and sent to Sandline in Hong Kong. He abused both the letter and the spirit of the Public Finance (Management) Act with regard to tendering procedures by, as the enquiry put it, 'resorting to the extraordinary device' of causing 100 waivers to be issued under subsection 40(3)(c) of the act. He wrongly advised the prime minister that the contract money would come from the proceeds of the Orogen float when, in fact, in the end, it came from cuts to the recurrent budget allocations of government departments. These cuts exposed PNG to further heavy criticism from the IMF and the World Bank for going back on its formal commitments to those institutions in respect of maintaining budgetary allocations deemed critical to numerous sectors of the economy including health, welfare, and education.

The enquiry summed up its view on Haiveta's evidence by saying that 'suspicion hangs over Mr Haiveta in respect of a number of matters'. Further, the enquiry 'remains suspicious of Mr Haiveta's actions and motivations and, in parts, rejects his evidence as untruthful'. So much, it might be said, for the enquiry's stated aim of establishing the facts and arriving at the truth surrounding the engagement by the state of Sandline International. If Haiveta's evidence was seen as being untruthful in key respects and if he was the main driver for the engagement of Sandline, as he was, then the aim to establish the truth was never going to be met. In addition, the enquiry was unable to positively identify who was behind the purchase of Bougainville Copper Ltd shares when Haiveta, Ijape, and Violaris were in Hong Kong with McCowan, Grunberg, Spicer, and Buckingham (see the following section). Nor was it able to determine who the beneficial owners and shareholders of Sandline International were.

That said, the enquiry did not find any evidence of secret commissions or corrupt payments being made from Sandline International to any PNG ministers, including Haiveta, or to any PNG public officials. It was, however, critical of aspects of Tim Spicer's evidence. He refused to say, or was unable to say, who the beneficial owners or shareholders of Sandline were. And his evidence in respect of the relationship between Executive Outcomes and Sandline was found to be 'not correct'. Spicer described Executive Outcomes as nothing more than a subcontractor to Sandline International. But when the enquiry examined the signing authorities on the Sandline Holdings Ltd bank account in Hong Kong through which the contract money had been sent, it discovered that the account signatories were two directors of Executive Outcomes, Luther Eeben Barlow and Lafras Luitingh, plus Simon Mann of Defence

Systems Ltd and Anthony Buckingham of Heritage Oil and Gas (but, interestingly, not Spicer himself).

The enquiry investigated, at some length, the question of possible insider trading in BCL shares on the Australian Stock Exchange but was unable to come to any conclusions. Someone who was in a position to know that PNG was about to sign a contract aimed at the recovery and reopening of the Panguna mine purchased a significant quantity of shares in BCL at the very moment that Sandline officials (Buckingham, Grunberg, Spicer), plus Rupert McCowan from Jardine Fleming, were in Hong Kong along with Haiveta, Ijape, and Nick Violaris.

The dates and sequence of events were as follows. On Thursday, 13 February 1997, Haiveta flew to Hong Kong for a meeting with Rupert McCowan of Jardine Fleming to discuss the possible purchase by the state of Conzinc Riotinto of Australia's majority shareholding of BCL shares and the financing of such a purchase. Ijape accompanied him but paid his own way, suggesting that his interests in the trip were privately motivated rather than official. Earlier that day, Haiveta—in his capacity as minister for finance—had instructed James Loko, acting secretary for finance and chairman of the PNG Public Officers Superannuation Fund (POSF), to sell one million of its shares in BCL. The POSF board signed off on this request the same day but did not actually instruct its share brokers to act either out of dilatoriness or, more charitably perhaps, to protect the minister from unwelcome claims of unlawfully seeking to manipulate the share market. The shares in a mine that had not operated for nine years were sitting at a bargain basement share price of forty-three cents. The very next day, a mystery buyer purchased 156,706 BCL shares, driving the price up to sixty-two cents. A further 486,000 shares in BCL were traded on the following Monday at around sixty cents. The Australian Stock Exchange took note of the unusual level of activity and enquired from BCL majority shareholder CRA if it knew anything to explain the jump in price. CRA denied all knowledge.

The Andrew commission dismissed the possibility of the sudden surge in trading as being mere coincidence. The trading in BCL shares took place at the very moment when a small group of people who knew about the Sandline contract were gathered together in Hong Kong.

Of these people, one of them (Haiveta) was in a position to direct the dumping of BCL shares belonging to the POSF to drive down the market price. The Andrew commission found Haiveta's testimony about the Hong Kong meeting 'not very satisfactory' but chose not to speculate further on who might have been the insider who was trading in BCL shares. Whoever it was, it must have been someone who was very confident of the efficacy of the services contracted from Sandline International. Had the mine reopened, its share price might well have reached AUD 2–4 in the near term and much more when (and if) the mine actually became profitable. The POSF had purchased its BCL shares at AUD 1.40, so it was looking at taking a hit if it offloaded at AUD 0.40–0.60 a share. In the event, it did nothing, preferring to await developments in the market and wishing perhaps to protect its minister from an unwise and possibly illegal intervention in the Australian Stock Exchange.

These events happened more than twenty years ago. If the mystery purchaser held on to his share parcel, it would now be worth less than one-third of what was paid in 1997. BCL shares are currently trading at around AUD 0.18 (at December 2018 prices).

It should be stressed that, although the enquiry expressed suspicions about the truthfulness of certain aspects of Haiveta's evidence, it stopped well short of fixing blame on him, or indeed on anyone, for insider share trading. The trading may not have been initiated by anyone on the PNG side. There were others in Hong Kong associated with Sandline in one way or another and, of course, many behind-the-scenes operatives putting together the personnel and equipment required under the Sandline contract. So there was a widening pool of knowledge in Africa, Britain, Europe, Australia, and elsewhere that might have led to the sudden interest in BCL shares. It need not have been Hong Kong based.

The remainder of Andrew's report was received with relief in some quarters and misgivings in others. In broad terms, the report exonerated PNG ministers and officials from corruption and illicit dealings over the engagement of Sandline. It criticised me for doing too little to prevent the Sandline engagement and Haiveta from doing too much to advance it. It expressed surprise that Haiveta should have caused a cheque to be issued, and purportedly guaranteed by the state, before there was a contract even in place. It criticised officials for doing nothing to check on Sandline's pricing of the equipment to be supplied under the contract. It was also critical of the fact that the contract was allowed to be drafted by Sandline and presented only after the state had guaranteed payment and was effectively committed. However, Andrew described this as commercial 'naivety' rather than corrupt dealing.

To conclude this account of Justice Andrew's commission, I will add a personal note. I was on the witness stand for nearly five full days that April 1997. It was personally and professionally discomforting to be taken backwards and forwards over the history of every aspect of the Sandline engagement and of the reasons for my decision to arrest and deport the mercenaries. I had the support of Peter Donigi, my counsel, through all this and will always be grateful for his wisdom and guidance. The most trying moments were during the questioning by Marshall Cooke, QC, counsel for Sir Julius, who took a very adversarial approach to the advancement and protection of his client's interests. I withstood this for as long as anybody reasonably could, but his slow, ponderous, and condescending air eventually began to get the better of me. There are only so many different ways that the same or similar questions can be answered. Every question that I answered, to the best of my ability, was met by yet another question, backwards and forwards, over the same ground again and again.

Questions about my own actions and motives were fine up to a point. But when he got onto a line of questioning about the failure of Operation High Speed II, the Kangu Beach massacre, and the assassination of Theodore Miriung, with the obvious intent of showing how poorly trained and motivated the troops were under my command, I could feel my self-control starting to slip. After I had struggled with recollecting accurately some detail or other, he said, 'That is a lie, General. I put it to you that you are lying. You are a liar. You have been lying to this commission the entire time you have been offering testimony.'

That did it. I stood up and demanded an immediate apology. He refused. I repeated my demand. He stood his ground. I turned to Justice Andrew and said, 'Your Honour, unless counsel apologises to me and withdraws his remarks, I will leave the room.' Still no apology. So with a bow to the justice, I left. And that was that. I was not recalled. Nor would I have returned until Marshall Cooke withdrew his remarks.

At no point during the hearings did I think that Justice Andrew was particularly in my corner. Perhaps he would have been failing in his duty to maintain strict impartiality had he displayed anything but the most correct behaviour. Therefore, I was surprised, a good deal later, to see in his report on the work of the enquiry the following brief reference: '[General Singirok] ultimately left the Commission and refused to answer any more questions which is a matter which goes to his credit.' So much for Marshall Cooke, QC! Given a choice, I would rather lead my men back into the Panguna mine or attempt another helicopter casualty evacuation into enemy territory than endure another commission of enquiry.

The Los Commission

The report of the Andrew commission had a mixed reception at the political level. Some saw it as vindication, others as a whitewash. When Bill Skate's government replaced Sir Julius Chan's administration on 22 July 1997, one of its first actions, on 11 August, was to announce the establishment of a new board of enquiry, with greatly extended terms of reference and a less restrictive reporting timeline, to look into additional aspects of the Sandline affair. The terms of reference of the new enquiry went through a couple of iterations. When eventually issued, on 11 September 1997, they were seen to deal mainly with issues arising from the Andrew commission. For that reason, Justice Sir Kubulan Los's commission of enquiry into the transparency in government dealings and accountability of public office holders is generally referred to as the second Sandline enquiry.

Justice Los was assisted by two senior magistrates, Raphael Apa and Mekeo Gauli. Counsel assisting was again Ian Molloy. Hearings were held from mid-October to mid-November 1997; in January, February, and March 1998; and in June and July 1998. In July 1998, Chris Haiveta applied to the commission to disqualify itself, arguing reasonable apprehension of bias. When the LOS commission refused to disqualify itself, Haiveta followed up with an application to the national court for a judicial review of the draft findings of the commission.

Pending an outcome from the application for judicial review, the LOS commission filed an initial report on its findings. This initial report, which can be read online, was never proofread or edited to the standards normally expected from an official enquiry.[2] The initial report notes that, given Haiveta's application for a judicial review, it was decided that no reference should be made to any of the issues or the evidence that might have prompted the application for such a review. This means that none of Haiveta's evidence or the conclusions reached by the LOS commission on that evidence are contained in the initial report.

It is not clear if, or when, this initial report was submitted to Parliament. It was submitted to the prime minister, with an undated covering letter, on 28 August 1998. But what happened to it thereafter, if anything, is unclear—nothing apparently.

Whether the national court ever dealt with the application for a judicial review is not clear either. But on 28 September 1998, the LOS commission filed a follow-up report to the prime minister dealing with matters concerning its terms of reference (specifically no. 10) and the actions of Chris Haiveta as deputy prime minister and finance minister in pushing through, and signing, the Sandline contract. No action was taken on this follow-up report either. For all these reasons, the LOS commission can only be regarded as a work in progress for which the undated draft initial report and draft follow-up report are all there is, or may ever be, as a record of its proceedings. This is highly unsatisfactory.

---

2   PNGi, 'Initial Report of the Commission Inquiry into Transparency in Government Dealings and Accountability of Public Office Holders', 28 August 1998, retrieved 28 June 2021, https://pngiportal.org/directory/initial-report-of-the-commission-inquiry-into-transparency-in-government-dealings-and-accountability-of-public-office-holders.

From scattered references, it appears that the Los commission had eleven terms of reference to report against. The draft initial report does not include a list of these, nor does it report its initial findings against these, so the reader needs to make a series of inferences about the subject matter going along.

Matters explored by the Los commission included the application of the Public Finance Management Act to the Sandline contract (it held that the head of state should have signed the contract, not the minister of finance), the question of insider trading in BCL shares (on which the commission made no progress; it records its disappointment at the unwillingness of the Australian Securities Commission to share its findings on the matter), and the nature of Nico Violaris's relationship with Sir Julius Chan. (It held that Sir Julius's evidence to the first Sandline enquiry denying that they were business associates was not correct and that Sir Julius and Violaris were, in fact, business associates in January and February 1997.) That said, the commission could find no reason why Violaris was in Hong Kong at the same time (mid-February 1997) as Rupert McCowan and Sandline executives Buckingham, Grunberg, and Spicer, as well as Ministers Haiveta and Ijape. It found no evidence that Violaris was trading in BCL shares either on his own behalf or on behalf of any other person or entity. The reason for his association with Sandline and others at that time remains unexplained.

A lengthy section of the interim report deals with the question of whether there was some wider intent behind the operational orders for Operation Rausim Kwik. Counsel for Sir Julius and Ijape argued that there may have been a wider plan to topple the government through intimidation and threats of force. On this issue, the commission found that 'the orders speak for themselves'. They called for the termination of the Sandline contract. If any removal from office was contemplated, that was limited to those ministers closely associated with the planning and execution of the contract and 'not to frustrating the democratic system of government in Papua New Guinea'.

This is an important conclusion as it goes to the question of whether I was, at any point, planning the overthrow of a legitimate government, in short a military coup. I was not. My intent was solely limited to terminating the Sandline contract and expelling the mercenaries. I called for an official enquiry into the circumstances around the engagement of Sandline, and I called on the three key ministers to resign or step aside pending conclusions from that enquiry. But I was certainly not advocating the overthrow of the government. I am glad to have the support of the Los commission on this key point.

The commission then went on to examine the legality of my actions in terminating the Sandline contract and detaining and then expelling the mercenaries. The commission found that I exceeded my lawful authority as commander in ordering these actions as there was no lawful justification in either military or civil law for this conduct.

The commission noted my view that the engagement of Sandline constituted a breach of section 200 of PNG's constitution, which prohibits the raising of unauthorised military or paramilitary forces. The commission said that it would deal with the underlying point about the legality or otherwise of the Sandline contract of engagement at some later point but that, in the meantime, it was necessary to observe that 'a breach of the Constitution by one person does not thereby authorise criminal conduct on the part of another'. The commission elaborated:

> It is ludicrous to say that . . . the representatives of a
> party to an allegedly illegal contract may be summarily
> imprisoned and deported. The former Commander
> should have protested in the normal way to the
> Government to abort the engagement of the Sandline.

In dealing with the legality of the Sandline contract in terms of section 200 of the constitution, the commission noted that what the constitution prohibits is the use of foreign military forces in a combat role. It observed that the intention of the contract was for foreign personnel to take the leading role in Bougainville operations. If this had been allowed to happen, then the legality of the contract could have been questioned 'when the events unfolded on the operational level'.

Any military commander worth a grain of salt, if confronted with such a desultory line of argument, would throw their hands up in despair. This advice, if followed, would not have prevented Sandline operations in Bougainville before they happened. If anything was to be considered ludicrous as a course of proposed action, this was. It was the moral equivalent of knowing that a murder was to be committed but waiting for the crime to happen before apprehending the criminal or considering questions of legality. That would be to make oneself an accessory to the crime.

The commission then attempted to deal with a series of other matters including whether Sandline had charged a fair market price for the military equipment supplied under the contract. However, it was unable to reach a conclusion as Sandline refused to cooperate with the commission in providing the necessary documentation. Similarly, the commission was unable to make much progress with determining how (or on what) the initial payment of USD 18 million under the Sandline contract had been spent. It did observe, however, that 'there was no contest that a payment of US$500,000 was made by Sandline International to Benais Sabumei in late February 1997 out of the Sandline contract payment'. Benais Sabumei was a former defence minister, and his evidence was that this was a consultancy fee paid out by Sandline for his having made the introduction between DSL and Mathias Ijape; DSL then introduced Spicer to Ijape. The commission found this explanation 'unconvincing'. It then made the following finding:

> The Commission finds from all the circumstances . . . that the payment to Mr Benais Sabumei was corrupt and that he was used as a conduit for one or more recipients of the money.

The commission recommended 'that the appropriate authorities consider charges of perjury and other possible offences against Benais Sabumei'.

The commission then considered the possibility that others in PNG might have benefited improperly from Sandline payments. In respect of Mathias Ijape, the commission

> believes that Mr Ijape received payment from Sandline through Sabumei. We do not know whether Benais Sabumei kept some of the money for himself. But we find that the money, meaning the US$500,000 paid by Sandline to the credit of Sabumei's Citibank account in Brisbane, was meant for Matthais Ijape and probably most of it, if not all, went to Matthias Ijape or his interests.

The commission noted that the Sandline account disclosed another payment of USD 500,000 that remained unexplained. The commission concluded that it believed that

> [i]t is reasonable to suspect that apart from the payment received by Mr Sambumei and through him Mr Ijape, there were others in PNG who may have received such improper payments or commissions.

It should be noted, in fairness, that none of these findings of the Los commission have been tested in court. Ijape passed away in May 2017 and Sabumei shortly afterwards. The commission made no recommendation in respect of its belief about Ijape having received an improper payment through Sabumei. It merely expressed the hope that investigations would continue, including into payments that it said had gone to unidentified beneficiaries in the United States. So far as I know, this did not happen.

Finally, the Los commission dealt with the question of payments, inducements, and commissions received by members of the PNGDF over the three years before its sitting. It noted that I had made a voluntary disclosure of payments into my Visa card account by Sydney Franklin, a UK-based military equipment supplier, totalling GBP

31,000 in 1996–97. I admitted to the commission that it was wrong to take this money but denied that it was intended for any improper purpose. As noted elsewhere in this book, the matter was subsequently dealt with, under the provisions of the Leadership Code, in March 2000 before Justice Moses Jalina. It was a very short hearing as I had already willingly provided all the details of the transactions through my Lloyds Bank Visa card account. There were no questions of fact to be contested about the payments, and I accepted the decision of the tribunal that it had been wrong to accept the payments from Franklin, even though it was also shown that he had not profited in any way as a result of decisions made while I was commander or subsequently. So far as I am aware, this was the only actual outcome from the extensive hearings held by the Los commission.

In summing up the work of the two commissions of enquiry, it cannot be said that either of them got very far in determining the real truth of the matters before them. The Andrew commission criticised me for not doing more to prevent the Sandline contract, and I have accepted that criticism. Justice Andrew criticised Minister for Finance Chris Haiveta for bending the rules under the Public Finance (Management) Act and for what he saw as Haiveta's commercial naivety in guaranteeing payment of contract monies before there was even a contract to consider. Andrew found much of Haiveta's evidence to be untruthful and, therefore, was unable to get very far in establishing the truth behind the Sandline contract. He was unable to discover who was guilty of insider trading of BCL shares and made no findings of corruption on the part of PNG ministers or officials.

The Los commission only got as far as filing an initial draft report on its work. It found that former defence minister Benais Sabumei had received a corrupt payment from Sandline and recommended that he should be prosecuted for perjury and other charges, but no action was taken by government.

The Los commission believed that Minister for Defence Matthias Ijape had also received a corrupt payment from Sandline through Sabumei. It made no finding of corruption against Chris Haiveta, pending an application by him for a national court review of its draft findings. That review has gone nowhere.

The Los commission found no adverse evidence against Sir Julius Chan but recommended that investigations continue, including into payments channelled to unidentified beneficiaries in the United States. In its initial report, the Los commission did not imply in any way that those beneficiaries were linked to Sir Julius. So far as I know, the investigations recommended by the Los commission did not continue.

The only finding that was followed up on was in respect of my transgression of the Leadership Code, which I have accepted. In the aftermath of the Sandline affair, Sir Julius and Ijape both lost their parliamentary seats in the June 1997 national elections. Haiveta retained his seat and returned to Parliament before being defeated in a subsequent national election. He is now serving a third term as governor of Gulf Province. Sadly, Justice Sir Kubulan Los passed away in August 2012, closing all aspects of the second enquiry.

I was reappointed commander of the PNGDF by the Skate government in October 1998 before being removed from command by the Morauta government in 1999 and dismissed from the defence force in March 2000. After protracted legal wrangling, Sandline received its full contract payment of USD 36 million from government, but all the equipment held at RAAF Base Tindal was destroyed by Australian authorities. On Bougainville, the civil war has finally stopped. On 16 April 2004, Sandline International announced that it was ceasing all operations. It is therefore defunct.

A referendum on Bougainville's political future, supported by the United Nations, was conducted between 23 November and 7 December 2019, with over 97.7 per cent of voters supporting independence. The processes of peace and reconciliation for Bougainville's people are ongoing. Many small arms and home-made guns have been destroyed as people want peace. As expected, as I conclude this book, the Panguna mine remains closed.

CHAPTER 10

Operation Rausim Kwik:
What Have We Learnt?

We get the government we deserve in a democracy.

—Deval Patrick

All that is necessary for the triumph of evil is for good men to do nothing.

—Edmund Burke

The time is always right to do what is right.

—Martin Luther King

It is now twenty-five years since Operation Rausim Kwik. What have we learnt? Where do we need to go next as a society? What did I get right? What did I get wrong? In concluding my account, I offer some personal reflections with the experiences described in this book.

Operations Rausim Kwik was a professionally executed military operation, from planning to conduct to conclusion to debrief. I say 'professionally' because, critics aside, it was properly thought through using a classical military appreciation process whereby all the factors were considered, including implications of various categories. But most importantly, not one single shot was fired, and there were no fatalities.

No military commander in modern times under a legitimate civilian regime would have dared to do what I did, given the nature of the military operation itself and its unimaginable consequences, because what I did was considered illegal and unconstitutional and bordered on gross insubordination. It was indeed a staged and planned revolt. The country was at the brink of collapse at the height of Operation Rausim Kwik, with observers predicting that the government would be overthrown by the military as was the trend in most developing democracies. Instead, under my leadership and command, the military allowed the rule of law to prevail throughout the operation.

In my personal view, the central government's handling of Bougainville to that point was regrettable. The fluidity of the nature of politics in Papua New Guinea, where the political system allows constant change in leadership, meant that every elected prime minister's statement that Bougainville was their top priority to resolve was mere hot air. Sir Julius Chan was no different from the others. When he took over as prime minister, he seemed more determined, and he publicly stated that he would reopen the mine. That was his priority. He also promised to bring services into Bougainville. Did he accomplish these aims? Of course not.

Sir Rabbie Namaliu was PNG's fourth prime minister (1988–92). He had served under Sir Michael Somare as foreign minister and later as finance minister. As leader of the Pangu Pati, he was a well-liked, consultative politician whose leadership was generally well regarded by both Papua New Guineans and the international community.

Sir Rabbie had gained the prime ministership on 4 July 1988 after a parliamentary vote of no confidence in Paias Wingti and by promising to negotiate better deals for landowners in resource-rich areas of PNG. He was able to deliver on that promise in two important projects in the highlands, but his efforts to renegotiate with Bougainville Copper Ltd on behalf of the landowners were unsuccessful. This was a major disappointment for the landowners. Rio Tinto was not prepared to give a better deal to the landowners due to their corporate greed, and regrettably, Sir Rabbie was unable to change the status quo.

Sir Julius had earlier attempted to negotiate a better deal with BCL—a classic case of too little, too late—and this made Sir Rabbie's task next to impossible. Trust had been destroyed. The destruction of assets belonging to the Panguna mine began in late 1988. It was then that Sir Rabbie's patience began to run out in spectacular and ill-fated fashion but not before he tried a more conciliatory route—sending a ministerial delegation to Bougainville in an attempt to negotiate with the Bougainville Revolutionary Army. Unhappily for Bougainville, this attempt failed as completely as earlier attempts at a peaceful resolution had failed.

In December 1988, Sir Rabbie—by now frustrated at the lack of progress in his attempts at conciliation—threatened arrest and retribution against the perpetrators of any further violence in and around the mine. On Boxing Day 1988, his cabinet declared a state of emergency in Bougainville; and in March 1989, in response to further killings, the defence force was called on to assist the police under the provisions of the Defence Force Act. At the same time, a bounty was placed on the head of Francis Ona from Guava Village on the outskirts of Panguna mine as he was identified as the main perpetrator of the rebellion against Rio Tinto and PNG. This was rapidly followed up, in April that year, by the declaration of a full-scale state of emergency, which gave the defence force additional powers under the PNG constitution. The violence then escalated with killings, retributions, and property damage on all sides.

A full-scale civil war was the inevitable result of political instability in Port Moresby, government inaction, government indecision, and finally, in desperation, a government direction to fight fire with fire. What might have been treated as a series of isolated, small incidents that could have been addressed through an appropriate mix of compensation and rights to self-government was allowed to drift and then escalate into a full-blown civil conflict. This conflict can only be described as being as needless as it was reckless and bloody, destroying a province and affecting the lives and livelihoods of thousands of families and, in so doing, crippling a country.

My opposition to the proposed engagement of Sandline and my thoughts on the likely consequences for the people of Bougainville have been fully documented. My fear is that the lessons that we should have learnt as a result of the mishandling of the Bougainville crisis may not have been learnt. Landowners in resource-rich provinces in PNG are still being denied a proper voice in airing their grievances over land and environmental issues. Worse still, a mere 2 per cent of royalties seem to be the figure favoured by politicians in deals with developers. It seems that the lessons on Bougainville may never be learnt.

Consistency of approach is especially important in dealing with the sorts of issues that Bougainville presented and, indeed, still presents. Thinking back, it is easy to fall into the trap of simplification and caricature. While Sir Julius Chan and other key ministers of state such as Chris Haiveta and Mathias Ijape came to the mistaken belief, thanks to the Sandline sales pitch, that a military solution to Bougainville was possible, Sir Julius had, at an earlier period as foreign minister, put a lot of personal effort into trying to find a peaceful solution. Almost his first act on assuming the prime ministership on 30 August 1994, after taking over the defence and police ministerial portfolios, was to fly to Honiara for face-to-face talks with Sam Kauona, the BRA commander. These talks resulted in the Honiara Commitments and an agreement to hold peace talks. It could be said that Sir Julius was driven to find a military solution as a result of the failure of the BRA military leaders to attend the Arawa Peace Conference and by his broader frustrations with the peace process.

The key point, though, is that the underlying reason for the long-drawn-out war on Bougainville, and the inability to find a peaceful solution in the period from late 1988 to 1997, was the inconsistency of approach on the part of successive governments in Port Moresby. As a consequence of vacillating between periods of negotiation and military pressure, between peace and war, trust between the parties was continually undermined on both sides. In addition, it could be argued that Port Moresby never took a long enough view on what eventual outcome would best serve the interests of both PNG and the province of Bougainville. In Port Moresby, there was a fixation on reopening the Panguna mine and on Bougainville an equally strong fixation on keeping it closed. Similarly, there was a perception in Port Moresby that any talk of autonomy for Bougainville, let alone its independence, would tear the fabric of PNG apart and open the door to other breakaway provinces. This fear may have been understandable, but it was also overstated.

Looking back at my own involvement at various points in the conflict, what did I get right, and what did I get wrong? Hindsight is a wonderful commodity. Knowing what I know now, I will outline what I think I could, and perhaps should, have done differently.

At the beginning of October 1995, when Sir Julius called me, a very junior colonel, into his office and said that he was looking for somebody young and competent in military tactics and leadership to take over the defence force who 'could hit the rebels hard' and deliver on his promise to the people of PNG and international investors to reopen the Panguna mine, warning bells should have sounded. What he wanted from me was a 'new operational concept' for Bougainville. In retrospect, I should have said that, while the defence force could no doubt put a battalion into the mine and possibly hold it there for a period, given sufficient logistic support and sustainment, to actually reopen the mine was quite a different matter.

In October 1995, the mine had already been closed for five years or more, its machinery wrecked, and its buildings vandalised. Reopening the mine was a very different prospect from simply holding ground. Sitting there in his office, I perhaps thought that, as prime minister, he would understand that, and so he didn't need me to tell him what should have been obvious. Or perhaps I thought that my job was just to secure the mine site and, after that, the surrounding high ground, Espie Highway, Loloho Harbour, the power pylons, and the power supply to the mine—and of course, Arawa Township. Looked at from a purely military perspective, the list of security requirements that would need to be fulfilled before the mine could be 'reopened' was not endless, but it was certainly very demanding, calling on considerable manpower and generating a very long, and potentially unsustainable, logistic tail.

Did I fail the prime minister in that first conversation about the need for me to come up with a new operational concept for Bougainville? At that point, having already completed three full operational tours in Bougainville (1989, 1993, and 1994), I believed that there was no total military solution to the problems on Bougainville. solution to the problems on Bougainville. The military could be used to put additional pressure on the BRA—yes, absolutely. The military could be used to secure the actual mine site—yes, up to a point. But armies do not run copper mines. Mining companies do. And mining companies need specialist staff and a massive and well-trained labour pool. Supplying and sustaining the labour requirements of the mine would be dependent on the willing cooperation of the local community. And that was not something that the military could ensure. On Bougainville in 1995, that was a deeply complicated political and social issue. And indeed, it still is.

These thoughts, and others, were running through my mind as I sat in the Prime Minister's Office. Should I have given voice to them as a young colonel? At the time, I did not think so. In hindsight, though, I think I should have voiced my concerns. Viewed narrowly, the job of a military adviser starts and ends with military questions. However, in an age when we talk about the 'strategic corporal', the task of military advisers cannot be viewed so narrowly. I now think that I was wrong not to at least open up the larger question of 'what's next?' Once the mine site was secured, what was the sequence of actions that the government was planning to secure the cooperation of the Bougainville civil authorities and the community to actually reopen and run the mine? Or failing to engage the prime minister at that first meeting, I should have put a very large footnote in the operational concept, drawing attention to the other factors that would need addressing as part of a larger military operation. In doing neither of those things, I think I am open to the charge that I failed the prime minister. I responded to him at the tactical level, where a degree of military success could perhaps be offered, but I failed to engage him at the broader and deeper strategic level.

That was the first thing that I got wrong and, with the benefit of hindsight, would do differently. The second thing that I got wrong was my assumption that the Sandline proposals, when they were first aired, would come to nothing because of their sheer unaffordability. As commander of the PNGDF, I had to scramble, beg, and borrow for every last kina I could find. Sir Julius had promised me all the resources that I needed when we first talked. Those promises had come to nothing. Under my command, the defence force was as chronically underfunded as it had always been. Consequently, talk of a Sandline military operation costing USD 36 million looked to me to be completely unrealistic. I thought it would never secure government funding. Moreover, I was aware of Noel Levi's written advice to the prime minister to reject the Sandline proposal and the prime minister's endorsement of that advice. But this meant that I didn't take Sandline seriously enough.

I had a full plate of operational matters to deal with and was content to let the Sandline proposals fall over under their own weight. This was a mistake. I should have consistently argued against the Sandline approach from the outset, and I should have opposed it on military, operational, and ethical grounds on every occasion that it was aired. Instead, I took the easy way out, dealing at the tactical level with what was actually a much deeper strategic issue.

Looking back, what are the lessons that need to be drawn? Two come to mind. First, military commanders need to be aware that political leaders are likely to come to their ministerial portfolios with a very simplistic notion of what the military instrument can offer. They have little or no appreciation of how fragile the military instrument can be and the extraordinary logistic requirements that accompany even the simplest of deployments.

Helicopters break. So do troops. Helicopters need fuel, and troops need feeding. The army may not depend on mule trains anymore, but the same age-old principle applies. Seven mules are needed to carry the feed for the one mule that carries anything useful. More often than not, the effort is not worth a damn.

It is all too easy for ministers to ignore the cost of using the military instrument while they focus on the benefits. And because armies everywhere are trained to have a 'can do' attitude, there is an in-built tendency on the part of military advisers, when talking to politicians, to make light of the difficulties when discussing the potentialities. Lesson one: never assume that ministers have any understanding of logistics and sustainability issues or that ministers have thought about the downside of deploying the military instrument to sort out what is, in most respects, a social, political, and environmental issue. Just because armed rebels are defying authority and challenging the established order does not mean that an armed response by the state is likely to be the best or only choice. Often, it will be the one choice that guarantees to make matters worse. The warning sign? When a minister asks for a military operational concept without demanding a full suite of accompanying political, economic, and social initiatives.

The obvious caveat is that I am discussing the use of the military instrument in the context of a civil war involving an internal armed uprising against the state or the emergence of armed criminal bands with some loosely defined ideology but only the partial support of the population. External aggression is a much more existential matter in which different and more urgent assumptions will apply. But for use internally, the military instrument should never be thought of as the primary response. It is only ever an adjunct and should be mainly held in reserve. The deployment of an army internally is a sure sign of earlier failures by the state. Those failures need to be addressed—not swept under the carpet by the use of the military.

The second lesson concerns the assumptions that all of us make just to get us through the daily round. In the context of Bougainville and Sir Julius Chan's request to me as his incoming commander to draw up a new operational concept to 'hit the rebels hard' and seize the Panguna mine, I *assumed* that he was talking to a range of his ministers and departmental advisers about all the other matters that would require attention and that my role was purely the military one. I also *assumed* that he would make good on his promise to meet the operational expenditures involved, and my military planning and logistic arrangements were based on that assumption.

In the case of the Sandline proposals, I *assumed* they would never be seriously entertained because of the extravagant scale of the costs involved and also because the prime minister had already accepted in writing with the single word 'reject' his departmental head's advice that accepting the Sandline proposal would be 'contrary to our long-term political and constitutional interest'. Nothing could be plainer than Sec. Noel Levi's advice on 19 September 1996 to reject the Sandline proposals or the prime minister's one-word written acceptance of that advice the following day. This underlines my point that *assumptions*, even the most certain and dependable looking of them, should never be the only basis for planning. They always need to be kept under review, and they should always be made explicit. And having been made explicit, having been written down and underscored, they need to be tested by asking what might happen if they are not borne out in practice.

Looking at the assumptions discussed here, what should I have done differently? First, instead of concentrating on the military concept planning that turned into Operation High Speed II, I should arguably have asked the National Executive Committee to convene a wide-ranging departmental committee at permanent heads' level to assist with the associated political, social, economic, and environmental initiatives that were needed to accompany increased military pressure on the rebels.

Second, in respect of my assumption that the operational costs of Operation High Speed II, estimated at PGK 10 million for a one-month-long military operation aimed at the seizure of the Panguna mine, would be met with additional funding from the Department of Finance, I should have insisted on having that funding in advance of the operation so that I could take care of the logistic and other costs. In the event, despite an instruction from the NEC to the Department of Finance, the funds were never allocated to me. What was already a shoestring operation came down to a single eyelet—with no shoestring.

Third, in respect of my assumption that the prime minister's acceptance of Noel Levi's advice about Sandline signalled the end of any serious entertainment of Sandline proposals, I should have kept a closer eye on what Chris Haiveta, the finance minister and deputy prime minister, was up to on his subsequent travels to Hong Kong and London. When Haiveta reported to me on his meetings with Branch Minerals in Hong Kong and Sandline's parent body, Executive Outcomes, in London, I should have made the full range of my objections to employing Sandline on military and many other grounds much clearer. Instead, I *assumed* that Haiveta would be aware that the prime minister had already firmly rejected the Sandline proposals. Arguably, therefore, I let both Haiveta and myself down at this key juncture.

My point—and the essential learning—is that, while all of us have to make assumptions to get us through the business of the day, assumptions can be extraordinarily dangerous if they come to be depended on as the *only* basis for planning. To guard against surprise, the only remedy that I know of is to make the assumptions explicit, write them down, underscore them, and test them as often as circumstances dictate.

Despite all the criticism that it has engendered from various quarters, I remain convinced that my eventual decision to launch Operation Rausim Kwik to arrest and deport the mercenaries and my public demand that the prime minister, his deputy, and the defence minister should all resign their office were absolutely the right thing to do. I could have just dealt with the mercenaries and left it at that. But I knew that I would be instantly dismissed, as indeed I was, for arresting and expelling Sandline; therefore, I thought that I might as well make a proper job of it and demand the resignation of the three key ministers who had decided to employ the mercenaries and demand, too, a full public enquiry into all the circumstances, including whether and to what extent there were corrupt dealings. I believe earnestly that there were.

Did I have any other options? Yes. I could have resigned as commander and left the government to find a replacement who would go along with the employment of the Sandline mercenaries. In circumstances where a department head or a military commander cannot, in good conscience, support the decisions of the executive, resignation is the only widely accepted path.

However, the mercenaries were already at a jungle training camp at Urimo, and their command elements were in Port Moresby. Their heavy equipment, including attack helicopters and massive quantities of firepower, was due to arrive at Jacksons Airport by Russian heavy-lift aircraft within a day or two. If anything was to be done, it had to be done immediately. My resignation would not have solved the problem. It would only have guaranteed widespread destruction on Bougainville and the permanent alienation of Bougainvilleans from PNG.

I could have done nothing and waited for the Sandline operation to end in failure, a fiasco. I was already getting twice daily reports from the Urimo camp where the African mercenaries were supposed to be training my own Special Forces Unit. According to those reports, the Africans—while impressive enough looking on the face of it— were, in fact, physically unfit and unfamiliar with jungle operations and had very poor weapons safety training and handling procedures. Moreover, their communications security protocols were extremely unprofessional.

However, doing nothing was not an option and not in my nature because it would lead to massive loss of life both for the Bougainvilleans who would be caught up in the operations and for my own men. Although Sandline talked a big game about surgical operations and precision attack, a glance at their weaponry and the hundreds of thousands of rounds of ammunition they were importing made it clear that, in the context of the intended attacks on rebel concentrations, these would inevitably result in high numbers of casualties. With the BRA intermingled with ordinary Bougainvilleans, precision attack was an impossibility, particularly from the air and even on the ground.

This was the sort of case that Edmund Burke must have had in mind when framing his famous dictum: 'All that it needs for the triumph of evil is for good men to do nothing.' I had to do something, but what? Neither of the two options outlined above was palatable. As we all know, life can be, and very often is, a messy business. Options do not present themselves like the slogans on a Furphy WWI Australian Army water cart. They are not good, better, and best. More often, they are bad, worse, and worst. The aim is to pick the least bad option from a thoroughly bad bunch. And that is what I believe I did.

The arrest and deportation of the mercenaries was a decision taken by me, and on my own responsibility as commander, at the strategic level. To implement it required a proper military appreciation process and good operational planning. With a professional army background that included being an instructor at Australia's leading Land Warfare Centre, that was a relatively straightforward matter for me. In fact, as sketched in an earlier chapter, this was a classic textbook case in military appreciation and detailed operational planning. To make it work, I needed the best team that I could find. I could not have been more fortunate in my choice of Maj. Walter Enuma as the man who would run the operation.

So those were two more things that I got right—the military appreciation and operational planning and the choice of my operations officer and his team. In taking credit for these two things, I am, of course, conscious of Justice Sir Kubulan Los's finding, in his draft initial report, that my actions in arresting and deporting the Sandline mercenaries had no justification in military or civil law, that I exceeded my lawful authority, and that the apprehension and deportation of Sandline personnel was therefore unlawful. The Los commission's findings were challenged by Chris Haiveta and placed under judicial review. With the review still pending, the Los commission presented its follow-up findings to the prime minister.

More than fifteen years later, so far as I am aware, no action has been taken on either of these two reports, which remain in draft form and therefore carry no legal weight. Should the report of the Los commission ever be finalised and the view of the commission sustained that my actions in ordering Operation Rausim Kwik were unlawful, I would have to say that the law is an ass. Section 200 of the PNG constitution states, in part, that it is strictly forbidden to establish, organise, equip, or take part in or associate with a military or paramilitary or to organise or take part in military or paramilitary training except such as is provided for by the constitution or to plan, prepare for, or assist in the raising or training of such a force or in such training. Thus, in engaging Sandline, the government was complicit in an illegal act. Although the mercenaries were never actually sent to

Bougainville, had they been, as described in the contract between the PNG government and Sandline, it would have been in strict violation of the constitution.

Part 3 of section 200 provides a potential waiver *but only for* the armed forces of another country *and then only if* duly authorised by an act of Parliament. But Sandline was not an armed force from another country; it was a contracted group of irregulars not subject to the discipline and control of an armed force belonging to another state and therefore well outside anything envisaged by the framers of the constitution, whether sanctioned by act of Parliament or not. In the simplest of terms, the Sandline contract was illegal in terms of PNG's constitution, and it could not be rendered legal by the device of signing Sandline personnel in as special constables, by act of Parliament, or by the pretence, much depended on by Sir Julius Chan, that Sandline was only a group of military consultants involved in training activities.

I would like to be able to say that, as a nation, we have learnt a great deal from those momentous days in March 1997, when the Sandline operatives were rounded up and deported, and ordinary people came out in mass protest to surround Parliament and demand the resignation of the government. But have we? In terms of good governance, resource management, rampant corruption, and leadership, the results look grim. The leading social indicators around poverty, law and order, and rural infrastructure and the ability to access basic services, employment, and job creation all confirm that our governance in PNG is failing us—not just at the margin but completely.

The Sandline contract was a corrupt deal. It was also illegal. To employ mercenaries to conduct combat operations contravenes the PNG constitution. The lethality of force provided for under the contract was grossly disproportionate to the threat. Further, the manner in which government funds were secured for the contract contravened the provisions of the Financial Management Act in a scandalous fashion. No one has been held responsible for any of these matters.

Operation Rausim Kwik was planned and executed in an extremely proficient and professional way. No lives were lost in the conduct of the operation. Not one shot fired. The officers and soldiers selected to lead and conduct the operation were among PNG's finest. I am proud of what they achieved. Some have gained fame, and others have faded into the shadows as is often the way. But we will go down in history as having conducted a successful operation. We believed in a cause. Our cause was just. History will judge us, but I am confident of the judgement. We did what had to be done. As Martin Luther King said, 'The time is always right to do what is right.'

PNG endured nine years of civil war in Bougainville. I served three operational tours there, and my time as commander of the defence force was dominated by civil war. The psychological effects of the war in Bougainville, especially among those who served there, are incalculable. Many good lives were lost.

Apart from Bougainvillean leaders and ordinary men, women, and children, I think of the fatalities of 2nd Lt Steven Yandu and Private Romas and other good and some outstanding men such as Maj. Henry Kekeboge and Private Pando, killed in the capture and seizure of the Panguna mine in August 1994, and Maj. Paul Panau and 2nd Lt Michael Jim, killed along with many others at Kangu Beach in September 1996. I think of the wives who survive these men, such as Henry Kekeboge's widow, Eunice, and the children without a father. I think of genuine Bougainvillean leaders like Premier Theodore Miriung, whose assassination gave rise to calls for peace and reconciliation and a way forwards for a political future for Bougainville.

I think of and value all the good men whom I led, who assisted me to execute Operation Rausim Kwik: Walter Enuma, Gilbert Toropo, Tokam Kanene, Michael Tamalanga, Belden Namah, Chris Mora, Charlie Andrews, Phil Emeck, Eddie Miro, Kamona Falaniki, Bola Renagi, Linus Osoba, Edy Yodu, Francis Jakis, John Wilson, Allan Nangoromo, Koisen Boino, Lee Palaso, Wyne Thomas, Siale Diro, Michael David, Richard Sond, Ben Wafia, Koisen Boino, Johanes Bakangili, Nick Henry, John Keleto, John Koraia, Joseph Fabila, Tom Ur, Max Aleale, Isaiah Keme, Craig Solomon, Liliak Lem, Patrick Waeda, Blaise Afara, James Pima, Paul Boga, Eric Aliawi, and many others.

As I say to my children, life in the defence force is tough and demanding. We go into harm's way with very little support and recognition. Yet it is because our soldiers are out on patrol, sleeping rough, enduring danger, tiredness, and hunger, and because our sailors are on the high seas and because our airmen are flying in what must be among the toughest bush and mountain terrain anywhere that we can sleep well at night. Churchill expressed a similar thought: 'We sleep safely at night because rough men stand ready to visit violence on those who would harm us.' Joining the defence force is a choice. Those who choose it volunteer to defend the motherland at whatever cost.

Operation Rausim Kwik was planned with precision and executed with a highly motivated and professional team without whom it would have failed. Therefore, I take no personal credit. There was no influence from within or from outside. Evidently, it was my own decision based on my conscience that led me to plan and execute the operation. Conscience is indeed a gift from God.

GLOSSARY

AA	assembly area
ABC	Australian Broadcasting Corporation
ABCA	American, British, Canadian, Australian, and New Zealand armies
ADC	aide-de-camp
ADF	Australian Defence Force
AO	area of operations
ASIO	Australian Security Intelligence Organisation
ATS	Air Transport Squadron
BCL	Bougainville Copper Ltd
BRA	Bougainville Revolutionary Army
CATT	command, administration, and training team
CIA	Central Intelligence Agency
CO	commanding officer
COA	course of action
CP	command post
CRA	Conzinc Riotinto of Australia
DSL	Defence Systems Limited
EO	Executive Outcomes
EW	electronic warfare
FSM	force sergeant major
HALO	high altitude, low opening
HF	high frequency

ICRAF	Individual and Community Rights and Advocacy Forum
MAP	military appreciation process
MELSOL	Melanesian Solidarity Group
MP	member of Parliament
NATO	North Atlantic Treaty Organization
NBC	National Broadcasting Commission
NEC	National Executive Council
NGO	non-governmental organisation
NIO	National Intelligence Organisation
NOTICAS	notice of casualty
NSAC	National Security Advisory Committee
NSC	National Security Council
OPSEC	operational security
PNG	Papua New Guinea
PNGBC	Papua New Guinea Banking Corporation
PNGDF	Papua New Guinea Defence Force
POSF	Public Officers Superannuation Fund
RAAF	Royal Australian Air Force
RAN	Royal Australian Navy
RPNGC	Royal Papua New Guinea Constabulary
SFU	Special Forces Unit
SIGINT	signals intelligence
SOG	Special Operations Group
TCV	troop-carrying vehicle
UHF	ultra-high frequency
UPNG	University of Papua New Guinea

APPENDIX A

THE SANDLINE CONTRACT
AGREEMENT FOR THE PROVISION OF MILITARY ASSISTANCE

DATED THIS 31 DAY OF JANUARY 1997 BETWEEN THE INDEPENDENT STATE OF PAPUA NEW GUINEA AND SANDLINE INTERNATIONAL.

This Agreement is made this day 31 of January 1997 between the Independent State of Papua New Guinea (the state) of the one part and Sandline International (sandline), whose UK representative office is 535 Kings Road, London SW10 OSZ, of the other part.
WHEREAS..
Sandline is a company specialising in rendering military and security services of an operational, training and support nature, particularly in situations of internal conflict and only for and on behalf of recognised governments, in accord with international doctrines and in conformance with the Geneva Convention.

The State, engulfed in a state of conflict with the illegal and unrecognised Bougainville Revolutionary Army (BRA), requires such external military expertise to support its Armed Forces in the protection of its Sovereign territory and regain control over important national assets, specifically the Panguna mine. In particular, Sandline is contracted to provide personnel and related services and equipment to:

- Train the State's Special Forces Unit (SFU) in tactical skills specific to this objective;
- Gather intelligence to support effective deployment and operations;
- Conduct offensive operations in Bougainville in conjunction with PNG defence forces to render the BRA militarily ineffective and repossess the Panguna mine; and
- Provide follow-up operational support, to be further specified and agreed between the parties and is subject to separate service provision levels and fee negotiations.

IT IS THEREFORE AGREED AS FOLLOWS:

The State hereby agrees to contract and utilise and employ the services of Sandline to provide all required and necessary services as are more particularly described hereafter.

1. **Duration and Continuation.**

The duration of this contract shall be effective from the date of receipt of the initial payment; (as defined in paragraph 5.2 below, for a maximum initial period of 3 calendar months, the initial contract period) or achievement of the primary objective, being the rendering of the BRA militarily ineffective, whichever is the earlier. The State shall have the option of reviewing this agreement either in part or in whole for further periods as may be required.

273

1.2   Notice of renewal, termination or proposed variation of this agreement is to be served on Sandline in writing by the State at least 45 days before the expiry of the current period. Non-communication by the State shall be regarded by Sandline as automatic renewal of the relevant parts of this agreement for a further three month period on the same terms and this precedent shall continue to apply thereafter.

2.   Service Provision

2.1   Sandline shall provide the following manpower, equipment and services:

(a)   A 16 man Command, Admin and Training Team (CATT) to deploy in PNG and establish home bases at Jackson Airport and the Jungle Training Centre at Wewak within one week of commencement of this agreement, which is deemed to be the day on which the initial payment relating thereto in accordance with paragraph 5.2 below is deposited free and clear in Sandline's nominated bank account. The role of the CATT is to (i) establish links with PNG defence forces, (ii) develop the requisite logistics and communications infrastructure, (iii) secure and prepare facilities for the arrival of the contracted equipment, including air assets, (iv) initiate intelligence gathering operation, and (v) commences SFU training.

(b)   Further Special Forces personnel which will deploy to PNG within ten days of the arrival of the CATT, together with helicopter and fixed wing aircrew and engineers, intelligence and equipment operatives, mission operators, ground tech and medical support personnel. This force will absorb the CATT as part of its numbers, therefore bringing the total Strike Force head count to 70. This Strike Force shall be responsible for achieving the primary objective as specified in paragraph 1.1 of this agreement and the full complement will remain in country for the initial contract period as defined in the said paragraph.

Note: At no time will Sandline personnel enter the sovereign territory of another nation nor will they breach the laws and rules of engagement relating to armed conflict. Once the operation has been successfully concluded, Sandline personnel will be available to assist with the ongoing training, skills enhancement and equipping of the PNG defence forces.

(c)   Weapons, ammunition and equipment, including helicopters and aircraft (serviceable for up to 50 hours flying time per machine per month), and electronic warfare equipment and communications systems, all as specified or equivalent to the items listed in Schedule 1. Upon termination of a contractual relationship between the State and Sandline and once all payments have been received and Sandline has withdrawn from theatre any remaining stock of equipment shall be handed over and become the property of the State. Selected Sandline personnel will remain in country to maintain and supplement such equipment subject to a separate agreement relating thereto.

Note: Delivery into theatre of the contracted equipment shall be via air into Jackson Airport or such other facility as may be considered appropriate. The equipment will be delivered in full working order, in accordance with manufacturers' specifications. After its delivery, any equipment lost, damaged or destroyed during Sandline's deployment shall be immediately replaced at the cost of the State.

(d) Personal kit, including US pattern jungle fatigues, boots and webbing, for Sandline personnel.

(e) All international transport arrangements for the shipment in/out of equipment and deployment in country of Sandline personnel but not for the movement of such equipment and personnel within the country if this needs to be achieved by way of commercial service providers.

(f) The provision of medical personnel to treat any Sandline casualties and their evacuation if necessary.

(g) A Project Coordinator, who, together with the Strike Force Commander and his Senior Intelligence Officer, shall maintain liaison with and provide strategic and operational briefings and advice to the Prime Minister, Defence Minister, NEC, NSC, the commander of the PNG defence forces and his delegated officers as may from time-to-time be required or requested.

2.2 Sandline shall ensure the enrolment of all personnel involved in this contract as Special Constables and that they carry appropriate ID cards in order to legally undertake their assigned roles.

3. Responsibilities of Sandline

3.1 Sandline will train the SFU in tactical skills specific to the objective, such as live fire contact, ambush techniques and raiding drills, gather intelligence to support effective deployment and plan, direct, participate in and conduct such ground, air and sea operations which are required to achieve the primary objective.

3.2 Both parties hereto recognise and agree that the force capability to respond to all emergency and hostile situations will be constrained by the manpower and equipment level provided within the terms of this agreement. The achievement of the primary objective cannot be deemed to be a performance measure for the sake of this agreement if it can be demonstrated that for valid reasons it cannot be achieved within the given timescales and with the level of contracted resources provided.

3.3 Sandline shall supply all the personnel and maintain all services and equipment as specified in paragraph 2.1 above to the appropriate standards of proficiency and operational levels as is generally expected from a high calibre, professional armed force.

3.4   Sandline shall further provide a project coordinator to act as the liaison officer between the company's management and the nominated representatives of the State. This individual will convene and attend regular meetings at such venues as he may be so directed.

3.5   Sandline shall be responsible for any expense resulting from the loss or injury of any of its personnel for the duration of the agreement unless same is caused by the negligence of the State, its personnel or agents in which case all such costs will be fairly claimed against the State by Sandline and promptly paid for the benefit of the persons involved.

3.6   Sandline will ensure that the contents of this agreement shall remain strictly confidential and will not be disclosed to any third party. Sandline will not acknowledge the existence of this contract prior to the State issuing notifications in accordance with paragraph 4.11 below and will not take credit for any successful action unless this is mutually agreed by the parties. Furthermore, Sandline and its personnel are well versed in the requirement to maintain absolute secrecy with regard to all aspects of its activities in order to guard against compromising operations and will apply the necessary safeguards.

4.   Responsibilities of the State

4.1   Immediately on signing this agreement the State automatically grants to Sandline and its personnel all approvals, permissions, authorisations, licences and permits to carry arms, conduct its operations and meet its contractual obligations without hindrance, including issuing instructions to PNG defence forces personnel to cooperate fully with Sandline commanders and their nominated representatives. All officers and personnel of Sandline assigned to this contract shall be enrolled as Special Constable, but hold military ranks commensurate with those they hold within the Sandline command structure and shall be entitled to give orders to junior ranks as may be necessary for the execution of their duties and responsibilities.

4.2   The State will ensure that full cooperation is provided from within its organisation and that of the PNG defence forces. The Commanders of the PNG defence forces and Sandline shall form a joint liaison and planning team for the duration of this agreement. The operational deployment of Sandline personnel and equipment is to be jointly determined by the Commander, PNG defence forces and Sandline's Commander, taking account of their assessment of the risk and value thereof.

4.3   The State recognises that Sandline's Commanders will have such powers as are required to efficiently and effectively undertake their given roles, including but not limited to the powers to engage and fight hostile forces, repel attacks therefore, arrest any prisoners suspected of undertaking or conspiring to undertake a harmful act, secure Sovereign assets and territory, defend the general population from any threat, and proactively protect their own and State Forces from any form of aggression or threat.

The State agrees to indemnify Sandline for the legitimate actions of the company's and its associated personnel as specified herein and to assume any claims brought against the company arising out of this agreement.

4.4 The State shall pay or shall cause to be paid the fees and expenses relating to this agreement as set out in paragraph 5.1 below. Such fees and expenses to be paid as further specified in paragraph 5.2, without deduction of any taxes, charges or fees, and eligible to be freely exported from PNG. All payments to be made in US dollars.

4.5 The State shall cause all importation of equipment and the provision of services to be free to Sandline (and any of its sister or associated companies as notified to the authorities) of any local, regional or national taxes, withholding taxes, duties fees, surcharges, storage charges and clearance expenses howsoever levied and shall allow such equipment to be processed through Customs without delay. Further, all Sandline personnel will be furnished with the necessary multiple entry visas without passport camps and authorisations to enter and leave the country free from hindrance at any time and shall be exempt from tax of any form on their remuneration from Sandline.

4.6 The State will promptly supply at no cost to Sandline and its sister and associated companies all End User Certificates and related documentation to facilitate the legitimate procurement and export of the specified equipment from countries of origin.

4.7 The State will provide suitable accommodation for all Sandline personnel together with all related amenities, support staff to undertake roles such as messengers and household duties, secure hangerage and storage facilities for equipment, qualified tradesmen and workmen to clear and prepare operating sites, all aviation and ground equipment fuel and lubricant needs, such vehicles and personnel carriers as reasonably specified for the field and for staff use, foodstuffs and combat rations, fresh drinking water, and sanitary and other relevant services and ancillary equipment as Sandline may specify from time-to-time to undertake its activities without hindrance.

4.8 If any service, resource or equipment to be supplied by the State in accordance with paragraph 4.7 above is not forthcoming then Sandline will have the right to submit an additional invoice for the procurement and supply thereof and may curtail or reduce operations affected by its non-availability until payment has been made and the said equipment is in position.

4.9 The State agrees and undertakes that during the period of this agreement and for a period of 12 months following the date of its expiration, it will not directly or indirectly offer employment to or employ any of the personnel provided hereunder or otherwise in the employ of Sandline and its associates.

Any such employment will be construed as a continuation of the contract for the employees concerned and Sandline shall be entitled to be paid accordingly on a pro-rata basis.

4.10   The State and the PNG defence forces will ensure that information relating to planned operations, deployments and associated activities is restricted to only those personnel who have an essential need to be briefed in. Appropriate steps will be taken to prevent press reporting, both nationally and internationally, or any form of security breach or passage of information which may potentially threaten operational effectiveness and/or risk the lives of the persons involved. Sandline's commanders have the right to curtail any or all planned operations which they determine are compromised as a result of a failure in security.

4.11   If deemed necessary due to external interest, the State shall be responsible for   notifying and updating the international Community, including the United Nations and representatives of other governments, at the appropriate time of the nature of this contract and the underlying intent to protect and keep safe from harm Papua New Guinea's Sovereign territory, its population, mineral assets and investing community. The content and timing of all such formal communications will be discussed and agreed with Sandline before release.

5.   **Fees and Payments**

5.1   Sandline's inclusive fee for the provision of the personnel and services as specified in paragraph 2.1 above and also in Schedule 1 attached for the initial contract period is USD36,000,000 (thirty-six million US Dollars).

5.2   Payments terms are as follows: All payments to be by way of cash funds, either in the form of electronic bank transfers or certified banker's cheques;

On contract signing 50% of the overall fee, totalling USD18,000,000 is immediately due and is deemed the "initial payment".

Within 30 days of deploying the CATT, the balance of USD18,000,000.

5.3   This contract is deemed to be enacted once the initial payment is received in full with value into such bank account as Sandline may nominate therefore. Payments are recognised as being received when they are credited as cleared funds in our account and payment receipt relies on this definition.

5.4   All fees for services rendered shall be paid in advance of the period to which they relate. Sandline reserves the right to withdraw from theatre in the event of non-payment of fees for any renewal of the original contract period.

5.5 The financial impact of variations, additions or changes to the personnel provision and equipment supply specified herein will be agreed between the parties and any incremental payment will be made to Sandline before such change is deemed to take effect. There is no facility for rebate or refund in the event of a required reduction or early termination of service delivery within a given contracted period.

6. Applicable Law

6.1 In the event of any dispute of difference arising out of or in relation to this agreement the parties shall in the first instance make an effort to resolve it amicably, taking account of the sensitive nature of this arrangement.

6.2 The aggrieved party shall notify the other by sending a notice of dispute in writing and, where amicable settlement is not possible within 30 day thereafter, refer the matter to arbitration in conformity with the UNCITRAL rules applying hereto.

6.3 This agreement shall be construed and governed in accordance with the Law of England and the language of communication between the parties shall be English.

7. Amendments and Supplements.

7.1 This agreement may only be altered, modified or amended by the parties hereto provided that such alteration, modification or amendment is in writing and signed by both parties.

7.2 Schedule 1 ("Oyster" Costings) forms part of this agreement.

IN WITNESS, WHEREOF the parties hereto have set their hands on the day and year first written above.

(For the Independent State of Papua New Guinea: Chris Haiveta, M.P.)
(Witness: Vele Iamo, Acting Deputy Secretary)

(For Sandline International: Tim Spicer, O.B.E.)
(Witness: J.N. Van Den Bergh, Consultant)

Schedule I			Oyster Costing	

Serial	Item	Quantity	Cost	Totals
	Helicopter/EW package			
1.1	Mi-24 helicopter	2	8.200	
1.2	Mi-17 helicopter	2	3,000	
1.3	Mi-24 ordnance	below	2,500	
1.4	Mi-17 ordnance	n/a	400	
1.5	Night vision equipment	18	610	
1.6	Mi-24 aircrew	6	680	
1.7	Mi-17 aircrew	6	860	
1.8	Surveillance platform (SP)	1	2,400	
1.9	On-board systems	1	4,850	
1.10	SP aircrew	4	280	
1.11	Ground System	1	600	
1.12	Mission Operators	5	480	
1.13	Ground Staff	6	270	
1.14	Air recce aircraft	1	inc	
1.15	EW trainers	inc	120	
1.16	SP trainers	inc	120	
1.17	Project co-ordinator	1	inc	
1.18	Personnel eqipment	30	250	
1.19	Personnel movement	pack	250	
1.20	Insurances for personnel	inc	inc	
1.21	Logistics support	client	client	
1.22	Asset positioning	4	1,200	
1.23	Spares - helicopters	pack	1,500	
1.24	Spares - SP	pack	600	29,170
	Special Forces Team			
2.1	Manpower (40 plus doctors)	42	4,500	
2.2	Equipment	below	2,500	
2.3	Positioning	pack	100	7,100
	Communications Equipment			
3.1	HF radio system	1 + 15	400	
3.2	Hardened tactical radio system	1 + 16	500	
3.3	Satellite comms units	15	200	1,100
	Contract Totals			**37,370**
	Package price reduction			-1,370
	Contract Fee to Client			**36,000**

1.3	**Mi-24 ordnance**	
1.3.1	57mm rocket launcher pods	6
1.3.2	57mm HE	1,000
1.3.3	12.7mm ball	40,000
1.3.4	12.7mm tracer	10,000
1.3.5	12.7mm links	50,000
2.2	**SF Team Equipment**	
2.2.1	AK-47	100
2.2.2	PKM	10
2.2.3	RPG-7	10
2.2.4	Makarov pistol	20
2.2.5	60mm mortar	10
2.2.6	82mm mortar	6
2.2.7	DsHK	4
2.2.8	AGS-17	4
2.2.9	7.62x39	500,000
2.2.10	7.62x54	250,000
2.2.11	12.7mm ball	100,000
2.2.12	12.7mm tracer	25,000
2.2.12	PG-7V	1,000
2.2.13	30mm grenade	2,000
2.2.14	Illumination flare	200
2.2.15	Smoke/frag grenade	800
2.2.16	AK-47 magazines	1,000
2.2.17	60mm HE	2,500
2.2.18	82mm HE	2,500
2.2.19	12.7mm links	125,000
2.2.20	Personal kit and uniforms	100

Office of the Commander

Headquarters Papua New Guinea Defence Force, Murray barracks, Free bag Service, Boroko, Papua New Guinea
Telephone: 324 2840 Ext: 2428 Telex: NE 22170

OPERATIONS ORDERS

OPERATION RAUSIM KWIK 03/97

ENEMY

1. There are few threat scenarios to be addressed;

Sandline

2. May take a discreet counter ops to prevent the operation to continue. Their strength is the personnel weapons, use and access to attack helicopters and aircraft that are being supplied, However it must be taken note that all equipment including aircraft, helicopters, weaponry are all state property as part of the contract and all efforts must be taken to prevent their use. The CEO of Sandline Tim Spicer is to be isolated throughout the operations and kept away from PM. Minister for Defence and Deputy PM.

Network International and The Corps

3. Network International is a security company owned by Sir Julius's children and employs two Australian brothers Mark and Cedric Rodrigues. It is not an enemy but can pose serious opposition to our mission because of the relationship with the PM and Sandline International and the state They could be armed and may pose resistance. Network was reported to be supported by serving and former soldiers. They are not to have access to our troops or enter military bases to seek support or hide.

4. The Corps is a British based security company and may become involved if there are possible threats against its foreign citizens mainly British subjects.

5. A clear line of communications is to be established with the Police as in the event of their involvement the Police with elements of the Defence Force are to contain and prevent these threats from escalating.

Royal Papua New Guinea Constabulary (RPNGC)

6, My greatest gamble is the Police Force. The Police Commissioner has been briefed on the circumstances surrounding the whole contract and will be informed along with PNGDF officers on D Day about my opposition. His senior officers, Chief of Operations and Commander NCD will be briefed concurrently on the day either to stand on our side or be neutral during the operation. The Police will either assist or prevent our operations from fulfilling its Mission. It is imperative that we have a clear line of communications and our troops must not take law into their own hands.

Dissident Groups

7.   These are mainly senior PNGDF officers who have been retrenched or sidelined awaiting the fate of their future. They may want to conduct counter operations and must be restricted from entering HQPNGDF fixtures . We must conduct surveillances on their movements and their residences. There are serving members who are linked to retrenched officers and politicians. Any suspicious movements must be reported.

Outside Intervention

8.   It is common knowledge that ADF 3rd Brigade is on short notice to move as they did in Fiji crisis on Operations Morris Dance in May 1987. USA and New Zealand may come into the paly due to their security alliance and especially now when over 30,000 troops are on Exercise at Shoalwater Bay in Queensland. Their objective would be secure safe passage for their citizens out of the host nation safely. Therefore, the key to the whole success of the operations in orderliness, discipline and conduct that represent nationalism, pride and protection of our sovereignty.

Motive of other rival groups within Papua New Guinea

9,   There are many dissident groups throughout Papua New Guinea who would want to take advantage and opportunity to destroy members of the government and property. Those intending to come into Murray barracks and support us are to be closely screened and referred to the Commander. There may be current politicians who will use the opportunity to take sides. In all cases they must be screened.

10.   I will use the media, particularly radio and TV to appeal for peace and allow us to complete our mission for the people to appreciate and be heard without bloodshed.

MISSION

11.   **PNGDF is to deport Sandline mercenaries out of Papua New Guinea**

EXECUTION

12.   General Outline

The operation will be conducted in three phases;

12.1	Phase 1-	Arrest and detention of Sandline Executives on D minus 1 (D-1).
12.2	Phase 2-	Arrest and expulsion of the main Sandline body and expose the secret operation plan for Bougainville and including the Contract (5-7 days).
12.3	Phase 3-	Review and consolidate and debrief of the operation and damage control immediately after expulsion of merceries.

13.   Four senior Sandline executives will be detained in Port Moresby and held in military custody. The CEO Tim Spicer will be isolated in a naval vessel under guard and out in the sea, while the remaining troops will be detained in Wewak and escorted to Port Moresby ready for expulsion. The isolation of Tim Spicer and his executive team from the PM and Minister for Defence and other executives and bureaucrats of PNG government is very critical to the whole operations. At no time during and after the operations should he be allowed to contact and communicate with the government authority.

14.   All the company equipment is to be searched and confiscated while personal belongings are to be searched and released. All weapons and recoilless propelled grenades and ammunition are to be accounted for and secured in PNGDF Armouries.

TASKS

15.   1RPIR

15.1   The Afrikaners executives are to be housed at Taurama Barracks Officers Annex awaiting deportation and guarded by a strong security team. DIB is to attach a small detachment for intelligence task.

15.2   A very effective ready reaction force is to be assigned to respond to any unexpected threats and deployed at short notice.

15.3   1RPIR as an infantry regiment is to be out of bound for unauthorised visitors throughout the operation

16.   2RPIR

16.1   Disarm and secure in armoury all confiscated small arms and RPGs. Provide security and search and ensure all Sandline members embark on the aircraft without being hassled.

16.2   Send the mercenaries to Port Moresby on order to Jacksons airport and SFU patrol ion company and ready got deportation.

17.   GOLDIE RIVER TRAINING DEPOT

17.1   Prepare a platoon strength of troops as reserve to be deployed at short notice.

17.2   Provide a security team to be based at Air Movement Shed (AMS) at all times an ensure that no unauthorised person enters the military base

18.   MURRAY BARRACKS AREA

18.1   Tighten up full security checks on vehicles and personnel moving in and out of Murray Barracks and HQPNGDF. Only the gate closest to the guard house and Fire Station is to be used, while the main gate is closed at all times.

18.2   Worksop, TTU troops are to provided personal security for Commander.

18.3   A Ready Reaction Group (RRG) of no more than a platoon is to be on standby and positioned at TTU area for any immediate action on order from Force Operations Centre.

19. **HQPNGDF**

19.1 The remainder of MBA and HQPNGDF staff are to be operationally ready and in direct command and control of the Chief of Staff.

19.2 There is to be no access of unauthorised people into HQ Murray Barracks

20. **SIGNAL SQADRON**

20.1 Is to provide the following:

20.1.1 An extra shift at Force Operations Centre to support the operations

20.1.2 Provide a full time operator when Commander is mobile

21. **MILITARY POLICE**

21.1 Are to support troops at respective deployment points and area. They are to ensure Sandline mercenaries arriving from Wewak are properly screened, processed for outbound travel.

22. **DEFENCE INTELLIGENCE ENGE BRANCH (DIB)**

22.1 DIB will provide two operators to be Tim Spicer and a cell of no more than 5 operatives to be stationed at Kiki Barracks to monitor Sandline activates until completion of operations.

22.2 DIB will monitor with assistance from Military Police the movement of Network International and foreigners assign to the company. They are to remove any weapon that may pose threat to the lives of troops and the public.

22.3 Tim Spicer is also to be interrogated and the Intelligence officer of Sandline Carl Deats is to be also isolated and interrogated.

23. **SPECIAL FORCES UNIT (SFU)**

23.1 Provide security for the transfer of mercenaries and their trainers out of the country commencing at Wewak.

23.2 Prepare two patrols as standby for special operations as commanded by the Commander and Operations Officer.

23.3 Leave a patrol back at Wewak for special duties as directed by the Commander through CO 2RPIR.

24. **LANDING CRAFT BASE (LCB)**

24.1 Proved a naval vessel on orders for special operations and able to be out in the sea for up to 21 days or more. Details to follow from D Mar Ops.

24.2 Provide commutations with SFU and

24.3 Provide naval personal for special operations and

24.4 Ensure the naval base is out of bound for the duration of operations

25. AIR TRANSPORT SQADRON (ATS)

25.1 Preposition the Casa aircraft before D Day to extract mercenaries and SFU patrol out of Wewak to include MP escort.

25.2 Prepare a dedicated helicopter for special operation on D Day and ensure it is serviceable and refuelled and a security team of SF members on board throughout the operation.

25.3 Provide security for hanger and ensure there is no access into the hanger by Sandline personnel or unauthorised personnel including media.

25.4 Assist in general security of Jacksons Airbase including SFU Operations Room.

25.5 Assist in the deportation exercise.

25.6 Prevent access into hanger and tarmac by Sandline pilots and ground crew.

25.7 Provide security for remainder of Sandline personnel.

GOVERNMENT AGENCIES

26. RPNGC

26.1 The involvement of the Police will have a very big bearing of the success or failure of the operations and a clear line of communications based on mutual respect and trust is to be maintained from the commencement of the operations.

26.2 The Commander is to inform the Commissioner for Police, Chief of Operations and Commander NCDC on the background of Operations Rausim Kwik. A request for a mobile squad will be presented.

26.3 They're to be requested to facilitate the deportation of the Sandline mercenaries.

27. Foreign Affairs

27.1 A dedicated Foreign Affairs officer Mr Simon Namis will coordinate all consular arrangements and liaison with Department of Immigration with the movement details of each mercenary.

27.2 If there are any difficulties the Commandeer will speak to the Secretary for Foreign Affairs.

28. Customs and Immigration

28.1 Movement staff are to liaise directly with Immigration for the safe passage of Sandline personnel to depart PNG shores without delay and difficulties.

29. **Air Niugini**

29.1   Major Barley is to coordinate all inbound flights and outbound to fly Sandline mercenaries out of PNG.

30. **CO- ORD INSTRUCTIONS**

30.1   Timings: TBA

30.2   D Day TBA

30.3   Phase 2 to commence immediately after Phase 1 followed by Phase 3.

30.4   Deportation Orders; To be coordinated with line departments.
Transport to be coordinated by Captain Chris Siroi in and out bound transport is to be coordinated by Major Bartley.

30.5   Nominal roll is to be maintained by all units and including troops participating on Operations Rausim Kwik.

30.6   No information is to be released to the public without being sanctioned by the Commander, Only the Commandeer and selected officers will provide information to the media. However, the Commandeer and his nominee must keep the public informed frequently to prevent misinformation

31. **ADMIN AND LOGISTICS**

31.1   Except for troops providing escort for Tim Spicer all troops will be in their uniforms. This includes DIB Operatives. All other troops are to wash. And iron their uniforms. No personnel will appear in public with our properly presented.

31.2   All troops are to be warned in for rations, while hot boxes for approximately 20 personnel are to be provided at the Force Operations Centre every evening.

31.3   All vehicles are to be serviced and refuelled the previous day and be ready for tasking at short notice.

31.4   There will be limited use of land transport and where possible all vehicle movement should be coordinated with Operations Officer.

31.5   Operations Officer is to allocate vehicles to troops on essential tasks do specialised task.

31.6   Normal feeding is to continue for Sandline personnel at respective holding units.

32. **COMMAND AND SIGNALS**

32.1   Commander PNGDF is the overall commander of Operations Rausim Kwik 03/97 and only him alone will cancel the operations if there are circumstances beyond the control of the PNGDF.

32.2   `**Appointments:**

32.2.1 Operations Officer; Major Walter Enuma

32.2.2 Deputy Operations Officer: Major Giblet Toropo

32.2.3 Ready Reactions Force Commander: Captain Beldon Namah assisted by Sgt Chris Mora.

32.2.4 Int Offrs (SFU); Captain Siale Diro and Lt Ed Yodu

32.2.5 Tim Spicer will be detained and guarded by Captain Namah and Sergeant Chris Mora and two Int Operators.

32.2.6 Logistics and Movements Officer: Major William Bartley

32.2.7 Comms Offr: Lt Michael David

33.3 Communications

33.3.1 Comms Officer: Lt Michael David

33.3.2 Troops disposition: SFU at Goldie Barracks and Operations unit at Air Movement Shed (AMS).

33.3.4 Lt Michael David is the Communications Officer for this operations throughout.

33.3.5 HF Racal radios will be used but to maintain radio silence throughout the actual operations period.

33.3.6 Satellite Communications provided by Tim Spicer will be used for high level communications by Commander and Operations Officer only.

33.3.7 There is to be radio silence on D-1 and on D Day.

33.4 All telephone use is to be restricted due to lack of proper security.

34. CODE WORDS

34.1 D Day: WETIM ONEM

34.2 Executive address to units: TOKSAVE

34.3 Arrest of key personnel: TIME OUT

34.5 Success of each phase: KOL WIN

Authentication

(Jerry SINGIROK, MBE)
Brigadier General
Commander
14 March 1995

(W. SALAMAS)
Lieutenant Colonel
Acting Chief of Operations

Commander of Operation Rausim Kwik:
General Jerry Singirok
March 1997

Operation Rausim Kwik command team:
Left- Navy Lt Commander Aleale, Capt Namah, Capt Emech,
Sgt Mora, Sir Barry, Gen Jerry Singirok, Mr Donigi, Maj Enuma,
Commander Ur, Maj Toropo, Capt Diro, WO Gubag
26 Mar 97

Operation Commander
Major Enuma and OC SFU Major Toropo
26 Mar 97

Operation troops:
Troops with Sgt Guina and Cpl Isaiah ith Joes Malam, Koisen
Boino, Alan AIma, Keme Isaiah, Pte Peso, Amatus, Kepas Hiviki,
Mickey Kiapen Cpl John Koraia, and Tom Namnai 26 Mar 97

Gen Singirok with Capts Namah, Graig Solomon and John Keleto

Maj Enuma and Comd Max Aleale hug 26 Mar 97

Commonwealth Secretary General
Chief Emeka Anyoku received by Peter Donigi at Flag Staff House
25 Mar 97

Capt Namah hugs Singirok after Sir Julius steps down 26 Mar 97
Looking on Comd Aleale and Sir Barry 26 Mar 97

Sgt William and Cpl John Koraia reconcile the $UD400,000.00
cash from Tim Spicer's safe for court exhibit 8
Apr 97

PART B

CONTENTS

CHAPTER 11

Early Beginnings, 1956–75

In 1968 I had to repeat my Standard 6 school year as my Dad said I was too small. I was awarded a prize for the most improved pupil. The prize was a book titled Terry the Jungle Boy. *It was the first book I had ever owned. It was the only book in my house growing up.*

—Jerry Singirok

Beginnings

I am a Karkar Islander. Karkar is a small but populated island in the Bismarck Sea in the Pacific Ocean. I was born in my family's small thatched-roof house just before daybreak on 5 May 1956. The family house was in a small hamlet called Dagadag, not far from the village of Did. My three cousin sisters Madek, Sileng, and Minem—daughters of my dad's close relatives—assisted Mum during my birth.

Within a few days, Mum was strong enough to take me with her, walking along a bush track to Gaubin Lutheran Hospital, about 8 km away, to get me immunised. She was afraid of losing me as she had some of her earlier children. She said I was a chubby baby and fair for a Karkar Islander.

Karkar Island

Karkar Island sits across a narrow piece of water some 30 km off the coast of Madang on the north coast of Papua New Guinea. The island is small, 25 km long and 19 km wide, and dominated by a volcano called Bagiai. The highest peak is called Kanagioi. Bagiai is an active volcano over 1,800 metres (6,033 feet) high, and on most days, its peak is hidden by cloud. The narrow plains surrounding the mountain consist of rich black alluvial volcanic soil that is excellent for farming. Coconuts, cocoa, betel, and mustard are the main commercial crops.

The population of Karkar is small. There has been no recent census, but I would guess the population today is over 80,000. (Madang, the provincial capital, numbers 27,000.) The main religions on Karkar are Lutheran and Catholic, with Lutheran being the predominant faith. There are two main languages spoken locally: Waskia in the north-west and Takia to the south-east. These two local languages are believed to have very few words in common. Most islanders also speak Tok Pisin or pidgin, and English is taught in all the schools.

The volcanic soil being very fertile, fruits and vegetables thrive on the island. Breadfruit is a staple part of the diet, particularly while the villagers wait for the rainy season. The island also has *galip* nuts (the fruit of the *Canarium indicum* tree), which are dried and the oil extracted and mixed with taro, banana, or breadfruit pudding. It is served as a dessert after the main meal. The *galip* nut has a taste somewhere between that of a macadamia and an almond.

My Family

There were seven children in my family growing up. My eldest brother is Willie, and after him is Kabun. I also have three elder sisters, Pirik, Balim, and our adopted sister, Dig. My younger sister is Amin Katuk. An elder sister, Maib Kumai, died of natural causes when she was 7. Mum loved her so much and hardly ever talked about her. My adopted sister, Dig, was given to Mum to bring up when her natural mother died after she was born.

My mum, Yeiwo Pesi Waibibi, was born in around 1925 in Wihun Village in the West Yangoro District of East Sepik Province. She met Dad, Singirok Mudan Langong, when he was on a gold prospecting expedition to East Sepik before the war with a former patrol officer from the territory administration, Gerald Michael Keogh. My dad was born in around 1920 and is from the Painane clan of Did Village. With our parents coming from such different parts of PNG, others regarded our family as being 'mixed race'.

Willie, my eldest brother, was born just before World War II broke out in PNG; sadly, Willie passed away in late 2019. My parents had just arrived in Madang from Wewak in 1942 when they were caught up by the war. This prevented them from returning to Wewak, where Dad's boss and companion, Gerald Keogh, an Australian ex-patrol officer who had left the Australian administration to go into gold prospecting in the Maprik and Yangoru area in East Sepik, resided.

Dad told us the story of how he and Gerald had met. He was working as a crew member on a Catholic mission trading boat operating between Madang, Sepik, and West Hollandia (Jayapura) when they took on cargo for the trading post at Angoram. That evening, some goods were stolen by the crew, which led to the whole crew being arrested, along with Dad. But as Dad's work ethic on the boat was so outstanding, Gerald got him out of prison and made him a local constable and helping hand.

Soon after this, Gerald was drafted into the Royal Australian Air Force and then seconded into the United States Air Force. He died in an aircraft crash near Mount Diamond after taking off from Jacksons Airport on a resupply run during the war. When I was born, I was named Gerald. But all the people who knew Gerald called him Jerry. I have since been called Jerry. I do not have a village name.

Growing up around the fringes of the virgin forest in Karkar was exciting and many times adventurous. The forest was littered with fuel drums and trailers and other wreckage left over from the Japanese occupation during the war. Dad was a master at trapping and hunting bandicoots, possums, and other wildlife. There were many wild fowl eggs that supplemented our diet. I liked wild fowl eggs, which were wrapped in leaves and cooked over the fire. The staples in our diet consisted of root crops, taro, cassava, banana, and many fruits, particularly *galip* nuts and breadfruit with wild meat and plenty of fish.

At the age of 6, I was still clumsy in picking up hunting skills, weaving coconut mats, or climbing trees and coconut palms. Instead, I spent most of my early days with Mum and my sisters in the gardens or around the house. I was well looked after by my mum and sisters, and I grew up in a humble and pleasant home. Dad was not a particularly religious man, but he did insist that we practise our Christian faith in the local Lutheran church.

Our village is situated about 5 km from the shoreline at Karkar, where Dad maintained close links with his relatives. Apart from his hunting skills, he was skilful at fishing, using both handlines and skin diving. What I enjoyed most was going fishing with Dad in his dugout outrigger canoe. When Dad took me fishing, my job was to remove the hook from the fish he caught while he threw fresh lines into the sea. I would sit at the rear of the canoe for hours without any word being exchanged with Dad as he never spoke unless the subject was important. In between unhooking the fish that Dad caught, I would throw my own fishing line into the sea and catch my share of fish to take back home. I have never lost my love of fishing since those early days with Dad.

One day we were returning to the village from the beach and walking along a bush track. We were resting under a large tree when Dad picked up a branch the size of a rifle and showed us his rifle drills. Being a former policeman, he started going through the arms drill, from slope arms to order arms and then salute. I was impressed. It is a memory that has never left me. I realise, looking back, that Dad had so much practical knowledge and skill. And he was a very hard worker. We children learnt so much from him.

Another time that I remember was when there had been a long drought on Karkar Island. It must have been in about 1966. Mum, Dig, and I were off to the garden; and as we passed through our coconut plantation, I felt thirsty and wanted to drink a fresh coconut. I asked Mum to climb the coconut palm. Mum said she could not. She had never learnt how to climb. I then begged Dig to climb, and she said she had never climbed a coconut palm either and that it was outrageous for me to ask. I couldn't cope with this. I stood under the coconut palm and cried. Then lo and behold, a bundle of coconuts fell all around me. Twelve fresh nuts were in the bundle, and they scattered all around, leaving me untouched.

Mum and Dig thought I must have been injured and rushed over to me. Startled, I was standing there, rooted firmly to the ground. Mum said it must have been God who heard my cry and provided what neither she nor Dig could give. Later on, when Mum was sharing the experience with my family, she told them that I was a very special child and that such a present could only have been a blessing and a very promising sign from God.

Our sleeping arrangements really depended on where Mum slept every night. We always slept next to a fire as most nights were cold. Mum or Dad would sleep with their back towards the fire so that when they turned, they would provide us kids with their body heat. I always slotted myself between Mum and whichever was the sister who slept between Mum and the wall. There would be bitter fights between Balim, Dig, and Katuk about who would sleep next to Mum. None of us wanted to sleep next to the wall as we believed the nights were filled with bad spirits.

The thought of being consumed by night spirits used to frighten me badly as a kid. This meant many preliminary manoeuvres before sleep. Well before last light, I would visit the toilet. Then I made sure that all the sleeping mats and pillows were arranged neatly nearby. Finally, I made sure that there was a suitable gap between the palm floors within reach in case I need to go in the night.

We were lucky that our dad was a man of vision. He did not want us to become ordinary villagers. His earlier exposure to the outside world and being in the company of Australian administration officers had convinced him of the importance of education and the planting of cash crops such as coconut and cocoa.

Dad sent Willie to a Lutheran boarding primary school at Narer and later on to a couple of schools on the mainland before sending him to Lae Technical College to learn joinery as his trade. Willie would become a senior public servant with the Department of Transport and Marine and a specialist in boatbuilding before becoming the chief marine surveyor for the department. My sister Balim would excel at Asaroka Lutheran High School before going to the University of Papua New Guinea, where she graduated with an arts degree, majoring in political science. She continued her postgraduate studies at London University before becoming a senior department budget officer and, later, assistant secretary in Madang and the East Sepik provincial government. Today Balim is a widow and a self-made businesswoman, entrepreneur, and Christian spiritual leader.

I stayed home all my childhood days and helped Dad clear the forest and plant coconut and cocoa. The larger of our coconut plantations was near the village of Did and was about fifteen hectares in size. The plantations of coconut and cocoa became the sole source of our small family income to pay for our school fees and other expenses, while Mum would sell vegetables at Gaubin Lutheran Hospital market from time to time.

Dad was elected village councillor and president of Takia Local Government Council. He spent many days helping resettle villagers and carrying out government policies throughout the Karkar Local Government Council area. He was a councillor for fifteen years and retired in 1968.

On many occasions, the Australian patrol officer from the district office at Miak would arrive at our village and conduct village court mediation, land demarcation, or population surveys. All these meetings would take place near our house. The patrol officer would be accompanied by at least two policemen. We children were scared of the policemen as they carried .303 rifles. Along with our cousins, we would hide in an upstairs room of our house and make small peepholes through the bamboo wall to spy on the policemen with the rifles, hoping that a shot might be fired. But nothing ever happened.

Being of mixed parentage, with our mum being from another province and raising us in Dad's village, was not easy. Mum had to learn Dad's language, customs, genealogy, and land boundaries. She was sensitive and was aware of our lack of genuine acceptance into Dad's clan. Mum never left her own customs behind, and she taught us kids her own language, Dagua. We often used it when other relatives visited us and when she wanted to communicate with us on matters that only we should know.

Primary Schooling

In May 1962, I turned 6 and was enrolled at Dangsai Primary School. The school was new and was located about 5 km from Did. My sisters Pirik and Dig took turns walking me to school every day until I was big enough to walk to school on my own or sometimes with other children.

In 1967, Dad transferred me to Kavailo (Lillberg) Primary School, which was farther away from Dangsai again. The reason for moving me, as I was informed much later, was a direction from the administration to mix Karkar Islanders together to develop unity and understanding because Papua and New Guinea were to be united in a new nation. Whatever the reason for the transfer, it did not matter to me all that much, though the distance we now had to walk to school was about a 20 km round trip five days a week. I must have developed pretty good aerobic fitness after a few weeks of that.

Our day commenced at about five thirty, and it took us around two and a half hours to walk to school. During the mornings, we would walk through bush tracks to the school. I feared the jungle as flying foxes, huge trees with buttresses, and large birds flying around frightened us. But the jungle was cool most of the way past Daup Village before we arrived at Babel Village, where we followed the main road. On our return leg, we would follow the main road as it would be getting dark. If we arrived at school after eight o'clock, we would be held back at school on punishment. On those days, we ended up leaving the school at about five in the afternoon. By the time we got home, it would be well past dark. This was the daily pattern for three years.

Occasionally, I got a break from the early morning walking routine. Late in 1967, through Mum's arrangement, I was invited to stay with

Joseph Kara and his wife, Francisca, both of whom were from Murik Lakes in East Sepik Province. Joseph Kara had just arrived as a teacher at Kaivailo. This was a sigh of relief at least for 1967. Another teacher from Gulf Province, Lawrence Karawa, a single man, also invited me to stay with him, which assisted me greatly as he lived in the precinct of the school.

Mr Karawa was very kind, looking after me with great care. He took me for the first time to Madang Town. I was so excited because we could only see the mainland and the twinkle of the town lights from the island.

It must have been Easter of 1967 when we set sail on MV *Lilung*, a small boat owned by Noel Goodyear, a British trader who was stationed at Biabi Plantation. It took us about four hours to reach Madang. Seeing many vehicles, speedboats, and planes landing and taking off fascinated me. We stayed at the place of Mr Karawa's friend. I saw many foreigners, particularly in Chinatown.

One unforgettable night, Mr Karawa took me to a cinema to watch a movie along Modilon Road. He bought me my first ever ice cream, Pauls Hava Heart. It was a heart-shaped chocolate-coated vanilla ice cream on a stick. I will never forget eating that first ice cream. I not only ate the ice cream but also sucked the stick until it broke in half in my mouth. We went back to the movies later that weekend, and I was treated to another ice cream.

A few months later, Dad took me to Madang. We visited a relative who had installed an electric stove in his house. I walked past the stove and saw the red-hot element. Not being aware of the danger, I touched the element out of curiosity. I burnt a large patch of skin in the palm of my right hand. Dad was not impressed.

In 1968, I was to have gone to Tusbab High School in Madang, but Dad said I was too young to go, so I repeated standard 6 at Dangsai Primary School, this time under the guidance of John Ferrier, a caring, fair-minded, and very astute Australian teacher. Mr Ferrier constantly reminded us of the importance of working and studying hard as he said that, sooner or later, we would have to run our own country. He also motivated us to plant a big peanut patch opposite the school, as well as raising pigs in the school grounds to sell.

I can still remember the impression that John Ferrier made on us with the fact that the country was going to gain independence and that it was important that we get a proper education so that we could run our own country one day. My class was a rather big group, and perhaps uncommonly at that time, over 80 per cent of us made it to high school. In my class were Madako Suari, Dudui Kasu, Kambei Kasu, Mait Kulil, Bagiom Kautil, Babir, Agai Tangoi, Magai Kubailon, and Akoi Buk. Many of my relatives who started school with me dropped out early as they preferred village life with its hunting, gardening, ceremonies, and traditional dancing, while others whose parents were unable to meet the cost of further education dropped out also.

The last day at Dangsai was memorable as we had many sweets, balloons, and presents. I was awarded a prize for the most improved pupil, and a book titled *Terry the Jungle Boy* was presented to me. It was the first book I had ever owned. It was the only book in my house growing up.

Asaroka Lutheran High School, 1969–72

The following year, most of my class went to Karkar High School. However, Dad wanted me to get a mission education along with my sister Balim, who was already at Asaroka Lutheran High. He approached Edwin Tscharke, the doctor at Gaubin Lutheran Hospital, to ask if he could contact his brother, the Reverend Len Tscharke, the principal at Asaroka, to accept my enrolment. We celebrated Christmas with the good news of my acceptance.

As usual, that Christmas, there was hardly any break for us as, under Dad's leadership, we had to collect and dry copra and sell wet cocoa beans for our school fees and pocket money. Dad preferred selling his dried copra at the Copra Marketing Board in Madang. On a good day, he would sell about ten to twelve bags of copra, which would be sufficient to enable him to buy new clothes and other essentials for the family, including our suitcases and some reading and writing material.

Processing the coconuts into copra is very hard work. The dry nuts are gathered up and split open with an axe or by holding the nut in both hands and driving it down with great force over an upright iron spike planted in the ground. The white meat is extracted from the split shell, laid out on racks to dry over an open fire, and smoked for about four days before being put into sacks for shipping. It is a hot, thirsty, laborious way to make a small living.

With the new year approaching, I became more and more anxious as I knew I would miss Mum and my sisters and relatives. I could make copra but had not even learnt how to wash my own clothes and cook for myself. That said, I was hugely excited at the prospect of going on my first ride in an airplane. In the first week of January 1969, the whole family came to Kurum Mission Wharf as we boarded the Lutheran mission vessel MV *Simbang* for Madang. Mum and Dig cried when we said goodbye. I also cried as I boarded the ship. But as Balim was sailing with me and many other students from school, I soon overcame the feelings of loss and separation from my mum and my sisters.

We sailed into Madang Harbour at the Lutheran Mission Wharf and were loaded onto a truck to Baitabag Lutheran Mission Station to be billeted for the night before flying to Goroka in Eastern Highlands Province. I sat up that night listening to the other students who were a year or so ahead of me and tried to learn as much as possible about Asaroka. I was excited about being a boarder and being taught by overseas teachers, but none of the students told me about the hardships that I would face at the school.

Two days later, the student nominal roll was finalised and the manifest prepared, and we boarded a school charter, an Ansett DC3, and flew from Madang to Goroka. I was frightened as we took off but was comforted with having Balim in the same aircraft, and I saw that the other students were relaxed and chatting away happily. The ride in the aircraft, with the ground many thousands of feet below us, fascinated me. I spent the flight with my nose glued to the window.

After claiming our luggage at the terminal, we were crammed together onto the school lorry. This was an old green Bedford open-tray truck. We sped off on a dusty, winding, and bumpy ride to Asaroka

High School, about 30 km west of Goroka Township. The road led to Iufiyufa before taking a left turn into a feeder road to Notofana Village. We arrived at Asaroka Lutheran Station before driving down to the site where the high school itself was located.

The school was situated on a long and wide ridge line running north to south along the edge of the Asaro Valley. Daulo Pass towers over the school to the west and the Finisterre Ranges to the north-east. The Asaro River is distinctly visible as it runs through the valley below.

Rev. Leonard Tscharke established Asaroka Lutheran High School in 1963. It was one of the first ever Lutheran mission high schools to be established in the highlands region; the other was Kitip in the Western Highlands. We were shown our dormitories and allocated a bed each. There were no such things as mattresses, and we had to make do with blankets and bed sheets. Although I had two blankets, it was always cold and miserable. On enrolment day, we had to bring essential items. These were a Holy Bible (the King James Authorised Version), a spade, a plate and cup, and school fees. I had all the required items except the school fees as Balim was the only one required to pay under the scheme.

The meals were dreadful. There was no breakfast. Most of us attended the early morning routine of communal gardening on an empty stomach. Lunch was brown rice and tinned fish mixed in boilers and scooped out with huge wooden scoops into a bowl big enough for ten students per table; dinner consisted of sweet potatoes with skins boiled and centrally served in the same bowls. Many students would bring in supplements like tinned fish or meat and vegetables or even some Vegemite to add to their meal to make it more interesting. To this day, I still do not know why we could not have breakfast, always the most important meal of the day.

After about a week of the same diet, I refused to eat and ended up with diarrhoea and typhoid. I missed my parents, particularly my mum and my sisters, and cried constantly. I thought of leaving the school. Balim continued to do my laundry but, in the end, told me that I must toughen up and do it myself because she had her own to do, and her studies were taking up her time.

It was not a good start. But I was determined to be strong and self-reliant, and I wanted to achieve good academic results. Asaroka was a leading school in district sports and many religious activities, and before long, I participated in many school activities and began to settle in.

Our roll call was at five thirty, and we would all be assembled in front of the mess. If we were in luck, we could grab a cup of dark tea with no sugar. Then we'd go to the gardens down in the valley about a kilometre away and weed, dig new ditches, or plant new sweet potatoes. This was a one-hour job, and we'd climb back up the ridge and take thirty minutes to shower and be at class.

The first period started with devotion and a prayer. Each student took turns to lead the devotion and say a prayer. When it came to my turn, I would tremble as I had not been to a mission primary school, and the routine was unfamiliar. But after a few opportunities, I began to enjoy leading class devotions.

In the evening, our meal was sweet potatoes from our own gardens. We would harvest all the sweet potatoes, put them in bags, and carry them to the kitchen where we'd weigh them and register our names. We never had other vegetables cooked with the sweet potatoes. Looking back at it now, our diet could have been far better and more interesting had the teachers and the cooks been a bit more imaginative. But that was the order of the day for the remaining four years that I spent at Asaroka.

At the end of the day, there was evening devotion in the school chapel, where we had to sit in our classes. After roll call, the final-year students would lead devotion. Then we would go to our classrooms for another two hours of private study supervised by student monitors. About nine or half past nine, we'd go to our dormitories; and by ten, the lights went out as the school generators were switched off.

Saturday evenings were the only free evenings. Most students would go and stay in town with friends, and those who were local would go back to their villages. Those of us who had nowhere to go stayed at school and attended Scripture Union classes or took part in choir practice.

Every Sunday during school term, church was compulsory, and we were required to attend wearing our best clothes. The church service would go for hours. Preachers came from neighbouring districts to preach. In the evenings, if we were lucky, movies would be shown using 35 mm projectors and scratchy film prints.

Strangely enough for a mission school, many of the films were westerns in which John Wayne always acted the tough guy. One Sunday evening, the school principal's attention must have slipped, and we were shown *The Dirty Dozen*, a WWII film starring Lee Marvin, John Cassavetes, Ernest Borgnine, and Charles Bronson. Another memorable Sunday evening, we were treated to the 1956 Cecil B. DeMille blockbuster, *The Ten Commandments*, with Charlton Heston unforgettable in the role of Moses. The film also starred Yul Brynner, Edward Robinson, Anne Baxter and Yvonne de Carlo. That was an evening to remember.

At lights out, everyone, without exception, had to be physically present in bed. There was no wandering around at night as the teachers enforced maximum rest before the day's routine. On most Saturdays, we spent a good two hours in the coffee plantation in the morning either weeding among the coffee bushes or picking the coffee 'cherries' and pulping them for the beans.

I was punished once, and my privileges were taken away for being nasty to a girl who was annoying me in class. My punishment was to shift gravel from in front of the school office to other parts of the school ground using a spade and a wheelbarrow. As the classrooms were arranged in a semicircle, I could be seen from all parts of the school, making it an extremely humiliating experience. I made sure that I never got punished after that.

Asaroka was active in many sports including athletics. I played Australian Rules and soccer but did not get into the school team until my second-last year. From our Australian Rules team, we had students who went on to represent the province, such as the late Wesley Kikesung, who was the Lutheran head bishop; Andrew Columbus; Harry Hitaro; and a South Pacific long-distance runner, Wallace Hofagoe.

The school by then had introduced school uniforms. We each had two pairs. For the boys, the uniform was a yellow shirt and blue trousers, while the girls had a yellow blouse and grey and white striped skirts.

In my second year, I was selected to teach Sunday school in the surrounding villages. The area I was allocated to was Asaro Mando. We'd get ready on Sunday mornings as early as six o'clock and would be dropped off by the school lorry along the main road from where we'd walk into the villages. I enjoyed these mornings, not only conducting Sunday school but also because the villagers would give us sugar cane or food such as sweet potatoes and other root crops.

In 1971, my third year at Asaroka, I had my first ever high school sweetheart. Dupain Damun also came from Madang, but she was two years behind me at school. We saw each other constantly, but as the school rules were strict, we only passed notes and took the opportunity to see each other at Goroka Town on a Saturday. She would remain my girlfriend for another eight years before we decided to get married. After I graduated from Asaroka in 1972, Dupain left to train as a nurse at Angau School of Nursing in Lae, Morobe Province.

The year 1972 was a critical year for me. It was my last year at Asaroka, and our final exams dictated where we went in life. Many of us had little choice as either the teachers dictated our career paths or we'd gain positions based on academic performance. Asaroka was an outstanding school in terms of academic achievements mainly because of Reverend Tscharke's leadership. He was made a Companion of the Star of Melanesia in 2018. He sadly passed away in May 2019. When he left Asaroka in late 1971 for further study, he was replaced by Erhard Pinno.

Our teachers were the greatest assets we had. They were the best in their teaching professions and created a great study environment for us. They were a mix of Australians, Americans, Canadians, and Dutch. Some of the teachers who helped us were Paul Breddin, Bob Brown, Rhoda Carlstedt, Judith Finkenbine, David Star and his wife, Paul Hombrom, Leslie Kolbjensen, Graham Cole, Lionel and Irene Worrall, Mark Steinmuller, Christine McKenzie, Rosemary Jasper,

Hugh Langdale, Joyce Dodge, Lionel and Irene Worrall, and Iek and Ann Collet. Erhard Pinno, a Canadian, would replace Len Tscharke as headmaster in 1971. Tony Flyn was our fresh food farm manager. All I can say and be thankful for in my reflections is that they blessed us by rendering the best style of teaching with a wealth of specialised knowledge provided to prepare us for our future academic achievements.

My home teacher, Joyce Dodge, told me I had talents in public speaking. I was just beginning to master the skill, and she thought I would make a good preacher. This would mean going to the Martin Luther Seminary in Lae. I dreaded the idea of being a preacher and avoided close contact with my home teacher from then on.

It was sad to depart Asaroka High School at the end of 1972. As our driver, Tore, manoeuvred the old green Bedford truck out through the entrance for the last time, we held back tears from our shared memories of hardships, friendships, and discipline. Indeed, the experiences gained at Asaroka over four years would play a large role in my grounding for the bigger world. I would not return to Asaroka for another twenty-six years.

Back at Karkar Island, Dad had prepared the grass knives and bush knives that we used when we came home for the summer vacation. There was no time for rest. The very next day, we were up early and out in the plantation, making copra or cutting grass. Balim and I spent Christmas of 1972 helping Dad as usual in the plantation, making copra.

It was a tense period of waiting as I did not know which tertiary college I would be going to the following year. In those days, the high school results were published in the *Post-Courier* as were the listings of which institutions we were selected to attend. There was much relief when I was informed that, along with five others from my class, I had been accepted to attend Sogeri Senior High School.

It was an exciting proposition getting ready to go to Port Moresby for schooling. By then, Balim had completed her first year at the University of Papua New Guinea and was able to tell me about life in Port Moresby and at Sogeri. Our big brother, Willie, was a senior tradesman at the

Department of Transport and Marine, so I was comforted that two of my own siblings would be with me in Port Moresby.

Sogeri Senior High School, 1973–74

In January 1973, my nephew Wakon Luan and I departed Madang for Port Moresby bound for Sogeri Senior High School. Wakon had completed form 4 at Karkar High School and was selected, along with other Karkar Islanders, to attend Sogeri. We both felt excited and privileged to be picked to attend Sogeri. Apart from being the first high school established in PNG after WWII, it had a reputation for being the place where the elites of PNG were educated. It maintained an outstanding record for academic excellence. Only the top 2 per cent of school leavers were selected for entry. Studies at Sogeri followed the New South Wales syllabus.

After landing at Jacksons Airport, we were loaded onto the school truck and dropped off at Hohola, the suburb where my big brother, Willie, was living. Mum, as usual, had sent some food and fruit for Willie and the family. The following day, we departed for Sogeri on the open back of the school lorry. As we meandered up the winding road to the Sogeri Plateau, I became increasingly nervous looking down into the steep ravines and the river many hundreds of feet below us. I recalled the Highlands Highway, but this seemed even steeper and more precipitous. We climbed up and up until we came to the famous S-bend. The lorry lurched sideways and shuddered as the driver struggled to change down for the last leg of the climb. As we slipped back towards the edge, I thought this was the end of all of us. With much grinding and protesting from the gearbox, the driver rammed in his gear at last and dropped in the clutch; and having aged several years at least, we finally reached the top of the plateau before dropping down into the Sogeri Valley.

The valley before us looked lush, beautiful, and green. The air smelt fresh and clean, and the Owen Stanley Mountains in the background reminded me of Asaroka. Unlike Port Moresby where it was hot, humid, and dusty, the climate was cool and pleasant.

When we arrived at the school, the duty teacher confirmed our names and showed us to our dormitory. Both Wakon and I were allocated dorm 7 near Evarogo Creek. Soon I was introduced to fellow Karkar Islanders: Peck Asafo, Alphones Banik, Samson Aiau, Kikereng Wargem, John Kulala, Gunip Wam, Bagilu Yafet, Wakon Luan, and Wil Akus. The only female student from Karkar was Rag Gubag. Bunam Lakasa, also from Karkar, was my classmate at Asaroka, and he joined us along with Kasi Akiro from Eastern Highlands Province.

As the months rolled on, I became acquainted with students from other parts of PNG. From Morobe, there were Brown Kiki, our basketball star; Nagora Bogan; Gaff Bonga; Dahu Mathew; Pama Anio; Nuri Towika; Tukubin Malang; Praio Oksap; and Naiu Apisa. Then there were the Central Province students Nau Badu, Sibona Kopi, Thomas Dirona Abe, Vagi Oala, Haraka Gabutu, Paul Luke, Patrick Ali, Arua Toa, Gerard Kassman, Miria Ikupu, and Joseph Kosi. Joseph was a survivor from a Caribou aircraft crash the previous year in which twenty-two school cadets lost their lives. The girls in my class whom I got to know well were Lila Tore, Govea, Sinepi Ila, Pepetua Haiveta, and Ruth Cowley.

There were other students too whom I befriended: Gabriel Saliau, Steven Nion, Memel Pohei, Alphones Kaluwin, and Lapun Porou from Manus and Tito Masken and Moses Tolingling from New Ireland. From East New Britain, they were Akwila Kanene and Joseph Malir and from Bougainville Frank Kapapal Torova, Moses Koiri, and Kapeatu Puaria. Among the Bougainvilleans, Kapeatu would become a lawyer for the Bougainville administration during the crisis period, Moses Koiri would become the company secretary for Bougainville Copper Ltd, and Frank Torova would become the director of health services and a surgeon in the defence force, operating on my left wrist when I was wounded in 1994 at the Panguna mine.

Those who shared dorm 7 with me were Vincent Warakai, Philip Kanora, Louise Bau, Tom Ur, Andrew Waliya, and Naplau Michael Waipo from East Sepik Province; Memafu Kila from Gulf Province; and Gibuma Salika and Auda Bamaga from Western Province. Gibuma (Gibs) Salika was appointed chief justice of PNG in late 2018.

There was much more freedom at Sogeri than at my previous school. There were no devotions or work parties. The food was good, unlike at Asaroka, and more importantly, there was breakfast with plenty to eat. I also saw that boys were allowed to walk hand in hand and even cuddle with their girlfriends openly. This would never have been permissible at Asaroka. But one thing I noticed at Sogeri was that you had to study to get good marks to continue to university. I had no problems getting into a good study discipline.

I started attending rugby training and soon was selected to play in the school rugby league team. The seniors who led us were Tau Maguuru, Gainama, and Sale Kumuna. That year, Sogeri entered the Under 19 Port Moresby Rugby League competition, and we finished the season undefeated.

What attracted me most was the Thirty-Five School Cadet Battalion in which Sogeri had a subunit. The Q-store was situated near the girl's dormitory, always a sound reason for joining up, especially at that age. The cadet unit would spend most of the latter part of the afternoon doing drills, both foot and arms drills.

I was envious of those in the cadet unit. Many who came to Sogeri had already been in their respective units with the Thirty-Five School Cadet Battalion the previous year, and it was easy for them to continue if they elected to do so. I was eager to enlist and so organised with John Kulala to see the deputy headmaster, Mr O'Hara, to ask if I could enlist as soon as there was a vacancy.

This was not difficult. There was a vacancy, and I was issued my initial uniform: long jungle green trousers; shirts, both short and long sleeves; boots, gaiters and puttees; two pairs of socks; and a beret with the sunrise badge of the Australian Army along with the school cadet badge. There were also a range of accessories, including a toilet bag, boot polish, toothbrush and toothpaste, shaving gear, a hand mirror, and a sewing kit. All this gear was more than I had bargained for, and I shifted some of my efforts from studying to perfecting my drills and uniform attire on weekends and undertook additional cadet unit activities after school periods (by the girl's dormitory, remember?).

We attended weekend bivouacs mainly at the national park at Variata, not far from the school. We laid cement platforms and made walking tracks. We spent one weekend at Owers' Corner at Uberi Ridge, replacing logs for 1,000 steps from the bottom to the top of the ridge. I loved the ration packs that we were issued when we went out on overnight bivouacs or training. (I may be the only person in the history of the world who has ever confessed to loving army ration packs, but then I was always hungry in those days.)

In around March 1973, we sat for our junior leadership non-commissioned exams, and I passed. I was promoted from ordinary cadet to the rank of sergeant and was identified to take over as senior cadet under officer the following year.

In August, while we were at Igam Barracks in Lae for the annual camp with all the other cadet units from around the country, the government announced the disbandment of not only the Thirty-Five School Cadet Battalion but also the Papua New Guinea Volunteer Rifles and any other auxiliary military organisations in the country in preparation for independence, which was anticipated within two years. Many of us were disappointed by the news of the disbandment of the school cadet programme, and we returned our .303 rifles and bayonets to the Q-store. After we returned to Sogeri, the only thing that reminded us of the school cadets were the uniforms we wore to school and the parade boots we were allowed to keep.

It was the end of 1973 and school holidays. Back on Karkar Island, Dad was delighted to see his two labourers return, Balim and me. After a day or so off, we spent most of the Christmas and New Year holidays making copra to help earn our allowances for the following year.

The following year, 1974, was my final year at Sogeri. I took up smoking for the first time, not so much for the taste, which I have always thought is somewhere between pretty average and downright vile, but because it was a big thing at school. A group of smokers would form to share one cigarette, which would be passed around by those in the circle. My style of clothes also changed. I started wearing jeans and open flared trousers and tank tops, and I let my hair grow into an afro. The music we preferred was all on cassettes from the 1960s and

'70s. Pop groups like CCR (or Creedence Clearwater Revival) were big back then with songs like 'Bad Moon Rising', 'Have You Ever Seen the Rain', and 'Willy and the Poor Boys'. Individuals and groups like Michael Jackson, Little River Band, the Beatles, and of course Elvis Presley were also popular. Listening to these singers and musicians made us feel like we were truly living. Maybe we were.

From our elevated perspective, the first-year students who arrived at Sogeri that year were a mixed bunch. I was often taken aback and amused by their attitudes and openness. Many had come back to PNG from Australian schools, smoked openly, and used slang words that I was not familiar with. The girls were much more outgoing and made friends with me through smoking. Fag mates—if you can imagine such a thing. They included Jenny Mae, Karau, Jenny Wesley, Kila Maioka, Aileen Kaisava, and Konio Vae. Another girl I got to know, though not as well, was Weni Moka of mixed Kerema and Central parentage. Weni was rather shy and introverted, not that I was interested in her back then (or her in me, it would be fair to add), but thirteen years later, Weni and I would marry.

I was voted deputy student president for boys, and Margaret Bagita was voted deputy head prefect for girls. Margaret was a very strong-willed girl from Central Province, and I enjoyed her leadership and commitment. We both assisted Michael Timbi, who was the head prefect. This additional responsibility required me to be active in organising school forums and rallies. With independence approaching, there were many political issues being debated in forums such as the Sogeri Bully Beef Club, which had been instigated by earlier students, including Michael Somare, Paulias Matane, and Albert Maori Kiki, who passed on their passionate interest in domestic and international politics.

In around May, we organised a school rally against Josephine Abaijah, the first Papuan female politician who was a strong advocate for Papuans to break away from New Guinea. She was running a movement to separate called Papua Besena (meaning Papua family or community). It was such a topical issue then. At Sogeri Senior High School, with students from all around Papua and New Guinea grouped together, we developed a strong sense of unity and togetherness. Many of us wanted a united country, not one that would be divided as proposed by Josephine Abaijah. The committee I formed organised placards and banners during one of her visits to the school. Maybe we went too far because, after one such demonstration, I was paraded in front of the school headmaster, Malcolm Gordon. A rather traditional type of no-nonsense English school principal, he reprimanded me for my role in leading the demonstration.

At that time, I had access to the school biology laboratory as it was my job to put away chemicals and other apparatus after class. Another student and I discussed the possibility of distilling methylated spirits and converting it into pure ethanol. So most Friday evenings, we'd distil methylated spirits until we had at least a litre of what we mistakenly thought was pure alcohol ready for the Saturday night school dance. We'd buy at least three bottles of Coke and mix the liquor and get ourselves fixed before we went to the mess for a dance. A few of us who still had our cadet boots would wear these with our army green shirts and dark sunglasses and crash into the mess hall. We terrified a lot of girls. I doubt that we picked up any. We told ourselves we were having a good time.

I masterminded this illegal spirit-making activity for a while, but I ceased when I realised that we were going too far. I reminded myself why I was at Sogeri. Besides, having progressed with my science studies, I had a better awareness of the extreme dangers of trying to convert methylated spirits into drinking alcohol. The methanol (or wood spirits) that is added to ethanol to 'denature' it can very readily cause blindness and early death. Its boiling point being very close to that of ethanol, it cannot readily be distilled to leave pure drinking alcohol. Depending on the composition, the pyridine that is added to methylated spirits to give it an unpleasant taste and the methyl violet to colour it blue can sometimes be removed by distillation, but the schoolboy chemist attempting this dangerous process will still have a potentially very poisonous methanol/ethanol mixture for his Saturday night dance. Not to be recommended, in fact downright stupid and potentially lethal.

One day a fellow student backchatted me, and I pushed him from the dormitory steps, and he hurt himself. The matter was reported to the duty teacher, Mr Roberts, and I was sent to the headmaster's office and suspended for a week. I received the strict warning that when I returned, there was not to be any more trouble. I decided to go to Goldie River Recruit Training Depot to see my distant relative and guardian, Cpl Macklay Munog, and his wife, Jill. I explained that I was suspended and needed to stay with them for the week.

It was while at Goldie that I saw the recruits and soldiers marching and drilling, and this deepened my interest in becoming a soldier. I asked so many questions to Macklay, and he was also eager to see me in the military. However, given my education, he said it would be better to enter the army as an officer cadet and not as an ordinary soldier.

After my week's suspension, I reported back to Sogeri. Mr Gordon informed me, in no uncertain terms, that if I got into trouble again, he would not hesitate to dismiss me from the school. I took good notice of this warning and settled down to my studies until final exams and graduation.

A few of us at that time began to show interest in studying law. There was Nagora Bogan, now Sir Nagora; Gibuma Salika, now Chief Justice Salika; and Moses Koiri, now a private lawyer.

Mr Gordon took a keen interest in me as, despite my troublemaking, I had shown leadership qualities that the teachers and he took notice of. He suggested that I apply for entrance to the Royal Military Academy, Sandhurst, near London, in the hope of getting a government scholarship. Although this was an attractive possibility, the timing was problematic. The next year, being 1975, PNG was due to be granted independence from Australia, and it was not clear whether the newly independent government would be making such nominations in its first year.

Mr Gordon told me about a school programme commencing at the end of the year and informed me that I had been selected to go to Melbourne for a few weeks to attend Eltham College on exchange, sponsored by the Port Moresby Rotary Club. I was excited about the prospect of going to Australia during the Christmas break. That year,

Mr Gordon allowed me to learn to drive his red Isuzu sedan in return for washing his car at the dormitory most weekends for some pocket money. So while at Sogeri as a student, I was able to obtain my driver's licence. Years later, I realised that, although Mr Gordon was tough on me, he wanted me to be responsible as he could see potential in me.

In the final term, we filled out our study applications for university. Although I applied to read law, I still had the military in mind as my second choice. My mates convinced me that I could do both. A lawyer can still be an officer in the military, they said. I replied, 'Yes, that may be true, but a lawyer doesn't go to war or go on patrols. They spend their days in court defending the military.'

At the end of October, Sogeri played in the grand final rugby reserve grade against our arch-rival, Port Moresby Technical College. We won the final match. Instead of attending the rugby party at Koitaki Country Club on the outskirts of Sogeri Senior High School, I decided to go with Macklay and Jill to attend a family function at Goldie River Barracks. And just as well because some of my rugby league mates got involved in a drinking bout that led to one of them, my best mate Akwila Tokanene, assaulting the school administrator for which, not surprisingly, he was dismissed and sent home immediately. It was a good warning to me to stay out of trouble and concentrate on my studies.

About this time, the Papua New Guinea Defence Force recruiting team arrived at Sogeri to recruit pilot cadets, engineers, and general officer candidates. There were many in my group who turned up to the interview room in the maths laboratory. An Australian Army officer addressed us on career options in the military, and we were shown a recruiting film at the end of his speech. His presentation was very professional, and I was keen to enlist immediately without seeking my parents' consent. The recruitment officer was Maj. Raymond Paul Stevenson (Gunner). Much later, after enlistment, I found out that he was a highly decorated Australian Army veteran, that he had been a prisoner of war in Burma, and that he had seen service in the Korean, Japanese, and Vietnam wars. After he retired from the Australian Army in 1979, he rendered his services to the Department of Defence in the Audit Division before finally retiring and returning to Australia in 1985.

After the career briefing and presentation by Major Stevenson, we completed the application forms. I stated that I wanted to be a land element cadet, with maritime midshipman as my second choice and pilot cadet as my third choice. I left the interview room anxious.

In early November, just before graduation day, Malcolm Gordon called me into his office to chat about my future. While he agreed that the military was a good option, he advised me to obtain a law degree first and then switch to the military. He said that in my early twenties, after a law degree, I would still be young enough to do that. In the meantime, as he had confirmed earlier, I was selected along with three other Papua New Guinean students to go to Melbourne on a study tour for two weeks before university.

I invited Jill and Macklay to attend my graduation in the last week of November. It was such a moving occasion as we said goodbye to those leaving and those staying behind. As we were driven out the following day to the airport to return to our provinces, I realised that Sogeri had given me a real chance to make some important life choices. I had drunk and smoked a bit and had been occasionally militant in the school rallies, but I had also developed real leadership potential. Being a boarder at school for a total of six years, four at Asaroka and two at Sogeri, allowed me to appreciate the dynamics of school bonding and mateship.

I flew back to Madang and took a boat to Karkar Island for a few days. As always, my parents were delighted to see me. They had mixed emotions when I told them that I would be leaving for Port Moresby in two days' time for Australia. That night, I was tempted to tell Dad that I had applied to join the army, but I was fearful that he might report me to the patrol officer and have him take me off the list. Dad was quite sure that I should do law, and I knew he would have reservations about the army. So I kept quiet about that as a possibility.

I left all my belongings at home and departed once again for Port Moresby, where I went to Goldie River Barracks to see Macklay and Jill, who prepared me for my trip to Australia. At the end of the week, two other students and I boarded an Ansett flight for Melbourne. Joyce Webb, a senior teacher at Eltham College, was my sponsor. She was a lovely person. A widow, she took care of me for the next two weeks and assisted me in the programme.

My two weeks in Melbourne went fast, and it was coming up to the new year. I flew to Sydney to stay with an ex–Karkar High School teacher from Sydney, Roger Gilkes. We had a good time visiting sites in Sydney and enjoying invitations from friends before I returned to Port Moresby. After collecting my suitcase, I reported to the University of Papua New Guinea information desk to see the list of students arriving for university. My name was listed as a first-year law student.

I looked across to the other side of the lounge and saw a military officer in full uniform talking to new recruits who were arriving from other parts of PNG. I walked across the lounge and looked at the list of new recruit intake for 1/75. Sure enough, my name was on the list. I made up my mind there and then to enlist as a soldier in the PNGDF. It was Saturday, 4 January 1975.

CHAPTER 12

Army Career Beginnings, 1975–89

It was good fun commanding a division in the Iraq desert. It is good fun commanding a division anywhere. It is one of the four best commands in the Service—a platoon, a battalion, a division, and an army. A platoon, because it is your first command, because you are young, and because, if you are any good, you know the men in it better than their mothers do and love them as much. A battalion, because it is a unit with a life of its own; whether it is good or bad depends on you alone; you have at last a real command. A division, because it is the smallest formation that is a complete orchestra of war and the largest in which every man can know you. An army, because the creation of its spirit and its leadership in battle give you the greatest unity of emotional and intellectual experience that can befall a man.[3]

—Field Marshal Sir William Slim, 1956

---

[3] *Defeat into Victory* (London: Cassell). Sir William (Bill) Slim fought with the Anzacs at Gallipoli. He served with the Sixth and Seventh Gurkha Rifles in India before commanding the Tenth Infantry Division of the Indian Army in Iraq. He led the Fourteenth British Army in the Burma campaign against the Japanese, fighting them to a standstill in Burma. He was brought out of postwar retirement in Britain to serve as chief of the Imperial General Staff, 1949–52, before being appointed governor general of Australia (1953–59).

I was freshly graduated from high school. Back then, I knew relatively little about military history and virtually nothing of leading an army platoon, much less a regiment, an army, or an entire defence force. I had enjoyed my time in school cadets, finishing as a sergeant. I had been nominated to become senior cadet under officer in the Sogeri subunit of Thirty-Five School Cadets, though this was before the incoming government disestablished the battalion. But to a young 19-year-old, despite my experiences in cadets, the prospect of full-time life in the army, while exciting and challenging, was also daunting.

To me, as a brand-new recruit in the Papua New Guinea Defence Force, the officer at the career desk at Jacksons Airport looked impressive. He was dressed in starched and ironed jungle greens and was wearing black jungle boots spit-polished to a mirror finish. He was a graduate from the Australian Army Officer Cadet School in Portsea, Victoria. Smartly turned out, he impressed me with his military bearing as I loaded my luggage into the back of the Australian Army Holden utility. As we were driving off to Goldie River Training Depot, I learnt that his name was Lt Walter Salamas from New Ireland Province. As chance would have it, twenty-two years later, Salamas—by then a lieutenant colonel—served as my acting chief of operations when, as chief of the defence force, I launched Operation Rausim Kwik.

As I was being dropped at the recruit barracks lines that early January day in 1975, eight months before Papua New Guinea gained its independence, I found out that the selection of officer cadets for the Joint Services College (JSC) was under way and that the following day was the last day for interviews. I had arrived just in time.

There were many recruits arriving at Goldie River Training Depot that day, and a handful were my colleagues from Sogeri Senior High School. I was relieved to see that I would not be on my own after all. Arriving with me were Frank Wi, Michael Timbi, Vagi Oala, and Auda Bamaga. My classmate Alois Tom Ur was already there. As we were standing around talking, Cpl Liliak Lem from Karkar Island came up to me. 'Come with me. You need a haircut. Now.' Like many of my young school friends, I was still wearing my hair in an afro. Back then, American music, 'fros, and cigarette smoking were all the rage. The

Black Power movement in the United States was alive and flourishing in Moresby. If you were cool, you wore an afro. But not, said Corporal Lem, looking at me with distaste, in the army.

As I sat on the stool near the shower room, Corporal Lem hacked my outstanding afro down to nothing. I hardly had any hair left. It was a massacre. As I looked at myself in the mirror, I hardly recognised myself; it wasn't me. I was physically transformed. I complained to the corporal about my appearance. 'Better to have short hair than long,' he said as he packed up his scissors and comb. 'You don't want to be singled out on your first parade, sir.'

Joint Services College, 1975–76

The following day was Monday, 6 January. With my hair now regulation length, if not shorter, I was the last to be interviewed by the Officer Selection Committee headed by the commandant of the JSC, Lt Col. Des Mealey, Australian Army.

I passed the interview and enlisted after taking the oath of loyalty and allegiance. I was given my military service number (86506), took my medical examinations, and was issued my uniforms. Two days later, my officer cadet intake boarded an Australian Air Force Caribou and was flown to Lae to join the JSC. There, we would commence our two-year full commissioning course.

Arriving at Igam Barracks and having received no prior drill instruction, we were paraded in two ranks. Confronting us was our regimental sergeant major (RSM), a tough-looking tall Australian Army officer named Tilbrook. Looking us over with evident scorn, in a broad Australian accent, he said, 'I'm Tilbrook, the regimental sergeant major. God help us all. And remember, I don't have to like you. You don't have to like me. But you will call me sir. My job is to turn you lot into officers—those of you who survive, that is. And for now, I'll just say this. If you girls don't smarten yourselves up as officer cadets, you might as well go back to where you came from. Forget the army. Join the girl guides. Do I make myself clear?'

'Yes, sir.'

'I can't hear you!'

'Sir, yes, sir!' we chanted, louder this time.

'All right then. Parade dismissed.' And turning on his heels smartly, off he marched without a backwards glance. And that was our first experience of the parade ground. Clearly, the army was not interested in popularity. Efficiency and combat effectiveness was all that mattered.

I was intimidated by this first encounter—which no doubt was the aim. Tilbrook was a hard-looking soldier. He had a long pace-stick under his arm and was always pointing and shouting something at somebody, mainly cadets.

Darcy Tilbrook, I later discovered, was a career infantry soldier with 2RAR (Second Royal Australian Regiment). He was recruited from the small New South Wales town of Kempsey, where he had been working on the railways, and saw service as an infantryman in Malaya, Borneo, and Vietnam before finishing up in PNG as RSM at the JSC. He retired from the Australian Army in 1978 and went on to work as a court bailiff in Townsville for another seventeen years. His duties as RSM at the JSC in Lae included discipline, dress, drill parades, and dealing with offences and charge sheets.

We were each issued linen and more uniforms, a metal trunk to hold our gear, and a very high-quality brown briefcase. We were permitted to help one another move our items from the Q-store back to the barracks, where we were shown our respective lines. I was allocated to Finschhafen Line, named after the town of Finschhafen, some 80 km east of Lae on the Morobe Peninsula. It had been the scene of prolonged battles between Japanese and Australian forces over the period September to December 1943. It was there that Australian and American forces turned the tide against the Japanese.

In those early days at Igam Barracks, one of our biggest difficulties was learning how to starch and iron our uniforms. These comprised juniper green shorts and shirts and jungle green uniforms. Getting access to sufficient quantities of starch and an electric iron was essential as a good part of our frequent individual assessments were based on smartness and personal cleanliness. It was absolutely mandatory to have stiff, clean, and smartly ironed uniforms every day of the week.

As junior cadets at JSC, there was a great deal of physical hardship, with early morning runs, physical training, and plenty of foot and arms drills. I was among over 200 or so officer cadets, and there was so much screaming and barking of instructions from the moment you woke up until you turned into bed that your head spun until you dropped off into a deep sleep. The daily programme was intensive, and there was never any spare time. Worse still, we had senior cadets who hounded us juniors like small warlords and who exercised influence over their subordinate cadets with patronage and a considerable degree of obsession. I just took one day at a time, and this became my motto in life: 'Take it as it comes.'

There were endless briefs on dos and don'ts and college regulations that were read out to us and then provided in handbooks that we were required to study. We were confined to the barracks for the first three months and not allowed to go to Lae City. On Saturdays, we were required to work in the college farm, digging a fish pond or planting vegetables under the guidance of our instructor, Lt John Gabigabi from Central Province. After Saturday work parties, we had the afternoon off. This was when we would wash and starch our uniforms, polish our boots, and clean and polish the tiled floors of our rooms.

Our boots had to be spit-polished by rubbing cotton buds on black Kiwi boot polish and making many circles on the black leather. We were assessed on the quality of our polished boots and the starched greens that we wore. There were no discussions on haircuts. Hair was worn short, and I mean *very* short. Our seniors would come around and attempt to pull out our hair if it was long, and then it was either a haircut or punishment time or both.

I was in class 1/75 of a mixed group of seventy or so police, correctional, and military cadets from both the land and maritime elements. In my class, we quickly got ourselves into a closely knit group that shared jokes and told stories and sometimes got into mischief, but it was all part of learning.

JSC ran a father-and-son system whereby senior cadets were allocated junior cadets to take care of. If there were any breaches of regulations, the 'father' would be punished by doing extra drills. The more mistakes made by a junior cadet ('son'), the more the father would be punished. My father was Correctional Officer Cadet Maru. He played his part in providing guidance, and I tried my very best to avoid small breaches of the JSC regulations. I was relieved that, after one month, he had not been punished for my mistakes.

The senior cadets in the graduating class were seen as the untouchables. Our leading officer cadet, the battalion sergeant major (BSM), was John Miria from Yule Island in Central Province. To many of us, he was the ideal role model. Always impeccably turned out, he demonstrated what the college demanded from us. Not only was he effective as a disciplinarian but he also provided high levels of leadership, particularly on the parade ground and in his after-hours bearing. His example motivated me to work harder to achieve good results and to be an effective officer once I graduated.

As a junior cadet at JSC, I was an active member of our rugby league team. I had played at Sogeri, mainly as a second rower, and I enjoyed the game. In our junior class, John Wagambie, a police officer cadet, was captain; later, he rose to head the Kumul national rugby league team that defeated *les Chanticleers*, the French national team. Our team remained unbeaten in the reserve grade in the Lae City competition. Vagi Oala and I had played at Sogeri, and we continued to play in the college rugby league town competition. Later, Vagi Oala played for the PNGDF team in Port Moresby, where he was known as the 'human bullet' for his daring mid-air tackles, leaping from the ground to tackle his opponents.

JSC was the ideal institution to bring all the disciplined forces together. Police and Correctional services were required to commence their officer cadet training at JSC on a common syllabus in the first year. The subjects studied were drill, field craft and minor tactics, weapons training, leadership, and land navigation. After this initial year, they passed out to their respective service colleges at Bomana, a few kilometres out of Port Moresby. There were two intakes per year, in January and again in June, and this had been the pattern since the inception of JSC in 1974.

The police officer cadets in my intake were a mixed group headed by Lua Vanua. He had worked as a bank teller before enlisting. He was bright and tall (just under 6 feet or around 180 cm) and was outspoken in the pack. With his height, Lua was always the right marker of our class on parade; sometimes he used his height to dominate the other cadets, some of whom feared him.

The other police cadets in my class were Willie Embrose, John Bonot, John Wakon, Francis Ali, Augustine Guau, Edward Kinamun, Bartley Yarume, Harry Rakara, Mark Yangin, and Peter Manga. The correction services cadets were Henry Wavik, Richard Sikani, Gimana, and Oma.

The attrition rate in the college was very high. As we went through quarterly boards of studies, cadets were regularly removed for lack of academic or core subject achievement. They would be posted out of the college, either back to Civvy Street or, for some, as regular soldiers in the security forces. Many opted to go back to university to further their tertiary studies.

Towards the end of the first year, my intake had been reduced to just under thirty people or a little less than half our starting out number. The standard of instruction was excellent. Most of our instructors were from the Australian Army, and many of them, both officers and senior weapons and field craft instructors, were ex-Vietnam veterans with substantial real-life experiences to draw on. We had only two national instructors, Capt. Bill Kavanmur and Capt. Gordon Copper. Their inclusion as instructors motivated us to work harder.

In June 1975, the senior class—led by BSM John Miria—graduated, giving us junior cadets a goal to achieve ourselves in eighteen months' time. The graduating class was Second Lieutenants John Miria, Joseph Mocke, John Navi, Ben Norie, Duga Saira, Bob Yonomiho, and Elias Kamara. The maritime cadets, graduating as midshipmen, were Mathew Efi, Juda Yasi, and Tuain.

The following year, now as a senior officer cadet, I was determined to do even better than in my first year. My girlfriend, Dupain, was no longer at Lae School of Nursing as she had graduated and transferred to Madang General Hospital, so I was able to get my head down and concentrate on my studies.

In June 1976, the year after independence, the first Papua New Guinean national commandant was appointed. This was Lt Col. Anthony Huai. He replaced the Australian commandant who had recruited me, Lt Col. Des Mealey. Tony Huai was an up-and-coming officer in the PNGDF. He had graduated at Portsea in June 1969 and gone back there as an instructor in 1973. It was a significant change. Lt Col. Des Mealey was the last Australian Defence Force commandant at JSC.

The next graduation was in June 1976. The 2/74 graduating class were Second Lieutenants Francis Agwi, John Kinivi, Tenny Pakawa, James Taureko, Samson Masuin, Romano Yangomina, Raphael Keto, Daniel Patoi Mitau, Paul Vuluamat, Bill Daniel, Peter Dringo, Miri Osi, Peter Sudan, and Ernest Aki. From the maritime element were Kim Soso and Immanuel Gabu. The police officer cadets who continued police officer training at Bomana Police College from that intake and graduated as sub-inspectors were Peter Aigilo, Gari Baki, Joseph Kupo, and Samson Inguba. Years later, all the police officer cadets from that intake were appointed police commissioner in succession—a feat that will surely never be repeated.

After their graduation, my class, 1/75, became the senior class. We resumed training for the last six months of an intensive tactics syllabus while continuing with our main academic subjects of mathematics, science, English, and geography.

Senior Officer Cadet Alois Tom Ur was appointed BSM, and the cadet under officer was Aba Bina. I was given a platoon sergeant portfolio. This was not as demanding as the two other appointments as I was merely responsible for my platoon, Finschhafen Platoon.

I ensured that the platoon areas of responsibility were clearly designated and that troops were assigned to them. Every morning our toilets had to be cleaned—no wet floors, and all toilets had to be flushed and scrubbed. Our rooms also had to be put into inspection order according to standard operating procedures (SOPs). I exercised a very basic level of leadership and had three section commanders working with me. We worked as a team to conform to the higher authorities' demands and expectations.

In October, a few of us senior cadets involved in the motorbike club took an ambitious motorbike trail trek from Lae to Madang, a round trip of some 670 km. Our team leader was Bonnie Tanikerei. I rode a Suzuki 200, Bonnie was on a Honda 450, and Philip Gasuat and drill instructor Sgt Tony Wupu were both on Honda 100s.

We returned to JSC the following day. The return trip was faster as we knew where the bends in the trail were and what rivers we needed to cross. When we arrived back, there appeared to be an unusual silence. We soon learnt that, during our absence, two colleagues from the motorbike club, Joseph Marum and Silas Kehari, had had a terrible accident. They were riding back from Lae to the college when they crashed into an oncoming Volkswagen. Their injuries were terrible, and Joe Marum, whose right hand was ripped off, died. Silas Kehari was seriously injured and bedridden at Angau Hospital for a very long time.

Apparently, Joseph Marum had decided to stay at the college and assist with the dance that was organised for the Friday evening that we departed for Madang. All this was a great shock to me as I was a close friend of Joe Marum. He had played rugby with me, and I had taken him to Karkar Island the previous Christmas. His death was a loss to his family, his friends, and the defence force as, no doubt, he would have graduated with the rest of us.

A few days later, the land element cadets went to Bulolo for our final practical exams. These are known as TEWTs (tactical exercise without troops). In November, the final exercise for the graduating class was held at the Buso River area east of Lae. Upon our return from this exercise, the senior instructor from the Australian Army, Maj. John Dwyer, informed me that I had achieved excellent grades, passing all my practical and academic exams and coming in the top three of the class. He assured me that I would graduate. I was delighted and encouraged by this. My class filled out our application forms and placed our preferences for postings. Mine was to be an infantry platoon commander. I had my eyes on Second Battalion, located at Moem Barracks, Wewak, East Sepik Province.

The first week of December 1976 was very busy, with parade rehearsals for graduation on 17 December. Eighteen of us from an initial class of over 100 were to graduate as second lieutenants. The five maritime cadets who graduated were Sub Lieutenants (navy) Alois Tom Ur, Max Sundei (Aleale), John Selau Yanis, Klark Konigala, and Nason Moat. The land element cadets who graduated as second lieutenants apart from me were Tony Jamea, Sam Ifid, Vincent Tadigu, Eki Nalau, Jarry Jaribanu, Aba Bina, David Pote, Bonnie Tanikerei, Vagi Oala, Michael Tamalanga, Albert (Seah) Rolman, and John Yawa. Silas Kehari was 'back squatted' (held back) due to injuries sustained in October.

Regimental Duties, 1977–81

My official regimental assignment commenced on 5 January 1977, when I departed on Air Niugini from Madang for Wewak after spending some time with my parents on Karkar Island. With an army career laid out in front of me, I was anxious and very excited about the prospect of becoming a member of the regiment.

Second Pacific Islands Regiment (2PIR, later 2RPIR) was raised in 1965 at Cape Moem, a few kilometres out of Boram Airport and Wewak Township. The drive from the airport to the barracks is very scenic. A long stretch of road runs alongside a white sandy beach from Boram Airport before arriving at a prominent landmark. This is a big bend they call Petrus Point. Then it's a 2 km drive among green foliage and coconut plantations before approaching the main gate. The driver pressed a single horn to signify the presence of a commissioned officer in the vehicle below the rank of major. As I looked on, one soldier on duty raised the security bar while the other saluted me and shouted, 'Pass through, sir!' He was carrying a self-loading rifle (SLR). These were my first impressions of the very distinguished and highly disciplined infantry regiment where I would remain and serve for the next four and half years.

The aura and the pride of being in such a regiment needs to be experienced to be fully understood. All things appeared so orderly and precise in their execution. The bugle sounded every hour on the hour until the last post was sounded. This was my introduction to the 2PIR, as it was known until 1984, when it was granted the Royal prerogative.

2PIR was based around a battalion-sized infantry unit, plus headquarter elements. The battalion was well kept and managed and very ably led by our commanding officer, Lt Col. Tom Tau Naona from Central Province. He had graduated from Portsea in 1966. In 1974, he took over command from the last of the Australian commanders, army lieutenant colonel Mike Jeffery, a very distinguished officer who had served in Malaya and Vietnam, where he was awarded a Military Cross. Mike Jeffery served as commander of Second Battalion, 2PIR from 1974 to 1975. On his return to Australia, Jeffery assumed command of the Australian Special Air Service Regiment in Western Australia (1976–77) before being promoted to major general and deputy chief of general staff. On his retirement from the army, he was appointed governor general of Western Australia. In 2003, he was appointed Australia's twenty-fourth governor general, serving in that role until 2008. He was the first Australian infantry officer to receive such a distinction.

I was shown to my room on the top southern side of the officers' mess and settled down quickly as I was informed that I should report to the adjutant the following morning at 0830 hours. That night, I was joined by three other officers in my intake, Sam Ifid, Jarry Jaribanu, and Seah Rolman. I spit-polished[4] my boots from college, which were still in superb condition, and pressed my juniper shirt and shorts, both starched and very stiff. I polished my black leather belt, and by midnight, I turned into bed. I was content that, the next day, I would be a member of a very elite infantry regiment.

At 0815 hours, I reported to 2nd Lt Bill Daniel, who was a year senior to me and now assistant adjutant at battalion headquarters (BHQ). He

---

4   Readers who have not had the advantage of a proper military education and who want to learn how to spit-polish their boots or shoes to a mirror shine should check out YouTube. When I last looked, there were at least four instructional videos guaranteed to make your adjutant, drill instructor, and mum very proud indeed.

checked my dress and my personal file. Happy with my turnout, he said that CO Tom Naona would speak to me. Daniel took me upstairs to the adjutant, Kapinias Toumong (who would later change his name to Carl Marlpo). I was uneasy in the adjutant's office and stood rigid for a while. Marlpo instructed me that he would march me into the CO's office. I was to remain at attention unless the CO told me otherwise. When the CO was ready, I was marched inside in quick time and commanded to stand at attention as if I was in trouble. I was mortified to think that the regiment could hear the bellowing of commands by the adjutant and assume that there was a problem with me already.

The CO was a gentle but focused senior officer who called me Singi. He reminded me of my responsibilities as a platoon commander and the need to look after my men. He reiterated the importance of leading and posted me to Four Platoon, B Company. He wished me well in my junior leadership role.

At the BHQ, the staff officers were busy. The operations and training officer was Maj. Phil Joyce from the Australian Army. Joyce was a Vietnam veteran and former platoon commander with First Battalion and Recruit Company who had mastered pidgin as his medium for communicating with soldiers. He was very well respected. The battalion intelligence officer (IO) was Lt Bernard Maris from New Ireland. As mentioned, the adjutant was Lt Carl Marlpo, and his assistant was 2nd Lt Bill Daniel. The battalion second in command (2IC) was a tall, sharp-looking, and well-built major from Bougainville, Peter Anisis, and the RSM was Paul Kuia. As he was missing a finger, his nickname was Nine Finger among the soldiers.

It was a full day of introductions when I reported to B Company. Our company 2IC was Lt Elias Kamara from East New Britain. My platoon sergeant, Iru Yandua, was from Southern Highlands; and my three section commanders were Charles Poseliau, Peter Grangory, and Henry Tanga. They were all experienced soldiers and made my job easy from the start. Another of my graduate mates, 2nd Lt Sam Ifid, was also posted with me to B Company. He commanded Five Platoon, and an in-service officer, Lt Willie Wagera, was posted to Six Platoon.

As I settled into the battalion routine, there was always something happening. Troops were on deployment for border duties, companies were off for weeks of training exercises outside the barracks, and troops undertook civil action programmes.

The battalion also hosted fifteen surveyors from Australian Eight Field Survey Squadron, a part of the Royal Australian Survey Corps, whose motto was *Videre parare est* (To see is to prepare). They added to the battalion's strength and were involved, along with other survey sections elsewhere in the country, in the production of detailed maps of the PNG interior and coastline. Maj. Patrick Wood led Eight Field Survey. Squadron members resided at the officers' married quarters, with single men living in quarters just off the Cape Moem Golf Course.

This golf course was very well kept and a centre of attraction, bringing in visitors from far and near. Along with the regiment's other sporting complexes, such as the gymnasium, squash court, and swimming pool, it was the pride of the regiment. In addition, the Australian Rules, rugby, and soccer ovals attracted local teams and brought much community spirit to the base.

The regiment celebrated its birthday in March. After the celebrations, my platoon was deployed to the Angoram area where the country's first prime minister, Sir Michael Somare, came from. My mission was to construct a series of timber bridges from Ariapan to Waskurin, Kis, and Kaup Villages along a timber track. This was part of a government plan to construct a proper road through the area to accompany the planting of a large rubber estate at Gavien. Sir Michael came from the Murik Lakes at Karau Village, not far from our civic action site.

A section of pioneers attached to my platoon was led by Sgt Herman Chouka from Manus Province. He was a capable and very experienced soldier, and I relied on him for technical advice for the bridge and culvert construction. During this period, I learnt how to use explosives, including P4 primer and a detonator cord. While the thought of transferring to a pioneer platoon was tempting, I decided to remain an infantry officer as working with men was still my desire. Besides, as an infantry officer, there were many opportunities to go on patrols and training rather than becoming too specialised.

The civic action patrol was for three weeks, and we constructed five bridges, each of which were over nine metres in length. Towards the end of the civic action patrol, I got word that Prime Minister Somare would visit us with the battalion 2IC, Maj. Peter Anisis.

Prime Minister Somare arrived with a long convoy of vehicles, and I was introduced to him for the first time. In pidgin English, he asked me, 'Yanpela, yu bilong weah?' (Young man, where are you from?)

I replied, 'Karkar Island and part Sepik.'

'I know your parents,' he said. 'Your mother is from Yangoru, and your father was the president of Takia Local Government Council, Karkar Island. I also met them when I was teaching at Namau Primary School.'

It was a rare opportunity for a very junior officer to meet and speak to the prime minister. I would maintain a personal relationship with Sir Michael Somare until his passing on 26 February 2021.

First Border Patrol, 1977

After we returned to the barracks, I was detached to Support Company, the largest of the battalion's companies, which was stationed in Vanimo. I took my detachment orders and flew to Vanimo in Sandaun Province across the border from the Indonesian city of Jayapura.

I was informed that an urgent patrol had to be conducted in the Skotiaho area in Bewani District for three weeks. It was standard operating procedure that all patrols conducted along or near the international border must be commanded by a commissioned officer. I took my first steps into Bewani District from the end of the road at Kilipau. This was my first patrol, and I was determined to answer as many of the questions that the battalion's IO, Lt Ben Marris, had given me as possible.

Preparing for a border patrol as the patrol commander was very demanding. A comprehensive patrol preparation and checklist had to be followed. Items on the checklist included dress and equipment, ammunition and explosives, weapons, PNG flag, ropes, medical kit, marker panels, high-frequency radio and spare batteries, border SOPs, entrenching tools, machetes, an axe, spare uniforms and fresh socks, foot powder, shaving razors, and spare shaving blades.

Each soldier was issued a British-manufactured L1A1 SLR with three full magazines. The calibre was 7.62 × 51.00 mm, which is the standard NATO round. The SLR had an effective firing range of 800 metres and weighed 4.337 kg empty. The gunners carried a light machine gun, commonly known as the Bren gun, which weighed 6.58 kg and fired a standard NATO 5.56 × 45.00 mm round. With a full F1 patrol pack, the gross weight a soldier would carry into the field would be about 50 kg. Before the patrol, many of us would break open the ration packs and carry only the most essential food, leaving the rest behind. Many of us would exchange our rations with locals for food and vegetables. An item in high demand among the locals was a can opener. Many soldiers told of how they could bargain and trade with can openers, even to the extent of exchanging ten can openers for a village chicken. Before the actual patrol, the soldiers paraded, and their equipment was physically inspected. These were the SOPs that I instigated and enforced from the day I joined my platoon.

On the second week into our patrol, after receiving a resupply by helicopter and a brief visit by our officer commanding (OC), Maj. Mino Taeni, I made an error by ordering the troops to make their own way back to Skotiaho Village. It was nearly dark. I was with the last lot of troops, and by last light, I had lost control of the platoon. Only one lot arrived back; the rest, split into small groups, spent a miserable night in an unknown forest infested with huge mosquitoes. For my troops, it was a night without their leader along the international land border.

There were eight soldiers in my group. The next day, we followed a riverbed down to the main track junction that led to the Bewani government station. I was relieved to see most of my men at the station. They were eagerly waiting for our return, but I had my tail between my legs as I recognised that I had not been sufficiently clear in directing my troops. I explained the incident in my written debrief, much to the amusement of the operations officer, Maj. Philip Joyce, who was happy to treat it as a much-needed lesson from which I would most certainly learn.

One month later, I took another patrol into the Iau Kono area north of Bewani where we tracked and located over thirty refugees from Indonesia who had escaped from the harassment of Indonesian troops And came to the Papua New Guinean side of the border, seeking safe haven, shelter, and food. They were malnourished, and many of them had ulcers and were in urgent need of medical assistance and proper nutrition. I sent an urgent encrypted message to Support Company HQ. They instructed us to remain in contact with the refugees until a medical team was sent in. We spent the next three days with the refugees, assuring them that a medical team with government officials was on its way. After briefing the medical team, I withdrew the patrol to Bewani before we were extracted by trucks back to Vanimo.

After a few days' rest, I reported back to B Company at Wewak. Next, my platoon was attached to D Company for three weeks' training in close jungle warfare at Goldie River under revised tactics introduced by the Australian Army following lessons learnt in Vietnam. Our company commander was Maj. Mineva Pohonu, a Portsea graduate and very professional officer who had his finger on the pulse during training.

After two weeks of training, we were given a weekend to rest. On the Friday after a debrief with my platoon, I accompanied fellow officers to the command officers' mess at HQ Murray Barracks. After what turned out to be too many drinks, I accompanied Officer Cadet Ted Braun and Warrant Officer Roson Bateng, both from Madang, to the University of Papua New Guinea. On our return trip, Ted Braun drove so fast under the influence of liquor that we crashed into a signpost along Waigani Drive near Boroko Motors. Careening off the signpost, we carried on and plunged into a nearby creek. The accident resulted in Ted Braun having a fractured skull while Roson Bateng, who was an outstanding physical instructor, suffered a broken limb and dislocated hips. I had internal bleeding in my chest. We all ended up in hospital, with Bateng being the worst out of the lot of us.

I was discharged a week later from military hospital at Taurama Barracks and rejoined my platoon at Goldie River Barracks. Major

Pohonou was not impressed when I reported to him. As expected, he grounded me until we returned to Moem Barracks.

In October 1977, B Company—now under a new company commander, Capt. Bill Kavanamur, former instructor at JSC—was deployed back to Vanimo to relieve A Company. I looked forward to another border tour as my first two patrols had given me good experience in patrol planning and conduct.

Our resupply procedures back then were pretty old-fashioned. We would prepare a clearing with bright marker panels, and a DC-3 would approach after detecting the panels. We would then throw a smoke grenade to confirm our position, and loadmasters would push out our resupply with a parachute strapped to it. If the chute opened, well and good—that meant minimal damage to our resupply. However, sometimes the chutes did not open, and rations would be scattered and damaged. At one resupply, the parachute was trapped on the branch of a large tree. Our poor soldiers spent hours chopping the tree down to recover the rations and other supplies. Sometimes if the dispatchers were kind, they would include cigarettes, tobacco, or even smoked fish in the resupply packages. The most disheartening part of aerial resupply was the need to carry the heavy parachute canopy with us for the remaining period of the patrol. However, many of us subalterns found ways of relieving our troops. We would hire local porters with C rations and small amounts of cash and send them early to our extraction point, normally a small airstrip like Amanab, Imonda, or Green River. We never ran out of volunteers, and it was good public relations (PR) for us to be able to provide a little casual employment for the locals.

During this period, my platoon was dispatched to Imonda in the Green River area. After some days on patrol, I was struck down by pneumonia and malaria and had to be carried out by stretcher, a two-day journey from Iafar Village, before being medevacked to Moem Barracks. I was bundled into a small Cessna aircraft with our regimental medical officer, Captain Bailey from the Australian Army, on board. I was so sick and drugged that I remember nothing of the convulsions I went through from the fever and little of the flight.

Angoram Survival Training, January 1978

Our training was intensified with the introduction of jungle fighting based on lessons learnt in Vietnam. Subsequently, survival training came to be regarded as an important component of the training objective. Maj. Phil Joyce, in his role as our training officer, established a training cell at the Gavien rubber plantation, a few kilometres from Angoram in an area that I was familiar with as I had commanded a civic action platoon there the year before. The Gavien rubber estate was a government-run farming project. Farmers planted rubber, which they sold to a centrally located factory for processing.

The survival training centre was well thought out. Companies came through the centre for two weeks at a time for both theory and practical training. The whole regiment went through the training in company lots. My company participated in January 1978. The idea was to teach and train us in jungle survival. While many of us, including myself, came from a jungle and rural background, the training was still exciting and relevant. Major Joyce demonstrated how to catch snakes and cook them, how to fish and make traps for wild animals, and which plants were edible and which could be used for medicine. Theory lessons occupied three days, and the final four days comprised a survival exercise based on escape and evasion. We were the escapees, and a platoon from another company along with military police was to look for us. Our goal was to evade capture and survive in the jungle before reaching a secret rendezvous point where we would be picked up.

We were broken into five teams of escapees. Other ranks were paired off into teams of five while groups of three were established for commissioned officers. My group consisted of 2nd Lt Bill Daniel and Lt Willie Wagera. We were blindfolded and taken along the Gavien Road towards Ariapan Village before being dropped off at night on an isolated stretch of road. That night, we hid in a hut in an overgrown garden, drenched by torrential rain and tormented by mosquitoes. The mighty Sepik River was only a few kilometres to our west, and the high number of ponds and creeks made it a perfect breeding place for mosquitoes. Mosquitoes are a real menace in the Sepik Plains; it can take a broom to brush them from you. In addition, we were only too conscious that the area was massively infested with crocodiles.

With sleep impossible, we sat the whole night telling stories and waiting impatiently for dawn. When daybreak finally arrived, we snuck out to the main road to orientate ourselves and then darted back into the forest, avoiding unsuspecting civilians. Using a small blunt bush knife, we made a hut and built a fire. We split a cane, took the fibre out, and rubbed the soft, dry wood together (a million times!) until it caught alight. The fire was mainly to keep the mosquitoes away as, even in the daylight, they were fierce and merciless. Seriously hungry and miserable, we started using our survival training. The first things we found were jungle ferns and mushrooms. Then we made an important discovery. Near our makeshift camp was a creek in which the villagers had chopped a sago palm to make sago. The end of the palm was still intact but was rotting. Fortunately, Wagera was from Western Province where sago is their staple diet, so he commenced chopping open the trunk to get at the fibre. While Daniel and I took turns on sentry duty, Wagera got stuck into the trunk, which gave us plenty of food.

We collected banana leaves, stole an unripe banana from a garden, and put ferns and mushrooms into the banana leaves with the sago and made a big fire. This was completely contrary to our training, but we took the gamble. Within thirty minutes, our tropical jungle food was cooked. Wagera then cooked more food on the charcoal, adding to the taste and reigniting our hunger.

After putting out the fire, we relocated to eat our meal for the day. We knew that Major Joyce had spoken to the villagers about the exercise and, as part of his PR, had given out C rations to villagers and asked them to report any sightings of escapees to the mobile patrols that were on the beat.

Thinking that we might have been compromised—having made a fire, stolen a banana, and hacked open a sago trunk—and rather than risk being caught and spending a few miserable days and nights in a military jungle cell with no shelter, toilet, or other amenities, we decided to go to Angoram where Daniel's cousin sister lived. We used all the special training and techniques we had learnt to get close to

Angoram Town. It took most of the afternoon to reach the compound of Daniel's relative. We waited until nightfall for Daniel to make his move while Wagera and I covered him. He was away for a long time—it felt like forever as we were still fighting off mosquitoes. Finally and much to our relief, he returned laden with water, a potful of rice and tinned fish, and a large used, partly torn mosquito net.

When we finished our dinner, I recalled that 2nd Lt John Kinivi Bishop—who had been my senior at JSC and a classmate of Daniel's—was in Angoram as he had applied for leave to be best man at my wedding the following month. I proposed that we track him down. Daniel and Wagera agreed that we should go into town, freshen up, maybe have some beers, and enjoy ourselves. We thought Bishop would be at the Biwat camp along the Sepik River and so headed there once night fell. However, we soon learnt that Bishop had gone to Angoram Tavern to play pool and watch videos. Yes! With thoughts of cold beer filling in our heads, we raced up the small knoll to the back of the hotel; and sure enough, Bishop was there. In his excitement, he called out to us, blowing our cover. Soon after our first sips of cold beer, we turned around to see soldiers in uniform at the front door with their SLRs trained on us. We ducked through the back, ran straight into a crocodile pond, struggled out, and ran towards our preselected location. This time, it was every man for himself.

Daniel and Wagera disappeared into the darkness, but I was surrounded under a house not far from the tavern. Five soldiers manhandled me, dropped me to the ground, fastened my arms with a toggle rope, and shoved me into the back of a military police (MP) vehicle. For the soldiers, there was the promise of a reward for catching a commissioned officer. It was a big bounty. Or so they thought. Then their team leader started interrogating me. He asked where the other two officers were and where our hiding place was. I said, 'Go to Biwat compound along the Sepik River.'

They started the Land Rover and drove a few metres to the Sepik River. Three of the soldiers doubled down to the river, while the driver kept the vehicle running, and the MP sat smoking. Escape was on my mind. I had to escape.

I was a smoker back then, so I asked the MP for a cigarette. I realised that he was unarmed and had only a baton. The weapon was in the front seat close to the driver. Little did the MP know that I had managed to undo the toggle rope in the dark. My heart was racing because the soldiers could return at any minute. I had to make my move. The MP got out of the vehicle and placed a cigarette in my mouth. As he lit the match and with the light between him and me, I kneed him hard in the belly. He fell to the ground, winded, and his face smacked into the dirt. I ran into the darkness across the field to the market side of Angoram. I was very fit, being just out from college and having played rugby in the regiment-town competition. And I was B Company's sports officer. The MP was no match for my fitness and determination. From my hiding spot and with the town asleep, I watched as the MP and soldiers drove away without their prize.

Eventually, I made my way back to the other end of the small town. Following a path to our hide, I saw two lots of long grass lying criss-cross, telling me that both Daniel and Wagera were back in our hiding place. I arrived unannounced, and they both sat up with surprise. They had been worried stiff at my capture. I was bruised from the knocks and kicks I got from the MP and soldiers, but otherwise, I was fine. It was a close shave. But my colleagues teased me and said it was my idea that led to us being compromised and me being captured. I accepted the blame. After another night of high drama and mosquito bites, we made our way, undetected, to the rendezvous point where we were to be picked up as the exercise was ending that day.

The same MP I had kicked was in the troop-carrying vehicle that came to pick us up. He was not impressed when he spotted me. Pointing to his badly swollen lips, he said he would lay formal charges against me for assault. However, such talk was soon dropped as it was all in the spirit of training and comradeship. And I think a drink or two and a laugh in the mess afterwards may have helped. But I did owe him a cigarette.

Marriage

We arrived back from Angoram in late January 1978. Dupain Damun, my fiancée, had transferred to Wewak Boram General Hospital from Madang General Hospital. We planned to get married on 18 February 1978, and I applied to take February off in preparation.

As was customary, I wrote to our new CO, Lt Col. Lima Dotaona, for permission to marry. This was granted. Maj. Joshua Mule was to be our master of ceremony, Lt James Pokasui the coordinator, and 2nd Lt John Bishop my best man. Both my parents and Dupain's mother came to the wedding, which took place at the chapel at Moem Barracks. Our celebrant was Chaplain David Piso. After seven years, Dupain—my high school sweetheart—and I finally tied the knot. The reception was organised by the regimental caterer, Warrant Officer Arnfried Brendecke from the Australian Army, who was married to Helen, a mixed race Papuan woman from Hula. The reception was held at the Sergeants Beach at Moem Barracks. It was well attended, and there was plenty to eat and drink. The setting was beautiful, and we had a lovely day before retiring back to our quarters.

Resuming normal life, Dupain continued her work at the hospital while I was fully engaged in regimental duties as a junior officer. There was a lot of work in the regiment at that time. The security situation along the PNG-Indonesian border was very unsettled, and this meant that we had to spend many weeks and months on border patrol protecting PNG sovereignty and acting as a deterrent to both Indonesians and Papuan rebels from the Organisasi Papua Merdeka (OPM), the Free Papua Movement.

As mentioned, it was a requirement that all border patrols within 5 km of the international border be commanded by a commissioned officer. As many junior officers of my seniority as possible were needed for these patrols. Unfortunately, there were too few available, and I had to stand in for numerous patrols, including on detachment from my company to others who were on border duties in West Sepik Province, where the regiment had an outstation post sufficient to hold a company strength.

The following month, B Company deployed back to the border, and the year was very busy as Indonesian soldiers were once again on the offensive against OPM rebels. By now, we had settled into Vanimo Camp, though without Sam Ifid, who had been posted to Infantry Wing at Goldie. We were joined by another two platoon commanders, 2nd Lt Ted Braun, posted to Five Platoon, and 2nd Lt Jacob Pawia, posted to Six Platoon.

Halfway through our tour, another round of major clashes were reported between Indonesian troops and the OPM. In response, headquarters ordered that the battalion be deployed from Vanimo to Green River and along specific pockets of the border at Imonda. The higher command deployed the whole regiment, meaning that a battalion tactical headquarters under the CO Lt Col. Lima Dotaona was deployed. He set up his forward tactical headquarters at Vanimo Army Barracks. We were further reinforced by A Company First Regiment from Port Moresby under the command of Maj. Thomas Niaga. This operation was code-named Operation Rausim Kwik 1.

The regiment extended its area of operations from Vanimo to Green River and made a series of arrests after cordon and search operations. B Company was dispatched to Imonda and concentrated at Kembaratoro and Wasengla Catholic mission stations where there were reports of incursions by Indonesian troops searching for OPM rebels. My colleague 2nd Lt Seah Rolman of D Company led a patrol right along the border, gathering evidence of Indonesian incursions by retrieving empty packets of rice, canned meat, and fish, as well as empty ammunition shell cases. These finds were critical as they were used later in Port Moresby during talks aimed at building dialogue and understanding between Indonesia and PNG.

After my return from the field, I was posted as assistant adjutant to BHQ at Wewak. Among other responsibilities such as bookkeeping, I was in charge of the unit piggery. I was required to conduct a weekly stocktake of pigs and ducks and provide for their feeding. This did not go down all that well with me as I felt I was trained to look after men, not pigs and ducks. But in the end, the additional responsibilities were rewarding as the regiment sold the pigs for additional funds to support sports and other activities.

1979–80

After a short stint as assistant adjutant, I was relieved when I was posted back to Support Company as 2IC of Mortar Platoon as mortar line officer. My Mortar Platoon commander was Capt. Joseph Pais from Bougainville. He did not remain long with Mortar Platoon as he was soon posted to command D Company on promotion and later posted to Port Moresby. Ironically, Joseph Pais would go on to join the Bougainville Revolutionary Army in 1989 and would be on our wanted list until the peace process that followed the Sandline crisis in 1997.

I was excited by my posting, knowing that I would learn how to handle all aspects of fire control and the use of mortar bombs. The regiment was using old F1 81 mm mortars. Within weeks, I taught myself plotting board procedure, firing tables, and adjusting and controlling elevation on the mortar bipods. Mortar Platoon also had responsibility for manning the battalion's medium machine guns or GPMG (general-purpose machine gun) M60s, a crew-served weapon effective out to 1,200 yards. This gave me a greater chance to handle machine guns, and I became competent in their operation, including their effective deployment, along with mortars during a defensive role play exercise protecting battalion tactical headquarters.

In mid-August 1979, 2nd Lt Michael Tamalanga and I were selected to attend a Mortar Platoon commander's course at Singleton, New South Wales, Australia. The course was held over six weeks. We learnt everything about mortars—from the mortars themselves to the C2 sights and command post operations, finishing off with a series of live field firing exercises.

Most weekends, we would pool our resources, catch a bus to Newcastle, rent a room for five, and go pub crawling until all our money was gone; then we would sneak back to our room to sleep before getting the last bus to Singleton on the Sunday evening. One time, I was lucky to get a trip to Sydney to meet Phil Joyce's brother, Geoff, who showed me around Sydney with his family who were on a business trip.

After I returned to PNG, I was promoted to full lieutenant and went about reorganising Mortar Platoon with my newly acquired skills. The command post procedures had to be brushed up as the Australian Army was computerising command procedures, and scales for the firing tables were being changed due to significant modifications in motor bomb manufacturing.

In 1980, I was promoted to the rank of captain and posted as adjutant of the regiment. I replaced Capt. Puri Idau, who was posted back to Port Moresby. The job was demanding as it required attending to personnel administration, as well as handling disciplinary and ceremonial matters. The new CO was Lt Col. Rochus Lokinap, and the new 2IC was Maj. Ian Glanville, a former officer from the Australian Army who had transferred into the PNGDF. The battalion training officer was Australian major Steven Lind, who replaced Maj. Phil Joyce, who returned to Australia on promotion.

It was sad to see Maj. Phil Joyce leave for Australia as he had so much experience, spoke pidgin, and was popular among the troops and their dependants. Major Joyce spent as much quality time with me as he could before he left. He reminded me to remain focused on my job, to maintain a positive attitude, and not to compromise as a result of social pressures. He predicted that, if I continued my performance, one day, I would command a regiment. Many of us junior officers felt that Major Joyce was a real mentor and an inspiration.

My earlier experience of indulging in liquor had taught me of the dangers of overindulging. On many occasions, I opted to return home when drinking sessions grew heavy. This was more critical for me as Dupain had accepted a midwifery course for a year at Nonga Hospital in Rabaul, East New Britain, and I had to preoccupy myself with domestic activities in the regiment.

Operation Wantok Durua, Vanuatu, July–September 1980

The Santo Rebellion or 'Coconut War'

In the run-up to Vanuatu's independence in 1980, a Ni-Vanuatu nationalist leader and politician named Jimmy Stevens, also known as Moses by his followers, emerged to declare the island of Espiritu Santo, the largest island of the former New Hebrides group, the independent State of Vermerana. Stevens, it turned out at his subsequent arrest and trial, was being financed behind the scenes by a US-based entity called the Phoenix Foundation, a libertarian group that had previously attempted to set up an independent tax haven on Abaco Island in the Bahamas. He also had support from a number of French planters on Espiritu Santo.

A former bulldozer driver, Stevens was a colourful character of part-European, part-Melanesian, and part-Polynesian descent. He claimed that his father was Scottish and his mother Tongan. He is said to have had twenty-three wives and forty-eight children, and if this claim is anywhere near accurate, which hardly seems probable, it may have been partly to escape this menagerie, as much as on the grounds of *kustom* and cargo cult beliefs, that he got himself involved in an independence movement.

Whatever the motivation, Stevens's declaration of independence for Santo immediately before the independence celebrations was an outright challenge to the incoming government of Vanuatu, led by Fr Walter Lini, the new prime minister. Political negotiations with Stevens having failed and lacking sufficient police or armed forces of his own, Walter Lini turned for assistance in crushing the rebellion to Sir Julius Chan. From then on, events moved quickly. Sir Julius was happy to be seen as the regional leader or 'big man' of the newly independent states of Melanesia, and in the PNGDF, he had a suitable instrument to assist him in this aim.

Even before the PNG government could obtain the necessary approvals from Parliament for a deployment of the PNGDF, preliminary orders had already been issued to the commander of the PNGDF, Brig. Gen. Ted Diro. He appointed Col. Tony Huai as his operations commander and Lt Col. Ian Glanville, now director of land operations, as the contingent commander. They were sent ahead to Vanuatu to scope out the size and shape of a proposed deployment before final approvals from the National Parliament could be obtained. The intervention force was to consist of two rifle companies (or a battalion minus worth of troops), two DC-3s, two patrol boats, one landing craft heavy, and one Nomad aircraft to support the operational effort.

Sir Julius convened an emergency meeting at the old House of Assembly in Downtown Port Moresby on 5 August. Sir Michael Somare, the opposition leader, opposed the deployment on the grounds that the Constitution of the Independent State of Papua New Guinea made it illegal to deploy the PNGDF outside the country. He argued that it would be preferable, and potentially wiser, to assemble a peacekeeping force from a broader array of Pacific Islands Forum countries. After three days of debate, the Parliament voted in favour, 55–40, of legalising the first deployment of PNGDF troops overseas since independence. A Papuan infantry battalion had been actively engaged in the Pacific campaign in WWII, but this was in the context of a wider allied effort against Japan in which Australia was one of the key players and at a time when PNG was a dependent territory administered by Australia.

Kumul Force, as the battalion minus group was named, was to be based on two companies drawn from the first and second battalions of the Royal Pacific Infantry Regiment. A contingent headquarters was to be based at Luganville Police Station after the Luganville airport on Santo was handed over to the Kumul Force from a temporary holding detachment of 100 French paratroopers and an equal number of Royal marines.

Apart from Colonel Huai and Lieutenant Colonel Nuia, the other senior officer was Lt Col. Ian Glanville, whose role was to coordinate all land operations and other support services involving aircraft and naval vessels. He was also the coordinator and liaison with the new Vanuatu government based in Port Vila. The director of transport and supply was Lt Col. Robert Dademo. He was based in Port Vila to coordinate all the logistics efforts to support the Kumul Force operating in Santo and the surrounding atolls.

PNG's national census was also conducted in 1980. I was visiting Support Company in Maprik, East Sepik, in connection with PNGDF support for the census when the CO of Second Battalion, Lt Col. Rochus Lokinap, instructed me to return as soon as practical to accompany him and Maj. Steve Lind to Vanuatu. I was anxious for the opportunity to go to Vanuatu as part of Kumul Force and was delighted to get the call. I returned to Moem, and soon after, we departed for Port Moresby. Along with another Australian officer, Maj. Les Trentor from Taurama Barracks, we departed for Port Vila on a chartered Gulf Stream aircraft.

At Port Vila, we billeted at the technical college before departing for Espiritu Santo the following morning by Nomad aircraft. At Santo, I was detached to B Company, which had occupied Bougainville Hotel on the outskirts of Luganville. After a few days of operational and intelligence briefings, I was asked by Maj. Jeff Key to lead night patrols in an area where supporters of Jimmy Stevens were known to be gathered, mainly in a French-owned coconut and cocoa plantation.

I was allocated ten men for the patrols. I divided them into two five-men patrol teams, and they conducted two patrols each. We raided a plantation where a defence force officer was caught with a Frenchwoman and another couple. In one of the raids based on local intelligence, we detained a French planter found with ammunition and explosives and brought him back to Luganville. Three weeks later, I returned to Moem, content with my contribution.

Subsequently, the main operations were centred at Vanafo, where the headquarters of Stevens's Nagriamel movement was based. On 31 August, PNGDF troops surrounded the headquarters and arrested Stevens and seventy of his followers. Mopping-up operations were held elsewhere on Santo, and the secessionist movement quickly collapsed. During operations, PNGDF troops shot and killed one of Jimmy Stevens's sons, Eddie Stevens, who drove through a checkpoint and refused to stop. Support for Jimmy Stevens quickly collapsed after this incident, which was the only fatality. The rebellion was quashed, government control was restored, and Jimmy Stevens was convicted and sentenced to fourteen years in prison. No casualties were sustained by the PNGDF. The Kumul Force returned to PNG on 27 September, having successfully quelled the rebellion.

A week later, the Kumul Force assembled in parade formation at the National Broadcasting Commission at Five Mile before marching back to Murray Barracks. Sir Julius Chan received the troops with pride. The parade was addressed by Brig. Gen. Ted Diro; Col. Tony Huai, the commander of the Kumul Force; and Gerega Pepena, the minister for defence. While no campaign medal was struck by the PNG government, Vanuatu struck a campaign medal for Kumul Force and an independence medal for the officers and men of B Company 1PIR and the pipes and drums who had participated during the independence inauguration day in July 1980.

Exchange Officer with Twenty-Fifth Infantry Division, Schofield Barracks, Hawaii, September 1980

After the Kumul Force deployment, I returned to Moem Barracks, where I continued to serve as adjutant of the regiment. At the end of September, I was selected as an exchange officer with the Twenty-Fifth Infantry Division at Schofield Barracks in Hawaii for six weeks. The division's nickname is Tropic Lightning. It served with distinction in WWII, the Korean War, Vietnam, Iraq, and Afghanistan. It has combat brigades based on the Stryker light-armoured vehicle, plus combat aviation and airborne and artillery units.

This was a prestigious opportunity, and I had to make the best of it. Along with Capt. Ben Norrie from Engineers Battalion and WO Alois Mone, we departed for the United States via Sydney. I was attached to A Company Twenty-First Infantry. After a few weeks of close quarter training in and around Hawaii, my company departed on a C-131 for cold weather training and training in the conduct of military operations in urban terrain, as well as special forces training at Fort Lewis, Washington.

Fort Lewis is situated west of the Rocky Mountains and 14 km south-east of Tacoma. A garrison unit, it is integrated with the US Air Force base McChord, a logistics, training, and mobilisation base for the US Army. Upon arrival and after settling into vacant barracks accommodation, we began intensive training in infantry weapons systems, followed by highly specialised and carefully regulated military operations in urban terrain. This ran for two weeks. Next, we deployed to a special forces training camp at Huckleberry Creek at the base of Mount Rainier, a few kilometres out of Seattle. There, we lived in snow and practised using snow boots and skis as part of our cold weather training. When it rained at night, which was often, close surveillance operations became extremely demanding. I endured the freezing temperatures as best I could, but some nights, I had to move closer to the central heater to complement the cold weather clothes I was wearing. While at the training camp, I had the opportunity to operate heavy machine guns and other weapons systems and experience the use of night-vision devices (NVG) not in the PNGDF inventory.

After six weeks, I returned to PNG, having had the rare opportunity of seeing how the world's leading military operates. This gave me a solid foundation on which to progress in my own military career. In early December, I was posted to the PNG Defence Academy at Igam Barracks, Lae, Morobe Province, as the instructor in tactics. So after four and a half years and after most of my colleagues had been posted out of the regiment, I was finally posted out of Second Battalion, this time to a training institution.

Defence Academy, 1981–83

At PNG Defence Academy, I was posted as an instructor of tactics. The subjects were shared with New Zealand Defence Force Artillery officer Paul Southwell. We alternated subjects, covering topics such as patrolling, land navigation, tactics (both defensive and offensive), and the four phases of war. A new subject we introduced was anti-insurgency operations based on the Vietnam model. Our senior instructor was Maj. Matthew Tovebae, who was rigidly doctrinaire and very critical of everything we did. In my second year at the academy, Maj. Matthew Tovebae replaced Lt Col. Peter Schumann on promotion, while Maj. Francis Agwi, my senior and a close colleague, replaced Matthew Tovebae.

Feeling that my career in the army was in danger of stagnating, I decided to apply to read law at the University of Papua New Guinea. As I had matriculated, all I needed to do was brush up on basic subjects like maths and English. I was excited about the prospect of pursuing a schoolboy dream of becoming a lawyer. As required by the defence force, I filled in an application to do civil schooling, first on the basis of sponsoring myself and then, based on satisfactory progress with my studies, to ask the defence force to sponsor me. I waited and, months later, finally got a response from the HQ training directorate. My application was denied. I would later discover (when I was appointed commander in 1995) that my change in career was considered a 'waste of a good infantry officer' by Lt Col. David Josiah, then director of training in the personnel branch.

I was downhearted but determined to work even harder to be more proficient in my work. I never reapplied to do law. Instead, I concentrated on reading military history, tactics, and manoeuvre warfare based on Australian and US doctrines, with the view that one day we would need to work side by side with other countries in coalition operations.

I attended the 1/82 junior staff duties and tactics promotion courses along with over thirty other career officers at Igam Barracks for two months, ending at Goldie River Barracks. I was given the following course report by the chief instructor:

> Captain Jerry Singirok was a competent, co-operative and confident student who fully applied himself to every aspect of the course. He was determined to succeed and he did. He gained first place in all three major assessed exercises conducted, a feat not before achieved and not likely to be repeated again. His quiet and confident manner served as a guide to other

students. He produced excellent results and topped the course. Well done.

We were given married quarters at Ten Mile, a few kilometres from Igam Barracks along the Highlands Highway at the junction of Wau Bulolo and Nadzab Airport. Dupain had been on a bridging course at Simbu Hospital and was expecting our first child. On 11 June, Arnfried (Alfred) Brendecke Singirok was born at Angau Hospital. He brought much joy and pride to both of us.

My two years at the defence academy went quickly. I had participated in all the courses and been the subject master for tactics and leadership. In 1983, I was posted back to Moem Barracks, Wewak, as 2IC of Support Company. This was an important posting as Support Company was still engaged along the Indonesian-PNG border. After settling Dupain and Alfred at Moem Barracks, I joined the company, flying by a DC-3 Dakota aircraft to Vanimo and then straight into Bewani on a resupply run. The border being the main area of operations for the regiment, I was not surprised when I was dispatched to join the company on operations in the field in Vanimo. The company was commanded by Maj. John Gaera. After we returned to Vanimo, he was suspended for an operational mishap, and I took charge of the company.

That year, the Hong Kong–based Seventh Duke of Edinburgh Regiment, a British force, sent a company including a detachment of Gurkha engineers to Vanimo; and within four weeks, they built a new company headquarters. The company also assisted in dismantling the old company offices that were built after WWII.

This was an interesting time as I had always wished to command a company of my own. When we returned to Moem Barracks, we learnt that the CO had also changed. Lt Col. Herman Komeng, an impressive non-commissioned officer from East Sepik, was the new CO. He was passionate and very caring but a disciplinarian who had no time for half-hearted officers and soldiers.

In 1984, I was posted within 2PIR as acting OC of D Company, replacing Maj. Dagi Demarcus (Delta Mike), who was suspended for an operational incident. D Company, also known as Senior Company, was the original company raised in 1965 when Second Battalion was formed, so this was a real honour. This was the year that the title Royal was bestowed on the Pacific Island Regiment after the visit and presentation of new regimental colours by Charles, Prince of Wales.

During battalion celebrations that year, D Company, under my command, won major trophies from tactics to shooting and sports and was named champion company of the year. Not only did D company carry the Regimental colour for Trooping the Colour but the company also was selected for a month-long exchange with a company from First Royal Australian Regiment (1RAR), Townsville.

I was still a captain and was content with the conduct of the men under me. I controlled and led the company with passion and concentrated on looking after my men and their welfare. I drank less and continued to remain fit. I made sure that D Company was the model company in the regiment.

In May 1984, along with over 150 soldiers, I boarded a Royal Australian Air Force Hercules for Townsville. I was met by the CO of the regiment, a very fit and tall lieutenant colonel, Peter Cosgrove, MC, and his 2IC, Ian Flawith. The company we replaced was D Company 1RAR under Maj. Dougal MacMillan; they spent the same period in Wewak. Lt Col. Peter Cosgrove would later progress to command Sixth Brigade, then First Division. In 1999, he achieved international prominence as commander of International Force for East Timor (INTERFET). This was followed by his appointment as chief of army (2000–2) then chief of defence force (2002–5). As Gen. Sir Peter Cosgrove, AK, MC, he was Australia's twenty-sixth governor general. He published his autobiography, *My Story*, in 2006. He retired as governor general in March 2019 to be succeeded by Gen. David Hurley.

I had visited Townsville and made recommendations on the type of training I envisaged for the troops before D Company's arrival. We spent a week at the Field Force Training School at Tully, north of Townsville, and a week training in armoured personnel carriers and a few days undertaking helicopter training. We returned to PNG with a new spirit of enthusiasm as the troops were exposed to another and more advanced soldiering environment with a consequent urge to do better in their careers.

I was deployed once again with D Company to the border station in Vanimo. The year was memorable because refugees from Indonesia, now stationed at Black Water Camp, went on a rampage in Vanimo Town, resulting in the militants or ringleaders being deported to Jayapura. On the way to Jayapura, one of the ringleaders attempted to slit the throat of the pilot. He was overpowered by Government Officer Moses Poi, but the aircraft was required to return to base. On their arrival at Vanimo Airport, I was called on to take control of the situation, which I did. With the seven militants secured so that they could cause no further trouble, we escorted them, all male adults, to Jayapura—a twenty-minute flight across the international border.

I attended another course at the Infantry Centre (now called the Australian Army School of Infantry, Lone Pine Barracks) in Singleton, New South Wales, in February 1985. The aim of the course was to 'prepare officers in the corps for aspects of command and operational staff appointments in the rank of major'. Lt Col. D. A. W. Webster made the following remarks in his course report:

> Captain Singirok's attention to detail was adequate and his presentations were of an acceptable standard. His contribution to syndicate discussions was pleasant and honest and displayed a positive attitude. He always displayed a willingness to learn and was thoughtful in the application of knowledge and his own experience. His desire to contribute to discussions was enhanced by his high standard of English which is a credit to him. Captain Singirok was an excellent representative of his country and its Armed Forces.

On my return to PNG on 26 October, I got an urgent signal conveying my promotion to the rank of major and posting as operations officer and training officer for 2RPIR. I was to localise the last Australian operations officer, Maj. Barry Ryan. It was a challenge, and as I handed over D Company to Francis Agwi, who had just completed his time as senior instructor at the defence academy in Lae, I felt a sense of regret. The D Company troops were sad to see me go as well. We had bonded together closely in my year as their company commander.

The outgoing CO for 2RPIR was Lt Col. Parry Iruru. He served for less than a year before taking up a posting as director of land operations at HQ PNGDF and was replaced by a Bougainvillean from Buka Island, Lt Col. Andrew Trongat. Trongat was a graduate of Portsea, Victoria, in 1972 and was a company commander in 1RPIR before being promoted and posted to 2RPIR as CO. A disciplinarian, Trongat took no chances with subordinates. He paid particular attention to tactics and proper procedures, and as operations officer, I was able to learn a lot from him. As my CO, Trongat allowed me a lot of freedom to develop training conditions, fixtures, and facilities to train the battalion in a variety of realistic scenarios, mainly close quarter combat and jungle settings.

I was allowed to convert the Urimo Field Firing Range into a modest live firing range where I developed firing templates for all weapons and hand grenade ranges. I modelled my approach on the Jungle Training Wing of the Australian Army Field Force training centre at Tully, north Queensland.

Later that year, I qualified on the 2/86 intermediate operations course, which aimed to 'instruct students in Tactics and War Administration to enable them to plan Brigade Operations in a Divisional setting'. Col. P. M. Arnison, commandant of the Land Warfare Centre, Canungra, Queensland, presented me with my course report, which included the following comments:

> Major Singirok worked consistently on the course and the amount of effort he put into the tactical problems was evident in his solutions and accurate work. His prior attendance at the Australian Army Infantry Company Commander's Course enabled him to be more familiar with the Australian terminology and demonstrated an understanding of Brigade tactics and war administration. Major Singirok's capacity to work

hard, his polite manners and sense of humour showed him to be an excellent ambassador, both professionally and socially for his country.

Desk Posting, HQ PNGDF, 1986

At the end of October 1986, I was posted to HQ PNGDF, Port Moresby, on a desk job as staff officer grade 2 land operations. By then, I had put in over ten years in the field and was ready for a staff posting. I arrived with mixed feelings. At HQ, I met very senior officers I had never seen before in my career. Most wore immaculate uniforms with ribbons displayed on their chest. Some ended up at the officers' mess every day after work. I noticed that quite a few stayed on drinking until the small hours of the morning, obviously heavily intoxicated. I did not find such habits reassuring as there were serious problems with maintaining high levels of discipline and protecting individual integrity. But this trend continued unabated, and it seemed to me that the professional edge of the military at the higher levels was diminishing as many decisions were apparently being made over drinks. Worse still, confidential issues affecting individuals and the defence force in general were being subjected to open arguments and debates in the mess. As I occupied a room upstairs from the mess, I could hear such nonsense continue, sometimes with laughter and scuffles, at odd hours of the night. So much for setting high standards.

The year 1987 went by quickly. Dupain and Alfred joined me in the first part of the year, but it was apparent that, with so many months of separation in the field, our marriage was not working. Dupain and I separated. She took our son back to Madang, where we both had roots. Dupain was a midwife, so she was able to secure a job at Madang General Hospital and continued to raise Alfred.

In 1987, I had another opportunity to go to Hawaii for a field training exercise where visiting forces were introduced to joint operations between air force and ground troops. We were billeted at Hickam Air Force Base. Maj. Ignatius Lai from the air element, and the first DC-3 PNG pilot, was selected to go with me. The trip was significant as George Konrote,[5] then a decorated Fiji Army major, was also with us, and it coincided with Fiji's first military coup, led by Col. Sitiveni Rabuka. Expecting significant political changes after the coup, George Konrote departed early for Fiji but not before sharing his insights, which gave us first-hand information on the background of the coup and the people behind it.

After returning to Port Moresby, I began to see more of Weni Moka as my marriage with Dupain had all but collapsed. Weni was a prominent radio journalist at the National Broadcasting Commission. A senior reporter, she was in charge of programmes. She became pregnant, and it was decided by my superiors that I should be posted away from Port Moresby to save my career and marriage. Rochus Lokinap was commander of the defence force, and both he and Lt Col. Perry Iruru, my immediate director, agreed that I should be posted out of Port Moresby.

A position became vacant at the defence academy in Lae as senior instructor of Officer Cadet Wing to replace Maj. Geoffrey Wiri, who was being posted to headquarters on promotion as director of training. I was posted to the defence academy at the end of October 1987. My prominence as a middle-ranking officer had not diminished despite the appearance of a degree of chaos in my personal life. Along with CO of Goldie River Depot, Lt Col. Ben Tasia, I was selected to represent the PNGDF at a Pacific Armies Management Seminar sponsored by the US Army in Dhaka, the capital of Bangladesh. This was a high-profile seminar in which participating countries gave country briefs on military activities. There were a great many opportunities to meet senior military and defence and security officials from other countries.

Ben Tasia and I transited through Singapore, spending a night there, and the following day, we departed for Bangladesh through

---

[5]   Jiorji Konrote, OF, MC, also known as George Konrote, was elected president of Fiji in October 2015. He had a distinguished military career, retiring from the Fiji military force as a major general. He served as UN assistant secretary general and force commander of Lebanon before entering politics from his home island of Rotuma in 2006 and again in 2014. After his election to the office of president of Fiji, he retired from his seat in Parliament.

Thailand. During our nine days stay in Bangladesh, after attending the seminar, I took time off to see the country and visit the crowded streets of Dhaka. I was appreciative of the opportunity to see what real overcrowding and poverty looks like close-up.

After we returned, I was instructed to go to New Zealand and Australia to open up new posts for exchange instructors at both the Royal Military College, Duntroon, Canberra, and Waiouru Military Camp, New Zealand. I returned from Canberra and handed my report to the director of training, Geoffrey Wiri; and later, we both travelled to Waiouru in New Zealand. Our subsequent reports gave full endorsement for PNG cadets to be trained on full commissioned courses in both Australia and New Zealand.

The PNG Defence Academy was required to conduct a bridging course for six months, including basic training such as foot and arms drills, field craft and minor tactics, and other relevant subjects. As a result, the officer commissioning course at PNG Defence Academy was suspended, and commissioning courses reverted to the Officer Cadet School of New Zealand at Waiouru and Royal Military College, Duntroon.

On 14 April 1988, Weni and I were delighted to welcome the arrival of our daughter Maib Kumai at Port Moresby General Hospital. I was completing a three-month course in management studies at the Administrative College, and this gave me a chance to be with Weni, Futua, and Maib before I returned to the defence academy.

That year, Capt. Mac Grace from the New Zealand Defence Force arrived in Lae. He added significant value to my management and teaching team of capable instructors in preparing selected officer cadets for the officer cadet commissioning courses at Duntroon and Waiouru while the remainder were to be commissioned in Lae.

In mid-1988, I led our senior officer cadets in walking the Kokoda Trail for our military history exercise. We were walking from Kokoda to Owers' Corner in Central Province when Capt. Mac Grace fell critically ill after suffering a severe attack of malaria and pneumonia. The onus was now on my cadets and me to rescue him as his medical condition was fast becoming life-threatening. We made a stretcher, and despite the difficulty of carrying a body in steep and slippery terrain, the officer cadets carried him over 10 km to Templeton's Crossing before we were able to radio for assistance. Much to our relief, an Australian Army Black Hawk helicopter was in the area. It got our SOS and, after pinning down our location among thick canopy, slung down the loadmaster who winched Capt. Mac Grace into the helicopter and medivac him to Taurama Barracks field hospital. Capt. Mac Grace would return a few years later, after my tenure as commander, to be the New Zealand military attaché to PNG. When anyone asked Mac Grace about me, he would tell them I had saved his life along the Kokoda Trail.

While we continued to conduct officer cadet courses at Igam Barracks, the security situation in Bougainville was fast becoming a political problem and dominating national life. Constant rebel actions were disrupting operations at the Panguna mine, which was partly owned by Bougainville Copper Ltd and operated by the majority shareholder, the giant mining company, Conzinc Riotinto of Australia.

In December 1988, the rebel group now known as the Bougainville Revolutionary Army intensified their activities against the state and CRA operations in Panguna by felling power pylons along the Espie Highway past Tunuru Junction using explosives stolen from the mine. In March 1989, a prominent Bougainville politician, John Bika, was murdered, prompting the central government to take immediate action to address the prevailing security situation. In April that year, PM Sir Rabbie Namaliu declared a state of emergency on Bougainville, a decision that would trigger a chain of unprecedented disasters for the next decade or more.

As a result of the sharply deteriorating security situation, the Panguna mine was closed on 15 May 1989 and has remained closed ever since, depriving both central and provincial governments and landowners of any further share in tax and revenue from the mine. Up until the mine's closure, the PNG government, as a 19 per cent shareholder in BCL, had received returns from the mine totalling an estimated AUD 1 billion in tax and revenues while the provincial government had received AUD 83 million in royalties, and landowners had received a total of AUD 33 million. Offsetting such economic benefits was widespread evidence of environmental degradation, increasingly severe health issues among the local population, and significant complaints over the treatment of landowners and the unequal share in revenue.

In June 1989, while I was still the senior instructor at the Officer Cadet Wing and conducting a field exercise with officer cadets in Madang at Malala, Bogia District, I was called for operational duties on Bougainville to relieve the first operations officer, Maj. Allan Pinia. The chief of PNGDF operations, Col. Leo Nuia, directed that I be placed on short notice for active duties on Bougainville as the contingent operations officer for four months. Given the deteriorating security situation on Bougainville, I recognised that this appointment was a critical one. Still, I was surprised to be called up for this role as, normally, officers in the regiments would have been appointed.

Nevertheless, as it was a command appointment from headquarters, I welcomed the opportunity. I departed Lae on Air Niugini and arrived on a late flight to Port Moresby. It was the last week of June 1989, and after two days of briefings and access to highly confidential intelligence assessments and analysis, I was ready for operational deployment on Operation Blueprint as the contingent operations officer.

As I waited to deploy, I reflected on my career and on Gen. William Slim's thoughts about command in his book *Defeat into Victory*. In my fourteen years of service in the PNGDF, I had commanded at both platoon and company levels, so I understood what General Slim meant about the joys and challenges of high command. I had extensive patrol experience on the PNG-Indonesian border and over ten years in the field, learning my trade. I had also instructed at senior levels in tactics and leadership and had been given numerous training and development opportunities with both Australian and US forces.

But now that I was to be contingent operations officer in Bougainville, in the midst of a seriously deteriorating security situation, and with significant expectations on the part of government, I recognised that I was about to face an altogether more serious set of challenges than any I had encountered so far. Training and coursework, no matter how well it is designed and no matter how diligent and able the student, can only prepare one so far for actual combat operations.

Extensive patrol experience, which I had, would be vital. Knowledge of the jungle operating environment and of the necessary survival skills was also essential. But past experience and current knowledge would only take me so far. In Bougainville, the tests that I knew I was about to face would be of a different and more demanding order altogether. That they would be as much political as military I had no doubt. Whether I would be able to meet those tests with the resources at my disposal, and to the satisfaction of my military superiors as well as government ministers, was another matter. That I would give it the best shot that I could I had absolutely no doubt. The stage was now set for my long-term connection with the Bougainville crisis. It was June 1989.

CHAPTER 13

Bougainville Crisis, 1989:
Operation Blueprint

Your time is limited, so don't waste it living someone
else's life. Don't be trapped by dogma—which is living
with the results other people's thinking. Don't let the
noise of others' opinions drown out your inner voice.
And most important, have the courage to follow your
heart and intuition.

—Steve Jobs

Vast quantities of copper-, gold-, and silver-bearing ore, estimated at a
conservative 1 billion tonnes of reclaimable deposits, were discovered
in the Crown Ranges of Bougainville by prospecting geologists in
1963. Excavation soon commenced, and a mere three years later,
the fabulously wealthy Panguna mine was opened. Operated by
Bougainville Copper Ltd, a subsidiary of Australian-owned Conzinc
Riotinto, it soon became the largest open-cut mine in the world. From
1972 to 1989, when the mine was closed by rebel action, it produced
an enormous amount of wealth for its owners: some 3 million tonnes
of copper, 306 tonnes of gold, and 784 tonnes of silver were extracted.

However, little of this wealth flowed through to landowners, sowing a very large field of dragon's teeth.[6]

The Papua New Guinean government held a 19 per cent share of BCL, while Panguna landowners received 5 per cent of the 1.25 per cent royalties on production paid by BCL, and the balance of 1.25 per cent went to the national government until 1977 and the North Solomons provincial government after that. The Panguna landowners also received land rents and compensation for the damage to land under lease to BCL.

Bougainvilleans were supposed to receive, but seldom did, a share of the profits from the mine, varying between 0.50 and 1.25 per cent, a very paltry share, even when paid. At full production, the mine accounted for 45 per cent of Papua New Guinea's national export revenue. Over the seventeen years of its operation, the total value of profits received by the PNG government from its share in the mine is estimated to have been PGK 5.2 billion (AUD 2.2 billion at current conversion rates).

Local landowners in the vicinity of the mine, never happy at the vast amounts of spoil and tailings dumped into the Kawerong River, which flows into the Jaba River, destroying all life in both rivers, were becoming increasingly dissatisfied with the severe environmental and social impacts of the mine. They were also unhappy with their allocated share of the mine profits, which they saw as being grossly inadequate compensation for the disruption to their land and traditional ways of living. These dissatisfactions eventually boiled over into labour disputes at the mine and sporadic outbreaks of violence, threatened and actual attacks on mine personnel, and sabotage of mine property and installations.

The approach of PM Sir Rabbie Namaliu's government to the deteriorating security situation was initially very restrained. In December 1988, a ministerial delegation led by Deputy PM Akoka Doi and including Police Commissioner Tohian was sent to Bougainville

---

6   In Greek mythology, a dragon's tooth, once planted, will grow to become an armed warrior.

in an attempt to negotiate with Francis Ona, the rebel leader. An undertaking was given to rebel landowners gathered at Guava Village on a ridge above the mine that police action would be confined to protecting local villages and the Panguna mine. But the police, who were apparently not advised of this policy of restraint and acting on what they said were instructions from the prime minister, moved to search villages around the mine in an attempt to recover stolen explosives and arrest the saboteurs. A local youth, caught throwing stones at a police Land Rover, was detained, beaten, and died in custody. From there, the security situation boiled over.

In March 1989, in response to a spate of isolated killings, the Papua New Guinea Defence Force was called in to assist the police under section 204 of the Constitution of the Independent State of New Guinea, which deals with 'call-out' and 'aid to the civil power'. A state of emergency was declared the following month, giving the defence force additional powers under the constitution. A contingent based on a battalion-sized group was formed under the command of Lt Col. Geoffrey Key. This was supported by a forward tactical headquarters with a contingent of engineers, transport, supply, intelligence, logistics, military police, and air wing personnel.

Their orders supposedly[7] were to move into the jungle; find Francis Ona, a former mineworker and local landowner from Guava Village who was identified as the main ringleader of the dissident militia, and his men; and hand them over to the police who would arrange for them to be tried for murder, theft, and damage to public and private property. While all this was being put into place, Port Moresby–based troops left their barracks and marched to Parliament House to protest over pay and conditions. The PNGDF commander, Brigadier General

---

[7] I say 'supposedly' because the actual orders under which the defence force was then operating, if they ever existed, have never been published. Operation Blueprint was the name given to these initial operations, but even as operations officer, I was never briefed on their content. In hindsight, one wonders if operational orders were ever actually written for the initial defence force deployments on Bougainville; it would be an astonishing oversight if they were not.

Lokinap, was suspended; and Col. Joseph Bau Maras, a logistician who was then PNG's defence adviser in Indonesia, was called in to take over as acting commander.

Under Maras's leadership, weaknesses in command and control, operational planning, and strategic direction setting soon became evident. Decision-making was left in the hands of a few senior officers who were incompetent and lacked sufficient cohesiveness and unity to address the rapidly deteriorating security situation in Bougainville.

The contingent commander, Lt Col. Geoffrey Key, was a veteran infantry officer from Finschhafen, Morobe Province. As a platoon commander, he had walked from Wewak to Port Moresby with a platoon of selected soldiers in 1975. Later, he was company commander of B Company Second Battalion for Kumul Force, the defence force operation in Vanuatu.

The first defence force casualties in Bougainville were incurred on 6 April 1989, when 2nd Lt Steven Yandu and his batman, Pvt. Martin Romas, were killed at Orami Village in the Kongara area of central Bougainville. Their deaths, the first defence force casualties since WWII, inflamed the emotions of their fellow soldiers who were already under extreme operational pressure and very restrictive rules of engagement.

When the PNGDF was called on to assist the police force in Bougainville in April 1989, I was on exercise with the senior officer cadet intake in Bogia District, Madang. We followed the news of developments in Bougainville as closely as we could. While I was very keen to get involved, I didn't expect to be called on as I was heavily involved in a training command environment.

We arrived back at Lae from our field exercise and completed the final selection board of officer cadets to be sent to the Royal Military College, Duntroon, Canberra, and Officer Cadet School of New Zealand at Waiouru. Once this was finalised and seemingly out of the blue, I got a confidential deployment call from HQ Operations Branch telling me that I was to relieve the operations officer, Maj. Allan Pinia, in June 1989 for a three-month tour in Bougainville. It was something I had not expected. Apart from Lt Col. Andrew Trongat, a

Bougainvillean from Buka Island and former CO of Second Battalion who was now director of land operations, I did not really know many senior officers who I thought might have confidence in me. However, Maj. Francis Agwi—my closest mate who was now staff officer grade 2 land operations—told me that Trongat had recommended me to replace Maj. Allan Pinia. I was required to travel within twenty-four hours to Port Moresby for preparation and briefing before deploying to Bougainville.

I arrived on the late afternoon Air Niugini flight out of Nadzab Airport, Lae, to Jacksons Airfield, Port Moresby. At headquarters, I met Francis Agwi who made signals and a few other highly confidential files available for me to read. This I did before departing for Tokarara, where Weni, Futua, and Maib were staying in a National Broadcasting Commission unit.

On Wednesday, 12 July, I departed on a chartered flight along with another company from 1RPIR, who were being deployed for the first time to Bougainville. We arrived at Aropa Airport in central Bougainville, and I could see concern and anxiety in the faces of the people in the airport terminal buildings as they watched the arrival of more soldiers. The defence force base was located at the south-east end of Aropa Airport, separated by sea and swamp and the road leading to Koromira Catholic Mission. The military checkpoint was at the north-west end of the airstrip. To my critically trained eye, the site selected for the base was tactically unsuitable, apart from the security cover provided by the sea.

I was shown around the base and also saw the command post manned by Capt. Bulina Airo. It was not long before I realised that if command and control was to be effective, we had to lift our operational game. The controller of the state of emergency was the police commissioner, Paul Tohian. Col. Lima Dotaona had been appointed deputy controller, and he was based in Arawa at the Nafik Club, some thirty minutes away from Aropa.

I waited to meet the operations officer I was to replace. When Maj. Allan Pinia appeared, it was obvious that he was tired, frustrated, and cut up by the loss of his two soldiers and also by the lack of coordination between the various stakeholders he was working with. Even after the state of emergency was declared, the restrictions and limitations imposed on the military made it difficult to plan and act effectively. For example, villages could not be searched unless there were reliable intelligence reports backed up by police reports, and there was to be no deployment into new areas unless approved by the deputy controller.

We began my handover with a helicopter flight over Kongara, Sipuru, and Guava Villages and then the giant Panguna mine. The site of the Panguna mine, high up in the Crown Range, far from the coast and surrounded by impenetrable jungle, was unbelievable, and the size of the opencast excavation was absolutely stunning. We refuelled at Panguna before continuing our aerial tour, taking in Buin Station and then Torato Island. A defence force strategic post, Torato Island provided a vital base for operations near the border with Solomon Islands.

The new contingent commander on Bougainville was Lt Col. Walter Salamas, the officer who had been detailed to pick me up at Jacksons Airfield when I first joined the military fourteen years earlier. I waited patiently for him to arrive at Aropa. As both of us were new to Bougainville, we relied on the briefings by Maj. Allan Pinia. The CO said he needed more time with Deputy Controller Colonel Dotaona so that we could plan our operations from the briefs.

Colonel Dotaona's Joint Force HQ was staffed by three disciplined services liaison and intelligence officers. The PNGDF was represented by Lt Col. Ben Maris, who was director of military intelligence. Maris and the others were supposed to provide forward tactical headquarters, in which I was the operations officer, from which we were to develop operational plans for vetting before directing our limited military operations.

The frustrations that Maj. Allan Pinia had warned me about were already taking a toll on me. I have always had an active, impatient disposition, and I could not wait around forever. It was fundamental to get on the offensive and launch aggressive patrolling operations designed to give the defence force the upper hand over the rebels, now styling themselves as the Bougainville Revolutionary Army. In reality, they were not an 'army' so much as a ragtag bunch of dissidents and rebels.[8]

I convinced Lieutenant Colonel Salamas that the ground of tactical importance[9] was the Panguna mine and that dissident groups were not spread across the whole island of Bougainville but were limited to a few locations around the Panguna mine. It was therefore critical that forward military operations be relocated to Panguna to provide security for strategic installations in and around the mine pit and as a base for mounting patrols in the immediate surrounding area. For obvious security reasons, a logistics unit would remain at Aropa Airport to secure the point of entry away from the immediate front line. After another few frustrating days, I finally got the nod to move a small forward operations group to the Panguna mine to establish a forward tactical headquarters before moving the main tactical headquarters.

I took Sergeant Siroi, a long-time signaller from Second Battalion, with me. After we arrived by helicopter at Panguna, we got down to setting up the first operational base. The following day, I met with Bob Cornelius, BCL general manager, and sought his permission to move into single quarters, Block D, taking the top two floors for the command post. This he readily agreed to, and I immediately set to work to establish our communications links to both HQs, using very high-frequency radios and landlines. This was completed within two days, and I reported back to Lieutenant Colonel Salamas, who was still at Aropa Airport.

---

[8]   Intelligence estimates differ, but it is generally accepted that, even at its height, the BRA never exceeded more than a couple of hundred armed insurgents, operating in loosely associated groups of a dozen or so men at a time.

[9]   In military tactics, the GTI is different from the centre of gravity. The GTI is the ground that needs to be held from a narrow military operational perspective. The centre of gravity often has a wider meaning, reflecting the political and social realities within which military operations are unfolding. Properly speaking, the Panguna mine was never the centre of gravity for reaching a proper understanding of Bougainville's many problems or for thinking about how best to resolve the civil war.

At this time, the Panguna mine was the largest open-cut copper mine in the world. When the mine was fully operational, it operated twenty-four hours a day, and there were many different nationalities involved with various disciplines and professions. Industrially, it was a very busy site with massive excavation and ore-crushing machinery, equipment, noise, clouds of suffocating dust, and movement of people in and out of the mine pit. Standing on the ridge at the edge of the pit and looking down into its vast expanse was an incredible, awe-inspiring, and Dantean experience.

Next, I was joined by two subalterns—Lt Dick Kandapaki, communications officer, and Lt Yauka Liria, intelligence officer—and also Capt. Bulina Airo, the administration officer responsible for logistics for the tactical headquarters. Within seven days, the operations centre was fully operational. A map of Bougainville was put up, and more specific maps for the main area of operations were also placed on plastic-covered talc papers for marking-up objectives and the disposition of troops. Rooms were allocated for intelligence and administrative use, an interrogation room was set up, and rooms for sleeping were also assigned.

The Panguna mine management, after consulting with BCL management in Port Moresby and no doubt further up the chain with the owners of CRA, made an important decision to allow the military to tap into their logistics supply and support chain. This included transport, rationing, petrol, oil and lubricants, medical support, and accommodation. Many families were leaving the mine area as safety concerns mounted. However, others took a gamble and stayed as negotiations with warring parties and landowners showed positive signs of potential success.

I was determined to concentrate military operations in and around the mine and the rear supply area at Aropa Airport and to keep the Espie Highway open. To secure mining operations, I was also determined to increase security around the other satellite townships along the Espie Highway from the Crown Prince Range back to Loloho, which was the road down which the crushed ore travelled to be converted into slurry at Panguna and piped down to Loloho not far from Arawa, where the Joint Force HQ was located; all these places needed to be secured. My main areas of operational interest were Kupei, Guava Ridge and Paruparu, Mananau and the Jaba River, and Sianke area in Bana District, where one of our young subalterns, Lt Tony Oawa, came from.

In thinking about my operational responsibilities, I was conscious of the many military lessons I had learnt about the futility of chasing ground as opposed to defending ground: it was much better to lure the opposing force to come and fight in the place and time of one's own tactical choosing. To me, as the operational commander on the spot, this was the obvious strategy to pursue. Moreover, as the PNGDF was manpower strapped (our contingent was operating at little more than 50 per cent of about 300 troops, plus support staff including a handful of civil staff) and support services were at critical levels or non-existent, the importance of concentration of effort was all the more evident.

It was clear to me from my discussions with HQ at Aropa, and from what they were being told by Port Moresby, that the hierarchy of military planners at Murray Barracks had decided that, to defeat the insurgents, the BRA had to be engaged all around the island. In effect, it was a strategy of having no strategy. Inevitably, it would result in a dilution of effort and the handing of operational initiative to the BRA, which could make its own choices over where and when to strike. This was a decision and an operational approach that would backfire months later.

It was now one month after I had established my command post at Panguna. I had managed to get some respect from the subunits operating under the contingent HQ. It was now decided to deploy a composite contingent as opposed to a complete unit. On the first call-out, Lieutenant Colonel Key deployed with two companies from First Regiment, and the others came from Second Battalion. A new company, put together as D Company, changed its name to Delta Force. This was commanded by Maj. Peter Dringo, who was later replaced by Maj. Donnie Bauwie. Having Donnie Bauwie, Joseph Fabila, and Capt. Kessy Rovae on my team gave me a lot of personal comfort as we had been officer cadets together. These relationships continued in the operational theatre and were excellent for teamwork and comradeship.

I also continued to work closely with the mine management at Panguna and with their support services, including Horst Alman from Heli Niugini, a helicopter company on contract for air support for BCL. During our quieter operational periods, some of the officers, including me, would be invited for family dinners and BBQs around the residences in Panguna, signalling a level of respect for our work. The catering manager, Joe Fregnito, was very helpful; he catered without complaint for our increasing troop numbers, including providing cut lunches when troops were out on day-long deployments around the mine and its surrounds.

At this time, I established a close personal relationship with Peter Comerford and his wife, Marian. Comerford was a long-time teacher who had taught in New Ireland, Oro Province, and was now headmaster of Panguna International Primary School. A keen photographer, Peter sometimes accompanied me on resupply runs on the chopper to take photographs of soldiers in action as we did not have our own dedicated photographer.

The intelligence officer Lt Yauka Liria[10] and I decided to collect our own intelligence information about the BRA as the intelligence we received from the Joint Intelligence Unit in Arawa was very slow in getting to us. This was the most critical tactical move we made; from then on, we based the planning of our military operations on our own intelligence. I trusted Liria. He had been trained by me at the defence academy in 1982 and served under my command in D Company 2RPIR in 1984. I was very pleased with his commitment and the quality of the intelligence estimates being compiled by his small cell.

He was assisted by Cpl Jack Aria, who had been my dedicated batman in 1984, and Sgt Joseph Igo, who was one of my soldiers in B Company in 1977. I thought our intelligence cell was very effective as its operators were extremely professional and dedicated. The CO,

---

10   After a few years as a captain, Liria elected to be discharged from the defence force and published a book on his experiences on Bougainville, *The Bougainville Campaign Diary* (1993).

despite initial misgivings, reluctantly endorsed the operations in and around the Panguna mine, including ensuring the security of the Espie Highway. He gave me the flexibility to plan and execute these operations, which—amazing as it seems looking back—resulted in very few losses of life on either side.

Lt Col. Jethro Usurup, the director of health services from HQ PNGDF, flew to Panguna to assist in planning for medical evacuations so that injured soldiers' lives could be saved. His personal interest was invaluable. The lives of many soldiers, policemen, and civilians were saved by linking our medivac directly to three sites: Arawa General Hospital, another medical facility owned and operated by BCL at Arawa, and the Panguna Medical Centre. As operations officer, I stressed the importance of doing everything humanly possible to save the lives of anyone injured on operations—soldiers, rebels, and civilians alike. No distinctions were to be made.

As we settled into our operations, it became increasingly obvious that there was a growing conflict of view between Col. Leo Nuia, the chief of operations at HQ PNGDF back in Port Moresby, and some of the senior command team at Arawa and Aropa. Loyalty to Nuia from Lieutenant Colonels Salamas and Maris was obvious, while Colonel Dotaona's command authority as the deputy controller in Arawa was being undermined. This growing conflict of view over how operations should be conducted began to take its toll on us as the subordinate officers in the field.

Colonel Dotaona was a kind, approachable, and consistent senior officer. He was my CO in 1978, and I learnt a lot under his command as did many others. Fit, sober, and intelligent, he served as a role model to many of us. His quiet manners and willing ear always served as an example to us. He was articulate in his public relations, and his daily news conferences in Arawa became the conduit through which the general public gained confidence in what the state was doing.

The arrival of four Australian-donated helicopters on 31 July provided a welcome boost to our morale. Painted in PNGDF colours, the Iroquois flew from Australia via Rabaul and Buka and were received in theatre with great jubilation by our forces. In providing these helicopters under the Defence Cooperation Program, Australia insisted on certain restrictions being agreed on and respected. The helicopters were to be used for resupply and general troop mobility, logistics support, and medevac operations only. They were not to be fitted out as gunships or used in any offensive capacity. These restrictions would become a source of contention in defence relations between Australia and PNG, especially in the face of Australian media reports claiming that the helicopters were being used as primitive gunships.

In reality, while weapons were strapped onto the frames of the helicopters during resupplies, these were for self-defence purposes. Matters grew more complicated when the Australian media claimed that the helicopters had been used to dump the bodies of executed BRA insurgents at sea. In an interview on Australian television, Col. Leo Nuia—then in charge of field operations in Bougainville—admitted such atrocities, earning him the label 'the butcher of Bougainville'. Nuia's revelations jeopardised further support from Australia, a major donor partner, and dampened public opinion in the region. Nevertheless, my air mobility was greatly enhanced, and we began to use the helicopters for patrol insertions and extractions, resupply, and medivac. My prior training in using helicopters for such operational purposes was paying dividends.

As the terrain around Mount Kupei and Paruparu provided very restricted landing zones, I incorporated scaling and abseiling practices using the safety division in the mine. A classmate from Madang, Sama Menambo, was in charge. He, along with 2ⁿᵈ Lt Charles Samalas, put in a training team and began an intensive in-house training programme using, first, the concrete towers in the mine pit and then, after confidence was built up among the troops, real-life deployments using the Iroquois helicopters to rappel into their patrol insertion points. Sadly, Lieutenant Samalas would be killed in 1990 during a clearance operation on Buka Island.

As this training was getting into full swing, the troops at Panguna were visited by a parliamentary committee headed by Sir Hugo Berghauser and Philemon Embel. After lunch with the delegation,

I organised A Company under Capt. Kessy Rovae to meet for a field demonstration in the top part of the mine pit. I had been informed that the committee had already been sanctioned by Joint Force HQ to meet with the troops to gather impressions and report back to Parliament.

In the meantime, however, Lieutenant Colonel Salamas had arrived at the mine from Arawa. Asking for me at the command post, he was informed that I was with A Company, who were running a demonstration for the parliamentary committee high on one of the surrounding ridges. For some reason, upon hearing this, Salamas blew his top. Getting on the high-frequency radio, he made it clear, in no uncertain terms, that he objected to the committee's presence at the mine and was unhappy with them meeting my men and seeing a field demonstration. He demanded that they be removed from the mine.

I was caught between my civil duties to a parliamentary delegation and my need to respect and obey orders from my military superior. I informed Philemon Embel about the sudden intervention by my commanding officer. As he was not far from the radio, he had heard every detail of the conversation between Salamas and me, including the use of coarse language by Salamas in demanding the immediate removal of the delegation. After an embarrassing and abrupt end to the briefing of the parliamentarians, I was further grilled by Salamas in his room about the event. At no time was I given the opportunity to explain to him the background to the meeting and the direction from Joint Force HQ.

A few days later, Colonel Dotaona, Salamas, and I were called to appear before the Parliamentary Privileges Committee in Port Moresby. Salamas went into damage control. He had to acknowledge that the military was subordinate to civilian authority. I prepared my statement to the Privileges Committee as carefully and as precisely as possible. Attempting to protect my senior officer, I explained that Salamas's language was not directed at the visiting parliamentary delegation in any way; instead, he had wanted to find out what (the bloody hell!) was happening with A Company at the top of the mine. This was not exactly true, but hopefully, it was a way out. I was required to appear before the committee, which chose to take my words as being essentially a correct description of what had happened, which saved Lieutenant Colonel Salamas's immediate future.

Towards the end of July and at the discretion of HQ PNGDF, the combined Mortar Platoon was deployed to Bougainville with 81 mm mortars and high-explosive (HE) rounds to support the troops. Being a former Mortar Platoon commander, I was perplexed at this decision as mortars are an area weapon, not a pinpoint weapon. I was a professionally trained mortar officer, and I knew of the high probability of lethal effects and significant collateral damage when using mortars against rebels mixing with unarmed civilians. This would be yet another decision that was made in Port Moresby without a proper appreciation of the actual situation on the ground and the likely consequences of this indiscriminate use of force.

Early on the morning of 17 July, twenty troops raided a suspected BRA camp at the back of the plantation and airport at Aropa. This was a result of intelligence information that the BRA was stockpiling food supplies. The H-hour was 3.30 a.m. as first light in Bougainville is 4.30 a.m. Colonel Dotaona was present. While the cordon and search operations were under way, a junior officer was seen pointing his rifle and threatening suspects in an unnecessarily harsh manner. Colonel Dotaona intervened and told the officer to stop his harassment.

The officer then lifted his carbine and, in a very dangerous and unprofessional way, shouted back at Colonel Dotaona. The whole scene was very tense. After the junior officer had backed off, I relieved him of his command and told him to report to me at Panguna. Later, the CO—Lt Col. Walter Salamas—told me that Dotaona had no right to intervene during the operations. I thought otherwise. I stood the junior officer down and sent him back to Port Moresby on the first flight out of Bougainville. In doing so, I saved his career as I saw he had great potential if he could learn to moderate his behaviour. He rose to the rank of major, including a posting as an instructor at the Royal Military College, Duntroon. After resigning from the defence force, he was headhunted by a leading bank to be their regional security manager.

From my standpoint as operations officer, I could see that a decline in troop and unit discipline was already setting in. When casualties increased among the troops, so did the level of indiscipline. There was a breakdown in command and control at all levels, and inevitably, this had a significant impact on troop morale and affected the progress of the operations. Our particular challenges were not so much the troops with me in the field and forward at Panguna but with the rear echelons based at Arawa with the Joint Force HQ and the supporting units stationed at Aropa Airport. They ended up in uncleared villages or hanging around at Keita or the Loloho clubs or mixing with civilians in and around Arawa. This was mainly attributed to a lack of proper chain of command and the incompetence of officers appointed to take control of the rear echelon troops.

The issue of discipline was brought to my notice so many times that I raised it with the CO and asked him to give directives for undisciplined troops and their immediate superiors. I said that our smooth operations depended on the contingent being brought forward on the line as additional manpower from the supporting units would enable us to conduct operations with greater ease and enable valuable lives to be saved with effective leadership at all levels of command. As there was still an abundance of liquor in the province, we sent out an instruction that each subunit would have the opportunity to stand down on a Friday or Saturday and have a hot meal and three beers per soldier. This worked very well. Despite the fact that many units were composite or lacked the full complement of troops, we managed to keep the troops together. However, command and control was still an important challenge.

On the night of 17 August, I got an SOS from the Kobuan checkpoint near Kieta from Sergeant Manase, 2RPIR, to inform me that soldiers had fired at the driver of a speeding utility that had failed to stop at the military checkpoint. Upon searching the vehicle, they found a soldier from the engineer detachment, Private Mena, deceased from gunshot wounds and a colleague who had sustained injuries. I took off for the checkpoint to take control of the situation. Driving at speed, I fumed at the needless loss of life. I had tried my best to minimise deaths, and now this futile incident had happened.

At the checkpoint, there were confusion, anguish, and despair. The circumstances were reported to me as follows: a soldier in a civilian vehicle, allegedly under the influence of liquor, had failed to stop at the roadblock, and the senior non-commissioned officer in command had given the order to shoot as the vehicle appeared hostile. It was an unfortunate incident involving the loss of a valuable life. I stood down the soldiers on duty at the checkpoint and immediately reported the matter to the CO and to Deputy Controller Colonel Dotaona.

Not long afterwards, the CO—whom I was having great difficulty in contacting—arrived, having been informed of the incident. I stood down the platoon for a few days until further notice. The deceased soldier was sadly boxed home. The number of accidents now began to rise further, bringing much concern at battlefield discipline, command and control, and leadership at all levels of command. The death of Private Mena took a toll on the morale of the engineer detachment and the rest of the contingent. In the face of these problems, the personal leadership of Maj. Joseph Fabila, who was the engineer liaison officer, was superb. He was able to calm the soldiers by providing counselling and remained with them until they were relieved after three months of continuous operation.

In addition to my other duties, I was responsible for orderly staff duties at the command post. As such, I was shown all the paperwork that came in and was responsible for the situation reports (sitrep) that were sent to HQ PNGDF and Joint Force HQ at Arawa. My instructions were clear. I was to report to Colonel Dotaona at Arawa and not to send correspondence directly to Port Moresby.

Unfortunately, as the operations progressed, the CO Lt Col. Walter Salamas appeared to place himself on a personal war footing with Colonel Dotaona. He regularly paraded me in his office to inform me that, on all operational matters, I was to report to him and not Dotaona or even HQ PNGDF. He made it clear that he called the shots and not me or any other person at the forward tactical headquarters. He was rude and frequently held me responsible for issues that were beyond my control. In my annual evaluation, he downgraded my performance rating, a matter that I put down to personal bias as I knew from feedback I was getting from company commanders that I was performing well above expectations. I tried to remind myself that Lieutenant Colonel Salamas was working under extreme pressure, torn between two demanding senior officers, Colonel Dotaona at Joint Force HQ and Col. Leo Nuia at HQ PNGDF. Despite these difficulties and disappointments, I remained calm and continued to serve Salamas regardless of his vindictiveness towards me and others in our team at forward tactical headquarters.

As I read the changing tactical situation on the ground, I came to appreciate the dynamics of dealing with the Bougainvillean villagers, who were beginning to be displaced from their homes by the increase in military pressure on the BRA as well as rebel propaganda and oppression. My approach to battlefield leadership was to be as far forward as possible. Field commanders need to be with their troops at all times to give directions and to monitor the operational situation as it progresses. Keeping troops informed in changing tactical and security situations requires leaders who are cool and not easily swayed by the emotions of their troops. The responsibility of the leader is to make sure that the mission is never compromised by hasty decisions or ill-conceived reprisal action.

As we pushed forwards with military operations in August, the inevitable happened. Civilians who lost their homes put pressure on the authorities to provide them with safe areas to live away from the BRA. To meet this pressure and to provide greater freedom of action to the military, government care centres were created. The concept was good, but with insufficient troops and police to administer them, the centres became a drain on manpower. They would also become a source of BRA support for the supply of food and intelligence gathering. Ultimately and through lack of appropriate funding quite apart from anything else, they proved counterproductive and, at times, fatal for the security forces in years to come.

Meanwhile, the security forces applied more pressure, mainly through the surveillance of civilians who were known or suspected of being in contact with rebels, resulting in increased rebel activity. The Espie Highway, which ran from the mine all the way down to Loloho

Harbour, experienced a sharp increase in rebel activity. The rebels used the dense jungle cover on either side of the highway to shoot at mineworkers and security forces. Another effective method adopted by the BRA was to blow up the power pylons carrying electricity to the mine using explosives stolen from the mine magazine.

One evening, about 7 September, just before I returned to Port Moresby to be relieved, I was ordered to instruct Engineer Liaison Officer Maj. Joseph Fabila to booby-trap selected power pylons along the Espie Highway. The order came from HQ PNGDF, Murray Barracks Operations Branch, without any prior analysis or assessment. Major Fabila told me that the order, while possible to fulfil, would not easily be achieved as booby-trapping was not a skill readily available in the Engineer Battalion. He told me that he would need to reorganise his men, train them, and then select a highly specialised team to lay the booby traps. It was indeed a very tall order and near impossible.

One of the difficulties was that the engineer company was being deployed as a light infantry unit. This was contrary to their initial task for assisting in engineer-related activities. It had been forced on us by the shortage of manpower in infantry companies, at that time running at barely 50 per cent of strength (around 60 men per company out of the usual strength of 110). Under the circumstances, the engineer detachment performed remarkably well, and no doubt, many of their junior non-commissioned officers stood out as very committed and with a lot of leadership potential. Major Fabila played a crucial role by using his own personal skills and leadership to direct his engineer troops who were not only deployed in infantry tasks but also used for many non-core tasks, such as the provision of escorts and other limited operations around the mine.

The setting up of booby traps required many years of training, and only those with special aptitude could be detailed to deal with double-edged explosives. I was uncomfortable and apprehensive, but the directive from higher headquarters (HQ PNGDF) was definite: we were required to execute. It was undeniable that unless we could stop the rebels from blowing up the power pylons, mine operations would not be able to recommence as power to the ore crushers and other mine equipment was vital to the mine. Fabila and I took the gamble.

By then, my replacement as operations commander had arrived. Maj. Seah Albert Rolman, my classmate from Joint Services College, was eager to take over the task of field operations, but he was instantly taken aback with the level of intensity in operations as contact with the rebels had intensified. I was at the Panguna mine when I got an urgent call that a major incident had happened near Morgan Junction towards the Rorovana Village back road. The incident was very unfortunate. A member of the engineer splinter team, Cpl Francis Wasali, while setting up the first of the planned booby traps, accidentally applied pressure to the mechanism of the booby trap and exploded the ordnance, instantly killing himself. We were all shocked over the loss of a valuable life. The mood of the men and the maintenance of their morale depended on Major Fabila's personal skills in holding his troops together, a task he performed extremely well.

Major Rolman was badly affected. Neither psychologically nor emotionally prepared for active operations at this level of intensity, he developed high blood pressure overnight and couldn't sleep. The regimental medical officer, Capt. Louie Samiak, reported that he had no option but to medically downgrade the new operations officer. He advised that Major Rolman was not medically fit to remain in the front line and had to be removed from Bougainville as soon as practicable. Having prepared myself for such an eventuality and having often been in similar situations, especially along the Indonesian border when my colleagues were mentally or medically unable to lead border patrols, I volunteered to stay on to fill the gap. Unfortunately, the chief of operations, Colonel Nuia, overruled this, and said I was to leave Bougainville within twenty-four hours and return to Port Moresby to report to him at HQ PNGDF.

It was now 21 September 1989. I had spent eighty-four days on Bougainville. I had done what I could and was reassured by Colonel Dotaona that I had set an appropriate standard for my predecessors to continue. But I also knew that I personally would not be able to save Bougainville, at least not as a middle-ranking officer, and that the downward spiral in security was likely to accelerate as police and defence force operations intensified.

I boarded the Air Niugini flight from Aropa Airport in central Bougainville, anxious about what was waiting for me in Port Moresby. As we flew over the Crown Prince Range westwards, I felt for the troops I was leaving behind. Over a cold drink, I took out my diary and entered a few more memories of my time on Bougainville, knowing very well that we were in for the long haul. I was safe, at least for the time being, and was flying thousands of feet above Bougainville and away from the pressures of the situation there. I was content with my own personal command experience and with the fact that no soldiers had died under my command, apart from the incident at Kobuan in which Private Mena had been shot dead at the roadblock and the booby trap accident that had cost Cpl Francis Waslai's valuable life. Our medivac plans worked well, and I hoped that no other lives would be lost on active operations. I concluded by writing, 'Thank you, Bougainville, for 84 days of operational experience.' It's mildly embarrassing to think of it now, thirty years later, but I signed off as 'Soldier Boy'.

I arrived at Jacksons Airport with my field pack and an echelon bag with my M16 rifle, field-stripped into its four major pieces. Weni was waiting for me at the arrival lounge, and we departed for her flat at Tokarara. I waited for four days to see Col. Leo Nuia, only to be told that he did not have time to see me, and I was to return to Igam Barracks to continue my job as senior instructor for the cadet training wing.

I wrote my post-operation report and sent if off to HQ PNGDF. I was critical of what I saw as the likely outcome of the current defence force operations in Bougainville. I said that our doctrine was not well matched to the nature of the internal threats we were facing. In my view, standard brigade and battalion formation operations and tactics were inappropriate to the close quarters warfare we were experiencing on Bougainville. Instead, stealth, a high level of bushcraft, advanced skills in weapons handling, and highly trained and well-motivated small teams of no more than ten men, led by active and politically aware junior commanders, were the paramount requirement. In countering insurgents, we needed to use and adapt to their own modus operandi and get inside and disrupt their own decision cycles. Whatever they did, we needed to do it better but in a way that discriminated carefully between active insurgents on the one hand and a frightened and oppressed civilian population on the other, whose own choices were very limited. In the same report, I reiterated the importance of civil affairs. The defence force needed to operate openly and in close partnership with the civilian authority as their backing was essential to success, especially when trying to enforce government policies and expectations and when using only some of the elements of force open to us.

On Bougainville, even, or perhaps especially, in these very early years, psychological operations were paramount. As early as 1989, it was evident that the defence force was failing to understand the dynamics of civilian support to the militants. The role of the defence force as an aid to the civil power was misapprehended, and the hierarchy had no immediate remedy to retrain and prepare our troops for a protracted operation in Bougainville. Police and defence force mistreatment of suspects and civilians did not in any way give us the needed psychological and tactical advantage over the civilian population. As Mao Zedong said that the people are like water, and the rebel is like a fish; thus, separating the guerrilla from the people renders the guerrilla ineffective and exposed. The difficulty, though, was how to achieve this separation as the rebels would always seek to integrate with their civilian support bases, which they needed for their food, sanctuary, psychological support, reinforcement, and intelligence. It follows that our operations had to be focused as much or more on civilian centres and villages than on insurgent forces away from villages. Frightened and oppressed villagers would align with whichever side, insurgent or government force, was stronger, more active, more present, and more caring. But this required manpower, strict discipline, restraint, money and other resources, and a well-thought-out set of policies as well as a long-range vision on the part of government. We were very short on heart and mind, which was central to gaining public support.

I was also critical in my report of the defence force standing orders, which had very little relevance to the local conditions on Bougainville.

Deficiencies in operational planning, logistical planning and support, and crucially funds were overwhelming the morale of the troops and weakening the fighting spirit of our soldiers. The quest to control operations in Bougainville from HQ PNGDF was a clear obstacle and hindrance to the smooth running of the state of emergency by the controller and his deputy. Such weaknesses in the command and control structure and delegation of powers affected the integrity of many decisions.

With my experiences and observations, I offered the following comments regarding the overall command and control of the operations on Bougainville to that point:

a. The appointment of Col. Lima Dotaona from the military as deputy controller of the state of emergency gives him all the powers and responsibilities of the controller, Police Commissioner Paul Tohian. He should be allowed to command and control the state of emergency without interference by the chief of operations or even commander PNGDF as this undermines the intergrity of the appointment and the state of emergency. They can collectively coordinate efforts but not undermine his position.

b. The call-out of the defence force must strictly be in accordance with the call-out provisions, and the rules of engagement (ROE) must be clearly promulgated to the commanding officer and the subordinate commanders. The command structure, including chain of command and reporting lines of communication, should be clearly visible and laid out. This includes the linkages to the civilian's authority and respective government agencies.

c. At the operational and tactical level on the ground, all subordinate commanders and supporting subunits must be fully familiar with reporting channels, tasking, and the importance of disseminating information down to the troops.

d. Bougainville is a 'hearts and minds' operation, and winning the support of the local population is indeed central to the overall success of the government presence and military operation.

e. The PNGDF has to step up on discipline and enforce the Defence Force Code of Military Discipline as a very important aspect of soldiering.

I was never able to get any explanation for two issues that troubled me: the use of 81 mm mortars and the use of booby traps. There was no doubt headquarters had the authority to issue directives about what they perceived would give the tactical edge to our troops to achieve a desired military outcome. My fear was that the use of such force would quickly become normalised and considered appropriate by the troops and their subordinate commanders. They would rapidly become dependent on the use of excessive force and see it as an important part of future military operations. Many of us down the line disagreed with the deployment of 81 mm mortars and the use of booby traps, believing instead that strict regard to proportionality in the use of force was the only way in which we could achieve anything like military success in the Bougainville context, where our opponents were never more than a ragtag bunch of lightly equipped irregulars carrying old WWII rifles and handmade weaponry, augmented occasionally with explosives stolen from the mine or the local quarry.

We were not facing North Vietnamese regulars, the Vietcong, or Chinese communist guerrillas in the Malayan jungle—which is not to say that the BRA posed no danger, just that they were not an organised army. Therefore, battalion-, brigade-, or even company-sized formations were not required. Instead, section- or, at most, platoon-sized engagements led by officers with skills and training in command and leadership, not heavy weaponry, were needed.

I continued my role as senior instructor at the Officer Cadet Wing, placing extra emphasis on junior leadership, man management, discipline, and restraint in the use of force. I also took the opportunity to conduct officer training and share my experiences on Bougainville with junior and senior officers as well as non-commissioned officers, underlining as often as I could the importance of the lessons I had learnt.

In May 1990, I was officially informed from the Office of the Governor General that I was to be awarded a medal from the Queen for my services to the PNGDF and the North Solomons provincial government, as it was then known. I was to be made a Member of the Military Division of the Most Excellent Order of the British Empire (MBE). The award was on the advice of Col. Lima Dotaona and Lt Col. Ignatius Lai, who recommended that I be recognised for my service to the defence force and to Bougainville. I have never been an advocate of receiving such awards as I have always thought that it was the troops, rather than the officers, who deserved the government's support and recognition. Hence, I felt that my MBE belonged to the troops. Nonetheless, it was a pleasure to have my work recognised.

I sent for Mum and Dad to come to Port Moresby and accommodated them at Granville Motel for the investiture. I felt that the award was also for them. I wanted them to see it as the fruit of all their pains and struggles to see their children successful in their individual lives.

On an afternoon in June 1990, the award recipients paraded at Government House and were given their respective medals. Mum and Dad had the chance to shake hands with the acting governor general, Dennis Young, a naturalised citizen formally from Australia who congratulated me on my award. Col. Lima Dotaona was awarded a CBE (Commander of the British Empire) for his service to Bougainville's peace efforts, an award he truly deserved.

On 14 June that year, Weni gave birth to our son Moka Kauru at Angau General Hospital, adding joy to our small family. In October I was cleared by the Selection and Appointments Committee, a senior defence committee at HQ PNGDF, to attend the prestigious Australian Army Command and Staff College at Fort Queenscliff, Victoria, in 1991. Weni and I agreed that she should take leave without pay and accompany me with our children—Futua, Maib, and Moka—to Queenscliff. But her request was not approved by the chairman of the National Broadcasting Commission, Prof. Sir Renagi Lohia. Despite having been awarded Journalist of the Year in 1987, she was forced to resign, ending her fourteen-year career as one of PNG's most outstanding radio journalists and cutting short what could have been an even more remarkable career.

By December 1990, the armed insurrection on Bougainville had escalated with no sign of peace in sight. The defence force continued to stagnate. Soldiers continued to lose their precious lives, and civilian fatalities also increased. Failures in logistics support, and leadership became so appalling that troop morale inevitably faltered, with troops becoming careless both on and off duty.

As I prepared for my one-year period of study at the Australian Army Command and Staff College in Queenscliff, I was quite sure that my personal commitment to Bougainville was not over. Now as I reflect and write about the events of 1989 and 1990, the conflict on Bougainville dominates my thoughts. In my first operational tour from July to September 1989, I had my share of tactical-level operational successes. The Panguna mine, though shut intermittently through loss of power and labour disruptions, nonetheless continued to function. By pushing my tactical operational base forwards to the mine, I was able to achieve at least some kind of limited operational dominance. Equally important, I was able to tap into the Panguna mine's logistical supply chain. We were on the offensive, even if it was only in a limited way. We had elements of the BRA on the run. Our casualties were surprisingly light considering the amount of ground we were covering. And very importantly, we were on reasonable—even good—terms with the villages we were covering. However, I knew that much more work was required to win hearts and minds.

A curiosity of this deployment to Bougainville is that I deployed under orders for an operation that was styled 'Operation Blueprint'. Although I was the operations officer in charge of devising the tactical-level operational deployments and objectives for Blueprint, Lieutenant Colonel Salamas never saw fit to share these orders with me; and to this day, I have not seen them. Exactly what Blueprint was designed to achieve I can only speculate. While this is a hell of a way to run anything, it gives full scope for individual initiative, which I certainly exploited to the full.

Despite the limited gains that the troops under me were able to achieve, the medium- and longer-term outlook at the end of my first operational tour was not good. We were running a stop-start campaign with muddled objectives. Government direction was uncertain and, at times, plainly contradictory. The senior leadership of the PNGDF were at odds with each other.

And the war was about to take an ominous turn. The PNG government, having failed to negotiate with Francis Ona, the original landowner at Panguna mine, put a price of PGK 200,000 on his head. Then on 11 September 1989, Minister John Bika was assassinated. The provincial member for Nasioi and Pirung and minister for commerce and liquor licensing in the North Solomons Provincial Assembly, Bika had not been afraid to make his personal views known and had openly opposed the breaking away of Bougainville from PNG. Just ten days before I left Bougainville, Colonel Dotaona was told by Minister for State Ted Diro, the first indigenous and former defence force commander, that the government wanted him to institute tougher measures against the rebels, akin in effect to a search and destroy mission. This intent was further reinforced when the sensible and conciliatory colonel Dotaona was recalled in October and replaced by hardliner Col. Leo Nuia, soon to be branded by the Australian media as the 'butcher of Bougainville'. As David Lloyd George is reputed to have said of General Haig, Nuia was an absolutely brilliant man, to the very top of his boots.

Any prospect of a conciliatory approach to the problems of Bougainville was now well and truly over. Those who believed that a military solution was achievable were now in the ascendancy. In short, the scene was set, tragically, for a real PNG-style FUBAR—that is, fucked up (or fouled up) beyond all recognition (or repair)—in which thousands of lives would soon be lost. What's more, the mine was closed, seemingly forever or at least until Bougainvilleans could run their own affairs.

CHAPTER 14

Training and Instructing with the Australian Army, 1991–93

Self-control is the chief element in self-respect, and self-respect is the chief element in courage.

—Thucydides, 404 BC

Learn to obey before you command.

—Solon of Athens, 638–559 BC

Special orders to No. 1 Section:

1. *This position will be held and the Section will remain here until relieved.*
2. *The enemy cannot be allowed to interfere with this programme.*
3. *If this Section cannot remain here alive it will remain here dead. But in any case it will remain here.*
4. *Should any man through shell-shock or such cause attempt to surrender he will stay here dead.*
5. *Should all guns be blown out the Section will use their standard issue M1915 Stielhandgranates, captured Mills bombs, sticky bombs and other novelties.*
6. *Finally the position as stated will be held.*

—Notice found in a German pillbox at Passchendaele
in 1917 after its recapture by Allied troops and
subsequently translated into English

*If I go on, I shall die. If I stay behind I shall be dishonoured. It
is better to go on.*

—Ashanti war song

I. Australian Army Command and Staff College, Fort Queenscliff, Victoria, 1991

I arrived at Australian Army Command and Staff College, Fort
Queenscliff, Victoria, with my family in early January 1991. At that
time, joint training not being the requirement that it now is, the army,
navy, and air force staff colleges were all separate institutions: the army
college was at Fort Queenscliff, the navy college was at HMAS *Penguin*
in Sydney, and the air force college was at the Royal Australian Air
Force base, Fairburn, Canberra.

Fort Queenscliff has a long and distinguished history. Fortifications
were first installed there in 1859, when the Victorian government
placed guns on Shortland's Bluff to command the entrance to Port
Phillip Bay. Construction of the fort itself began in 1882, the result of
increased activity in the Pacific by the Russians. Many of the present red
brick buildings of Fort Queenscliff date back to a major construction
programme in the 1930s. The Australian Staff College was established
at the fort in 1947. It was renamed the Australian Army Command and
Staff College in 1982.

Its motto—borrowed very unimaginatively from the British Army
Staff College at Camberley and used at similar staff colleges elsewhere,
such as Quetta in modern-day Pakistan, the Indian Defence Services
Staff College at Wellington in Tamil Nadu, and the Canadian Army
Command and Staff College at Fort Frontenac, Kingston, Ontario—is
'Tam marte quam minerva.' This has various translations; for example,
'As much by war [Mars] as by wisdom [Minerva],' 'As much by the pen
as the sword,' and more simply but rather less accurately 'Wisdom is

strength.' Symbolising wisdom, the unit insignia for each of the above-named defence colleges has the owl prominently incorporated, recalling the legend that Minerva—the Roman virgin goddess of music, poetry, medicine, and wisdom—kept an owl perched on her right arm as her sacred symbol of knowledge and wisdom. The role of the Australian Army Command and Staff College is to prepare selected army officers for senior command and staff appointments. More specifically, it aims to 'create an environment which encourages . . . systematic habits of the mind and which develops the ability to read critically, think analytically and communicate lucidly' about the profession of arms.

I was looking forward to this year of study and reflection away from the pressures of service life in Papua New Guinea. Our arrival into Australia was marred by the fact that a small portable iron I had bought in Singapore a few years earlier and a small, but priceless, Sony transistor radio were both stolen while staying at Randwick Hotel in Sydney on the eve of 8 January 1991. Putting the incident to the back of our minds, the following day, we took the bus to Sydney's Kingsford Smith Airport for our flight to Melbourne, where we were met by Directing Staff Lt Col. Mike Shaw. We drove through Geelong and Leopold and then to Point Lonsdale, where we were shown the house at 7 Sara Street, in which we were to live for the year.

Point Lonsdale is a small coastal town on the Bellarine Peninsula near Queenscliff. Located 103 km south-west of Melbourne and 28 km south-east of Geelong, Point Lonsdale is one of two headlands that frame the entrance to Port Phillip Bay. It was a very convenient and pleasant place to live and concentrate on my studies, with good beach access and a public facilities business centre nearby. Also close by was Swan Island, where the Army Reserve First Commando Regiment administered a training area and other facilities.

The facilities for study and sports at Fort Queenscliff were extensive. Within the grounds were a historic black lighthouse and disappearing gun, a massive flagstaff, a nineteenth-century keep and underground magazine, and a sports oval. Towards the northern part of the college were tennis courts, a museum, and the officers' mess and function rooms. The main theatre was called Blamey Theatre after Field Marshal

Sir Thomas Alfred Blamey, who served in the Australian Army in both world wars and took command of the New Guinea Force during the Kokoda Trail campaign and later the Salamaua and Lae campaigns. Blamey is the only Australian soldier to have risen to the rank of field marshal. Adjacent to the Blamey Theatre was a well-stocked library with a computer laboratory below it.

The officers' mess was a cosy spot, well stocked with drinks of all sorts and newly renovated living-in accommodation. The mess was a good place to continue discussions started in the syndicate rooms. Invariably, solutions were discussed and problems solved in the cellar bars, where no lines were drawn between directing staff and students. Queenscliff was indeed an excellent facility, well set up with the infrastructure and amenities necessary for achieving the objectives and charter of the college.

Futua was enrolled at Point Lonsdale Primary School, Maib was enrolled at a Queenscliff preschool, and Moka remained at home with Weni as he was only nine months old. The main shopping centres were at Queenscliff, Point Lonsdale, Ocean Grove, and Geelong.

The commandant in our year was Brig. Gen. Jim Townley, a former battery commander in the 106th Field Battery, Royal Australian Artillery. The director of studies was Col. Ernie Chamberlain, a very articulate and smart officer from a military intelligence background. He was supported by over twenty directing and other staff, including Lieutenant Colonels Gary McKay, author of *In Good Company*, and Alastair Ross, a New Zealand artillery officer and Vietnam veteran with a very wry sense of humour.

Opening the academic year, the commandant encouraged us to make the most of the opportunities offered by the college. He said that, in its fifty or so years of existence, the college had produced many generals, improved many golf handicaps, and converted innumerable numbers of non-golfers to the royal and ancient game. He said that the year would be broken up with a variety of activities including academic work, visits to Australian institutions, and lots of social interactions. He made specific welcome to the foreign students and appointed Lieutenant Colonel Kanokchot from Thailand in charge of us. Maj. Mike Trafford was the overall head of the student body for the year. The aim of the course was to 'produce officers who can fulfil command and staff appointments at all levels in a single service or in multinational or interagency environments'.

Our syllabus was divided into several main parts: strategy and tactics, including military history; operational planning; peacekeeping and enforcement; international relations; communications skills; and elective studies. The students were divided into eight syndicates, with ten in each group. I was allotted to syndicate 3. My team members were Majors Brendan Sowry, Mark Patch, Paul Straughair, Mike Corne, Bruce Scott, Steve Barr, Craig Gillette, Karl Ernest Strachwitz (from Germany), and Mike Mutton, a civilian.

Our syndicate directing staff were Lieutenant Colonels Richard Howell and David Smith. Smith was my guidance officer, and he and Howell spent much of their free time coaching me through my studies. I owe them a great deal as they motivated me to work hard at my studies, gaining results that enabled me to be transferred to the Australian Defence Force the following year.

After two weeks of settling in, I drove into Leopold, a few minutes away from Queenscliff, to purchase a sedan for my family's use. At Cityside Cars, I bought a second-hand blue Mitsubishi sedan for a reasonable price. But as it was relatively old and kept breaking down, I kept in touch with the dealer at Cityside Cars, David Fernyhough.

David Fernyhough came out to Point Lonsdale a few times, and during the course of our conversations, he realised that I had served in Bougainville. He was interested in this and invited me around to his place along with Weni and the children. Later, he invited me to join the Leopold Lions Club, and I became an active member. When I wasn't studying, I spent most weekends in and around Leopold and Geelong on working bees and fundraising for the club. I was even invited to be a guest speaker at the Melbourne Lions Club.

This was a rewarding experience as many questions were raised about Bougainville and the future of PNG. In my encounters with Australians, I discovered a strong affection for, and interest in, PNG. Some had relatives who had fought in PNG during WWII, others were former public servants with the Australian administration, and still others had worked in the Panguna mine or had shares in Bougainville Copper Ltd. It confirmed to me that PNG enjoyed a very close and important relationship with Australia, both because of geographic proximity and because of the rich history that we shared.

The foreign staff and students formed a tight social and sporting group. We formed our own soccer team, in which Karl Earnest from Germany and I were the key players. Both of us played as forwards. Our main aim was to score two or three goals quickly in the first half and then to defend our goalmouth. Mardi, our Malaysian student, controlled the backline. We remained undefeated throughout the year, playing against fellow Australian students, staff, and even visiting colleges from other states. Unfortunately, the Australian students at the college defeated us in the grand finals. Did I say Australians are competitive?

My nights were long and cold as I often had to read and complete my assignments into the early hours. Not having a good grasp of computers at this time was a hindrance, and I would spend many hours at WO Les Terret's place, our quartermaster, using his computer. Les Terret lived only a few houses away.

A few of us from overseas got together and planned two nights away exploring the Great Ocean Road that runs through Anglesea at Point Addis Marine National Park and along the coast to Port Campbell National Park, where the famous Twelve Apostles landmark can be seen. Our close student friend from New Zealand, Gordon Milward, and his wife, Katrina, would camp out with us in caravan parks. Those weekends were greatly enjoyed by our families, and the kids got on very well with one another.

Lt Col. Gordon Milward, ONZM, has gone on to have a distinguished career in the New Zealand Army, commanding the 2/1st Infantry Battalion and serving as chief of staff operations in East Timor, chief of the observer group in the Golan Heights, and New Zealand defence adviser to PNG, Solomon Islands, and Vanuatu. He returned to the Army Staff College to serve on the directing staff in

1996–97 and is currently programme principal lead capability at the New Zealand Defence Force Institute for Leader Development.

On our first study break, I took the opportunity to drive to Canberra with Weni and the children to spend time at the Australian National University, researching a paper, 'The Use of Helicopters for Manoeuvre Operations in Close Country Using Vietnam as the Case Study'. While in Canberra, we were assisted by Col. David Josiah, PNG's defence attaché. It was an enjoyable week as, with my research finished, we were able to visit a number of museums and landmarks before returning to Victoria.

In June, the college organised an excursion around Australia called Full Circle. It started in Melbourne and then went to Sydney, Brisbane, Townsville, the Northern Territory, and Western Australia before heading back to Victoria. The trip enabled us to fully appreciate Australia's vast size and relative emptiness—in other words the true flavour of what Prof. Geoffrey Blainey, in his 1966 book, termed *The Tyranny of Distance: How Distance Shaped Australia's History*.

In October, there were five vacancies at the Tactics and War Administration School at Kokoda Barracks, Canungra, Queensland, a part of the Australian Army's Land Warfare Centre. While waiting for my academic and military studies results, I was shortlisted among the graduating students from Queenscliff to take up a posting. Eventually, the commandant, Jim Townley, after an interview, officially informed me that I was recommended along with four other Australian students to take up a lecturing position in military strategy and tactics the following year. I was humbled by such an important offer, and pleased, as it would enhance my learning and experience in the Australian Defence Force. My whole perspective on life, military science, and the art of war would be changed by this appointment. I would come to understand the many dimensions of conflict resolution, international relations, peace enforcement, and the management of battlefield logistical planning and intelligence as these were critical tools in the successful conduct of land warfare operations.

Graduation day from the Australian Army Command and Staff College was 10 December 1990. We gathered at the Blamey Theatre, and the commandant presented us with our graduation certificates and read out our postings. I invited Weni and my civilian sponsor, the late lieutenant colonel John Dixon, and his wife, Diane, to the graduation. The graduation reception was held at the officers' mess. We shared moments of happiness and sadness, parting after a very enjoyable year both professionally and socially. Many of us openly shed tears as it was likely to be the last time we would see one another again.

With Commandant Brig. Gen. Jim Townley's farewell speech still echoing in my ears, I departed Queenscliff having spent not one day or even a single hour at the Point Lonsdale Golf Course, unlike the majority of my classmates, who had no doubt improved their golf handicaps. A handful would make it to the rank of general. But so far as I am aware, I was the first non-golfer in my class to be promoted to brigadier general—and less than four years after graduating.

Walking out of the Australian Command and Staff College for the last time that December day, I knew that I was very privileged to be a graduate of a highly respected military institution that produced senior army officers and generals across Australia and the Commonwealth. I was even more grateful for the confidence the Australian Army had shown in me as a foreign student to be given the rare opportunity of a follow-on posting as an instructor at the Australian Army Land Warfare Centre, Canungra.

II. Australian Army Land Warfare Centre, Canungra, 1992–93

The Australian Army Land Warfare Centre is a direct descendant of the Jungle Warfare School established at Canungra during WWII for Australian troops posted to the Pacific theatre (including, notably, for the campaigns against the Japanese attempting an overland attack on Port Moresby in 1942 via the Kokoda Trail, from their initial lodgements in Lae and Salamaua after the Japanese defeat in the Battle of the Coral Sea). The Tactics and War Administration Training Wing, to which I was to be posted, was a battle command school in all but name, dedicated to teaching all aspects of tactics and operations for officers up to and including battalion- and brigade-level appointments. It was an exciting and demanding prospect and one that I was looking forward to with great enthusiasm as a learning opportunity that could hardly be equalled and probably not bettered anywhere.

We spent two days packing before checking into Point Lonsdale Lodge near the Point Lonsdale Lighthouse. On 15 December, after the removal agents picked up our belongings, we packed our station wagon for the long drive from Victoria to Queensland via Sydney. Our first night was spent at Batemans Bay. The next day, we arrived in Sydney before departing for a holiday at Coffs Harbour on the north coast of New South Wales.

We arrived at Canungra early in the new year and, after reporting in, were billeted at Mermaid Waters on the Gold Coast. I commuted to Canungra until our house was fully renovated and the white goods installed. We were allocated a very modest married quarter in Canungra at 11 Mahoney Crescent. After settling in, we took leave back to PNG.

The commandant of the Australian Army Land Warfare Centre was a rather slightly built but very experienced Vietnam veteran, Col. J. (John) R. Paget. Colonel Paget had graduated from the Royal Military College, Duntroon, in 1966 and served in the Royal Australian Infantry, 7RAR in Vietnam and 2PIR Papua New Guinea before attending the Malaysian Armed Forces Staff College in 1983. He then served as assistant defence adviser and later as defence advisor to Kula Lumpur before taking up his current command. John welcomed Weni and me to the Canungra community and informed me that I was to be part of a unique and dynamic team of instructors at the Tactics and War Administration Wing. The wing prepared students as operations officers and battalion commanders, and it also conducted advanced tactics courses for lieutenant colonels.

Our senior instructor was yet another capable officer and former CO of 1RAR, Lt Col. J. (John) D. Petrie, AM. Petrie had only just arrived at Canungra from his previous posting as CO of 1RAR (15 December 1988–14 December 1991). He assisted us in our professional development and also took time out when we were instructing in the field with students on TEWTs.

I was part of the defensive operations team. Our team leader was Maj. Mike Hindmarsh from the Australian Special Forces. Hindmarsh was a very experienced and impressive infantry and special forces officer who had already served as a platoon commander with Second/Fourth Battalion Royal Australian Army (RAR) and as a troop commander and squadron commander with the Special Air Service Regiment (SASR). He later went on to command the SASR and Special Operations Command. He also commanded the Anzac special operations force in Kuwait in 1998 and the special operations components of Operation Bastille and Operation Falconer in the Iraq War and Operation Slipper in the Afghanistan War. In 2008, as a major general, Hindmarsh took over the command of all Australian forces in the Middle East area of operations. He retired from the Australian Army in 2009 and later joined the Army of the United Arab Emirates as commander of the UAE Presidential Guard and special forces adviser, in which capacity he is still serving. His awards and decorations include Officer of the Order of Australia, Distinguished Service Cross, and Conspicuous Service Cross.

The methods of instruction led by Maj. Mike Hindmarsh were very specific, with each phase of war being centrally prepared in the theatre before students were broken up into syndicates of about ten officers. Two instructors shared the leadership of each syndicate from syndicate discussions to the conduct of TEWTs. All TEWTs were based on scenarios involving large formations, up to brigade level in size, of fictitious enemies. Syndicates were provided with the enemy order of battle (orbat) and information on the tactics used in both offensive and defensive operations. Friendly forces, led by the syndicates, had their own integral orbat, including service support units, with information provided on the weapons available to the fighting units. The syndicates then had to come up with detailed scenarios in which the tactics to counter the opposing forces were devised along with detailed orders to implement the proposed operations.

During our courses, we would take students on day-long trips, looking at different topography and ground features and discussing tactical scenarios; for example, in the event of an invasion by outside forces through the northern approaches of Australia with the intention of capturing major Australian cities such as Brisbane, Sydney, Canberra, or Melbourne, how would one mobilise to prevent such an invasion and so forth? In mid-1992, a new subject was added to the syllabus: vital asset protection (VAP). A fellow instructor from New Zealand, Maj. Graeme Williams, and I shared the syllabus development and writing of instructions and teaching materials. Williams's experiences in the New Zealand Army included a variety of regimental, staff and training appointments, postings with the New Zealand Special Air Service, and a number of peacekeeping assignments including, from 2006 to 2008, as the UN chief military liaison officer in Timor Leste. Williams and I used our very different operational experiences to develop the VAP course syllabus, introducing scenarios for students to discuss and then plan solutions for the protection of strategic infrastructure and buildings in and around the Gold Coast from a wide variety of possible threats, including terrorist incursions.

The overall setting that we developed was to imagine that several terrorists had made their way into Australia. The terrorists were supported by elements drawn from dissident citizen groups living in Australia and were funded and supported by overseas groups. They were holding Australian citizens hostage in a variety of high-profile public places, including airports, harbours, and hospitals, both to publicise their demands and to terrorise the general public.

At that time, the concept of a terrorist attack on Australian soil was perceived as a remote possibility. This meant that our students, while taking the scenarios and proposed responses seriously enough, could still relax at the end of the exercise, which they did, enjoying a three-course meal and a few bottles of wine on the last day of their module. It has probably always been true that Australia, given its geography, sees itself as the 'lucky country'. Back when we were developing VAP scenarios, the threat of the spread of extreme ideologies seemed quite remote, and the risk of cyber threat was equally remote. There was serious debate in Australia about the future of the defence force, and public opinion was running high on the need for making savings on defence so that more money could be spent on much-needed services in areas such as education, health, and research and development. Nevertheless and despite the undercurrents of scepticism over defence spending that were a part of Australian public debate at that time, I took every opportunity to educate myself on Australian tactical doctrine and continued to network with my fellow Australian and New Zealand officers and to see as much of Australia as I could.

On the family front, Futua was enrolled to do grade six at Canungra Primary School, less than a kilometre away from the barracks. Maib was enrolled at the Canungra Preschool, and Moka spent a few hours a week at the local playschool.

I was still a non-golfer. Despite the fact that there was a well-kept nine-hole, par 70 golf course at the Canungra Army Golf Club and another nine-hole course at the Canungra Area Golf and Country Club, I preferred to drive to Tweed Heads, just across the Queensland–New South Wales border, or to Currumbin to fish for bass, a local delicacy. I also played in the local rugby touch club and, led by our team leader, the ferociously fit and legendary Maj. Mike Hindmarsh, had taken up hiking along with the rest of the tactics wing instructors.

One Friday, five of us set out to climb Mount Barney (elevation 1,359 metres), part of the McPherson Range and one of the highest mountains in Queensland. Mount Barney is close to the Queensland–New South Wales border, and we chose to climb it via Logan's Ridge to the east peak summit, rather than by the more leisurely Peasants Ridge. Before the climb, we had a BBQ and a few drinks. As usual, I took a bottle of Bundaberg rum ('Bundy' with its distinctive white polar bear mascot on the label to 'ward off any chill'), and we drank into the night. The following morning as we were climbing up Logan's Ridge with its spectacular views, we could all feel the effects of the liquor in our systems. After an eventful and lung-busting five hours and much to our delight (we were sober by then), we arrived at the summit. We reached the bottom of the mountain before last light and, pretty stiff and sore, called into a motel for a few rounds of beers before driving back to Canungra.

In June, I was instructed to return to Port Moresby to follow up on a proposal to conduct a command post exercise for the Papua New

Guinea Defence Force. This exercise was not pursued, but I took the opportunity to find out how things were going in Bougainville. It was apparent that the defence force was doing it tough as there was no clear political direction, and the security forces were desperate for logistics and other essential support to sustain operations. All other tasks like border patrol and civic actions were suspended for the year. Money was scarce, and the PNGDF was struggling in all aspects of force maintenance. I returned to Canungra disheartened but with a new appreciation of the real difficulties affecting the operational and combat readiness of the PNGDF.

I took Weni's mother, my mother-in-law, back to Canungra to show her a bit of Australia and continued instructing and enjoying the challenges. In December, Weni and her mother along with Maib and Moka returned to Port Moresby while I waited for Futua to finish school before joining them. In January 1993, we flew back to my hometown of Madang and took my father to come with us to Australia for a few months.

Dad was excited. I showed him around the Gold Coast and Brisbane, and we also took him to Hervey Bay for a weekend to do a spot of fishing. Unfortunately, I could only take Dad because Mum had been ill and was unable to travel. But I wished I could have also blessed her with the opportunity to see Australia.

After we returned from Hervey Bay, I developed pneumonia and was admitted to Canungra Hospital at Kokoda Barracks. While I was there, Chief Instructor Lt Col. Peter Persey visited me with an immediate signal from Canberra directing my recall to PNG for operational duties on Bougainville. The signal directed that I must return to PNG within fourteen days.

The commander of the PNGDF at that time was Brig. Gen. Robert Dademo, former chief of logistics, from Northern Province. The minister for defence was the former commissioner for police, Paul Tohian. As the situation in Bougainville was further deteriorating, Commander General Dademo called his counterpart at the Russell Defence Offices in Canberra—Gen. Peter Gration, the chief of the

ADF—to request my release from the Land Warfare Centre due to urgent operational requirements back in PNG. There was no argument.

After I was discharged from hospital, I told Weni, Dad, and the children that we were to return to PNG due to pressing issues in Bougainville. Meanwhile, as I would learn later, our chief instructor, Lt Col. Peter Persey, had been negotiating with defence headquarters in Canberra for an extension to my instructor's appointment or even a permanent transfer to the Australian Army. My team leader, Maj. Mike Hindmarsh, was visibly disappointed about my sudden recall. But in my own mind, I was determined to return to PNG and do what I had always been trained to do. While it was tempting to think of continuing in my current role as an instructor at the Australian Army's Land Warfare Centre, it was clear to me that service to my own country had to be given priority. I was reminded of my oath on joining the PNGDF to serve my country. On this, there could be neither debate nor argument. It was early April 1993, and my desire to serve my country and respond to the call of duty was paramount.

CHAPTER 15

Bougainville Operations with 1RPIR, 1993

Whatsoever thy hand findeth to do, do it with thy might; for there is no work, no device, no knowledge, no wisdom, in the grave, whither thou goest.

—Solomon, Ecclesiastes 9:10

Nothing will be wanting on my part towards the success of the common cause. I have eight Sail of Frigates under my command; the service I have to perform is important, and, I am acting not only without the orders of my Commander-in-Chief, but in some measure contrary to them. However . . . I am doing what is right and proper for the service of our King and Country. Political courage in an Officer abroad is as highly necessary as military courage.

—Admiral Lord Nelson, 24 July 1795

My family and I boarded an Air Niugini airbus from Brisbane International Airport on Friday, 2 April 1993. At Jacksons Airport we were met by Maj. Francis Agwi, rear echelon commander of First Regiment Taurama Barracks. I was to be the new operations officer for 1RPIR and would deploy to Bougainville as soon as arrangements could be made.

Major Agwi generously vacated his married quarters, which were always reserved for the regiment's operations officer. As we drove through the main gate at Taurama Barracks, I could feel the neglect of a unit whose regiment was on operations in Bougainville. The rear echelon was reduced to skeleton strength—the bare minimum required to do garrison duties. I noticed that the sentry was casual in his conduct as we passed through the gate—never a promising sign.

In the afternoon, I was informed of the death of Private Palike from Karkar Island. The mourning house was at the residence of Capt. Tony Belong Dibul, a fellow Karkar Islander, and not far from our new married quarters. I walked down to meet those who had gathered to arrange the funeral and repatriation of Private Palike's body to Karkar Island. The death of Private Palike on operations in Bougainville was a sharp reminder of the difficulties that lay ahead.

I had been overseas for two and a half years, and many things had deteriorated in my absence. Our married quarters were run-down, water hardly trickling out of the tap, and white goods were non-existent. We had to make do with what was there. Weni and I collectively agreed that we had no choice.

On the evening we returned, there was a further reminder of the volatility surrounding a defence force that was underfunded and suffering from neglect and low morale. Newly returned soldiers from Bougainville were out of the barracks and on rest and recreation in the city. The Germania Soccer Club on Waigani Drive was loud with music and drink and revelry when matters got out of hand. Pvt. Jack Adam from Milne Bay met his fate after drinks got the better of him and his companions, and he was murdered outside the club. As soon as news of his death reached Murray and Taurama Barracks, the troops mobilised on trucks and converged on the club, setting it on fire.

Major Agwi picked me up, and we made our way to the Germania Club to assist the police in restoring order and getting the troops back to barracks. It was a sad day for the defence force. We lost the life of a soldier, and the public display of drunken and disorderly behaviour by the troops did very little for public sympathy and respect for the defence force.

On Monday, 5 April, reporting for duty, I was given my deployment orders and informed that I was to depart for Rabaul on Thursday, 8 April, travelling with my new CO, Lt Col. Davey Ugul from Western Highlands Province. Lieutenant Colonel Ugul was one of the first graduates of Joint Services College in December 1974. He was a fair-minded CO, and I would enjoy working with him as our tour of duty progressed in Bougainville.

After farewelling Weni in the morning at Jacksons, we checked into Kaivuna Hotel in Rabaul and met with the CO of Second Battalion, Lt Col. Allan Pinia; his operations officer, Maj. Seki Berapu; and Intelligence Officer Capt. Mark Goina. The Second Battalion command team were on their way to Bougainville to visit their troops serving alongside 1RPIR under a contingent arrangement for manpower sharing. Rabaul, the capital of East New Britain Province, was the most forward logistics and staging base. It had the amenities and logistics required to support operations in Bougainville while capacity was being built up in Buka after the total withdrawal of security forces in Bougainville in 1990, when a ceasefire had been agreed to by all parties.

For the record, it was the Buka Liberation Front (BLF), a quasi-rebel group of former Bougainville Revolutionary Army members with the support of community leaders on Buka Island, who formed a resistance movement against the BRA and requested the national government to send the defence force back to Buka in September 1990. The BLF provided significant assistance, helping pacify Buka locals and making the general security situation conducive for the defence force to build up Buka and adjacent Kokopau across the Buka Passage for a staging and logistics base to support the operations on the main Bougainville island. Today Buka still remains the most important government and trading post for Bougainville and the atolls.

The following day, 9 April, we boarded an Airlink flight from Rabaul to Buka Island, touching down in just under an hour. The obvious presence of troops and the air of uncertainty could be sensed as we stopped by the Air Transport Unit's post, where air element soldiers had set up their camp to support the air effort. They were well set up, with running water, flush toilets, a small outdoor kitchen, and as usual a decent-sized refrigerator.

The Air Transport Unit at Buka had an IAI Arava light utility aircraft piloted by Timothy Narara and a Bell UH-1 Huey helicopter piloted by Capt. Sam Ono and Maj. Dennis Gareitz from Petas Island close to Buka. The IAI Arava was one of three such aircraft purchased by Papua New Guinea from Israel. The Arava is a twin-engine, high-wing, short-take-off-and-landing turboprop built by Israeli Aircraft Industries. It has a crew of two and can carry up to twenty-four fully equipped troops.

From the airport, we drove down to Ieta Village along the Buka Passage where the rear maintenance base (RMB) was set up close to the local wharf. The RMB was responsible for all administrative efforts to support the troops throughout the main island of Bougainville. Across the Buka Passage, Bonis Plantation was less than five minutes away on a speedboat. In past years, Bonis had been a profitable coconut and copra plantation. It was now the designated transit accommodation area; a sea of tents accommodated troops moving into the area of operations or awaiting repatriation back to their parent units after a tour of duty.

Late in the afternoon, we boarded the Huey (so-called from the Bell helicopter designation of UH-1) and departed for Wakunai. This was an ideal location for the field hospital. It was close to Asitavi High School and Numa Numa Plantation, one of the largest coconut plantations in the South Pacific. The Red Cross had set up there to take care of overcrowding in the government care centres. Pauline Onsa, a prominent and hard-working lady, was in charge of the Red Cross relief operations throughout Bougainville, a truly daunting and demanding task.

The forward operating base was located at Kiviri Point. This was a secure location at the end of the airstrip and next to a cove not far from the Numa Numa Wharf. I met Capt. Otto Pandum, the battalion intelligence officer and acting operations officer. The former operations officer, Maj. Duga Saira, whom I was replacing, had been suspended. It was good to see Otto Pandum again. I had been his instructor at the defence academy in 1983, when he was a young officer cadet from

East Sepik Province. I was shown my tent and, tired after a long day of travel, settled down for a short nap.

In the evening, Chaplain James Singi introduced me to Bishop Ray Rasuwe and Pastor Masail Baude. They were at Wakunai for a week, running a revival spiritual crusade for the care centre and soldiers. WO Robert Lek and Giwe then briefed me on the tempo of operations, discipline, and general administration. It is always a good idea to try to get along with senior non-commissioned officers as they are often very experienced and have useful contacts with other ranks and officers. What was already very apparent from my brief encounters in Rabaul, Buka, and now central Bougainville was that there was a general need for good leadership, for plenty of discipline, and for the troops to be led by competent officers.

It rained that night—all night—and my low-quality tent leaked. As I lay in bed, wet and miserable, I pondered how I could assist the troops in good decision-making and be of value to operational planning and conduct. I was determined to make an impact the next day by having a muster parade to introduce myself and to inform the troops of my expectations. I needed to make a list of priorities and enforce orders and protocol.

After breakfast, the troops paraded in front of the command post for my address and introduction. I laid down my requirements as clearly and plainly as possible. The first of these was respect for civilians, adhering to orders and instructions, and the need for greater self-discipline. Suspicious incidents were to be reported. Many soldiers, knowing that I had been the operations officer in 1989 when the first state of emergency was declared, were happy that I was in the role again. They also knew that I was the first officer from the Papua New Guinea Defence Force to have been posted to the Australian Defence Force as an instructor at the Land Warfare Centre.

After the parade, I went into the command post to familiarise myself with troop dispositions throughout the area of operations and the locations of the care centres. At lunchtime, the CO, Lt Col. Davey Ugul, called me to report to him on an urgent matter that had cropped up overnight. He said that Sean Dorney was reporting on

ABC Television and also on radio that our troops had crossed into the Solomon Islands and had destroyed a trading post at Kamalia and that some lives may have been lost. He wanted me to fly to the furthermost border post at Torato Island and get first-hand information from the small boat team (SBT) that was established there. He informed me that Cdr Brig. Gen. Dademo and Chief of Operations Col. Andy Trongat were both jumping down his throat, seeking information on the incident, and PM Paias Wingti was also demanding to know what had happened.

The incident made my message to the troops that morning about the need for personal discipline all the more important. The incursion into the Solomon Islands may have been triggered by an overreaction or by sailors acting without regard for their rules of engagement. My team consisted of the CO of 2RPIR, Lt Col. Allan Pinia; Majors Berapu and Mark Goina; Warrant Officer Lek; and Corporal Wayne. As soon as the typical torrential rain subsided enough for the Huey to fly and navigate safely, we departed for Torato.

At Torato, we were met by Sub-Lt. Philip Kaski Polewara and the chief of Lamuai Village, Joseph Buago, who briefed us on the incident that, by now, was attracting intentional attention. I instructed Kaski to prepare an incident report and to take it to Wakunai to brief General Dademo and others in the defence and foreign affairs hierarchy.

Pending Kaski's detailed report, I compiled my own brief preliminary report and returned with it to Wakunai via Arawa Township. Our flight path followed the road from Koromira Catholic Mission. We stopped to refuel at Aropa Airport, where a detachment of Support Company was based. We continued to Toniva and Kobuan and then to Arawa. The township of Arawa was held by elements of Support Company along with C Company First Battalion. C Company was commanded by Capt. Michael Kumun, and B Company was commanded by Major Demarcus, universally known as Delta Mike.

At Arawa, I was relieved to find a special service vehicle—a bulletproof vehicle bought by the PNGDF from Short Brothers in Belfast. It was a versatile light-armoured vehicle that enabled the troops to secure and control parts of the Espie Highway between

Arawa, Kobuan, Morgan Junction, and Loloho. I decided to stop over at Arawa to get additional briefings from Captain Kumun and his officers and Major Demarcus and his platoon commanders. I needed to recommend to the commanding officer that we should reposition ourselves to meet our mission requirements, including taking account of the complexities of the operations, the civilian mood, and actions by the rebels. I then proceeded to Morgan Junction, which is based at the foothill of the Panguna mountain range and is the junction leading to Manatai and Wakunai and back to Kokapau. At Morgan Junction, I was happy to meet Lt Jobi Ala and Corporal Lofena, who were tasked with controlling this strategic post.

On our return journey, we stopped at Loloho, where the main wharf and power station servicing the Panguna mine were located. While many fixtures had been vandalised, the structures were mostly still intact. We then drove to the far end of the cove at Loloho. The dongas and kitchen mess hall in the cove were only lightly vandalised, and the common toilet and showers were still in good condition. Apart from the high ground separating Rorovana Village from Loloho, this appeared to be an ideal place to relocate the forward tactical headquarters, currently at Wakunai, Kiviri Point. I needed to consult the CO about this and seek his earliest possible agreement.

My party returned to Arawa with Capt. Michael Kumun, and we were soon joined by several junior officers: Lieutenants Belden Namah, John Manuai, and Craig Solomon, platoon commanders with C Company. With their experiences, they informed me about the pattern of rebel operations and the pressures and demands on a growing civilian population, mainly for health services but also for safety as the rebels were making unrealistic demands on the village chiefs, in particular for young males to join them.

At mid-morning, the Huey returned from Torato with Lieutenant Kaski on board. It picked me and my team up at Arawa and took us back to Wakunai. By then, commander of PNGDF General Dademo was present with his aide-de-camp, Capt. Moses Jenjet, along with Maj. Penial Nilingur, the officer commanding D Company, now based at Manatai Catholic Mission.

With the operations and tactical maps and overlays set up, General Dademo was fully briefed on the Kamalia incident. Afterwards, I requested approval to relocate battalion tactical headquarters to Loloho. My main reason was that Loloho was closer to Arawa in central Bougainville and that Wakunai and the Red River area had been effectively pacified. The government wanted us to be in and around Arawa, Kieta, Kongara, and the Panguna area. The CO agreed and enabled me to issue administrative orders for a shift of personnel, assets, and the field hospital to Arawa.

I then sent for the resistance force commander for Rorovana, Peter Sepe, who was a former diesel mechanic and operator with Bougainville Copper Ltd. Peter Sepe was about my age, and I liked him for his positive mindset. He was a good man, and he assured me that he knew of about twenty villagers who could easily be mobilised to form a Rorovana resistance force that would be prepared to work alongside Capt. Otto Pandum and myself at Loloho and Arawa.

Peter and I discussed the possibility of the resistance force using Rorovana Village as their base in the hope that large numbers of villagers from Rorovana who were being held captive by rebels in Kongara, up in the Kupei area, could be freed to return to the village and resume their normal lives. It was a big gamble, but after briefing the CO, he agreed with all my requests. These were to establish our forward operations base at Loloho and scale down Wakunai, move the field hospital from Wakunai to Arawa in partnership with the Department of Health, and deploy the Rorovana Resistance Force at Rorovana Village to provide local area village defence.

Not wanting to lose a moment, that evening, I briefed Capt. Otto Pandum to mobilise the Rorovana Resistance Force and have them ready for sailing to Loloho the following day. HMPNGS *Basilisk* was tied up at Numa Numa Plantation Wharf, so I drove over that evening to give early warning to the ship's company. The *Basilisk* was captained by Stanley Terupo, a Polynesian and Mortlock Islander from the Takuu atoll group east of Bougainville. The 2IC was Lt John Wilson, and the two navigation officers were Martin Taririn and Peter Forova. It worked out well as all three naval officers had been officer cadets at the defence academy when I was instructing. I gave them a warning order to sail for Loloho at 0900 hours on 14 April, the next day. That evening, we were busy undoing tents and organising other essential equipment and personnel to be moved to Loloho.

As the *Basilisk* set sail for Loloho, Capt. Otto Pandum organised speedboats to ferry Peter Sepe and the Rorovana Resistance Force along with Sgt Francis Bia and a handful of soldiers to provide the initial support team. Meanwhile, I flew by Huey to Boku in South Bougainville and returned to Sikoreva and then to Loloho and Rorovana to ensure that the place was safe and that we could settle in without rebel action. The task of cleaning up and making a security analysis and assessment of Loloho, Rorovana Village, and Tunuru Junction was given to Capt. Otto Pandum, assisted by Major Demarcus. Arawa was left to the care of C Company under Capt. Michael Kumun.

On Friday, 16 April, I loaded my field gear on a speedboat assisted by Maj. Penial Nilingur and departed for Loloho via Mabiri. Nilingur disembarked at Mabiri to make his way to Manatai, where D Company was operating. I continued to Rorovana Village and stopped there for about two hours, checking the work that Peter Sepe was doing in the defence of the village.

Rorovana Village is divided into two parts separated by a creek and a swamp that provides a natural barrier for would-be intruders. The village had not been destroyed by the BRA. Instead, the villagers had been rounded up and taken to Kongara, where they were used as forced labour by the BRA to make coconut oil and establish farms to support the BRA's war efforts.

After lunch, I arrived at Loloho and was pleasantly surprised to find a large work party—Major Demarcus, Captains Kumun and Pandum, and soldiers and members of the Rorovana resistance force—cleaning up Loloho Camp. I selected four holiday flats for the forward tactical headquarters and two units for the command post and intelligence cell.

The Signal Platoon commenced setting up an aerial while I took a small reconnaissance patrol to plan our area defence as we needed to secure our tactical headquarters. The only high ground and ridgeline ran north-east and southwards, and it needed to be occupied. Up at Tunuru Junction, the area was held by Belden Namah's platoon from C Company; and to the west, Rorovana Village was now being occupied. We issued shotguns, a few M16 rifles, two MAG 58 machine guns, hand grenades, and a few claymore mines for village defence at Rorovana. That done, I felt confident that our overall area defence, including the security of Loloho, was adequately covered. The seafront lay to the east. Any intrusion from the sea was ruled out as there were permanent sentries, and our accommodation blocks faced the sea. I allocated areas for a fuel dump (close to the middle of the camp near the beach) and a helipad (near my accommodation hut and co-located around the corner from the maritime liaison officer's building, which also coordinated SBT operations).

The next day, Saturday, 17 April, was very tense. The rebels directed small arms fire into our troops at Barima School, Corporal Lofena reported that a power pylon had been destroyed near Morgan Junction, and four houses at section 16, Arawa Township, were set on fire. Lt Col. Yaura Sasa was conducting special infiltration operations with both reconnaissance platoons, assisted by Maj. Ivan Iamo and Lieutenant Budiara. I met with Sasa so that he could conduct limited operations in and around Kieta. We had limited resources, reserves, and backup plans. Therefore, all operations had to be planned and centrally coordinated in case we encountered unexpected levels of resistance or greater offensive operations mounted by the BRA.

That evening, I decided to dominate the immediate area by conducting an aggressive patrol and ambush programme. The plan was to pacify the area and deny the rebels freedom of movement. I had access to Support Company, C Company, and elements of specialist support from HQ PNGDF, including workshop personnel, SBT, cooks, and medics. During my operations group meeting, headquarters staff were represented by Sgt Joseph Ginal and Corporal Kaluvia. They said that, for identification purposes, they wanted to be known as the Foodland Tigers while the Loloho contingent wanted to be called the Loloho Marines. I had no difficulty with either name if they felt they needed distinct identities. Thus, the names Foodland Tigers and Loloho Marines were born.

Within as little as seven days, we began to see the benefits of the aggressive ambush and patrolling programme aimed at dominating the areas around Arawa, Lonsiro, Rorovana, and Morgan Junction. I arranged to take a section of ten soldiers on an ambush party out to Barima School overnight. I had to prove to my subordinate officers that, even as the contingent's operations officer, I was prepared to share the same risks as them.

As our presence became further established in Loloho, our caterer, Sgt Roger Mua—a devoted bulky soldier from Simbu Province— established a first-class field kitchen. Mua was an innovative and energetic man, baking scones and bread and roasting anything he could get his hands on. There were spare buildings at the back of the mess hall at Loloho that I authorised for conversion into a care centre to cater for the stream of civilians who were now escaping from rebel-held areas. Among the civilians were respected elders Chief Francis Baria and his wife.

Chief Baria was from Arawa, and his wife was from Panguna. They would develop close relationships not only with me but also with many soldiers. The civilian numbers gradually built up to about 100. I gave them permission to make gardens, and soon fresh vegetables were grown and harvested to supplement food that was supplied by the Bougainville Restoration Authority and Red Cross. The care centre at Loloho was connected to the Rorovana Resistance Force as there was a jeep track and footpath linking the villages.

Having brought my fishing gear, including rods and reels, I took up my usual hobby. There were many evenings when I slipped out to the small islands off Rorovana to go fishing, and sometimes in the early mornings, I would go trolling. I shared the fish I caught with the care centres and soldiers, including soldiers in the field, to give them some relief from their field rations.

Towards the last week of April, having successfully established the command post and with Arawa Township and its surrounds and Rorovana Village generally secure, I commenced a programme of visitations to South Bougainville and places inland to direct new initiatives and check the tempo of operations and state of civil-military relations in each area.

I also made use of the milk run by the Huey captained by Maj. Dennis Gareitz and Capt. Sam Ono. The southern part of Bougainville was controlled by 2RPIR, and Maj. Bill Nende was in charge. Soldiers called him Smoking Bill as he always had tobacco in his mouth. I then departed with the Huey to visit the big care centres at Tonu and Torokina and then over the range to Wakunai before being dropped off at Loloho.

On 23 April, Cdr Gen. Robert Dademo arrived with the foreign affairs secretary, Gabriel J. K. Dusava. They were on their way to Torato to continue the investigation of the alleged intrusion and killing of Solomon Island subjects by the SBT based at Torato and June Island. I boarded the helicopter, which also carried much-needed supplies for a small section of soldiers headed by a very capable non-commissioned officer, Sergeant Kwaragu of Central Province, at Motupena Point. At Motupena, Capt. Sam Ono told me that we were running out of fuel and that we must immediately depart for Torokina to refuel.

We departed for Torokina at the extreme northern end of Empress Augusta Bay, only to discover that there was no aviation fuel there. With our fuel situation now desperate, the pilots decided to fly over the Crown Prince Range into Wakunai. On board, we had a soldier with gunshot wounds from Boku and three others returning to Buka for various reasons. As we flew towards Mount Bagana, the Huey began to sound a fuel alert. Convinced that we were not going to make it across the mountain range, I began to reposition myself for a forced landing. Finally, after a very tense few moments and with less than fifteen minutes of fuel left in the Huey, we landed at Wakunai. I could not thank Sam Ono enough for the safe landing. It was already last light, so the pilots decided to extract the commander and his team from Torato Island the following day.

We experienced another border skirmish on Saturday, 24 April, when a Solomon Island patrol boat opened fire on our SBT at one of our observation posts. The nature of the engagement was unknown, so I dispatched HMPNGS *Basilisk* under Capt. Stanley Terupo and

Lieutenant Kaski to investigate and report back. With the incident report in hand, I flew to Buka, where I compiled a series of border incident reports for Operations Branch and the commander's staff officer.

Because of our patrolling programme, the rebels were now under pressure. Moving into Kerei and Kobuan, the rebels occupied the high ground behind Arco Motors on the fringes of Arawa Township. From there, they had a clear view into Arawa and beyond and were able to monitor our movements. I planned to capture and dominate the high ground behind Arco Motors to deny it to the rebels.

I directed Captain Kumun to conduct a patrol up to the high ground overlooking Kerei as it was reported that the rebels had set up a radio station and were monitoring and reporting on our activities in Arawa. While the operation was being conducted, I boarded a speedboat with Sgt James Koiba, Signaller Palike, Sgt Steven Koa from Pioneer Platoon, and William, my batman from Rorovana, to monitor the operation from offshore.

As we were drifting offshore, not too far from Kerei Village, three rebels crept onto the beach unobserved and took an aimed shot at us from behind cover using a self-loading rifle. The round missed me and penetrated the speedboat. We all hit the floor of the boat and then returned fire. It was a very close shave, particularly for me, as I was standing at the stern of the speedboat and must have stood out as an easy target. We abandoned our trip and returned to Loloho. But the principle of dominating ground through aggressive patrolling was now proving its worth as we had reasonable freedom of movement in and out of our area. After the speedboat incident, C Company sent a section patrol up to the high ground behind Arco Motors, where they captured a radio, home-made guns, and a quantity of assorted ammunition.

Meanwhile, our troops' alleged intrusion into Solomon Island territory was being investigated by Col. David Takendu from HQ PNGDF. This meant that I had less to worry about on that score, which was a relief as I had many other pressing issues on my hands. As we continued to dominate the area around Arawa Township, villagers who had been hiding in the jungle began to come out in family groups, no doubt causing the rebels some concern. For our part, we continued to stress the importance of civic action and winning hearts and minds.

During this campaign, another very important and well-respected paramount chief of Arawa, Nanao Taninung, made contact with Capt. Michael Kumun to ask for our help in leaving rebel territory. After gathering further intelligence, I made an operational plan for a rescue operation to be conducted by the Rorovana Resistance Force led by Peter Sepe. Cpl David Ban from the intelligence cell was the only soldier to be attached to the patrol. As planned, the resistance patrol departed just after midnight. Risking my M16 carbine, I handed it to Peter Sepe and pleaded with him not to lose it; if he changed his mind during the mission, I told him to escape into the jungle. The party worked their way carefully through Bovo Valley and Pavaire and finally made contact with Chief Nanao Taniung.

The chief was returning with three other families when the party was engaged by the rebels. Three resistance members received gunshot wounds including Peter Sepe. But the mission was successful, and my carbine was safely returned. This patrol and many similar ones around Arawa and surrounds would pave the way for civilians, including the whole village of Rorovana, to escape from rebel captivity. This gave government agencies the clear message that, given a chance, the civilian population wanted peace and not war.

Paramount chief Nanao Taniung introduced himself to us at Loloho and made a personal commitment to foster friendly relations and work with us to bring peace to Bougainville. I felt that, with this and other indications we were seeing, the tide was beginning to turn in favour of restoring peace and normalcy on Bougainville. Our CO, Lt Col. Davey Ugul, was very particular about the behaviour of our troops and the need to show respect for those who had already been traumatised by the hard realities of living in fear and lack of proper healthcare and education for their children.

As operations officer, it was my job to maintain the battalion operations and patrol programme. By keeping the rebels under sufficient pressure, the hope was that they might surrender their arms as many of them had young families at the care centres at Loloho and

Arawa. The care centres were experiencing a big influx of civilians, and there were plenty of houses available. Some returning families chose houses that—apart from a lack of white goods, power, and running water—were reasonably modern, having been left behind by BCL staff.

By the end of April, our intelligence had gathered information on a clandestine radio station being used by the rebels at a place called Nulendi or Tamaisi. This was behind the Rumba Seventh-Day Adventist Mission, up in the hills about 10 km behind Arawa Township. With Capt. Michael Kumun and some of his reconnaissance elements, I set to work to come up with an operations plan to capture the radio station. I would be the patrol commander for the operation, code-named Operation Rumba. Our mission was 'to capture and destroy the radio station at Nulendi'.

My general outline for the mission was as follows:

> I will require a reinforced platoon supported by elements of the Resistance Force for the operation. We will depart by midnight using tracks from Arawa Section 6 along the Rumba Road up to Nulendi. Once at the location troops will secure the ground and the raiding party will surround the house where the radio station is located and capture it. Loloho Marines and elements of C Company and Reconnaissance platoon will provide cut offs and a firm base as we withdraw and wait for any counter attack. A helicopter is to be on standby for medivac. A Recon section will provide a dedicated reserve with sufficient firepower and medical support for the backup.

I prepared a mud model of Nulendi Village and went over the operations plan, ensuring that the troops fully understood what was intended. We checked all our equipment including machine guns, M16A1 with grenade launchers and night-vision goggles, radio, medical kits, and explosives. We issued camouflage cream for the troops to use to break down the outline of their faces. Our signaller checked the radio set and ensured we had spare batteries as the ability to communicate is one of the most critical elements in operations of this kind.

Capt. Michael Kumun was my 2IC, and Peter Sepe, who had proved to be a very gifted and highly spirited person, was in charge of a small band of resistance fighters. The Loloho Marines composite unit comprised cooks, mechanics, drivers, and clerks who also got their orders to provide a firm base during our extraction and were shown exactly on the mud map and sketch where they would be deployed during the extraction phase.

H-hour was eleven in the evening. First light was around 4.10 a.m. and I did not want to run into unexpected resistance and delays, which could be disastrous. We slipped through the sleeping township of Arawa and Rumba Mission and up along a clear bush track behind the mission. As we walked towards our objective, we came across a small hut where a fire was burning outside in a clearing. Around the fire, which was just about burning out, were six rebels sleeping on the ground. With the assistance of night-vision googles, our forward scout was able to spot them from a little way away, and he requested me to move forward as I was only four soldiers behind him in the single file patrol line-up.

I crept up as close as possible and told the forward point scout team not to disturb them and to pass the message down to Captain Kumun and the rear troops not to disturb them either but rather to walk as stealthily as possible past them as our mission was to capture the radio station. This we achieved but with some apprehension in case they woke and we needed to take immediate evasive action. We arrived at the main road and, using the cover of night and the surrounding jungle, continued further into the hills towards our target. The timing was critical. We were all on edge and at maximum alert.

As we approached the village, Peter Sepe told me with a whisper in my ear that the hamlet was on the right of the track about twenty metres from our current location. I took a section forward and switched on my night-vision goggles, which turned the night into day effective to about fifty metres as it was also misty and foggy. I had a good view of the track leading into the hamlet at Nulendi. As we neared the hamlet, the soldiers crept around behind the huts as low and as quietly as possible. But dogs started barking, prompting a firefight. We lost the element of surprise, and the rebels were able to flee with the radio, disappearing into the cover of the dark amid a hail of bullets.

We entered the target house and found two suspects with gunshot wounds, apparently dead. A very young girl, barely 6 years old, had been caught up in the firefight. She had a bullet wound to her left wrist and was screaming frantically and also bleeding out fast. She spotted me standing a few metres away and, crashing between my legs, passed out on the spot. As soldiers continued to fire, I yelled out not to shoot and to leave her alone. I called out, 'Medic, medic, over here now!' I asked Peter Sepe to stay with the injured girl while she was with the medic. I then left the hut to check what the troops were doing.

We searched the houses and the hut and came across thousands of kina coins in bags. I instructed the soldiers not to burn down any of the houses and ordered them to take care of the girl and two small boys who had emerged from their hiding place. The boys were obviously shaken by the noise and violence of the firefight.

The troops continued their search of the hamlet but could not locate the radio. By now, it was close to six o'clock and therefore well after first light before we commenced our planned withdrawal. I ensured that the young girl's injury was attended to by our medic, and Peter Sepe placed her over his shoulder. We dug a proper grave for her father and the other dead man. I offered a short prayer of respect for the two dead men, and the troops buried them with all the honours we could muster in the time available. We then started an agonisingly hot withdrawal as the sudden firefight had woken the whole of Bovo Valley, and rebels were coming from all corners to engage us. It was the first time since 1989 that a security force patrol had taken the initiative to infiltrate into the stronghold of a rebel-controlled area.

My greatest asset as we made our fighting withdrawal was Capt. Michael Kumun. Not only competent but also very articulate in tactics and command and control, he took charge of the main body. I was in the advance team. As we slowly withdrew from one road bend to the next, we encountered numerous contacts from rebels on both sides of the track. But we were ready for counter-attacks, and our soldiers in the lead positions fired shots into possible vantage points to keep the rebels' heads down.

Before long, we encountered our backups, and they provided a firm base as we continued our withdrawal down to the Rumba Arawa River. It was there, on high ground, that we encountered our first casualty. Pvt. Charles Pejikere was shot by a .22 from the left flank, the bullet entering his left cheek and exiting the right without damaging his mouth. It was a clean shot and a very unusual one. We went to ground and got the medic to patch his mouth. He was instructed to hold the dressing pressed with both hands on his head. A loincloth was tied around his head to prevent bleeding. The troops shared the weight of his gear including his personal weapon, day pack, and webbing.

Around midday, as we were crossing Rumba Creek, the rebels targeted Cpl Henry ToValuve of Field Engineer Platoon. He was just in front of me. The .22 bullet hit ToValuve in his stomach, and the force of the shot threw him into the river, which was flowing fast. He screamed and said many things including his wife's name and then yelled, 'I am going to die! Please help me!' Instantly, with three other soldiers, I jumped into the creek to rescue him. There were blood and guts everywhere. I panicked as he was losing blood fast through his stomach wound.

The troops returned fire. Once again, Captain Kumun took control of the situation and deployed troops all around our position, including holding the high ground where the shot had come from. Shortly afterwards, the Loloho Marines turned up and started clearing the immediate area of rebels.

Lifting ToValuve from the river was a most difficult task as the East New Britain man weighed well over 100 kg. We managed to lift him to the bridge and then to a safe area where the medic could stabilise his wound. It was one of the biggest challenges I have ever faced. With Captain Kumun and the medic, I used whatever skills I had to help save his life. I kept calling his name. 'Henry, Henry, be strong. You will live. You are a very brave soldier. Your wife and kids love and care for you.

We all love you. Henry, Henry be strong.' I continued yelling at him as he passed out, but his heart was still beating. I thanked God for that.

ToValuve was bleeding furiously and lost consciousness a few times, and each time, the medic worked hard to revive him. Time was against us, but he was pulling through. As we carried his huge body up the slope, the rebels melted away and vanished into the jungle.

By then, we had been joined by Reconnaissance Platoon sergeant Jackson and his troops. A makeshift stretcher was constructed, and we transferred the two soldiers to a waiting ambulance to be extracted by the helicopter that was already on its way.

At the Arawa Airstrip, as we waited for the helicopter, I spent time reassuring ToValuve. He was barely awake, but his heartbeat had stabilised, and the medic was at his side. His bleeding was also under control. Shortly after the helicopter arrived, he and Pejikere were airlifted to Wakunai Field Hospital. Later that day, I organised a speedboat from Loloho and went around Mabiri Point to Wakunai and visited ToValuve and Pejikere in hospital. ToValuve was stabilised at Wakunai before being flown to Rabaul. Years later, I would learn from a relative of the rebels at Rumba that the rebels had deliberately targeted Henry ToValuve because he was so big and looked like an officer. I was just wearing body armour and looked like an ordinary soldier, so I was spared on this occasion.

Peter Sepe took the girl to Wakunai, where he handed her over to the Red Cross under the care of Pauline Onsa. The two boys were left in the hands of Francis Baria at the care centre at Loloho. Twenty years later, as I was relating to the story, I found out the identity of the small girl whom we rescued; she is now the mother of two children.

It had been an eventful day. After returning from Wakunai Field Hospital and while quietly sipping my coffee, I entered the events of the day into my Bougainville diary. It was only then that it dawned on me that it was 5 May 1993, my birthday. I was 37 years old and serving on Bougainville as a volunteer soldier for my country.

The responsibilities I was carrying as the operations officer for the contingent and the First Battalion were heavy, and there were many expectations on me. As I sipped my coffee, I reflected on the nature of command. It was not just about leadership or tactical ability or an active disposition or even courage in the face of adversity and danger. It was all those things, yes, but at its heart, command involved political courage above all else—the ability to make sense of the situation on the ground and then to act in the best way possible to further the interests of one's country as best as one understands them, which is not necessarily the same as the way one's political or military instructions are framed at any given time.

The news of our operations into Nulendi gave confidence to civilians in the Bovo Valley who had been held against their will since 1990 that it might be safe to surrender to us so that they could have access to basic services. Soon after this, I got an urgent signal to be ready with the tape recordings we had picked up of rebel radio conversations. Major Nilingur and I were to accompany a government delegation to Torato Island to meet with Solomon Island officials to sort out the outstanding issues surrounding border violations and incidences. The government delegation was led by foreign affairs senior diplomat Tarsisius Tarcy Eri and included international lawyer Camillus Narokobi, younger brother of the late Sir Bernard Narokobi; chief of operations at HQ PNGDF, Col. Andy Trongat; and the ABC's Sean Dorney.

Our patrol boat was already at Torato for the meeting, and it was good to see the commanding officer for the patrol boat base at Lombrum, Cdr Fred Siroi (now at the National Maritime Safety Authority), on the ship. The maritime officer on the ground was Lt Cdr Peter Ilau. He delivered two fast catamaran speedboats that enabled us travel to Mamola Island, where our SBT was providing surveillance near the Solomon Island border. I was offered a bed on board HMPNGS *Tarangau* (later renamed HMPNGS *Rabaul* and recently scrapped), for which I was grateful as I had not slept well after the operations into Nulendi.

The following day, the Solomon Island delegation headed by Deputy Police Commissioner Fred Siretehi and including John Homelo, acting field force commander, and a handful of government officials arrived on the Pacific patrol boat *Lata*. We were also joined by the chief of Torato

Island. Col. Andy Trongat, a Bougainvillean from Buka Island, chaired the meeting. Our lawyer, Camillus Narokobi, stressed the importance of mutual respect and the rule of law, especially the international conventions that guide diplomatic relationships in times of conflict. He noted the difficulties that PNG was facing with gun running and smuggling from the Solomon Islands to Bougainville in aid of the rebels, which was prolonging the conflict and leading to the loss of innocent lives. The border meeting agreed to establish communication protocols and liaison officers who were to be responsible for briefing each side from time to time and for reporting on any incidents. Later, we shared a meal—a BBQ of steak and fish—and refreshments, and the Solomon Island delegation departed, apparently content with the meeting.

While sailing back to Loloho with Sean Dorney, Colonel Trongat pulled me aside and asked if I had planned the raid on Kamalia and ordered the SBT to fire at passing Solomon Islanders. I denied any responsibility for the incident. I told him that I would not have planned such a thing outside my direct operational area unless directed by higher command. I had served under Colonel Trongat as operations officer in 1987. He never raised the issue again. I was conscious of the fact that General Dademo was taking a keen interest in my leadership and tactical ability and that any further international incidents, however inadvertent, would involve me as the operations officer for 1RPIR.

Back at Loloho, I provided lodging to the government delegation. Sean Dorney sat up quite late. He wanted to talk through numerous unresolved issues. I had established a good relationship with him when he interviewed me at the Panguna mine in 1989. And of course, he had worked with Weni at NBC, so we were able to respect each other's positions.

I also had to deal with another Australian, Ken Morgan, who was a builder and owner of Aropa Builders. He had decided to return to Arawa from Rabaul, where he was based, to recover some of his company's property. I assigned Capt. Otto Pandum to deal with him. As reported to me, he returned to his former residence and undid the panel at the back of his electric stove where he recovered a substantial quantity of kina notes, much to the amusement of our soldiers. He also gathered up some other equipment and a truck, and I authorised him to move them back to Rabaul on MV *Kingfisher* on its return leg.

Towards mid-May, I was informed that higher command wanted me to conduct limited patrols to Aropa Airport, Sipuru, Rororeng, and Koromira Catholic Mission. In discussing the patrols, it was quite clear to me that, even though I was the operations officer for the regiment, I had no control over the independent operations of the Reconnaissance Platoon under the command of Lt Col. Yaura Sasa. Sasa acted as if he had some independent authority and often conducted his own operations. It was irritating and frustrating, but I had to leave him to get on with his job as the troops serving under him were some of our best-trained and most highly disciplined soldiers. Much later, in December 2012, Colonel Sasa made headlines when he led a group of mutinous soldiers against PM Peter O'Neill; subjected the commander of the PNGDF, Brig. Gen. Francis Agwi, to house arrest; and demanded the return of Sir Michael Somare to the prime ministership. Sasa was arrested and tried for sedition but later acquitted when the Crown prosecutor failed to substantiate the charges.

I discussed the impending operations with my team to see what could be accomplished before our scheduled relief by the Second Battalion. I planned a preliminary operation leading up to a major deployment at a later date of troops into Aropa, Kieta, and Koromira Catholic Mission. These areas were effectively controlled by a rebel commander named Sam Kauona. Known to his supporters as Gen. Sam Kauona, he was a fugitive from justice and an absconder from the PNGDF. As a junior officer, he was said to have received explosives training by the Australian Defence Force. As a member of BRA, Kauona was waging well-coordinated small-scale attacks on our security forces that were frustrating government efforts for peace.

Kauona was from the Kongara area, and his village was not far from the mission. In planning operations into the area, one of my main motives was to show the rebels that we retained the operational initiative—even in Kauona's home area. I employed Capt. Otto Pandum and Maj. Ivan Iamo to conduct limited reconnaissance between Sirowai,

Koromira, Aropa, Pokpok Island, and Kieta. One of my first moves was to set up an observation post off Kieta on a sandy island. Our troops did an excellent job of deterring rebels from using the route in and out of Kieta by speedboat.

By the end of May, I had developed the general concept of what we were to call Operation June Special. The concept was to insert a company at Tavatava Village at night while another company landed at Koromira, and the reconnaissance patrol held Aropa Airport. The insertion was to be done by naval vessels. The company landing at Tavatava was to clear the road and village and then marry up with troops at Koromira Catholic Mission. It would be a five-day operation. I convinced CO Davey Ugul that we had sufficient information to be sure of the security of the southern part of central Bougainville while we put pressure on Koromira. I added that any operations inland would be extremely difficult to sustain because of the lack of reliable helicopter support. The CO left it to me to work up the concept of operations, which he then forwarded to headquarters for concurrence. This being received, Lieutenant Colonel Ugul gave me the go-ahead to deploy an expeditionary force into central Bougainville from Aropa Airport, Tavatava, and Koromira, consolidating our position at Sirowai.

On Monday, 7 June, at nine in the morning, the helicopter that I had requested to conduct a preliminary reconnaissance arrived. It was flown by Capt. James Pima and co-piloted by Capt. Eric Aliawi. With my team on board, we flew along the beach to Kieta, Aropa Airport, and Koromira and then back towards Panguna. From Panguna, I asked the pilots to follow the Espie Highway back to Loloho. While approaching the coast at about 700 feet, I noticed smoke on a ridge at Lonsiro Village and asked the pilots to check it out as I knew that C Company was operating in the area.

Captain Kumun of C Company was conducting search and clear operations. As we flew lower, we spotted yellow smoke, and the pilots brought us in towards a very tight landing zone. I jumped from the hovering craft and discovered that a soldier had been wounded in the face and chest. I signalled the pilots to give us time to create a better landing spot. We quickly cut down some trees and threw them into the gully. Thirty minutes later, the Huey returned. As we were loading the injured soldier into the cabin, rebels concealed in the verge of the clearing shot at the helicopter, shattering the visor on Cpl Peter Sere's helmet.

While the troops secured our defensive perimeter and attended to the ground threat, we left, arriving less than five minutes later at Loloho, where the injured soldier was stabilised before being evacuated to Wakunai Field Hospital. My day ended with mixed results. I had completed a reasonably successful aerial reconnaissance of the intended operational area and a successful evacuation of an injured soldier. Cpl Peter Sere, who had been acting as our loadmaster, was pretty shaken up and said he would keep the helmet with the shattered visor and ball round embedded in it as a souvenir.

Insufficient manpower was a constant problem. I appointed Capt. Otto Pandum to put together about thirty troops, drawing on the remnants of our support troops including cooks, drivers, mechanics, medics, and resistance forces from Arawa, Wakunai, and Rorovana. This he was able to do. The resistance forces were headed up by our loyalists Paul Akoitai, Maibiri, and Vito, with numbers from the Rorovana and Arawa areas.

The arrival of three naval vessels to assist in the operation boosted our morale. These were HMPNGS *Tarangau*, commanded by Lt Comd Stanley Terupo, with Commander Fred Siroi, the CO of Patrol Base Lombrum, on board; HMPNGS *Salamaua*; and another patrol boat, *Basilisk*, captained by Lieutenant Commander Verani.

On Tuesday, 8 June, at six in the evening at Loloho, I issued the operational orders for Operation June Special. The duration of the operation was to be for a maximum of five days but shorter if the objectives were met earlier. The operation was to be supported by the heavy landing craft *Salamaua* and the patrol craft *Tarangau*. With a mud model constructed for the purpose, I got all the subunit commanders to go through their insertion points with me and to establish each of their beachheads. I always ensured that my operational plans were complemented by mud models and charts as nothing is worse than troops being unclear about their role and the geography and detailed layout of the areas they are to operate in.

At last light on Wednesday, 9 June, troops boarded the *Salamaua* supported by *Tarangau* and *Basilisk*. Two reconnaissance patrols under Maj. Ivan Iamo and Lieutenant Budiara were disembarked at Aropa Airport beach and immediately secured the landing point. The next troops ashore were the Loloho Marines at Tavatava Village, which included the support elements under Capt. Otto Pandum and the resistance force. Last ashore were elements of A Company and Lt Willie Saim to secure the area around Koromira Catholic Mission.

There were a few enemy contacts at Tavatava and Koromira, but after three days, the area appeared quiet. I ordered Maj. Kessy Rovae to consolidate between Koromira and Sirowai. I remained on board HMPNGS *Tarangau*, from where I was able to maintain direct contact with all the commanders on the ground. Each night, under the low lights of the cabin of the ship's captain, I sat with Fredrick Punangi and our team of defence intelligence analysts to reappraise the rebel situation at Kongara, Aropa, and Koromira, knowing that the self-proclaimed rebel general, Sam Kauona, came from this part of Bougainville. On the third day of operations, I landed at Koromira to take personal stock of the situation before ordering a withdrawal, all being quiet.

Operation June Special officially ended on Thursday, 10 June, at Loloho. The troops, sailors, and resistance force members enjoyed a meal of steak, lamb chops, and plenty of fruit provided by our support staff before redeployment to their respective locations. In the meantime, an advance party from Second Battalion led by Maj. Seki Berapu with veteran intelligence operator Sgt Julius Gilgil, Sergeant Idigel from the Mortar Platoon, and Acting Regimental Signals Officer Sergeant Siroi arrived from Buka. They were to survey the area of operations before A Company under Kessy Rovae arrived for our planned changeover.

In mid-June, I gave more briefings and site visits with Major Berapu and his party on board HMPNGS *Tarangau*. We visited troops at Koromira Catholic Mission, Sirowai, and Torato Island, where we picked up Lieutenants Phillip Kaski and Kase before sailing to Motupena overnight. Guarding Gazelle Bay, Motupena Point was a strategic location where we had to have troops stationed as it covered the long stretch of black sandy beach along the bay from Laguai and the mouth of Jaba River to Torokina. An outstanding non-commissioned officer, Sergeant Kwaragu from D Company, was stationed there with a section and a handful of local resistance force members. The swells and waves were unrelenting, and torrential rain hammered us all night and continued the following day. As our return trip to Loloho would take time, I organised the Huey to pick up Major Berapu and his party to return to Buka while I continued to Torato Island with Lieutenants Kaski and Kase.

Meanwhile, the commander of the PNGDF, Brigadier General Dademo, had returned for more briefings, obviously as a result of political pressure from Waigani. He was just getting to know me as I had never worked with him before. I briefed him on the results of Operation June Special and cautioned him that, if we chased ground, we would lose the focus of our mission, extend our lines of supply, and lose unnecessary lives. I enjoyed my relations with General Dademo and found him to be a fair commander. We trusted each other.

General Dademo was frank with our CO, informing him that government was desperate to reopen the Panguna mine. However, given the complexities of the political and social aspects of life on Bougainville and the lack of political will, logistics, and credible intelligence, it did not know how to go about this. My preference was to bring services to the people of Tavatava and to let the Catholic church continue their service and mission work at Koromira while reopening the schools and aid posts. I said that, from an operational perspective, Aropa Airport was not immediately needed. Therefore, to conserve troops, Koromira should be regarded as a strategic location just like Wakunai, Buin, and Tonu. A few days later, Chief of Operations Col. Andrew Trongat arrived at Loloho, and we discussed a major intelligence brief prepared for him by the battalion IO, Capt. Otto Pandum.

As Bougainville was the main issue affecting the region, I was informed that I was required to travel with the chief of operations to brief Administrator Sam Tulo and an Australian and New Zealand ministerial team led by Development Cooperation and Pacific Islands

Affairs Minister Gordon Bilney, a former dentist and Australian diplomat, later a minister in the Hawke and Keating ministries. This briefing was important. We needed to open Bougainville to the rest of the world as PNG could not solve the crisis on its own. In any case, it was in the best interests of Australia and New Zealand to be actively engaged to help secure peace in the region. The briefing took place at the Buka administration office. In attendance was Gordon Bilney; the Australian high commissioner to PNG, Bill Farmer; Lt Col. Gary Young, deputy head of defence staff; the New Zealand high commissioner to PNG, Maarten Wevers; and the New Zealand defence attaché, Squadron Leader Kevin Firth. Sean Dorney and Frank Mills from the ABC and AAP reporter Belinda Goldsmith also travelled to Buka to be briefed.

The meeting was inconclusive. I thought it instructive that no PNG minister attended. This seemed to signal a lack of interest on Port Moresby's part—or perhaps a lack of fresh ideas about the future of the North Solomons Province (called the Autonomous Region of Bougainville since the negotiated peace agreement of 2000). Equally, the arrival of the Australian minister may have ruffled certain feathers in Port Moresby, and PNG ministers may have decided to leave Bilney to it.

According to academic accounts, the PNGDF had the upper hand during this period when it came to running day-to-day affairs on Bougainville. However, with my own experience at the time and later, I don't think this is correct. Academic accounts tend to overlook the fact that the administrator responsible for all aspects of ordinary life on Bougainville from 1990 to 1995 was Sam Tulo, a civilian, who reported to the minister for Bougainville affairs in Port Moresby. Overlooked, too, is the important role of the churches, the Red Cross, and other aid organisations. Nevertheless, the view of the defence force as having the upper hand begs the question about what our senior commanders believed our actual mission on the ground was at this time—security, certainly; helping out with the lives of ordinary Bougainvilleans where we could; keeping the BRA under pressure and, where possible, on the run; search and clear but not search and destroy. In any case, this was how I interpreted my role as operations officer in 1993.

Meanwhile, the handover with the Second Battalion continued with the arrival of the commanding officer, Lt Col. Allan Pinia, and his regimental sergeant major, Paul Mate, a long-time friend of mine from my Mortar Platoon days. I spent the next few days at Rorovana inspecting their village defence system and encouraging families to restart their normal lives as their village was more secure than other villages. I also visited the care centres at Arawa and continued to reassure the people of peace and the need to create a climate of trust. I was saddened to see young children play and smile, knowing that war and conflict had denied them the opportunity to attend school. I knew that many had missed out on even the most basic of education.

By now, MV *Kingfisher* had arrived from Wewak with the remainder of Second Battalion for the handover. We extracted our troops from Manatai and Koromira, and others further inland were extracted by helicopter to Buka. For my last act, I organised a fishing trip to a sandy island off Rorovana Village with three members of the Rorovana resistance: Moses, Greg, and Tomato.

We secured the area by setting up claymore mines and established an observation post before diving for seashells; we also did some night diving. We feasted on fish as well as bananas and fresh coconuts that we had brought with us. We had a good night of comradeship before returning to Loloho early the next day.

On Friday, 2 July, the remaining elements of the forward battalion tactical headquarters and Support Company boarded MV *Kingfisher* for Buka. Civilians led by Chief Nanao Taniung and Chief Francis Baria and his wife came down to the wharf to see us off. The captain blew the departure horn for the last time as they waved their farewells. We sailed out of Loloho, central Bougainville, for Buka to regroup before sailing on to Port Moresby as a regiment. We felt that we had made many lifelong friends at Loloho, and in many ways, we were sad to leave.

On Wednesday, 7 July, I paid a courtesy call on Administrator Sam Tulo and thanked him for his support. Over the last few months, I had developed a close working relationship with him and the leaders of all the sectors reporting to him. I told him that the replacement battalion under the command of Lt Col. Allan Pinia and his operations officer, Maj. Seki Berapu, fully supported the various peace initiatives that we had been pursuing and that he would enjoy working with the new team. At five in the afternoon, I ensured that the manifest was complete. The company commanders reported to me in the wheelhouse of MV *Kris* that their men were all complete and accounted for. Just before sunset, with darkness blanketing our vessel, we sailed out. The only sounds were waves hitting the ship, which gently rocked as darkness overtook our journey.

I was offered a bunk on the lower deck of the ship but could not stand the thick air and the bunker fumes and so spent most of my time in the wheelhouse with soldiers who were either asleep or telling stories. On Saturday, 10 July, we finally sailed into Basilisk Passage, the entrance to Port Moresby named by Capt. John Moresby after his HMS *Basilisk*, and docked at the landing craft base. Our CO, Davey Ugul; Maj. Francis Agwi; and other senior non-commissioned officers of the regiment, along with our spouses, were there to greet us. Weni and our three children were among them.

We embussed for Taurama Barracks, unloading at the main gate, from where we marched with the assistance of the regimental pipes and drums, forming up on the parade ground for the official welcome home parade. Each company had their own reception areas set up by the wives and soldiers who had remained back as rear echelon support staff.

I was thankful to God for having given our troops and myself his protection, guidance, and care. Regrettably, on its return voyage to East New Britain from Lae, MV *Kris* sank with many passengers and crew unaccounted for. Many times have I wondered whether this could have been our fate coming home; I remember trying to sleep below decks and seeing evidence of leaks and rust and being worried about the ship's seaworthiness and the troop's safety.

The remaining three months of 1993 was a very low period. Many soldiers were granted rest and recreation leave and most elected to take the opportunity. I used the time to conduct debriefs with the officers of the regiment, looked at lessons learnt during our deployment, and coordinated a new training programme with the CO so that we could commence a new battalion training programme to focus on leadership, civil-military affairs, patrolling, and night operations for the 1994 training year.

In the last week of November, we were visited by Brig. Gen. Robert Dademo, who came out to the regiment to meet with the CO, Lt Col. Davey Ugul. I was asked to report to them in the CO's office. The commander informed us that the Promotion and Selection Committee had approved the posting of Lt Col. Davey Ugul to headquarters as director of land operations and that I would replace him as CO of First Battalion on promotion. I was paraded at the HQ PNGDF conference room on Thursday, 9 December, and promoted by General Dademo to the rank of lieutenant colonel along with Alphonse Oae'efa, who was to command the Air Transport Squadron.

As the year 1993 came to a close, I thought back on my time as operations officer and attempted to organise my thoughts about what I had learnt. I tried to be systematic and organised about this, but my mind kept going back to the Nulendi operation and the abortive attempt to seize the rebel radio station on 4–5 May. What had I done right? Where did I go wrong?

Looking over my operational orders, I thanked God that I had followed the book and put in place troops from the Loloho Marines, C Company, and Reconnaissance Platoon to provide cut-offs and a firm base to look after our rear in case we needed to mount a fighting withdrawal. And I thanked God that I had arranged medical support and a standby medivac helicopter—all of which we needed. I also thanked God for the quality of command and cool courage and tactical sense shown by my deputy, Capt. Michael Kumun, and by the leader of the resistance forces, Peter Sepe.

As I ran through the events of that night and the following day in my mind, I kept asking myself what, if anything, I might have done differently. When my lead scout came across the fire and the six rebels sleeping by its embers as we moved up the track towards the radio station, I directed that we leave them sleeping. Were those the rebels who hit us hard as we were withdrawing the following day? Should I had them taken into custody, disarmed them, and escorted them back to our rear? I can't honestly say that I thought of it at the time. I was totally focused on our objective—the radio station—and a bunch of sleeping rebels was just a distraction. Plus, the patrol was already at minimum strength, and weakening it further by detaching a couple of soldiers to take the rebels under armed escort to the rear was not an attractive option.

A second question that I found difficult to answer concerned the operation around the house with the radio station. Our attempts at stealth were disrupted by dogs barking as we crept close. A firefight broke out. Two rebels died of wounds sustained in the firefight, holding off the attacking party long enough for their comrades to make off into the night with the radio. What could we have done differently? Perhaps the obvious answer is that we should have thrown a protective cordon around the entire hamlet before making our approach to the house. This might have prevented the loss of the radio (a portable SB radio receiver and transmitter that had been mounted on a wall inside the house), but it might also have widened the area of the resultant firefight. And there was still the problem of the dogs barking and waking up their owners, to which there was no ready answer.

Looking back on my operational orders, I see that they required the ground to be seized before the house with the radio was approached by the raiding party. In our haste and in the event, we approached the house before 'seizing the ground'. Could we have seized the ground without waking up more dogs? Impossible to say. But if an error was made over that aspect, as the operations officer on the spot, the blame was mine.

A third question concerned the delay in leaving the hamlet while we were burying the two rebel fighters who had given their lives to allow their comrades to make their escape. I did not regret doing what any ordinary soldier would want to do, namely, honour the dead and see them given at least a basic burial and farewell prayer. But the time taken over this rite gave rebel fighters in the valley the opportunity to organise an effective harassing operation as we withdrew.

The final question in my mind concerned the extreme shock and horror I felt when Cpl Henry ToValuve was shot in the stomach immediately in front of me and knocked screaming into the river. Instinct takes over at such moments. Four of us launched into the river to grab him and pull him out. His injuries were shocking, and there was blood everywhere.

Some things are impossible to train for, and I think the sight and sound of an injured soldier who has taken a bullet right in front of you and is screaming for help and in mortal danger from blood loss and drowning is one of them. At that moment, I thanked God for the steadying influence of Michael Kumun, who directed the troops to throw up a defensive barrier while the soldiers and I did what we could to get ToValuve out of the river, across a flooded causeway, and to a safe area where the medic could patch the wound roughly and try to save him from going into immediate shock.

Then we had the task of getting ToValuve down the track and out of the valley and into a waiting ambulance. Without my having stationed troops to act as cut-offs and to look after our rear and without effective comms support to call in the ambulance and helicopter, we would have been in even worse trouble. We needed the manpower just to stretcher Henry out and also to look after Pejikere, who had sustained bullet wounds to his cheeks and mouth.

So thank God for that part of my planning. Still, as Mike Tyson, the 'baddest man on the planet', once said, 'Everyone has a plan until they get a punch in the mouth.' The point of army training and discipline is to help you absorb and deal with the immediate shock and horror of battle and then get on with recovering the situation as best you can.

You are alone with your thoughts and hopes and fears. Danger, injury, and death come suddenly, shockingly, and without warning. But with the right team around you and when the training kicks in, much can be done to recover even the most daunting situation.

I know that I would have been in real trouble that day without the backup troops, medical help, communication support, and calming and steadying influence of people like Michael Kumun and Peter Sepe who looked danger calmly in the face and got on with it. The ultimate operational lesson? You absolutely can't do it all on your own. Soldiering is a team game. And it is not a teddy bears' picnic.

CHAPTER 16

Bougainville: Operation High Speed I

Now is the hour, Aeneas, for the dauntless spirit—now for the
stout heart.

— Virgil (70–19 BC), *Aeneid*, vi. 261 (Jackson
translation)

Taking Command, First Royal Pacific Islands Regiment, 1994

Taking command of First Battalion as a brand-new lieutenant colonel was an honour and a challenge. I was in my prime, 37 years old, and felt that I was more than ready, having had two postings as operations officer for both battalions. I had a strong training background in Papua New Guinea, having been trained at the Joint Services College and the defence academy; had enjoyed rewarding training experiences with US and Australian armies; and had worked as an instructor at the Australian Army Land Warfare Centre.

I also had a young family and a professional working wife. All this allowed me to set my personal goals to ensure that my military ability, culture, and values were visible to my subordinates who would be encouraged to seek my counsel and guidance. To operate cohesively, unity of command based on trust and respect is essential. I had served as operations officer for the Papua New Guinea Defence Force in 1989, when the Panguna mine was on the brink of closure. In many ways, those were the glory days before indecision and lack of coordination from government, coupled with sharply deteriorating social and economic conditions on Bougainville, led to a complete impasse. My more recent experiences as operations officer in Bougainville had prepared me for the challenges that lay ahead. Many of these would be truly daunting. But this time, taking the lead from the front as commanding officer would put me in a position to influence events more decisively, or so I hoped.

As I thought about the challenges that lay ahead, I ran through in my mind some of the fundamental aspects of warfare that I needed to focus on before we deployed as a fighting unit. One of these was the need to put real emphasis on the development of our civil-military relationships on the ground in Bougainville. Without local support, cooperation, and mutual respect, no progress in resolving the conflict was possible. Other important principles of war that have remained constant throughout recorded history include selection and maintenance of the aim of war, economy of effort, operational security, offensive action, surprise, flexibility, and the maintenance of morale. Within the context of a limited war, our focus had to be on ensuring that the lives of our troops were conserved, that they were always backed up, and that they were not committed unnecessarily. And how pregnant this final thought was!

The first quarter of 1994 was to be a very busy year. First on the calendar was a training exercise with a US Special Forces combat diving team based in Okinawa. Then we were to host a battalion open day and Trooping the Colour in March, followed by pre-deployment training before deployment to Bougainville in May to relieve the Second Battalion for another year.

The first step was to reorganise my management and leadership team. I negotiated with the commander to secure the services of Maj. Tokam Kanene as operations officer. He was then serving as staff officer grade 2 with defence intelligence. Tokam and I were both platoon commanders in the Second Battalion in 1979 and 1980. He was later posted as my second in command with the Mortar Platoon as mortar line officer.

I was always impressed with Tokam Kanene's abilities, knowledge, and composed character. He was a devoted family man and his wife, Penny, was very supportive. My 2IC was Maj. Job Kasa, one of the pioneers of JSC in 1974. Just as I was securing their services, the battalion lost Maj. Peniel Nilingur, a very effective and intelligent officer, and Capt. Otto Pandum, both of whom were posted to defence intelligence at Murray Barracks.

The adjutant was Capt. Tony Dibul, a fellow Karkar Islander who would later takeover D Company, and the intelligence officer was Lt Belden Namah, who was posted out of C Company. My company commanders were Maj. Airo Bulina of A Company; Maj. Henry Kekeboge of B Company; Major Kumun of C Company on promotion; Capt. Paul Panau, acting, of D Company; and Major Demarcus of Support Company. The regimental sergeant major was Robert Lek.

As all the company commanders were JSC graduates with extensive experience in Bougainville, I was comfortable with the line-up of my new subordinates. The regiment was also blessed with new subalterns from the Royal Military College, Duntroon; Officer Cadet School, Waiouru; and PNG Defence Academy. The young officers were Martin Bure, Nick Henry, Craig Solomon, James Kadiesany, Andrew Kopada, Freddie Aile, Emmanuel To Dick, Steven Tolikun, John Keleto, Oscar Oksap, Kenny Ere, Jonathan Sembesen, Michael Jim, Jobi Ala, Mahlom Lahep, Willie Siam, John Manuai, Eram, Alex Hanema, Ben Kawio, Eric Pawiong, Moses Jenjet, and Herman Inahembi.

It was fun taking over the command of such a talented group of young officers, and I set about creating the right conditions in which to develop their tactical and leadership skills. I had been involved in most, if not all, of their careers from when they enlisted as officer cadets. Having been the senior instructor in the Cadet Wing at the PNG Defence Academy, I took a close personal interest in the welfare and careers of all the subalterns. Wanting them to maximise their tactical and leadership development ability, I made sure that everyone had every opportunity to excel. This was especially important now that the Bougainville crisis was showing every sign of going from bad to worse, mainly through the lack of political wisdom and clarity.

I discussed with Majors Tokam Kanene and Job Kasa the internal posting of officers and shared insights with them on which of the company commanders would be the best to nurture our junior officers. In working with my company commanders, I emphasised the importance of junior officers since both the success and operational tempo of small team operations were intimately related to the quality of our junior officers. I also underlined the importance of self-discipline and leading by good example. Working under the trying conditions of Bougainville and fostering civil-military relations required high levels of self-discipline, restraint, and patience.

Our battalion celebrations were set for 11 March with an open day, followed by Trooping of the Colours. PM Paias Wingti was pencilled in to be the parade host. On the Wednesday before the open day, I got an urgent call from my sister Balim to tell me that Mum had finally succumbed to cancer and would be buried the following day. I was distressed and deeply saddened by the news. My mother had done so much for me. She had always been my comforter and source of love, and now she was gone. My family understood why it was impossible for me to attend her funeral service and burial, but it was a sad and upsetting time.

On the Saturday morning after the open day, the troops prepared for the Trooping of the Colours at two o'clock. As Commander General Dademo and PM Paias Wingti sat watching us on parade, it occurred to me that, with the polish and precision of the troops on parade, both men must have been thinking about the possibility of using the regiment in reopening the Panguna mine. For my part, I was only too aware of the difference between an orderly parade ground and the realities of the jungle. On the parade ground, in a way that is hardly ever experienced in ordinary life, one can be totally in command of events. And this, undoubtedly, was one of the best parades I had ever commanded. Only an infantry battalion CO understands the sacred synergy that exists between a commander and his troops in the giving and receiving of commands during the Trooping of the Colours.

A few days later, Weni and the children and I arrived on Karkar Island to complete post-funeral activities. I was overwhelmed by feelings of loss and absence. Knowing that the one and only woman who had held me close to her bosom in my moments of despair and loneliness had now departed forever was heartbreaking.

Deep down, though she seldom said much, I knew that Mum was proud of me in her own special way. Mum was buried in the precinct of our family property at our humble village of Did on Karkar Island. After meeting family obligations and feasts and giving gifts to Malisa Toviai, my elder cousin brother from Yangoru, Wihun Village, we said goodbye to Dad and the rest of our relatives and made our way back to Port Moresby. It was a very emotional time; apart from the loss of my mother, my relatives were equally concerned about my safety on Bougainville, where events were so unpredictable.

Soon after my return from Karkar, I was thrown into arrangements for a reception and training mission with a US Special Forces training team based out of Okinawa. The team consisted of twelve troops from Special Forces Operational Detachment Alpha (SFODA) Combat Divers. The plan was for the training team to be inserted by parachute from the rear ramp of a special forces Hercules C-130 into the sea off Taurama Bay complete with all their combat gear. Majors Kanene and Job Kasa organised with the US Embassy and Immigration Department to set up an ad hoc office at Taurama Beach to process the US troops once they parachuted in. It was an exciting event. At 0730 hours, after establishing the location of the landing zone as marked by a yellow smoke grenade, the team parachuted out along with their Zodiac and other supplies. Once in the water, they recovered the parachutes, loaded the Zodiac, and made their way to the shore.

The training with the US Special Forces detachment was code-named Exercise Balance Passion. We settled the team at the officers' mess and then proceeded to Goldie River Training Depot where, with the assistance of the Warrior Wing, we had planned a battalion-level training programme for ten days. The training was based around enhanced junior leadership for small team operations, including advanced medical and explosives training. Training stands were set up, and the companies rotated through. At the end of the training, the regiment did a lightly loaded speed march from Goldie to Taurama Barracks, a distance of around 40 km, for which the training target was three hours or under.

The last week of Exercise Balance Passion saw the battalion deployed to Kupiano in Abau District, Central Province, for a civic patrol. We conducted medical patrols in the area with the PNGDF Preventive Medical Platoon, which worked closely with the director of health services, Col. Frank Torova. As a goodwill gesture, the US Embassy fully funded the renovation of Kupiano Health Centre. This involved the use of the US troops and an element of field engineers from the PNGDF. The civic action patrol was very successful. Indeed, the whole training with SFODA was a great success. On their departure, we shared gifts and well wishes, and many long-term friendships were made.

By the end of April, the battalion was ready for redeployment to Bougainville. We were blessed with three new officers joining us, Second Lieutenants Freddie Aile, Andrew Kopada, and Michael Jim. Before they could go on leave, I sent them to Bougainville for a month to command a platoon each to get them ready for operational deployments.

So far as my order of battle was concerned, I was reasonably content, having restructured the battalion manning from officers down to senior non-commissioned officers. Logistics were a headache, however, and gave me many misgivings, but we did at least have three sets of uniforms issued for each member of the battalion, plus personal weapons and assorted ammunition. Under General Dademo's guidance, we were also issued with Fabrique Nationale MAG 58 Belgian medium machines guns firing the standard NATO 7.62×51.00 mm round, replacing the US GPMG 60 Vietnam-era general-purpose machine gun, and a supply of automatic grenade launchers.

For mobility on Bougainville, we had sufficient soft-skinned vehicles, a bulletproof special service vehicle, and fast speedboats. For medium weapons, we had 81 mm standard-issue mortars. One of the more immediate challenges was to preposition sufficient fuel of all sorts throughout the island so that land, sea, and air transport fuel supplies were available.

During April and the early part of May, Major Kanene and I worked on the development of our operational concept for the battalion's redeployment. The superior commander's intent, towards which we were working, had been spelled out to us in simple terms as follows:

a. capture the Panguna mine
b. neutralise the Bougainville Revolutionary Army's factions as soon as possible and disrupt their logistics and supply
c. continue the national government's 3R strategy (restoration, reconstruction, and reconciliation) for Bougainville

To support the development and implementation of our operational intent, we brought up to date, so far as possible, our intelligence information on the structure and personnel of the Bougainville Revolutionary Army in its political, military, and administrative wings.

It was important for us to appreciate that the crisis on Bougainville had deep-seated political roots that, along with the associated and very real social and economic aspects, made the crisis an unimaginable quagmire. Full autonomy from PNG followed by political independence was the ultimate aim of the rebels. So long as this continued to be the case and the rebels enjoyed at least a minimum level of support from the people and so long as the national government was unwilling to contemplate secession, the armed struggle would continue.

With these various forces at play, the task ahead was daunting. From as early as April 1989, when the government declared a state of emergency in response to a sharply deteriorating security situation, the use of military force as a means of ensuring security for the civilian population of Bougainville and eventually overcoming the rebels was seen by the national government as a realistic option. That school of thought, namely, the possibility of imposing a military solution on Bougainville, never left the minds of our politicians, even in the midst of the various rounds of peace talks that were held.

Within the context of the superior commander's intent, I worked up a general concept of operations and an outline for the approach to be taken by the battalion when it deployed. In developing this approach, my assumptions were as follows:

a. The BRA will continue to fight and disrupt the government's 3R strategy and undermine our operations wherever possible.

b. Local support to the rebels will continue to hamper our ability to develop a comprehensive intelligence picture throughout the island.

c. The rebels will seek to distract us and prolong the crisis wherever they can, but the centre of gravity for military operations remains around the Panguna mine.

d. The rebels will continue to receive international support and sympathy including critical support from the Solomon Islands.

e. The BRA leadership is based around Sam Kauona, Joseph Kabui, Ishmael Toroama, and John Tari supported by Martin MirIori in the Solomon Islands. central Bougainville is the area of greatest strategic importance to the security forces and the government of Papua New Guinea both because of the Panguna mine and because it is the centre of BRA military, administrative, and political resistance.

f. The Bougainville Interim Government (BIG), the political arm of the BRA, and hardliners will continue to advocate for political autonomy and eventual secession from PNG.

With these considerations, my general concept of operations for the battalion was as follows:

a. Plan and implement an aggressive fighting patrol programme supported by fire support and logistics.

b. Deploy troops in and around the Panguna mine and hold the ground there as long as possible.

c. Tighten the Solomon Island border through aggressive maritime patrols and presence in our new border outposts.

d. Plan and implement a modest communications, logistics, and supply chain to support our troops in outposts and while on patrol.

e. Upgrade our medical support including provision for medivac.

f. Have fresh troops in reserve.

g. Enhance our psychological operations by seeking increased community support and confidence at the local level.

h. Give more recognition and support to the resistance force throughout Bougainville.

i. Work closely with the Bougainville provincial government and non-governmental organisations.

j. Consolidate our command and control team at Arawa and Loloho. The forward supply base will remain at Buka but be scaled down in Wakunai.

k. Enforce personal and subunit discipline.

In developing this concept of operations, my key assumptions were the following:

a. Logistics including air support will continue to limit our operations.

b. Manpower available to assist with maintaining security in rebel-controlled areas will be a concern.

c. Fostering confidence through hearts and minds operations must be seen as being of central importance to the peace process over the longer term. It cannot be seen as a distraction as in many instances in the past.

d. Significant manpower will be taken up with static duties looking after the thirty-one care centres spread throughout central Bougainville, South Bougainville, and the south-west, Bana and Telei areas. Over 20,000 civilians have to be looked after mainly by providing static security while the Red Cross and Bougainville administration will continue to provide for health, education, and other needs.

With these various assumptions very much in mind and within the concept of operations outlined, the battalion mission was simple: '1RPIR is to continue to re-establish Papua New Guinea government control in Bougainville.'

To accomplish this mission, the concept of manoeuvre was set out as follows:

> A battalion group will be inserted into Bougainville by sea and the remainder inserted by air, and each company will take over and relieve Second Battalion positions while Battalion Forward Tactical Headquarters will be based at Loloho and the remainder at Arawa. Battalion operations will be conducted in four phases:
>
> Phase 1. Insertion.
> Phase 2. Conduct of operations in respective areas of operations.
> Phase 3. Consolidation of operations including fostering of public relations and winning hearts and minds by assisting in medical, hygiene, and spiritual programmes.
> Phase 4. Preparation for relief by Second Battalion after one year.

The important dates were as follows:

a. 7 May: advance party deployment led by battalion second in command
b. 15 May: deployment of main body to Buka
c. 19 May: insertion of main body of troops to Arawa and Loloho
d. 21–29 May: complete relief of all locations held by Second Battalion

The main body of the battalion sailed out on 15 May. I had to remain back for a commander's conference and more briefings from the Department of Foreign Affairs due to the fragile security agreements with Solomon Island government officials and members of the Solomon Islands Field Force, who were also operating along their international borders.

The day before I departed, I met Capt. Walter Enuma at Hohola at his relative's place. He was completing the post-burial arrangements for his late wife, who had died of natural causes. After our days together at the defence academy in 1983, he had been posted as aide-de-camp to Gov. Gen. Sir Kingsford Dibela before resigning to pursue a civilian career. However, he volunteered to re-enlist in the PNGDF in 1991. I knew his tactical and leadership skills from first-hand experience; he was exactly the type of officer we needed to command and lead the troops in Bougainville. I asked Enuma if he wished to transfer from Second to First Battalion. He was pleased to be considered for a transfer as he had small children who needed to be close to his relatives including his dad, the retired sergeant Enuma.

I made an appointment to see Brigadier General Dademo. Like Enuma, Dademo's ethnic tribe was Binandere from Oro Province. The commander instantly approved my request and directed his staff to prepare the posting and transfer of Enuma as acting company commander of First Battalion. We were booked to travel to Bougainville on a chartered aircraft with John Momis, the regional member for Bougainville, a week later. When we arrived at the hangar, all the seats were taken, but we managed to remove a staff member travelling with Momis and slot Walter Enuma in his place. I provided a new lease to Enuma's life and career, and we became solid comrades once again, this time for a long time.

My command team settled into our command post and forward tactical headquarters at Loloho. This time, I had Pvt. Patrick Kero from Warumo Village, Sandaun, as my batman, replacing the two civilian youths I had in 1993. Moses Piri had moved to the village at Rorovana and enlisted with the resistance, and William had been killed at Morgan Junction by rebel fire in October 1993.

We reorganised the command post by erecting a conference room and sand model area and put up military maps of Bougainville, noting the locations of troop dispositions, care centres, and suspected rebel camps. Other aspects of camp administration were looked after by Maj. Job Kasa, including securing running water for our toilets, shower, and laundry; mess facilities; and various amenities for the civilians who had joined us. When we arrived, the number of civilians seemed to have grown. The Rorovana Resistance Force had completely taken control of Rorovana Village, providing a good example of what a village defence system could look like given effective leadership and support.

At Loloho, at the insistence of Major Kasa and Lt Belden Namah, both of whom were Seventh-Day Adventist (SDA) members, I approved the construction of a chapel to be used by the SDA and any other church denomination that wanted access for spiritual activities. Our supporting agencies were also at work, ensuring that they were prepared to meet our operational needs when called on.

I made a very important decision, and I stuck to it, which was not to carry a personal weapon in Bougainville. Instead, I decided to carry my pointer or swagger stick, originally presented to me by my brother Willie. I used this in all my day-to-day activities, outlining key features of maps that we were discussing and for emphasis when I gave instructions. As I had no weapon on me, women, children, and even the most disadvantaged in Bougainville society could talk and approach me without being apprehensive. The whole operation was focused on winning hearts and minds; therefore, it was important to show that we believed that most ordinary Bougainvilleans were peaceful in intent. If there was any danger from enemy fire or action, I had sufficient troops around to protect me. Not carrying a personal weapon did not place me in danger.

Our medical centre was soon operational, along with our Small Boat Team and the maritime liaison officer's headquarters. The workshop responsible for our vehicle and speedboat maintenance was also soon up and running. It looked after the upkeep of the 50 kVA generator (ex–Bougainville Copper Ltd) we set up near the Loloho power station. Our communications links were established after a visit by Telekom officials who set up direct lines via satellite, giving us good data, telex, and high-frequency links up and down our military command chain.

No commander will go into battle without a comprehensive communications system. Our high-frequency military radio gave me direct communication with subordinate commanders and the headquarters at Murray Barracks. All in all, I was content with our preparations before we commenced an active patrolling programme.

The Bougainville civilian administration was also functioning. The administrator was an experienced public servant called George Lesi. I made it my business to drop by from time to time to give him briefs on rebel activities, the Solomon Islands, and the care centres. He was well respected.

In early July, I was recalled to Port Moresby to meet the commander and the new acting chief of operations, Col. Paul Dala. I was given a new concept of operations with the code name Operation Dynamo IV. The general concept was to plan for the capture of the Panguna mine inclusive of the villages of Guava, Sipuru, and Kongara. My instructions were that this must be completed by the end of August.

I was informed that PM Paias Wingti and his cabinet had made the capture and securing of the Panguna mine before September a top priority as 16 September would mark PNG's twenty-ninth anniversary of independence. It was paramount that all necessary resources, including intelligence, were put before the defence council and further up the chain for approval. The Field Intelligence Company under Capt. Paul Kaliop and the Defence Intelligence Directorate under Fredrick Punangi, Terence Flawrey, and Doreen Joel were tasked with preparing intelligence analysis reports for the National Security Advisory Council and the cabinet's Security Council.

While I understood my superior commander's intent, I returned to central Bougainville with a series of unanswered questions. The first concerned the availability of resources, including very importantly air mobility, in particular the essential helicopter support and logistics supply to sustain our troops and maintain their continuous presence in and around the Panguna mine. My other main concern was the choice of Col. Paul Dala as chief of operations to handle planning at the Port Moresby end. Dala was a very likeable senior officer, but he was not cut out for this demanding job. He had spent most of his career as a diplomat and had no prior field experience, let alone exposure to the operating realities on Bougainville. There were other senior colonels available, such as Allan Pinia, who had been overlooked. In my view, this was a critical weakness in the operational planning chain.

As a result, I started to rely on my own tactical planning and analysis to come up with a general concept of operations to secure the Panguna mine once the troops were ready and we had in place the necessary mobility assets and intelligence reports. I sat with my operations team, Major Kanene and Lt Belden Namah and the three company commanders, Majors Henry Kekeboge and Airo Bulina and Capt. Tony Dibul, to develop our operations planning and appreciation. We all understood that the Panguna mine, long since deserted and with no extraction or ore-crushing machinery intact, was the immediate tactical-level military objective.

Back at Loloho, Capt. Paul Kaliop was my anchor for tactical intelligence. He was an able officer, having had his first taste of action in April 1989 at Sipuru under Lt Col. Jeff Key, and his earlier exposure and contacts helped him in his assessments. He also had excellent field intelligence soldiers, such as Pvt. Philip Waibauru and Corporal Riken. Private Sarin completed our intelligence cell headed by Lt Belden Namah.

We were further supported by our intercept radio station at Manatai Catholic Mission that passed on valuable intelligence of rebel movements between Solomon Islands and Bougainville. These movements were organised through Joseph Kabui, who was based in his village at Paruparu, west of Panguna mine. I was truly blessed as both Captain Kaliop and Lt Belden Namah provided me with up-to-date intelligence. I kept them on their toes as I made it mandatory that no fighting patrol was to be conducted without proper intelligence, and every patrol had to have a good backup plan.

We finally made contact with a reliable source who informed us of the need to make contact with the people at Paruparu, where Joseph Kabui was based. Kabui's elder brother, Martin Miriori, was operating out of Honiara, the capital of Solomon Islands. Determined to make progress, I issued an early warning and tasked Major Kasa to arrange for second-hand clothes, medicines, sporting equipment, and food to be dropped off at Paruparu and to seek an opportunity to create a care centre so that we could bring in the Red Cross and Bougainville administration. This would allow us to bring government services to the periphery of the Panguna mine.

On a Sunday morning, with the assistance of the helicopter operating out of Loloho, we loaded up ten soldiers, boxes of medicine and food, and battalion headquarters staff, including my driver, Pai, from Oro and flew towards Paruparu under a beautiful midday sun. The pilots were Captain Pak from Korea and Charlie Andrews.

We flew along the Espie Highway at a safe height and, after reaching the Pakia Gap, turned westwards over the ridge from where we could spot Paruparu School. I pointed downwards, and the pilot lowered the chopper close to the high ground, the creek, and the SDA church area. After the troops had secured the immediate area of the landing zone and as we were in the process of offloading, the rebels opened fire. We returned fire. I was caught between Major Kanene, Belden Namah, and Job Kasa. RSM Robert Lek grabbed me by my webbing and flung me back into the chopper, and we took off. We were now in the air and cut off from the remainder of my forward tactical headquarters staff: Major Kanene, my operations officer; Belden Namah, the intelligence office; two resistance force members from Rorovana Village; and five soldiers along with my driver, Corporal Pai—all were stranded at Paruparu.

As they recited the story to me later, they made their way to the ridge high up behind Paruparu Village, established an ambush site to catch any rebel fighters who might be following, and hoped for the early return of the helicopter. The rebels were, of course, well aware by now that there was a patrol isolated in no man's land. We were able to confirm this by monitoring radio conversations between Joseph Kabui, Sam Kauona, and Martin Miriori in the Solomon Islands.

I was very uneasy that night and wondered how the patrol would survive the cold and lack of food and the need to defend themselves against enemy action. Early the following day, I flew back to the area in the hope of locating them; and sure enough, I spotted them along the ridge. While there was no clear area on the ridge for even a rudimentary helicopter landing zone, I managed to drop C ration packs and fresh radio batteries to them.

Fortunately for the patrol, when they took shelter near the church after being engaged, Major Kanene spotted a bush knife against a wall and instructed one of the resistance force members to take it. Later, this knife would save their lives. With only one bush knife between them, when they reached the ridge, they decided to stay in one spot and try to chop down a tree to create a rough landing zone where the helicopter could land or at least hover.

The approach to their position by air was safe enough as the helicopter could approach via a deep ravine from the south, where it would be difficult for the rebels to position themselves. Overnight, the patrol set out a number of 1.6 kg M18A1 claymore anti-personnel mines and placed a FRONT TOWARD ENEMY marking, allowing them to dominate the ridge. I returned with pilots Captain Pak and Charlie Andrews and dropped more C rations and fresh radio batteries and then returned to Loloho, still worried about how best to attempt their retrieval. With the fresh batteries, they were able to give us the situation on the ground, which by now was manageable and consolidated.

Meanwhile, they continued taking it in turns to chip away at the tree until it fell early in the morning. As soon as the clouds lifted and while still holding ground, they called for extraction. It was now the third day. I immediately dispatched the helicopter. The pilots held the helicopter in a hover position above the ground while the patrol clambered on board, stepping off the skids into the cabin. Belden Namah, the last on board, fired the remaining claymores to keep the rebels' heads down as he sprinted to the chopper and hung onto the skids, dangling in mid-air as the patrol was extracted from the ridge.

The patrol arrived back at Loloho, much to our delight. I vowed never again to venture into unknown country with the complete battalion forward tactical team. I also took a lot of flak from the closest members of my staff about putting my own life at risk. Meantime, there were plenty of lessons to ponder over the Paruparu operation. Had our arrival that Sunday been anticipated? Were our secure communications compromised? Was our reliable intelligence source as reliable as we thought, or had we been set up? Were we too casual in securing the landing zone? Had we given sufficient thought to the possibility of enemy action? Plenty of room for thought and plenty of room not to take security too lightly in the future. Meanwhile, the tactical value of the ordinary bush knife as well as the M18A1 claymore mines with their iconic labelling FRONT TOWARD ENEMY was certainly reinforced as was the vital need for helicopter support and effective communications links.

By the end of July, we had completed our intelligence picture and were visited by General Dademo and Col. Paul Dala, which meant that the operation to capture the Panguna mine was imminent. General Dademo and I promoted Lt Belden Namah to the rank of captain and Tony Dibul, the officer commanding D Company, to the rank of major.

The operation to seize the Panguna mine, originally called Operation Dynamo IV, was now code-named Operation High Speed I. Its final outline was as follows:

> **Mission:** 1RPIR is to capture and seize the Panguna mine.
>
> **General Outline:** The operation will be conducted in three phases: Phase 1 is the deployment and seizure of critical locations and approaches; Phase 2 is the conduct of aggressive patrolling; Phase 3 is the consolidation of gains made by the regiment.
>
> It will be a three company operation with B Company deployed by helicopter to Kupei Gap with the Mortar Section and A and D Company to be deployed by trucks along Espie Highway. A Company to hold Moronei Village and control the Pakia gap approach and D Company to deploy and hold the main office called the Pink Haus. Support company and elements of forward tactical headquarters to be established at Panguna International School and to control all operations in and around the mine.

The resistance force units from Buin, Rorovana, and Wakunai were to complement our manpower. The operation period would be three weeks.

As designated, Major Kanene was inserted by helicopter at Panguna International School to establish the forward tactical headquarters. B Company under Maj. Henry Kekeboge was inserted by helicopter into the Kupei Gap and, not encountering any immediate resistance, successfully sent a reconnaissance party to patrol and secure the area from Kupei Gap to Guava Village. Rather than leaving a patrol on the high ground, the rest of B Company then made their way down to Guava Village and camped on the flat area overlooking the mine from the eastern side. With B Company's immediate objectives apparently achieved, I planned to use D Company to aggressively patrol around Jaba River and the Kewarong gully to control the exit road out to Mananau along the Jaba River.

Before last light on 23 August, I was able to report to HQ PNGDF that the troops had successfully completed phase 1 of the operation, namely, the deployment and seizure of critical locations and approaches, including the establishment of forward tactical headquarters at Panguna International School. The next step would be to initiate phase 2, aggressive patrolling, before moving to phase 3, consolidation of tactical gains.

On the morning of 24 August, we resupplied B Company by chopper at their location above Guava Village. I was with Major Kanene at Panguna International School to discuss the battalion patrol programme. Major Kekeboge, commanding B Company, had received a letter, sago, and fish from his wife, Eunice, at Port Moresby in our early morning helicopter resupply. He did not have his helmet or flak jacket on and was reading his letter outside. Unbeknown to us, he was being watched by a sniper using a rifle fitted with a telescopic sight from about 100 metres away on the high ground to the north-east. The bullet struck Kekeboge in his head, dropping him to the ground. His batman, Private Pando from East Sepik Province, jumped on top of him to cover him, and he, too, was shot in the head. Both died instantly.

Our regimental medical officer, Capt. Raphael Kaule, could not do anything as he was at forward tactical headquarters in the mine. The situation was critical. We did not know if this was a lone sniper operating or a rebel group massing for an attack. I instructed Captain Kaule to remain at forward tactical until we saw how the situation developed.

B Company was now without their company commander. The troops, initially in disarray, were steadied and reorganised by Lt Martin Bure. With the threat of further enemy action, it was not safe to try to retrieve the bodies. The developing situation at Guava Ridge was relayed to us by Corporal Kila, the signals officer. All communications were transmitted in Motu language rather than pidgin and passed on to me by Lt Craig Solomon. With the light fading and the tactical situation extremely uncertain, I decided not to try an immediate night extraction.

Meanwhile, D Company under Maj. Tony Dibul, initiating their planned patrol programme the following day, spotted an abandoned Toyota Hilux, presumably the property of Bougainville Copper Ltd workers. All it appeared to need was a fresh battery and some petrol. I flew back to Loloho on 25 August, found a fresh battery, acquired about twenty litres of petrol, and returned the next day, Friday, 26 August, dropping off the supplies at Panguna International School. I took Pvt. Joe Kimin from Enga Province and flew across to Guava Ridge in an attempt to recover the bodies, which had been lying out in the open for two days. The security position around B Company's location was still extremely uncertain, but I judged that an attempt at recovery had to be made before making a decision about how best to reinforce and stabilise the company's position.

As we were attempting to land on the ridge, the rebels sprayed the helicopter with a heavy burst of automatic fire, hitting Joe Kimin in his thigh. I was crouching between the pilots to direct them to their landing spot. Hearing Joe Kimin cry out, I turned and reached back to help him dress his wound. As I did so, a second burst of fire into the rear cabin through the empty side door area caught me, a bullet going through my left wrist and arm. I didn't feel the impact immediately, but as I turned back, blood sprayed from my severed artery all over the windshield and floor. The helicopter generator was also damaged by a stray shot. Captain Pak, a veteran pilot from South Korea who had clocked many hours of combat mission in Vietnam, was the captain of the Huey, and Charlie Andrews was his co-pilot. Pak immediately aborted the landing and set an emergency course for Arawa Field Hospital while I did what I could to strap a field dressing over my wound and stabilise Pvt. Joe Kimin's gunshot wound.

As we were coming into land at Arawa, the engine failed, and we lost all power. The pilots managed a semi-controlled descent with autorotation, and we crash-landed heavily near the field hospital. By now, I was bleeding profusely. The standard white 4 × 7 inch field dressing I had strapped on my left wrist had not done much to stem the flow of blood. Bleeding out from a severed artery in my arm, I ran into the hospital and told the medic to take the stretcher to the helicopter to assist Private Kimin. Those were the last words I said before passing out from loss of blood and shock. I blacked out at the door, and by the time I regained consciousness, it was about three in the morning. As I lay drifting in and out of sleep, I heard women's voices beside my bed and realised that the women's group from the care centre of the SDA church were there to support me.

The women started singing hymns of faith and other songs in their own local language. It was the most soothing, beautiful, and unexpected outpouring of goodwill. I was operated on by the defence force director of health services and surgeon, Lt Col. Frank Torova, who was also my schoolmate from Sogeri. He reassured me of my recovery but referred me to Port Moresby and then to Australia for further medical tests as the main artery and several of the nerves in my arm and wrist had been severed.

The commander of PNGDF, General Dademo, immediately flew into Loloho to take stock. He took time out to call Weni to let her know that I was wounded but had been operated on and that my injuries were not life-threatening. I was very thankful to General Dademo for this gesture; even though working under extreme political pressure, he still found the time and presence of mind to keep my wife and children informed of my medical condition from the front line. This attention to detail was typical of the care that he showed towards his men.

Meanwhile, as soon as they heard the news of my injury, D Company under Maj. Tony Dibul and his able company sergeant major, WO2 Thomas Biaun, took firm tactical control of the situation. Lt James Kadiesany, who was Ten Platoon commander, assembled a handful of selected troops, deployed with the assistance of Maj. Tokam Kanene, to link up with B Company at Guava Ridge. While the rest of D Company provided a firm base at the bottom of Guava Ridge, B Company carried out the bodies of their late company commander, Maj. Henry Kekeboge, and his batman, Private Pando. The chopper flew into the mine pit and extracted the bodies to Arawa and then to Buka for an onward flight to Port Moresby.

B Company now withdrew from Guava and regrouped with forward tactical headquarters at Panguna International School. In the meantime, I was flown by medivac to Port Moresby and then to First Military District Hospital, Brisbane, for further surgery to the artery and nerves in my left arm and wrist and also to my right eye.

News of the deaths of Major Kekeboge and Private Pando hit the battalion hard. Major Kekeboge was related to Weni, so it was all the more difficult for me. In our culture, we take such deaths personally, and family pressure added additional strain. Mandatory traditional burdens were a feature of all the deaths of soldiers and policemen from the beginning of the crisis. Major Kekeboge's married quarter was next to my own commanding officer's house, increasing my family's exposure to the shared grief at the loss of a husband, father, and very fine officer.

In my absence, Operation High Speed I was left in the capable hands of my operations officer, Major Kanene. He was soon directed to commence withdrawal from the Panguna mine and associated positions. The reason for this sudden reversal of government policy would eventually become evident, but in the short term, the battalion was left in the dark about why it had first been ordered to take the Panguna mine and then, having successfully done so at the cost of two fine lives and associated injuries, withdraw just a few days later.

The operation to seize the mine and associated strategic points had been confirmed in a personal visit to me and my command team at forward tactical headquarters in Loloho by PNGDF commander Gen. Robert Dademo and Chief of Operations Paul Dala at the end of July. It was stressed that the operational orders for Operation High Speed I had been drawn up and issued under secrecy and urgency. We were told that PM Paias Wingti and his cabinet were determined to be able to report the seizure of the mine by the end of August, in time to mark PNG Independence Day celebrations on 16 September.

My injuries at Guava Ridge above the mine and the death of Major Kekeboge and his batman made news headlines. But within defence headquarters, there were mixed reactions. Many senior officers, especially the stay-at-home colonels who had chosen not to take operational commands or were medically unfit for the field and were classified either formally or informally as unfit for battle, criticised me, saying that the place for a commanding officer was not in the front line and that I should be disciplined for interfering with the progress of the operations. In my defence, I positioned myself in the front line so that I could direct operations and be physically with the troops rather than rely on radio communications. I was the commanding officer and the man on the ground. Also, I was the accountable senior officer, so where I positioned myself during operations was my call and my call alone. Besides, it is a standard part of tactical doctrine for field commanders to position themselves as far forward As far forward as possible as they can be physically seen by troops can be physically seen by the troops but also so that they can evaluate and react to the evolving tactical situation on the ground.

While I was aware of these criticisms, I was not immediately involved in responding to them because, at that point, I was receiving further surgical care at First Military District Hospital, Brisbane. While recovering from surgery, I became aware of a major political development in Port Moresby. PM Paias Wingti, after a Supreme Court ruling on the legality of one of his parliamentary manoeuvres, lost the support of some of his key coalition partners in Parliament and was replaced as prime minister after a vote of no confidence by his deputy,

Sir Julius Chan, minister for foreign affairs and trade and minister for finance.

I saw the news of this change in prime minister on a TV set in my hospital ward in Australia just four days after being shot. I wondered what the implications of this might be for the PNG government's policy in Bougainville. I did not have long to wait for the answer.

As a postscript, I was later to learn that, at the very moment that I was ordering my men forward into the Panguna mine on Operation High Speed I at the personal urging of Cdr Robert Dademo, officials in government, under the direction of Sir Julius Chan, were commencing talks with Sam Kauona in the Solomon Islands to thrash out the details of what would become the Honiara Commitments to Peace, signed at a conference in Arawa in October 1994. These officials were led by Brown Bai, head of the Department of the Prime Minister, and Gabriel Dusava, secretary of foreign affairs. No one from the PNGDF was present at this secret high-level meeting, and it is not clear whether Robert Dademo was even aware that the talks were taking place.

The talks occurred on 26 and 27 August. Major Kekeboge and Private Pando were shot and killed on 24 August. Pvt. Joe Kimin and I were shot and wounded while trying to retrieve their bodies on 26 August. While we were risking our lives, government officials were sitting in air-conditioned comfort in the Solomon Islands, holding talks with the BRA senior commander, whom we had orders to 'neutralise'.

Why am I even raising the matter? Because, at the very least, this looks like a case of extreme disarray and lack of coordination among government departments in Port Moresby. Alternatively and less charitably, it could be seen as a case of extreme cynicism on the part of ministers and departmental heads. Allowing a military operation to proceed with its attendant risk of life and limb to one's own soldiers, not to mention enemy combatants, in the middle of peace preliminaries is either the result of cynicism or a lack of coordination and carelessness of a very high order. It is little short of scandalous. In the end, Dademo was relieved of his command on 30 August, the wives of Major Kekeboge and Private Pando were condemned to a long widowhood, and Pvt. Joe Kimin and I were both left with permanent and serious injuries.

How hard would it have been, I wonder, for someone from the Department of the Prime Minister or the National Security Council or the Department of Foreign Affairs and Trade to have picked up a phone and told General Dademo to put Operation High Speed I on hold for a few days? No explanation need have been given, though that might have been a reasonable courtesy. One phone call to save the lives of two very fine men is not much to ask. What a waste. What a fucking needless waste.

CHAPTER 17

Last Days as Commanding Officer, 1RPIR

Now let us understand the situation. We are going into battle against a tough and determined enemy. I can't promise you that I will bring you all home alive. But this I swear, before you and before Almighty God. That before we go into battle, I will be the first to set foot on the field, and I will be the last to step off, and I will leave no one behind. Dead or alive, we will all come home together. So help me God.

Lt Col. Harold G. Moore and Joseph Galloway
(1992)[11]

Lt Col. Hal Moore is my kind of leader—not the stay-at-home colonels at Murray Barracks who criticised me for leading Operation High Speed I from the front line. Against such criticism, I say, what would they know? They were never there. I was. And my troops were, two of whom gave their lives, Maj. Henry Kekeboge and Private Pando. They should be remembered. They *will* be remembered.

Sir Julius Chan, upon taking over the prime ministership on 30 August, announced that his key priority was to solve the Bougainville conflict. He took control of the police and defence ministerial portfolios

---

[11] *We Were Soldiers Once . . . And Young* (Random House Publishing). This book has been on the Commandant of the Marine Corps' professional reading list since its original publication in October 1992.

461

and, on his first day in office, removed Brig. Gen. Robert Dademo from command of the Papua New Guinea Defence Force, replacing him with his old friend Gen. Tony Huai. He then flew to Honiara for face-to-face talks with Bougainville Revolutionary Army military commander Sam Kauona. After two days of talks chaired by Solomon Island prime minister Francis Billy Hilly, they signed a piece of paper styled the Honiara Commitments, dated 3 September 1994, under which they agreed to hold a peace conference at a date and place to be determined by both parties (i.e. by Chan and Kauona) but preferably no later than 10 October, involving all sides of the Bougainville conflict, with security for delegates to be provided by a South Pacific Regional Peacekeeping Force (SPRPKF), to be set up especially for that purpose.

Article 1 of the Honiara Commitments stated:

> Peace is hereby declared immediately at Honiara on this Third day of September 1994 following which all forces will maintain strategic positions, and the Cease-fire shall be declared by both parties at a time and date to be agreed and announced within seven days of this commitment.

Article 2 provided as follows:

> That a South Pacific Peace Keeping Force will be deployed to Bougainville as soon as practicably possible after the declaration of ceasefire when mechanisms and arrangements for the Force are finalised in consultations with participating governments and through consultation between the Commanders of the Forces of both sides.

Events now gathered pace quickly. The ceasefire provided for in Article 2 of the Honiara Commitments was declared on 8 September. Whether this followed actual consultations between the parties is unclear.

What we do know is that difficulties over the nature of the peacekeeping force immediately surfaced. The difficulties involved a range of practical issues including who was to pay for the force, who was to provide the logistical support, and who was to command it. Kauona made it clear that, because of Australia's history of ownership of the Panguna mine, as well as their role as the colonial power pre-independence, the BRA could not agree to Australia commanding the force or having too prominent a role in it. The force had to be a *regional* peacekeeping force (meaning a force formed mainly from the smaller countries in the region). Yet realistically, Australia was the only country that could pay for such a force, the only country with the muscle to organise it; and if Australian troops were to be involved, it would therefore have to retain national command responsibility.

There were other difficulties as well. Deployments of this kind always need a status of forces agreement to be negotiated and agreed by lawyers. Sam Kauona was insistent that, as a party to the Honiara Commitments and as the commander of one of the two forces mentioned in that document, he needed to be a signatory to the status of forces agreement for the SPRPKF. This proved to be a sticking point. Whether the real sticking point was with Australia, Sir Julius, their respective defence lawyers, or all of them, I don't know. But in the end, all that was agreed was that Kauona could be invited to observe the signing ceremony, if he wished, which was to be held at South Pacific Forum Headquarters in Suva. He chose not to attend. No doubt he felt, perhaps with some justification, that merely being an observer would diminish his standing as one of the two main parties to the Honiara Commitments.

Dragons' Teeth

Other difficulties soon crowded in. Francis Ona and other commanders of the BRA insisted on guarantees for their personal safety while travelling to, from, and around Arawa, where the Bougainville Peace Conference was to be held. They also wanted guarantees of neutrality on the part of the SPRPKF, and they continued to object to Australia leading the force or playing too prominent a role in it. Further, they wanted pre-commitments from the Papua New Guinea government in respect to the ultimate independence of Bougainville, pardons and exemptions from prosecution for members of the BRA for all extrajudicial crimes that may have been committed by them, reparations for damage to the Bougainville economy and environment, and agreements on a range of other issues. I was on medical leave while all this was being discussed and argued over, so I don't know what commitments were entered into and how much airy hand-waving went on to try meet these demands.

To try to accommodate the BRA's insistence that the peacekeeping force must be a regional one, Tonga agreed to provide the chief of operations for the SPRPKF, a patrol boat, and 135 personnel from His Majesty's Armed Forces; Fiji provided the land force commander and 200 troops from the Fiji Military Force; and Vanuatu provided 65 personnel drawn from its field force. New Zealand provided a C-130 Hercules, twelve personnel, and two liaison officers while Australia provided the commanding officer for the SPRPKF, two ships for logistical support, HMAS *Tobruk* and *Success*, three Sea King helicopters, a number of Black Hawk helicopters, four C-130s, two Caribou, and 230 service personnel. In short, Australia provided a very substantial and highly visible contribution—and one that was bound to raise objections from the BRA.

Australia formally confirmed that it was willing to meet the costs and logistical hurdles of mounting the force. Col. David Hurley, then chief of staff to Australia's First Division, was appointed commander of the SPRPKF; later, he would be promoted to general and appointed chief of the Australian Defence Force (2011–14) and governor general of Australia (2019).

On Saturday, 10 September, though still formally on medical leave, I was ordered back to Bougainville to provide a ground and security brief to Colonel Hurley, who was making immediate arrangements to travel to Arawa and Loloho to conduct a preliminary reconnaissance. I provided the required brief from my forward tactical headquarters in Loloho on Monday and Tuesday, 12–13 September. Wg Cdr Kevin

Firth, the New Zealand defence adviser in Port Moresby, and Paul Bengo, senior government adviser in the Bougainville Restoration Office, Waigani, were also present for the briefing.

The Papua New Guinean government chose Arawa as the site of the Bougainville Peace Conference. Despite being the former capital of Bougainville and its largest town, the population of Arawa never exceeded 30,000 or so; and its facilities, never extensive, had been devastated by the civil war. Hosting a major conference, plus the peacekeeping force, posed a sizeable logistical and command challenge that Colonel Hurley, assisted by Brig. Gen. Peter Abigail, in charge of logistic arrangements for the Australian Defence Force, and representatives from the other contributing countries and the PNG government needed to face up to—quickly.

Meanwhile, back at Murray Barracks, veteran brigadier general Tony Huai also needed to move quickly to get his senior command team in place. Tony Huai had distinguished himself as the commander of Kumul Force in 1980 in Vanuatu and as commander of the PNGDF from 1985 to 1987, when he was succeeded by Brig. Gen. Rochus Lokinap. After leaving the military, Huai found employment as the chief security officer for the National Parliament. He had been a close associate of Sir Julius Chan since the Vanuatu operations. He had an advantage in terms of having the ear of the prime minister. However, having been out of the mainstream of PNGDF operations since his retirement in 1987, General Huai had no knowledge or experience of Bougainville operations, which had commenced at the beginning of the crisis in 1988–89.

The Bougainville Peace Conference in Arawa took place from 10 to 14 October 1994. Sir Julius opened the conference with Sir George Lepping, former governor general of the Solomon Islands, in the chair. Lt Col. Davey Ugul, director of land operations, represented the PNGDF. As this was the Bougainville Peace Conference mandated by the Honiara Commitments, the two main parties to the conference were the government of PNG, represented by Sir Julius and senior officials from Waigani, and representatives of the BRA and the Bougainville Interim Government. The senior commanders of the BRA had stated that they would attend from 12 October, but in the event, the only BRA commander who turned up was Ishmael Toarama, who wandered in as if to see what was up, and Theodore Miriung, a former acting National Court judge who represented the political (rather than the military) wing of the BRA. Frances Ona, Sam Kauona, and Joseph Kabui— the three most senior commanders of the BRA—all boycotted the proceedings. Nevertheless, Ishmael Toroama and Theodore Miriung's participation was applauded and, in hindsight, proved significant to the peace process for Bougainville.

The prime minister was infuriated by this humiliating turn of events. He had put his personal reputation on the line and had been stood up in front of his own people and the countries of the region. The political capital he had expended in Canberra, Wellington, Nukualofa, Suva, Honiara, and Port Vila to set up the peacekeeping force at very short notice was considerable. He had been made to lose face. He would not forget the insult. And he would make somebody pay.

I was not party to the negotiations with Kauona over the implementation of the Honiara Commitments nor the setting up of the SPRPKF. Therefore, it is difficult to know where to apportion the blame. Did the PNG officials misread the strength of Kauona's objections to Australian participation, let alone leadership, of the force? Did they miscalculate the snub they were offering in refusing him the opportunity of signing the status of forces agreement, or were Kauona's objections more fundamental? Did the PNG officials fail to convey the depth of Kauona's objections to Sir Julius, or did they choose to gloss over them and hope for the best? Did Sir Julius choose to ignore the advice he was getting, or was he getting bad advice?

Perhaps it was a little of all of the above. We will probably never know the truth. What we do know, however, and as I was soon to learn, is that Sir Julius, having come into office bent on peace with the BRA at any price, would very soon be bent on war.

On Friday, 14 October, the day that the Arawa conference was due to conclude, I was visiting a contingent of my troops at Torato Island near the border of PNG and Solomon Islands. I had barely gotten off the boat when I received an urgent radio message informing me that

I was needed back at headquarters at Loloho. Upon returning by fast speedboat, I was handed a confidential telex. It advised me that I was to be relieved of my command of 1RPIR and was to hand it over as commanding officer to Lt Col. Elias Kamara, on promotion from major. Kamara was from East New Britain and was my senior at Joint Services College, having graduated in June 1975.

In the same signal, I was advised that I was being promoted to full colonel and posted to headquarters as chief of staff. I was stunned and read the signal over and over again. I had hardly spent any time as a lieutenant colonel and was just getting the battalion organised to my liking. Further, I was all too aware that, as a brand-new colonel, there were a number of colonels senior to me who could have expected to be appointed to the role of chief of staff. I thought that a mistake may have occurred.

My promotion to full colonel came as a big blow to some officers who were more senior to me. I had been a lieutenant colonel for only ten months. I was now a target for serious backchat by senior officers who had been passed over. Maj. Geoff Wiri wrote to the commander and acting chief of staff, Col. David Josiah, to say that my promotion was not in the best interests of the PNGDF as it would 'destabilise the force'. He also intimated that there were serious security implications. What these were I had no idea. The letter was circulated among Portsea graduates and others seeking support against my promotion.

In the meantime, I was happy enough to let events at Murray Barracks take their course. On Sunday, 16 October, I flew back to Brisbane to resume medical treatment. I spent four days at One Military Hospital in Yeronga, Brisbane, from 17–20 October, where I received further treatment for my damaged wrist, arm, and right eye.

Returning to Port Moresby, I handed over my command of 1RPIR, with some regret, to Lt Col. Elias Kamara and, with Weni and the children, exchanged married quarters with Kamara on Brigadier Hill at Murray Barracks. Our new residence was well situated. We could look down into Basilisk Passage and enjoy the cooling breezes that blew in from the sea while watching the sun set. As I pondered my fairy-tale posting as CO of First Battalion, I realised that my time as CO was less than ten months, the best time in my career. To command an infantry battalion is the dream of any aspiring infantry officer. And now the dream was over.

What I loved best was working alongside soldiers and providing the right environment for junior officers as they progressed in their career. Junior officers below the rank of major are a rare breed. They were fun to work with. At the beginning, many could hardly tell left from right. They needed plenty of attention and opportunity to excel. Most of them were single men. They were no different from me at that stage in my career. All the subalterns who worked with me in the battalion were individually brave and showed their willingness to put their lives on the line for their troops and comrades.

The battalion had glowed under my command; the troops had marched smartly and attended to their duties and training, including keeping the barracks nice and tidy. I had insisted that company commanders take disciplinary action against soldiers for breaches of good order and service discipline. The barracks were kept clean, and church activities were encouraged. Weni had provided guidance and leadership to the wives, helping organise a group to represent their interests when we were away on operations. As I relinquished command and left the battalion for the last time as CO, I felt a certain emptiness of spirit.

Chief of Defence Intelligence, 1994–95

I was now in limbo, waiting for resolution of the protests that had erupted over my proposed appointment as chief of staff. A number of senior officers informed General Huai that they would not work for me in that capacity. I holed up in a spare office on the ground floor below the Department of Defence and waited for the commander and secretary for defence, Rupa Mulina, to review my posting with the minister. Finally, General Huai called me in to his office and informed me that my posting as chief of staff was revoked and that I would be posted to the Department of Defence as chief of defence intelligence (CDI).

Inshallah! I was to be given a real job—not just a glorified senior clerk position. Intelligence was an area I had always enjoyed and been reasonably competent in, both at the tactical and strategic levels, especially intelligence estimates and analysis. The year 1995 was going to be a busy one. I replaced Emos Daniels as CDI. Daniels, who was secretary to Sir Julius Chan's People's Progress Party (PPP), moved to the Prime Minister's Office as an adviser.

First on my agenda was a return to the Land Warfare Centre, Canungra, Queensland, for a refresher course in intelligence. Canungra was an old stomping ground of mine, and after two weeks there, I had refreshed myself on the fundamentals of intelligence management and application. Returning to PNG to fill my appointment as CDI, I began work by restructuring the Field Intelligence Company (FIC), identifying outstanding non-commissioned officers to be posted as defence security liaison officers in all four regions, and drafting training courses to upskill our intelligence operators.

My travels were now quite frequent. I attended a range of security conferences and border liaison meetings, both in country and abroad, on behalf of the defence council. I also spent a good deal of time overseeing the preparation of intelligence estimates, working alongside civilian analysts from the Department of Defence, which had some very capable officers, including Ambrose Takafoin, Terrance Frawley, Doreen Joel, Fred Punangi, and Vali Asi. All university graduates, they had become indoctrinated and enneltured into the PNGDF and had become competent in their analytical and intelligence work.

I also continued to work on strengthening the FIC. As both operations officer and commanding officer, I knew first-hand how important good tactical intelligence was to the strength of operational planning and the conduct of operations. I got concurrence from both the commander and the secretary for defence, and technical and funding support through the Australian Defence Cooperation Program, to conduct a series of three-week-long intelligence courses for soldiers and officers in Port Moresby. With some degree of freedom, I repositioned and raised the status of defence intelligence to the extent that it became well recognised for its work on Bougainville and later throughout the country.

Early in 1995, I had been recommended for a US Army professional academic fellowship programme associated with Harvard University. I completed a series of psychology and aptitude tests at the American Embassy for processing through the US Army's International Military Education Training programme. Factors that were helpful to me at this time were my record as the first PNG exchange officer to the US Army in 1980 and my exposure as battalion commander to the US Special Forces training team out of Okinawa in 1994. Being a graduate of the Australian Army Command and Staff College and the Australian Institute of Management Studies enhanced my chances. After some months, I was finally cleared for an eighteen-month degree programme in the United States, commencing in March 1996.

In the meantime, I was nominated as the PNGDF candidate to participate in a US State Department–funded tour of US security installations in the region called the Southeast Asia Security Symposium (SEAS). This tour, which commenced in September 1995, would take me into the region with a group of selected senior defence service personnel and civilians drawn from a wide range of countries around the Indo-Pacific.

The SEAS programme commenced with calls on a number of senior US commanding officers in Hawaii, including the chief of US Pacific Command at Camp Smith; a briefing by the admiral in command, US Seventh Fleet, Japan; a visit to the UN command and demilitarised zone (DMZ) at Panmunjom in South Korea; a call on Ministry of Defence officials in Singapore; and a visit to Cambodia. The month-long programme provided an excellent introduction to a range of US security installations in the region as well as networking opportunities with other defence officials from participating countries.

At the Carlton Hotel in Singapore, a few of us were having drinks in my room at the end of a long day. I was on the floor, challenging my Australian colleague, Col. Micky Crane, to the gorilla stretch—a beer drinking game in which the challenge is to see who, heels against the wall, can put a full can of beer on the carpet farthest away from the wall without allowing any part of the body to touch the floor. The game requires a combination of great upper body strength, balance, and agility. I was at full stretch and carefully placing my beer can with the tips of my outstretched fingers when the phone rang. Dr Lance Beath, a close friend from New Zealand's Ministry of Defence, took the call. He listened and then said, 'Jerry, it's the prime minister's chief of staff on the line from Port Moresby. He wants a word.'

I was not entirely surprised. Weni had called the previous day to say that the prime minister's chief of staff, Prof. Renagi Lohia, wanted to get in touch, and she had passed on my contact details. I wondered what Lohia might want from me. He said, 'Colonel, the prime minister is on the line for you.' There was a pause and dead silence as I waited for the call to be transferred to Sir Julius.

A cultured voice that I recognised at once from radio and TV interviews came on the line. 'Commander Singirok?'

'Yes, sir. Good afternoon.'

There was long pause, then Sir Julius asked, 'When are you coming back to Port Moresby?'

I replied, 'In about a week, Prime Minister.'

Then came the bombshell. 'Commander, I intend putting your name forward to the cabinet as my choice for promotion and appointment as commander of the defence force.' The prime minister continued, 'I want a young blood in the defence force to sort out Bougainville. Your name has been mentioned as a younger officer of particular promise. We have been impressed with your performance, especially on Bougainville. And I know that you are very popular and well respected by troops throughout the defence force. As soon as you return, you must come to my office at Morauta Haus, and we'll talk further.'

I said, 'Yes, sir, thank you, but—' There was a click on the line. Sir Julius had hung up.

Professor Lohia came back on the line. He asked me if I had heard what the prime minister had said. I replied, 'Yes, sir, but—'

'But what?' Lohia interrupted.

'I have been accepted to do my MBA in the United States, commencing in March next year.'

Lohia advised, 'You had better explain that to the prime minister when you come back to Port Moresby. But I think you'll find that he will be quite firm. It will be your studies or the country.'

I was momentarily stunned when I got off the phone. Mike Crane, Lance Beath, and Cambodian general Chuchi Chum gathered round. Then Lance broke in, 'Congratulations, Jerry. Gentlemen, we have a brand-new general in the room. Call room service for bottles of champagne and buckets of ice!'

What an evening! I had mixed emotions about the news. I had just turned 39. It was barely ten months since my promotion to full colonel. I had not yet put in significant time in rank, and I still had courses that I needed to attend before taking on responsibilities at senior executive leadership level in the defence force. And I hadn't even met the prime minister.

In Port Moresby, the news that I would be replacing Brig. Gen. Tony Huai broke very quickly. I was no sooner home than I learnt that a group of senior colonels at Murray Barracks were looking to block my appointment by laying trumped-up charges against me. They had apparently written to the chief of staff and were seeking to have me charged for going on the SEAS programme and abandoning my duties, among the more onerous of which was acting as president of the command officers' mess. *Good god!* I thought.

When confronted with this, I told the acting chief of staff, Col. David Josiah, that I had been properly released for the SEAS assignment by the secretary for defence, Rupa Mulina, as the Defence Intelligence Branch, which I directed, came under the jurisdiction of the Department of Defence, not the PNGDF. A little later, when I had access to PNGDF files as commander, I was amazed to read about a plot to have me charged and disciplined for the injuries I had sustained two years earlier when on operations in Bougainville. These had resulted in permanent damage to my left arm (the result of taking a bullet through my wrist) and right eye. They wanted me charged because, as CO, they said my place was in the rear of the battlefield, not the front line. But leading from the front is what I have always done when on operations. Further, I am a believer in the ethos of never leaving a dead or wounded officer behind on the battlefield, regardless of personal risk. That was how I had sustained the automatic gunfire wound to my left wrist and arm—trying to recover the bodies of the major commanding one of my companies who had been shot dead along with his batman.

In mid-October 1995, I got a call from the Prime Minister's Office to come in for a formal meeting. I arrived in my colonel's uniform. This was only the second time I had met Sir Julius Chan. After being served with refreshments, I joined him in his rather large office overlooking the road to Parliament House and beyond.

'Colonel,' he said, not wasting time on small talk, 'I will be making a change in the appointment of the commander shortly, and as I said to you on the phone, I believe it is time for a young and competent officer like you to take over an ageing defence force. As you know, after the former prime minister was voted out of office, I removed Brig. Gen. Bob Dademo and gave the opportunity to General Huai to bring the Bougainville conflict to a close. But we are still chasing the rebels in Bougainville.

'I have turned over every stone, and still, there is no progress on the ground. I believe you are the right choice to hit the rebels hard. When I formed this government, I promised the people of Papua New Guinea and our international investors that I will reopen the Panguna mine. I have made that promise, and now I have selected you to help me. I want you to come up with a new operational concept for Bougainville so that we can hit the rebels hard. Bougainville is my number one priority. Do you understand?'

I nodded.

Looking at me sharply, he went on, 'We will do everything possible to bring an end to this conflict. I want a draft operational plan from you by the end of the week spelling out how we are going to end this war. And don't forget to provide me with a breakdown on the budget that you require.'

Stunned by the directness of his approach, I said, 'Yes, sir.' I saluted and stepped out of his office. As I was driving back to Murray Barracks, I could recall clearly what Sir Julius wanted me to do. He spoke clearly, slowly, and precisely. He was articulate and knew how to deliver his instructions. I had no chance of raising the issue of my impending study in the United States. And I knew instinctively that my rise in the PNGDF had every prospect of coming to a sudden and premature end. The next few days, as rumours circulated about the appointment of a new commander, I started drafting the general concept of operations for Operation High Speed II.

On Thursday, 16 October, news of my appointment was released by the Prime Minister's Office. I was to be appointed over Colonel Dotaona and four other senior colonels including Col. Joe Maras. To this day, I still have a lot of time for both Dotaona and Maras. I had served under Col. Lima Dotaona as a junior officer when he was CO of 2RPIR in 1978–79. I also served under him when he was joint forces commander on Bougainville in 1989 during the state of emergency there. An editorial published the next day gave me a sober assessment:

> The newly appointed Commander has an enormous task ahead of him. He takes over an army that is barely functioning. The Air and Sea element exist but only in name. Due to lack of funding most of their equipment is already unusable.
>
> The massive 200 mile exclusive economic zone is now open to infiltration by illegal fishing boats and other illegal activities.
>
> The Defence Force is also stretched to the limit in trying to meet its commitment to patrolling the Indonesian PNG border—the subject of the joint border committee discussion in Goroka today.
>
> A report found a few years back that the Terms and Conditions of employment the Defence Force offers to its members dates back to the late 70s and a massive upgrading is now required to bring it on a par with other disciplinary forces in the country. In the time of former Defence Minister Benias Sabumei

and Commander Lokinap, a 10 year development plan was put forward. That plan which took into account all elements of the PNGDF and which opted for new sources of assistance, is now virtually forgotten as the force concentrates solely on maintaining its presence on Bougainville.

The Bougainville crisis has been a sticking point for the PNGDF right from the word 'go'.

The Force has to put up with frustrating and life-wasting political interference. Its advances have rarely been backed up by logistical support. Its proposals and strategies for a resolution to the Bougainville crisis presented by various commanders have rarely found favour with the civilian government.

The problems have collectively provided the backdrop for a massive drop in morale, the full extent of which cannot be estimated.

Indiscipline has set in at all levels of the force. We have seen manifestations of this in several controversial raids on settlements, street marches by soldiers, unruly behaviour at the airports and the burning of the Germania Club amongst other incidents.

In addition, the force has been saddled with a court decision to pay out huge amounts of money totalling K28 million to ex-servicemen who were discharged under a 1982 government retrenchment exercise.

Even everyday needs like food are sometimes hard to come by in some of the barracks today.

These are the problems the young colonel from Karkar Island, Madang, will inherit. He is going to need all the help he can get. There is little doubt that there is support from troops for Colonel Singirok and that is important.

Equally important however is cooperation from his fellow and more senior colonels in the army. Here he is going to have a problem. It has been the problem faced by almost all Commanders after Ted Diro.

If Colonel Singirok can somehow get the cooperation of his fellow officers, the big task ahead of him will be easier.

He is a career officer and one who obviously has the future of the force at heart. He will do well to keep out of politics. That too, he will find a rule that if he were to follow strictly, will stand him in good stead.

The prime minister sent me a letter confirming my appointment:

My dear Commander,

On behalf of the national government, may I now offer you our warm congratulations on your appointment as the new Commander of the Papua New Guinea Defence Force.

I realise this marks a significant step forward in your professional and personal life and, therefore I take this opportunity to also reassure you of my Government's continuing confidence in you and the Defence Force.

As I have already stated publicly, your appointment as an up and coming young career officer, to the post of Commander, has become necessary to allow the Government and the people of Papua New Guinea the benefit of having a capable man inherit the important task of rebuilding the Force at this crucial point in time, when as you are well aware, we all are desirous of reaffirming and reassessing our territorial sovereignty and providing effective policing of our international borders.

Once again, on behalf of the Government, I welcome and congratulate you on your appointment and

I look forward to working closely with you, especially on matters affecting the security of our nation.

Yours sincerely

Julius Chan

17 October 1995

I discussed the letter with Weni. We were both aware that no commander in recent PNG history had survived a complete term without being made a scapegoat on matters beyond the control of the defence force. The job of commander had come early for me as I had been accelerated ahead of time, outranking many colonels more senior to me in the PNGDF. That discomforted me as I have always believed in the merits of a gradual progression based on rank, experience, and academic ability.

That night, officers close to me visited us at home and offered well wishes and, as usual, brought dishes of food to share. I slept late. To be honest, I had mixed feelings about the job. The most serious issue was how to go about addressing the massive challenges that the defence force had in store for me. These challenges had defeated every one of my predecessors.

The next morning, Thursday, 19 October, was the handover parade and change of command ceremony. General Huai had been my commandant when I was an officer cadet at JSC in 1976, twenty years earlier. I felt for him as he was now another scapegoat for the government's inability to bring the Bougainville crisis to a close using military force. Tony Huai was a good man who always took the time to listen and get advice. But like every other commander before him, he was unable to deliver the expected outcomes. I could only sympathise with him.

I rose very early in the morning and spit-polished my black service shoes, ironed my uniform, polished my Sam Brown belt, and shined my ceremonial sword. As I was having breakfast, the telephone rang. Weni answered. She said, 'It's an urgent call from Gaubin Lutheran Hospital on Karkar Island.' It was unusual to receive a call so early in the morning. It was six forty-five. It was my brother Kabun. He informed me that Dad had passed on at five o'clock that morning and that his body would be held in the mortuary until we could get to Madang.

Numbly, I stood for a while with the handset in my hand. I sighed and cried, 'No! No!'

As tears started to stream down, I called out, *'Wai, wai, wai* [dad, dad, dad], why today?' Weni and our children rushed to me and embraced me as I sobbed uncontrollably for the loss of a person I had loved and adored all my life. My mentor, counsellor, and pillar had passed on at the very hour that I needed him to witness my achievement. But I knew Dad would be happy and proud of me, and the thought of that gave me some comfort. Dressing quickly and putting my emotions to one side for the moment, I got ready to be sworn in as the seventh commander of the PNGDF.

The defence force and dignitaries were already making their way to the Murray Barracks parade ground as the troops would march there at precisely nine o'clock. The ceremony was well attended by hundreds of well-wishers, official dignitaries, and members of the diplomatic corps, including defence attachés. Australia was represented by Col. John Edwards and his deputy, Lt Col. Gary Young; New Zealand by Wg Cdr Athol Forrest; and Indonesia by Col. Edie Butabuta.

After the parade, my family and I boarded an Air Niugini flight for Madang, where Sir Peter Barter, the governor of Madang, picked us up in his helicopter and flew Weni, Maib, and me across to Karkar Island, while the remainder travelled on a light aircraft. We laid Dad next to Mum's tomb in our private cemetery in my village of Did. After a few days spent exchanging gifts and making customary obligations according to Dad's life and the blessings he brought on so many families, we bade farewell to our relatives and departed for home.

Back in Port Moresby, there was a lot of defence force housekeeping to do. Many colonels who had been in their jobs for long periods had to be replaced with up-and-coming middle-ranking officers. I recommended wholesale changes in the senior officers' ranks, including retrenchment of the most senior colonels. I posted Col. Jack Tuat as chief of staff and Walter Salamas as acting chief of operations. Col. Philip Playah was appointed chief of personnel, and I confirmed navy captain

Fred Aikung as chief of logistics. Col. Bau Joseph Maras was posted as commandant of the defence academy while navy captain Reginald Renagi remained as chief of plans. Among the senior colonels whom I had to put on the retrenchment list were Colonels Dala, Trongat, David Josiah, and Paul Batman. A number of lieutenant colonels were also retrenched. Colonel Dotaona was posted as New Ireland administrator as compensation for not being appointed commander.

Two lieutenant colonels, John Litus and Gabriel Tamegal, distinguished themselves by flatly refusing to serve under me. 'Why should we serve under the commander when he was only a high school student when we were already commissioned officers?' Others, like Lt Col. Bernard Maris, just refused to come to work and opted to take extended leave, hoping for my demise down the track (and, indeed, actively working towards this end). He probably wouldn't have long to wait, I thought, as I surveyed the problems lying ahead of me.

Gaining senior officers' loyalty and building team spirit in the defence force would be a huge challenge in the months ahead. In the infantry battalions, 1RPIR was already commanded by Lieutenant Colonel Kamara, who had replaced me in 1994. In 2RPIR, I replaced Lt Col. Yaura Sasa with Lt Col. Michael Tamalanga.

My appointment as commander marked a new era for the next generation of middle-ranking officers. I was the first graduate of JSC in 1976 to be appointed as commander, phasing out the older crop of officers from the Australian Army Officer Cadet School at Portsea and the Royal Australian Naval College at HMAS *Creswell*, Jervis Bay.

Unattached and awaiting discharge was Col. Leo Nuia, in many ways a very interesting challenge. He had a reputation of always challenging new commanders on their appointment, and I was to prove no exception. When I took over command, he was awaiting a posting to Jakarta as defence adviser. But the word coming back from the Indonesian Embassy in Waigani was that he was not seen as an acceptable choice by the Indonesian government. He was to remain unattached—and a considerable problem.

Having sorted out my senior staff appointments, I then considered my own position. As the *National* editorial had remarked, I was only going to be as good as the political support I could get from government. The first commander of the PNGDF, Brig. Gen. Ted Diro, resigned to contest the national elections, entering Parliament in 1982. He was replaced as commander by a PPP affiliate, Gen. Gago Mamae, who was replaced by a Pangu Pati affiliate, Gen. Kenneth Noga. General Noga was replaced by Huai, and Huai was replaced by Lokinap, who in turn was replaced by Dademo, an appointee of the People's Democratic Movement. Dademo was replaced by Prime Minister Sir Julius's favourite general, Huai, who served for a second term. I was replacing Huai. Surveying this sorry record of political patronage, I was profoundly grateful that I had, to that point at least, escaped the tarbrush of political affiliation.

An issue I had to face was how to enforce personal discipline in the PNGDF. The image of the force was constantly being tarnished by the actions of a minority of ill-disciplined troops when off duty. The psychological and emotional stress on troops serving in Bougainville took a toll on troop behaviour, especially as the PNGDF had no counselling or rehabilitation services.

Many other issues, while apparently trivial in themselves, were having a disproportionate impact on morale. For example, there were issues with outstanding leave, including paid return tickets for soldiers and their families, and shortfalls in pay, housing, food supplies, and medical services. All these were taking a toll.

I also looked at the career path for officers, including how to offer educational and personal development opportunities. In my own case, I had been privileged to serve with the US Army, the Royal Gurkha Rifles, and the Australian Army. I had seen how they groomed their officers and troops for higher command. I determined that I would make it my priority to send officers to higher military institutions so that they, too, could contribute meaningfully when they returned to PNG. I also intended to pave the way for university studies for officers who had the aptitude so that the defence force developed a cadre of highly trained and well-educated officers.

Then I reviewed our operational platforms. With only four Australian-supplied Bell UH-1H Iroquois helicopters and an ageing fleet of fixed-wing aircraft, this was a particular area of concern. The Air Transport Squadron was barely surviving, although the young pilots supporting our Bougainville efforts were some of the most daring and experienced pilots I had ever worked with. They were adventurous and very skilful. There was no recorded fatality involving any aircraft, either fixed or rotary wing. And they performed some of the most daring rescues and insertions of troops and supplies. They were well-trained, well-led, and highly motivated.

My biggest challenge was how to sustain the Bougainville operations given the fact that there were body bags returning to Port Moresby every week of soldiers killed in action (KIA). The tasks of sending fresh troops and resupplying arms, ammunition and explosives, food, uniforms, fuel, and medical supplies were among the biggest challenges I had. As the CO on the ground in Bougainville in 1994, I had viewed our needs very differently. But now as commander, I had a broader perspective on Bougainville, taking into consideration political directives, international views, and the Bougainvilleans' own plight. I was committed to their future destiny and the need to bring back peace and normalcy to their lives without violence and the use of disproportionate force.

Then I had to reappraise our commitment to ensuring that the PNG-Indonesian land border was free from rebel and Indonesian troop activities. Our border patrol programme had been shelved as the situation on Bougainville became all-consuming. Intelligence reports coming from Vanimo in Sandaun Province pointed to ongoing border incursions by Indonesian troops. The hamlets between Bewani and Yapsie in Sandaun Province were now experiencing a major security threat. Reports from Weam in PNG's Western Province suggested that Indonesian Army and Navy units continued to patrol PNG's Torasi River and that Indonesian hunters were often sighted well into PNG territory, hunting for deer using trail bikes for their transport. Reports of illegal trading and the movement of contraband were alarming, to say the least, as the international border was indeed very porous.

Equally concerning was PNG's ability to maintain sovereignty over its 200-mile (321 km) exclusive economic zone, with constant reports of foreign vessels, mainly of Asian origin, anchored for days and fishing illegally among our pristine reefs and waters. The defence force patrol boats supplied by the Australian government under its Pacific Patrol programme were out of action due to maintenance issues and crew shortages as a result of budgetary pressure.

Such was the reality of the defence force I had taken over. When addressing the troops on my inaugural parade, I described the PNGDF as a sinking ship. I added that we needed to plug the holes and obtain a new crew. We could still sail and get to our destination, but we needed a good captain and a committed team with guaranteed political support.

For now, all eyes were on me. Settling into the commander's office, I was consumed by its size compared with my tiny office downstairs. Having been a full-time field officer, it was awkward for me suddenly to be grounded in an office with a desk. I had served for nearly twenty years, eighteen of which had been in the field. The other two years had been as an officer cadet. It was a steep learning curve; staff routine, conferences, visits, report writing, defence council attendance, frequent meetings at government offices in Waigani, and endless travelling in and out of the country consumed my time. I reorganised my office staff, appointing Capt. John Keleto as my aide-de-camp, Maj. Michael Kupo as my research officer, and Cpl John Koraia as my bodyguard. For my military adviser, I appointed Lt Col. Mark Noga.

On Christmas Day in 1995, amid all the challenges I knew would come the following year, I set my mind on establishing and raising a special forces unit. Based on National Executive Council decision 149/83, a long-overdue strategic force was needed with highly specialised skills in long-range ground operations and with airborne and seaborne capability. I had Capt. Gilbert Toropo in mind as the first officer commanding of the SFU. Gilbert comes from the Ialibu-Pangia District in Southern Highlands, and he was the first PNGDF soldier to complete special force training at Fort Benning Ranger School, Georgia. On 25 December 1995, I promoted him to the rank of major and appointed him OC of the SFU. He was more than ready to take up the challenges ahead of him. I appointed a highly respected lieutenant colonel, Jeffrey Key, to draft the mounting instructions for raising the

SFU. Providing him with specific terms of reference, I gave him one month to complete the paper that I wanted on my desk no later than the end of January 1996.

On the home front, Weni was recruited as news director with the newly established radio station NauFM. Futua was attending Gordons High School, and Maib and Moka were attending Korobosea Primary School. Fred was enrolled in the upper primary class at Good Shepherd Primary School in Madang.

We celebrated Christmas 1995 by serving dinner to the troops at the other ranks' mess, Murray Barracks. That night, I penned in my 1996 work diary my priorities for the coming year. One such priority was to visit major military bases throughout the country and our troops in Bougainville.

In the first part of 1996, I re-emphasised the importance of unit training and reinstated the border patrol programme to address the number of reports I was seeing of illegal activities, including incursions by Indonesian troops along the border. The retrenchment programme for senior officers also took off. Of all the colonels who were retrenched, Col. Andrew Trongat was the only one to return to my office to pay a courtesy call and wish me well. A Bougainvillean, he graduated from Portsea in 1972 and spent time in intelligence before being appointed CO of 2RPIR in 1986–87. I served under him as his operations officer.

Meanwhile, Major Toropo was making good progress in raising the SFU. He recruited Capt. Bola Renagi as operations officer and 2IC. Captain Renagi was a Waiouru graduate (1990 class) who had also attended Ranger School at Fort Benning. I left the recruiting and training of the SFU to these two officers, but I demanded that very high standards were set for the unit, and regardless of other issues competing for my time, including the pressures of Bougainville and a very demanding prime minister and minister of defence, I made sure that the SFU got as much of my personal attention as it needed.

In April 1996, an upcoming overseas trip was approved by the minister of defence, and my staff prepared my travel documents, visa, and itinerary. I was informed that the secretary for finance, James Loko, a schoolmate of mine from Sogeri, had approved his deputy, Vele

Iamo, assistant secretary for finance, to accompany me. The itinerary included visits to Singapore, London, Belfast, and the United States. We organised cash and traveller's cheques.

We arrived in Singapore on Saturday, 13 April, and checked in at the Mandarin Hotel. On Monday, we visited Unicorn Industries, a supplier of ammunition and weapons to the PNGDF. We met Sydney Franklin that day and confirmed that he was travelling with us to London. He had been a supplier of uniforms, tents, and other field equipment to the defence force since 1987.

On Tuesday, 16 April, we flew to London. We arrived at Heathrow Airport and checked in at the Royal Horseguards, a central city hotel on Whitehall Court between the Thames and Trafalgar Square. After settling in, we visited factories that manufactured military accessories. We took a day trip to Coventry and paid a courtesy call on the Ministry of Defence, where we discussed, among other things, the possibility of one of our officer cadets enrolling at the Royal Military Academy, Sandhurst, in 1997.

On the morning of 19 April, needing to turn my traveller's cheques into US dollars, I called at Lloyds Bank, London. Sydney Franklin accompanied me to the bank, where I also opened a Visa card account in my own name and residential address back in Moresby. I deposited GPB 1,000 into this account, which was duly activated on 24 April 1996. While I did not know it at the time, opening this account would become a major leadership issue, ultimately leading to my suspension and dismissal from office as commander during my second term.

That evening, back at the hotel in London, I met with Tim Spicer and Michael Grunberg to discuss the proposed engagement of Executive Outcomes for military assistance with the PNGDF in Bougainville. They came with a list of inventories, weapons systems, and air capabilities, including a spotter aircraft, an electronic surveillance aircraft, and both attack and troop deployment helicopters. I was deeply concerned about their proposal for a quick-fix military offensive on Bougainville that was being sponsored by the minister for defence, Matthias Ijape. Tim Spicer would soon register a new company called Sandline International in the Bahamas. A year later, I would rebel against the government of PNG and Sandline International, leading to Sandline's expulsion from PNG in March 1997.

On Saturday, 20 April, Vele Iamo and I flew to Belfast for the day to meet with the executives of Shorts Belfast. They were the suppliers of armour-plated Land Rovers to the PNGDF. I had a technical report from the PNGDF's Directorate of Technical Services on the performance of these special service vehicles and their limitations, and I wanted Shorts to make the necessary modifications to suit PNG conditions.

Vele and I departed for the United States, landing first in San Francisco and then taking a domestic flight to New Orleans, where we met up with our PNG team, Lt Col. Carl Marlpo and Legal Officer Steven Raphael, to inspect military equipment from an arms dealer for possible investment in small arms and tracked wheeled vehicles. We returned to PNG via Singapore.

Arriving back in PNG, I checked on Maj. Gilbert Toropo's progress with the SFU. Reasonable, though still limited, funding had been provided by Minister Chris Haiveta through the government's special operations vote, enabling Toropo to develop the SFU's critical capabilities. Both Toropo and I agreed that the intelligence and training sections of the SFU were critical to the development of the operational unit. We appointed Sergeant Gan and Lt Eddie Yodu to the intelligence section and Warrant Officer David to the training cell that we merged with Warrior Wing. A logistics support unit headed by Warrant Officer Magola and including Cpl John Kulila was also established.

The first graduation of SFU patrols was set for Saturday, 1 June. We held an SFU open day at the Warrior Wing, 2 km along the Open Range Road, not far from Goldie Training Depot, at the same time. We organised for Chris Haiveta, deputy prime minister, and other senior ministers and dignitaries to visit the training facilities. As they arrived, the SFU trainees greeted the official team with a mock attack demonstration and other specialised drills not normally seen or trained for by ordinary soldiers. Warrant Officer David caught a two-metre-long python and cut its head off in preparation for cooking as part of SFU survival skills.

Meanwhile, I was being pressed at the political level to get on with Operation High Speed II to exert additional military pressure on the rebels in Bougainville. I issued my commander's concept of operations and superior commander's intent to the chief of operations, who in turn instructed the CO of First Battalion, Lt Col. Seki Berapu, providing him with support services: a patrol boat, two helicopters, and the complement of a battalion minus to deploy into central Bougainville. A beachhead was to be established at Aropa Airport, and the troops were to patrol into the Sipuru and Kongara areas. The navy was to block the sea approaches and cut off resupply and the logistic chain to and from Solomon Islands for the rebels. I dispatched a veteran lieutenant colonel from land operations, Allan Pinia, former CO of 2RPIR, to oversee the deployment.

On 6 July, after a few days of deployment, the troops patrolling the fringes of Aropa Airport came into contact with the BRA. One soldier was wounded, and another was KIA. Without the approval of his battalion commander, Lt Col. Seki Berapu, the company commander, withdrew his company back to the battalion headquarters.

On Monday, 15 July, Lieutenant Colonel Berapu informed the chief of operations that the battalion would withdraw to Arawa and the forward tactical headquarters to Loloho. I was deeply disappointed and concerned about all aspects of battlefield leadership. The inability to sustain prolonged military operations and to develop an effective intelligence system to strike the BRA was an indictment on the officers concerned. We had lost the initiative and the will to fight.

Battlefield leadership, particularly in the toughest of moments, requires the officers in charge to remain composed and on top of the situation, which will inevitably change due to various controllable and uncontrollable factors, such as weather, the tactical situation, intelligence, logistics, mobility, and enemy actions. All aspects of command, control, communications, and intelligence—also known as C3I—come into play. If the battlefield commander is not physically on the ground and in immediate touch with the troops, snap decisions cannot be made, seriously affecting all elements of command and control. Hands-on leadership is not possible in such circumstances, and the inevitable result is demoralised troops and unnecessary loss of life. The enemy will gain an immediate psychological advantage.

I launched an immediate enquiry into why the CO had decided to withdraw his troops. I was informed that the CO, Seki Berapu, had established his command post on a patrol boat just off Aropa Airport with his colleague Peter Ilau, CO of the patrol boat base at Lombrum. Berapu was immediately relieved of his command and the chief of staff was directed to conduct an investigation to establish the causes of the withdrawal and to take the necessary disciplinary action against the battalion commander for his evident failure in leadership.

The failure of Operation High Speed II became leading news in PNG, Australia, and New Zealand. I gave reporters a detailed account of the events leading up to the withdrawal of the troops. There was no cover-up. The PNGDF was poorly prepared and underfunded. There were failures in leadership on the ground, and the troops had lost the will to fight. There were no hiding and no excuses. I admitted the truth to the public. While the PNGDF's only two operational helicopters had been assigned in support of the operation, both had suffered rotor damage from enemy gunfire and had to be withdrawn, creating major problems for troop mobility and support. However, this was not the primary cause of failure.

After the investigation, the CO was found guilty of inefficiency and incompetence. He had contravened the code of military discipline and was referred to me for punishment. I demoted Seki Berapu from the rank of lieutenant colonel to major and posted him to the unallotted list HQ. This was the first time I had demoted a senior officer, and it was a difficult decision to make as I had known Seki Berapu since officer cadet days when he was my junior. He was liked by many, but the obvious failure in battlefield leadership was inexcusable. As I handed him my judgement, I intended it to be a lesson for future commanders and officers who needed to appreciate that we had a real war on our hands.

Kangu Beach Massacre

September 1996 was the darkest month in the history of the Bougainville crisis and one that would haunt PNG for a long time. In the lead-up to the twenty-first anniversary of independence, Sunday, 8 September, would be the bloodiest day in our short history as a country. The day started early. It was just an ordinary Sunday.

Kangu Beach was strategically linked to the Solomon Islands by boat for trading and traditional crossings. It was also linked to Torato Island, where the PNGDF's forward-most border outpost was manned by members of the Small Boat Team. A vehicle track connected Kangu Beach with Buin District and the rest of Bana District to the west about 8 km away. An area of high ground called Kangu Hill dominated the location. Around 300 feet high (91 metres), it offered an excellent vantage point. A sharp escarpment ran north-west on Kangu Beach, making any approach up the hill difficult.

After a series of close encounters with the BRA and suspicions about the loyalty of the local resistance force, the OC, Capt. Paul Panau, instructed 2nd Lt Michael Jim (Jimbo)—Twelve Platoon commander and a 1993 Duntroon graduate from Eastern Highlands—to take his platoon up Kangu Hill and remain there until further notice. Among the troops in Twelve Platoon relocating to the top of Kangu Hill were Cpl Junias Keri and Pvt. Koisen Boino, who happened to be Junias Keri's uncle.

The care centre at Kangu Beach had about 300 civilians, some men but mainly women and children and about 20 resistance force members who worked closely with the troop detachment. The centre was situated a few metres away from D Company HQ and Support Section. From the centre, numerous tracks ran into the jungle. Villagers used the tracks to get to the beach for fishing, and they gardened and hunted in the jungle.

The Support Section at Kangu Beach had the task of providing firepower for D Company, including direct and indirect fire support. It had three MAG 58 machine guns and three 60 mm mortars and assorted ammunition and explosives. All these were being held in D Company's ammunition bunker.

A resupply helicopter arrived at ten o'clock on Sunday morning with food and other stores organised by company sergeant Maj. Allan Kopa and Insp. Titus Pamben. Second Lieutenant Jim sent a party of five soldiers down from Kangu Hill to carry their resupply back up the hill. The party was led by Cpl Junias Keri. When they arrived at the command post, they discovered that a speedboat was departing for Torato for the day. The five men—Corporal Keri, Corporal Gamoga, Private Godua, Private Meaforo, and Const. Midi Mitmit—volunteered to go to Torato to take the SBT supplies and trade for dried fish to supplement their rations, a delight they looked forward to each week as part of their normal routine.

Later that morning, some of the troops attended church service while others cleaned their weapons and did their laundry. Corporal Iramu, a dedicated radio operator (RO), manned the radio in the command post. A Sunday afternoon game of volleyball had been prearranged for 1400 hours. It was supposed to be a mixed game involving a team of soldiers and resistance force members. The volleyball net was tied, the ball was pumped up, and the stage was set for the game. Troops and resistance force members drifted slowly towards the centre of the camp for the game.

At about 1430 hours the game started, with soldiers taking part, leaving their weapons unattended. About thirty minutes into the game, at precisely 1500 hours, the resistance force members rushed for the soldiers' weapons, taking hold of the M16 carbines and SLRs. They started shooting indiscriminately at unarmed soldiers, first on the volleyball court and then at those who were unprepared around the camp.

Two resistance force members rushed to the command post where Captain Panau was having a midday nap. He and Corporal Iramu were shot multiple times. Captain Panau had no chance to defend himself. The sudden bust of gunshots scattered the entire care centre, and people fled into the jungle with whatever they could grab, while resistance force members looted the armoury of spare weapons, 60 mm mortars and assorted weapons, hand grenades, and hundreds of rounds of ammunition and pyrotechnics.

Three soldiers and two policemen who were having lunch with families at the care centre took cover with the fleeing civilians and were rounded up, isolated, and held as hostages by the BRA commander, Thomas Tari, for the next ten months. They were Cpl Arnold Makabia, Pvt. Sava Korren, and Pvt. Alphonse Yuaken, all from East Sepik Province; Const. Tony Kalinau from East Sepik and Manus; and Sgt Andrew Ponda from West New Britain.

The hostages' lives were only saved because Private Koreen's sister was married to a man from Buin who had taken refuge at the care centre along with others. She pleaded with the rebels for the soldiers' lives to be spared, saying that if the rebels intended to kill the hostages, she should be killed in their place. She was a very courageous and brave woman.

From their vantage point on Kangu Hill, Twelve Platoon witnessed the mayhem and destruction of D Company HQ and Support Section. Second Lieutenant Jim ordered his platoon to dig in and reorganise their defence system with interlocking machine-gun fire positions to cover the most likely approaches by the rebels. They knew that the rebels would turn to attack them next since they had captured sufficient firepower from the D Company armoury.

The natural geographic features of Kangu Hill aided their defence. Second Lieutenant Jim told the troops that they would hold their ground no matter what until reinforcements came. Although Twelve Platoon was massively under-strength, with only Second Lieutenant Jim, Corporal Patrick Valuka, Pvt. Stanis Buliau, Pvt. Koisen Boino, Denise Waibauru, Clement Mangaia, and Freddy Asua, they had sufficient firepower. They had a GPMG 60 with over 2,000 7.62 mm rounds and a MAG 58 machine gun. With these weapons, plus their rifles, they had sufficient firepower to hold their ground and fight off any attack, no matter how determined the enemy action was.

The platoon's RO, Pvt. Stanis Buliau, tried desperately to contact Torato to prevent Corporal Keri and party from returning but could not raise them. The situation was desperate all around. Second Lieutenant

Jim knew that he was now in charge of the remnants of D Company and what was left of Twelve Platoon with him on Kangu Hill.

As expected, just after 1545 hours, Junias Keri and his small party bade farewell to their colleagues at Torato Island and returned by speedboat to Kangu Beach, unaware of the massacre and what was waiting for them. As they were about to land, the rebels, who had been waiting for their return, gunned them down mercilessly. Private Meaforo and Constable Mitmit jumped overboard but were shot and killed, and their bodies were never recovered. They both were declared as missing in action (MIA).

The following day, Monday, 9 September, BRA soldiers—under instruction from their commander, Thomas Tari—took two hostages up Kangu Hill and shouted to the platoon commander that if he surrendered, their lives would be spared. Second Lieutenant Jim flatly refused and prepared himself and his men to fight to the end.

The RO on Kangu Hill, Pvt. Stanis Buliau, with very little life left in his radio batteries, attempted in vain to alert the battalion forward tactical headquarters in Loloho or any other call signs in Bougainville. He was not successful. However, back in Port Moresby at Taurama Barracks, Cpl Paskal Wandia picked up the SOS; and from there, the rest of the PNGDF was alerted to the situation. By then, Twelve Platoon was on its last fresh battery, and the situation confronting Second Lieutenant Jim was becoming more pressing by the hour. Yet as his surviving platoon members recounted afterwards, he remained cool and collected, providing inspirational leadership, guidance, and counselling to his troops whose lives now relied entirely on his leadership, courage, and training.

Meanwhile, the command post at Loloho had received news of the massacre and set about organising relief reinforcements from Buin Station. Lt Herbert Wally was at Loloho and volunteered to lead the rescue operations. He took the resupply helicopter to Buin, about 8 km west of Kangu Beach, to appraise the situation and organise operations. He was assisted by Privates Kili and Kobel, who also volunteered along with a section of trusted resistance force members from Buin. They come from the village of a defence force pilot, Lt John Imaka, and they volunteered to join Lieutenant Wally to undertake the risky operations by foot from Buin to Kangu Beach.

On Wednesday, 11 September, three days after the massacre and with 2nd Lt Michael Jim and what was left of his platoon still holding out on Kangu Hill, Lieutenant Wally and his party made their way by foot through hostile and unknown territory towards the scene of the massacre. They had one enemy contact on the way but managed to fight the rebels off. Shortly after that, they met a mute civilian who was known to be living in the Kangu Care Centre. They took him with them; later, he was able to show the rescue party where the shallow graves were and assist in the recovery of bodies.

Lieutenant Wally's patrol made contact with Twelve Platoon. They brought in food and fresh batteries and spent the night with them on Kangu Hill. That night, the officers planned an operation to retake the command post on Kangu Beach. On the morning of Thursday, 12 September, the now reinforced Twelve Platoon made their way tactically down the hill to the end of Kangu Beach, where they commenced a clearance process through leap frog movements supported by a patrol boat that had been dispatched from Loloho for close fire support to the shore. At this moment, fresh tragedy struck. Second Lieutenant Jim was on a clear stretch of beach, giving orders to his men, when he was shot through the back of his head by an enemy sniper situated somewhere on Musuru Point.

By midday, Thursday, 12 September, two patrol boats under the command of Lt Cdr Clement Tele, elements of C Company 1RPIR under Operations Officer Maj. Bill Nende, and Regimental Sergeant Major Lem arrived on the shores of Kangu Beach and undertook the extraordinarily painful task of searching for the bodies of the fallen soldiers. Ten soldiers were KIA: Capt. Paul Panau, 2nd Lt Michael Jim, Cpl Jubilee Gamoga, Cpl Oa Iramu, Cpl Otto Gamoa, Cpl Junias Keri, Cpl Anton Nopau, Pvt. Andrew Papura, Pvt. Paul Gadoa, and Private Godus. Const. Midi Mitmit and Private Meaforo were declared MIA. The five hostages were taken to Laguai, where they were held as political prisoners for the next ten months.

Some years later, talking to the surviving soldiers, I was told about all the terrible things they had seen. The most horrifying sight was the body of their OC, Captain Panau. He had been so good and kind to the civilians under his care, and the sight of his mutilated body was painful to see. The death of Second Lieutenant Jim, whose cool courage and leadership was so inspiring to his men, added to the pain felt by the remaining soldiers. Indeed, the loss of Jimbo, as the regiment called him, was a blow to all of us. As was the loss of Maj. (awarded posthumously) Paul Panau and all the other excellent soldiers who died so tragically. Even today as I write this book, the regiment and I still feel the trauma of those events.

I had flown into Vanimo on Saturday, 7 September, for an NEC meeting with the minister and secretary for defence. When news of the massacre reached me and after consulting with the minister, I chartered a single-engine Cessna from the Mission Aviation Fellowship and returned to Wewak to catch the afternoon flight to Port Moresby. I took refuge at my sister Balim's place at Wewak Hill while I tried to gather myself together. I had never been at a lower point in my spirits and wondered what I could possibly say on my return to Port Moresby.

On Friday, 13 September, the bodies arrived from Buka on the defence force CASA flown by Major Berobro. Weni accompanied me as did Sir Peter Barter, Minister for Defence Ijape, Minister for Police Castan Maibawa, and Ben Micah, member for Kavieng. The airport was packed to capacity with grieving relatives and onlookers. While there, we were alerted to a possible threat against Sir Julius Chan and his cabinet. Once the bodies were secured and escorted from the airport, I instructed Major Toropo to organise an armed escort back to Parliament House with the remaining members of Parliament and myself. Ben Micah, a dear and long-time colleague, was visibly upset by the turn of events and urged me to be strong, which I appreciated.

At the Prime Minister's Office, Sir Julius's personal assistant, Louise (Lulu), prepared glasses of champagne and red wine, which was the normal way Sir Julius had of saying thank you. After he was assured of his own personal safety and was told that the bodies had arrived and were being secured at the mortuary, he passed the wine and champagne around. I abstained from this totally inappropriate indulgence as I was still overtaken by the scenes of wailing and mourning of the relatives and troops at Jacksons Airbase. I couldn't stop thinking about the late captain Paul Panau's wife, Augusta, and their two young children, who would grow up without a father.

The funeral for the victims of the Kangu Beach massacre was a mass service held at First Battalion parade ground on 23 September. It was the most moving funeral service I had ever attended. The coffins were laid out in a long row, each draped with the PNG flag. Next to me were Sir Peter Barter, Minister Paul Tohian, and Police Commissioner Bob Nenta. Lady Stella Chan represented Sir Julius.

After the mass funeral service, I stood outside at Brigadier Hill on my own, staring into Fairfax Harbour as the sun set. Tears flowed once again as I thought about my fallen soldiers. I knew every single soldier who was killed at Kangu Beach. Company commander Capt. Paul Panau was to have been promoted to major that month, and Corporal Iramu was my signaller at Support Company in 1985, when I was OC of Second Battalion. Lt Michael Jim was a good-looking young officer, stocky in built, and a Duntroon graduate who was posted to First Battalion. I was his CO in 1994. He was full of potential and had his whole life in front of him when he led the patrol down from Kangu Hill to clear the Kangu Beach area. He lost his life from a single gunshot on the beach strewn with bodies. The Kangu Beach massacre was the biggest single loss of lives from the defence and police force.

One aspect that troubled me at the time was the behaviour of the prime minister. Sir Julius did not come out to Jacksons Airbase to be with the official party when the bodies arrived from Buka. Did he not understand that he must be seen by the nation and the relatives? He was one of the fathers of the nation, and he had children of the same age as the fallen soldiers. Even more surprising was the fact that he did not attend the mass funeral at Taurama Barracks, where senior ministers, the diplomatic corps, defence attachés, soldiers, and many families joined to express their respect for the fallen. Instead, he sent his wife, Lady Stella. Sir Julius's absence on both occasions was noted by many. This is PNG after all, and before long, there were murmurings and rumours about his absence. His absence could be interpreted in many ways according to the customs and expectations of Papua New Guineans—none of which were complimentary.

In the meantime, my attention was directed towards a proposal for acquiring new military capability, including much-needed helicopters, from Germany. Funds identified to purchase the new capabilities were to be drawn from the Public Service Superannuation Fund and Defence Force Retirement Fund. I had been informed that I was to be part of an official delegation to travel to Germany to inspect helicopters, roadwork equipment, and communications facilities. This would be under a government-to-government agreement. But when I wrote to Sir Julius seeking approval to travel with the delegation, he responded curtly, 'Rescue the hostages [from the Kangu Beach massacre] and then you can go overseas.'

Assassination of Theodore Miriung

In October, another hammer blow to the credibility of the PNGDF on Bougainville was struck with the assassination of Theodore Miriung, the transitional premier of Bougainville and a lawyer for the administration before the crisis. In 1994, he had come out of hiding along with chiefs from Nasioi in central Bougainville and Arawa to commence dialogue on behalf of the Bougainville leaders still in hiding and to try to bring peace. He spoke with me then about how we could resolve the crisis without more loss of life. As the operational commander of the PNGDF on Bougainville at that time, I guaranteed him freedom to move around Bougainville to mobilise support for a peaceful end to the crisis. I gave him space on our helicopters and patrol boats to visit wherever he wanted to go in Bougainville And go to Port Moresby and back.

I was deeply distressed when I was informed of his death. He was gunned down at Konga Village in Tonu while having dinner with his wife and children. Upon instructions from the PNG government, a state funeral was conducted in his honour in Port Moresby. Along with senior members of Sir Julius Chan's cabinet, I had the distressing task of receiving the body at Jacksons Airbase when it arrived with his daughter and widow. The body arrived on Monday, 14 October, and a requiem mass at St Mary's Cathedral was held in Downtown Port Moresby. The funeral service was well attended, and a moving eulogy was given for a leader who was a selfless and simple man totally committed to his cause. The following day, we all gathered at Jacksons Airbase to take a chartered aircraft back to Bougainville to attend the burial service at his village of Rumba at the back of Arawa Township.

At Sir Peter Barter's urging, Sir Julius agreed to approach the Commonwealth secretary general for help in finding a suitable person to head up an independent coronial enquiry into the assassination. A retired Sri Lankan judge, Justice Suntheralingam, was appointed to head the enquiry. Neither Lieutenant Colonel Kanene, Major Wiri, nor I was summoned to give evidence. Justice Suntheralingam's findings pointed to an unidentified group of defence force soldiers stationed at Tonu Camp as the probable guilty party, assisted by resistance force members, some of whom he named. Justice Suntheralingam concluded his report with a recommendation that the police commissioner pursue his investigations into the murder with a view to arresting and laying charges against the guilty parties. Twenty years later, that has still not happened.

Meanwhile, I was conscious of the plight of the five hostages taken during the Kangu Beach massacre. I directed Lieutenant Colonel Kanene to try to find a way to attempt a rescue mission. We had good intelligence pinpointing their location at Laguai, south-east of Buin. Kanene told me that a rescue operation had been planned very early on in their capture using the Reconnaissance Platoon operating out of Torato Island, but it had been aborted due to poor weather conditions. I pressed him to remain alert to remounting a rescue mission as soon as circumstances looked favourable. This did not occur, and the hostages remained in the hands of the BRA until July 1997. They were released after successful negotiations led by the New Zealand government and Sir Michael Somare, then in opposition, and John Momis, the regional member for Bougainville, from the PNG government.

Bougainville Visit

Towards the end of November, I paid a visit to Bougainville. I took with me the director of maritime operations, navy captain Tom Ur; force sergeant major Raymond Maisu; ADC Capt. John Keleto; Capt. Siale Diro, intelligence officer of SFU; my bodyguard, Cpl John Koraia; and communications officer Lt Michael David. We visited the troops by helicopter, travelling from Torokina to Boku and Kangu Beach and then to our maritime outpost at Torato Island before returning to Loloho, our forward tactical headquarters. In the evening, I took a speedboat around to Rorovana to visit the villagers and resistance force members there. It was heart-warming to see the villagers getting back to their routines, even though with all the uncertainties around them they restricted their activities to a much more limited area.

On Friday, 29 November, I departed on my last leg to Torokina and Buin and across to Wakunai, where I met with the local chiefs to give them what assurances I could for their safety and welfare before heading to Buka. On Saturday morning, Capt. Tom Ur and I met with our schoolmate Kapeatu Puaria from Mortlock Island. He was now the principal legal officer in the transitional administration, and he was waiting to take us to see Gerard Sinato, the premier who had been voted in to replace the late Theodore Miriung.

After lunch, my team boarded Air Niugini for our return flight to Port Moresby. As I sat back to reflect on the previous few days, I cherished the brighter moments in Bougainville—the smiling women who found moments of joy in the midst of uncertainty and the playing children who, innocent in their own world, seemed happy. For all its troubles, Bougainville had made men out of those of us lucky enough to serve among its people. Though I had been seriously wounded on operations in Bougainville, I counted myself fortunate to have spent so much of my operational life there.

December 1996

Earlier in December, the findings of Justice Suntheralingam on the assassination of the late Theodore Miriung were published. While the nation stopped to read and hear the outcomes of the enquiry, I called a meeting with my chief of staff, Colonel Tuat, and PNGDF legal officers for counsel. I was left on the wrong end of the findings as I had not been interviewed by Justice Suntheralingam to represent the soldiers implicated. I got a call from Capt Alphonse ADC at Government House. The governor general wanted to see me as soon as possible.

I reported to Sir Wiwa's private study, and he looked at me and said, 'I am disturbed about the newspaper reports of Justice Suntheralingam's findings on Theodore Miriung's assassination. Please explain as I am the honorary commanding officer of the regiment, and I need to know what happened.'

I explained that the findings were potentially biased as no soldier implicated had been asked to give evidence. I had been told that this was because witnesses to the killing were scared of reprisals. The commanding officer of troops in the area, Lt Col. Tokam Kanene, and the military intelligence officer, Major Wiri, had not been summoned by the enquiry. I added that I had not been asked to give evidence nor to make the soldiers who were suspected of the murder available for the enquiry.

I doubt that Sir Wiwa found this a very satisfactory answer, but it was the best that I could offer. The governor general was certainly entitled to know what was happening, and more importantly, as the Queen's representative and honorary commanding officer of the regiment, he was entitled to have all the available facts. I suggested to him that, as the matter was now in the hands of the police, we could no doubt expect the accused parties to be identified and put on trial. I would certainly cooperate fully with any police enquiry and murder investigation that was launched.

Reflecting on this visit and on the whole matter of Theodore Miriung's assassination, I regret now that I did not take a more active role as commander. I could have asked the justice to interview my CO,

Tokam Kanene, and defence intelligence officer, Maj. Geoff Wiri, who were on the ground in Bougainville. And I certainly would have cooperated fully with the justice had he been interested in my views.

Early on Monday morning, 6 December, I got a call to say that the prime minister wanted to see me in his office at Morauta Haus at ten in the morning. I was there early with my ADC, and we went up to his office on the third floor using the lift. As I entered, I met Police Commissioner Bob Nenta and Emos Daniels, adviser to the prime minister. Among other issues, the prime minister was concerned about lost weapons in the PNGDF; he wanted to know what I was doing about stolen weapons making their way into the wrong hands. Further, he said that he was hearing from his sources that the five hostages taken during the Kangu Beach massacre had been killed. That was news to me.

As I looked at Nenta and Emos Daniels, I saw an awkward look cross Daniels's face. He had become well known to me and the rest of the defence council as the possible instigator of most of the misinformation concerning the defence force that reached the prime minister. I said to the prime minister that I had not heard of any losses of weapons, other than those taken after the Kangu Beach massacre, and that, to the best of my knowledge, all five of the hostages were alive and well.

Meanwhile, I was hearing that our founding father and former prime minister, Sir Michael Somare, was planning to go to Bougainville in December in an attempt to free the hostages. This report alarmed me. It would be very difficult, if not impossible, to guarantee the well-being and safety of Sir Michael Somare if he went to Laguai in Buin to negotiate with the rebels for the release of the hostages. I could understand why he wanted to make the attempt as three of the hostages were from East Sepik Province in Sir Michael's constituency. But if he was taken hostage, the government would be in a nightmare scenario. We all agreed that it was not a good time for Sir Michael to attempt personal negotiations as the BRA leaders holding the hostages were known for their unpredictability and aggression. I resolved to talk to Sir Michael as soon as I could.

On 12 December, I had to deal with yet another adverse news headline in the *National*, PNG's leading newspaper. This time, I was being accused of organising a raid on Choiseul Island in the Solomon Islands in 1994, when I was the CO and contingent commander in Bougainville. I was given no chance to respond, and when I called the news editor to ask why I had not been given the opportunity to comment on the story before it was printed, he hung up.

Enraged by this discourtesy, I demanded to see the *National*'s general manager. The allegations of an armed incursion were entirely baseless. We had merely aided a Solomon Islander who had been swept into PNG waters by a strong current when out fishing. He was spotted by defence sailors at Torato Island. I directed that our sailors provide an escort party and sufficient fuel to get him safely back to Choiseul, check in with the local authorities, and then return and report to me at my forward tactical base at Loloho. That was in 1994. I demanded and got a retraction. But in the way of such things, the damage had already been done. I found out later that somebody senior in the Prime Minister's Office was the source. He wanted to tarnish my name, thereby justifying my removal as commander before the close of business in December 1996. This was infuriating beyond belief. Again, politics by so-called advisers PNG-style.

I had three important events coming up on my calendar. The Commander's Annual Parade on Friday, 13 December; a recruit passing out parade on Saturday, 14 December; and Christmas lunch on Wednesday, 25 December, at which senior non-commissioned officers and commissioned officers would serve lunch to the junior soldiers. The Commander's Annual Parade featured Lt Col. Paul Yareki as the parade commander. It was a well-organised parade for troops from all the surrounding Port Moresby units. I told the troops that 1996 had been a very difficult year marked by a lack of funding to maintain the defence force and our efforts in Bougainville. The Kangu Beach massacre had left a very big scar, and the lives lost reminded us that we had a duty to protect our country and the constitution. I asked all present to pray for the safe return of the five hostages, and I reiterated the importance of maintaining personal discipline and showing respect to fellow citizens and colleagues.

The following day, I attended the recruit passing out parade at Goldie River Training Depot. The theme of my address was on the need to recognise that complacency and idleness had no place in the defence force. I made it clear that if anyone did not welcome that thought, there were others who could take their place. They were all volunteers in an all-volunteer defence force, not conscripts in any sense of the word.

I then headed over towards Sir Michael Somare's residence at Four Mile as prearranged. Sir Michael had known my dad well as he had been on the committee for Pangu Pati on Karkar Island in the early days. Sir Michael had always asked after my parents. This morning, I wanted to brief him on the status of the five hostages being held in Laguai. He offered me refreshments, and I did my best to discourage him from travelling. I told him that the rebel leader he would be dealing with, Thomas Tari, was heartless. Finally, Sir Michael relented and agreed that the timing and conditions in Buin were not favourable for his trip. With Christmas approaching, I suggested waiting until the festivities were over. Then we could use John Momis and the other members of Parliament from Bougainville to negotiate on our behalf. Although unconcerned about his personal safety, Sir Michael agreed to hold off until after Christmas.

I was happy that I had spoken to him. He gave me a sense of belonging and fellowship that I badly needed, especially after the previous few days. Yes, Bougainville was an intractable national issue, but people of Sir Peter Barter and Sir Michael's calibre would surely help us find a peaceful solution. Thankfully, the five hostages were released on 10 July 1997. This was orchestrated by the New Zealand government. Sir Donald MacKinnon, New Zealand's foreign affairs and trade minister, and John Hayes, former New Zealand high commissioner to PNG, deserve high praise for the personal conviction and empathy they showed during the hostage negotiations.

On Christmas Day 1996, the entire group of commissioned and non-commissioned officers from HQ PNGDF and Murray Barracks garrison gathered at the sergeants' mess and marched to the other ranks' mess on the eastern side of Murray Barracks. As we marched across Wards Road, the traffic stopped to allow us to cross. The traditional lunch was served by the officers to the soldiers. I was glad to see that it was well organised and that the troops behaved well and in an orderly manner. This is the only time in the whole year that officers and senior non-commissioned officers served a meal for the ordinary soldiers. It was a small act of appreciation with a long tradition, and the soldiers always looked forward to it. In my Christmas message, I reiterated the need for self-discipline and, just as importantly, for continued loyalty to the defence force, the country, the Queen, and God—per the oath they all took upon enlistment. Then I wished them and their families all the best for the festive season.

Reflections on 1996

It was Tuesday, 31 December 1996, the last day of the old year. Weni and I had decided to take our children and spend New Year's Eve at Saroa Babaga Village in Central Province, about 60 km south-east of Port Moresby on the Magi Highway. The children wanted to be with their grandmother, and we were looking forward to a break away from the pressures of Port Moresby. While the children were busy setting up the BBQ for the evening, I made myself comfortable on a mat under the shade of mango trees and reflected on the year that was ending.

My family had a small but significant occasion to celebrate. Our son Futua had won a New Zealand government scholarship, the Aotearoa Scholarship, to complete his remaining high school years at Wesley College in Auckland over the period 1997–99. We counted it as a wonderful blessing and a tribute to his hard work.

This had been the toughest year in my entire twenty years in the defence force. The year started with Ijape's crazy idea of engaging Sandline. As far as he was concerned, this was the only way to solve the Bougainville crisis militarily and reopen the Panguna mine. Operation High Speed II, the thirty-day operation to flush out the rebels as demanded by the politicians, had proved a failure. The early damage and grounding of two of our helicopters to enemy action and the harsh geographic and physical difficulties of mounting military operations in Bougainville made it an impossible task. The morale of the troops was very low due to the loss of so many lives in the Kangu Beach massacre and ongoing funding difficulties. Five security force members were still being held hostage, and there was no indication of their early release. The assassination of Premier Theodore Miriung had tarnished the name of the defence force. The patrolling programme for the PNG-Indonesian land border had been curtailed. Many border incidents and incursions had gone without a response due to a shortage of troops and funding. The prime minister was ill-informed about the PNGDF due to the misinformation he was receiving from his own advisers. Consequently, my hopes for the future development of a smart, well-trained, and well-led defence force seemed likely to remain frustrated.

But there were some achievements for which I could be proud. My appointment as commander had initiated a change in high command in the defence force as middle-ranking officers were pushed up into the higher ranks to replace the older generation of officers, an important number of whom had been retrenched. I had successfully overseen the establishment of a new strategic entity, the SFU, which—thanks especially to Maj. Gilbert Toropo and Captain Renagi—was extremely well staffed and efficient. I had opened new study positions with Indian, Singaporean, and Chinese staff colleges. My personal relationships with the Australian and New Zealand defence forces were also good. Our first-ever officer cadet to be accepted by the Royal Sandhurst Military Academy was in place (Dalos Umul). We had hosted a very successful exercise with a US Special Forces detachment. I had commenced the recruitment and training of the first professional women into the PNGDF, and I was planning to enlist them in other ranks later. I had successfully encouraged university education for all officers with a diploma or above. I had introduced into service a basic inventory of 60 mm and 120 mm mortars. And I had continued a programme of spiritual meetings throughout the military establishments of the PNGDF.

As I thought about the year, there were three key areas of concern. First, I had lost, or was in the process of losing, much of the confidence of PM Sir Julius Chan and his minister for defence, Mathias Ijape. I did not rate Ijape, whose effectiveness as a minister was close to zero and whom I found difficult to respect as a person. But trying to rebuild the confidence of key ministers needed to be a personal priority. The second area of concern related to the serious lack of funding and the long-term sustainability of the defence force in a situation in which morale was dangerously low among the troops and some of the officers. Third and finally, I was extremely concerned about the danger posed by the Executive Outcomes/Sandline people. This looked like being my major challenge early in the new year.

As I sat there under the mango trees, I prayed to God for wisdom and guidance. My spirit was troubled as I sensed the uncertainty ahead and waited to see in the new year. The skies were dark that night, and there was not a star to be seen. I took this to be an especially inauspicious omen on which to end one year and see in the next.

The following year, 1997, was a turbulent year. Dramatic events unfolded as the government of Papua New Guinea—through the office of the deputy prime minister, Chris Haiveta, who was also the finance minister—signed a commercial contract to engage Sandline International Ltd singularly on behalf of the Independent State of Papua New Guinea to deploy with elements of the PNGDF (mainly SFU) into Bougainville with the objective of opening the Panguna mine and hope to render the BRA leadership and organisation ineffective.

As commander, I was troubled by such orders and refused to carry them out as such heavy military actions would further devastate an already suffering population and doubtless bring serious human right abuses, compromising PNG's national security and international standing. I decided to cancel the contract, arrest the Sandline executives and mercenaries, and expel them from PNG, having weighed all the options available, analysed advantages and disadvantages, and had a deep examination of my inner spirit. In doing so, I pressured PM Sir Julius Chan and two of his key ministers to step aside. Two commissions of enquiry were ordered by the government to enquire into the circumstances and the background of the Sandline engagement and why I defied government orders. Part A of this book gives an exclusive account of detail planning, conduct, and aftermath of Operation Rausim Kwik in 1997.

CHAPTER 18

Reappointment as Commander of PNGDF, 1998–99

Here's to the crazy ones. The misfits. The rebels. The troublemakers. The round pegs in the square holes. The ones who see things differently. They're not fond of rules. And they have no respect for the status quo. You can quote them, disagree with them, glorify or vilify them. About the only thing you can't do is ignore them. Because they change things. They push the human race forward. And while some may see them as the crazy ones, we see genius. Because the people who are crazy enough to think they can change the world, are the ones who do.

—Rob Siltanen

As the new year opened in 1998, the future looked bleak for us as a family. I had been dismissed as commander the year before by Sir Julius Chan's government, and we had very few means on which to survive. Weni was our breadwinner, and we relied on the rents collected from the two flats below our house to repay our mortgage with the bank. We managed to save a little money by being careful with our outgoings.

Our son Futua was on a New Zealand government scholarship and was continuing at Wesley College. Fortunately, Futua was a good child whose needs were fairly basic, and he helped us keep our expenses low.

Maib and Moka continued their schooling at Korobosea International Primary School.

National politics in Papua New Guinea are always unpredictable, but they seemed especially so at this time. Bill Skate of the People's National Congress party, a popular and effective governor of Port Moresby's National Capital District, had succeeded Sir Julius Chan as prime minister on 22 July 1997. He made a number of immediate changes at the top of the public service. Peter Aigilo replaced the outgoing commissioner of police, Robert Nenta, who was posted as PNG's high commissioner to Singapore. This was welcome news as Peter Aigilo was my senior police officer cadet at Joint Services College in 1975, and I believed that he would be more open and transparent in his handling of the police force. Michael Gene was appointed secretary for justice and attorney general, replacing Sao Gabi, while John Kawi was appointed solicitor general.

Meanwhile, legal issues stemming from my challenge to the Chan government over the Sandline affair were still very much alive. I had been hoping that the charge of sedition brought against me by Sir Julius would eventually be dropped since, as a number of very senior state lawyers had told me, such a charge could not be made to stick as the elements that constitute sedition were not present. The police prosecutor, Insp. Thomas Eluh, had been instructed to defer the sedition charges sine die (Latin: without day, i.e. indefinitely) due to the fluidity of the political landscape; however, the threat of a trial was still very much alive. The Ombudsman Commission had also deferred a possible leadership referral, but investigations continued unabated. In addition, Sir Julius had a PGK 1 million suit for defamation against me for remarks about him and his family in my public address in 1997. I was determined to fight off every case against me one by one.

The first sign of my possible reappointment as commander came when Sam Tasion— a prominent businessman, chairman of the Lands Board, and close confidant of the prime minister—asked to see me. I did not know why he wanted to see me, but I dropped by his office after work one day. He told me that the prime minister and a few senior cabinet members had suggested their desire for me to be reappointed as commander given that I had proven leadership abilities and was also very popular among the troops. He said that he had talked to the prime minister and that I was seen by government as being capable of restoring confidence in the Papua New Guinea Defence Force and bringing lasting peace on Bougainville.

On the afternoon of Wednesday, 3 September, I was working in my vegetable garden at Gordons when I got a visit from a courier from the Prime Minister's Office. He said that the prime minister wanted to see me at his office in Morauta House. I was in my gardening clothes and muddy boots and was not in a presentable state to see the prime minister. I said that I needed to wash and change, but the courier insisted that I was to go as I was.

Very reluctantly and trying not to get mud everywhere, I got into an unmarked vehicle. When we arrived at Morauta House, I wondered what was waiting for me. The prime minister was seated comfortably in his inner office with some of his senior cabinet ministers, including the member for the Port Moresby North-East Electorate, Philip Taku; the member for Kundiawa, Peter Waieng; Alotau Open member, Iaro Lasaro; and the police minister, Thomas Pelika. I was comforted when I saw Philip Taku and Thomas Pelika. Both were former senior police officers whom I had come to know and respect. This was the first time that I had met the new prime minister.

The prime minister offered me a glass of his favourite drink, Johnnie Walker Red Label, and I settled into my seat, hoping to calm my nerves while all ears and eyes were focused on me. I listened intensely to the casual conversation of the prime minister and his colleagues about the affairs of the nation, which carried on well into the night. As they talked, I reflected that, in March last year, they had all been holed up in the Parliament, barricaded in by a crowd of students and demonstrators who had come out in protest over the Sandline crisis. The protestors had been held back from storming Parliament by a determined group of soldiers and policemen.

Finally, the prime minister turned to me. He said, 'General, my government and cabinet have already discussed important national security issues and matters, and we want you to return as commander and regain control of the defence force. It is a matter of national importance to the country and to the security and well-being of the defence force. Quite frankly, Commander Nuia has lost the confidence of cabinet and the people. He is not trusted. That is why I wanted you to come and meet some of my cabinet members so that they can get to know you. What do you think?'

It was then that I had my first opportunity to apologise for my physical state and to protest that I was not dressed appropriately as I had been gardening when I was summoned to see him.

The prime minister waved away this apology. He continued, 'General, you know that I promised the voters, the policemen and women, the soldiers and their families, and the public servants that if I won the National Capital District Regional seat and took control of government, I would recall you to take over the defence force as commander again. And you know that, on the floor of Parliament, I vigorously opposed the engagement of Sandline International. It's all on the record in Hansard.'

I said that I had been grateful for his support over Sandline and was aware of the current tense situation orchestrated by the so-called Special Operations Group within the PNGDF. This was no more than an illegal entity set up by Leo Nuia and Carl Marlpo to counter the Special Forces Unit. The prime minister agreed, saying that he knew very well that when Nuia and Marlpo had been put under house arrest, the defence force had not rallied around them and removed the SFU. That showed that the defence force had very little confidence and regard for Nuia and Marlpo. I did not comment on this remark, but I agreed with his assessment.

Then the prime minister brought our conversation to a close. 'General, you may leave now if you want to, but I want us to talk again in private this weekend to see if we can find ways in which to restore the defence force and put a stop to all the nonsense that has been happening. My priority is to bring peace on Bougainville, not like previous prime ministers.'

I was glad to be able to take my leave. I thanked the prime minister and his ministers and, hoping that I had not left too much mud behind on the prime ministerial carpet, stepped into the escalator and took my leave.

Weni and I discussed all the advantages and disadvantages. She said I had to be the one to make the final decision. Understandably, she was not too keen on me resuming the role of commander, given the emotional stress that we had both been through in the past year and the three legal charges that were still pending. As I contemplated the prospect of being reappointed, I found I was actually quite uncertain. I had to acknowledge that, while I had been pivotal in holding the defence force together, inadvertent though it was, I had also split the force. The defence force had strong regional and ethnic groupings, a situation we all wanted to avoid. Loyalty and respect was always guaranteed to the commander and the state. It was always part of our doctrine and our make-up as soldiers to place the state first. But the strength of tribal and local loyalties were an inescapable fact in PNG.

As the weekend approached, I was called by the prime minister's assistant, Joyce Komeng, the daughter of former lieutenant colonel Herman Komeng from Kairiru Island in East Sepik Province, to meet with the prime minister at his private residence at Pari Village in South Port Moresby Electorate at one o'clock on Saturday afternoon. On 3 October, I drove to Pari, a few kilometres outside the city. Situated on a hill overlooking the village, Bill Skate's house had a magnificent view of the ocean. The prime minister and his wife, Rarua, were expecting me. Rarua had prepared light refreshments.

This time, the prime minister was not drinking, but he was in a jolly mood, chewing betel nut and very relaxed. He was a complete contrast from Sir Julius, who was very formal and rigid. Sir Julius always offered red wine if he was socialising. This was my second encounter with Bill Skate. And I immediately came to respect his simplicity and openness and his down-to-earth character and approach when meeting people.

The prime minister raised issues about General Nuia's seeming inability to communicate with him and how he appeared to get his directions from opposition party politicians, mainly from the ranks of Sir Julius Chan's People's Progress Party. It seemed that Nuia was not welcomed in Bougainville peace meetings; his record on Bougainville had been tarnished by his admission to extralegal killings and the dumping of civilians into the ocean in 1990 and his branding by the ABC as the 'butcher of Bougainville'. The prime minister said that the Bougainville Interim Government and Premier Joseph Kabui had raised serious concerns about Nuia during meetings in December 1997. Kabui had made it very clear that the Bougainville Revolutionary Army leaders would not meet to discuss peace if Nuia was involved in any way. On the other hand, because of my track record during 1989–94, because I had been active in fostering peace, and because it was under my leadership as commander that Sandline had been expelled, they would be happy to deal with me. 'Simply put,' Skate said, 'they prefer you over Nuia.' The picture was quite clear.

I raised three issues that could be a hindrance to my reappointment. First, I had a charge of sedition registered against me, currently adjourned sine die. Second, I had admitted to receiving financial assistance from Sydney Franklin, and this was the subject of a leadership tribunal referral that was still being investigated. Also pending was a major defamation suit against me by Sir Julius.

Regarding the last, Skate laughed. 'Consider that as a character reference,' he said. 'It will come to nothing. Defamation is when you tell a porky about someone. You told the truth. The truth cannot be defamatory.' On the two more serious matters, Skate was direct. He said the new secretary for justice, Michael Gene, had already briefed him. Prima facie, there was no case of sedition to answer. It would fail if it ever came to court because my actions in demanding the resignation of key ministers over their role in promoting the engagement of Sandline fell well short of the prerequisites for such a charge. The advice he had received from the solicitor general, John Kawi, regarding the money I had received from Sydney Franklin was that, while quite possibly ill-advised, it did not constitute a serious crime as it was not directly linked to the proceeds of a contract. To the contrary, Skate understood that Franklin's business had not received any contracts from defence during my time as commander. In the circumstances, a fine appeared to be the most likely outcome, considering that I had cooperated fully with the ombudsman's office in their investigations.

My last concern was with politics and what might happen to his governing coalition if I was reappointed. The prime minister laughed that off, saying that either his coalition partners would listen to him or he would kick them out. Besides, the secretary for justice and the solicitor general had already been instructed to prepare a National Executive Council submission for my reappointment, which would be taken by cabinet the coming Wednesday.

Surprisingly sombre, I bade PM Bill Skate farewell and, starting my vehicle, meandered down his driveway. I was both anxious and overwhelmed with the proposition of being back in uniform. The challenges would be immense. I can't say that Weni was overjoyed with the prospect either as we both knew what the pressures of the job were. Less vegetable gardening, that was for damn sure.

The next day and early the following week, I revisited my MBA electives with Southern Cross University at Air Niugini Training Centre. I wondered if I would ever complete my MBA. I had invested my savings and time in between fighting a series of court battles to study, and I had looked forward to completing the programme in eighteen months. Regrettably, my MBA remains unfinished.

Meanwhile, news of the possible sacking of Cdr Brig. Gen. Leo Nuia was spreading. Well before the announcement of my appointment by the government, many of my critics began an anti-Skate and anti-Singirok campaign. Undeterred by such criticism, the prime minister forged ahead. Gene made the NEC submission for my reappointment, and Skate brought it before cabinet. On Wednesday, 14 October, I was contacted at home and asked to report to Parliament House for a press conference at one thirty.

When I arrived, the prime minister and his senior ministers were there to announce my appointment. No mention was made during the press conference of the reasons why outgoing commander, Brig. Gen. Leo Nuia, was being replaced. While waiting for my official letter of appointment, I called Wg Cdr Athol Forrest, the New Zealand defence adviser, to inform him of my reappointment, so the New Zealanders were the first to get the news. My letter of appointment from the prime minister was dated 14 October 1998, and it read:

My dear Commander,

I am pleased to inform you on behalf of the National Executive Council, the Government and the people of Papua New Guinea that the Cabinet at its meeting this morning reappointed you to the Office of the Commander of the Papua New Guinea Defence Force. In order to facilitate your re-appointment, Cabinet has further rescinded its earlier decision and re-commissioned you to your previous rank as Brigadier General.

I further advise that Cabinet did consider other candidates within the rank and file of the Defence Force and upon actual consultation with the Public Service Commission as required under Section 193 of the Constitution. Following deliberation, Cabinet decided to re-appoint you to the Office of Commander of the Defence Force.

This decision was indeed not easy. Having considered the present prevailing security issues within the Defence Force and the serious allegations raised against the incumbent, Cabinet decided to make the changes in the best interest of Papua New Guinea. Your appointment will be made effective as soon as the necessary instruments including the Oath of Office and Declaration of Loyalty are executed and taken to the Government House today.

I take this opportunity to sincerely congratulate you on your re-appointment and wish you well in your endeavour to lead the Defence Force into the next millennium. I trust and believe that you will uphold the Constitution and serve the people of Papua New Guinea in the Office of the Commander PNG Defence Force with undivided loyalty, commitment and dedication.

Yours sincerely

Bill Skate, CMG, MP. Prime Minister.

My swearing in ceremony was held on Thursday, 15 October. I was sworn in by Gov. Gen. Sir Silas Atopare. The CO of 1RPIR, Lt Col. Peniel Nilingur, was notably absent, having chosen to organise a range practice rather than attend the ceremony. He was summoned to my office the next day, and I showed him the door. I told him that his services were no longer required due to lack of loyalty. It was sad as I had worked tirelessly with Nilingur in Bougainville in 1993. To ask an officer of his calibre to resign was regrettable, but disloyalty is never excusable, especially when demonstrated in such a public manner.

The news of my reappointment and Nilingur's sacking did not go down well. Soldiers loyal to Nuia and Nilingur crept into the historic First Battalion headquarters and set it alight in the early hours of 19 October. The timber structure burnt down in less than an hour. News of the fire was aired nationally and internationally. This deliberate act of arson did very little for troop morale and nothing to enhance our already diminished image among the general public. I was particularly incensed as the First Battalion headquarters had so much history associated with it. Many senior officers from Australia and PNG had occupied it in their time, officers such as Pears, Lange, Irvine, Diro, Noga, Nuia, Huai, and of course myself.

I immediately reshuffled the senior officer's postings. Col. David Takendu, a veteran colonel, was replaced by Col. Joseph Kewa as acting chief of staff; Lt Col. Fred Kiriba was promoted to full colonel and appointed chief of intelligence; navy commander Peter Ilau was appointed chief of operations; Col. Ben Norrie was promoted and posted as chief of logistics; Lt Col. Francis Agwi was made commanding officer, Goldie River Training Depot, overseeing the re-establishment of SFU; and Captain Lofena was appointed acting officer commanding of SFU. I replaced Nilingur with Lt Col. Vex Mae. My personal staff officer was young captain Craig Solomon. I knew and trusted and liked him from our days together on operations in Bougainville; he was the perfect choice for my aide-de-camp.

To re-establish command and control, my first task was to sort out the mess that had accumulated over the year and a half or so since my sacking by the Chan government and to prevent further divisions in the defence force created by the SOG. I consulted senior officers and called Walter Enuma. Enuma suggested that members of Operation Rausim Kwik, SFU, and SOG should go on a retreat for a few days and walk the Kokoda Track, finishing with a BBQ. I agreed and ordered the staff to go ahead and issue instructions. We achieved some degree of success, but the SOG went underground for a while as they had other plans.

Lt Col. Geoffrey Wiri led a faction of officers and soldiers from the highlands who were opposed to me. He had written numerous letters to senior officers seeking my removal, but I knew that he was only pursuing his own narrow interests as he was running out of time, having graduated from the Australian Army Officer Cadet School at Portsea in 1973. His chances of reaching the highest echelons in the PNGDF had been diminished by his own malicious intent. But he was desperate to grab every chance to remain in the mainstream. He never relented and would pursue his self-interested agenda at every opportunity, using political connections to remain in the force and appear untouchable despite his age and time in rank. And regrettably, he eventually succeeded—as much as such a man ever succeeds.

Other opposition forces were also at play. A group led by retired former commander Brig. Gen. Kenneth Noga called for my resignation due to the various allegations laid against me. And then there was Acting Police Commissioner John Wakon, a classmate of mine from Joint Services College. He told a media conference that the charge of sedition against me would be reactivated. He further alleged that I had pressured Bill Skate to get the police off my back. John Wakon loved publicity and wanted to appear like a tough cop, yet he lacked even the most basic understanding of the legal definition of sedition and the elements that might constitute such a charge.

Police Commissioner Peter Aigilo was away on a study break in America when Wakon stirred this particular hornet's nest. Sam Inguba was the police force's chief of operations and a personal friend of mine. He told me that the political undercurrents were such that one could not tell who was on your side and who was not. The charge of sedition had not been dropped; however, it had been put away sine die and would not be resurrected until 2004, a full six years later, by Insp. Thomas Eluh before Justice Cathy Davani. The media hype that John Wakon hoped for came and went as did his own career when he was sacked in 1999 after heading up a special task force to investigate charges of fraud brought against PM Bill Skate that were subsequently dropped.

In the meantime, I continued assisting the office of the Ombudsman Commission over a possible leadership charge. I was informed by Ila Geno and Joseph Waugla, both commissioners at the time, that they would review my case as I had provided all the bank details of my Lloyds Bank Visa account. Ila Geno, who was also a former police commissioner, later testified that I was the first departmental head to surrender all the documents they sought and that I had continued to assist the Ombudsman Commission in their investigation until they decided to refer me to the leadership tribunal in 2000.

Stephen Mokis from New Ireland was a close friend of mine and an outstanding public servant. He had been defence secretary in 1987–88 and was now working with the Ombudsman Commission. He assisted in the interviews and gave me all the support I could ask for to resolve the allegations of misconduct against me while in office.

By now, it was early December 1998, and I decided to revisit Bougainville. I had not left Port Moresby since my reappointment. The prime minister was constant in his insistence that, rather than signing peace agreement after peace agreement, we should actively engage with the warring factions. True to his word, Skate had spent the previous Christmas at Paruparu Village with Joseph Kabui, the very same village where I nearly lost my entire battalion forward tactical team in 1994. The prime minister's jungle visit in 1997 triggered an unprecedented peace process that would allow unarmed New Zealand–led international peacekeepers to be deployed into Bougainville under Brig. Gen. Roger Mortlock (the Brig), deputy chief of army general staff of New Zealand. Skate maintained that his position on Bougainville was to make peace using peaceful means, and there would no longer be any thought of military action or offensives.

My small party visited the troops and civilians, many of whom were glad to see us. Many troops openly cried when they thanked me for expelling Sandline. They said that their personal security and safety on the ground was now guaranteed by the BRA and other former hardliners. We stopped at Loloho, and I took the opportunity to go to Rorovana to visit the villagers and the resistance force members I had spent so much time with in 1993 and 1994. I was pleasantly surprised to see Moses Piri, my former batman, and he was happy and emotional to see me. He eagerly introduced his wife and baby, Jerry, who was named after me. I was overwhelmed.

As the peace process was now coming along in a big way, the troops were restricted to static duties. This allowed the Truce Monitoring Group and the follow-on Peace Monitoring Group to intercede and United Nations ambassador Noel Sinclair to coordinate the peace process with the warring factions. I had the opportunity to meet Sam Kauona at Arawa and have a one-on-one conversation with him in Ambassador Sinclair's office. Sam Kauona asked if he had won the battle, and I replied no, the people had won the peace process. I said that the war was still far from over, but as the prime minister was saying, peace would now be pursued through peaceful means. And that meant by all the parties involved. He thanked me personally and said that if I had not stopped Sandline, it would have been mayhem, and peace would never have been possible. I agreed with him.

It was obvious that the decision by the Chan government to engage the Sandline mercenaries had taken a toll on the people of Bougainville, whose trust in the national government and its agencies needed rebuilding. My own popularity in Bougainville was striking. Even the hardliners now wanted peace and were taking the opportunity to open dialogue in rebel-controlled areas. This was supported by women community leaders throughout Bougainville. Personally, I took no credit for the popularity I was getting over the expulsion of Sandline. As I said repeatedly on Bougainville, I merely performed my duty as a responsible soldier and commander.

Once back from Bougainville, the immediate priority was to present to government through the defence council a far-reaching White Paper to address our urgent needs for rebuilding and modernisation. The intended scope of the paper was to look at PNG's strategic setting, consider the implications for defence policy and the military considerations flowing from that policy, and examine the full range of defence capability, management, funding, and implementation issues. In short, I wanted a paper that would provide a blueprint for the rebuilding of the PNGDF over both the medium and longer term. To get the ball rolling, I presented to the defence council a policy paper on the terms of reference and intended scope of the White Paper. I outlined the need for a technical advisory team, the budget required to engage a reputable security analyst from the region, and the timeline within which to publish the findings.

I recommended that we engage Dr Lance Beath from the Centre for Strategic Studies at Victoria University of Wellington to assist the defence council. Beath had worked in the New Zealand Ministry of Defence and had extensive experience in the preparation and writing of such papers. I had known him and his work in this area for some years. His role, in close consultation with both myself and the secretary for defence, Vali Asi, would be to assist in scoping and presenting a draft White Paper to the defence council. In terms of time frames, I wanted to complete our work by the end of the first quarter of 1999 and to present our findings to the defence council and cabinet before the end of May 1999. We met those timelines.

Another important development in the new look of PNGDF I was working towards was the establishment of an Engineer Battalion forward operational base in the highlands of PNG. This was an important move for the Skate government. To accomplish this, I discussed the matter with all five governors from the highlands to get their support for basing the battalion in Western Highlands, being the centre of the region. The Western Highlands governor, Fr Robert Lak, and I staked out some government land at Kerwil near Banz along the old highlands road linking Jimmy District and the famous bush track from Madang to Jimmy Valley. This was where the first pioneer

Catholic priest, Father Ross, had walked up from Madang to spread Christianity to the highlands just before World War II.

On 12 December, I flew to Mount Hagen with Captain Mopang, the surveyor from the engineer directorate, and headed out to the site. Fr Robert Lak joined us at Kerwil for the initial reconnaissance. As we made our way up to the hilltop, I instructed Captain Mopang to sketch out the location for the officers' and senior non-commission officers' mess, other ranks' barracks, and married quarters. I also pointed out where the hardstand for the workshop for heavy equipment and Q-store should go. On the opposite side of the road, I indicated where the airstrip should be built.

As we headed back to Highlander Hotel, I emphasised that this project would now be a top priority. Upon return to Port Moresby, I made a submission to Secretary for Defence Vali Asi for funding to be transferred to the Engineer Battalion from the civic action vote. I called the CO of engineers, Lt Col. Joseph Fabila, and directed him to regard the project at Kerwil as the Engineer Battalion's top priority project for 1999. I then wrote to the highlands governors to ensure that at least PGK 1 million was allocated yearly in their project budget for the civic action vote so that work could commence on building the base. In the meantime, the director engineer, Lt Col. Daba Rakagaro, was given instructions to commence the drafting work with Captain Mopang.

On 20 December, PM Bill Skate was invited by the highlands governors for a ceremony to break the ground at Kerwil with the local member, Fabian Pok. We were given a warm welcome Western Highlands–style. I was accompanied by a strong contingent of engineer officers. In the presence of the Western Highlands governor, Robert Lak; the governor of Simbu, Fr Louie Ambane; and the Southern Highlands governor, Anderson Aigiru, the site was officially declared as state land for use by the Engineer Battalion as a base for all civic activities in the highlands region.

After speeches by the prime minister, Western Highlands governor, and Fabian Pok, the local member, we adjourned to Banz Golf Course for more entertainment. Weni had accompanied me on the trip. Our next stop was Wewak for a visit to 2RPIR.

With the peace process now under way in Bougainville, Sandline issues were a thing of the past; and the change of government meant that the troops could now be rested, retrained, and redeployed. Others would be made redundant and assisted with redundancy and resettlement back into their communities.

Our ongoing relations with the Australian government through the Defence Cooperation Programme continued to be very important to us. The posting of the new defence attaché, Col. Richard Howell, was most welcome as he had been my DS (directing staff) in 1991 and my guidance officer while I attended the Australian Army Command and Staff College. First on Howell's agenda was to get to know my personal staff, including my aide, Capt. Craig Solomon. While the relationship at the personal level was welcomed, I cautioned young Solomon about the importance of remaining sensitive to the possibility of competing interests when it came to national security and integrity.

Christmas came with a lot of mixed newspaper headlines, especially over the handling of the economy and the public service machinery. The PNGDF's ongoing duty to maintain and secure the international land border as well as maritime surveillance and looking after the troops on Bougainville presented numerous challenges. After the traditional Christmas lunch to serve other ranks at Murray Barracks, I took the family to Jayapura in acceptance of an outstanding invitation by the Trikora army commander, Gen. Amir Sembiring, for Christmas and New Year. We boarded an Air Niugini flight to Vanimo and overnighted there before going on to the Wuting checkpoint at Batas. There, we met General Sembiring and his wife and staff officers for a short welcome and drive to Jayapura.

The highlight of our trip was a flight on an Indonesian Army CASA to Manokwari and then to Biak Island, where we spent the New Year. It was a good way to finish the year and gave me an opportunity to reflect on current challenges and find the best way forward given the political climate and uncertainties ahead.

Public Apology to Sir Julius Chan

As the year 1999 opened, Sir Julius Chan's suit against me for defamation increased in pace. Of course, the former prime minister was entitled to sue; however, the amount he was seeking in damages, PGK 1 million, was completely unrealistic. Also, one might have wondered what good could come from raising the Sandline issue when the public perception of Chan's handling of the affair was entirely negative. Sir Julius was represented by Mr Paterson of Paterson Lawyers. He instructed Paterson to liaise with my counsel, Moses Murray, regarding a public apology. Sir Julius wanted me to take out an advertisement publicly apologising, following which he would drop the charge. We welcomed the news and immediately set about developing the text of the apology. This duly appeared in the *National* and the *Post-Courier* on Thursday, 18 March 1999, two years to the day after Operation Rausim Kwik:

SINGIROK APOLOGISES PUBLICLY FOR SANDLINE–CHAN COMMENTS

PORT MORESBY: Papua New Guinea Defence Force (PNGDF) Commander Jerry Singirok publicly apologised to former Prime Minister Sir Julius Chan today for alleged defamatory remarks he made during 1997s Sandline mercenary crisis.

Brigadier Singirok said he had asserted that Sandline—which had been hired by the Chan government to assist the PNGDF in ending the Bougainville secessionist crisis—had used the defence force as a front and was equipping a security company that belonged to Sir Julius's family.

'If such a statement was construed by members of the general public to mean that Sir Julius Chan was dishonest, corrupt, abusing his position as Prime Minister for personal gain and for members of his family, and that he was selling his country to foreigners for economic gain at the expense of Papua New Guineans, then I am sorry because that was never my intention,' Brigadier Singirok said.

'I therefore unreservedly withdraw each and every one of those statements and any inferences those statements may have attracted and fully apologise to Sir Julius and members of his family.'

In an editorial, *The Nation* commented that Sir Julius had sued Brigadier Singirok for defamation but the National Court was informed earlier this week that the parties had agreed to settle out of court and that Brigadier Singirok would apologise to Sir Julius.

After Sir Julius saw the article, a close confidant of his, Joseph Asaigo, a long-serving foreign service officer and former high commissioner to Solomon Islands, organised a reconciliation dinner for Sir Julius and me. I hired a private room at Airways Hotel and had my defence intelligence officers comb the area. I arrived at about seven o'clock, and sure enough, Sir Julius was there, waiting with Asaigo. It was remarkable how well we got on that night—after two red bottles of wine and a wonderful dinner of roast beef.

As we parted, we were both content that we had at least put some differences aside. Moreover, as I saw it, while he was out on the streets, I was back in as commander. When paying for the meal, I nearly choked. Sir Julius had chosen the most expensive red wine on the wine list. He was a seasoned master at his games, I thought ruefully. Still, I was content that I could continue my job as commander not worried by Sir Julius looking over my shoulder. I still have the greatest respect for him. Unfortunately, he had surrounded himself with incompetent advisers (not including his head of department, Noel Levi, who is a brilliant, very decent, and hard-working man). Yet ultimately, Sir Julius's advisers could not be blamed for his decision, along with Chris Haiveta and Ijape, to engage Sandline. That disaster must rest where it belongs—firmly on their shoulders.

In April, I was given an official invitation to visit New Zealand and tour their defence force establishments. I was accompanied by Wg Cdr Athol Forrest, the New Zealand defence adviser; Director of Training Lt Col. Paul Mai, and my aide-de-camp, Capt. Craig Solomon. Our trip took us to Linton Barracks and Waiouru to the Officer Cadet School of New Zealand, where my former ADC, Capt. John Keleto, was posted as instructor. I was also able to visit Futua at Wesley College, where he was completing his secondary schooling. My party took some time off to stay overnight with Dr Lance Beath at his farm south of Taihape, a few kilometres from Waiouru. From there, we organised a trout fishing excursion to Lake Taupo. Being a keen fisherman, it was an interesting experience, and I enjoyed my first go at fly fishing.

On the last leg of my New Zealand visit, I was contacted by foreign affairs officials in Wellington who advised me that PM Bill Skate was on his way to Rotorua to meet with delegates from BIG, led by Joseph Kabui, and a number of BRA commanders. Skate was accompanied by the minister assisting on Bougainville affairs, Sir John Kaputin, and I was required to meet with them in Auckland and then drive to Rotorua. We spent three days at Rotorua, and the meeting paved way for further progress on the peace process. John Momis, a veteran politician and icon in PNG politics and Bougainville matters and the regional member for Bougainville, was very particular on the question of autonomy. He argued forcefully that Bougainville should be allowed to administer itself through a system of autonomous government.

The White Paper was ready upon our return to Port Moresby. Dr Beath presented the manuscript to the defence council for their approval and publication. Under the guidance of Minister Peter Waieng, Secretary for Defence Vali Asi and I agreed that the White Paper met our needs and should be authorised for official release.

Operation Selamat, May 1999

In early May, I was preoccupied with a major international incident caused by West Papuan rebels, the Organisasi Papua Merdeka. Over twenty OPM rebels seized a small resettlement outpost called Arso a few kilometres from Jayapura, the capital of Irian Jaya. They killed four civilians and took as their hostages seven women and four men who had been attending the local first aid post, fleeing with them towards Bewani inside PNG. Among the female hostages was a nurse, Yolando, who had been ministering to the sick. The incident, which occurred on 4 May, attracted major regional and international headlines. I was given an operational staff briefing and then consulted with the CO in Vanimo, 2RPIR's lieutenant colonel Earnest Aki. I ordered Aki to be ready to deploy a company into the area within twenty-four hours. Meanwhile, we worked on the operational planning details with the governments of PNG and Indonesia.

On 5 May, I was summoned to a National Security Council meeting chaired by the prime minister at Morauta Haus. The Indonesian government was very concerned about the welfare of its citizens. I took Col. Fred Kiriba, the chief of defence intelligence, to the meeting. After briefing the prime minister and the council, I was directed to use all the resources available to ensure that we rescued the hostages safely and as soon as practical. Back at Murray Barracks, I put in place an immediate operational order aimed at the release of the hostages.

Operational Orders Operation Selamat Mission

To locate and release the Indonesian hostages.

The General Outline of Operations

The operation will be mounted by a company minus group of 2RPIR supported by one SFU patrol complemented by the Reconnaissance Platoon section from Support Company 2RPIR. The operation will be based at Skotiao and a coordinated patrol program using local guides and trackers will fan out over the suspected area.

SFU patrol is to be deployed from Port Moresby commanded by Captain Belden Namah and Sgt Chris Mora.

DIB will attach Warrant Officer Ravu Mareva who will link the field intelligence provided by DSLO David Yim and Sgt Jack Aria based out of Vanimo. A DF Huey helicopter will be despatched to support the operation. I will be briefed on the hour every hour on progress of the operation or more frequently as required. I will be directing all operations from Skotiao village and will redirect the operation according to the intelligence gathered and disseminated.

All available air and land mobility assets will be used. A Secure High Frequency (HF) link is to be established to Vanimo base and 2RPIR.

Operation Selamat will be monitored by the National Security Council and in Jakarta. All troops participating must exercise constraint, self discipline and apply tactics to track, apprehend the rebels and negotiate for the safe release of the hostages.

Police Chief of Operations Gari Baki was tasked with making police officers and the police helicopter available for the operation. Capt. Belden Namah, a local from Somboi Village near Bewani Government Station, was highly respected by his people. He spoke fluent Bahasa, having studied the language at James Cook University in Queensland in 1992, and would be pivotal to the success of Operation Selamat. The terrain around Bewani was mountainous with dense forest, tropical vegetation, and fast-flowing rivers. It was infested with leeches and spiked native cane, and torrential monsoon rains were common all year round. It was the worst imaginable place for operations. I was very familiar with the area and its geographical challenges as I had conducted numerous border patrols there in my earlier years.

Before departing from Port Moresby, I gave an intelligence brief to Indonesian ambassador Benny Mandalika and Defence Attaché Col. Edie Butabuta. I assured them that I would take over Operation Selamat myself and that I would be based at Skotiao Village in the Bewani area. I flew to Vanimo with Colonel Kiriba. We were driven to

Jayapura as prearranged to meet with Indonesian government officials. We overnighted in Jayapura and the following day, along with a heavy military escort and commander of Trikora Maj. Gen. Amir Sembiring, drove to Arso to meet the families of the hostages and those who had lost their loved ones.

We returned to Vanimo on 21 May, and I joined Police Chief of Operations Gari Baki and Sgt David Terry, media officer. We flew to Skotiao in the police force's Eye in the Sky helicopter, captained by Capt. David Inau, a former defence force pilot. After receiving situational briefs, I reorganised the tactical plan based on credible intelligence now coming in and then used helicopters to insert five small patrols surrounding the main area of interest.

On the third day, Captain Namah and his brother, Bob Namah, established contact with the OPM leader and the local informants as they closed in on the hostages. On 27 May, I took the police helicopter for a reconnaissance of the area. We were flying along a small tributary at about 200 feet when we spotted a civilian waving on the bank of the river. I signalled the pilot to land. The civilian came up to the helicopter and said that he knew where the hostages were being held.

We took him on board and flew to the area, which he pinpointed for us. We established a firm base on the riverbed and then ferried troops into the area to cordon it off. Bob Namah moved forward towards the location among thick jungle foliage with Sgt Chris Mora and made contact with the rebels and the hostages. Captain Namah and I met with the OPM rebel leader and negotiated for the release of the hostages. As had been reported, there were seven females and four males, all of Javanese origin and all accounted for. The OPM rebels, around ten of them, disappeared into the forest in haste towards the Indonesian border.

The inclusion of Captain Namah in the operation was the key to its overall success. He knew the terrain and the area and was well respected, so the locals readily assisted in narrowing down the location of the hostages. The hostages were bundled into the helicopter and flown to safety at the operations base in Skotiao. They were held for a few hours until a medical team from Vanimo General Hospital and consular officials were flown in. The medical team was led by former PNGDF doctor Capt. John Noveti and two nurses.

At last light on 27 May, I walked into the Indonesian Consulate in Vanimo and reported the release of the hostages to Col. Edie Butabuta and Consul General Marcus Budi Suanto. I showed them the video of the hostages. They were happy and relieved and could not thank the defence force enough for all its efforts. I rang the defence minister and the prime minister and confirmed the success of the operation.

On Sunday, 30 May, Gen. Amir Sembiring flew into Vanimo with the West Papua governor, Freddy Numberi, and we took the hostages back to Jayapura. Minister Peter Waieng and the member for Nuku, Andrew Kumbakor, represented the government and officially handed the released hostages to Gov. Freddy Numberi. An open invitation to the troops and policemen who had participated in the operation was issued to accompany the released hostages to Jayapura and spend the weekend there.

A welcome reception and military parade was held on Tuesday, 1 June, along with a news conference. The news coverage was unprecedented. This was one of the highlights in my military career—planning and directing a successful military operation involving foreign citizens and military.

Extensive coverage of the operation featured in the *Jakarta Post* and on major TV stations throughout Indonesia, the rest of Asia, and CNN. We were officially farewelled by General Sembiring on Wednesday, 2 June. I flew back to Wewak with Capt. David Inau and my bodyguard, Sgt John Koraia, to board an Air Niugini flight to Port Moresby.

The prime minister and his cabinet were pleased with our efforts and announced to the nation that Operation Selamat was successful. In an official news release, Skate said:

> I would like to thank Commander Brigadier General
> Jerry Singirok personally for his outstanding leadership
> in taking control of a very important operation which
> successfully resulted in the release of the 11 hostages.
> I want to also thank the troops and policemen who

participated. The deeply entrenched dispute the hostages were caught up in has existed for some time and I urge all involved to address the problems faced through peaceful means.

The Indonesian ambassador, Benny Mandalika, wrote to Skate in gratitude for the rescue and the release of the hostages:

I have the honour on behalf of the Indonesian Government and the people of Indonesia and the people of Irian Jaya specifically to express our heartfelt thanks and gratitude to you for your strong support and assistance to free the 11 hostages.

When I think back to the joy and the tears shared by the hostages, who had been in the hands of the rebels for over twenty-one days, I treasure the memories of this operation. Their treatment—like the treatment of anyone who has been oppressed and denied freedom, such as Bougainville's civilians—was a scar on humanity. It was a privilege to work with others to secure the release of the hostages and to be reminded of the true meaning of freedom. As commander, it was a pleasure to share the success with all those who were involved in the operation from start to finish, especially Capt. Belden Namah, Sgt Chris Mora, and Bob Namah, who played such critical roles. This was the last successful military operation that we, as a team, played post-Bougainville and Operation Rausim Kwik.

As anticipated in the Defence White Paper and taking note of the perceived increase in our roles and functions under section 202 of the Constitution of the Independent State of New Guinea, cabinet promoted me to major general (two-star). The rank was conferred on me by Gov. Gen. Sir Silas Atopare in a ceremony at Murray Barracks on Monday, 7 June. I was happy to accept the promotion, but I considered it secondary to the greater task that lay ahead, namely, 'service to others', as detailed in the White Paper.

Though completely unaware at the time, this ceremony at Murray Barracks would turn out to be the high-water mark for me in my role as commander of the PNGDF. From early June onwards, the politics of the nation went through another period of turbulence. The economy took another downturn. Bill Skate's government began to come apart with the firing and departure of key members of his administration. Finally, on 14 July, a vote of no confidence was taken in Parliament, and Sir Mekere Morauta emerged as the new prime minister. Bernard Narokobi was appointed speaker.

Skate should be remembered as the prime minister who took an olive branch to Paruparu and Joseph Kabui on Christmas Day in 1997 and who reassured the BRA command of his willingness to bring peace to Bougainville by withdrawing security forces. Skate can also be remembered for spearheading the release of the five hostages from the Kangu Beach massacre in a high-level collaboration with the New Zealand government. A maverick leader, many of his speeches and actions were unorthodox. Not surprisingly, his favourite song was 'My Way' by Frank Sinatra.

PM Sir Mekere Morauta, when addressing the media on 15 July 1999, said:

> We have chosen order over chaos. We have chosen hope over despair. We have chosen pride in our young country over mindless pursuit of narrow interests. We have chosen to give our children the chance of a decent life in their own country, in place of fearful descent into poverty, poor health and disorder.

There was no doubt that Morauta had wide support among the general public and foreign interests. International financial institutions saw him as a proven economist and manager with the ability to resurrect PNG's failing economy through tight fiscal planning and monitoring. But his elevation proved very problematic for the security sector.

Far from maintaining the credible security policy framework as laid out in the Defence White Paper of 1999, Morauta's government took drastic measures that resulted in the crippling of the PNGDF. The White Paper had recommended a process of modernisation and renewal, starting with the construction and careful costing of a series of force models. The first was the status quo model, in which the cost of maintaining the force at current manpower levels (4,591 at that point) would be determined but at a rate that allowed the force to be fully fed, clothed, trained, exercised, and deployable. To be clear, the objective was to develop an accurate cost picture of the current force—fully trained, maintained, and deployable—not the force 'standing in its socks' as it were.

The second costing model was to have been based on a force structure held at current establishment levels but where manpower would be managed down through a process of attrition and early retirement of all those defence force personnel who were classified as left out of battle or medically unfit for further service. In this model, manpower was to be reduced until the costs of a fully maintained, trained, and deployable force met current budgetary allocations. The consequences in terms of roles, tasks, deployability, and sustainability were to be outlined for government *before* any action was taken.

Two more drastic costing models were proposed, by way of illustration, to determine where the expenditure floor, as distinct from the ceiling, might be. These costing models were based on a 25 per cent reduction to current manpower levels (down to 3,440 personnel) and a 50 per cent reduction (2,295 personnel). The White Paper made it clear that these were *illustrative models only* and that each of them, if seriously considered, would require maximum use of commercial support and capital expenditure on force multipliers such as IT, C3I, intelligence, surveillance, force troops, and the like before proceeding.

This was how an orderly and rational process would have unfolded. But so far as I know, none of these cost models were constructed. The Morauta government simply slashed the defence force's numbers from 4,591 to 2,000 overnight. It did not institute any of the investments recommended in the White Paper that would be needed by such a small force if it was to retain, let alone enhance, its effectiveness.

The Morauta government blew out the lights in the PNGDF by ordering the reduction of manpower by over 50 per cent and the destruction of hundreds of small arms, medium machine guns, and assorted weapons systems that had originally been provided or funded by the Australian government. There was no fallback plan to sustain the operational and combat capability of the defence force.

The new prime minister replaced all those he saw as impediments to his coalition government. Among the first to go was Peter Aigilo, the police commissioner, replaced by John Wakon. I was in Milne Bay for naval exercise Paradise 99 in which naval ships from around the Pacific were exercising. Aigilo called me and told me that he had been replaced and that he believed I would be next. The new defence minister was Alfred Pogo from the highlands. A former district manager in Finschhafen, Pogo had resigned from the public service to contest and won the Finschaffen Open seat. At face value, he appeared confident, but he experienced great difficulty in translating political vision into military and strategic outcomes. It was sad to see the outgoing defence minister, Peter Waieng, being posted as a minister assisting the prime minister in state matters.

On 4 August 1999, I was passed a drop copy of a top-secret information paper prepared for PM Sir Mekere Morauta. Its stated purpose was to inform the prime minister 'of the current situation in the Defence Force' and to seek NEC endorsement for a leadership change in the defence force. I knew at once who the authors of this so-called information paper were. After my promotion to major general, it became apparent that the SOG had become active again. Working closely with selected politicians, they embarked on something they called Operation Rescue PNG and commenced a campaign to oust me as commander and replace me with Lt Col. Carl Marlpo.

I called my senior officers in to discuss the contents of the paper. My team included Acting Chief of Staff Col. Joseph Kewa from Western Highlands, Colonel Kiriba, and Colonel John David, acting chief of logistics. The contents of the information paper were typical of the misinformation that was being funnelled out of the defence force by members of the SOG. The paper listed several things that I was allegedly responsible for. For example, it reported unauthorised weapons training at Goldie River Barracks; weapons missing from Port Moresby Supply Company, with over 2,500 ammunition rounds unaccounted for; the eviction of senior officers from Murray Barracks; and the arbitrary discharge of certain senior officers. It also reported that Maj. Walter Enuma and a senior government minister were celebrating a court victory, having been exonerated from a charge of forming an illegal army.

Further, the paper stated that under my leadership there was a breakdown in command and control, nepotism, malpractice, and misinformation. It stated that there had been no changes in terms of defence force development and that I was only preoccupied in pursuing my own agenda. It said that, as long as I was commander, I would be a threat to national security and stability and urged the prime minister to replace me forthwith. It also stated that the revolt against the national government to remove Sandline in March 1997 had not been done in isolation but was inspired with political backing and that I had serious criminal charges still pending.

The paper concluded with two recommendations: first, it called for the NEC to take note of the current situation in the defence force, including internal insecurity and instability; second, it asked the NEC to take note of the options to effect my immediate removal as commander. It was a well-calculated but extraordinarily ill-motivated letter based on fear, uncertainty, and patently false allegations spread by the SOG and my opponents. It was obvious that my further employment as commander was in serious jeopardy. Lt Col. Carl Marlpo's name was being floated as my replacement, and I had serious doubts about his ability to command. He was physically unfit, had been medically downgraded, and had no prior experience as a battalion commander or a senior branch head at PNGDF headquarters. His appointment as commander would be a seriously retrograde step.

Events now moved extremely swiftly, suggesting a high degree of collusion between Carl Marlpo, Geoff Wiri, and a group of highland soldiers and politicians, including the defence minister. On 5 August, Gov. Gen. Sir Silas Atopare signed my suspension notice, bringing my military career to an end. Lt Col. Carl Marlpo replaced me as acting commander. The appointment of Carl Marlpo was a disaster for the defence force and the country as he had no ability or experience in translating policy issues at the strategic level into military outcomes.

After Colonel Marlpo was appointed as acting commander, he received a letter from SOG that restated the importance of appointing Lt Col. Geoffrey Wiri as chief of operations and suggested a list of junior- and middle-ranking officers for important postings. It stated that the postings were endorsed by the leadership of the People's Democratic Movement (the prime minister's party). Extraordinary! It further stated, 'We hope these requests are not demanding and pray that you will respond to us favourably.' The majority of its eight signatories were officers from the highlands region.

The acting commander was now trapped in an abject corner of his own making; he had no choice but to appoint Wiri as acting chief of operations and the other officers to the postings requested. This thoroughly craven act destroyed any chance the acting commander had of exerting any influence of his own during his tenure as commander. He would be a creature of the SOG until his eventual demise two years later.

Lt Col. Francis Agwi, who had only recently taken command of Goldie River Barracks, was replaced on suspicion of being pro-Singirok and SFU. Meanwhile, the PNGDF was in serious trouble over lack of cohesiveness, professionalism, and loyalty, not to mention being in a state of crisis over overt politicisation—the death knell for defence forces everywhere.

My family and I departed Murray Barracks for the last time on 12 August. We closed the door on Flagstaff House and returned to our residence at Nuana Street, settling in once more as ordinary citizens.

My suspension meant that I would continue to remain as a soldier until the charges under the Leadership Code were determined. I was contacted by Peniel Mogish from the Office of the Public Prosecutor on 10 November. He referred to a letter he had written to me on 23 October, advising that the chief justice had appointed an appropriate leadership tribunal to enquire into allegations of misconduct when I was commander of the PNGDF between 1995 and 1997. I was being charged under sections 27(1), 27(2), and 27(5)(b) of the Constitution of the Independent State of New Guinea and sections 12(1)(a) and 4(6)(b) of the Organic Law on the Duties and Responsibilities of Leadership.

The leadership tribunal was chaired by Justice Moses Jalina and assisted by senior magistrates Regina Sagu and Cosmas Bidar. It would be a very short tribunal as I had already willingly provided all the details of my Lloyds Bank Visa card account, transactions, and balance. My counsel assisting was Moses Murray.

On 22 March 2000, I was found guilty of receiving money from J. and S. Franklin in July 1997 in a newly opened Visa account, which sum I had not declared in my annual returns of income as required by the Leadership Code. Justice Jalina, in reading his verdict, said that 'public policy demanded the Commander be dismissed from office as Commander'. While I accepted the decision, there was lobbying from different quarters on the grounds that the payment was not a form of bribery. However, I told my supporters that it was actually a win-win situation as my dismissal would put to rest those critics who wanted me dead for expelling Sandline and for forcing Sir Julius to step aside, resulting in him losing his seat in Parliament to his cousin Ephraim Apelis.

As I reflect back on my second stint as commander, I am content that during my brief period in office I was able to accomplish a number of important things. I obtained cabinet approval for the establishment of the Engineer Base at Kerwil (now Jiwaka Province) and was successful in initiating the Commercialisation Support Programme. I contributed to a lasting peace in Bougainville and the complete withdrawal of security forces from that war-torn province. With assistance from the SFU, 2RPIR, and policemen, I planned and executed Operation Selamat, resulting in the successful rescue of eleven Indonesian hostages. And I was able to dampen down, though not eliminate, the long-drawn-out infighting between the highly professional and respected SFU and the amateur clowns in the so-called SOG.

I am extremely proud of my achievement in organising and contributing to the writing and editing of the groundbreaking Defence

White Paper of 1999, subtitled 'Service to Others'. After twenty years, this White Paper is still the leading example in the region of how to think through and write a strategic assessment.

On the staff development front, I was successful in increasing the number of officer cadets sent to the Royal Military College, Duntroon. I also signed a memorandum of agreement for officers in the PNGDF to undertake training in China. I completed a policy paper to enlist generalist female soldiers in the PNGDF and was able to make a number of merit-based appointments for some especially talented officers. I recommended the appointment of Col. Tokam Kanene as director general of the National Intelligence Organisation. He was the officer who, as a young major, had shown the coolness and tactical ability to fight our forward tactical team out of trouble at Paruparu Village in 1994. I sent Maj. Michael Kumun, who as a captain had been so steady under fire in our fighting withdrawal from the raid on the radio station at Nulendi in 1993, to Singapore Staff College. And Major Pandum, who as a young captain had been battalion intelligence officer and acting operations officer when I joined 1RPIR in 1993 and who was such a help to me in setting up the support section troops at Loloho, was sent to the Defence Services Staff College at Wellington in the Nilgiris District of Tamil Nadu, India. Second Lieutenant Dalos Umul returned from Sandhurst, the first Papua New Guinean to graduate from the Royal Military Academy, Britain's most prestigious officer training college.

Finally, my own rank had been upgraded by the government from brigadier general to major general to signal an increase in my responsibilities in accordance with section 202 of the constitution. While there had been intense debate on the floor of Parliament, in the media, and among the legal profession and certain interest groups regarding my reappointment as commander, I had accepted the position as a loyal soldier. In doing so, I enabled others to find opportunities to build their own potential so that one day they, too, would make our community better.

I learnt the hard way that neither I nor any other single officer could save and transform the military. The success of any military force is based on loyalty and trust between the military arm and the political machinery of government. But this is a commodity that is difficult to sustain, especially in the face of political disarray, patronage, and extreme politicisation of the public service.

CHAPTER 19

Life beyond the Army

Ὦ ξεῖν', ἀγγέλλειν Λακεδαιμονίοις ὅτι τῇδε
κείμεθα, τοῖς κείνων ῥήμασι πειθόμενοι.
[Go tell the Spartans, thou that passeth by, that here,
obedient to their laws we lie.][12]

Moving on with Life

While waiting for my discharge from the army in 2000, Weni and
I accepted an invitation from her close relatives, the Tua tribe from
Tubuserea Village a few kilometres out of Port Moresby, to build
our house in their hamlet known as Mauru near Bautama. As it was
traditional land, I asked my cousin brother Paul Bereria, a private
surveyor by profession, to survey the site. After the survey, we registered
the land with the Department of Lands before we commenced building.

The setting and site selected for the house was exceptional. From
the hilltop, there was a panoramic view looking south over to Loloata
Island and beyond and to the west looking over Taurama Bay and the
barracks. To the east, we looked towards the Owen Stanley Ranges,

---

[12]   This inscription is engraved on the monument to the Spartans who fell at the
       Battle of Thermopylae, 480 BC. Ascribed by Herodotus to Simonides of Ceos.

including Variarata National Park. The sunsets were spectacular; they had a mystical feeling.

We settled happily at Mauru and rented out our town property. It was from the rental that we were able to service the mortgage with the bank. I also started a poultry farm and a vegetable garden in the gully as there was plenty of farming land. Most weekends, I would join family members fishing in the bay.

I needed to take time to consolidate before I could seek public office again. Under the leadership provisions in the constitution, there was a mandatory stand-down period of three years before I could seek further public office. In addition, I had to deal with the charge of sedition that had been adjourned sine die. Despite the hype by the outgoing commissioner for police, John Wakon, the police prosecution team were dragging their feet on this for reasons best known to them, but they were nevertheless determined to put me behind bars.

In April 2002, I was engaged as a security consultant by the Electoral Commission to make a risk assessment of the possibility of violence, including the use and movement of illegal guns, at the June general elections. The brief required me to travel throughout Papua New Guinea, concentrating mainly on the highlands region. I had just finished meeting with community leaders in Wabag, the capital of Enga Province, when I got a call from Reuben Kaiulo, the electoral commissioner. He sounded distressed. The Prime Minister's Office, presumably at the direction of Sir Mekere Morauta, had advised him to cancel my engagement on the grounds that I was a high-security risk and that I was there to support opposition members standing against the prime minister's People's Democratic Movement candidates.

Kaiulo was quite upset with this instruction. The allegations against me were obviously baseless. I had no involvement in political patronage or, at this point, political activities of any kind. I returned to Port Moresby and was given a copy of an intelligence brief that had been passed to the minister for defence and the prime minister. The brief contained serious allegations against me by members of the Special Operation Group who were deeply rooted in the Defence Intelligence Branch. Ignoring this further example of politicisation of the Papua New Guinea Defence Force, I completed my general threat assessment and passed it to the Elections Security Steering Committee, where it formed the basis for operational planning for all security forces engaged in the 2002 general elections.

In late 2003, my marriage with Weni got into difficulties, and we parted company in early 2004. Our children were suddenly faced with the most stressful period in their lives. I continued to provide my undivided commitment and love to them by supporting them as much as possible to complete their studies. Futua was studying at Waikato University, New Zealand, having completed high school at Wesley College, Auckland; Maib was at Gordons Secondary School; Moka was at Port Moresby International High School; and Alfred had returned to Madang to be with his mother. Weni was working for Sir Peter Barter, the regional member for Madang Province, who was serving in various capacities with the Somare government, mainly as provincial affairs minister and minister responsible for Bougainville.

Upon the insistence of my counsel, Moses Murray, the charges for sedition were finally brought before Justice Cathy Davani in early March 2004. The prosecutor, Senior Inspector Thomas Eluh, asked the judge to adjourn the case further. Moses Murray objected to the case being delayed yet again. Justice Davani, intervening from the bench, told Thomas Eluh they had had seven years to work on the case and gave him *one further hour* to complete the case for the prosecution. We returned to the court room after lunch, and Eluh informed the judge that they did not have a case. On 4 March, seven years after I was first charged, I was finally acquitted and walked out of the packed courtroom a free citizen. Whatever the findings of Justice Davani, as a soldier, I would have been fully ready to obey the court knowing 'that here obedient to their laws we lie'. A soldier has no other choice nor, indeed, does anybody else, from the governor-general to the lowest in the land.

Upon hearing the verdict, a Bougainville Revolutionary Army spokesman, David Sisisto, issued a media release thanking me for the stand I had taken against Sandline and the government of Sir Julius Chan. He said:

When the leaders started talking, the BRA found it easier to accept peace because they realised that even you as Commander PNGDF cared for them and their people. God will bless your wife and your children.

Bill Skate, the former prime minister and now speaker, released a press statement congratulating me on the acquittal:

It has been a long drawn out ordeal for Mr Singirok and his family, but justice has prevailed in the end. I have the greatest respect and admiration for Mr Singirok for contributing towards restoring peace and normal life on Bougainville. I wish him and his family full recovery from any stigma associated with the Sandline crisis of 1997.

Peter Donigi, one of my former lawyers, wrote this in the *Post-Courier*:

There is one thing people seem to forget—Jerry Singirok made a move no one else could have. He sacrificed his career for a greater good. He was also restrained enough to know when to stop so as to preserve the Constitution. At the end of the day, we all sat back and congratulated Papua New Guinean resilience and our inherited Melanesian values. We forget he was the man who did it all. He was the catalyst.

Congratulations, General Singirok!

J. K. Semos, PhD
Goroka, EHP.

Another supporter wrote:

Congratulations to General Jerry Singirok for allowing justice to run its course in the courts. The people of Papua New Guinea and especially of Bougainville would greatly acknowledge and celebrate your acquittal and freedom.

I salute you General Singirok and your team of lawyers. You and your trusted team of soldiers, who drove the Sandline out of PNG, will go down in history as cross-road martyrs and heroes of the Bougainville conflict and the subsequent peace and reconciliation processes and agreements.

Personal and public sacrifices for the national interest at the level you showed are rare and far between.

With God's guidance and wisdom, you are the reason why all my nephews, nieces and liklik bubus long ples Buka and Bougainville are back in school and happily playing around again.

Bravo General Singirok! Bravo PNG! Bravo Bougainville! Bravo PNG Judiciary!

When I was interviewed by the media at the courthouse, I said, 'I was the special weapon God used to put a stop to the killings and sufferings on Bougainville. I thank God for the wisdom, resilience, and the courage and strength to prevent a major catastrophe on Bougainville after nine years of civil war. Only God gets the glory. The past seven years have been tough for my family, but it was worth the fight.'

The Use of Illegal Guns and Security Implications for Papua New Guinea

Upon my exoneration by the court, I received an invitation from Dr Sinclair Dineen at the Research School of Pacific and Asia Studies, the Australian National University, Canberra, to come to the school as a visiting fellow. I took the opportunity and departed for Canberra on 1 July 2004 for six weeks. During my stay, I was assisted by Col. Philip Playah, who was just completing his time as defence attaché in Canberra. As a result of this stay, I published a discussion paper (no.

2005/5) titled 'The Use of Illegal Guns: Security Implications for Papua New Guinea'.

While in Canberra I was invited to participate in an Australian Aid–funded police assistance programme to support the PNG police. Police Minister Bire Kimisopa, the vibrant and intelligent member of Parliament for Goroka, invited me to chair a new gun control committee that he intended to establish to investigate and report to cabinet on the prevalence and use of illegal guns throughout PNG.

In late September, I was given the proposed terms of reference for the new committee. I established a gun control secretariat, and we went to work to assist the minister in seeking out nationwide views on the impact of illegal guns on civil society. Sir Barry Holloway was appointed deputy chairman. The committee comprised Oseah Philemon, Prof. Betty Lovai, former assistant police commissioner John Toguata, lawyer John Kawi, and Trevan Clough from the Brian Bell Group.

On 3 March 2005, a gun control campaign was launched with press statements from the prime minister, Grand Chief Sir Michael Somare, and the leader of the opposition, Peter O'Neill. Grand Chief Sir Michael Somare said:

> My government has acknowledged the seriousness of the impact of the use of illegal guns on innocent people and has taken the initiative to find ways to assist the government in addressing this issue and making realistic decisions on guns control. The breakdown in the law and order sector, the proliferation of violence now increasingly associated with guns, and the state institution's inability to exercise authority because of various excuses, are among the more obvious features of the current state of affairs in Papua New Guinea.

In response, Peter O'Neill said:

This is an issue for the whole community, not only
for the Government or the Opposition. If we are to
make a real impact on the problems created by the gun
culture in our society, then we must develop solutions
and strategies that transcend politics, and in which the
whole community can embrace and have confidence.
Crime in our society is perhaps our greatest problem.
Believe it or not, it has gone from being a major problem
in urban areas to an even greater problem in our rural
communities.

Given everything I had experienced on Bougainville, I accepted
with alacrity the appointment of advocating for a peaceful community.
We toured the country to investigate and consult before reporting our
findings to the prime minister.

It took our committee five months to complete the community
consultation, culminating in a gun summit at the University of Goroka
campus in Eastern Highlands from 4 to 8 July. In September 2005, we
gave Grand Chief Sir Michael Somare a total of 244 recommendations
relating to the issue of illegal guns in the community. As I write this
book, successive governments have ignored the people's cry in relation
to the proliferation and use of illegal guns throughout PNG. In the
highlands and the metropolitan cities, guns have become an accepted
way of life and a menace to society.

No government has had the courage to take the gun culture
seriously. Illegal guns are the single most dangerous weapon in society.
Port Moresby is regarded as the hijack capital of the South Pacific.
The police report that most incidences of carjacking involve the use
of illegal guns.

The gun culture in PNG is escalating unabated and has brought
the economy in many parts of the country to its knees. The highlands
region is particularly problematic. There, the use of illegal guns has
become a symbol of tribal power, replacing the bows and arrows that
were a traditional feature of tribal warfare. In other parts of the country,
illegal guns are used daily by thugs and criminals.

Of course, it will be wrong to say that nothing has been done about the proliferation of illicit guns in PNG. Rather, the picture is one of sporadic action, followed by prolonged periods of inactivity. For example, after a PNGDF stocktake of weapons and ammunition in 2002, Australian Defence Force staff assisted the PNGDF with the destruction of surplus small arms and ammunition. The weapons were cut into pieces using Gas Axe and were sealed into 200-litre drums of wet concrete. That dealt with that problem. Soon afterwards, the Australian Defence Cooperation Program funded the construction of modern, state-of-the-art armouries at each of the main bases of the PNGDF. This helped tighten up the control of weapons and ammunition belonging to the defence force.

In 1994–96, the Royal Papua New Guinea Constabulary had initiated a programme designed to assure greater accountability over the ownership of guns. After an extensive nationwide search, a total of 4,300 illegal firearms were seized and then destroyed by dumping them at sea at a sufficient depth to make retrieval impossible. Despite these efforts and a subsequent AusAID-funded programme to establish a central firearms registry and system of photographic firearm licences, large numbers of illicit guns remain in circulation, including several hundred stolen police firearms, machine guns, automatic assault rifles, pistols, and shotguns, along with thousands of rounds of ammunition.

The 2017 national election was the most violent in the history of PNG. Over thirty people were killed as a result of gun violence, and numerous houses and businesses were burnt. Southern Highlands, Hela, and Enga remain the most dangerous of the highlands provinces as neither the politicians nor the security forces seem to know how to approach the question of getting rid of the illegal guns held by tribal warriors and warlords. The situation will not improve unless this or some future government chooses to make gun control a real priority. Until then, PNG will continue to grow more and more like the *Gunfight at the O.K. Corral*. It will become like Tombstone, Arizona, and the Wild West on steroids. How much razor wire will it take before we agree that we need to sort this problem out once and for all?

Professional Consultancy Services

In 2001, I registered a consulting company, Premium Concepts Ltd, which specialised in security analysis and risk management. When needed, I brought in other professionals to assist me. Among other jobs, the company was engaged to review PNG ports, formerly the PNG Harbours Board, under Chairman Job Suat. This review involved a professional survey of aspects of compliance and the International Ships and Ports Security Code. I completed a major security consultancy with PNG Customs, which involved the rewriting of more than thirty of their standard operating procedures and a comprehensive analysis of the security structures of state enterprises. I also investigated a robbery of the Metals Refining Operations by PNG's most infamous bank robber, William Kapris, and his accomplices. Kapris was jailed in May 2011 for thirty years but was killed in a shoot-out involving police in July 2013 after escaping from Bomana Prison by 'walking out of the front gate'.

In 2004, I began living with Vasity Abau. She bore Paul Gevas, our first son, and Tyla, our only daughter. Vasity was a senior bank officer with Westpac Bank, working in the Bills and Overseas Department. She took long service leave in November 2005 as she had been with the bank for eighteen years. In April 2006, she resigned from the bank to support the small enterprise that I had set up and, at the same time, began a diploma in business accounting. Vasity's newly acquired skills along with many years of experience in the banking sector have been useful as we work to sustain ourselves was a bonus for us.

Commission of Enquiry into the Department of Finance

On 29 June 2009, I received a letter from Steven Kassman (now Justice Kassman), counsel assisting the commission of enquiry into the Department of Finance in respect of illegal and corrupt payments and out-of-court settlements. The issue they wanted me to assist with concerned a claim by Network International Security Services (WS125 of 1997). They asked me to appear at the commission of enquiry hearing room located on the top floor of the Government Printing Office on Kumul Avenue, Waigani, on 7 July at 0900 hours.

The enquiry was investigating a deed of release for PGK 3 million paid by the state to Network International Security Services as the result of a defamation action or threat of action. Defamation by whom? Me? It couldn't be me as I would have been involved in the action at the time if I was the instigator. I was interested as this was the first time it had been reported that Network International, the company owned by Sir Julius's children, had been allegedly paid PGK 3 million for defamation.

I arrived early, and as I looked around the car park, I saw a group of very serious-looking men with dark glasses loitering with menace. Byron Chan spotted me and waved as I made my way up to the enquiry room. After my introduction, I was told that the relevant file was missing along with other files on matters the enquiry was investigating. I was advised that, as soon as the files were located, I would be recalled.

As I stepped out of the building, I reflected on the action for defamation Sir Julius had filed against me. He had demanded PGK 1 million in damages. I had published an apology as the price of getting him to drop his suit. And now it appeared that Network International had obtained from the state and the people of PNG a cool PGK 3 million for allegations of defamation against the company's name. Why should the taxpayers required to pay for this extraordinary bill? On the face of it, this had the appearance of corrupt behaviour, but by whom was not clear.

I got a call the next day from the finance enquiry secretariat advising me not to return to the enquiry as the file relating to Network International had gone missing under mysterious circumstances. So the facts, wherever they led, were now hidden by the loss of stolen file. I got no other calls from the commission of enquiry, so I assume the matter was dropped. I was incensed at how a security company could be awarded PGK 3 million for doing nothing. It was daylight robbery. Yet this trend continues.

The commission uncovered many instances of illegal, incorrect, or improperly documented payouts and out-of-court settlements by the Department of Finance against bogus and unsupported claims. The commission reported its findings on 29 October 2009. I do not know what action, if any, was taken by government to implement the many recommendations of the enquiry, including the issue of criminal proceedings and disciplinary action against many named officials, lawyers, and private sector individuals suspected of defrauding the state. My friend Peter Yama was one such accused, and like many others caught up in the enquiry, he has not been given the opportunity of clearing his name.

Haus Karkar, 2010

Around this time, Vasity and I decided to build a homestead at her mother's place near Matairuka Village in the Rigo District of Central Province. I needed space and wanted to go back to farming, which is in the blood of Karkar Islanders. We flew in my relatives from Karkar Island: my nephew Bara Mai, an experienced Lutheran mission–trained carpenter, and Charles Singirok, an experienced timber miller. There was plenty of hardwood all around the new site. We moved all our logistics onto the site of the new house away from the main village. After setting up our base camp, we lumbered local hardwood timber with assistance from Vasity's relatives. We spent most of 2010 building our homestead. By end of 2010, we had completed the house, which sits on top of a ridge overlooking the valley and beyond. We called our new homestead Haus Karkar, in memory of the Karkar Islanders who spent nearly two years with us building the house and cultivating the unused land for farming.

Farming

Toiling on the land and farming are some of the skills and strengths I gained from my upbringing among the village gardeners and owners of coconut and cocoa plantations on Karkar. The same skills and strengths were instilled in me at Asaroka Lutheran High School. At Aran farm at Matairuka, we planted bananas and vegetables of different varieties. We also raised chickens and ducks.

I was introduced to a tree called the tree of life, moringa, a health-giving plant that has a very wide array of health benefits. Originating in India and Africa, its botanical name is *Moringa oleifera*. It is named after the Tamil word for 'drumstick', *murungai*, and is said to have 125 medically proven health-giving properties. Vasity bought four small moringa trees as pot plants in 2015, and today we have propagated and planted, which continues to provide us food nutrients and supplements. Envisaging their commercial potential, we continue to look after our moringa plantation very carefully.

Jeredin Wilfred Singirok

In January 2010, I went to Singapore on a business trip. On my return to Port Moresby, Vasity was at the airport to pick me up. I sensed that she was anxious to tell me something. I waited. She said, 'You will not believe it, but I am pregnant.' She was 45 years old, which is past childbearing age for most women in PNG.

On 26 October, she was admitted to Pacific International Hospital with high blood pressure and labour complications. I was at her bedside along with her sisters, Alise, Monica, and Cheryl, when she was wheeled into the operating room by Dr Mathias Sapuri for a caesarean operation. At 0900 hours, Jeredin Wilfred was delivered. He was tiny, weighing only 1.8 kg. Along with Sr Tamate Alu, we rushed Jeredin to Port Moresby General Hospital, where he was placed in an incubator. He would be in special care in the nursery for the next six weeks.

After about six weeks, we noticed that Jeredin was not responding to noise, and we realised that his hearing was impaired. Regardless, we gave all we had to raise him until we could afford to find specialist care for his hearing difficulties. Currently, he resists wearing a hearing aid, but we continue to take him to the ear doctor. Apart from raising our own three children—Paul, Tyla, and Jeredin—we also adopted Diane, who was just 10 years old from my nephew back on Karkar Island.

We treat Diane exactly like one of our own, and we will give her every opportunity to excel in life.

Conversion to the Seventh-Day Adventist Church

I experienced a spiritual turning point in 2012. It came after attending a two-week evangelical meeting led by international Seventh-Day Adventist preacher John Carter. Vasity and I decided to be baptised, and this was done on 19 April 2013. Today we are both elders and support community services at our local Faole Memorial SDA Church.

I took on a personal ministry in the church and felt that life could not have been better. I got involved in a programme to replace pit toilets in settlement churches with modern septic toilets, running water, and showers as a way to encourage healthy living and good hygiene. I found it very satisfying and fulfilling to be able to use my practical skills to serve the Lord.

These days, I use my free time to support church outreach meetings and to assist our local evangelist preacher, Pastor Karl Jack. His tribal affiliations go back to the Taburi clan in Koiari District, one of the first districts to receive missionaries from the SDA church in the very early years of last century.

Commissioning of Singirok Barracks, Engineer Battalion Forward Operation Base, Jiwaka Province

Early in August 2015, I received a very pleasant and welcome surprise. I was contacted by the staff of Cdr Brig. Gen. Gilbert Toropo's office to inform me of an official invitation from the defence council and minister for defence to accompany them to Kerowil in Jiwaka Province for the official opening of the Engineer Battalion Forward Operation Base. It was to be named Singirok Barracks.

I was humbled by this gesture and accompanied Brigadier General (now Major General) Toropo and his party of senior officers on Wednesday, 19 August, to Mount Hagen for the commissioning of the barracks the following day. The Engineer Base was the result of an initiative that I had taken in 1999. I had worked with highlands regional governors to establish a forward engineering base to assist in civic action and emergency tasks.

Politics 2007, 2012, and 2017

As I was now cleared to run for public office, after consulting with my family and my supporters, I arranged for a nomination to contest the Sumkar Open seat, Madang Province, under Pangu Pati endorsement in 2007 and 2012. The seat includes Karkar Island, my birthplace. While I worked hard in both campaigns, I lost to Australian businessman Kenneth Fairweather, a local resident.

I ran again in 2017, this time in the Madang Regional seat. I was nominated with the support and under the banner of Pangu Pati. Pangu Pati is PNG's oldest political party. Its campaign slogan is 'Pangu Pati save long rot', which is pidgin for 'Pangu Pati knows the road.' The longer Pangu Pati slogan is 'Givim gavman bek long ol pipol na strongim Ward na LLG [local-level government]'. This translates roughly as 'Give government back to the people.' My individual campaign was built around a promise to work for the people to make Madang a 'safe, secure, beautiful and prosperous place'. My emphasis during the campaign was on law and order, security, youth development, quality education, health, agriculture, business, and roads.

My campaign was vigorous and well-received, but on the initial count, I was placed third after Peter Yama and James Yali. The losing candidates disputed the manner in which the final elimination was being conducted by the counting officials and asked me to lead them to the counting venue at Holy Spirit Catholic Church Hall, Madang, at about six thirty in the morning to protest.

When Peter Yama saw us at the counting venue, he confronted me and began to argue. He then assaulted me. He even threatened Vasity, who was in our support vehicle. His supporters broke the window and side glass of the support vehicle and, at the same time, assaulted James Yali. Yama told me to take him to court if I wasn't happy, so that was what I did. I'm not a gangster or a street fighter; my integrity is important to me. It was amazing to see how desperate Yama was to re-enter politics. I told him that I would dispute his purported election win, and I did.

My counsel, Brendan Lai, the son of my very close army colleague Lt Col. Ignatius Lai, was instructed to commence legal proceedings against Peter Yama and the Electoral Commission. My election petition case was heard by Justice Terence Higgins, judge of the National and Supreme Court of PNG and a former chief justice of the Supreme Court of Australia. On 1 March 2018, Justice Higgins ruled in my favour and ordered that the Madang Regional seat be recounted on the basis that James Yali, a convicted rapist and prison parolee, was not eligible under the Constitution of the Independent State of New Papua Guinea and Electoral Law to nominate.

The constitutional provision we relied on was section 103, subsection 3(e), which prohibits any person who has been convicted for over nine months or more to stand for public office. The final election result had inevitably been affected by being split three ways rather than two. As a consequence, Peter Yama was no longer eligible to remain governor for Madang. Yama applied for leave to review Justice Higgins's ruling; this was granted by former CJ Sir Salamo Injia. In June 2020, Yama's review application went before the full Supreme Court, headed by CJ Sir Gibs Salika, Justice David Cannings, Elinas Batari, Penuel Mogish, and Thomas Anis. The court ruled in Yama's favour. Only Justice Thomas upheld Justice Higgins's ruling.

On my instruction, my counsel filed a slip rule application to challenge the verdict on the basis that neither I nor any other candidate nominating for the Madang Regional seat had the authority or jurisdiction to prevent a candidate with a conviction from nominating. The slip rule application was heard by Justice Canning, who dismissed it, citing abuse of process. The final verdict by the Supreme Court set a new precedent. By allowing Yama to remain in office as governor, it shifted the onus to candidates to prevent convicted felons from nominating. To this date, I am perplexed about how the court reached this decision. All I can say is that sometimes justice can be spiteful.

Passing of Grand Chief Sir Michael Thomas Somare (1936–2021)

Great Grand Chief Sir Michael Thomas Somare was known as the father of the nation. He was born on 9 April 1936 and passed away on 26 February 2021. He was PNG's first prime minister in 1975–80 and then again in 1982–85 and 2002–11.

Many of us had joined Somare's journey and followed his political career at various points in our respective lives. As the nation mourned his passing, many of us reflected on the highs and lows of his political career and the experiences that we, as a young nation, had endured.

Somare's political career came to an abrupt end in 2011, when he was unceremoniously removed from office while on medical leave in Singapore. Even after the Supreme Court ruled that Somare had been unlawfully removed as prime minister, the new government headed by Peter O'Neill continued to rule unabated.

A state funeral was held for Somare at Sir John Guise Stadium on Friday, 12 March 2021. During the funeral, Somare's youngest daughter, Dulciana Somare-Brash, delivered a powerful eulogy before a capacity crowd that included PM James Marape, senior ministers, dignitaries, and members of the diplomatic corps. Dulciana spoke with vigour and passion as she described how her late father had been removed from Parliament as a villain. She said, 'The Sana spirit of peace and the dream to build a strong democratic society based on equality, justice, respect, well-being, and prosperity of our people must live on. This is the opportune time to take stock of our life as a nation as leaders and as a diverse people unified and PNGnised by the Sana purpose. For the last ten years, when my father was confronted with the most public opposition he had ever faced in his entire political life, he handled it with the grace and patience as a saint.'

Duliana said that her father was unlawfully removed as the legitimate prime minister but that he did not care about revenge or retaliation. 'He exercised incredible caution despite his frail state after he returned from Singapore after his surgery. He feared that any bad decisions on his path would have such lasting and adverse effect on the nation that he merely accepted his fate, and he never defended himself beyond that certain point. My father upheld parliamentary and constitutional democracy over himself enough to contest another election in 2012 before his retirement in 2017 on his own terms.'

She continued, 'Many have asked why? The answer is that the true essence of the Westminster system of democracy was his guiding light from before independence and well after he achieved much of his dreams for us, his people. He allowed his journey to be broken so we would continue ours. In retrospect, I consider my father's deepest love was for his country. I strongly believe now that he believed that knowing when to stop conflict is not defeat. It was his leadership.'

In closing the curtains on Grand Chief Sir Michael Somare's life and selfless service to PNG, Dulciana summed up the manner in which the country was run from time to time. Her words stand as a stark reminder for the next generation if the country intends to make positive progress in the interest of all.

Where to Now?

What have we learnt from the story of my early life, military career, and encounters in the higher echelons of PNG? Where do we need to go next as a society? Here, I will offer some personal reflections based on the experiences described in this book.

Emperor Hirohito's acceptance in a radio broadcast on 15 August 1945 of Allied demands for the unconditional surrender of Japan, seven days after the bombing of Nagasaki and nine days after Hiroshima, in which he said, 'The war situation has not necessarily developed to Japan's advantage', marked the end of WWII. I was born in 1956, ten years after the devastation in Japan, when Papua was still a possession of the Crown under the authority of Australia, and New Guinea was administered by Australia under a trusteeship agreement with the United Nations 'pending its progressive development towards self-government or independence in accordance with the wishes of the peoples concerned'.

As citizens of Australia (if living in the Crown territory of Papua) or as inhabitants of the Australian-administered trusteeship of New Guinea, we were free to roam our shores, explore the virgin forests, swim for hours in pristine streams and rivers, breathe clean air, and spend night after night counting thousands of stars in the Milky Way. We all had our own space to roam. The world was truly ours. Natural resources were in abundance, and we were blessed in a land of plenty.

Many of us chased our dreams. But that was more than fifty years ago. As I write these pages in mid-2021, we have enjoyed forty-five years of self-government since gaining independence from Australia in 1975. We are now at the crossroads. It is time to take stock of what we have achieved as a nation, and what we need to change if we are to leave a legacy that we can be proud of for the next generation to enjoy. My generation were the founding fathers of PNG. Can we be proud of what we have achieved? I say yes but only in part. Could we have done more? Yes, absolutely. Can we do more looking ahead? That is the question.

Two things mark a happy island nation. First, the ordinary people need to be able to enjoy the fruits of their labour free from oppression and want. They need to be able to generate wealth in their own small world—a world that is made safe and secure from criminal behaviour and free from excessive taxation or unjust laws, a world in which the government meets basic health, welfare, and educational needs and provides security for its citizens.

Second, we need to insist on a caring and transparent government that translates opportunities for all by ensuring that the laws are fair and observed by all. Corruption in government must be totally stamped out. This will ensure confidence in the public sector, which in turn will encourage foreign investment and stimulate the market economy in an open and transparent way.

The question that needs to be asked is this: Can we say that any recent PNG government, at either central or local level, has met these two most basic tests of a well-governed society? Or is the record mixed? Or is it, in some important respects, a national disgrace? Many decisions made at the national government level since PNG's independence have been questionable. The one that stands out for me—because it blighted my ability as a soldier and military commander on Bougainville to find a peaceful way forward—is the decision to militarily intervene in Bougainville in 1989. I wholeheartedly believe that we failed the people of Bougainville big time from the start as we literally destroyed a province and a community, negatively affecting thousands of families. In so doing, we ruined our economy.

As a nation, we have barely progressed in fulfilling the dreams and aspirations of our people. The social indicators are appalling, and the future looks bleak. Middle- and low-income workers are poorly paid, and poverty is rampant. They have limited access to good healthcare, the education system is stagnating, and basics such as clean running water and proper sanitation are lacking. Unemployment is high, housing is scarce, and security against crime is worsening and, in some areas, non-existent.

Why should this be? We have plenty of labour and plenty of land. We are not overpopulated. The soil is good. We have an abundance of natural resources, vast areas of untapped agricultural land, and virgin forests. Yet the national economy is barely breaking even. Successive governments have turned us into a country with high taxes due to massive foreign loans, a country that relies on charity and handouts and partnering with unscrupulous foreigners. Violence is endemic throughout the county, and with state agencies underfunded and stressed, hope of intervention is little more than an incredible proposition.

Politics has become a race towards personal enrichment. Anyone doubting this need only look at any number of official enquiries into aspects of government in Port Moresby. A good place to start is the commission of enquiry into the Department of Finance published in October 2009 in which criminal proceedings and disciplinary actions were recommended against many named officials, lawyers, and private sector individuals suspected of defrauding the state. What happened as a result of this enquiry? Nothing. One of the named parties filed an injunction to halt consideration of the recommendations pending a judicial review, and there the matter rests, a full nine years later.

Defrauding the state should not be thought of as a white-collar crime that doesn't affect individual citizens. Nothing could be farther from the truth. When the state is defrauded, so are individual taxpayers and citizens. When the state is defrauded, there is less money to spend on the basic services that are in such short supply in PNG. It is the hard-pressed individual citizen who misses out.

Fraud, corruption, and waste eat away at our society. The decision by government to import forty Maserati Quattroporte luxury cars by airfreight from Italy for use by APEC leaders at a cost per car of around AUD 210,000 is just the most flagrant and recent example of government waste. A Lowry Institute director called the decision 'tin-eared', which is the kindest possible dismissal of an extraordinary piece of misjudgement in the management of what had been described, erroneously as it turned out, as a Pacific-style APEC summit. Can you imagine a Maserati saloon lasting very long on a typical stretch of PNG road? Stupidity writ large.

This leads to my second question. Where do we need to go next as a society? If we want to lift the quality of our government, we need to find better candidates to stand for election—candidates who will put their electorates' needs before their own; candidates for whom service is a core value and personal ethic; candidates who will not tolerate corruption, who will be honest and transparent, and who will work tirelessly for a better PNG; candidates who know the needs of their electorates; candidates who have tilled the land, taught in schools, worked in hospitals, struggled to raise families, been active in communities and who know what it is like to be poor, to struggle, and to work long hours; and candidates who are also aspirational, who want to create a better life—not just for themselves but also for their children and the PNG people at large.

There are plenty of good men and women out there who meet this prescription. I see them in my church. I saw them in the military. I see them on Karkar Island and in Madang Province, and I see them nationwide.

It is not an accident that the 1999 PNGDF White Paper that I submitted to the defence council was subtitled 'Service to Others'. Service is the key ethic, not personal enrichment or power.

The need for political candidates to come forward for election with a strong service ethic is the first biggest lesson to be drawn at both national and local government levels. Second is the need for more consistency of approach and a longer-term view in dealing with the intractable problems that plague all developing countries but particularly PNG. PNG shows all the indicators of a failed nation—high levels of corruption, ethnic alienation, failing health and education services, widespread poverty, and gun violence and propagating gun culture. Further, if we continue to condone the criminal behaviour by corrupt officials and by some elements of the police force, PNG could find itself becoming a police state. These are the real social and security issues that raise a number of red flags that we must not ignore and that we, as a nation, are confronted with. We have to take ownership and do something, like now.

Karkar Island, 2021

Putting all the weight of the nation aside, I arrived on Karkar Island in September 2021 knowing too well that my elder brother, Willie, lay in a grave not far from my parents' tomb and that my late sister Dig is also laid next to her husband's graveyard. Vasity, Jeredin, and I arrived mid-afternoon at a stretch of black sandy beach at Dumad Village, where I had started my journey many years earlier. Our relatives offered us fresh coconut juice, and we sat on the black sand, telling stories from our past along with few jokes. As we looked across the straits to the mainland some twenty nautical miles to the west, we tried to spot places we thought we knew over a misty horizon growing dim in the fading light—pretty much what our own future looks like.

The world seemed so far away—and was getting farther away, drifting at a fast pace. The sudden arrival of gale force winds signalled a possible storm coming our way. We said goodbye to our relatives and walked slowly up the vehicle track to our village of Did, about 5 km inland.

As we neared the village, the memories of my family's love and the absence of my parents, Willie, and Dig filled my empty spirit. I missed them so much as I reflected on what their own dreams may have been like. My parents' unadorned tomb lay close to our house. As I looked at it, I realised that theirs was most likely a very simple dream. They wished for us to have the chance to be educated, to excel in our lives, and to become worthwhile members of the community.

As we approached our nicely kept lawn, the dogs raced towards us to welcome us home. Darkness had suddenly fallen, and we settled down for the evening routine. A single solar light bulb hung centrally to break up the darkness in the main upstairs room, casting shadows into the far corners.

Memories rushed in. It felt like only yesterday—not fifty years ago—that I had decided to follow my own dreams, choosing the army over studying law. I have no idea what the future will hold for my family and me. Only my Lord knows. And he is not saying. All that I know with any certainty is that, like the Spartans at Thermopylae, I fought to my last breath for what was right. And in the end, like them, obedient to their laws, I will lie.

EPILOGUE AND
ACKNOWLEDGEMENTS

This is our story and theirs. For we were soldiers once, and young.
Lt Gen. Harold G. Moore and Joseph L. Galloway,
1992[13]

I could not have put these memoirs together without the encouragement of the tightly knit small team of professional soldiers who assisted me in the execution of Operation Rausim Kwik. They urged me to write a book to tell not only our story but also that of my own career as a soldier.

This story is for our children and the new generation of soldiers and Papua New Guineans. My hope is that it may contribute to a searching re-examination of the way we approach politics in Papua New Guinea, as well as a better understanding of the events that surrounded the Sandline crisis.

I pay tribute to the key members of Operation Rausim Kwik, whom I hand-picked based on their merit and exceptional professionalism. I trusted their instinct and abilities and knew that, together, we would execute the operation successfully despite all the obstacles that would be put in our way.

This book owes much to late Dr Lance Beath, a long-time personal friend and colleague who gave me valuable professional assistance.

---

13 *We Were Soldiers Once . . . and Young.*

He was a senior fellow at the Centre for Strategic Studies, Victoria University of Wellington. Lance had a long history of involvement in PNG. He assisted the defence council and me with the writing of the 1999 Defence White Paper, 'Service to Others'. Lance passed away on 21 August 2021.

No book of this kind can be written without the prior research and efforts of others. I acknowledge the lifetime of study and work that our friend and colleague Sean Dorney has brought to his writing on PNG and the Pacific. When in doubt about the sequence of events, the names of people, or the correct interpretation to place on specific issues, we often found ourselves turning to Sean Dorney as our authority. His 1998 book *The Sandline Affair* (ABC Books) retains its reputation as a well-deserved classic of contemporary reporting and analysis.

This book could not have been written without the financial support provided by Stuart Bruce, managing director of Combat Clothing of Australia. Believing that this was an important story that deserved to be told, Stuart made a personal commitment to fund the editing of the book. I am very grateful to Stuart for his generous financial support and encouragement.

Other friends who have provided important support include Lt Col. (Retd) Mac Grace of the New Zealand Army, who taught alongside me at the defence academy in Lae and whose friendship over the years has been an important source of succour and support. Many other friends in the Australian and New Zealand Armies assisted me in various ways, helping with my legal expenses and providing encouragement in my long and ultimately successful defence against the charge of sedition brought by the government of Sir Julius Chan.

The chief of operations for Operation Rausim Kwik was Maj. Walter Enuma. Without his commitment, determination, and extraordinarily tough professionalism, Operation Rausim Kwik would have failed. Walter earned his nickname 'the Walker' early in his days in Bougainville. He was named after the Ghost Who Walks and the Man Who Cannot Die in the *Phantom* comics of Lee Falk. Walter would appear silently and unexpectedly, making his presence felt deep on jungle patrols throughout the Bougainville theatre of operations. He attended Command and Staff College in New Zealand and, after his promotion to colonel, the Department of War Studies, Kings College, London. He last commanded Reserve Force before electing to retire.

Maj. Gilbert Toropo was an important source of support to me in my two tours as commander of Papua New Guinea Defence Force. Gilbert is a quiet, very tough, very determined, and extremely professional soldier from the highlands. He was the first PNGDF officer to successfully complete US Army Ranger training at Fort Benning, Georgia. I appointed him as officer commanding of Special Forces Unit in 1995. He was later appointed as commanding officer of 1RPIR and is now a major general and the chief of PNGDF, completing his second term in office. I am proud of his achievements.

Cdr Alois Tom Ur joined the defence force with me in 1975 after completing Sogeri Senior High School. As the director of maritime operations during the Sandline crisis, he ensured that naval assets were available to detain Tim Spicer and secure him safely at sea and in complete isolation from the rest of his Sandline command team. Tom was promoted to the rank of captain (navy). He was a scholar and served loyally as chief of staff for three consecutive commanders before retiring from the defence force, after which he ran a very successful real estate company. Regrettably, he passed away on 27 February 2021.

Capt. Charlie Andrews joined the PNGDF in 1982 under my command and became a fixed-wing pilot before converting to rotary wing. He flew the Bell UH-1 Iroquois (Huey) and its civilian variant, the Bell 205, in Bougainville on endless missions. Later, during Operation Rausim Kwik, he flew observation and contingency missions over Parliament House on the day that Sir Julius stood aside as prime minister. In 2001, he graduated from West Sydney University with a degree in aviation management before being promoted to lieutenant colonel and appointed as director of air operations. He is one of the best and safest rotary-wing pilots the defence force has ever produced.

Cpl Alan Nangoromo, nicknamed 'the Terminator' in the press, was in charge of gate security at Murray Barracks during Operation Rausim Kwik. Wearing a non-regulation pink T-shirt, camouflage trousers, dark glasses, and pistol, which he waved around to reinforce his message, he provided one of the more flamboyant and enduring images of the operation. His manning of the main gate to the barracks and his commanding physical presence contributed much to the success of the operation. Alan is now company sergeant major of the Port Moresby Supply Company.

Sgt Francis Jakis was an inspired pick who turned out to be a top soldier deeply skilled and thoroughly at home in jungle warfare operations. He was the platoon sergeant with Special Forces Unit when he trained alongside Sandline at Urimo Training Camp and was instrumental in rounding up the African mercenaries before their expulsion. He was later recruited by the Australian Defence Force with my full support. He is now on active service with the ADF as an instructor at the Jungle Training Wing of the Combat Training Centre in Tully, Queensland. He has participated in Australian Army training exercises in Indonesia, Malaysia, and Brunei and is undoubtedly one of the most experienced jungle warfare instructors anywhere in the region.

Those who were discharged from the PNGDF include WO Chris Kalik Mora, who is now staff officer with the Department for Information and Communication. Sgt John Koraia, who was my personal bodyguard from the Military Police Unit and who always wore his maroon UK para beret with quiet pride, is now a security manager with the Brian Bell Group.

Maj. Francis Agwi was promoted to lieutenant colonel and posted as commanding officer of the Goldie River Training Depot. He was later promoted to the rank of colonel and appointed chief of intelligence before being promoted brigadier general and commander of the PNGDF. He was last completing his term as PNG high commissioner to New Zealand. Francis has been a close friend and comrade of mine for many years.

Capt. Otto Pandum rose to the rank of colonel and was posted as defence attaché to Indonesia before being nominated to take over as director general of the National Intelligence Organisation. Regrettably, Otto passed on 8 April 2021. Capt. Michael Kumun rose to the rank of lieutenant colonel and had recently returned to Port Moresby after a posting in New Zealand. He too passed on in September 2021.

My loyal friend and fellow officer Maj. Tokam Jethro Kanene rose to the rank of colonel and was appointed director general of the National Intelligence Organisation. Later, he was appointed military attaché in Jakarta. Capt. Bola Renagi is a highly respected security manager in the commercial security business in Port Moresby.

Capt. Belden Namah, a Duntroon Military College graduate, is now the Honourable Belden Norman Namah and doing his third term as a member of Parliament for Vanimo Green Open. He was deputy prime minister and acting prime minister in 2012 and was involved in an abortive attempt to arrest CJ Sir Salamo Injia. This resulted in a set of findings by the leadership tribunal, including a recommendation for his dismissal from public office; however, he won his case on appeal and remains the opposition leader and member for Vanimo Green.

Belden Namah was a truly unorthodox but highly effective soldier. Unconventional in his thinking and ways, he earned the nickname Skull. He may still hold the long-distance, high-altitude record for a Bell 212 helicopter evacuation by hanging on to the skids with his bare hands while dangling mid-air. He will undoubtedly be remembered, though not necessarily with much affection, by Tim Spicer, who came off the worse for wear when he was forcibly arrested and restrained in my office by Belden in the opening stages of Operation Rausim Kwik.

Collectively, the operational team behind Rausim Kwik were solid, reliable, trustworthy, and effective. They were the best. They were a team that any commander would be proud to have by his side in times of trouble.

I am privileged to have mentored many junior and middle-ranking officers and ordinary soldiers in both regiments and at the defence academy, a number of whom have progressed to the middle and higher ranks of the defence force. Many have since been discharged and have become active and valuable members of their communities. The soldiers whom I served with were some of the finest that I have known. It was indeed an honour to serve in an institution that brought good men and women together.

I must mention the defence force pilots, both fixed and rotary wing, who undertook daring missions to support our land operations.

They were 'bush pilots' in the best sense of the term, flying in and over terrain that was very unforgiving of mistakes. Most of them exited the defence force and were highly sourced by both domestic and international airlines. I must thank, too, the sailors who manned our ships and patrol crafts, providing maritime surveillance and patrol, resource protection, interdiction, and heavy transport requirements.

I owe much of my professional development to the ADF. I was coached, groomed, mentored, and trained by some of the best military officers and trainers in the world. Among the many who taught me, I must single out some truly outstanding officers who provided me with excellent role models and mentoring—but on whose shoulders none of my subsequent errors of judgement should be blamed. The list begins with Col. Terry O'Neil and Maj. Ross Eastgate, both of whom spent many hours at the Land Warfare Centre mentoring me and who have remained good friends and close supporters over the years. I am eternally grateful for the constant interest and encouragement that they offered me.

Among my instructors and mentors, I should mention Lt Col. Des Mealey; RSM Darcy Tilbrook; Maj. Phil Joyce; Lt Col. John Dwyer; Lt Col. Peter Cosgrove (as he then was); Brig. Gen. Jim Townley; Col. Ernie Chamberlain; Lieutenant Colonels Richard Howell, David Smith, and John Paget; Lt Col. John Petrie; and Maj. Mike Hindmarsh, now major general commanding the UAE Presidential Guard.

And from the New Zealand Defence Force, I would mention Col. Graeme Williams, Lt Col. Mac Grace, and Lt Col. Gordon Milward, all of whom were wonderful friends and colleagues, as were Col. Richard Taylor and Wg Cdr Athol Forrest.

The opportunity to prove my worth by serving in the ADF enabled me to withstand the pressures of command at all levels. I was also fortunate to train with US forces in Hawaii (Twenty-Fifth Infantry Division, 'Tropic Lightning') and with the Special Operations Command Group at Fort Lewis and Huckleberry Creek in Washington State.

In speaking of the ADF, I would like to highlight the value gained through developing personal contacts at senior levels between our forces. When I was chief of defence intelligence, I got to know Gen. John Baker, then vice chief of the ADF. He had previously been the inaugural director of defence intelligence. John's first regimental appointment had been in PNG, and his continuing interest in PNG affairs enabled us to form a close personal working relationship. When the Sandline crisis blew up, I was able to phone John, who was then chief of the ADF, and provide him with assurances and briefings on what was going on in Port Moresby. I am sure these briefings were instrumental in preventing the crisis from boiling over further. Should it have proved necessary, I think I might have been able to arrange, through John, to have the Russian and Sandline arms shipments intercepted by the RAAF in mid-air and diverted to Australia. This would have been a big call, and I don't know whether John and the Australian government would have gone that far, but at least I had the necessary contacts in Australia to try.

Special mention should also be made of the highly respected role that New Zealand played in the peace efforts in Bougainville. The New Zealand government provided troops, aircraft, and naval vessels, the last as neutral venues for peace talks, and helped win the confidence of the Bougainville Revolutionary Army in hostage negotiations.

Within the PNGDF, I was fortunate in having a small group of supporters, role models, and mentors who helped me with advice and guidance at key moments in my career. I am thinking of Col. Lima Dotaona, Herman Komeng, Parry Iruru, Andrew Trongat, Ignitius Lai, Davey Ugul, Joseph Fabila, and Philip Playah. In addition, there were many others who helped establish the professional standards that we all aspire to in the PNGDF.

I must pay homage to those who assisted me in dealing with the challenges that form the basis of my story. Three people stand out. The late Sir Barry Holloway was my mentor, my closest friend, and a brutally frank adviser. At times, I am sure he thought that I had taken leave of my senses. Perhaps I had. But he was my rock.

The late ambassador Peter Donigi—my tribesman from West Coast, Dagua, and the Aropes in East Sepik Province—was someone on whom I leant heavily for legal advice on numerous occasions. Sir

Barry and Peter were two of the three immortals whom I could not have done without. Both have sadly passed on, Sir Barry in 2013 and Am. Peter Donigi in 2014.

I pay special tribute to the third immortal, my counsel Moses Murray, who showed absolute commitment and professionalism from the time he replaced Ralph Saulep and Peter Donigi as my lawyer. Moses Murray represented me with skill and passion. He was very quick to learn the military terminologies, customs, and traditions that animate our life, and he was indeed my anchor from 1997 until 2004. Both he and his wife, Maria, provided a buffer for my family when the chips were truly down. Moses had the final laugh when I was acquitted of the charge of sedition in 2004.

I am privileged to have seen more of the legal profession than most military officers. It is fitting to pay tribute to the legal professionals I have encountered over the years as their jobs are never easy. I include here the judge who found me guilty of a breach of the Leadership Code, Justice Moses Jalina. I think also of Justice Warwick Andrew, Justice Sir Kubulan Los, and senior magistrates Raphael Apa and Mekeo Gauli of the first and second commissions of enquiry into the Sandline affair. Their combined labours to throw light onto the Sandline affair took many months and resulted in thousands of pages of legal transcripts but ultimately threw little real light on ministerial involvement.

And then there was the controversial Justice Mark Sevua, who evicted me from Murray Barracks and sentenced the so-called mutineers to long and extremely punitive prison terms, having promised in public before their trials that he would do so. He was found dead on a beach in Manus Province in August 2014, apparently from a stroke. I do not suggest there was any connection.

I also acknowledge the personal sacrifice and commitment shown by the late Bill Skate when he opposed the engagement of Sandline on the floor of Parliament in 1997 and later offered an olive branch to the BRA and Bougainville Interim Government, paving the way for lasting peace on Bougainville. He masterminded the release of the five hostages in collaboration with the New Zealand government. Sir Donald MacKinnon, New Zealand's foreign affairs minister, and John

Hayes, former New Zealand high commissioner to PNG, played key roles in the negotiations.

My immediate family from Karkar Island, Dagua, and Yangoru in East Sepik Province offered essential support during 'the troubles' as did Col. Francis Agwi and his wife, Martina; WO Maclay Munog and his wife, Jill; WO Pinser Gubag and his wife, Noreen; and WO Liliak Lem and his family. I am grateful to all of them and many others who stood by me and my family. PM Hon. James Marape Colonel (Retd) Ian Glanville, the late Sir Brian Bell, Sir George Constantino, Michael Yaipupu, the Honourable Bryan Kramer, Pila Niningi, Gary Juffa, the Honourable Wera Mori, and William Duma provided much-needed assistance, guidance, and help with my legal expenses at various times.

I am grateful to Justice Cathy Davani, our first female judge in 2004, who found me not guilty on the charge of sedition that had hung over me for seven long years. And I acknowledge Justice Terence Higgins, judge of the National and Supreme Courts, very recently retired, who heard my electoral petition in March 2018 and awarded a recount in the Madang Regional seat that never eventuated due to a series of appeals by Peter Yama until he won the Supreme Court appeal and would continue as governor of Madang. Sadly, under his tenure, he along with some of his family members and his administration are facing series of criminal charges on public fund embezzlements.

I am indeed equally grateful for Minister for Communications and Information Technology, Honorable Timothy Masiu whose Department assisted toward funding of the printing of the autobiography. Minister Masiu is now the Member for South Bougainville in the national parliament. In his earlier career as a journalist and reporter for National News paper he was covering the Bougainville crisis working out from East New Britain. He covered many events in Bougainville risking his own life, He was also the journalist that scooped the headlines in August 1997 when the five hostages were released at Laguai in Buin District Bougainville in August 1997.

The care of my family during my time in the military was shared briefly with Dupain and then with Weni. They carried the burdens of my military career. I was away for many days, weeks, and months on training, schooling, and active duty. Thankfully, Dupain and Weni took our children under their wings and gave them comfort, something I was not always very good at doing as I readily acknowledge. Weni took much of the burden of the backlash on the family from the Sandline crisis; she understood the consequences of war and stood behind my decision as a soldier's wife and mother.

Vasity and our four children form the foundation and strength of my post-army life. We have dedicated our remaining time to serving our community through the Seventh-Day Adventist church. We hope to make whatever small differences we can to enrich the spiritual lives of our people.

Apart from my immediate family, the person who stands out in my mind as a long-time supporter, friend, and critic is Sir Peter Barter, former member of Parliament and governor of Madang. Sir Peter was minister for health and minister for provincial and local government affairs (a portfolio that included Bougainville among its responsibilities) in Sir Julius Chan's government. His early opposition to the Sandline contract was one of the catalysts that sparked my own opposition. His friendship, encouragement, and support since my removal from office as commander have been invaluable to my family and me. The late Noel Goodyear was another of my constant supporters. He had known and encouraged me from my earliest years. I am proud and honoured that his children call me 'Uncle' whenever I visit Karkar.

As I think back on the conception and planning of Operation Rausim Kwik, I view it as having been a necessary but thoroughly thankless task for everyone involved. Nevertheless, it has produced some positive and lasting legacies. For example, I think it is true to say that Operation Rausim Kwik served as a conduit and circuit breaker for peace on Bougainville. The ultimate test came in December 2019 when over 97.7 per cent of Bougainvilleans elected to be independent. My colleague—and once a bitter rival in the Bougainville conflict— Ishmael Toroama was unanimously voted in as president of the Autonomous Region of Bougainville. The SFU, which I founded in 1995 and which played a key role in Operation Rausim Kwik, is another legacy. Renamed the Long Range Reconnaissance Unit, it was given prominence as a strategic strike force during APEC 2018. Finally, the Engineer Battalion Forward Operation Base at Kerowil in Jiwaka Province, named Singirok Barracks in memory of my service to the defence force, should also be seen as a legacy of Rausim Kwik.

I was awarded Vanuatu campaign medal in 1981 made a Member of the British Empire in 1989 for my services on Bougainville and was awarded a Distinguished Military Service Medal in 2012 in recognition of my service to the PNGDF.

There is no shortage of adventure in the life of a soldier. I am thankful to the defence force and the government for having given me the opportunity to follow my dreams as a soldier and twice reach the pinnacle of service as commander of the PNGDF.

It was an honour and a pleasure to volunteer for service when I enlisted into the army as a 19-year-old in 1975. I took an oath to serve God and the Queen and to protect our resources and safeguard the people of PNG and defend the constitution. My military service number is 86506. I was once a soldier.

GLOSSARY

ADC	Aide-de-camp
ADF	Australian Defence Force
BCL	Bougainville Copper Ltd
BHQ	battalion headquarters
BIG	Bougainville Interim Government
BLF	Buka Liberation Front
BRA	Bougainville Revolutionary Army
BSM	battalion sergeant major
CDI	chief of defence intelligence
CO	commanding officer
CRA	Conzinc Riotinto of Australia
DS	directing staff
FIC	Field Intelligence Company
GPMG	general-purpose machine gun
HE	high-explosive
HF	high-frequency
IO	intelligence officer
JSC	Joint Services College
KIA	killed in action
LLG	local-level government
MIA	missing in action
MP	military police
NEC	National Executive Council

OC	officer commanding
OPM	Organisasi Papua Merdeka
orbat	order of battle
PNG	Papua New Guinea
PNGDF	Papua New Guinea Defence Force
PPP	People's Progress Party
PR	public relations
RMB	rear maintenance base
RO	radio operator
ROE	rules of engagement
RSM	regimental sergeant major
SASR	Special Air Service Regiment
SBT	Small Boat Team
SDA	Seventh-Day Adventist
SEAS	Southeast Asia Security Symposium
SFODA	Special Forces Operational Detachment Alpha
SFU	Special Forces Unit
SLR	self-loading rifle
SOG	Special Operation Group
SOP	standard operating procedures
SPRPKF	South Pacific Regional Peacekeeping Force
TEWT	tactical exercises without troops
VAP	vital asset protection

Pre-deployment training Goldie Trg Depot
1RPIR 1994

PM Sir Julius Chan Capt Jerry Singirok and
Gerega Pepena Minister for Defence
2PIR Bn Ex Dagua
Pre- deployment
Vanuatu
1980

Chatting with Capt Kaliop, Lt Bure, Lt Kadiesany , Capt
Paul Panau and Maj Tony Dibul after Ops High Speed
1 Aug 1994.

Lt Col Jerry Singirok Commanding Officer
1RPIR
1994

Staff and students Australian Army Command and
Staff College Fort Queenscliff Victoria
1991

Last outgoing Australian Commander PNGDF Brigadier General Jim
Norrie(75) and Maj Garry Young and Major Jerry Singirok Canungra
1992

Maib Kumai Singirok with grandparents Pesi (Mum)
and Singirok (Dad) at Igam Barracks 1989

Guard of Honor Fort Bonifacio Metro Manila
Feb 1997

Looking on is PNG Ambassador James
Pokasui and staff of General Acedera
Feb 1997

With Vasity at home
2015

Maj. Jerry Singirok Ops Offr Panguna mine
1989

Advance Tactics Course School of Infantry Singleton NSW
1985

Field trip to Oil fields Lake Kutubu with COP Aigilo and C Ops Gari Baki
1999

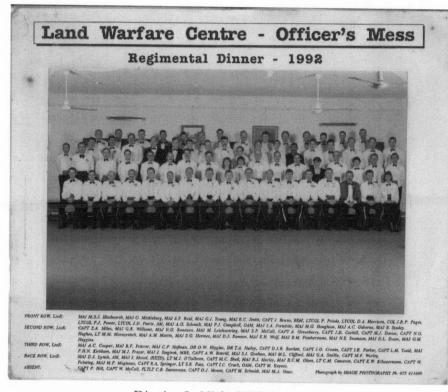

Land Warfare Centre - Officer's Mess
Regimental Dinner - 1992

FRONT ROW, L to R: *MAJ M.S.J. Hindmarsh, MAJ G. Mickleberg, MAJ S.F. Reid, MAJ G.J. Young, MAJ R.C. Smith, CAPT J. Bruno, BEM, LTCOL P. Priede, LTCOL D.A. Morrison, COL J.R.P. Pagn.*

SECOND ROW, L to R: *LTCOL P.J. Power, LTCOL J.D. Petrie, AM, MAJ A.G. Schmidt, MAJ P.J. Campbell, OAM, MAJ S.A. Ferndale, MAJ M.G. Houghton, MAJ A.C. Osborne, MAJ B. Spaley. CAPT S.A. Miles, MAJ G.R. Williams, MAJ N.G. Swanson, MAJ M. Leichsenring, MAJ S.P. McCall, CAPT A. Greenberry, CAPT J.D. Coxhill, CAPT M.J. Davies, CAPT N.G. Hughes, LT M.M. Morozreuch, MAJ A.M. Martin, MAJ S.G. Hermes, MAJ D.J. Rawson, MAJ E.H. Wolf, MAJ B.M. Featherstone, MAJ N.E. Swanson, MAJ D.L. Evans, MAJ G.M. Huggins.*

THIRD ROW, L to R: *MAJ A.C. Cooper, MAJ R.F. Peirrer, MAJ C.P. Hofman, DR D.W. Higgins, DR T.A. Natley, CAPT D.J.R. Bartlett, CAPT J.O. Cronin, CAPT J.R. Parker, CAPT L.M. Todd, MAJ F.H.N. Kirkham, MAJ M.J. Frazer, MAJ J. Singirok, MBE, CAPT A.W. Bottrill, MAJ S.J. Graham, MAJ M.L. Clifford, MAJ G.A. Smillie, CAPT M.F. Worley.*

BACK ROW, L to R: *MAJ D.J. Lynch, AM, MAJ J. Heost, (RETD), LT M.J. O'Sullivan, CAPT M.C. Shell, MAJ R.J. Morley, MAJ B.C.M. Olsen, LT C.M. Cameron, CAPT K.W. Scheuermann, CAPT W. Pointing, MAJ M.P. Maginnes, CAPT R.A. Springer, LT S.R. Pato, CAPT I.C. Crack, OAM, CAPT M. Keynes.*

ABSENT: *CAPT P. Hill, CAPT W. McColl, FLTLT C.B. Santariosa, CAPT D.J. Mount, CAPT M. Schmidt, MAJ M.A. Haus.*

Photograph by IMAGE PHOTOGRAPHY Ph: 075 421690

Dinning In Night LWC Canungra
1992

Ops High Speed 1 briefing using mud model Loloho Bougainville
with Ops Offr Tokam Kanene, Beldon
Namah, Tony Dibul and Airo Bulina
Aug 1994

Extracting Pte Walome 2RPIR Bougainville
1989

PM Bill Skate , BIG President, Joseph Kabui and General
Singirok peace talks Rotorua New Zealand Apr 1999, Lt
John Kinivi Bishop and 2Lt Jerry Singirok2PIR
Feb 78

Singirok with young girls from Bana High School
Apr 2019

Maj Fabila with Lt Tony Oawa, Sgt Gavuri, Lt ben
Moburau, Pte Ou and others at Sipuru Bougainville
Jul 1989

Singirok Mudan Langong
(1910-1995)

Cadet Sgt Singirok 35 School Cadet Battalion Sogeri Cadet Unit
1973

Officer Cadet Nason Moat, Police Cadets Willie Embros,
Cdt Piuk, General Bamaga Mark Yangiin, Michael Timbi,
Jerry Singirok, Harry Rakara, CIS Cdt Richard Sikani
1975

Singirok reconciles with BRA Commander Ismael
Toroama Bana witness by Evangelist Karl Jack
Apr 2019

Joint Service College with Police Cdt Willeie
Embros and CIS Cdt Henry Wawik
1975

INDEX

D

I

Moka (son) 60, 129, 168-9, 172, 388, 394, 402-3, 483, 507, 539

Moka, Weni 318, 360

Mokis, Stephen 516

Molloy, Ian 238, 247

Momis, John xxv, 93, 230, 447, 496, 501, 523

Moore, Hal 461

Moore, Harold G. 461, 559

Mopang (captain) 519

Mora, Chris xv, 169, 202, 219, 268

Mora, Chris Kalik xv, xx, 134-5, 140, 154, 157, 169, 202, 207, 210, 219-20, 268, 524, 526, 528, 562

Morauta, Mekere 529, 531, 538

Moresby, John 113, 326, 433, 472, 484

Morgan, Ken 425

Mori, Wera 567

Morrison, Alastair 5

Mortar Platoon 106, 347, 429, 439

Mortlock, Roger 516

Mua, Roger 415

Mule, Joshua 345

Mulina, Rupa 18, 49-50, 468, 472

Munog, Macklay 320-2, 567

Murray, Moses xxiii, 521, 534, 539, 566

Mutton, Mike 395

MV *Kingfisher* 432

MV *Kris* 433

MV *Lilung* 306

N

Nalau, Eki 333

Namah xix, 105, 135-6, 146, 149, 151-5, 157, 181, 210, 231, 526

Namah, Belden 104, 133, 135, 140, 148, 154, 156-7, 169, 202, 205, 213, 268, 411, 414, 439, 448, 450-2, 524-5, 528, 563

Namah, Bob xix, 105, 135-6, 146, 149, 151-5, 157, 181, 210, 231, 526, 528

Namah, Norman 563

Namaliu, Rabbie xix, 93, 224-5, 228, 232, 256-7, 362, 366

Nangurumo, Alan 209, 268, 561

Napu, John 216, 225

Narara, Timothy 408

Narokobi, Bernard 57, 59, 76, 93, 424, 529

Narokobi, Camillus 425

National Broadcasting Commission (NBC) xiv, 60, 143, 163, 185-6, 188, 352, 360, 369, 388, 425

National Executive Council (NEC) xi, xv, 4, 7, 41, 199, 201, 263, 512-13, 532

National Intelligence Organisation (NIO) 25, 27, 49, 88, 121, 126, 202, 535, 562-3

National Security Advisory Committee (NSAC) 121, 272

National Security Council (NSC) 4, 21, 44, 48, 120, 124, 460, 525

Navi, John 330

Nelson, Lord 69, 405

Nende, Bill 416, 492

Nenta, Bob xi, 30, 93, 121-2, 171, 494, 499

Nenta, Robert 143, 168, 170, 507

Network International Security Services 545-6

New Ireland 146, 197, 315, 335, 374, 479, 516

New Zealand xxv, 86, 105, 130, 158, 190-1, 212-13, 271, 361-2, 394, 396, 401, 431, 464-5, 478, 487, 496, 501-2, 506, 512, 516, 523, 529, 539, 562, 565-6

New Zealand Army 136, 396, 401, 560

609

9781543768824